LEARNING
CONFLICT OF LAWS
...

Thomas O. Main
William S. Boyd Professor of Law
William S. Boyd School of Law
University of Nevada, Las Vegas

Stephen C. McCaffrey
Carol Olson Endowed Professor of International Law
McGeorge School of Law
University of the Pacific

LEARNING SERIES

WEST ACADEMIC PUBLISHING

© 2019 LEG, Inc. d/b/a West Academic
  444 Cedar Street, Suite 700
  St. Paul, MN 55101
  1-877-888-1330

West, West Academic Publishing, and West Academic are trademarks of West Publishing Corporation, used under license.

Printed in the United States of America

ISBN: 978-1-63459-497-4

*We dedicate this book to our students, whose perspective,
curiosity, and insight remind us that we are students, too.*

ACKNOWLEDGMENTS

The authors express their profound gratitude to Professor Symeon C. Symeonides, Alex L. Parks Distinguished Professor of Law and Dean Emeritus at Willamette University College of Law. Professor Symeonides is one of the world's leading authorities on the subject of conflict of laws, and all scholars and teachers of the subject benefit from the breadth and depth of his knowledge, which he shares generously and modestly. Professor Symeonides' many books and articles exploring the theory, doctrine, context, and practice of conflicts have informed the authors' understanding of this complex and important subject.

The authors thank Seleste Wyse for her research assistance. The authors also thank Louis Higgins, Gregory Olson, and the editorial team at West Academic Publishing for their professional advice and assistance.

Excerpts from the Restatement (Second) of Conflict of Laws, copyright 1971 by the American Law Institute are reprinted with permission. Portions of Chapter 10 borrow liberally from Thomas O. Main, *The Procedural Foundation of Substantive Law*, 87 Wash. U. L. Rev. 801 (2010). Portions of Chapter 18 borrow liberally from Thomas O. Main, *The Word Commons and Foreign Laws*, 46 Cornell Int'l L.J. 219 (2013). Portions of Chapter 21 borrow liberally from Thomas O. Main, *Arbitration, What Is It Good For?*, 18 Nev. L.J. 457 (2018).

PREFACE

This is not a traditional casebook.

Traditional casebooks reprint court opinions and encourage students to extract the important doctrinal principles from key cases that have shaped the law. The traditional approach has its virtues: students are immersed in the conventions of legal discourse and learn to identify key issues, appreciate procedural history, observe the use of precedent, engage with legal reasoning, and develop domain knowledge. The traditional case method is an effective technique for constructing the scaffolding necessary to understand law and to understand legal process generally.

This book assumes that you have already learned these basic skills, the hallmarks of a legal education. This book treats you like a new lawyer who is unfamiliar with the field of Conflict of Laws. Each chapter reads like a lecture from a partner of a law firm. Hypotheticals then force you to apply the doctrine—thereby reinforcing the basic concepts, and revealing the complexity. Advocacy plays an outsized role in Conflict of Laws, and the hypotheticals allow you to develop and leverage that skill.

Each chapter includes some court opinions, but their pedagogic purpose here is limited. Indeed, your professor may not even assign or discuss them. The opinions that are included—often trial court opinions—were curated to illustrate applications of the doctrine. Each opinion is something of a pinpoint on a grand map that plots the outcomes of all case law that comprises a particular doctrine. The opinions exhibit both good and bad advocacy by lawyers—and also exhibit both deep and superficial understanding by judges. You will be encouraged to second-guess lawyers' strategic choices. And you are encouraged to assume that any court opinion that you read may well have been reversed on appeal.

Preparation for class should feel like preparing for a seminar for practitioners. The reading is straightforward, but dense. This approach assumes that you are a careful and deliberate reader who can be told something once.

The classroom experience should feel like you are learning how to be a good lawyer, as opposed to learning how to be a good law student. You will think strategically, perceive and leverage ambiguity, impose clarity, reason deductively and inductively, envision all sides of an argument, and pay attention to detail while recognizing which issues are more important than others.

One useful metaphor for this course is three-dimensional chess. You will learn how to think spatially, dynamically, and in stages. Where should you file: State A or State B? State court or federal court? How do not only the laws, but also the choice of law rules of the various alternatives affect your choice? And what are the ethical dimensions of preferring the jurisdiction in which you are qualified to practice? One of the nagging superficialities of legal education is the separation of topics into distinct silos. Because in fact, when practicing law, many different doctrines are engaged at once, and strategic decision-making does not allow for compartmentalization. This book puts you in the position of a lawyer who must navigate the contours of various doctrines, and make non-obvious strategic choices.

The focus of this book is on the contemporary practice of law, and the conflict of laws in particular. Accordingly, this book is not a treatise that captures the history and nuances of all doctrines. In fact, it deliberately aims to spare you the complexities of notes and comments that often distract students' attention away from the core questions. That said, we highly recommend consulting a treatise when you want more historical context or nuance. The most comprehensive and authoritative treatise in the field is Hay, Borchers, Symeonides, CONFLICT OF LAWS (5th ed. 2010). Other, compact and excellent treatises and study aids include Robert Felix & Ralph Whitten, AMERICAN CONFLICTS LAW (6th ed. 2011); William Richman, William Reynolds, and Chris Whytock, UNDERSTANDING CONFLICT OF LAWS (4th ed. 2013); Clyde Spillenger, PRINCIPLES OF CONFLICT OF LAWS (2d ed. 2015); Kermit Roosevelt, CONFLICT OF LAWS: CONCEPTS AND INSIGHTS (2d ed. 2014); Patrick Borchers, CONFLICTS IN A NUTSHELL (4th ed. 2015); Michael Hoffheimer, EXAMPLES & EXPLANATIONS FOR CONFLICT OF LAWS (3rd ed. 2016).

Finally, we want to address two administrative matters. First, the book contains quite a few cross-references. To be sure, it can be distracting when reading Chapter 5 to be told that you will learn more about some tangentially relevant doctrine in Chapter 8. Although the advance notice may be as confusing as it is reassuring when you read the cross-reference in the first instance, that cross-reference will be extremely helpful to you when, later in the course, you are re-reading earlier chapters as you become more sophisticated and can apply multiple doctrines simultaneously.

Second, the hypotheticals in this book present conflicts between the laws of different states and countries. To put the focus on the multi-dimensional nature of the strategic questions with respect to the choice of law, we will manufacture a conflict between, say, the employment laws of Kansas and the employment laws of North Carolina. Do not learn the employment laws of either state from a hypothetical in this book. They are, indeed, hypotheticals.

We hope that you find this book engaging and provocative. The field of Conflict of Laws is fascinating. Realize that you may be the only person in your law office or company (or, dare we say it, judge's chambers) that understands it.

Thomas O. Main

Stephen C. McCaffrey

Summer 2018

SUMMARY OF CONTENTS

TABLE OF CONTENTS

TABLE OF CASES

The principal cases are in bold type.

TABLE OF STATUTES

TABLE OF RULES

TABLE OF RESTATEMENTS

LEARNING
CONFLICT OF LAWS

1

Introduction

Key Concepts

- Laws vary from state to state, and country to country
- When the question of what jurisdiction's law applies is posed you may have some normative intuitions about what law *should* apply when transactions or occurrences transcend borders

Much of contemporary life transcends territorial boundaries. Students travel to other states and countries for education. Consumers purchase items over the internet from sellers in faraway places. Individuals work remotely for employers that are located elsewhere. People purchase property in distant places as investments or vacation homes. Air travel is ever safer, faster, and more affordable than ever. And technology minimizes the burdens of geographic distance.

Businesses, too, have taken advantage of a "flat" world where geographic constraints are increasingly less relevant.[1] Rarely would one find a company's headquarters, manufacturing facility, inventory, employees and customers concentrated in just one place. It is common for goods in production to cross the U.S.-Mexico border multiple times before they are ready for market. Even a so-called local business ordinarily contracts with suppliers that are located elsewhere, enjoys financing provided by a distant bank, and maintains a presence on the worldwide web. People and goods and communications are in constant motion at a speed, and in quantities, that would not have been imaginable only several decades ago.

Of course some of these interactions do not go as planned: people are injured; businesses lose money; disasters occur; diseases spread; people act carelessly and

---

1   The metaphor of a flat world was popularized in Thomas L. Friedman, The World is Flat: A Brief History of the Twenty-First Century (2005). Friedman wrote of a level playing field in terms of global commerce where history and geography are increasingly less relevant.

even maliciously; unforeseen events surprise; and relationships unravel. And in these unfortunate circumstances, often there are questions about the rights and responsibilities of the parties. When your clients turn to you, these prospective plaintiffs and defendants will wonder aloud: "They can't get away with that can they?" "What are my rights?" "Did I do anything wrong?" "What can you do?"

If every jurisdiction had the same laws (and also interpreted those laws in the same fashion), we would not need a discipline called conflict of laws. But in fact laws (and the interpretation of laws) differ across jurisdictions. Sometimes those differences are dramatic, as when one jurisdiction recognizes a cause of action or an affirmative defense that others do not. But even subtle and nearly imperceptible differences between the laws of two jurisdictions (or different applications of the "same" law) can be dispositive of the outcome in a particular case.

Your first task in studying conflict of laws, is to appreciate that—and how—laws can differ. For example, in law school you have learned about substantive matters where there is a "majority rule" that is followed by many states and a "minority rule" that is followed by others. You have studied sections of the Restatement of Torts (or Contracts or Property) that restate the common law in most or many states, but these generalized depictions often mask important variations. Further, many of the "note cases" that follow the principal cases in law school casebooks are included to illustrate alternative approaches and different laws. Each jurisdiction has its own court system, procedures, traditions, regulations, statutes, and case law. Indeed, even when the laws in two jurisdictions are textually identical, they may be applied differently in practice.

Importantly, then, whenever a transaction or incident implicates more than one state (or country), there lurks an important question: what law applies? Consider the following hypothetical.

Hypothetical 1-1

Devlin Enterprises, Inc. (Devlin) is a small company that is incorporated in Delaware, and has its headquarters and only manufacturing facility in North Carolina. Devlin manufactures camp stoves, and sells them to a wholesaler that is also located in North Carolina. Devlin does not control the wholesaler's sales markets nor set the prices that the wholesaler charges its consumers.

Plaxico is an individual who has spent her whole life in Utah. Indeed, she has never left the State. One day she was seriously injured in Utah by a camp stove that she purchased in Utah from a Utah retailer.

The camp stove that injured Plaxico was manufactured by Devlin. The wholesaler bought this stove from Devlin, and then sold it to a retailer in Utah who, in turn, sold it to Plaxico.

If Plaxico sues Devlin, which state's law should establish Devlin's responsibilities as a manufacturer? Or, put another way, which state's law should establish Plaxico's rights as a consumer? Should the answer depend on where suit is brought?

The question concerning what law governs the rights and responsibilities of the parties could be a significant one. Plaxico might be entitled to punitive damages under one state's law, but not the other. Or Plaxico might have to prove negligence under one state's law, but enjoy a regime of strict product liability under the other. Or contributory negligence might be a defense available to Devlin under one state's law, but not the other. Or the lack of privity between Devlin and Plaxico could be fatal under one state's law. The differences could be much more subtle than these examples, yet no less consequential.

From the perspective of system design, neither of the two most obvious answers to the choice of law question in Hypothetical 1–1 is attractive. Applying *Utah* law makes sense so long as one looks at the dispute only through the eyes of Plaxico. After all, she purchased the product in Utah, was injured there, and has never left the state. From this perspective it naturally follows that the available causes of action, the available defenses, or the remedy could only be prescribed by the state of Utah. Yet viewed through Devlin's eyes, the company should not be subject to the laws of every state (and country) to which their product just happens to travel. After all, they sell their products only in North Carolina, and they cannot control the distribution or movement of their products. (You may note similarities with the law of personal jurisdiction.)

Applying *North Carolina* law makes sense so long as one looks at the dispute only from Devlin's perspective. Devlin needs to know the standards to which its products will be held when it is manufacturing and selling them. If North Carolina law does not prescribe the company's rights and responsibilities, then the company cannot even know what law prescribes their rights and responsibilities. How could it satisfy our notions of due process to deny Devlin meaningful notice of the standard to which it will be held until after it's too late to modify its conduct? But of course the application of North Carolina or any law other than Utah's seems unfair to Plaxico, who has never left the state and therefore seems entitled to the protections of its laws. Imagine Plaxico's lawyer explaining to her that North Carolina law determines her right to recover.

How, then, do states make the choice between different laws which may be conflicting? Each state has its own choice of laws rules that guide the selection of the applicable law. The different methodologies that states use to select the applicable law are the principal focus of this course. Before we explore those methodologies, however, plumb your intuition on a few more hypotheticals. When answering the questions that follow, you are not constrained by what a court would choose as the applicable law (because we haven't studied it yet); instead consider what the choice of applicable law *ought* to be.

Hypothetical 1-2

Calore Enterprises, a Connecticut company, was involved in a contentious dispute with one of its vendors, Laskey Electronics, a New Hampshire company. Rather than rush to court, the principals of these companies hired a mediator to help them resolve the dispute. After seven days of mediating at a retreat center in New Hampshire, the parties terminated the session because they could not resolve their differences.

Calore subsequently filed suit in Connecticut against Laskey. During this litigation Calore seeks to introduce a statement that Laskey's chief executive officer made. Specifically, during the mediation, the CEO admitted certain mistakes that the company made. The issue now is whether those statements are admissible evidence in the Connecticut suit or are, instead, inadmissible and/or privileged.

The Uniform Law Commission has promulgated a uniform act that establishes a privilege of confidentiality for mediators and for participants in mediation. The State of New Hampshire has adopted the model legislation and therefore recognizes the statement as privileged and inadmissible. The State of Connecticut has not adopted the model legislation, and does not recognize the privilege. *Should* the statement be admitted?

Hypothetical 1-3

The State of California is unusually skeptical of non-compete clauses in employment agreements, and seldom enforces them. All other states, and especially Nevada, are much more sanguine about the value of non-compete clauses and tend to enforce them, provided they are reasonable.

When Dr. Dassar began working for a clinic in San Diego, California, her employer, Southern California Medical, insisted on an employment agreement that included (i) a strict non-compete clause, (ii) a choice of law clause requiring the application of Nevada law, and (iii) a choice of forum clause requiring that any dispute arising out of the contractual relationship be litigated in Nevada. Dr. Dassar, who was represented by counsel, understood these three clauses and, according to the employment agreement, received additional consideration in exchange for her willingness to agree to them.

A dispute between the parties arose, and Southern California Medical filed a breach of contract action against Dr. Dassar in a Nevada state court. *Should* the Nevada court apply Nevada law (or California law) to determine the enforceability of this non-compete clause?

Hypothetical 1-4

A tragic airplane accident took the lives of all forty-five persons aboard a flight. The airplane departed from Denver, Colorado. The plane, a Canadair CRJ 700, was destined for Devil's Lake, North Dakota, but crashed in Rapid City, South Dakota.

Among the deceased were fifteen passengers who were heading to Devil's Lake for a wedding celebration. These people haled from seven different states (three on the East Coast, three on the West Coast, and one from Texas). These relatives met in Denver to catch the connecting flight to Devil's Lake. Representatives of these fifteen individuals hired a lawyer who filed a lawsuit on their behalf against the airline in Denver, Colorado. The airline is a Delaware corporation with its principal place of business in Los Angeles, California. Denver is one of the airline's four main hubs.

This airline has recently been the target of whistle-blowers and undercover investigators who have described atrocious behavior in respect to repairs. It is possible, then, that the facts of this case could, depending upon the applicable law, support an award of punitive damages.

The laws in the East Coast states allow recovery of punitive damages only for "willful misconduct." The laws in the West Coast states allow recovery of punitive damages for "reckless or callous disregard." The law of Colorado permits recovery of punitive damages for "gross negligence." The laws of Texas, North Dakota, and South Dakota permit recovery of punitive damages for gross negligence in survival and personal injury actions, but prohibit recovery of punitive damages in wrongful death actions.

Which state's (or states') law(s) should govern the availability of, and the standard for recovering, punitive damages?

Hypothetical 1-5

Park died in a traffic accident while he was riding as a passenger on a motorcycle driven by Martin. The motorcycle collided with a car driven by Gonzales. The accident occurred in Texas, a few miles from the Oklahoma border. Park, Martin, and Gonzales were all lifelong residents of Texas. Neither Martin nor Gonzales had automobile insurance. However, Park had a policy (issued to him by A-Z Insurance Company in Texas) that covered three vehicles; none of those vehicles were involved in the accident, but the policy included uninsured motorist coverage at $50,000 per vehicle.

For years, Park had commuted daily to his job in Oklahoma. On the day of the accident, Park was not going to or from work (nor was he otherwise headed to or from Oklahoma).

Shortly after the accident, Park's husband moved to Oklahoma. The State of Oklahoma appointed him the personal representative of Park's estate. In that capacity, he filed an action against A-Z in the Oklahoma state courts seeking a declaration that the uninsured motorist coverage could be "stacked." A-Z acknowledges that it is liable to Park for damages suffered at the hands of an uninsured motorist, but argues that its exposure under the policy is capped at $50,000. Park's husband contends that the policy coverage for each of the three vehicles should be "stacked," and thus $150,000 is due. Stacking is permitted in most states, including Oklahoma, but not in Texas. Should the court apply Oklahoma or Texas law with respect to stacking?

With any of these hypotheticals your answer might be—perhaps should be—"It depends." That is a fair response, as these fact patterns are bare-bones. But do not let the absence of details be an excuse for failing to grapple with the issues presented. If your answer is that it depends, be ready to explain *on what* it depends. Identify the conspicuously-absent fact that prevents you from committing to an answer. In other words, the framework of such an answer should look something like this:

"It depends. I would need to know whether *x*.

If *x*, then Alabama law should apply.

If *not x*, then South Carolina law should apply."

Identifying the dispositive fact x is essential. Examples of an x might be "Artest is a Georgia resident," "Able is licensed to practice medicine in Georgia," "A files the action in Alabama," "Alabama's law is codified in a statute," or "Alabaster Concrete has more than 3 employees." Your conditional fact x is not dispositive unless it changes your answer; indeed, this is what means to say that your answer *depends* on something. Identifying the conditional fact x often takes considerable time and careful thought. Demand precision of yourself (and others).

In this course you will learn how courts determine what law applies. In this introductory chapter, however, we are deliberately avoiding any mention of those particulars (so as not to influence your intuition and reasoning). That said, embedded in the framing of the hypotheticals are two important assumptions that deserve your attention and criticism.

First, notice that several of the hypotheticals assume that the courts of one jurisdiction might apply the law of some other jurisdiction. In Hypothetical 1–5, for example, the action is filed in Oklahoma, yet the hypothetical implies that an Oklahoma court might apply Texas law. At this point in the course, you should be skeptical of whether an Oklahoma court would have the *authority* to apply some other jurisdiction's law. (After all, wouldn't the Oklahoma legislature expect its state courts to apply (only) Oklahoma's laws?) At this point in the course, you should also be skeptical of whether an Oklahoma court would have the *competence* to apply some other jurisdiction's law. (After all, lawyers and judges will often disagree about the content and meaning of laws with which they are familiar. How, then, can we expect the court to accurately apply some other jurisdiction's law? It might not be terribly taxing for an Oklahoma court to apply the law of Texas, its neighboring state. But what if the fact pattern called for the application of Pennsylvania law—or Panamanian law?) We will explore these issues later in the course.

Second, notice that all of the hypotheticals assume that the court confronts an essentially binary choice of applying its own law or the law of the other jurisdiction. In Hypothetical 1–5, for example, the choice is presented as either Oklahoma or Texas. One question we will revisit from time to time throughout the course is whether the court might apply some combination of the two alternatives—a combination that might fairly be described as "neither" or as "both" of the competing states' laws. Could the Oklahoma court allow "some" stacking to allow Park's husband to recover more than Texas's $50,000 but less than Oklahoma's $150,000? A recovery that compromises those two laws might allow Park's estate to recover, say, $100,000. Should the discipline of conflicts embrace these creative, third-way solutions?

This course will prepare you to identify and resolve issues regarding choice of the applicable law. Whether you are litigating cases or drafting contracts in the shadow of litigation, understanding (and influencing) what law determines the parties' rights and responsibilities may be profoundly significant. Conflict of laws is a discipline with several distinctive components. Each chapter in this book will broaden and deepen your understanding of the subject, and prepare you for practice. However, before you proceed to the next chapter, spend more time with the five hypotheticals above, as these will be the subject of class discussion.

2

Why Not Always Apply Forum Law?

Key Concepts

- Applying the law of the forum has intuitive appeal
- *Lex fori* has limitations as a choice of law methodology
- Substantive and procedural law are treated differently

One might fairly assume that the courts of a given state would apply only the laws of that state—and never the laws of some other state (or country). *Lex fori* is the Latin term for the law (lex) of the forum (fori). Although we will ultimately reject the notion that a court should always apply its own law, applying the lex fori has an intuitive appeal (and contemporary relevance) that merits examination.

In this Chapter we also introduce, even if only cursorily, several concepts that are helpful as orientation for the rest of the course. Conflicts can be a difficult subject to master, especially when it is unclear how different doctrines fit together. This chapter will give you some "big picture" perspective while also tackling some very specific questions.

Hypothetical 2-1

Parsons was cycling on a bicycle trail near his home in Moscow, Idaho, when a car driven by Larsen veered off a busy road, careened onto the bike path, and struck Parsons, critically injuring him. Larsen, also an Idahoan, was uninsured and is judgment-proof.

Just before the accident, Larsen thought she heard an emergency siren while she was driving. Responding to the siren, she was trying to pull over to the side of the road to allow the emergency vehicle to pass. She expected other drivers to slow down and pull over, and when they did not she panicked; an over-correction led ultimately to her losing control of her vehicle, in turn causing the accident.

The emergency siren that Larsen heard was, in fact, part of an advertisement that was playing on her car radio. A Pullman, Washington radio station KQQU was playing an advertisement for a personal injury lawyer—and that advertisement contains 20 seconds of an emergency siren. There is a voice-over for 15 of those 20 seconds, but the advertisement itself does not warn that, nor explain why, there is an emergency siren in the background.

A police officer later told Parsons that these radio advertisements were involved in a couple of other accidents in the area. Parsons' counsel is exploring a lawsuit against the radio station KQQU and/or the law firm mentioned in the advertisement.

Parsons' claims against these putative defendants would test the outer boundaries of proximate cause (or scope of liability). A defendant in a negligence case is only responsible for harms to individuals that the defendant could have foreseen. Even if Parsons can prove the other elements of the tort of negligence, he may have a difficult time proving that injury to a cyclist riding on a bike path is within the scope of risk that these defendants could have foreseen with their careless radio advertisement.

Although causation is generally a question of fact, the outer boundary of proximate causation (or scope of liability) is a question of law for the judge to decide. Some states are much more aggressive than others about finding—and policing—those boundaries; courts in the more aggressive states regularly grant motions to dismiss or motions for summary judgment on the element of proximate causation. Other states preserve a more robust role for juries.

Parsons lives in Moscow, Idaho, and was commuting to his job, when he was injured. His job is just across the border in Pullman, Washington. The radio station KQQU is a corporation that is located in Pullman, and is wholly owned by a conglomerate that is located in Chicago, Illinois. The law firm that is mentioned by name in the advertisement is a small Idaho personal injury law firm whose lawyers are licensed to practice in both Idaho and Washington. The law firm is a member of a nationwide consortium of personal injury firms that is located in Kansas City, Missouri. The consortium produced the advertisement, which runs nationally, but tailors it for each market to feature the name of the resident member.

Plaintiff's counsel might join the radio station and law firm as two defendants in one suit or, instead, sue them separately. Strategic considerations will also determine in which state(s) this suit (or suits) is (are) filed. Will—and should—courts in the forum state(s) necessarily apply forum law?

A. An Exclusively *Lex Fori* Approach Is Problematic

In many cases, the application of forum law is a sensible choice. Often the plaintiff and the defendant will be from the same state, and all of the important events leading up to the suit will also have occurred in that state. Imagine, for example, a breach of contract action between two Missouri businesses arising out of a contract entered into in Missouri, resulting in a failed joint venture in Missouri. Under such circumstances, a Missouri court is likely to apply Missouri law. That Missouri court would likely apply Missouri law to the breach of contract action even if one of the Missouri businesses involved in the dispute had a foreign vendor, foreign employee, or some other business project outside the state of Missouri; unrelated contacts of a party with other jurisdictions would be irrelevant.

But a *strict* lex fori approach means that the forum state *always* applies its own law. Fact patterns will not always be so neatly aligned where the forum state is the home of both parties and also the situs of all of the important events leading up to the suit. Imagine fact patterns like Hypothetical 2-1 where one (or some or many) of the important events leading up to the suit took place outside the forum. Or imagine fact patterns where many of the important *events* took place in the forum state, but one or even both of the *parties* are from another state or country.

A strict lex fori approach is indifferent to where any of the important events leading up to the suit took place; nor is it relevant where the parties are from. Rather, under lex fori, the court applies forum law simply because it is forum law. In Hypothetical 2-1, following this approach, an Idaho court necessarily would apply Idaho law to determine all of the rights and responsibilities of all of the parties; a Washington court would apply Washington law; an Illinois court would apply Illinois law; and so on.

In the following three subparts we explore some of the fundamental problems associated with a strict *lex fori* approach.

1. Personal Jurisdiction

One problem with a strict lex fori approach is that it outsources the deliberation of profound questions about what law should apply to another doctrine, namely personal jurisdiction. As you have no doubt seen in your Civil Procedure course, the doctrine of personal jurisdiction determines where litigation may take place; and the contours of that doctrine are defined by the constitutional doctrine of due process which enshrines considerations of access, fairness, convenience, and efficiency. A strict *lex fori* approach places an additional layer of consequences on to the personal jurisdiction inquiry, because the forum will necessarily apply its own law.

Personal jurisdiction doctrine, as presently constituted, may not be well-suited to bear the additional weight. You will recall from your Civil Procedure course that the personal jurisdiction doctrine defines the set of permissible forums, but gives the plaintiff considerable freedom to choose among that set of options. A strict lex fori approach allows plaintiffs to shop not only for their preferred *forum* but also for their preferred *law*. This approach could still be defensible as a policy matter— maybe even desirable—if personal jurisdiction doctrine reliably produced a limited set of permissible forums. But as our review will confirm, contemporary personal jurisdiction doctrine would allow litigation to proceed in a forum where the application of forum law would be illogical—and perhaps even unconstitutional.

Although the doctrine of personal jurisdiction is treated in depth in Chapter 20, a concise overview at the outset of the course will be helpful. The bases of personal jurisdiction include: (a) general jurisdiction; (b) specific jurisdiction; (c) personal service; (d) waiver; and (e) consent.[1]

a. General Jurisdiction

There is a limited set of affiliations with a forum that will render a defendant amenable to general (or "all-purpose") jurisdiction there. According to the Supreme Court, these are the paradigmatic examples:

- For an individual, the person's *domicile*.
- For a corporation, their **place of incorporation** and their **principal place of business**.

> **TERMINOLOGY**
>
> A person's **domicile** is the place that they were last both simultaneously present and intending to remain indefinitely—generally, their home. Although we will continue to use this term we will not give our full attention to domicile until Chapter 13.

---

1   Three additional bases, not discussed here, are reviewed in Chapter 20.

"Those affiliations have the virtue of being unique—that is, each ordinarily indicates only one place—as well as easily ascertainable."[2] And in each instance a defendant may be fairly regarded as "at home."

These paradigmatic examples are not necessarily the only forums where a defendant may be subject to general jurisdiction. The touchstone for establishing general jurisdiction is whether the defendant is "at home." Where a person or an entity is at home, they can, consistently with due process, be sued regardless of whether the lawsuit has any connection to the forum state. Such is the nature of general or all-purpose jurisdiction. Yet this inquiry requires more than an assessment of the gravity and character of the defendant's contacts with that state. "General jurisdiction instead calls for an appraisal of a corporation's activities in their entirety, nationwide and worldwide. A corporation that operates in many places can scarcely be deemed at home in all of them."[3] Accordingly, the ubiquitous presence of an oil and petroleum company like Chevron Corporation does not mean that they are "at home" in every state.

Hypothetical 2-2

Zoeing Aircraft, a Delaware corporation, is one of the world's largest manufacturers of commercial airplanes. For nearly a century, all of the company's design and manufacturing facilities have been located in the State of Washington. Approximately a decade ago, Zoeing moved its corporate headquarters from Seattle, Washington to Chicago, Illinois; the rest of its operations (research and development, manufacture, testing, sales, etc.) remained in Seattle. Since the move, all of the company's senior executives have worked out of the Chicago office.

Akram is a former Deputy General Counsel of Zoeing who was constructively discharged last year. Akram, who had an otherwise exemplary performance record, was demoted after he made certain statements to investigators from the Federal Aviation Administration. Akram left the job, claiming he was constructively discharged.

A patchwork of federal and state laws provides certain limited protections to "whistleblowers" who report violations of the law and are subject to retaliation by their employers. These laws vary in numerous respects, including (1) what kinds of reported violations trigger the protections; (2) what kinds of employers' activities constitute unlawful retaliation; and (3)

---

2   *Daimler AG v. Bauman*, 571 U.S. 117, 137 (2014).

3   *Daimler AG v. Bauman, supra*, 571 U.S. at 138.

what remedies are available for violations of the statute. Compared with other states, Washington's laws are especially protective of whistleblowers; Illinois's laws are less protective; and Delaware's laws even less so.

Where is Zoeing subject to personal jurisdiction on a theory of general or all-purpose jurisdiction? Notice the dearth of facts in this fact pattern. Does it matter where Akram worked, why the FAA was investigating Zoeing, what and where Akram told the FAA, or whether Akram's statements affected Zoeing?

b. Specific Jurisdiction

Even a defendant that is not "at home" in the forum state may nevertheless be subject to personal jurisdiction there. Indeed, a defendant that has only "minimum contacts" with the forum state may be subject to specific jurisdiction, provided those contacts have a sufficient nexus to the litigation. The exercise of jurisdiction also must not offend traditional notions of fair play and substantial justice.

Consider, first, the nexus requirement: the litigation must have a specific relationship with the forum state. In particular, the cause of action must *arise out of* the defendant's contacts with the forum.[4] The plaintiff must show more than that the cause of action is merely related to the defendant's forum activities. Indeed, the defendant's activities *in the forum state* must have actuated the plaintiff's claim.

Second, specific jurisdiction is proper only if the defendant has minimum contacts with the forum state. These contacts must not be fortuitous, accidental, or solely the result of the plaintiff's actions. Rather the contacts must demonstrate the defendant's *intention* to purposefully avail itself of the benefits the forum state. Put another way, the defendant must have purposefully and voluntarily *targeted* the forum state so that it should expect, by virtue of the benefits it receives, to be subject to the court's jurisdiction.[5]

Third, and finally,[6] the exercise of specific jurisdiction must not offend traditional notions of fair play and substantial justice. The factors of this so-called reasonableness test include the burden on the defendant, the interests of the forum state, the plaintiff's interest in obtaining relief, the interstate judicial system's interest in obtaining the most efficient resolution of controversies, the shared interest of the several states in furthering fundamental substantive social policies, and, in the in-

---

4   *See Bristol-Myers Squibb Co. v. Superior Court of California*, ___ U.S. ___, 137 S. Ct. 1773 (2017).

5   *See Walden v. Fiore*, 571 U.S. 277 (2014).

6   In Chapter 20 we will also discuss the role of long-arm statutes in exercises of specific jurisdiction.

ternational context, the procedural and substantive policies of other nations whose interests are affected by the assertion of jurisdiction.[7]

Hypothetical 2-3

Paul and Phyllis Pierce, a married couple, are life-long residents of North Carolina. Phyllis is a sales representative for Iguana Wear, a North Carolina wholesaler of outdoor clothing.

Approximately one year ago, Phyllis answered a telephone call from Dale Davis. Dale owns and operates a recreational equipment store in Indianapolis, Indiana. In response to Iguana Wear's national advertising campaign, Dale sought additional information about the company's product line, and called the company; Phyllis answered. In the months that followed, Dale and Phyllis talked on the telephone frequently—first weekly, then daily, then several times each day. Their relationship transitioned from professional to personal. Each of Dale and Phyllis initiated about half of the calls; they used both their work and personal telephones; and both were always aware that the other was married.

Dale and Phyllis eventually concocted a ruse so that she could visit him in Indiana. Dale contacted one of the vice presidents at Iguana Wear and falsely represented that he was sponsoring a regional expo in Indianapolis; he requested that a sales representative from Iguana Wear participate. The vice president obliged and Phyllis, who was the sales representative on this very successful account, was the obvious choice to attend. She traveled to Indiana about two months ago.

After spending four days with Dale in Indianapolis, Phyllis retuned to North Carolina. The day after returning, she called Dale and told him that their affair was over. Dale flew to North Carolina (his first and only visit to North Carolina) hoping to change Phyllis's mind. Phyllis was unwavering in her decision and Dale, after spending two days alone in a North Carolina hotel, returned home.

In a court in North Carolina, Paul Pierce filed a lawsuit against Dale Davis. North Carolina is one of only three states that still recognize the tort of alienation of affections. The tort allows a betrayed spouse to sue his or her spouse's lover. Juries in North Carolina have awarded million dollar verdicts for such actions on numerous occasions. Dale and Phyllis had sexual relations in Indiana, but never in North Carolina.

---

7   *Asahi Metal Industry Co. v. Superior Court*, 480 U.S. 102, 113–115 (1987).

Before reaching the question what law applies, the court must address whether it has personal jurisdiction. Would Davis be subject to personal jurisdiction in North Carolina on a theory of specific jurisdiction?

c. Personal Service

A third basis for establishing personal jurisdiction focuses on how and where the defendant was served with process. A natural person who is personally served while physically present in the forum state is subject to personal jurisdiction there.

A defendant's presence in the forum state at the time of service might be temporary and wholly unrelated to the plaintiff or to the subject matter of the suit, yet still suffice. For this reason, this basis is often referred to as "tag" or "transient" jurisdiction. The feasibility of effectuating in-hand in-state service on a prospective defendant constrains the utility of service as a method for establishing personal jurisdiction: a prospective plaintiff will seldom know exactly when and where an out-of-state defendant will be in the desired forum state.

Rooted in traditional notions of territorial sovereignty, tag jurisdiction requires that the defendant be physically and voluntarily present in the forum state at the time of formal service of process. Accordingly, personal service may not establish personal jurisdiction if the defendant's presence is acquired by force or fraud, or if the defendant is present in the forum as a party or witness in an unrelated judicial proceeding.

Hypothetical 2-4

Recall the facts of Hypothetical 2-3. Now consider personal service as an alternative basis for establishing personal jurisdiction over Dale Davis in North Carolina. Which of the following set of circumstances would suffice to establish personal jurisdiction by personal service?

(a) Phyllis called Dale and lied to him, telling him that her marriage to Paul was over. Dale flew to North Carolina to console Phyllis. When he arrived, he was greeted at the airport not by Phyllis, but rather by a process-server.

(b) Paul's lawyer noticed on Facebook that Dale Davis was in Chapel Hill, North Carolina, attending a basketball game between Indiana and North Carolina. Paul had Dale served as he exited the arena.

(c) Paul's lawyer noticed on Facebook that Dale Davis was hiking the Appalachian Trail. The lawyer had a sign posted at the Nantahala

Outdoor Center (in North Carolina) alerting Dale Davis that he had "won a prize." When Davis followed the instructions for claiming his prize he was given a $4 Starbucks gift card and served with process (at Nantahala).

(d) Dale is a member of the U.S. Marine Corps Reserve. Dale was required to participate in a training drill at Camp Lejeune in North Carolina. During his two weeks of service there, he was served.

(e) The company for which Dale works is a defendant in a collection action filed by a vendor in a North Carolina state court. This collection action has no relation or connection to the Pierces or to Iguana Wear. Shortly after appearing as a witness in the collection action, Dale was served with process (re Pierce's tort action) on the steps of the North Carolina courthouse.

d. Waiver

Waiver is another basis for establishing personal jurisdiction. An objection to the lack of personal jurisdiction must be properly asserted by the defendant; failure to do so will, itself, establish personal jurisdiction.

In federal court, a proper objection is made either by filing a motion to dismiss for lack of personal jurisdiction *prior* to answering or by preserving the motion by asserting the defect *in* the answer. If a defendant files a pleading or a motion without asserting the court's lack of personal jurisdiction, the defendant will be deemed to have made a general appearance before the court and, thereby, to have waived any objection to personal jurisdiction. Notice that this is an especially unforgiving interpretation of the word *waiver*; this species of waiver can be unknowing and inadvertent. State laws regarding waiver can be stricter still, requiring something called a special appearance to preserve the objection.

Hypothetical 2-5

Recall again the facts of Hypothetical 2-3. Assume that Dale Davis filed an answer admitting the affair with Phyllis but denying that any physical contact happened in the state of North Carolina. Two days after filing his answer, Davis filed a motion to dismiss for lack of personal jurisdiction. Based upon the facts stated here, Davis may or may not have waived his personal jurisdiction objection. What is the conspicuously absent fact that would allow you to determine whether Davis waived the objection?

In Practice

Noting and appreciating (and ultimately even exploiting) conspicuously absent facts is part of your progression from law student to lawyer. Law school tends to lull students into thinking that all of the relevant facts will be provided. In practice, however, it will be up to you *find* all of the relevant facts; the fact-*finding* process is hard to simulate in law school. But we can omit key facts from hypotheticals and exam questions to test whether you notice what is missing.

e. Consent

Contracting parties may designate a forum in which litigation is to take place. For example, a contract might include the following provision:

> Any dispute arising out of this agreement, its application, performance, or termination shall be litigated in courts of the State of Vermont.

A forum selection clause establishes personal jurisdiction in the designated forum.

Forum selection clauses are presumed valid. Although courts review forum selection clauses for their reasonableness and fairness, generally speaking, courts enforce them. To establish the unreasonableness or unfairness of a forum selection clause, the party resisting enforcement has the heavy burden of showing that trial in the chosen forum would be so difficult and inconvenient that the party would be effectively denied a meaningful day in court. State courts are somewhat less inclined than their federal counterparts to enforce a clause that inconveniences a party or that designates a state with only a tenuous connection to the parties or events.

Hypothetical 2-6

Dulles Rentals, Inc. (Dulles) is a Delaware corporation that rents and sells industrial equipment. Dulles's corporate headquarters is in Connecticut, but it has retail stores nationwide and four regional offices. Pruitt responded to a job posting at Dulles's Southwest regional office in Phoenix, Arizona. After a series of interviews in Phoenix, Pruitt was hired to manage a retail store in her hometown of Tucson, Arizona. Her salary is $48,000 per year. While in Phoenix, Pruitt signed an employment agreement that included the following clause: "The interpretation and enforcement of this Agreement shall be resolved exclusively in the state or federal courts of Connecticut." Notwithstanding the clause, all of Pruitt's interactions with the company (both before and after starting work) have been with corporate officials in the Phoenix office.

In her first eighteen months on the job, Pruitt has been denied all of her vacation requests. The parties now dispute whether Pruitt is entitled to additional compensation for these additional hours worked. The federal Fair Labor Standards Act (FLSA) provides certain guarantees to employees with respect to compensation. But the federal legislation is a floor, rather than a ceiling, and some states (like Arizona, but not Connecticut) have created higher standards to protect workers.

Pruitt has never been to Connecticut and has no connection with the state. If Dulles files a declaratory judgment action against Pruitt in Connecticut, do the courts of that state have personal jurisdiction over her?

f. Concluding Thoughts on Personal Jurisdiction

Revisit Hypothetical 2-1 in light of this brief survey of personal jurisdiction doctrine. The hypothetical involves two defendants, and the personal jurisdiction analysis must be undertaken separately for each of them. Could you get jurisdiction over both defendants in Idaho or Washington? Could you get jurisdiction over one or both defendants in Missouri, or Illinois? Could you get jurisdiction over one or both defendants in Florida—a state that is not even mentioned in the hypothetical?

Now imagine that Idaho and Washington (and/or other states where the defendant(s) may be subject to personal jurisdiction) have different case law with respect to the scope of proximate cause. Should Parsons be allowed to shop not only the *forum* but also the *law* that will determine the parties' rights and responsibilities? Under a lex fori regime, jurisdiction and the applicable law are linked. The courts of Florida could have personal jurisdiction even though the parties and the underlying events have absolutely nothing to do with Florida. Under such circumstances should Florida law also determine these parties' rights and responsibilities?

The application of Florida law by a Florida court when the parties and the underlying events have absolutely nothing to do with Florida is surely bad policy; it could also be unconstitutional. In Chapter 14 we will learn that the U.S. Constitution limits the ability of a state to impose its own law on parties and facts that have a tenuous connection to that state. Specifically, the Due Process Clause protects defendants against the unfair surprise of being subject to some law that they could not have reasonably foreseen would apply to them. Additionally, the Full Faith and Credit Clause protects the regulatory interest of a state from having its law undermined by another state that has no such interest.

The prospect of forum shopping for favorable law dooms lex fori as a comprehensive approach for determining the applicable law. Our intuition tells us that Parsons should not be able to research the laws of all of the possible states where he could sue the radio station, find the most favorable case law on proximate cause, and then, simply by filing in that jurisdiction, get the benefit of that state's laws.

But this may be an unfair criticism of a lex fori approach. After all, these dangers of forum shopping are caused by the contours of the doctrine of personal jurisdiction, not by a lex fori approach to choice of law. We could embrace a strict lex fori approach to choice of law if we restructured the doctrine of personal jurisdiction to minimize or eliminate the plaintiff's ability to forum shop. This is not a new idea. The primary proponent of a lex fori approach to conflict of laws proposed that the doctrine of *forum non conveniens* be converted from a negative mandate (negating jurisdiction in an inconvenient forum, see Chapter 21) into an affirmative mandate *forum conveniens* that would allow jurisdiction *only* where the application of forum law would be proper.[8] Absent this or some other dramatic restructuring of the law of personal jurisdiction, forum shopping presents a serious challenge for advocates of a strict lex fori approach.

A strict lex fori approach could also be manipulated by a *defendant's* forum shopping. If a defendant were able to avoid being subject to personal jurisdiction in a state, she would likewise be able to skirt the responsibilities imposed by that jurisdiction's laws (unless that defendant's home jurisdiction would also apply the other jurisdiction's law). When personal jurisdiction doctrine is expansive, plaintiffs have the ability to shop. But when personal jurisdiction doctrines contract, as is the current trend,[9] the *defendants* are in the better position to shop. Imagine, for example, that personal jurisdiction law allowed jurisdiction over a corporation only in the state of its principal place of business; by choosing the state of its principal place of business, the corporation would also be shopping for the law that would govern all actions against it by its employees or customers or investors or suppliers, no matter their location. Notice that this forum shopping by defendants would typically occur *ex ante*, meaning before the event giving rise to the litigation, whereas plaintiffs' forum shopping would occur *ex post*, meaning after the event.

---

8   *See* 1 Albert A. Ehrenzweig, Private International Law 107–110 (1967).

9   This is explored further in Chapter 20.

We might imagine a state embracing a lex fori approach to choice of law provided it were not strictly adhered to, but instead allowed for some exceptions. Indeed, that is the approach of a couple of states. (See Chapters 3 and 11.) Once the doctrine allows for some exceptions, however, every case becomes about the exceptions—because the parties dispute exactly *when* the forum state should depart from its general rule—and *which* law should apply. A theory other than lex fori is necessary to provide answers to these questions. Hence, the need for this course.

2. Choice of Law Clauses

A second challenge for advocates of a strict lex fori approach is the difficulty occasionally posed by choice of law clauses. The specific problem is revealed in the next hypothetical.

Hypothetical 2-7

Geering Construction Co. (Geering) is a builder that specializes in commercial and industrial projects for environmentally-conscious companies. Geering is incorporated in Delaware, has its principal place of business in Seattle, Washington, and has completed projects throughout much of the western half of the United States.

Reiter Cranes Inc. (Reiter) is a Portland, Oregon-based company that owns and operates boom trucks and tower cranes for construction companies that hire them as a subcontractor. Reiter, which is incorporated in Delaware, has successfully completed many construction projects with Geering.

Geering won the bid to construct a manufacturing facility in Sitka, Alaska, for a company that was expanding there. This was Geering's first project in Alaska. Further, because Sitka is accessible only by air or sea (i.e., not by land), the project presented a number of unique challenges. Geering contracted with a number of subcontractors, including Reiter, who similarly had never done work in Alaska.

Access to the construction site and development of the project itself implicated a network of environmental, tribal, and commercial laws that required vigilant compliance by all companies doing business there. Seeking to streamline matters and to avoid the possibility of inconsistent obligations, Geering included a choice-of-law clause identifying Alaska as the state whose law would govern the interpretation of all of the terms, obligations, and responsibilities of the subcontractor agreements. Reiter recognized the wisdom of that approach and signed the contract.

The construction project was completed several months ago, but Gearing and Reiter disagree about whether Geering is obligated to pay Reiter for $750,000 of cost overruns. Reiter has filed an action in a Washington court. Should the Washington court apply Alaska law?

Choice of law clauses can interfere with a strict lex fori approach to choice of law. The only way both to respect the Alaska choice of law clause and to embrace a strict lex fori approach would be to have this case heard in Alaska. However, this would be inconvenient not only for both of the litigants, but also for the State of Alaska which would likely prefer not to expend judicial resources resolving a dispute that now has little to do with Alaska.

Alternatively, the Washington court could ignore the choice of law clause, and instead apply forum law. But this undermines party autonomy and the reasonable expectations of the parties. How important are those values to contract law? We will study choice of law clauses in Chapter 9. At this point, however, it is important to see only that choice of law clauses can create tension within a strict lex fori approach.

3. Federal and State Law

In this part, we consider a third problem with a lex fori approach that is fundamentally different than the challenges described in parts 1 and 2 above. Here, the interplay of *federal* and *state* laws introduces complexity that even a resolute commitment to apply lex fori cannot trump. This differs from the circumstances contemplated above which focused instead on the interplay of two states' laws

The Constitution constrains the application of forum law in two additional respects. First, the *Erie* Doctrine obliges a federal court with diversity jurisdiction to apply state (not federal) substantive law.[10] And second, the Supremacy Clause obliges state courts to recognize federal law as the supreme law of the land.[11] This interplay of federal and state laws means that applying *only* "forum law" is not an option. Let us consider each of these two Constitutional complications more closely.

Federal courts have limited subject matter jurisdiction that falls into two fundamental categories: federal question and diversity. When a case arises under federal

---

10   *Erie R. Co. v. Tompkins*, 304 U.S. 64 (1938).

11   U.S. Const. Art. VI, cl. 2.

law, federal courts have federal-question jurisdiction; and in these cases, federal law—the lex fori—applies. But the federal courts also have diversity jurisdiction over certain cases that arise under state, not federal, law. In these cases, the federal courts must apply the state substantive law. The Court's famous *Erie R. Co. v. Tompkins* decision established that there is no general federal common law. In this respect, then, in diversity cases, the federal courts cannot apply lex fori strictly (i.e., they cannot apply only federal law) but must instead apply state law. (We will revisit this principle, the *Erie* Doctrine, again in Chapter 19.)

State courts are courts of general subject matter jurisdiction and thus hear cases that arise under federal law and cases that arise under state law. In all exercises of their jurisdiction, however, a state must recognize that federal law is the supreme law of the land. Accordingly, even in a state court case that involves only parties from that state, events in that state, consequences in that state, and where the court is principally enforcing a law of that state, that state court must recognize federal constitutional or statutory mandates that bear on the litigation process or on the resolution of the dispute. In this respect, then, the state courts cannot apply lex fori strictly (i.e., they cannot apply only their own state law), but must also apply federal law.

In sum, our system of federalism requires that federal and state courts apply their own and their counterpart's laws.

B. Authority to Depart from Forum Law

The idea that a state court would apply some other state's law is a curious proposition. After all, when taking office, judges pledge to uphold the laws of their home state, not of some other state. And isn't it an affront to the separation of powers if a state's judiciary does not enforce laws that were duly enacted by its legislative branch?

One way to resolve this dilemma is to read the home state's law (also referred to as "local" law) as incorporating the other state's law (also referred to as "foreign" law). State legislatures can pass legislation acknowledging that, in certain prescribed circumstances, the court should apply foreign law. For example, a state statute might provide that in tort cases where both the plaintiff and the defendant are domiciled in the same foreign state, the court should apply the law of the parties' common domicile.[12] The court thus applies the foreign law as part of the local law. In this sense, the application of foreign law is not really foreign law at all.

---

12 *See, e.g.,* Or. Rev. Stat. § 31.875(2)(a).

Yet statutes of that sort are rare. More often, the authority to apply the foreign law as part of the local law is a product of judicial fiat. As you will see, jurisdictions adopt one of various methodological approaches that lead them, in certain circumstances, to apply foreign law. Generally speaking, these methodological approaches are products of judicial decisions—i.e., case law—rather than statutes. Rationales for this practice of applying foreign law—and not applying forum law—tend to be rooted in the following theories:

> ┌─────────────────────────────┐
> │ **TERMINOLOGY**
> │
> │ The laws of another state are routinely referred to in this book and in practice) as "*foreign*" law. The laws of another country may also be referred to as "foreign" law, though context or some additional qualifying language will usually make that clear.
> │
> │ The word *domestic* is similarly deployed. Commonly, a domestic situation refers to something that occurred within a state. (E.g., "This Kentucky action arising out of an automobile accident is purely a domestic situation since all of the parties are domiciled in Kentucky and all relevant events occurred in Kentucky."). Occasionally, the word domestic refers to the United States as whole, in contrast to something with international connections.
> └─────────────────────────────┘

(1) The local law does not apply because, regardless of its textual mandate, the local law was not drafted with a multi-state situation in mind.

(2) Some superseding principle or law obliges the court to respect the foreign mandate.

The first of these two rationales builds from the premise that laws are constructed with certain unstated assumptions about the scope of their applicability. The text of most laws follow this basic form:

> If any person engages in conduct *x*, then the consequence is *y*.

For example, this could be a statute passed by the Colorado legislature to protect consumers from unfair and deceptive business practices. Importantly, state lawmakers seldom include text that imposes any geographic limit; instead, lawmakers write laws as though they are the only jurisdiction that exists. Such a statute might declare that "unfair or deceptive acts or practices in the conduct of commerce are hereby declared unlawful." Accordingly, by its *express* terms this hypothetical Colorado law has been violated if someone in Maine (or Madagascar) engages in the prohibited conduct even if the people involved in the incident and the incident itself have absolutely no connection to Colorado.[13] Yet it seems most unlikely that the lawmakers of Colorado intended to give a right to the citizens of Maine; and if a Maine citizen involved in a transaction in Maine tried to invoke this right we would construe the Colorado statute as inapplicable.

We can use this same interpretive rationale in a situation that has *some* (rather than no) connection to Colorado. Imagine that a Coloradan, while vacationing in Nevada, is the victim of a Nevada vendor's unfair business practice. The Coloradan returns home and sues the Nevada vendor in Colorado. On its face the Colorado statute might apply. But we can imagine a Colorado court avoiding the application of Colorado law by saying that its lawmakers did not intend to give a right to someone who was injured in Nevada by a Nevadan.

This first rationale can provide a compelling justification for *not* applying the local law: the local law does not apply because it was not drafted with a multistate situation in mind. It offers no justification, however, for applying some foreign law. For that, we need the second rationale.

The second rationale involves some superlaw that obliges the court to apply the foreign law. The U.S. Constitution, for example, provides that "[f]ull faith and credit shall be given in each state to the public acts, records, and judicial proceedings of every other state." Art. IV. § 1. The Constitution thus contemplates that each state will exert its own sovereign authority while also recognizing the sovereign authority of its sister states. The Constitution thus can be that superlaw. We will revisit these and other Constitutional questions in Chapter 14.

The second rationale is also supported by principles of comity. Comity is an expression of deference, granted out of respect, to the laws of a fellow sovereign. Comity is conferred with an expectation of reciprocity from the other sovereign, when their circumstances are reversed. Comity has a status that is famously described as something between mere courtesy and a legal duty.[14] This superlaw is not so much a mandate as simply a good idea. But what comity lacks in formal authority, it compensates with history: roots of the doctrine are traceable to at least the 17th century of European private international law.

---

13   In Chapter 5 we revisit this phenomenon of legislative drafting.

14   *See generally* Yntema, *The Comity Doctrine, in* 2 Vom Deutschen zum Europaischen Recht, Festscrhift fur Dolle 65 (1963), *reprinted in* 65 Mich. L. Rev. 1 (1966).

C. The Pervasive Influence of *Lex Fori*

This Chapter, titled *Why Not Always Apply Forum Law?*, is divided into three parts. Part A established why a *strict* lex fori regime is not workable. Part B established the basic justification for applying foreign law instead of forum law in certain (as-yet-unidentified) circumstances. In this Part C we return to the idea of applying forum law. Because even if a strict lex fori regime is not workable, for two principal reasons, courts frequently apply forum law.

1. The Homeward Trend

Even if courts may—and from time to time must—apply some law other than forum law, applying the law of the forum is a seductive option. One might fairly imagine that (lawyers and) judges are always tempted to apply more easily-ascertained local laws whenever it is defensible for them to do so. Indeed, "[j]udges tend to be biased in favor of forum law."[15] Several empirical studies have confirmed the prevalence of this so-called homeward trend.[16] Empirical studies likely understate the trend, since in many cases where the application of foreign law might benefit one of the litigants, the lawyer does not even spot, much less raise the issue. Moreover, judges rarely apply foreign law sua sponte.

Applying foreign law can be difficult. Understanding the precise contours of each element of a cause of action, navigating the available defenses, mastering the governing precedent—each of these tasks can be complicated and time-consuming. Practitioners disagree vigorously about the content of law in the context of entirely *domestic* cases; indeed, even familiarity with law does not remove its uncertainties. Of course the potential for disagreement is heightened when relative strangers to a law try to make sense of it. (We will revisit this in Chapter 18.) Throughout this course you should consider the extent to which the homeward trend may be influencing a judge's analysis.

Applying foreign law can be more or less complicated depending on the law to be applied and depending also upon what the application of that law would entail. With respect to the former, applying California law is easier than applying Cambodian law. With respect to the latter, understand that applying foreign law may involve different levels of engagement, as exemplified in the following hypothetical.

---

15 Andrew T. Guzman, *Choice of Law: New Foundations*, 90 Geo. L.J. 883, 893 (2002).

16 *See, e.g.,* Patrick J. Borchers, *The Choice-of-Law Revolution: An Empirical Study,* 49 Wash. & Lee L. Rev. 357 (1992); Stuart E. Thiel, *Choice of Law and the Home-Court Advantage: Evidence,* 2 Am. L. & Econ. Rev. 291 (2000); Larry DiMatteo et al., International Sales Law: A Critical Analysis of CISG Jurisprudence 2–3 (2005). *But see* Symeon C. Symeonides, *The Choice-of-Law Revolution Fifty Years After Currie: An End and a Beginning,* 2015 U. Ill. L. Rev. 1847, 1901 (finding no undue preference forum law in torts cases).

Hypothetical 2-8

One year ago Plutarch, a Georgian, sued Georgia State Hospital in a Georgia superior court for medical malpractice. Plutarch lost on a summary judgment motion because she was unable to produce any evidence of the defendant's liability. Now one year later, it appears that Trimble Co., a vendor to Georgia State Hospital, may have destroyed evidence that would have allowed Plutarch to survive that summary judgment motion. Trimble Co., a Tennessee corporation located in Nashville, was not a named party in the underlying litigation.

Plutarch has since filed suit against Trimble in Tennessee, alleging spoliation of evidence. Spoliation occurs when an individual or corporation violates its duty to preserve relevant evidence. Some jurisdictions allow spoliation claims against defendants like Trimble who were not parties in the underlying litigation; these are called "third-party spoliation claims." Other jurisdictions allow spoliation claims only against parties to the underlying litigation; these are called "first-party spoliation claims."

Version #1. Tennessee allows third-party spoliation claims. Georgia allows first-party but not third-party spoliation claims.

Version #2. Tennessee allows first-party but not third-party spoliation claims. Georgia allows third-party spoliation claims.

If the Tennessee court were inclined to apply foreign (i.e., Georgia) law, which of these two versions requires more entanglement with that (foreign) law?

2. Forum Procedure

Although courts may—and from time to time must—apply foreign law rather than forum law, the lex fori governs *procedure*. In other words, even when a state's choice of law principles direct a court to apply another jurisdiction's law, only the foreign *substantive* law will be applied. A jurisdiction typically applies forum procedure.

The application of forum procedural law—even in circumstances when the court is applying some other's jurisdiction substantive law—is justified by the fact that procedural law constitutes the "house rules" by which the operation of the court is governed, and by the time and expense that would be required to replicate the requirements of the other jurisdiction's procedural system. There could be tremendous complexity in trying to distill another procedural system's requirements about commencing an action, service, joinder, pre-trial dispositions, interim remedies, the scope of discovery, experts, evidence, and sanctions for misbehavior. Imagine the task of recreating another system's modes of case assignment, court management, trial with specialized courts and judges, juries, appeals, and so forth.

Yet the dividing line between substance and procedure is hardly obvious. Is a law that requires plaintiffs to disclose their names in a complaint substantive or procedural? Is a law requiring certain types of claims to be submitted to non-binding mediation substantive or procedural? (What about compulsory arbitration?) Is prejudgment interest a matter of substance or procedure? (And is it necessarily the same answer for post-judgment interest?) Many doctrines have long been difficult to classify as either substantive or procedural: testimonial privileges, fee-shifting statutes, burdens of proof, the availability of equitable relief, measure of damages and other remedial matters. With any of these examples, the substance-procedure classification could be significant to the parties—sometimes even dispositive of the case. We will revisit the substance-procedure dichotomy in Chapters 10, 14, and 19.

Hypothetical 2-9

Two years ago, Demand Magazine Co. (Demand) published a series of articles describing chiropractic medicine as the "greatest hoax of the century." The series challenged the theoretical foundation of the field (the spinal subluxation) and also exposed highly manipulative marketing practices of three practitioners, namely Cancellara Chiropractic of Dallas, Texas; Perfect Posture by Gilbert of Grinnell, Iowa; and Boonen Wellness of Plymouth, New York.

Recently the three practitioners jointly hired a lawyer to represent them in a libel action against Demand. Demand is a Delaware corporation with its principal place of business in New York, New York. The magazine has more than a million subscribers and is read worldwide.

With one exception, all states have a one-year statute of limitations for libel claims. Hoping to take advantage of Delaware's extraordinarily long three-year statute of limitations for libel claims, plaintiffs filed their suit in the only forum where their suit might be timely. Should Delaware courts apply Delaware's statute of limitations even if it does not apply Delaware's libel law?

Quick Summary

- The bases for establishing personal jurisdiction over a defendant include general jurisdiction, specific jurisdiction, personal service, waiver, and consent

- A court may have personal jurisdiction even when it would be nonsensical for the court to apply the substantive law of the forum

- The application of foreign substantive law raises questions of authority and competence

- The *homeward trend* refers to a jurisdiction's natural inclination to apply its own substantive law

- A court will apply forum procedural law—even when it applies foreign substantive law

3

Modeling Choice of Law Methodologies

Key Concepts

- There is no single methodology for determining what law should apply when transactions or occurrences transcend borders
- Choice of law methodologies can be simple or complex, and flexible or rigid
- Any choice of law methodology will have both strengths and weaknesses

---

In Chapter 2 we established that courts may—and from time to time must—apply foreign law rather than forum law. Consider a contract dispute between *A*, a Nebraskan, and *B*, a New Yorker, arising out of their joint real estate venture in Florida. This dispute could require any court where the action is filed to choose the applicable law.

In this Chapter we begin to examine *when* courts should apply foreign law and also, when there are multiple options, *which* foreign law. In practice there are many methodologies for answering those *when* and *which* questions, and the chapters that follow tackle each of those methodologies seriatim. But before studying any of those methodologies in depth, it is useful to look broadly at the range of options. Imagine that you are in a position to draft choice of law principles for your state courts. What principles would you advocate for when answering those *when* and *which* questions?

We encourage you to think of the universe of options along two axes. The first axis involves the simplicity/complexity of what you expect judges to do when they engage your principles to determine the applicable law. One crude measure of the simplicity or complexity of the methodology is the number of factors to consider. At one extreme, there could be but one factor in the decisional calculus. But as we add factors to the decisional calculus, we add complexity to the inquiry; the more complexity we add, the more that we move toward the other extreme. There are many factors that could be included among the principles to determine the applicable law. Those factors might also vary by type of action—with different choice of law rules for contracts and torts, for example. Among the factors that might conceivably be included are facts about the litigants, for example:

What is the citizenship/domicile/residence of the plaintiff(s)?

What is the citizenship/domicile/residence of defendant(s)?

A jurisdiction might also wish to delve into the facts giving rise to the underlying cause(s) of action. For example:

Where was the plaintiff and/or the defendant when the first element of the cause of action accrued?

Where was the plaintiff and/or the defendant when the last element of the cause of action accrued?

Where was the plaintiff and/or the defendant when the majority of the elements of action accrued?

A state might also consider as relevant factors details about the laws that are conflicting. For example:

Are either/both of the conflicting laws attempting to regulate the incident giving rise to the claim?

Which of the conflicting laws is more specific with respect to the incident giving rise to the claim?

Which of the conflicting laws is more recent?

Is each of the conflicting laws the product of a statute or of decisional law?

Which of the conflicting laws is more generous to plaintiff (or is more prejudicial to defendant)?

Which of the conflicting laws is easier for the court to apply?

Whether the plaintiff and/or the defendant were aware of one or both of the conflicting laws, expected one of the laws to apply, or reasonably believed that one of the laws would apply?

Any combination of these and many more factors could be included in the decisional calculus. The more factors that are included the more complex the choice of law inquiry becomes.

Complexity is not only about the number of factors; some factors may be simpler than others to derive. For example, the residence of the plaintiff would often be a straightforward inquiry for the court. But ascertaining whether a particular law is attempting to regulate the incident giving rise to the claim is a more nuanced inquiry; the judge might need to review legislative history and speculate about a legislature's intentions. When establishing a choice of law methodology, the quantum of *complexity* desired can be dialed up or down.

Simplicity has its virtue. When asked about his assertion that the laws of physics should be simple, Albert Einstein said that if they weren't simple, he would not be interested in them. Complex structures lack elegance and can appear temporary and, even if paradoxically, incomplete. Reformers may be drawn to simple frameworks because they may be more likely to work. And even when they do not work, a simple regime may be more easily repaired.

Yet in a complex world, simple solutions may be unrealistic. Simple may be a euphemism for crude and unrefined. And it may be naïve or even insincere to demand simple solutions to complex matters. We will study simple and complex methodologies.

A second axis involves the rigidity/flexibility of the framework for determining the applicable law. A *rigid* framework mechanically produces an answer; the judge need only apply the prescribed formula to get the preordained result. By contrast, a *flexible* framework guides a judge's inquiry but does not necessarily produce one answer. Instead, the judge has a certain amount of discretion to choose the best answer. Discretion can be express and intended; or it can be the unavoidable consequence of an inquiry about which reasonable minds could differ.

The choice between rigidity and flexibility tracks the familiar dialectic between "bright line rules" and "flexible standards" that surfaces in many legal contexts.[1] Rules are attractive because they evoke the virtues of predictability and uniformity. They are prone to create mischief, however, because life inevitably produces circumstances that mechanical tests never imagined. And they may produce results which, though predictable, seem unfair. Standards are attractive because they al-

---

1   *See* Pierre J. Schlag, *Rules and Standards*, 33 UCLA L. Rev. 379 (1985); H. Hart & A. Sacks, The Legal Process 155–158 (unpublished manuscript tent. ed. 1958).

low common sense and judgment to play a role in an important decision. But certainty—both *ex ante* and *ex post*—suffers.

A grid of the two axes reveals a taxonomy of the fundamental approaches for determining what law applies.

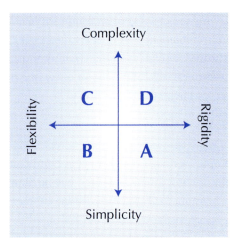

Methodologies that drift toward points in quadrant A embrace a simple inquiry with a mechanical application. In a strict lex fori regime, for example, the court always applies its own law. The approach is simple because the only factor that matters is: where is this court? And a strict lex fori regime is "strict" because it allows for no exception. The forum is the (only) triggering fact, and one need only apply the rule to that fact to determine what law applies.

Methodologies in quadrant B also embrace a simple inquiry, but are less prescriptive in their application. This approach might identify, say, two factors for judges to consider when determining what law applies, but would not describe which factor was more important. (*E.g.,* (1) place of plaintiff's injury; and (2) the location of the defendant.) When the factors point toward different laws, the exercise of judicial discretion, rather than the application of a formula, would determine which law applies. Discretion introduces flexibility.

To the extent that a jurisdiction identifies more factors (or more complexity) the jurisdiction shifts from the lower quadrants to the higher quadrants. A regime in quadrant C might identify numerous relevant factors that courts should consider—or may even authorize a judge also to consider unspecified factors. But like those methodologies that fall within quadrant B, judges would have flexibility to decide what law applies; the decision-making process is not preordained.

Finally, methodologies that fall in quadrant D are prescriptive yet involve more factors (or more complexity). An approach might, for example, list nine factors to be considered and require the judge to apply the law indicated by the majority of those factors. Or an approach might identify many factors but assign a hierarchy of significance to each of them.[2] These approaches seek the sophistication of multivariate analysis while retaining the virtues of a mechanical test.

Each of the four quadrants offers advantages and disadvantages as a methodological approach. Evaluate each quadrant relative to the others on each of the following values:

- ex ante predictability (for putative plaintiffs; for putative defendants)
- ex post fairness
- use of judicial resources (ex post certainty)
- legitimacy

With respect to choosing a methodology, which of these values is most important for determining the applicable law? (And which is least important?)

Each state or country has the authority to choose the methodology by which it determines what law will apply. These methodologies are the product of statutory and/or decisional law in each state. Although each state has its own unique set of choice-of-law principles, the various American approaches can be loosely grouped into seven basic types, each of which is represented with a column in the following table. We have already introduced the lex fori approach.[3] All of these types are explored in this course. The table captures the range of methodological approaches for torts (T) and contracts (C) cases, and the relative popularity of each approach. The approaches represented in the columns include: lex fori, traditional, interest analysis, center of gravity, Restatement Second, better law, and combined modern.

---

2   Imagine a test that assigned a weighted significance to variables. *E.g.,* (1) plaintiff's place of injury = 45%; (2) location of defendant = 35%; (3) forum state = 20%.

3   The two states listed are not *strict* lexi fori jurisdictions.

State	Lex Fori	Tradtl.	Int. A.	Ctr. of G.	Rest. 2d	Better L.	Comb. Mdn.
AL		T+C					
AK					T+C		
AZ					T+C		
AR				C		T	
CA			T				C
CO					T+C		
CT					T+C		
DE					T+C		
DC			T				C
FL		C			T		
GA		T+C					
HI							T+C
ID					T+C		
IL					T+C		
IN				T+C			
IA					T+C		
KS		T+C					
KY	T				C		
LA							T+C
ME					T+C		
MD		T+C					
MA							T+C
MI	T				C		
MN						T+C	
MS					T+C		
MO					T+C		
MT					T+C		
NE					T+C		
NV				C	T		
NH					C	T	
NJ					T		C
NM		T+C					
NY							T+C
NC		T		C			
ND				T			C
OH					T+C		
OK		C			T		
OR							T+C
PA				T+C			T+C
RI		C				T	
SC		T+C					
SD					T+C		

State	Lex Fori	Tradtl.	Int. A.	Ctr. of G.	Rest. 2d	Better L.	Comb. Mdn.
TN		C			T		
TX					T+C		
UT					T+C		
VT					T+C		
VA		T+C					
WA					T+C		
WV		T			C		
WI						T+C	
WY					T+C		
Total (52)	T 2 C 0	T 9 C 11	T 2 C 0	T 3 C 5	T 25 C 24	T 5 C 2	T 6 C 10

This table is reproduced from Symeon C. Symeonides, *Choice of Law in the American Courts in 2017: Thirty-First Annual Survey,* 66 Am. J. Comp. L. 1 (2018).

The above table is no substitute for research. Jurisdictions change their methodology, and tables become outdated. Tables of this sort also require generalizations that mask the uniqueness of each state's approach.[4] Finally, all discussions of "methodology" can inflate the role that methodology, in fact, plays in judicial decision-making.[5]

A range of approaches allows some plaintiffs (to wit: plaintiffs who could get personal jurisdiction over the defendant(s) in more than one state) to shop for a forum that offers the most favorable choice of law methodology. This kind of forum shopping could be minimized or even eliminated if all states followed the same choice-of-law methodology. Uniformity could be accomplished if all states voluntarily subscribed to one, predictable approach; yet that has not happened. Uniformity could also be accomplished by federal legislation nationalizing an approach that states would be obliged to follow;[6] however, Congress has declined to get involved.

---

4   The right-hand column of the table stands for the "Combined-Modern" approach Professor Symeonides assigns to this methodology those states that overtly, knowingly, and repeatedly combine more than one methodology. But as a practical matter, nearly every state could be assigned to that right-hand column; because all states have deployed, at least occasionally, some idiosyncratic combination of approaches. Again, do not take the data from this table (or any summary of a jurisdiction's choice of law methodology) too seriously. Notwithstanding the taxonomy, each state's approach is unique.

5   "[O]f all the factors that may affect the outcome of a conflicts case, the factor that is the most inconsequential is the choice-of-law methodology followed by the court." Symeon C. Symeonides, *Choice of Law in the American Courts in 1994: A View "from the Trenches,"* 43 Am. J. Comp. L. 1, 2 (1995).

6   On the constitutionality, practicality, and wisdom of federalizing choice of law, *see* Michael H. Gottesman, *Draining the Dismal Swamp: The Case for Federal Choice of Law Statutes,* 80 Geo. L.J. 1 (1991). *See also* Chapters 16 and 19.

Notice that forum-shopping for favorable choice-of-law rules is possible. The law that governs the parties' rights and responsibilities may differ if the methodology of State X leads to one result and the methodology of State Y leads to another. Hypothetically,

> Methodology X could provide: in tort cases, the law that governs the parties' rights and responsibilities shall be the state where the defendant's alleged wrongful conduct took place.

> Methodology Y could provide: in tort cases, the law that governs the parties' rights and responsibilities shall be the state where the plaintiff suffered injury.

Consider this simple hypothetical.

Hypothetical 3-1

> Rubenstein was injured while working in his garden in Lawrence, Kansas. The injury occurred when a rotary cultivating tool called a Garden Weasel broke, and a piece of metal struck Rubenstein in his eye.

> Rubenstein purchased the Garden Weasel over the internet from Garden Weasels, Inc., a company that is incorporated in and has its only place of business in the State of Maryland.

> You represent Rubenstein. Assume that the product liability laws of Maryland are much more generous than the product liability laws of Kansas. At this point you are considering only two possible forums for this action which alleges that the Garden Weasel was defectively designed: Kansas and Maryland. Your research reveals that Kansas follows a conflicts methodology that corresponds with approach "X" above (i.e., the law of the place of wrongful conduct). Maryland follows a conflicts methodology that corresponds with approach "Y" (i.e., the law of the place of injury). Based solely on this information, where would you file this action?

Of course there are reasons other than the applicable law that influence the decision to sue in one forum instead of another. But a forum's choice-of-law methodology can be a very important factor.

In Hypothetical 3-1, both approaches "X" and "Y" embraced simplicity and rigidity: their inquiries focused on a single fact (albeit a different triggering fact under each approach) and application of the rule was formulaic. Both approaches thus fell in Quadrant A mapped above. By complicating the relevant inputs and/or by tapping into judicial discretion, jurisdictions could instead move into one of the other three quadrants of that grid. For example, consider the following:

> Methodology X provides: in tort cases, the court shall consider the residence of the parties, the place of injury, and the place of wrongful conduct to determine which state's law defines the parties' rights and responsibilities.

> Methodology Y provides: in tort cases, the law that governs the parties' rights and responsibilities shall be the state where the plaintiff suffered injury, unless some other state has a substantially more significant relationship, in which case that other state's law applies.

Now where would you file this case (as far as choice of law is concerned) if you represented Rubenstein in Hypothetical 3-1?

Some lawyers fail to shop for a more favorable choice of law methodology because they fail even to see that their case may involve a choice of law issue. Imagine a Kansas lawyer who is approached by a Kansan who was injured in an accident in Kansas. Especially if the lawyer is licensed to practice only in Kansas, the lawyer may never even consider filing in any state other than Kansas. But this hypothetical is simply Hypothetical 3-1 again—albeit before the lawyer started using her knowledge of conflicts to benefit her client. She would think more broadly about the facts: although the injury occurred in Kansas, what else might be relevant that happened elsewhere? What started as a narrative that involved only Kansas details begins to expand. This thought process, in turn, reveals new causes of action and additional defendants that leads one to broaden the factual inquiry even further. If the product was designed in another state, what does this mean for our defective design claim? If the defendant hired a company in Pennsylvania to manufacture this tool, should we add a defective manufacture claim? If we bring a claim for failure to warn, where did this warning not occur? (Maybe it was when/where the product was boxed; or when/where corporate decisions about product warnings were made; or when/where the box was opened?) Was this product damaged in shipment, and if so where might that have occurred? At this point we are considering only possibilities. We have not yet begun to consider applying the mechanics of actual methodologies. But you should already appreciate that the presence of different methodologies creates an incentive to shop for a favorable methodology.

Although all stages of litigation occur in the shadow of a trial, most cases in fact settle. Accordingly, litigation strategy is often about positioning your client favorably for settlement. Settlement may occur before there has been any determination about what law applies. Understand, then, that if there is even a ten percent chance that, say, Maryland's law of punitive damages might apply (rather than Kansas's law which, let's assume, prohibits punitive damages under such circumstances), this will affect the parties' positions in settlement. The lawyer who never saw the possibility that Maryland law might apply squandered possible leverage in a settlement negotiation.

Neglecting to appreciate a subtle choice of law issue is foreseeable (maybe even likely) if someone has never taken this course. This is one reason that decades ago Conflict of Laws was a required course in many law schools. Even if Conflicts is now an elective course, transactions and occurrences are more likely than ever to transcend the boundaries of states and countries, thereby creating choice of law issues.

Yet there are also two trends that have made choice of law an increasing less relevant discipline over time. First, some state laws are preempted by federal law. For example, a claim that a jet ski was defectively designed might be preempted by the Federal Boat Safety Act. A claim against an employer based on terms of a labor contract might be preempted by the federal Labor Management Relations Act. Or a product liability claim against the manufacturer of a medical device might be preempted by the federal Medical Device Amendments Act. In these circumstances, differences among state laws can be irrelevant because the laws of both states are preempted by—rendered nugatory by—federal law.

Preemption occurs when (1) Congress enacts a law that explicitly preempts state law; (2) state law actually conflicts with federal law; or (3) federal law occupies a legislative field to such an extent that it is reasonable to conclude that Congress intended no role for state regulation. Preemption creates a uniform body of federal law that renders irrelevant differences among state laws. However, in the areas of traditional state regulation there is a presumption against preemption; absent clear Congressional intent to the contrary, the federal law operates alongside state law. This course is not about federal preemption; you will learn about that in your Federal Courts course. Our study of Conflict of Laws is simply revealing the significance of that doctrine.

Second, the spread of model laws minimizes the potential for differences among state laws. The National Conference of Commissioners on Uniform States Laws, for example, was formed in 1892 upon the recommendation of the American Bar Association for the purpose of promoting "uniformity in state laws on all subjects where uniformity is deemed desirable and practicable." The Uniform Commercial Code, The Uniform Probate Code, and The Uniform Fraudulent Transfer Act are examples of model laws that have been adopted by a substantial majority of states. The very purpose of these uniform laws is to eliminate (or at least minimize) differences among state laws.

At the international level, harmonization efforts are ubiquitous. International private commercial actors such as the International Chamber of Commerce and the International Institute for the Unification of Private Law (UNIDROIT) are especially active in arbitration, banking, commercial, insurance, intellectual property, securities, taxation, telecommunications, and transportation sectors.

The assimilating effect of model legislation should not be overstated, however. The versions of these laws that are actually enacted by the states (or by the United States, as the case may be) are rarely uniform, and even when the text is uniform, the case law interpreting these laws often introduces variance.

Quick Summary

- Choice of law approaches vary from state to state (and country to country)

- The six basic methodologies prevalent in the United States are lex fori, traditional, interest analysis, center of gravity, the Second Restatement, and better law

- The lex fori approach to choice of law was introduced in Chapter 2; the other methodologies are introduced in Chapters 4–8

- When different states would have personal jurisdiction over the defendant, litigators may shop for a favorable choice of law methodology

4

The Traditional Approach

Key Concepts

- Jurisdiction-selecting facts determine the applicable substantive law
- This approach (like several other approaches) requires the characterization of claims

---

In this Chapter we study an approach that is variously called the traditional, the territorial, and the *lex loci* method. In the United States, it is also the approach that is described in the First Restatement of the Conflict of Laws in 1934 (after 11 years of drafting). And because the principal behind the First Restatement was a law professor named Joseph Henry Beale, this approach is sometimes referred to as Bealean.

Whatever its label, this approach (1) features rules, rather than standards; and (2) anoints certain facts as dispositive to the choice-of-law inquiry. This approach dominated choice of law jurisprudence for the last half of the nineteenth and the first half of the twentieth century. Understanding the traditional approach is important in two different respects. First, it is an approach that many states follow; contemporary practitioners need to master it. Second, for other states, it was an approach that they once followed but have since abandoned; for these jurisdictions, the traditional approach is historically significant.

Hypothetical 4-1

Carroll was a brakeman for the Alabama Great Southern Railroad Co. (Great Southern). Both Carroll and Great Southern were located in Alabama, and they entered into an employment contract in Alabama, which is also where Carroll reported to work each day.

Carroll worked on a Great Southern freight train that ran regularly from Chattanooga, Tennessee, across the state of Alabama, to Meridian, Mississippi. Both Chattanooga and Meridian are cities that are just outside the state boundaries of Alabama—with the former outside the northeast corner of Alabama, and the other outside the southwest corner of Alabama.

One fateful day, a defective link that joined two railroad cars broke, eventually causing an accident that injured Carroll while he was doing his job on the train in Mississippi. Although the accident did not occur until the train was in Mississippi, the railroad car with the defective link was added to the train while the train was still in Alabama. The accident happened because one of Carroll's co-workers, in Alabama, negligently failed to properly inspect the link (in Alabama).

Workplace accidents raise a number of questions about whether and when an employer can be sued, what must be proven by the injured employee in order to recover, and what types of damages are recoverable. There may also be questions about whether or when an employer like Great Southern is liable to Carroll for the negligence of some other employee. The answers to these questions vary from state to state, including differences between Alabama and Mississippi. To which state's laws should we turn for answers to questions like these once Carroll sues the railroad?

One question that we need to begin thinking about is whether the *content* of the competing laws should influence the choice of what law applies? For example, the content of the competing laws may lead to different outcomes. So, for the purpose of determining whether Alabama or Mississippi law applies, *should* it matter that Carroll would be able to recover under one state's law, whereas under the other, he would as a practical matter have no recourse? The competing laws also likely have different histories, and may reflect different policy intentions; *should* any of that be relevant to the choice of determining which of the two applies?

The traditional approach provides a negative answer to all of the questions in the previous paragraph. The traditional approach is described as *jurisdiction*-selecting, which is to say that the content, wisdom, history, and consequences of the rules are irrelevant. Rather than a contest between *rules,* the choice of law question, according to the traditional method, is a contest between jurisdictions. Put another way, we will determine which jurisdiction will have its laws applied even before we know exactly which of that jurisdiction's laws apply (and what those laws prescribe).

The traditional method is a rules-based approach that favors *certainty* over flexibility. It is also a *simple* approach because it determines what jurisdiction's law applies based primarily on one fact. The dispositive triggering fact varies depending on the nature of the plaintiff's claim. The various rules include the following:

For tort cases, *lex loci delicti* (the law of the place of the wrong)

For contract cases, *lex loci contractus* (the law of the place of contracting)

For property cases, *lex loci rei sitae* (the law where the property is located)

For cases challenging the validity of marriage, *lex loci celebrationis* (the law where the marriage was celebrated)

Return to Hypothetical 4-1. If the plaintiff files in any jurisdiction that follows the traditional approach (whether that jurisdiction is Mississippi, Alabama, or Maine), that court would focus on the appropriate jurisdiction-selecting rule to determine the applicable law. Assuming that this is a torts case, that court would apply the *lex loci delicti*—the law of the place of the tort. In one sense, the place of the tort would seem to be the place where the defendant allegedly committed the wrong. (The negligent act occurred in Alabama.) Yet that is not how the methodology is applied. Instead, the focus is on the place where the last event necessary to create the defendant's liability occurred. Ordinarily, that last event would be the injury to the plaintiff. (Carroll did not have a cause of action until he was injured.) For this reason, *lex loci delicti* is often referred to as the place of injury rule (*lex loci injuriae*). A court following the traditional approach in Hypothetical 4-1 would thus apply the substantive tort law of Mississippi.[1] Mississippi law would answer those questions about who could be sued, under what circumstances, for which types of damages, and so forth.

The limitations of the traditional approach are obvious. What makes the place of injury a more important fact than, say, the place of alleged wrongful conduct (Alabama), the residence of the plaintiff (Alabama), the residence of the defendant (Alabama), the center of the parties' relationship (Alabama), or something else? Given the dominance of Alabama in these connections, would you have thought that Alabama law *should* apply?

The traditional method is designed to achieve certainty, predictability, and uniformity of result. Like a machine, you might imagine that **Tort=>Place of Injury=>Mississippi**. Are the values of certainty and predictability given too

---

1   The jurisdiction would apply its own *procedural* law, as we learned in Chapter 2. We will study the substance-procedure dichotomy in Chapter 10.

much weight in this case? The traditional approach surely does not presume that the place of injury is necessarily the most important fact in all tort cases. But what does it presume (about the place of injury, about jurisdiction-selecting rules)?

Hypothetical 4-2

Cora's Line, Inc. (Cora's) is an Iowa company owned and operated by an Iowa clothing designer who designs and sews apparel for patrons of dance academies in Des Moines, Iowa.

Yamamoto is a young dance enthusiast who lives with her family in Des Moines. At her local dance studio, she purchased a dance costume manufactured by Cora's. While competing at a contest in Little Rock, Arkansas, Yamamoto fell from a platform and was injured. Yamamoto and her parents have sued Cora's, alleging that the costume was defectively designed because it obstructed her vision when she was upside-down during her dance routine.

Under Iowa law, design defect claims require proof that the product was unreasonably dangerous as designed. Under Arkansas law, plaintiffs must prove that the product was not safe for its intended and reasonably foreseeable uses. (Even if the costume was not "unreasonably dangerous *as designed*," it might not have been safe for its foreseeable uses.) In other words, the Arkansas law gives this plaintiff some wiggle room to establish liability—and therefore some leverage in settlement.

Does the place of injury rule make sense? Should plaintiff be able to shop for Arkansas law by filing in a state that follows the traditional approach?

In fact, hypotheticals like 4-2 put such pressure on the place of injury rule that some jurisdictions following the traditional approach created a new rule for certain torts. For example, some jurisdictions assigned the place of wrongful conduct as the jurisdiction-selecting fact for defective design claims. In theory, of course, jurisdiction-selecting rules could be customized for every type of tort claim. What, for example, should be the triggering fact for a plaintiff who is libeled online by someone in another state? How about a plaintiff whose privacy is invaded by a hacker in another state?

Before considering the next hypothetical, think about what the triggering fact(s) should be for a contract dispute. Understand that if you want a rule (rather than a standard) you cannot have more than one triggering fact unless there is clarity about how to resolve circumstances where the multiple triggering facts point in different directions.

Hypothetical 4-3

Seleste Hamilton, a Californian, is a surfer who became famous at the age of 17 when she placed second at the Big Wave Invitational in Hawaii. Two days after excelling in that competition, and while still in Hawaii, she signed a three-year $500,000 endorsement deal with Wise, a popular brand of surfing apparel. The deal requires Hamilton to use/wear only Wise gear at all competitions and to appear at several Wise promotional events each year. Wise is incorporated and has its principal place of business in New York.

For the first 18 months of their relationship, Hamilton and Wise each performed their respective contractual responsibilities. In month 18, however, Hamilton won the World Surfing Championship. With this victory Hamilton has the potential to transcend her sport and to become a legitimate superstar. All of the major retailers in the ultra-competitive athletic apparel market are eager to sign her. Any of the deals would likely exceed ten million dollars. But she can't enter into a deal with any of these companies as long as she is under contract to wear/use only Wise gear.

Hamilton recently consulted a lawyer who advised her that the contract with Wise would be voidable under California law since she was only 17 when she signed it. Indeed, minors (those under the age of 18, in most states) lack the capacity to make a contract. Thus a minor who signs a contract can either enforce or (at any time) void the contract. However, in many states, including Hawaii, if the contract is to be voided, this must be done while the party is still a minor. Hamilton will be 19 years old in four months. Which state's law should apply?

Under the traditional approach the triggering fact in cases involving the validity of contracts is the place where the contract was made, to-wit: Hawaii.

Assume that this suit was filed in California, and that California follows the traditional approach. The court would apply Hawaiian substantive law. Is the fact that the contract was signed in Hawaii more important to the State of California than the fact that a contract signed by one of its residents, as a minor, is not voidable? That question may be important, but it is not a question that the traditional approach entertains. As we have seen, the traditional approach does not resolve a competition among *laws* (their policies, outcomes, etc.), but rather a competition among *jurisdictions*. The thinking here is that the place of contracting is the jurisdiction whose laws determine the rights and responsibilities of the parties.

The approach may be crude, but for its proponents it is also shrewd. In most cases applying the law of the place of contracting makes perfect sense; a methodology should focus on the typical case, not the atypical. The approach also has the virtue of eliminating forum-shopping. In every jurisdiction that follows the traditional approach, courts will apply the same substantive law—the law of the place of contracting in contract disputes, the place of injury in tort cases, etc. The First Restatement sought to curb the excesses of judicial discretion on choice of law issues that can undermine certainty, predictability, and uniformity.

In the eighteenth and nineteenth centuries, Friedrich Carl von Savigny described the goal of choice of law analysis as "discover[ing] for every legal relation that legal territory to which, in its proper nature, it belongs or is subject ."[2] Because of Savigny, the traditional approach is sometimes referred to as a *multilateral* approach: objective rules determine by neutral criteria which law applies. Under objective, mechanical rules, every jurisdiction following those rules would reach the same outcome (i.e., apply the same law).

The traditional approach embraces the qualities of simplicity and rigidity. But drafting unambiguous rules presents its own challenges. It is not always obvious, for example, where the place of contracting was. Imagine a variation of Hypothetical 4-3 where Hamilton left Hawaii with an unsigned contract. En route to another competition in Newport, Rhode Island, Hamilton signed the contract in the air over Colorado, and sent a pdf of the signed version to Wise as she changed planes at Chicago's O'Hare Airport. Wise's CEO acknowledged receipt of Hamilton's email in a reply from her home office in Greenwich, Connecticut. "Simple" rule schemes often require an auxiliary set of rules and fictions to resolve inevitable ambiguities. The place where the acceptance was sent is often presumed to be the place of contracting. This can resolve uncertainty, albeit at the expense of a coherent result; is there any reason that Colorado or Illinois or Connecticut contract law should govern the validity of this contract?

When the First Restatement codified the traditional approach it distinguished between disputes involving the *validity* of the contract and disputes about the *performance* of the contract. With respect to the latter, the place of performance (rather than the place of contracting) applied. Of course classifications like this invite controversy about whether the case belongs in one category or the other. This was not overlooked by the drafters of the First Restatement who warned: "[T]here is no logical line which separates questions of the obligation of the contract, which

---

2   Friedrich Carl von Savigny, A Treatise on the Conflict of Laws 133 (William Guthrie trans., 2d ed. 1880).

is determined by the law of the place of contracting, from questions of performance, determined by the law of the place of performance. . . ."[3]

Hypothetical 4-4

Plutonium Particles Co. (Plutonium) was sued after a toxic spill three years ago at its chemical plant in South Carolina caused its neighbor to suffer about $3.5 million in compensatory damages. In that South Carolina suit, which is ongoing, Plutonium also faces potential exposure to substantial punitive damages.

Plutonium is an insured under a liability policy issued to it by Dragmond Insurance Company (Dragmond) months prior to the spill. Dragmond does not contest its responsibility for any compensatory award that Plutonium may eventually be obliged to pay. However, the insurer denies any responsibility for punitive damages. The insurance contract indemnifies its insured for "damages," without distinguishing or mentioning liability for punitive damages.

Plutonium is a Nevada company with a principal place of business in Nevada. It has extraction and manufacturing facilities across the United States. Dragmond is a Texas company with a principal place of business in Arlington, Texas.

The contract law of Nevada prohibits insurance coverage for punitive damage awards. This public policy is premised on the notion that coverage for punitive damages awards transfers the burden from wrongdoers to innocent premium-paying customers of the insurer. Allowing for insurance coverage also undermines the deterrence effect of punitive damages.

Other jurisdictions are doubtful that the availability of insurance has any impact on the deterrent effect of punitive damages. And they are disinclined to allow insurers to avoid a risk that they contracted to assume. These states, including Texas and South Carolina, enforce insurance contracts as written, even if they include responsibility for the insured's punitive damages.

During the course of negotiating the insurance policy, Dragmond sent Plutonium a copy of its standard liability policy. Plutonium made some cosmetic changes and returned a signed copy with a check. The agreement never contained a choice of law clause because the parties could not agree upon which state's law would apply.

---

3   Restatement of Conflict of Laws § 358 (1934), Comment b.

In a jurisdiction that follows the traditional approach, which state's contract law determines the insurability of exposure to punitive damages?

Resolving the hypothetical requires, first, a characterization of the issue as involving an issue about the validity or the performance of the insurance contract. Second, in what state was the contract entered into or, alternatively, to be performed.

What if the contracts in Hypotheticals 4-3 or 4-4 contained choice-of-law clauses? For example, the parties might have agreed that "This agreement shall be governed, construed, and enforced in accordance with the laws of the State of *X*." Contemporary jurisdictions that follow the traditional method for contracts cases would typically enforce that choice of law clause. (See Chapter 9.) Historically, however, the traditional approach of the First Restatement was unmoved by choice-of-law clauses; the fundamental objection was that judicial enforcement of these clauses would give permission to the parties to do a legislative act; contracting parties could essentially make their own law.

The most intuitive of all of the traditional approaches involves the choice of law with respect to property claims. The triggering fact for claims involving immovable property is the location of that property. This is a good place to talk about the principle of territoriality. The thinking is that the territory where the property is located has the strongest claim to resolve disputes about that land. (Historically only the *forum rei sitae* had jurisdiction to try a case involving the title to land.) Although this reasoning may have less purchase in the context of tort or contract claims, this notion of territoriality helps explain why the laws of the state of the place of injury or the place of contracting have the strongest claim to determine the parties' rights and responsibilities.

This notion of territoriality is intertwined with the terminology of "vested rights," which is another vestige or hallmark of the traditional approach. The thinking here is that one state applies another state's laws because they are respecting a right that "vested" under the *lex loci*. The *lex loci* establishes the right because an act has legal significance only if the territorial jurisdiction where it occurred recognizes that act as something of legal consequence. If a legal right arises at the *lex loci*, this right vests in the injured party and she may enforce it not only at the locus but in the courts of other states and nations as well. In the language of vested rights, then, a forum state did not *apply another state's law* but rather *enforced rights and obligations created in the state where the injury occurred*. Some jurisdictions used the notion of vested rights to defend the traditional approach, while others used jurisdiction-selecting facts but without the philosophical commitment to vested rights.

Let us return to property claims in particular.

Hypothetical 4-5

A New York couple regularly spent weekends and summers at their second home in Massachusetts. Years later, the couple had marital problems and separated. Although there was much animosity between the two parties, the husband (Marvin) conveyed all of his interest in the Massachusetts home to the wife (Florence). The couple had physically separated, but divorce proceedings were never filed. The couple had a minor son (William).

Florence was later diagnosed with cancer. Concerned that, if she died, the Massachusetts house might somehow wind up in the hands of Marvin, Florence made a deal with her brother (Albert). Florence deeded the house to Albert for nominal consideration, and Albert orally promised her that he would, in turn, deed the house to William when William turned twenty-five years old.

Florence passed away. And now, nearly twenty years later, William has reached the age of twenty five. Albert refuses to deed the house to his nephew William. You represent William. A cursory review of your class notes from Property reminds you that the statute of frauds is likely to pose an obstacle to recovery on an action to enforce the oral promise. But you remember also from your Remedies course that some jurisdictions might view Albert's gain as unjust enrichment; of those jurisdictions, some might impose a constructive trust and order a transfer of title, while others might require Albert to pay restitution in the amount of the fair market value of the house. There may also be questions about whether the breach of a promise that Albert made to Florence can be enforced by William, who is only a third party beneficiary of that agreement.

Which state's law furnishes the answer to these questions? Marvin, Florence, William, and Albert are all New Yorkers. All of the pertinent conversations occurred in New York. Florence signed the deed in New York, and it was duly recorded in Massachusetts.

Under the traditional test for actions concerning title to property, the triggering fact is the location of the real property; the property laws of that jurisdiction would apply. In Latin, this is *lex loci rei sitae*. Accordingly, with respect to matters of property law, the law of Massachusetts would control in the above hypothetical. This simplicity, complexity, and predictability of this methodology comes at what cost?

Now consider movable (essentially what property law calls "personal") property. Should the same triggering fact—the location of the property—dictate the applicable law? Imagine that rather than disputing the ownership of a summer home, the parties in Hypothetical 4-5 disputed the ownership of a 1909–1911 T206 Honus Wager baseball card, which is worth at least $1 million. Unlike real property, the location of personal property is not fixed. Accordingly we need a supplementary set of rules to determine *when* the location of the (personal) property is relevant: in this hypothetical that might be where it was when Marvin transferred it to Florence, when Florence transferred it to Albert, when William turned 25, when Albert first refused to convey it to William, when William filed suit, or some other event. When drafting a rule to capture the appropriate event, we must also contemplate that the location of personal property may be unknown to one or even both of the parties; the baseball card, for example, might have been given temporarily and for safe-keeping to a collector or a gallery who might have it on display or in a secure vault in some geographic place that has no logical connection to these parties.

Personal property can also be nowhere or everywhere. Consider, for example, patents, trademarks, copyrights, and business methods. Or, where is a company's goodwill located? Computers store customer data, mailing lists, and research results; but where are these intangible assets located? If the location of these items of property is dispositive of the choice of law inquiry, again, a set of supplemental rules must prescribe how to resolve that inquiry.

The traditional test, then, features rules (supplemented by more rules) that prescribe a triggering fact for each type of substantive law problem. For torts cases, *lex loci delicti* emphasized the place of injury. For contracts cases, *lex loci contractus* emphasized the place of contracting. And for property cases, *lex loci rei sitae* emphasized the situs of the property.

The First Restatement also prescribed more or less rigid rules for other areas of substantive law. The validity of a marriage, for example, was usually determined by the law of the place of its formation—*lex loci celebrationis*. Another example is very important in the field of corporate law: the internal affairs of a corporation (which includes the rights and responsibilities of directors and officers, for example) is governed by the law of the state of incorporation You will see this again in Chapter 17.

The emphasis on a narrow set of triggering facts is both the strength and the weakness of this methodology. In many or most cases, the triggering fact is straightforward; and thus the applicable law is obvious. The traditional approach is often celebrated for achieving certainty, predictability, and uniformity, but this virtue is much more nuanced. Does the traditional approach achieve certainty and predict-ability *before* the key event (*ex ante*) and/or *after* the key event (*ex post*)? Answer that question separately for torts, contracts, and property cases. Which is more important—*ex ante* predictability or *ex post* certainty?

The certainty and predictability achieved by the traditional approach is also pre-mised on the divisibility of the jurisdiction-selecting rules. We observed in the contract hypotheticals the challenge of separating issues of *validity* from *perfor-mance* in contract law. Wherever there are overlaps with respect to categories, the stakes of the litigation will lead the parties to dispute in which category that case belongs. *Characterization* (or categorization) is a threshold matter that is hardly straightforward. For example,

> Hypothetical 4-1 involved an employee suing for an injury that occurred in the workplace. We discussed that case as a tort suit, but didn't the lawsuit arise out of his employment, *i.e.,* a contract?

> Hypothetical 4-2 involved the customer with the design defect claim against the designer of dancewear. We labelled that a tort suit, but couldn't this suit also be characterized as a breach of warranty claim?

> Hypothetical 4-3 involved the contract dispute between the surfer and her sponsor. We called this a contract claim, but what result if the company's behavior were instead characterized as fraud, *i.e.,* a tort?

> Hypothetical 4-4 involved the contract dispute between the insurer and its insured about the insurability of liability for punitive damages in tort. Moreover, this dispute involved insurance coverage of real property and was also about damage to real property.

> Hypothetical 4-5 exemplified the treatment of disputes about real property. But the key facts involved oral and written promises, *i.e.,* contracts.

These are the vagaries of characterization. Any choice of law methodology that we study in this course that relies on categories is vulnerable to strategic manipulation by able counsel.

These issues of characterization can create havoc for a rule-based system whose virtue is certainty and predictability. Certainty and predictability are undermined if characterization is a variable input. If one judge would label a Contracts matter what some other judge would label a Property matter, then issues about what law applies are uncertain (and thus litigable) until the judge makes that characterization. Of course a regime could also create rules to streamline this process—and even to remove uncertainty. Notice that the highly rule-based systems tend to require more and more rules.[4] Such a rule might establish a hierarchy of case-types; for example, if the hierarchy were established by the order Torts/Contracts/Property, then a case that is part-Torts and part-Contracts would always be treated as Torts. But how might such a rule be abused by parties?

Characterization is a "threshold" problem in the traditional approach because it must be resolved before we know which category of jurisdiction-selecting rule to consult. But that threshold problem has its own threshold problem: What law does one consult for the exercise of characterization? Whether a case is a Torts case or a Contracts case is not a category that exists in nature. Rather these are freighted words that can mean different things in different jurisdictions. One could resort to forum law for guidance about characterization, essentially treating the question as one of procedure. Or one could look to "general principles" to characterize the claim. These are the battle lines of a choice of law dispute. Of course once a claim is "properly" characterized, the appropriate law can then be consulted.

These issues (or, when you are a litigator, these *opportunities*) associated with characterization are relevant in every choice of law methodology that we study that involves characterization. To give you concrete guidance here about how courts handle these issues of characterization might be reassuring to you, but it would be misleading. Assume that every case is unique.

A problem similar to characterization arises when plaintiffs have multiple causes of action. For example, a plaintiff's complaint may include both tort and contract claims. In these circumstances a methodology *could* characterize the entire suit. If, say, the suit were predominantly a "tort" suit then the law of the place of injury would provide the law for the tort claims—and also for the ancillary contract claims.

But a methodology that relies upon characterization would not necessarily need to categorize a case as exclusively one type of case. Instead, if a particular case included both tort and contract causes of action, then the methodology could use the law of the place of injury to resolve the torts issues, and the law of the place of contracting (or performance) to resolve the contracts issues. This notion of applying different states' laws to different issues in one case is called **dépeçage,** a french word meaning "cutting up into many pieces." Depecage could mean that the law of Indiana would apply to one defendant while the law of Indonesia would apply

---

4   This is the phenomenon that creates the paradox where more rules can make a system look less rather than more complete.

to the other. Depecage could even mean that the law of New Mexico would apply to the plaintiff's claim yet the law of Vermont would apply to the defendant's counterclaims and defenses.

We will study depecage, which is available in all choice of law methodologies, in Chapter 15. Depecage can be problematic because the court applies a combination of laws that, as a set, do not appear in any jurisdiction. This approach runs counter to the idea that the corpus of laws in a particular jurisdiction is a coherent package. The combination of laws from multiple jurisdictions is often referred to as a synthetic hybrid that is half donkey half camel.

Remember from Chapter 2 that when we talk about one jurisdiction applying the law of another jurisdiction we are talking about the *substantive* law. The court will always apply the *procedural* law of the forum. (See also Chapter 10.) To the extent that depecage can be problematic, notice that there is an element of depecage in every conflicts case where the forum court is applying foreign substantive law with forum procedural law.

In order to classify the traditional method as a rule-based approach, its mechanics must be formulaic. The supposed virtues of a rigid rule are its predictability, certainty, uniformity, and ease of application. Yet the traditional method recognized that judges could depart from the use of *lex loci* in certain circumstances. Specifically, if the law to be applied was "against good morals or natural justice" or "offended public policy" of the forum, the court could refuse to apply the foreign law—and instead apply forum law. According to First Restatement § 612, "No action can be maintained upon a cause of action created in another state the enforcement of which is contrary to the strong public policy of the forum."

The virtue of such an escape hatch is that it allows the judge to incorporate policy concerns into the choice of law analysis—and preserve its own legitimacy and reputation. For example, should a court apply foreign law in a case involving a gambling debt if gambling is legal in the place of contracting but illegal in the forum? How about an extremely restrictive non-compete clause that is valid in the place of contracting but inconsistent with the policy of the forum? Or what if the forum has restricted recoveries in personal injury cases with legislation that caps damages and prohibits punitive awards, yet the place of injury is at the opposite extreme? In Chapter 11 we will revisit the "public policy exception" which, in some form or another, is part of all choice of methodologies. At this point in the course, you need know only that the traditional approach included such an "escape device." You learned of another escape device (of the traditional and all other choice of law approaches) in Chapter 2: choice of law is about applying foreign *substantive* law;

forum law applies to any issue that may be labeled *procedural*. (Is a cap on damages *procedural*? We revisit such issues in Chapter 10.) A third escape device is *renvoi*, which we will tackle in Chapter 12. One could also fairly characterize depecage and proof of foreign law as escape devices. (*See* Chapters 15 and 18, respectively.)

The traditional method was once applied in virtually all states, and is still applied in some states. (Revisit the table in Chapter 3.) Of course even states that follow the traditional method have each added their own gloss. In particular, contemporary states that follow the traditional approach in contracts cases are much more sanguine about enforcing choice-of-law clauses. You will study this in Chapter 9.

States that have clung to the traditional method have expressly rejected the alternative approaches that we will study in later chapters. Adherents to the traditional approach celebrate the method's stability, predictability, and ease of application. They describe the alternative approaches as confusing, unpredictable, manipulable, result-oriented, and incapable of providing guidance to the courts.[5] The traditional method is a good baseline to which each new choice-of-law method can be compared. States that have discarded the traditional for a "modern" approach are splintered among various alternatives. The traditional method was the last consensus choice. After studying all of the contemporary methods, we will consider whether the traditional approach may be poised to make a comeback.

Moreover, disputes about the applicable law in cross-border matters involving members of the European Union are resolved in a manner that resembles the traditional approach. For example, in tort cases (which, as "non-contractual obligations," are subject to a regulation (a binding E.U. measure) commonly referred to as "Rome II"), the law of the place of injury is the general rule. Specific rules also tailor outcomes for products liability, unfair competition, environmental claims, infringements of intellectual property rights, and some other torts. A different general rule governs, however, when the litigating parties are both from the same country; in these cases, the law of that country generally applies. The court departs from these general rules only where it is clear from all of the circumstances of the case that the tort is manifestly more connected with some other jurisdiction. Do you recall a hypothetical in which this was the case?

A separate European Regulation ("Rome I") deals with choice of law in contract cases. Rome I presumes that many contracts will include a choice of law clause, and most (but not all) of those expressions of party autonomy are enforced. When there is no (enforceable) choice of law clause, eight rules prescribe what law ap-

---

5   William M. Richman & David Riley, *The First Restatement of Conflict of Laws on the Twenty-Fifth Anniversary of Its Successor: Contemporary Practice in Traditional Courts*, 56 Md. L. Rev. 1196 (1997).

plies. For example, in a contract for the sale of goods, the law of the country where the seller has its habitual residence governs. A franchise agreement is governed by the law of the country where the franchisee has its habitual residence. As with torts, the Regulation departs from the general rules where it is clear from all the circumstances that the contract is manifestly more connected with some other jurisdiction.

FROM THE COURTS

RASKIN v. ALLISON

Court of Appeals of Kansas
30 Kan.App.2d 1240 (2002)

PADDOCK, SITTING JUDGE.

This is an interlocutory appeal by the plaintiffs from the partial summary judgment granted to defendants on a choice-of-law question. . . . We affirm.

The facts are brief and uncontroverted. Kaley Raskin and Jenna Turnbaugh, both minors, received personal injuries resulting from a collision of the water craft they occupied and a water craft operated by Chad Leathers in the ocean waters off Cabo San Lucas, Mexico.

Kaley's and Jenna's parents filed this action individually and as next friends to their minor daughters against Ken and Karen Allison individually and as guardians ad litem for their minor son and stepson, Chad Leathers. Plaintiffs' claims were framed on the theories of negligence and negligent entrustment. . . .

Kansas follows the rule that the law of the state where the tort occurred, *lex loci delicti,* should apply. *Ling v. Jan's Liquors,* 237 Kan. 629 (1985). Here, plaintiffs do not dispute the injuries were sustained in Mexican waters and that under the rule of *lex loci delicti*, Mexican law would normally control. However, plaintiffs argue the rule should not apply in this case because (1) all the parties are residents of Kansas, (2) Kansas has never invoked the rule in a case where a foreign country's law would apply, and (3) [applying Mexican law offends Kansas public policy].

Kansas residents

Plaintiffs argue that because all the parties are Kansas residents, Kansas has the greater interest in applying its substantive law; therefore, the case should be governed by Kansas law.

However, the Kansas Supreme Court has repeatedly applied the law of the place of the injury, even when all the parties were residents of Kansas. In each of those case, the law of the place of injury was less favorable to the plaintiffs than Kansas law.

For example, in *Kokenge v. Holthaus,* 165 Kan. 300 (1948), Kansas residents were traveling together in Iowa when an automobile accident occurred. The Kansas passenger sued the Kansas driver in a Kansas court. The Supreme Court held that because the accident happened in Iowa and the injuries were sustained there, the Iowa guest statute applied. Under that Iowa statute, the passenger was required to show reckless operation of the vehicle by the driver in order to recover. . . .

Because the Kansas Supreme Court has consistently applied the rule of *lex loci delicti* in tort cases, even when all parties are Kansas residents, plaintiffs' first argument fails.

Application to foreign countries

Plaintiffs also contend that because Kansas courts have never applied the *lex loci delicti* rule to apply the law of a foreign country, the rule should be rejected in this case. Plaintiffs are correct in asserting that neither of the Kansas appellate courts have applied the law of a foreign country in a tort case. This court, however, recently applied Canadian law in a contract case where the contract was made in Canada by applying the rule of *lex loci contractus. See Layne Christensen Co. v. Zurich Canada,* 30 Kan.App.2d 128 (2002).

Plaintiffs have not cited compelling authority that the rule of *lex loci delicti* does not apply in cases involving foreign countries. Kansas follows traditional choice of law principles largely reflected in the original Restatement of Conflict of Laws (1934). We have no hesitation in finding that the *lex loci delicti* rule would apply in tort cases notwithstanding the injuries were incurred in a foreign country. . . .

Public policy exception

[T]he thread that weaves through all of the plaintiff's arguments is that damage limitations purportedly contained in Mexico's laws are contrary to Kansas public policy and should not be enforced by Kansas courts. Plaintiffs seem to argue that public policy is defined by Kansas legislative enactments and since the Kansas Legislature had not enacted statutes with damages limitations similar to those in Mexico, Mexican laws are therefore contrary to Kansas public policy. Plaintiffs cite no authority establishing what damage limitations exist in Mexico. However, a recent case cited by defendants appeared to support the conclusion that Mexico recognizes that contributory negligence is a complete defense in a tort claim. *Spinozzi v. ITT Sheraton Corp.,* 174 F.3d 842, 844 (7th Cir. 1999). Also, Mexican law apparently limits recovery of damages in tort cases to the amount of the injured party's medical and rehabilitative expense and lost wages at the minimum wage rate. *See Hernandez v. Burger,* 102 Cal.App.3d 795, 799 (1980) (citing Civ. Code of the State of Baja California [Norte], art. 1793; Ley Federal del Trabajo, ars. 487, 491, and 495). Plaintiffs assert these damage limitations in their brief.

Kansas cases consistently hold that a Kansas court will not apply the law of another state to a claim if that other state's law is contrary to Kansas public policy. *See Safeco Ins. Co. of America v. Allen,* 262 Kan. 811, 822 (1997) (using *lex loci contractus* rule); *In re State of Troemper,* 160 Kan. 464, 469 (1945) (choice of law issue in probate case involving effect of divorce in Nebraska).

In *Brenner v. Oppenheimer & Co., Inc.,* 273 Kan. 525 (2002), . . . the Supreme Court held that a "strong public policy" is one "so thoroughly established as a state of public mind so united and so definite and fixed that its existence is not subject to any substantial doubt." . . . . The *Brenner* court found a strong public policy in the fact that the incorporation of New York law into the contract between a Kansas resident and a securities broker evaded Kansas' securities law prohibiting the sale of unregistered securities. . . .

The other Kansas cases refusing to apply the law of other states as required by traditional choice-of-law rules are *Dale v. Railroad Co.,* 57 Kan. 601 (1897) (refusing to apply New Mexico's penal statute); *Barbour v. Campbell,* 101 Kan. 616 (1917) (dismissing case seeking to enforce Idaho contract which violated Kansas' statute of frauds); *Peters v. Peters,* 177 Kan. 100, 106–07 (finding second wife was not a "legal widow" of decedent under Kansas law because remarriage occurred less than 6 months after Kansas divorce); and *Westerman v. Westerman,* 121 Kan. 501 (1926) (finding Missouri marriage contrary to Kansas public policy because marriage occurred less than 6 months after Kansas divorce).

None of these cases appear to set forth a public policy exception as broad as plaintiffs are arguing here. . . . The Supreme Court has repeatedly upheld the application of the law of other states in tort cases even when those laws impose a higher burden of proof on plaintiffs *before* they can recover damages. *See, e.g., Kokenge v. Holthaus,* 165 Kan. at 307 (applying Iowa guest statute which required a showing of reckless operation of the vehicle by the driver in order to recover); *Koster v. Matson,* 139 Kan. 124, 126–27 (1934) (Nebraska guest statute requiring gross negligence or intoxication applied in case between Kansas residents). The Supreme Court has even upheld the application of another State's wrongful death statute even though that statute excluded some types of damages allowed under Kansas law. *See McDaniel v. Sinn,* 194 Kan. at 625–26.

Thus, Kansas cases indicate the "public policy" exception in the choice-of-law context is limited and generally not triggered because of limitations on damages or higher burdens of proof.

Finally, plaintiffs cannot seriously contend that the application of Mexican law is unfair when they voluntarily vacationed there. As the Tenth Circuit once stated: "It is a firmly established principle of American jurisprudence that the laws of one state have no extra-territorial effect in another state. The forum state will give effect to foreign law as long as the foreign law is not repugnant to the moral sense of the community. The mere fact that the law of the foreign state differs from the law of the state in which recognition is sought is not enough to make the foreign law inapplicable. . . . Indeed, this Court is reminded of the oft-paraphrased advice of St. Ambrose, Catholic bishop of Milan in the fourth century, to St. Augustine, 'When you are at Rome, live in the Roman style; when you are elsewhere, live as they do elsewhere.' " *Brennan v. University of Kansas,* 451 F.2d 1287, 1289–90 (10th Cir. 1971). . . .

The trial court correctly determined that the substantive law of Mexico would govern the claims in this personal injury action.

COMMENTS AND QUESTIONS

1. The triggering fact under *lex loci delicti* is the place of injury, and these plaintiffs conceded that their injuries were sustained in Mexican waters. Is it relevant that that plaintiffs suffered (and continue to suffer) damages in Kansas?

2. Even a simple, rigid set of choice of law rules could include one more rule that, when the plaintiff and defendant are from the same jurisdiction, the rules of that shared jurisdiction apply (rather than the law of the place of injury, the law of the place of contracting, etc.). In fact, some jurisdictions have adopted such a rule for "common domiciliaries." The court says that Kansas has not adopted such a rule; what is the *reason*?

3. How difficult is it to find the applicable Mexican law with respect to negligent acts by minors, the liability of parents/guardians for the negligent acts of minors, possible affirmative defenses, limitations upon remedies, and any other Mexican legal doctrines that might be relevant? Try it. We will also address the difficulties of proving foreign law in Chapter 18.

4. Every time a court is faced with the application of some foreign law instead of its own law, the difference between the laws is the product of a contrary public policy. Accordingly, lest the exception swallow the rule, public policy exceptions require some heavy adjectives: for example, the foreign law must be *repugnant*, or must be contrary to *strong* public policy. Here the court concludes that the absence of limitations on damages in Kansas is not a strong public policy. Is that simply because there is no affirmative law on the subject? Would the absence of limitations on damages be a strong public policy if the Kansas legislature recently considered a bill to impose limitations and, after a thoughtful and purposeful session, rejected the bill? (Would the public policy be stronger or weaker if the vote count on such a bill was very close?) Again, we will revisit the public policy exception in Chapter 11.

5. Appreciate the dilemma of plaintiff's counsel when the defendant's motion for summary judgment is being argued. The core issue is whether the court will apply Mexican law. If Mexican law is so objectionable as to defeat Kansas's strong public policy, then the court won't apply Mexican law. Accordingly, it may be in the interest of plaintiff's counsel to put the

relevant particulars of Mexican law in their worst possible light. But what does plaintiff's counsel risk by doing that?

6. Is there a good explanation for why it is easier for courts to apply foreign law that denies or restricts plaintiffs' recoveries (*i.e.,* favors defendants) than to apply foreign law that creates or expands defendants' exposure to liability (*i.e.,* favors plaintiffs)? Revisit Hypothetical 2-8.

7. Plaintiffs may also have a claim against the Cabo rental company that rented the watercraft to the minor defendant. However, it is better strategy for plaintiff to pursue that claim separately. Because Mexican law most certainly applies to any claim against Cabo, joining that claim with the tort claims makes it even more likely that a court would also apply Mexican law to the tort claims against Allison. (Getting personal jurisdiction over the Cabo rental company in Kansas would also be difficult.)

8. Near the end of its opinion the court celebrates the "firmly established principle . . . that the laws of one state have no extra-territorial effect in another state." In light of the fact that a Kansas court is invoking Mexican law to resolve a dispute between Kansans, what exactly does *extra-territorial effect* mean?

9. The notion that "when in Rome" one should live like Romans suggests that one accepts the responsibilities of Roman law by visiting there. But it is surely a fiction that one would (or even could) investigate limitations of liability under Mexican law before vacationing there (or that ordinary citizens would know that Mexican law could apply to a Kansas law suit between Kansans). What should we do with legal fictions that are premised on such dubious reasoning?

BROWN v. KLEEN KUT MANUF. CO.

Supreme Court of Kansas
238 Kan. 642 (1986)

HERD, JUSTICE.

This is an action for strict liability in tort for the manufacture and sale of an allegedly defective product. This is an appeal from the district court's grant of summary judgment in favor of the appellees, Toledo Scale Corporation, Reliance Electric and Engineering Company, Reliance Electric Company, and Kleen Kut Manufacturing Company, defendants below.

The facts are not in dispute.

The accident giving rise to this action occurred in the summer of 1976. The appellant, who was sixteen years old at the time, was employed as a part-time cook in a restaurant located in Great Bend. On the evening of July 23, 1976, the appellant was directed to grind meat for hamburger. Although this task was not one of his regular duties, he began grinding meat using a meat grinder which bore the decal of Kleen Kut Manufacturing Company, Cleveland, Ohio, Model No. 5132A.

When the appellant attempted to push the meat into the auger, it caught his fingers and pulled his fingers and palm under the auger. His hand was so severely injured it required surgical amputation at the wrist.

Prior to December 15, 1955, Kleen Kut Manufacturing Company (Kleen Kut) operated a factory in Cleveland, Ohio, for the purpose of manufacturing food choppers, including Model No. 5132A meat grinders.

On December 15, 1955, Kleen Kut entered into an agreement with Toledo Scale Corporation (Toledo Scale) whereby Toledo Scale purchased Kleen Cut's assets for $405,650. Included in the assets were inventory, work-in-process, parts, components and raw materials relating to the manufacture and sale of food machines. Toledo Scale also acquired the exclusive right to the name "Kleen Kut" and agreed to enter into a two-year lease of the factory premises owned by Kleen Kut. [Toledo Scale also retained most of Kleen Kut's employees. Kleen Kut was dissolved on November 21, 1956.]

Toledo Scale continued to manufacture and sell parts for meat choppers previously manufactured by Kleen Kut and to manufacture and sell, under the name Toledo Scale Corporation, meat choppers and parts formerly manufactured and sold under the name Kleen Kut. Toledo Scale sold replacement parts for the Model No. 5132A Kleen Kut meat grinder; however, these parts were universal replacements and fit numerous grinder models.

Toledo Scale merged into Reliance Electric and Engineering Company on October 12, 1967, and Reliance Electric and Engineering Company merged into Reliance Electric Company on February 25, 1969.

Appellant filed the present action on July 17, 1978, against Kleen Kut, Toledo Scale, Reliance Electric and Engineering Company and Reliance Electric Company. On October 8, 1981, the district court granted Kleen Kut's motion to dismiss on the ground that appellant's action could not be maintained against an Ohio corporation on a cause of action filed twenty-two years after the date of [that company's] dissolution. On October 23, 1984, the court sustained the motion for summary judgment of Toledo Scale, Reliance Electric and Engineering Company and Reliance Electric Company on the ground that these corporations could not be held liable as successor corporations.

Prior to considering the substantive law relating to the corporate liability of both dissolved and successor corporations, we must first examine the conflict of laws question presented by this case.

The specific issue with which we are faced is whether the substantive law of Kansas or Ohio is applicable to the issue of the liability of either a dissolved predecessor corporation or its successor corporation for injuries resulting from a product manufactured by the predecessor. The appellant's injuries were sustained in Kansas. The machine, the use of which resulted in appellant's injuries, was manufactured in Ohio. The appellee corporations are all incorporated in the State of Ohio. Additionally, the transfer of assets from Kleen Kut to Toledo Scale was accomplished pursuant to a contract executed in Ohio.

The appellees argue that under the traditional rule of *lex loci delicti*, Kansas law is applicable. The appellant, however, argues the governing law is that of the jurisdiction where the transfer of assets between the predecessor and successor corporations took place.

We have traditionally applied the rule of *lex loci delicti* to choice of law for tort claims. *McDaniel v. Sinn,* 194 Kan. 625 (1965). Under this rule, the law of the state where the tort occurred is applied to the substantive rights of the parties.

We recently reaffirmed this rule in *Ling v. Jan's Liquors,* 237 Kan. 629 (1985). There, we held that, where injuries were sustained in Kansas as a result of a negligent act in another state, the liability of the defendant is to be determined by the laws of this state. . . .

Appellant here does not suggest we reject *lex loci delicti*. . . . Rather, appellant contends that, in an action against a dissolved manufacturing corporation and its successor, the law of the jurisdiction where the transfer of corporate stock and assets was made should govern, rather than the law of the place where the injuries occurred. In support of his contention, appellant cites *Bonee v. L & M Const. Chemicals,* 518 F. Supp. 375 (M.D. Tenn. 1981). There, a Tennessee plaintiff brought suit as administrator of the estate of Roy Bonee, who died from injuries he received when an oil drum exploded and severely burned him. The flammable construction sealer which exploded in the drum was manufactured by an Illinois corporation, which later transferred its assets to an Ohio corporation. The court noted that Tennessee follows the *lex loci delicti* rule and that under that rule the substantive law of the state in which the tort occurred governs. Rather than apply this rule, however, the court characterized the case as presenting a contract question— *i.e.,* what is the legal effect of the sale of the assets of one corporation to another corporation? 518 F Supp. at 379. Under Tennessee law, the rights of the parties to a contract are governed by the laws of the state in which the contract was entered into. Therefore, the Tennessee court determined that Ohio's substantive law was applicable.

The *Bonee* court stated [at pp. 379–80]:

> Because the basic question in this case is what is the legal effect of the sale of virtually all of the assets of one corporation to another corporation, under Tennessee conflicts rules the substantive law of Ohio applies. Although characterizing the case as contractual for the purpose of this issue and tortious for purposes of determining liability may seem disjointed. . . . One of the purposes of using choice-of-law rules is to ensure the uniform application of substantive law. The rights of a corporation that contracts in Ohio to purchase the assets of another corporation should be the

same with respect to assumption of liability for personal injuries regardless of where the personal injury occurs. For example, if the parties had specifically agreed that Dayton would assume liability for all injuries arising out of the use of BCS' product no one would dispute the characterization of the issue presently before the Court as contractual. The characterization should be no different simply because the parties did not expressly address the issue in their agreement." . . .

After examining the options, we are persuaded that the law of the jurisdiction where the corporation was formed, and where the transfer of corporate stock and assets took place, should govern the liability of a dissolved predecessor corporation and its successor corporation for injuries arising from use of a product manufactured by the dissolved predecessor corporation. Kansas tort law governs the nature of the cause of action available to the injured party, *i.e.,* strict liability.

Appellant first argues the trial court erred in granting summary judgment in favor of Kleen Kut. The trial court concluded that the filing of suit by appellant twenty-two years after the dissolution of a corporation is impermissible under Ohio law. . . .

In determining whether a dissolved corporation has the capacity to be sued, we look to the law of the state of incorporation. 26 Am.Jur.2d. Foreign Corporations § 446, p. 454. Thus, as previously held, we will consider Ohio law in determining whether appellant can maintain an action against Kleen Kut, a dissolved Ohio corporation. The applicable Ohio statute provides:

> (B) Any claim existing or action or proceeding pending by or against the corporation or which would have accrued against it may be prosecuted to judgment, with right of appeal as in other cases, but any proceeding, execution, or process, or the satisfaction or performance of any order, judgment, or decree, may be stayed as provided in section 1701.89 of the Revised Code.

Ohio Rev. Code Ann. § 1701.88(B) (Page 1985).

Ohio appellate courts have not considered this statute as it relates to the factual context at hand. . . . The trial court here . . . found that § 1701.88(B) extends a corporation's existence after dissolution only for a "reasonable" length of time. The trial court reasoned that such a finding is in line with the public policy of Ohio. Specifically, the trial court held:

> The public policy of Ohio is that continued corporate existence
> after dissolution exists as a concept for the purpose of facilitating
> corporate affairs and not for the purpose of providing relief for
> plaintiffs forever.

Thus, in the absence of any conflicting decision from Ohio appellate courts, we adopt the trial court's analysis and find that Ohio Rev. Code Ann. § 1701.88(B) (Page 1985) extends a corporation's existence after dissolution only for a reasonable period of time. In the instant case, appellant's claim was brought twenty-two years after Kleen Kut was legally dissolved. Such a claim was not within the scope of 1701.88(B) and the trial court properly granted Kleen Kut's motion for dismissal, styling it as a summary judgment.

Next, we must consider the issue of a successor corporation's liability for injuries resulting from the use of an allegedly defective product manufactured by its predecessor.

The trial court granted summary judgment in favor of appellees Toledo Scale Corporation, Reliance Electric and Engineering Company and Reliance Electric Company. The trial court ruled that under the traditional rule governing successor liability, the appellees were not liable to the appellant. As previously stated, Ohio law governs the issue of a successor corporation's liability for injuries arising from use of a product manufactured by its predecessor.

The general rule of successor liability is stated as follows:

> The general rule . . . is that where one company sells or otherwise
> transfers all its assets to another company, the latter is not liable
> for the debts and liabilities of the transferor. . . . An express agree-
> ment, or one that can be implied, to assume the other company's
> debts and obligations, is necessary; or the circumstances must
> warrant a finding that there was a consolidation or merger of the
> corporations, or that the transaction was fraudulent in fact, or that
> the purchasing company was a mere continuation of the selling
> company; the foregoing constitute two so-called exceptions to the
> general rule.

15 Fletcher, *Cyclopedia of the Law of Private Corporations* § 7122 (rev. perm. ed. 1983). . . .

This general rule was followed and applied by the Ohio Court of Appeals in *Burr v. South Bend Lathe, Inc.*, 18 Ohio App.3d 19 (1984). There, the plaintiff was injured by an allegedly defective and unreasonably dangerous mechanical press manufactured by Johnson Machine and Press Corporation. The defendant, South Bend Lathe, Inc., was a successor to Johnson Machine and continued to manufacture and sell "Johnson" brand machine presses. However, South Bend Lathe assumed no liability for products manufactured by its predecessor. . . .

The Ohio court held that South Bend and its predecessor dealt at arms [sic] length, there was no evidence of mixture of officers or stockholders and the two entities were separate and distinct. Additionally, the court noted that there was no evidence of inadequate consideration running from South Bend to its predecessor and South Bend assumed no liabilities of its predecessor. The court then concluded that all of these factors, particularly the absence of an agreement by South Bend to assume the liabilities of its predecessor, required a finding that South Bend was not liable for injuries caused by products placed in the stream of commerce by its predecessor.

The controlling facts in the present case are very similar to those in *Burr*. Here, there was an outright sale of assets from Kleen Kut to Toledo Scale, with no transfer or stock or continuity of ownership. Toledo Scale neither expressly nor impliedly assumed the liabilities of Kleen Kut. Moreover, there is no indication or allegation that the asset transfer was for less than adequate consideration.

While Toledo Scale continued to manufacture and sell meat grinders similar to the one which caused plaintiff's injuries, this factor alone is not determinative. Rather, following the Ohio court's analysis in *Burr*, the key factor in our determination must be the absence of an agreement by Toledo Scale to assume liability for products sold prior to its purchase of Kleen Kut's assets. Thus, we conclude that the appellees are not liable for injuries caused by products manufactured and sold by Kleen Kut, and the trial court properly granted summary judgment to the defendants.

We recognized that the application of the traditional rule of corporate successor non-liability sometimes leads to seemingly harsh results. Moreover, we are aware that a number of courts have attempted to deal with that harshness by relaxing or expanding existing exceptions to the general rule. *See Mozingo v. Correct Mfg. Corp.*, 752 F.2d 168 (5th Cir. 1985); *Cyr v. B.*

Offen & Co., Inc., 501 F.2d 1145 (1st Cir. 1974); *Polius v. Clark Equipment Co.*, 608 F. Supp. 1541, 1545–47 (D.V.I. 1985); *Bonee v. L & M Const. Chemicals*, 518 F. Supp. 375, 381; and *Rivers v. Stihl, Inc.*, 434 So.2d 766, 771–72 (Ala. 1983), for cases applying a "continuity of enterprise" theory. *See Ray v. Alad Corp.*, 19 Cal.3d 22 (1977); *Ramirez v. Amsted Indus. Inc.*, 86 N.J. 332 (1981); and *Daweiko v. Jorgenson Steel Co.*, 290 Pa. Super. 15 (1981), for cases applying the "product line" theory.

Our decision today is neither acceptance nor rejection of such exceptions since we are not applying Kansas law. The judgment is affirmed.

COMMENTS AND QUESTIONS

1. Imagine explaining to your client, the plaintiff Brown, that Ohio law rather than Kansas law determines his ability to recover for an injury that happened in Kansas. (What do you expect him to say? What will you say?)

2. The court's characterization of this as an (Ohio) "contract" case rather than a (Kansas) "tort" was not an inexorable conclusion. What was its authority for this characterization? Is that characterization more defensible with respect to the action against Kleen Kut or the action against the successor corporations?

3. With respect to the liability of successor corporations under Ohio law, the court relies on a traditional rule reflected in a decision of an Ohio intermediate appeals court. Since other jurisdictions are abandoning the traditional rule because of its "seemingly harsh results," could this Kansas court predict that the Ohio Supreme Court, if faced with the situation presented in the instant case, might also abandon the traditional rule for something more sympathetic to tort victims?

4. The quote from *Bonee* reveals one of the stock arguments in conflicts discourse: the rhetoric of uniformity. One of the most fundamental principles of justice is that similarly situated people should be treated similarly. Accordingly, it is often a compelling argument to position your client alongside other real or hypothetical litigants, and insist that they be treated uniformly. The quote from *Bonee* includes the following: "The rights

of a corporation that contracts in Ohio to purchase the assets of another corporation should be the same with respect to assumption of liability for personal injuries regardless of where the personal injury occurs." In other words, it would be unfair if a hypothetical Ohio company whose predecessor's product injured someone in Ohio *would not* be liable yet Reliance Electric Company, also an Ohio company, *would* be liable if its predecessor's product injured someone in Kansas. The two Ohio companies are similarly situated and should be treated uniformly.

But a paradox lurks in virtually all discussions of uniformity: there are many species of uniformity, and the pursuit of one type of uniformity invariably compromises another type of uniformity. For example, in *Kleen Kut*, the effort to treat similarly situated Ohio corporations similarly creates *dis*uniformity for similarly situated Kansas tort victims. As a litigator, allow your opponent to espouse the virtues of uniformity, but then argue that your species of uniformity is more important than theirs. Here, the argument would be that Kansas workers who are injured in Kansas by defectively-designed machines should be treated similarly by the law.

SAMPLE EXAM QUESTIONS

Question 4-6

You are a lawyer in Texas and one of your local clients manufactures a kit containing a small motor and battery pack that can invisibly transform any bicycle into an electronically-powered bicycle. The kit is designed to give enough power assistance to riders that folks who would not otherwise consider cycling will be induced to ride. As a practical matter, the kits have been more popular with experienced, including professional, cyclists rather than with novices. These experienced cyclists modify the kit by replacing the battery with a more powerful source that is available from other vendors.

The client brings you information about a new product liability law recently passed by the legislature in Wisconsin that will make it extraordinarily difficult for manufacturers to prevail in personal injury suits, even when the plaintiff uses the tool for something for which it was not intended. Your client has newspaper clippings containing stories about experienced cyclists who modified their kits and have been seriously injured in crashes caused by cycling at previously-unattainable speeds.

Your client has never manufactured or sold products in Wisconsin. The company's distributors and wholesalers have no present or former customers in Wisconsin. You are (appropriately) confident, then, that your client would not be subject to personal jurisdiction in Wisconsin. Is there any circumstance, then, under which Wisconsin tort law would prescribe the rights and responsibilities of your manufacturer-client?

Question 4-7

Wahlquist was severely injured when a tractor-trailer truck owned by Mt. Airy LLC ran a red light in South Brunswick, New Jersey and slammed into the side of Wahlquist's Tesla. An inspection by New Jersey State Police determined that the tractor's brakes failed.

Wahlquist filed a negligence action against Mt. Airy LLC, the driver Larsen, and Morton Service. Mt. Airy is a Maryland corporation with a principal place of business in Baltimore. Larsen is also a Marylander. Morton Service is a Maryland company that worked on the tractor's brakes (in Maryland) earlier on the day of the accident. Wahlquist sought both compensatory and punitive damages.

Under Maryland law, a plaintiff may be awarded punitive damages only upon a showing of actual malice. New Jersey law is more forgiving, allowing recovery if the defendant was grossly negligent.

What law will apply if Wahlquist files suit in a jurisdiction that follows the traditional approach? Does it matter where Wahlquist is domiciled?

Question 4-8

A factory in Windsor, Ontario (Canada) emits noxious fumes that are causing injury and damage to the people and property values of the factory's northern neighbors in Detroit, Michigan. A handful of the Detroit residents filed a lawsuit in Michigan against the factory, alleging nuisance. Nuisance is a tort that allows plaintiffs to redress harms that arise from the use of one's property. Is this a Torts or a Property problem? How would characterization affect the decision of what law is applied?

Question 4-9

Vega owns a luxury cabin on a lake in Michigan. Vega, until recently a longtime resident of Toledo, Ohio, used to vacation at her cabin regularly. A few months ago she retired to Arizona and now treats her Michigan cabin as a rental property.

Before Vega left Ohio, she talked extensively with her agent from Allco Insurance Co. (Allco) about insurance for the cabin. The amended insurance policy had a higher premium because the cabin was now an income-generating asset rather than just her vacation home.

Recently, while the property sat idle, vandals set fire to the property, causing $200,000 of damage. When Vega submitted her insurance claim, Allco denied coverage, citing an exception in the insurance agreement that disallowed coverage (and, in fact, cancelled the policy) if the property was vacant for a period in excess of 30 days. Insurers include clauses like this because a home is at much higher risk for damage when it sits empty.

Vega claims that she was misled by her insurance agent, as she never would have agreed to purchase a policy that included such an exception. But in any event, she also has records of rental payments that demonstrate conclusively that there has never been a gap of more than 20 days between renters. Under the circumstances, Vega finds Allco's denial of coverage inexplicable and indefensible. Most states have statutes that allow insureds to recover damages (and, sometimes, even treble damages) for an insurer's bad faith failure to pay insurance benefits.

In an Arizona court, Vega has filed a complaint that asserts claims using the language of both tort (for the insurer's bad faith) and contract (for breach of the insurance contract). And of course the root of the dispute involves real property.

On behalf of your client, the insurance company, you are preparing a motion to dismiss. If Arizona follows a traditional approach to choice of law problems, which state's laws define the available causes of action, the elements of those causes of action, the available affirmative defenses, and the available remedies?

Quick Summary

- In tort cases, courts adopting this approach generally apply the (substantive) law of the place of injury

- In contract cases, courts adopting this approach generally apply the (substantive) law of the place of contracting

- The situs of the jurisdiction-selecting fact (e.g., place of injury, place of contracting) may be contested

- The characterization of a claim (e.g., tort, contract) is a necessary part of the traditional approach but a particular characterization may be debatable

- Rigid systems invariably produce unintended results; such outcomes may be tolerated (as unfortunate mischief) or they may justify devices to escape from the rigidity (mollifying the situation at hand, but undermining the virtue of a rigid system)

5

Interest Analysis

Key Concepts

- Conflicting laws can be classified as false conflicts, true conflicts, or unprovided-for cases
- The domestic assumption constrains the scope of a government's interest

---

In the 1950s and early 1960s, Brainerd Currie authored a series of articles that launched a choice of law "revolution." Although commentators before him had exposed the limitations of the traditional approach, Currie's "governmental interests" test was not only a critique of the status quo, but an affirmative substitute. He was persuasive: interest analysis dominated the theory and practice of choice of law for several decades.

The table of approaches reprinted in Chapter 3 suggests that pure interest analysis is no longer a popular methodology and, in fact, is one of the least popular approaches. Yet it is essential that civil litigators master it—not because of its historical significance, but rather because of its contemporary relevance. Interest analysis has affected choice of law thinking in every jurisdiction and still lurks in every contemporary methodology.

Interest analysis embeds a strong preference for the application of lex fori. Currie believed that the job of the judge was to apply the law of the forum, except in the unusual case where a party could demonstrate that the forum had "no interest" in the application of its law.

Yet interest analysis is a more complicated methodology than either the traditional or lex fori approaches. To resolve choice of law questions using interest analysis, one must know not only the place of the forum, the place of injury, or the place of contracting, for example, but also the domiciles of the parties and much more. Further, unlike the lex fori and traditional approaches, the content of the competing laws is not an afterthought. Rather than a competition among jurisdictions (remember the traditional approach's *jurisdiction*-selecting rules), interest analysis resolves a competition among *laws*.

Currie envisioned a choice of law methodology that built upon an exercise of the kind of construction and interpretation that is undertaken in routine, purely domestic cases. The simplest of laws, for example, might prohibit vehicles in the park. Now, imagine that that mandate is silent on the question whether "vehicles" includes or excludes electric bicycles. In such circumstances we are familiar with the idea that some judge eventually will construe and interpret the prohibition to determine whether electric bicycles fall within or without the scope of the prohibition on vehicles.

Currie brought a similar interpretive approach to choice of law questions. When legal disputes transcend boundaries, these multi-state situations present questions about the scope of the respective mandates. You will recall the following fact pattern from Chapter 4:

> **Facts:** Carroll, an Alabama employee of an Alabama employer worked on a train that traveled daily from Tennessee through Alabama to Mississippi. One of Carroll's co-workers failed properly to couple two of the train cars at an Alabama way station. As the train reached its final destination in Mississippi, Carroll was seriously injured because the cars were not properly coupled.
>
> **Mississippi Law:** No employee may sue her/his employer for injuries arising out of a co-worker's negligence.
>
> **Alabama Law:** Any employee may sue her/his employer for injuries arising out of a co-worker's negligence.

Using an interpretive approach, the choice of law question asks whether the fact pattern falls within the scope of one, neither, or both of these mandates. Accordingly we ask: Does the scope of Mississippi's law include foreign employees and employers provided the injury happened in Mississippi? Does the scope of Alabama's law provide a remedy for local employees suing local employers even when the injury happened elsewhere?

The difficulty with this interpretive approach is that most state laws do not address multi-state situations. Legislatures usually write laws on the assumption that they will apply to "domestic" situations; after all, legislatures are responding to the needs of their constituents, who are, by definition, "domestic." " '[L]awgivers are accustomed to speak in terms of unqualified generality using words like 'all,' 'every,' 'no,' 'any' and 'whoever' because they ordinarily have given no thought to the phenomena that would suggest the need for qualification.' "[1] Unlike the exercise of interpreting the word *vehicle*, which is vague, words like *all* and *any* do not invite construction of their definitional parameters.

If one took this sort of unqualified generality at face value, it would seem that all laws were attempting to reach every litigant and every situation. By its terms, the Mississippi law purports to regulate a putative claim by an employee against her employer over a purely domestic action in, say, Oregon. Likewise, the Alabama law knows no bounds. Because our multistate situation falls within the scope of both Mississippi's and Alabama's laws, this interpretive approach is not helping us make the *choice* of law. (In fact, if Portugal's law is written with unqualified generality, should it be considered too?)

Of course we know that, regardless of their choice of words, Mississippi lawmakers have no intention of regulating the ability of an Alabama employee to recover against her/his Alabama employer over a workplace accident that took place in Alabama (*i.e.,* had nothing to do with Mississippi). Lawmakers are not trying to reach beyond their borders when they use sweeping language; rather they draft with sweeping language because it is as if nothing exists beyond their borders. In this sense, it is as if there is a silent geographic qualifier embedded into each state's legal mandate:

> **Mississippi Law:** No [Mississippi] employee may sue her/his [Mississippi] employer for [Mississippi] injuries arising out of a [Mississippi] co-worker's negligence.

> **Alabama Law:** Any [Alabama] employee may sue her/his [Alabama] employer for [Alabama] injuries arising out of a [Alabama] co-worker's negligence.

But this method of interpretation narrows the scope of a jurisdiction's law so severely that multi-state situations do not fall within the scope of either state's law. Surely, *some* law controls—lest all circumstances with a multi-state dimension fall outside the scope of every jurisdiction's laws. Absent anarchy, then, the court cannot grant or deny the plaintiff recovery without some body of law to determine the parties' rights and responsibilities.

---

1   Symeon C. Symeonides, *The Choice-of-Law Revolution Fifty Years after Currie: An End and a Beginning,* 2015 Ill. L. Rev. 1847, 1857 (quoting Currie).

Currie threaded the needle between the extremes of *always*[2] and *never*[3] recognizing conflicts. To avoid the *always*, Currie assumed that states, even when laws were drafted with unqualified generality, had a purely domestic interest ("the domestic assumption"). And to avoid the *never*, Currie assumed that in multi-state situations a state's laws could be applied (only) when that application benefited its own domiciliaries. After introducing the following hypothetical we will review the two steps of interest analysis. For hypothetical 5-1, the table would look something like this:

Hypothetical 5-1

Pinder is an Indiana domiciliary who was seriously injured in a workplace accident in neighboring Illinois. Pinder was injured when a lift that he was using to clean and repair streetlights tipped while he was inside it. The accident happened, at least in part, because Pinder had tools and supplies in the lift basket that significantly exceeded the allowable weight. The lift was manufactured by Keefe Co., an Indiana corporation with its principal place of business in Indianapolis.

Under Indiana law, misuse of the product bars recovery on a product liability claim. Under Illinois law, misuse merely reduces a plaintiff's award.

Pinder consulted a lawyer in his hometown, and that lawyer filed an action against Keefe Co. in an Indiana court. Assume that Indiana follows interest analysis.

Begin interest analysis by identifying the involved jurisdictions.[4] An *involved* state is not a key term, but it is very important not to confuse an involved state with an *interested* state, which is a term of art. A state is involved if any litigant is domiciled there or if any conceivably-important event occurred there; at this initial stage we are simply trying to get a comprehensive list of all of the jurisdictions whose law *might* apply. In Hypothetical 5-1, the only states mentioned in the fact pattern are Indiana and Illinois. Those are our involved states.

---

2   The *always* position refers to those statutes that seem to have no geographic limit. (*E.g.,* Any employee who . . . .)

3   The *never* position refers to the interpretation of statutes that presumes geographic limitations. (*E.g.,* Any [Ohio] employee who, while working for her or his [Ohio] employer, is injured [in Ohio] . . . .)

4   We are assuming that one of the parties urged the court to consider the application of something other than Indiana law. Currie did not expect the court to raise foreign law *sua sponte*.

In Practice

Beware of fact patterns with conspicuously absent facts. A party's domicile may go mentioned or the location of a key event may be unspecified. Absence of a detail does not make that missing fact irrelevant.

When applying interest analysis or any other choice of law methodology the construction of a table that charts the relevant facts and law can be helpful. Give every involved state its own column. The rows describe the relevant connections with the state. For Hypothetical 5-1, the table would look something like this:

	Indiana	Illinois
Facts	Forum Pinder (P) domiciled Lift manufactured Manufacturer incorporated and principal place of business	Plaintiff injured seriously in workplace accident on lift due to plaintiff's misuse
Law	Misuse of a product bars a product liability claim	Misuse of a product does not bar a product liability claim

Isolate the difference between the laws of the involved states. State the laws narrowly to bring the difference into relief.

Indiana: Misuse of a product bars a product liability claim

Illinois: Misuse of a product does not bar a product liability claim

Interest analysis focuses exclusively on where the respective laws *differ*. The many ways in which the laws are the same are irrelevant to this test.

Next, articulate the governmental policy(ies) behind each state's law—*i.e.,* why would the respective legislatures have passed these laws? Starting with Indiana, for example, ask: *Why* would Indiana bar plaintiffs who misuse a product from recovering on a product liability claim? You might find legislative history or case law helpful in answering the question, but you are not necessarily constrained by it. As you will later see, a lawyer's creativity at this stage can be rewarded. Remember that, at this stage of the analysis, it is not about the instant facts of the dispute; rather it is about the policy objectives that are reflected in the law. Also remember that your focus is on the choices that animate the difference between the laws of the involved states. (In other words, ignore the extent to which the Illinois and Indiana laws are the same.)

The policies behind the Indiana law might include: (i) safeguarding manufacturers' coffers from undeserving plaintiffs, (ii) discouraging people from endangering themselves or others by misusing products, or (iii) reducing frivolous litigation. But with each policy remember also Currie's assumption—central to interest analysis—that state policies have a purely domestic interest (*i.e.,* protecting or advancing the interests of its domiciliaries); hence the geographic qualifiers:

(i)   Safeguarding *Indiana* manufacturers' coffers;

(ii) Discouraging people from misusing products in *Indiana*;

(iii) Reducing frivolous litigation in *Indiana* courts;

Orthodox interest analysis includes this ruthlessly selfish and parochial perspective on lawmaking: lawmakers only enact laws to benefit their constituents.[5]

The next question is whether one or more of these policies would be advanced by the application of Indiana law in this case. That is to say,

(i)   Would Indiana law be safeguarding the assets of an *Indiana* manufacturer?

(ii) Was someone misusing a product in *Indiana*?

(iii) Are *Indiana* courts burdened by this litigation?

---

5   Interest analysis has long been—and still is—criticized for this depiction of policy-making that fails to account for altruism and ambition of legislators. But the domestic assumption is not a theory of policy-making. Rather it is an essential if artificial and crude assumption to limit the scope of a state's interest in order to facilitate a choice-of-law methodology.

An affirmative answer to any one or more of these questions means that the state is *interested.* That is a term of art. An interested state is a state whose laws embed policies that would be advanced by the application of that law in this case.

Indiana is an interested state because the defendant is an Indiana manufacturer. In other words, the answer to the question "Would the policy underlying the Indiana law safeguarding the assets of an Indiana manufacturer be advanced by the application of the Indiana law in this case?" is yes. (It is *also* an interested state because this case is pending in an Indiana court: Indiana courts would be burdened by this litigation.) The fact that the answer to the second question is negative (because the misuse occurred in Illinois) is immaterial; a state is interested because at least one policy would be advanced by the application of its law.

Although the application of Indiana law benefits one of its domiciliaries (the defendant manufacturer) it disadvantages another (the plaintiff). The detriment to a domestic plaintiff does not change the analysis. The issue, rather, is whether application of the law advances the policy for an intended (domestic) domiciliary. Here, it plainly benefits the Indiana manufacturer as intended. Application of Indiana law also benefits the Indiana *courts*, although that is surplusage since we need only one of its policies to be advanced in order to conclude that a state is *interested.*

Turn now to Illinois to see whether it, too, is an interested state. *Why* would Illinois allow plaintiffs who misuse a product to recover on a product liability claim? The most obvious policy behind the Illinois law is to ensure maximum compensation for persons injured by defective products. But remember Currie's assumption that state policies have a purely domestic interest. Hence, for purposes of interest analysis, this policy is:

> Ensuring that *Illinois* personal injury victims are fully compensated.

And in the next step of the analysis we would ask:

> Would Illinois law, if applied here, be ensuring the compensation of an *Illinois* personal injury victim?

Because the plaintiff, Pinder, is from Indiana, not Illinois, we could not (yet) conclude that Illinois is an interested state.

If only one state is *interested* (here, let us say that only Indiana is interested) then we have what interest analysis labels a **false conflict**. A court that follows interest analysis would apply the law of the only interested state. The notion of a false conflict is interest analysis's most enduring contribution to conflict of laws theory.

But before we label Hypothetical 5-1 a false conflict, you might feel uneasy about whether Illinois is or is not an interested state. After all, what exactly does it mean to ask whether a state like Illinois has an *interest*? Importantly, it does not mean a rooting interest. There may be many individuals in Illinois (plaintiffs' lawyers and safety advocates, for example) who are rooting for Pinder in his suit against Keefe, but this does not count in interest analysis. Interest analysis requires a policy to benefit its domiciliaries, and also an application that will in fact benefit the intended domiciliary.

Because the injury happened in Illinois, one might fairly presume that that state has some policy that discourages dangerous conduct that threatens the safety of Illinoisans. To be sure, Illinois domiciliaries would benefit if Illinois is a safe place to live and work. But the difference between the Indiana and Illinois laws is not really about safety. Revisit the mandates:

> **Indiana:** Misuse of a product bars a product liability claim

> **Illinois:** Misuse of a product does not bar a product liability claim

Illinoisans are no less safe under a regime where product liability plaintiffs cannot recover when they misuse a product. Put another way, the difference between these laws is not about trying to get more safety than Indiana. Rather, the difference is about ensuring that plaintiffs are fully compensated. That concern might be, for example, that plaintiffs who are not fully compensated wind up homeless, on disability, or on welfare; rather than having these individuals become wards of the state, Illinois would want them to be compensated by the manufacturers of the products that injured them. However, notice that Pinder, an Indianan, is not at risk of winding up homeless, on disability, or on welfare in *Illinois*. This is another way of appreciating that Illinois's policy interest would not be advanced by the application of its law on these facts.

It can be difficult to frame (and, in some circumstances, difficult to limit) the policies behind a law. Notice that a state's policy might be reflected through *inaction*: The difference between the policies of two states might be that one state has done something affirmative while the other has stood pat. Here, for example, Illinois has not curbed recovery of product liability plaintiffs as Indiana has. It is this not-acting, then, that constitutes Illinois's law, and the justification(s) for not acting are its policy. Especially when the policy is inaction, you may not find a statement of this policy agenda in legislative history or case law. But you can still state the policy reasons behind a law. Again: as you will soon see, creativity will be rewarded.

Although additional terminology is unnecessary, interest analysis differentiates *conduct-regulating* from *loss-allocating* (or "loss distributing") policies in tort cases. The distinction roughly tracks the twin aims of torts: deterrence and compensation, respectively. Conduct-regulating policies are about changing behavior—the rules of the road. The creation of a cause of action for tortious interference with contractual relations, for example, is passed to *prevent injuries from occurring*.

Loss-allocating policies, on the other hand, are about changing the consequences of a tort. The Illinois policy that allows plaintiffs to recover on product liability claims, even when they misuse a product, is not intended to incentivize the misuse of products; rather it is a rule about allocating damages once a tort has occurred. The distinction is controversial because in many circumstances an argument can be made that a policy is both loss-allocating and conduct-regulating. In any event, the place of injury is important when the policy is conduct-regulating because policies are directed to preventing conduct there; if the conduct occurred in that state, then that state's conduct-regulating policy should create an interest. When a policy is loss-allocating, the place of injury is often irrelevant.

In 1963, New York's highest court was the first to abandon the traditional method and to follow Currie, the scholar. In *Babcock v. Jackson*,[6] the court held that a New York auto passenger could recover from a New York driver under New York law even though the place of injury (and the place of wrongful conduct) was Ontario, Canada. Under Ontario law a "guest statute" barred a passenger from recovering on a negligence claim against his or her driver. Under New York law, the passenger could recover. The traditional approach would have focused exclusively on the law of the place of injury. But under interest analysis, Ontario had no *interest* in the outcome of a dispute between a New York passenger and her New York driver.[7] This was not about safety and was not about regulating conduct; this was a loss-allocating rule. The apparent conflict between the two laws was therefore, on examination, false.

Hypothetical 5-1 illustrates a false conflict because the State of Indiana has an interest that would be advanced by the application of its laws while the State of Illinois has no interest. Naturally, when there is a false conflict, the court should

---

6   191 N.E. 2d 279 (N.Y. 1963).

7   According to the New York court, the policy behind Ontario's guest statute was to prevent the fraudulent assertion of claims by passengers, in collusion with the drivers, against *Ontario* insurance companies. Because this case did not involve an Ontario insurance company, the application of Ontario law would not benefit an intended Ontario domiciliary. Accordingly, Ontario was not an interested state.

     New York did not have a guest statute. Instead, to ensure compensation for injured New Yorkers, passengers may sue negligent drivers. Because the driver and passenger were New Yorkers, New York was interested. And because New York was the only interested state, this case presented a false conflict.

apply the law of the only interested state. A false conflict is one of three possibilities contemplated by interest analysis. The next hypothetical introduces the second possibility.

Hypothetical 5-2

In a previous lawsuit, the music company JRX INC (JRX) sued the music group The Special Pleaders for breach of an exclusive recording contract. The Special Pleaders recorded only 2 of the 7 albums contemplated in the recording contract before negotiating a deal with another music company. JRX sued members of the band in a New York court. JRX is a New York company with a principal place of business in New York. The Special Pleaders is a band from Wabash, Indiana that performs nationwide. Also named as a defendant in this New York suit was the band's legal counsel, Rocky Callaskey, Esq., from Los Angeles, California. JRX sued Callaskey for fraud, but all of the claims against Callaskey were voluntarily dismissed nine months after filing. Litigation by JRX against the band members continued until summary judgment was granted in favor of the defendants about a year later.

Callaskey has now filed a suit of his own against JRX for malicious prosecution. That suit is pending in Los Angeles, and JRX has moved for summary judgment.

Callaskey has prima facie evidence of a claim for malicious prosecution under California law, namely that JRX (1) commenced a civil proceeding, (2) with malice, (3) without probable cause, and (4) that proceeding terminated in Callaskey's favor.

But JRX claims that summary judgment is appropriate because New York law applies, and New York law adds a fifth element to malicious prosecution claims. New York follows the "English rule" which requires that a plaintiff alleging malicious prosecution show interference with person or property, for example, by way of some remedy such as attachment or injunction. JRX didn't seek and the New York court didn't grant any equitable relief in the prior litigation Accordingly, Callaskey has no evidence of such interference; but he rejects the contention that New York law applies.

If California follows interest analysis, which law should it apply? The laws in question provide in relevant part:

California: Interference (with person or property) is not an essential element of a malicious prosecution claim

New York: Interference (with person or property) is an essential element of a malicious prosecution claim

What might be the possible policies underlying the respective state laws? (Why would one state require interference (with person or property) to sustain this cause of action but not the other state?)

One policy justification for California's approach is to make it more likely that persons who are victims of maliciously prosecuted claims will recover. Even if there was no injunction or no attachment, a maliciously prosecuted suit is still an inconvenience that California wishes to deter. But of course with Currie's domestic assumption, the policy is to ensure that *Californians* who are victims of maliciously prosecuted claims are more likely to recover. Here that policy would be advanced because the application of California law would benefit a California victim: Callaskey. Therefore, California is an interested state.

New York law denies recovery on malicious prosecution claims absent interference to person or property. The policies here could be: (1) to protect defendants from overly-litigious plaintiffs who were maliciously prosecuted (in an earlier action) but who suffered no real interference/harm; or (2) to rid the courts of claims unworthy of the courts' time. New York has an interest in having its laws apply if either (1) application of New York law on these facts would protect a *New York* defendant or (2) application of New York law on these facts would rid a *New York* court of litigation. Here the application of New York law would benefit JRX, a New York domiciliary. Therefore, New York is also an interested state.

When more than one state is interested, we have a **true conflict**. As conceived by its founder Brainerd Currie, interest analysis resolves true conflicts with an approach that is as unsatisfying as it is simple: apply forum law.

The application of forum law is a default position derived from the proposition that

TERMINOLOGY

Unfortunately, many contemporary judges use the terms **"false conflict"** and **"true conflict"** in a different sense than is described in the text. Sometimes the parties are arguing about whether, say, Rhode Island or South Dakota law applies, but it is not clear why they are arguing. If the pertinent laws of both states are identical, then it should not matter which law applies. Occasionally judges and others will refer to this situation as a false conflict. And similarly, after surveying two laws and finding a meaningful difference (e.g., Illinois allows product liability plaintiffs to recover even when they misuse a product, while Indiana does not), judges will occasionally refer to this as a true conflict. But this is not interest analysis, and this usage of these terms should be avoided.

courts either cannot or should not weigh governmental interests. Currie thought that the weighing of interests was a "political function of a very high order . . . that should not be committed to courts in a democracy."[8] Currie worried about the embarrassment and constitutional propriety of a judge nullifying the interests of its own sovereign on the ground that those of another state were weightier.

Interest analysis was popular and, in fact, was eventually adopted by the vast majority of states. But the solution to resolve true conflicts with forum law made interest analysis seem parochial and less-sophisticated. In disputes involving true conflicts, forum-shopping was rewarded. And in disputes involving what appeared at first blush to be false conflicts, parties could be rewarded with forum law by creatively finding some interest, however dubious, to convert a false conflict into a true conflict. For example, in Hypothetical 5-1 maybe Illinois's approach is, at least in part, a conduct-regulating rule that is about safety. Maybe manufacturers are so frequently able to avoid liability because it is so easy to prove that a customer misused the product that a non-bar is the only mechanism to deter manufacturers from selling defective products. Persuade the judge that this law was motivated, at least in part, by policy concerns about preventing *Illinois* accidents, and *voilà*, you have converted a *false* conflict into a *true* conflict.

Hypothetical 5-3

Peto Sagan, a Virginian, died while participating in a 300-mile, 4-day bicycle ride to raise funds for charity. His estate filed a negligence and wrongful death in Virginia against the Diabetes Charities Association (DCA), which sponsored and organized the bike ride, and the University of Virginia Medical System Corporation (UVMS), which provided the medical services in dispute. DCA is a Virginia corporation with a principal place of business in Arlington, VA, that operates runs and rides throughout the U.S. to raise funds for diabetes cures. Participants collect pledges and DCA handles logistics, including: finding corporate sponsors, selecting and securing the route, and arranging for services, including, as here, arranging for the UVMS to provide medical assistance to participants during the event.

Sagan died while participating in the fifth annual Washington D.C. DiabetesRide. This event had over 1,600 bicycle riders, beginning in Raleigh, North Carolina, crossing through Virginia, and ending on the National Mall in Washington, D.C.

---

8   Brainerd Currie, Selected Essays on the Conflict of Laws 182 (1963).

Before commencing the DiabetesRide, DCA required all participants to read and sign an entry form that included a section titled "Waiver of Negligence & Complete Release of Liability." The form calls for the signatories to acknowledge that they are "aware that serious injuries occur during bicycle riding" and that they "may be seriously injured or killed as a result." Participants agree to release and hold harmless DCA, UVMS, and other partners who "through negligence, carelessness or any other cause, might otherwise be liable."

The 31-year-old Sagan, who had participated in the DiabetesRide the previous year, executed this entry form in the District of Columbia (where he also worked) and began the ride a few weeks later.

Late on the first day of the ride, while traveling through Virginia, Sagan went to a medical aid station set up for the riders and complained that he felt nauseated and dizzy. He was given intravenous fluids by the volunteers at the station, but his condition worsened and he began vomiting, then lost consciousness as his blood pressure dropped. He died hours later. Plaintiff's experts will testify that Sagan was overhydrated by the aid station volunteers, and that his death from global brain hypoxia was preventable.

In Virginia, the release signed by Sagan has no legal effect. Virginia unambiguously rejects pre-injury releases as prohibited by public policy and thus, these releases are void.

In the District of Columbia, this release is enforceable. After all, any rule limiting the ability of consenting individuals to contract freely prevents mutually beneficial exchanges.

If Virginia follows interest analysis, is the release enforceable?

The heavy bias toward forum law made interest analysis subject to many of the criticisms that plagued *lex fori* as an approach to disputes involving multistate contacts. As interest analysis evolved, courts and scholars (including Currie himself) experimented with alternative resolutions for true conflicts. The jurisdictions that follow interest analysis now use one or some combination of the following four techniques to resolve true conflicts:

(1) Apply forum law (per orthodox interest analysis)

(2) Use the traditional approach to break the tie (apply the law of the place of injury, place of contracting, etc.)

(3) Balance the competing interests and apply the weightier of the two

(4) Supplement interest analysis with additional rules.

The third technique runs afoul of orthodox interest analysis because it puts judges in the uncomfortable position of weighing the forum state's interests against some other state's interest. Yet some courts (again, with Professor Currie's blessing) have embraced the notion that, in some circumstances, a "more moderate and restrained interpretation" of the forum's interest could allow for the application of foreign law.[9] After all, occasionally the forum state's interest is trivial or relatively insignificant. If only the foreign state had a legitimate interest in applying its policy then the "apparent" conflict was actually "false." Similarly, the adoption of "comparative impairment analysis" allowed judges to resolve true conflicts by applying the law of the state whose interest would be more impaired if its law were not applied.[10] Naturally this exercise resembles (if not requires) a weighing of interests.

The only difference between the third and fourth techniques for resolving true conflicts regards the level of formality. The state of New York, for example, has overlaid its so-called "*Neumeier* rules" onto interest analysis.[11] To promote a greater degree of predictability and uniformity, the *Neumeier* Court formulated three rules that apply to loss allocation conflict issues: (1) When the injured person and the tortfeasor are domiciled in the same jurisdiction, the law of that jurisdiction applies. (2) When the place of injury is also where either the injured person or the tortfeasor resides, the law of that jurisdiction applies. (3) When the place of injury, the domicile of the injured person, and the domicile of the tortfeasor are all in different jurisdictions, the place of injury ordinarily applies, unless some other state has a greater interest.

All of this experimentation ultimately led, in turn, to the invention of new methodologies that we will study in subsequent chapters. Before we leave interest analysis, however, we must acknowledge the third possible outcome: that no state is interested. These are typically referred to as the **unprovided-for** or **no interest** cases. That is illustrated below.

---

9   *See, e.g., Bernkrant v. Fowler,* 55 Cal.2d 588, 594–95 (1961).

10 *See, e.g., Bernhard v. Harrah's Club,* 16 Cal. 3d 313, 320, cert. denied, 429 U.S. 859 (1976).

11 *See Neumeier v. Kuehner,* 286 N.E.2d 454, 457–58 (N.Y. 1972) (with respect to loss allocating rules, applying the law of a common domicile, using place of injury to resolve true conflicts, and preserving a general escape).

Hypothetical 5-4

Rodowski, a Rhode Islander, was killed in an automobile accident in Rhode Island. The accident was caused by the negligence of Samuels, who is from Connecticut. Rodowski's live-in partner, Ives, sued Samuels in a Connecticut court for loss of consortium.

Connecticut law allows cohabitating (yet unmarried) partners to sue for loss of consortium, whereas Rhode Island law allows only family members to sue.

If the Connecticut court follows interest analysis then what law should it apply?

Connecticut's policy is to allow cohabiting partners to sue for loss of consortium. But per the domestic assumption, this must be a *Connecticut* cohabitor plaintiff. Connecticut has an interest in having its law apply *if* the application of that law would benefit *its* domiciliaries. But application of that law here would instead benefit Ives, a Rhode Islander. Accordingly, Connecticut is not an interested state.

Rhode Island's policy limits consortium claims to family members. This limits the exposure of defendants to suits by collateral persons. Rhode Island has an interest in having its law apply *if* the application of that law would benefit *its* domiciliaries. But application of that law here would instead benefit the defendant Samuels, a Connecticut domiciliary. Thus Rhode Island is also a disinterested state. So, if neither state is interested, can Ives sue for loss of consortium or not? (Appreciate how not-answering the question is not an option.)

For some, the failure of interest analysis to resolve the unprovided-for cases called the whole methodology into question. (Shouldn't a methodological approach produce an answer for every case?) Currie again suggested that the court should apply forum law under these circumstances. Once more this is a default that cannot be justified with interest analysis, thereby diminishing some of the luster of interest analysis.

SUPERIOR COURT OF SACRAMENTO COUNTY v. HURTADO

Supreme Court of California
11 Cal.3d 574 (1974)

SULLIVAN, JUSTICE.

. . . Real parties in interest, the widow and children of Antonio Hurtado (hereafter plaintiffs) commenced against Manuel Hurtado and Jack Rexius (hereafter defendants) the underlying action for damages for wrongful death, arising out of an automobile accident occurring in Sacramento County on January 19, 1969. Plaintiffs' decedent was riding in an automobile owned and operated by his cousin, defendant Manuel Hurtado. Defendant Hurtado's vehicle, while being driven along a two-lane paved road, collided with a pickup truck, owned and operated by defendant Rexius, which was parked partially on the side of the road and partially on the pavement on which defendant Hurtado was driving. Upon impact, the truck in turn collided with an automobile parked in front of it, owned by Rexius and occupied his son. Decedent died as a result of the collision.

At all material times plaintiffs were, and now are residents and domiciliaries of the State of Zacatecas, Mexico. Decedent, at the time of the accident, was also a resident and domiciliary of the same place and was in California temporarily and only as a visitor. All three vehicles involved in the accident were registered in California; Manuel Hurtado, Jack Rexius and the latter's son were all residents of California. Both defendants denied liability.

Defendant Hurtado moved respondent court for a separate trial of the issue whether the measure of damages to be applied according to the law of California or the law of Mexico. The motion was granted and at the ensuing trial of this issue the court took judicial notice . . . of the relevant Mexican law prescribing a maximum limitation of damages for wrongful death.[1] As a result it was established that the maximum amount recoverable under

---

[1]   Section 1889 of the Civil Code of the State of Zacatecas, Mexico, provided that a decedent's survivors may receive a maximum of 25 pesos per day for a period of 730 days. This section expressly makes the Federal Labor Law (of Mexico) applicable in determining the amount of damages recoverable in wrongful death actions. Section 1890 of the Zacatecas Civil Code provides that the court may, in its discretion, award an additional amount, not to exceed one third of the first amount, as extra indemnity.

Mexican law would be 24,334 pesos or $1,946.72 at the applicable exchange rate of 12.5 pesos to the dollar. After submission of the issue on briefs, the trial court announced its intended decision . . . and filed a memorandum opinion, ruling in substance that it would apply a measure of damages in accordance with California law and not Mexican law. . . . [T]he facts have been stipulated to and are not in dispute. The sole issue is a question of law as to which measure of damages should be applied. . . .

In the landmark opinion authored by former Chief Justice Traynor for a unanimous court in *Reich v. Purcell* (1967) 67 Cal.2d 551 . . . , we renounced the prior rule, adhered to by courts for many years, that in tort actions the law of the place of the wrong was the applicable law in a California forum regardless of the issues before the court. We adopted in its place a rule requiring an analysis of the respective interests of the states involved (governmental interests approach) the objective of which is "to determine the law that most appropriately applies to the issue involved." *Reich v. Purcell, supra*, at p. 554. . . .

The fact that two states are involved does not in itself indicate that there is a "conflict of laws" or "choice of law" problem. There is obviously no problem where the laws of the two states are identical. . . . Here, however, the laws of California and Mexico are not identical. Mexico limits recovery by the survivors of the decedent in a wrongful death action to 24,334 pesos. . . . California provides that the heirs of the decedent are entitled to recover such sum, as under all the circumstances of the case, will be just compensation for the pecuniary loss which each heir has suffered by reason of the death of the decedent. . . .

Although the two potentially concerned states have different laws, there is still no problem in choosing the applicable rule of law where only one of the states has an interest in having its law applied. . . . When one of two states related to a case has a legitimate interest in the application of its law and policy and the other has none, there is no real problem; clearly the law of the interested state should be applied. . . .

The interest of a state in a tort rule limiting damages for wrongful death is to protect defendants from excessive financial burdens or exaggerated claims. . . . [A] state by enacting a limitation on damages is seeking to protect its residents from the imposition of these excessive financial burdens. . . . Since it is the plaintiffs and not the defendants who are the Mexican residents in this case, Mexico has no interest in applying its limitation of damages—Mexico has no defendant residents to protect and has no interest in denying full recovery to its residents injured by non-Mexican defendants. . . .

California as the forum should apply its own measure of damages for wrongful death, unless Mexico has an interest in having its measure of damages applied. Since, as we have previously explained, Mexico has no interest whatsoever in the application of its limitation of damages rule to the instant case, we conclude that the trial court correctly chose California law. . . .

Nevertheless, . . . we deem it advisable to consider the argument addressed by defendant to the interest of California in applying its measure of damages for wrongful death. . . .

The creation of wrongful death actions insofar as plaintiffs are concerned is directed toward compensating decedent's beneficiaries. California does not have this interest in applying its wrongful death statute here because plaintiffs are residents of Mexico. However, the creation of wrongful death actions is not concerned solely with plaintiffs. As to defendants the state interest in creating wrongful death actions is to deter conduct. . . .

It is manifest that one of the primary purposes of a state in creating a cause of action in the heirs for the wrongful death of the decedent is to deter the kind of conduct within its borders which wrongfully takes life. . . . It is also abundantly clear that a cause of action for wrongful death without any limitation as to the amount of recoverable damages strengthens the deterrent aspect of the civil sanction: the sting of unlimited recovery . . . more effectively penalize(s) the culpable defendant and deter(s) it and others similarly situated from such future conduct. Therefore when the defendant is a resident of California and the tortious conduct giving rise to the wrongful death action occurs here, California's deterrent policy of full compensation is clearly advanced by application of its own law. . . . California has a decided interest in applying its own law to California defendants who allegedly caused wrongful death within its borders. . . .

Because Mexico has no interest in applying its limitation of damages in wrongful death actions to nonresident defendants or in denying full recovery to its resident plaintiffs, the trial court both as the forum, and as an interested state, correctly looked to its own law. . . .

COMMENTS AND QUESTIONS

1. Is this a false conflict or an unprovided-for case? (Why?) Does it matter which it is?

2. Interest analysis prescribes forum law as the resolution for both true conflicts and unprovided-for cases, and the law of the interested state for false conflicts. Is that the same thing as saying, as this court does, that, "California as the forum should apply its own measure of damages for wrongful death, unless Mexico has an interest in having its measure of damages applied."?

3. Plaintiffs argued that California's unlimited damages law results in more deterrence, and that the policy would be undermined if California law were not applied. Imagine that you made this argument on behalf of plaintiffs, after which the judge said: "California drivers whose negligent conduct injures another Californian will be liable for unlimited damages under California law. Are you saying that applying Mexican law here in *Hurtado* would lead drivers in California to drive less diligently because they know that if they have an accident with a Mexican national they will not have as much liability? Are you serious?" What is your response?

4. The court does not address the categories of "loss allocating" versus "conduct regulating" rules. Which is at issue in this case? Would a discussion of these terms have aided or undermined the court's reasoning?

5. The court says that "Mexico has no interest whatsoever in the application of its limitation of damages rule to the instant case." A more creative defense lawyer might have articulated an interest. What would you have said? (What law would the court have applied, per interest analysis, *if* Mexico was an interested jurisdiction?)

BERNHARD v. HARRAH'S CLUB

Supreme Court of California
16 Cal.3d 313 (1976)

SULLIVAN, JUSTICE.

Plaintiff appeals from a judgment of dismissal entered upon an order sustaining without leave to amend the general demurrer of defendant Harrah's Club to plaintiff's first amended complaint.

Plaintiff's complaint, containing only one count, alleged in substance the following: Defendant Harrah's Club, a Nevada corporation, owned and operated gambling establishments in the State of Nevada in which intoxicating liquors were sold, furnished to the public and given away for consumption on the premises. Defendant advertised for and solicited in California the business of California residents at such establishments knowing and expecting that many California residents would use the public highways in going to and from defendant's drinking and gambling establishments.

On July 24, 1971, Fern and Philip Myers, in response to defendant's advertisements and solicitations, drove from their California residence to defendant's gambling and drinking club in Nevada, where they stayed until the early morning hours of July 25, 1971. During their stay, the Myers were served numerous alcoholic beverages by defendant's employees, progressively reaching a point of obvious intoxication rendering them incapable of safely driving a car. Nonetheless defendant continued to serve and furnish the Myers alcoholic beverages.

While still in this intoxicated state, the Myers drove their car back to California. Proceeding a northeasterly direction on Highway 49, near Nevada City, California, the Myers' car, driven negligently by a still intoxicated Fern Myers, drifted across the center line into the lane of oncoming traffic and collided head-on with plaintiff Richard A. Bernhard, a resident of California, who was then driving his motorcycle along said highway. As a result of the collision plaintiff suffered severe injuries. Defendant's sale and furnishing of alcoholic beverages to the Myers, who were intoxicated to the point of being unable to drive safely, was negligent and was the proximate cause of the plaintiff's injuries in the ensuing automobile accident in California for which plaintiff prayed $100,000 in damages.

Defendant filed a general demurrer to the first amended complaint. In essence it was grounded on the following contentions: that Nevada law denies recovery against a tavern keeper by a third person for injuries proximately caused by the former by selling or furnishing alcoholic beverages to an intoxicated patron who inflicts the injuries on the latter; that Nevada law governed since the alleged tort was committed by defendant in Nevada; and that section 25602 of the California Business and Professions Code which established the duty necessary for liability under our decision in *Vesely v. Sager* (1971) 5 Cal.3d 153, was inapplicable to a Nevada tavern. The trial court sustained the demurrer without leave to amend and entered a judgment of dismissal. This appeal followed.

We face a problem in the choice of law governing a tort action. As we have made clear on other occasions, we no longer adhere to the rule that the law of the place of the wrong is applicable in a California forum regardless of the issues before the court. *Hurtado v. Superior Court* (1974) 11 Cal.3d 574, 579. . . . Rather we have adopted in its place a rule requiring an analysis of the respective interests of the states involved—the objective of which is "to determine the law that most appropriately applies to the issue involved." *Hurtado, supra,* 11 Cal.3d at pp. 579–80. . . .

The issue involved in the case at bench is the civil liability of defendant tavern keeper to plaintiff, a third person, for injuries allegedly caused by the former by selling and furnishing alcoholic beverages in Nevada to intoxicated patrons who subsequently injured plaintiff in California. . . .

We observe at the start that the laws of the two states—California and Nevada—applicable to the issue involved are not identical. California imposes liability on tavern keepers in this state for conduct such as here alleged. In *Vesely v. Sager, supra,* 5 Cal.3d at 166, this court rejected the contention that

> civil liability for tavern keepers should be left to future legislative action. . . . First, liability has been denied in cases such as the one before us solely because of the judicially created rule that the furnishing of alcoholic beverages is not the proximate cause of injuries resulting from intoxication. As demonstrated *supra* this rule is patently unsound and totally inconsistent with the principles of proximate cause established in other areas of negligence law. . . .

Second, the Legislature has expressed its intention in this area with the adoption of Evidence Code section 669, and Business and Professions Code section 25602. . . . It is clear that Business and Professions Code section 25602 (making it a misdemeanor to sell to an obviously intoxicated person) is a statute to which this presumption (of negligence, Evidence Code section 669) applies and that the policy expressed in the statute is to promote the safety of the people of California. . . .

Nevada on the other hand refuses to impose such liability. In *Hamm v. Carson City Nuggett, Inc.* (1969) 85 N.W. 99, the court held it would create neither common law liability nor liability based on the criminal statute banning sale of alcoholic beverages to a person who is drunk, because "if civil liability is to be imposed; it should be accomplished by legislative act after appropriate surveys, hearings, and investigations to ascertain the need for it and the expected consequences to follow." It is noteworthy that in *Hamm* the Nevada court in relying on the common law rule denying liability cited our decision in *Cole v. Rush* (1955) 45 Cal.2d 345, later overruled by us in *Vesely* to the extent that it was inconsistent with that decision.

Although California and Nevada, the two involved states . . . have different laws governing the issue presented in the case at bench, we encounter a problem in selecting the applicable rule of law only if both states have an interest in having their respective laws applied. "[G]enerally speaking the forum will apply its own rule of decision unless a party litigant timely invokes the law of a foreign state. In such event he must demonstrate that the latter rule of decision will further the interest of the foreign state and therefore that it is an appropriate one for the forum to apply to the case before it." *Hurtado, supra*, 11 Cal.3d at p. 581.

Defendant contends that Nevada has a definite interest in having its rule of decision applied in this case in order to protect its resident tavern keepers like defendant from being subjected to a civil liability which Nevada has not imposed either by legislative enactment or decisional law. It is urged that in *Hamm v. Carson City Nuggett, supra*, the Supreme Court of Nevada clearly delineated the policy underlying denial of civil liability of tavern keepers who sell to obviously intoxicated patrons:

> Those opposed to extending liability point out that to hold otherwise would subject the tavern owner to ruinous exposure every time he poured a drink and would multiply litigation endlessly in

a claim-conscious society. Every liquor vendor visited by the patron who became intoxicated would be a likely defendant in a subsequent litigation flowing from the patron's wrongful conduct. . . . Judicial restraint is a worthwhile practice when the proposed new doctrine may have implications far beyond the perception of the court asked to declare it. They urge that if civil liability is to be imposed, it should be accomplished by legislative act after appropriate surveys, hearings, and investigations. . . . We prefer this point of view.

Accordingly defendant argues that the Nevada rule of decision is the appropriate one for the forum to apply.

Plaintiff on the other hand points out that California also has an interest in applying its own rule of decision to the case at bench. California imposes on tavern keepers civil liability to third parties injured by persons to whom the tavern keeper has sold alcoholic beverages when they are obviously intoxicated "for the purpose of protecting members of the general public from injuries to person and damage to property resulting from the excessive use of intoxicating liquor." *Vesely v. Sager, supra*, 5 Cal.3d at 165. California, it is urged, has a special interest in affording this protection to all California residents injured in California.

Thus since the case at bench involves a California resident (plaintiff) injured in this state by intoxicated drivers and a Nevada resident tavern keeper (defendant) which served alcoholic beverages to them in Nevada, it is clear that each state has an interest in the application of its respective law of liability and nonliability. It goes without saying that these interests conflict. Therefore, unlike *Reich v. Purcell, supra*, and *Hurtado, supra*, where we were faced with "false conflicts," in the instant case for the first time since applying a governmental interest analysis as a choice of law doctrine in *Reich*, we are confronted with a "true" conflicts case. We must therefore determine the appropriate rule of decision in a controversy where each of the states involved has a legitimate but conflicting interest in applying its own law in respect to the civil liability of tavern keepers.

The search for the proper resolution of a true conflicts case, while proceeding within orthodox parameters of governmental interest analysis, has generated much scholarly examination and discussion. . . . The father of the governmental interest approach, . . . Professor Brainerd Currie, originally took the position that in a true conflicts situation the law of the forum should always be applied. CURRIE, SELECTED ESSAYS ON CONFLICTS OF LAWS (1963) p. 184. However, upon further reflection, Currie suggested that when under the governmental interest approach a preliminary analysis reveals an apparent conflict of interest upon the forum's assertion of its own rule of decision, the forum should reexamine its policy to determine if a more restrained interpretation of it is more appropriate.

> To assert a conflict between the interests of the forum and the foreign state is a serious matter; the mere fact that a suggested broad conception of a local interest will conflict with that of a foreign state is a sound reason why the conception should be reexamined, with a view to a more moderate and restrained interpretation both of the policy and of the circumstances in which it must be applied to effectuate the forum's legitimate purpose. . . . An analysis of this kind . . . was brilliantly performed by Justice Traynor in *Bernkrant v. Fowler* (1961), 55 Cal.2d 588.

Currie, *The Disinterested Third State* (1963) 28 LAW & CONTEMP. PROB., pp. 754, 757. . . . This process of reexamination requires identification of a "real interest as opposed to a hypothetical interest" on the part of the forum . . . and can be approached under principles of "comparative impairment." Baxter, *Choice of Law and the Federal System* (1963) 16 STAN. L. REV. 1, 1–22. . . .

Once this preliminary analysis has identified a true conflict of the governmental interests involved as applied to the parties under the particular circumstances of the case, the "comparative impairment" approach to the resolution of such conflict seeks to determine which state's interest would be more impaired if its policy were subordinated to the policy of the other state. This analysis proceeds on the principle that true conflicts should be resolved by applying the law of the state whose interest would be the more impaired if its law were not applied. Exponents of this process of analysis emphasize that it is very different from a weighing process.

> The court does not "weigh" the conflicting governmental interests in the sense of determining which conflicting law manifested the "better" or the "worthier" social policy on the specific issue. An attempted balancing of conflicting state policies in that sense . . . is difficult to justify in the context of a federal system in which, within constitutional limits, states are empowered to mold their

policies as they wish. . . . [The process] can accurately be described
as . . . accommodation of conflicting state policies, as a problem
of allocating domains of law-making power in multi-state contexts—limitations on the reach of state policies as distinguished
from evaluating the wisdom of those policies. . . . [E]mphasis is
placed on the appropriate scope of conflicting state policies rather
than on the quality of those policies. . . .

Horowitz, *The Law of Choice of Law in California—A Restatement* (1974) 21
U.C.L.A. L. Rev. 719, 753. . . . However, the true function of this methodology can probably be appreciated only casuistically in its application to
an endless variety of choice of law problems. . . .

Mindful of the above principles governing our choice of law, we proceed to
reexamine the California policy underlying the imposition of civil liability
upon tavern keepers. At its broadest limits this policy would afford protection to all persons injured in California by intoxicated persons who have
been sold or furnished alcoholic beverages while intoxicated regardless of
where such beverages were sold or furnished. Such a broad policy would
naturally embrace situations where the intoxicated actor had been provided
with liquor by out-of-state tavern keepers. Although the State of Nevada
does not impose such *civil* liability on its tavern keepers, nevertheless they
are subject to *criminal* penalties under a state making it unlawful to sell
or give intoxicating liquor to any person who is drunk or known to be an
habitual drunkard. *See* Nev. Rev. Stats. 202.100. . . .

> We need not, and accordingly do not here determine the outer
> limits to which California's policy should be extended, for it ap-
> pears clear to us that it must encompass defendant, who as alleged
> in the complaint, "advertis[es] for and otherwise solicit[s] in Cali-
> fornia the business of California residents at defendant Harrah's
> Club Nevada drinking and gambling establishments, knowing and
> expecting said California residents, in response to said advertising
> and solicitation, to use the public highways of the State of Califor-
> nia in going to and coming from defendant Harrah's Club Nevada
> drinking and gambling establishments." Defendant by the course
> of its chosen commercial practice has put itself at the heart of Cali-
> fornia's regulatory interest, namely to prevent tavern keepers from
> selling alcoholic beverages to obviously intoxicated persons who
> are likely to act in California in the intoxicated state. It seems clear

that California cannot reasonably effectuate its policy if it does not extend its regulation to include out-of-state tavern keepers such as defendant who regularly and purposely sell intoxicating beverages to California residents in places and under conditions in which it is reasonably certain these residents will return to California and act therein while still in an intoxicated state. California's interest would be very significantly impaired if its policy were not applied to defendant.

Since the act of selling alcoholic beverages to obviously intoxicated persons is already proscribed in Nevada, the application of California's rule of civil liability would not impose an entirely new duty requiring the ability to distinguish between California residents and other patrons. Rather the imposition of such liability involves an increased economic exposure, which, at least for businesses which actively solicit extensive California patronage, is a foreseeable and coverable business expense. Moreover, Nevada's interest in protecting its tavern keepers from civil liability of a boundless and unrestricted nature will not be significantly impaired when as in the instant case liability is imposed only on those tavern keepers who actively solicit California business. . . .

Therefore, upon reexamining the policy underlying California's rule of decision and giving such policy a more restrained interpretation for the purpose of this case pursuant to the principles of the law of choice of law discussed above, we conclude that California has an important and abiding interest in applying its rule of decision to the case at bench, that the policy of this state would be more significantly impaired if such rule were not applied and that the trial court erred in not applying California law. . . .

COMMENTS AND QUESTIONS

1. The court takes great pains to say that it is not weighing or balancing the conflicting state interests. Weighing and balancing are compelling metaphors because they vividly convey both the action to be undertaken and the terms of the disposition: weigh/balance the items and the heavier one wins. What is a metaphor that describes the court's approach—*i.e.,* their alternative to weighing and balancing?

2. The court's discussion of the defendant's contacts with California re-
    sembles a personal jurisdiction inquiry about a defendant's minimum
    contacts with the forum state. Is the court confused about the categories
    or transcending them?

3. In international law, the concept of "legislative jurisdiction" refers to the
    authority to regulate conduct (domestically and) abroad. Is that what
    the California court is doing here? *Should* California have jurisdiction to
    regulate the conduct of a Nevada casino?

4. The way that the court uses Nevada's criminal statute to reach its conclu-
    sion (to not apply Nevada law) is an excellent illustration of a stock ap-
    proach that you will want to master as a litigator: When two laws conflict
    and you want the law of State *X* to apply, argue that State *X*'s law, rather
    than being inconsistent with State *Y*'s policy, is an intensification of State
    Y's policy; you are doing State *Y*'s policy a favor by amplifying it! Here,
    Nevada has already criminalized serving alcohol to an intoxicated person,
    so applying California law is just adding consequence to something that
    Nevada is already trying to deter. The Court says that its imposition of
    California law on the Nevadan is not an "entirely new duty."

    Stock arguments usually have stock counter-arguments. Should Nevada
    be grateful that conduct that they have described as a misdemeanor will
    be further penalized?

    Also, the stock argument that the court uses to apply California law could
    instead be deployed as a justification to apply Nevada's law. What Califor-
    nia policy would be enhanced by the application of Nevada's law?

5. In a portion of the court's opinion that is not reprinted here, the court ob-
    serves that imposing the additional liability on Nevada tavern keepers who
    do substantial business in California is an expense that they can insure
    against. Is consideration of such practical consequences or workarounds
    laudable or irrelevant with respect to choosing the applicable law?

6. The court's mention of insurance conveys that Harrah's and other puta-
    tive defendants have alternatives to soften the impact of the application
    of California law. Does Bernhard have any alternative to suing a Nevada
    tavern keeper for injuries he sustained in a California motorcycle accident?

7. The court tells us that comparative impairment "can probably be appreciated only casuistically in its application to an endless variety of choice of law problems." Is Justice Sullivan (who also authored *Hurtado*) commending this methodology or apologizing for it?

8. In 1978 the California legislature granted immunity to purveyors of liquor by amending section 25602. The statute explicitly references the legislature's intention to abrogate the holding in *Bernhard*.

FROM THE COURTS

DOE v. ROE

U.S. District Court for the District of Columbia
841 F. Supp. 444 (D.D.C. 1994)

PRATT, DISTRICT JUDGE.

In this action, plaintiff seeks to recover for injuries allegedly resulting from the tortious communication of a sexually transmissible disease. Currently before us is defendant's motion for summary judgment under Fed. R. Civ. P. 56. This Court, sitting by diversity, is required to apply the choice of law rules of the District of Columbia. The sole issue for purposes of this motion is to determine which substantive law applies, *i.e.,* the law of the District of Columbia or that of Virginia. For the reasons given here, we apply the law of each jurisdiction to the events occurring within its respective territory.

I. Background

Plaintiff and defendant met on March 21, 1990, at a reception in the District of Columbia. At all times relevant to this litigation defendant Roe was a resident of the District of Columbia. Plaintiff Doe resides in Virginia, but was employed in the District of Columbia during 1990. The parties began a social relationship which developed romantically over the course of several contacts, the vast majority of which occurred in the District of Columbia.

On the night of April 26, 1990, the parties returned to plaintiff's home in Virginia after dinner in the District of Columbia. During the course of the evening, the parties engaged in sexual intercourse ("the Virginia encounter").

Complicating the legal scenario, on April 29th, the parties again engaged in sexual intercourse, this time at the Watergate Hotel in the District of Columbia ("the District encounter"). Two days later plaintiff Doe allegedly began to feel the pain associated with Herpes Simplex Type II ("herpes"), commonly known as genital herpes, and human papilloma virus, commonly known as genital warts. Because the incubation period for herpes is somewhere between two to ten days, it is difficult, if not impossible, to determine which encounter resulted in plaintiff's becoming infected.

Plaintiff's complaint alleges that defendant intentionally misrepresented to plaintiff that he was free from sexually transmitted diseases. She seeks relief under theories of negligence, fraud, intentional and negligent infliction of emotional distress, and battery.

II. Analysis

A. Standard of Review

Fed. R. Civ. P. 56(c) permits a court to grant summary judgment when the evidence in the record shows that "there is no genuine issue as to any material fact and that the moving party is entitled to a judgment as a matter of law." The moving party bears the burden of showing that there is no genuine issue of material fact or that the opposing party has failed to make a showing sufficient to establish the existence of an element essential to that party's case. *Celotex Corp. v. Catrett,* 477 U.S. 317, 322–23 (1986). . . .

B. Choice of Law Standard

This Court, sitting by diversity, must apply the choice of law rules of the District of Columbia. *GEICO v. Tetisoff,* 958 F.2d 1137, 1141 (D.C. Cir. 1992). The law of the forum is presumed to apply unless it is demonstrated that a foreign jurisdiction has a greater interest in the controversy than does the District. *Kaiser-Georgetown Community Health Plan v. Stutsman,* 491 A.2d 502 (D.C. 1985). . . .

C. Application of Governmental Interests Analysis

The choice of law question is central to this action because criminal statutes in both jurisdictions prohibit sexual intercourse between unmarried partners. *See* 22 D.C. Code § 1002 (fornication punishable by a fine of up to $300 and/or 6 months in jail); *see also* Va. Code § 18.2–344 (fornication punishable as Class 4 misdemeanor). Therefore, recovery is only possible [under laws] which allows damage awards for tort injuries incurred while committing a crime.

[In an earlier order in this case issued by Judge Boudin, who was elevated to the Court of Appeals while this suit was pending, this court] held that District law created an exception allowing recovery for a wrong resulting from an illegal act if plaintiff is less at fault than defendant. *See Doe v. Roe* Order filed September 23, 1991 (citing *Wagner v. Pro*, 575 F.2d 882, 885 (D.C. Cir. 1976)). While defendant contests Judge Boudin's holding, we assume his decision [is the law of the case] for purposes of this motion.

It is undisputed that recovery is barred under Virginia law. In *Zysk v. Zysk*, 239 Va. 32 (1990), the Virginia Supreme Court held that a plaintiff cannot recover damages for herpes infection when she consented to engage in an immoral or illegal act. This holding would apply to an injury caused by any tort, negligent or intentional. The *Zysk* Court concluded that

> when the consenting participant seeks monetary reward for harm resulting from the unlawful conduct, the public interest is protected sufficiently by criminal sanctions and does not require that the participant receive compensation. . . . [A] contrary rule would . . . encourage plaintiffs to engage in or permit illegal conduct.[8]

Therefore, plaintiff can recover only if District of Columbia law applies.

Plaintiff urges the Court to apply District law, noting that the relationship "was centered in—indeed, was almost entirely limited to—the District of Columbia." Plaintiff's opposition, p. 7. Defendant counters that Virginia has a compelling state interest in denying reward for injury resulting from illegal conduct within its borders.

Both parties err in attempting to apply one jurisdiction's law to what is essentially an injury resulting from at least one of two independent acts. Either sexual encounter may have caused plaintiff's injuries. In such a setting, a jurisdiction's interest in the case varies depending on where the alleged tort was committed. . . .

---

8 The Court believes this logic is flawed considering Virginia's apparent unwillingness to enforce section 18.2–344. *See Doe v. Duling*, 782 F.2d 1202, 1204 (4th Cir. 1986) (violators of fornication statute face "only the most theoretical threat of prosecution"). The *Zysk* holding, when combined with Virginia's failure to enforce the fornication statute, essentially immunizes from all possible liability those who consciously or unconsciously spread infectious and incurable disease. Concern over the spread of such disease is undoubtedly a pressing social concern it is own right. Nevertheless, we are bound by the Virginia Supreme Court's interpretation of local law.

While the Court of Appeals of the District of Columbia has renounced a *lex locus delicti* interpretation of choice of law, the place where the injury occurred always remains a factor to be considered under the governmental interests analysis. . . . If a jurisdiction's interest in a case is strongest when both the situs of the injury and the domicile of the plaintiff are within its territory, . . . then we believe the converse is also true, *i.e.,* other factors being equal, a state's interest is weakest when a foreign plaintiff suffers an injury outside the jurisdiction.

In such a context, the state's "significant interests" in the litigation must be substantial for its law to apply to both sexual encounters. In the case at bar, the interest of each jurisdiction in the extraterritorial application of its law is limited because both governments ban the conduct at issue. A jurisdiction has a diminished interest in its citizens being compensated in another state for engaging in conduct which it, at least theoretically, prohibits at home. Therefore, we discuss choice of law issues separately for each sexual encounter.

1. The Virginia Encounter

Plaintiff contends that the District has a compelling interest in holding its residents liable for the full extent of their negligence, even if the negligence occurs out of state. *See Kaiser-Georgetown Comm. Health Plan v. Stutsman*, 491 A.2d 502, 511–12 (D.C. Ct.App. 1985).[10] However, the District of Columbia's policy interest in allowing recovery for negligent acts is diminished when the conduct at issue is illegal in the District of Columbia. Consequently, the cases holding that the District has a special interest in protecting persons living elsewhere but working in the District of Columbia[11] do not apply to a situation involving illegal conduct. The District of Columbia has no articulable interest in the claim of a foreign plaintiff seeking relief for injuries arising from illegal sexual conduct occurring outside the borders of the District of Columbia.

---

10 Stutsman applied District of Columbia law in a medical malpractice case where plaintiff lived in Virginia and the injury also arose in Virginia, but defendant was a corporate resident of the District of Columbia.

11 *See, e.g., Dominion Caisson Corp. v. Clark,* 614 A.2d 529, 531–32 (D.C. Cir. 1992) (District has strong interest in deterring accidents protecting rights of employees in the District who live in Virginia); *see also Hitchcock v. U.S.*, 665 F.2d 354, 360 (D.C. Cir. 1985) (District of Columbia law applied when occurrence of the injury outside the District was "fortuitous" and the relationship was centered inside Washington). Although the relationship in this case was also centered in the District, and it is likely that it was fortuitous that the parties first engaged in intercourse in Virginia, the fact remains that the act was illegal. This implicates policy concerns not at issue in *Hitchcock*.

This Court remains bound by the determination in *Zysk* that Virginia has a public interest in preventing the illegal conduct at issue. As a result, Virginia has a greater interest in this encounter in Virginia than does the District of Columbia, the forum jurisdiction. District of Columbia substantive law cannot apply to any cause of action arising from the Virginia sexual encounter. Plaintiff is barred from recovery to the extent her cause of action arises from the Virginia encounter.

2. The District Encounter

The Court believes the converse of the above reasoning is also true. Virginia has a minimal interest in denying recovery to one of its citizens for actions in another jurisdiction if such recovery is available.

> [A] state whose only connection with this litigation is that it was the domicile of a plaintiff or victim has no interest in the imposition of punitive damage liability.

In re Air Crash Disaster at Washington, D.C., 559 F. Supp. 333, 353 (D.D.C. 1983). Instead, it is the District of Columbia which must absorb the strain on its health system of treating both the defendant and any other residents he might infect.

D. Determination of Whether Infection Resulted from the District Encounter

As a final line of defense to defendant's dispositive motion, plaintiff contends that there are material facts in dispute which raise a triable question as to which of the two sexual encounters resulted in infection. . . . [T]he evidence is strongly to the contrary. . . . [Both parties' experts] agree on the fundamental fact that the period of incubation is at least two to seven days. Plaintiff states that she began experiencing symptoms of the disease "within 48 hours of the sexual encounter with the defendant in Washington D.C." Declaration of plaintiff, p. 1. Two days after the April 29, 1990, encounter would have been May 1, 1990. This is only five days after the initial sexual encounter in Virginia, and well within the undisputed incubation period of seven days. . . . There are no genuine facts in dispute that would preclude summary judgment.

III. Conclusion

For the foregoing reasons the Court applies Virginia law to the Virginia sexual encounter and District of Columbia law to the District encounter. As a result, recovery would be possible only if plaintiff could trace her injury to the District encounter. Because we conclude that no reasonable trier of fact could determine which encounter resulted in infection, we are forced to grant defendant's motion for summary judgment. We regret this unfortunate result which, if plaintiff's allegations are true, shields from liability conduct which is not only despicable, but at the least is highly irresponsible. We hope plaintiff will appeal our determination that we are unable to grant the relief she seeks.

COMMENTS AND QUESTIONS

1. This is the first conflicts case that we have read that arises out of federal court. We will tackle this topic directly in Chapter 19, but, as the court observes: in diversity cases, federal courts follow the choice of law rules of the state in which they sit.

2. According to the court in its discussion of the Virginia encounter, one of the plaintiff's arguments was that D.C.'s policy was an anti-defendant policy that should be applied to the defendant, a D.C. domiciliary, while he was in Virginia. Is this orthodox interest analysis?

3. Interest analysis requires us to identify a state policy and then to assess whether that policy would be advanced by the application of the law to the instant facts. The latter step often turns on whether a party is foreign or local to the state. Doe argued that someone who works (but does not live) in the jurisdiction could be local. The court rejected this argument because the underlying conduct was illegal, but isn't this a non sequitur?

   In cases where the underlying conduct wasn't illegal, should someone who works in the jurisdiction be considered local for purposes of interest analysis? How about someone who visits the jurisdiction? What other kinds of relationships might qualify?

4. The opinion quotes the plaintiff's brief as arguing that the parties' relationship "was centered in—indeed, was almost entirely limited to—the District of Columbia." (How) Is that relevant to interest analysis?

5. The court observes that a state's "interest in a case is strongest when both the situs of the injury and the domicile of the plaintiff are within its territory." (Think *Bernhard*.) Will a state be interested when it is both the situs of the injury and the domicile of the *defendant*? (What would result in *Bernhard* if the plaintiff had been injured on a Nevada highway?) The court then uses this framing device to suggest that a state's interest would be "weakest" in the converse situation, "when a foreign plaintiff suffers an injury outside the jurisdiction." If weighing interests is anathema to interest analysis, why is the court talking about "strongest" and "weakest" interests?

6. Judge Pratt chides both parties for arguing that only one jurisdiction's law would apply to this case. The opinion offers two possible explanations for his approach: (1) we do not know whether the tort occurred in Virginia or in Washington, D.C.; and/or (2) both jurisdictions criminalize the underlying conduct. Why would it follow from either of these justifications that the case should be split into two cases for purposes of a conflict of laws analysis.

   What result would occur if the case is not split into two cases for purposes of a conflict of laws analysis? What are the respective policies of the two states and would the policies of neither/one/both state(s) be advanced by their application to a single fact pattern that contained both the Virginia and D.C. encounters? Which state's law would the court ultimately apply? Put another way, why did this plaintiff file her case in D.C. rather than Virginia where she lived?

7. In Part II.B. of its opinion the court refers to a presumption that "[t]he law of the forum is presumed to apply unless it is demonstrated that a foreign jurisdiction has a greater interest in the controversy than does the District." Did the court apply (and rebut) this presumption?

SAMPLE EXAM QUESTIONS

Question 5-5

Michael Margolis rented a truck to facilitate his move from Maryland to Mexico. While still living in Maryland, he decided to rent a U-Move truck after noticing a U-Move advertisement in a local newspaper emphasizing that by crossing the Potomac River (into Washington D.C.), Marylanders could rent the most reliable trucks, at the cheapest prices, from the most professional moving truck business. Margolis went online to www.umove.com, where he reserved a large truck and tow dolly for a seven-day rental. The website allowed him to input a zip code for his preferred pick-up location.

Shortly before the scheduled rental date, Margolis was informed that he should pick up the truck and dolly from a U-Move location in Washington, D.C. U-Move is a Pennsylvania corporation with a principal place of business in Philadelphia.

When Margolis arrived at U-Move he found the truck in disrepair and with an odometer reading 233,420 miles. Margolis expressed his dissatisfaction with the condition of the truck but was told there was no other option. U-Move also did not have Margolis's tow dolly, and directed him to another D.C. location to pick that up.

Margolis returned home and loaded the truck but, even before leaving Maryland, noticed that the truck leaked substantial amounts of oil and that exhaust fumes entered the cabin. Margolis called U-Move's roadside assistance, and they sent a mechanic the following day to make the necessary repairs.

Three days later, while Margolis was in Louisiana, the same problems with oil and exhaust fumes returned. Again he called roadside assistance, and U-Move said that it would take several days to make the necessary repairs. U-Move gave Margolis a replacement truck and a new rental contract.

Eight days after initially renting the (first) truck, Margolis returned the (second) truck to the return location in Texas specified on the second (but not the first) rental contract. His credit card was charged an additional $1,025 due to the late return of the truck, and for returning the truck to the wrong location.

Margolis filed an action against U-Move in a D.C. court seeking recovery under the District of Columbia Consumer Protection Act (CPA). Every state has a consumer protection act that is designed to protect consumers from unfair and misleading actions by businesses, but each state's law varies. The CPA (1) specifically includes deceptive advertising and pricing among its prohibitions, (2) does not require that the violation be intentional, (3) automatically awards plaintiffs their attorney's fees for any violation, and (4) permits judges to award injunctive relief in addition to damages.

Maryland's consumer protection law includes items (1) and (3) above, but requires plaintiffs to prove that the violation was intentional. Injunctive relief is unavailable.

Pennsylvania's consumer protection law includes (1) and (2) above, but does not allow plaintiff to collect their attorney's fees. Injunctive relief is unavailable.

What law applies if the D.C. court follows interest analysis?

Question 5-6

Plumlee and Parks, domiciliaries of North Carolina, were limited partners in a hedge fund partnership called Duke Investment Fund. Duke's executives, who are New Yorkers, made some dubious investments and engaged in unethical and illegal conduct. However, with only one possible exception, the statute of limitations on all federal and state causes of action against Duke and the alleged malefactors has run in all jurisdictions.

The one possible exception is a cause of action for fraudulent conveyance. This cause of action is designed to prevent debtors from transferring property in order to thwart or defraud creditors.

Under New York law, limited partners are not "creditors" of the partnership, and therefore the plaintiffs would have no cause of action. Under North Carolina law, limited partners may be classified as "creditors."

If New York follows the traditional approach to conflict of laws and North Carolina follows interest analysis, where should the plaintiffs file the suit to get the more favorable law?

Quick Summary

- A state is interested only when the application of its laws would advance the policy underlying that law

- False conflicts generally require application of the (substantive) law of the only interested state

- True conflicts generally require application of the (substantive) law of the forum state, absent a restrained interpretation of the governmental interest of the forum state

- Unprovided-for cases generally require application of the law of the forum state

- Governmental interest analysis assumes that a state passes laws only to advance the interests of its own citizens; this is the domestic assumption

- Orthodox interest analysis is committed to Currie's original vision; departures therefrom may be deliberate policy choices by a jurisdiction or inadvertent misapplication of interest analysis

- Interest analysis is incorporated within all contemporary choice of law methodologies

6

Center of Gravity

Key Concepts

- The center of gravity of the underlying transaction or occurrence is the locus of the key factual contacts
- Multi-factor tests

The center of gravity approach, which was something of a rival to the interest analysis approach we considered in Chapter 5, is a methodology with more factors and more flexibility than other methods we have studied. Judges can take a broader look at the factual history of the parties' dispute in order to render a more informed decision about what law should govern the parties' rights and responsibilities. Once enlightened by these details, a judge has considerable discretion to decide what law applies. There are no localizing rules, no Latin terms, and no academic concepts to master. Rather, a judge looks at the facts presented and applies the law of the place that she considers to be the "center of gravity" of the transaction or occurrence at issue. This approach is also referred to as a "grouping of contacts" or as an examination of "significant contacts." As demonstrated by the table in Chapter 2, this methodology does not have many subscribers.

Jurisdictions that have adopted a center of gravity approach typically circumscribe the facts that are relevant to the inquiry. In contract cases, for example, the court will consider:

- the place of contracting;
- the place of performance;
- the physical location of property that is the subject matter of the contract; and
- the domiciles or places of business of the contracting parties.

In tort cases, courts consider:

- the place of injury;

- the place of allegedly wrongful conduct;

- the domiciles or places of business of the contracting parties; and

- the place where the parties' relationship was formed.

Although the inquiry is broader than other methods, an enumerated list constrains the scope. It is not relevant, for example, that a party to the suit has a corporate affiliate or a familial relation in a state. Nor does the inquiry include, say, how wealthy or deserving of sympathy the parties are.

But when there is more than one relevant factor, these factors will often point in different directions. After all, choice of law questions arise from multi-state situations. The methodology does not prescribe how a judge (or a lawyer advising her client) should use the list of factors to determine (or to predict) the center of gravity of a transaction or occurrence. Upon review of the four facts listed above, is the center of gravity where there are quantitatively the *most* contacts? Is it where there are qualitatively the *most impactful* contacts? A formal answer to these questions would be inconsistent with the aspiration of a more discretionary methodology. The virtues of flexibility in choice of law models were introduced in Chapter 3.

The center of gravity approach emphasizes *facts*. In contrast to interest analysis, this approach is less concerned with the outcome or even the content of the law—and especially not the policies underlying those laws. One court called the identification and weighing (or non-weighing, as the case may be) of such policies "difficult and ultimately speculative."[1] Notice also that, with a gestalt test like this, there is no formal preference for forum law.

Now use the list of factors set forth above to determine the center of gravity in the following hypotheticals.

Hypothetical 6-1

Shawna Arthur of Grinnell, Iowa, contracted with Aidan Homes, a modular home dealer in Oskaloosa, Iowa, to purchase a modular home manufactured by Capra Homes of Somerville, Missouri. Arthur later established an internet website describing her dissatisfaction with the condition of the home and making unflattering statements about Capra Homes and

---

1   *Simon v. U.S.*, 805 N.E.2d 798, 803 (Ind. 2004), quoted in Peter Hay et al., Conflict of Laws Fifth Edition 109 (5th ed. 2010).

its business practices. Arthur drew attention to her website by placing an advertisement in an Iowa newspaper and by posting a sign on her family's pickup truck that advertised the website's address. She then drove the truck through Iowa communities and through the parking lot of a dealership in Kirksville, Missouri that sells Capra Homes.

Capra Homes filed a lawsuit against Arthur in a Missouri court, claiming that the website and sign were libelous. Capra Homes seeks damages for the harm to its business reputation.

Missouri law requires proof of actual damages to sustain a libel claim. Iowa adheres to the rule that damages may be presumed in an action for libel per se. It will be difficult, probably impossible for Capra to prove actual damages by a preponderance of evidence. Capra believes that they have lost customers and sales. But Capra's revenues are seasonal and so erratic that it will be hard to blame Arthur for any decrease in sales. Hiring an expert to do market surveys would cost at least $20,000 and, in any event, may not produce anything useful.

Arthur's motion for summary judgment looms. If the forum follows the center of gravity approach, which state's law will it apply?

Hypothetical 6-2

Gaultieri Studios Inc. (Gaultieri) is a California entertainment production company that has its principal place of business in Los Angeles. Four years ago, Gaultieri purchased an idea for a television series including character biographies, themes, and storylines from a freelance writer who lived and worked in Arlington, Texas. The concept was for a television show called "Greyhounds and Greyhounds," about a Greyhound bus driver in Arlington, Texas who also rescued greyhound dogs. Gaultieri immediately submitted this idea for a series to the Turner Broadcasting Network (Turner), a Delaware corporation that has its corporate headquarters in Atlanta, Georgia. Turner allowed Gaultieri to pitch their show at a meeting with executives in Atlanta. Other than superficial pleasantries, the parties had no further conversations thereafter.

Three years later, Turner produced and aired a television show called "Texas Greyhound" featuring a Greyhound bus driver who rescued greyhound dogs. Gaultieri did not consent to the production of this show and received no compensation from Turner for the use of its idea for the show.

In the entertainment industry it is well understood that writer-creators pitch creative ideas to prospective purchasers with the object of selling those ideas for compensation, and it is standard in the entertainment industry for ideas to be pitched with the expectation of compensation in the event of use. Accordingly, Gaultieri filed a lawsuit.

For reasons that are not important here, Gaultieri's claim does not implicate federal copyright law. Gaultieri's cause of action is for breach of an implied-in-fact contract. Turner argues that Gaultieri's claim is defective because, although contracts can be implied in fact, this so-called contract had no price term.

Under California law, an implied-in-fact contract can have an open price term to be filled in by industry standards. Under Georgia and Texas laws, price is an essential element of a contract, and no contract can be implied without it.

If the action is filed in a jurisdiction that follows the center of gravity approach, what law should it apply?

Navigating a multi-factor test is a skill worth taking time to master. Let us consider a multi-factor test in a non-legal context so that we can avoid the distraction of the doctrine itself. Imagine that you are part of a committee of nine that has been constituted to designate the Best American Situation-Comedy ("Sit-Com") Since 1980.[2] The committee has been told that four criteria should inform its deliberations and determine the ultimate winner. The published criteria are:

(1) **Longevity.** Total number of episodes.

(2) **Popularity.** Viewership ratings share at peak.

(3) **Critical Acclaim.** Total "Best Comedy Series" Emmy Awards.

(4) **Cultural Legacy.** Number of spin-offs generated by show.

The issues that would arise in the context of this discussion and ultimately, the designation of a winner have an analog in the context of the center of gravity approach (and other multi-factor tests you will see in law school and in practice).

First, there are arguments about whether the test excludes key criteria. Especially when the missing criteria would bolster the standing of the series that matches your preference or intuition, those missing criteria will come naturally to mind.

---

2   Think Cheers, The Cosby Show, Seinfeld, Friends, Modern Family, The Simpsons, Arrested Development, The Big Bang Theory, 30 Rock, The Office, Will and Grace, Rick and Morty, etc.

For example, the *number of years in syndication* could have been a fifth criterion, yet it is not included. Arguments that "fight the criteria" are often unsuccessful, however, because the decisional criteria are already decided. Unless you are in a position to rewrite the criteria, the better approach is to recast this objection in a form that is more palatable; we will see a version of this below.

Second, because the four expressed criteria inevitably overlap somewhat, the fact of overlap raises important arguments. *Longevity* and *Popularity*, for example, overlap to the extent that we would expect a very high correlation between the life-span of a television series and the number of people who watch that series. One could argue, then, that there is really one criterion here that is masquerading as two. If this is really a three-factor test rather than a four-factor test, then the series that wins one of three criteria is in a weaker position in the conversation than if it were instead the series that wins two of four criteria. Conversely, the fact of overlap could indicate that that the area of overlap is the crux of the entire inquiry. If the designers of this award are double-counting something, then one might argue that it is *because* this (overlap) is the essence of this award. In this line of thinking, we should find ways to maximize not minimize the television series that scores well in the overlapping criteria.

Another way to influence the outcome is to persuade the committee to commit to an overall procedure for considering and selecting the television series. Among an infinite range of options are these four:

Option A	Option B
Identify the sit-com that wins each of the four criteria. We will then discuss which of the series on that list (of ≤4) is "the best" before we take a vote; the series that gets the most votes wins.	Identify the top-five sit-coms in each of the four criteria. We will then discuss which of the series on that list (of ≤20) is "the best" before we take a vote; the series that gets the most votes wins.
Option C	**Option D**
Identify the sit-com that wins each of the four criteria. We will then discuss which of the series on that list (of ≤4) is "the best." We will discuss/debate until the committee reaches consensus.	Identify the top-five sit-coms in each of the four criteria. We will then discuss which of the series on that list (of ≤20) is "the best." We will discuss/debate until the committee reaches consensus.

The difference between the top and bottom rows emphasizes how the process of voting/selection can dramatically affect outcomes. Indeed there is an entire literature about voting techniques.[3] Of course one could also get the committee to agree to a specific weighted significance for each of the four criteria. (*E.g.,* Longevity could be worth 15% of the overall score; Popularity, 25%; Critical Acclaim, 50%; and Cultural Legacy, 10%.) The difference between the left and right columns in the table above emphasizes that determining the initial set of candidates to be considered can dramatically affect the outcome. For example, a sitcom that came in second-place in all four categories would not even be considered in Options A and C yet could win in Options B and D.

Another battleground for multi-factor tests is the broadening of the proxy for a(ny) criterion. The "total number of episodes," for example, is a proxy—a substitute for or an attempt to quantify—the real criterion, which is *longevity*. In our example, the proxy was stated. In other situations the proxy is unstated or assumed. But whether stated or unstated, the proxy can be broadened to affect the outcome:

> "Well, fellow committee members, if what we really care about is longevity, the total number of episodes is only one measure for that. We should also be considering the total number of years that it was on the air. A show that was on the air for 10 years but had 20 episodes per year arguably had more longevity than a show that was on the air for 7 years but had 30 episodes per year. We need to broaden the proxy for longevity to include not just total number of episodes but also the number of years that it was on the air."

Expanding the proxy for longevity would also be a way to incorporate *number of years in syndication* as a relevant metric. Expanding the proxy for cultural legacy is another option.

Criteria or their proxy might also have some discriminatory effect. At least three and perhaps all four of these criteria are systemically biased in favor of older television shows. Television shows that are still on the air have not had a full opportunity to log episodes, win Emmys, and develop a legacy. Should the committee take this into account?

Knowing how to navigate (or manipulate, as the case may be) a multi-factor test is an extremely important advocacy skill. All of the arguments that we have just

---

3   Techniques include Plurality Rule, Borda Count, Plurality with Runoff, The Hare Rule, Coombs Rule, Negative Voting, Approval Voting, Cumulative Voting among the many available options. *See generally* "Voting Methods," in Stanford Encyclopedia of Philosophy, available at https://plato.stanford.edu/entries/voting-methods/#2 (last visited July 31, 2017).

explored in the context of this best sitcom hypothetical have direct or indirect analogues in the context of the center of gravity test. Skillful litigators are aware of all of the tools at their disposal.

Hypothetical 6-3

Nikolai Bunk was a long-haul truck driver. He was hired by Camden Transportation (Camden), a large shipping corporation based in New Jersey, to drive Camden's tractor trailers along routes between several West Coast cities and Camden's Midwestern transit facility in St. Louis, Missouri. Bunk was hired after a telephone interview from his home in Vancouver, British Columbia. Bunk was a reliable and valued contractor who worked these same routes for the company for sixteen years.

One morning a Camden dispatcher in New Jersey noticed from a GPS tracker that Bunk's truck had not moved since the previous night. It was parked in an Oklahoma City, Oklahoma parking lot. When the dispatcher was unable to reach Bunk, she called the police. Bunk was found dead in the cab of his idling tractor. There was no obvious cause of death, but blood tests and an autopsy indicated that he died of carbon monoxide poisoning. Examination of the tractor revealed a faulty repair to the exhaust system.

Bunk was cremated and his wife scattered his ashes in New York Harbor. Bunk had never traveled east of the Mississippi River and it was his unfulfilled dream to visit New York City.

Camden is incorporated in Delaware. Bunk did not own his own truck, and instead drove different trucks provided to him by Camden for different routes. The truck that Bunk was driving when he died was purchased by Camden in New Jersey. That truck had last been serviced by Camden employees in St. Louis less than a week before Camden was assigned to drive that truck from Los Angeles to St. Louis. He was on the second day of that trip when he pulled over to nap in Oklahoma City and died.

Bunk's wife and one of Bunk's three adult children sued Camden. The conflicts issue arises only with respect to a loss of consortium claim by the adult child. The 28-year-old is disabled and is financially dependent upon his parents.

The laws of California, Oklahoma, and New Jersey do not permit loss of consortium claims by adult children. Under British Columbian law, dependent adult children may sue, but damages are capped at (Can.)

$100,000. Under the laws of New York, Missouri and all other states, recovery by dependent children is allowed and uncapped.

If plaintiff's counsel files this suit in a jurisdiction that follows the center of gravity approach, what law should it apply?

We cannot give you definitive guidance about how judges would resolve these hypotheticals. Some jurisdictions have imposed some order onto this methodology by anointing certain factors as possibly more important than the others. In contract cases, the place of contracting (and, sometimes, also the place of performance) enjoy this billing. And in tort cases, it is the place of injury (and, sometimes, also the place of the alleged wrongful conduct). Notice the pull of the traditional approach—or at least the shared intuition.

In Practice

Did you also find yourself influenced by the method (or intuition) of interest analysis? Or the traditional approach?

Recognizing the overlap of methodologies is important to an advocate. When the result that you are urging would also be the result under a different methodological approach, mention the alternative approach to demonstrate how intuitive and obvious your position must be. ("Your Honor, choosing the applicable law may look difficult here but this is something that even different methodologies would agree is the single right answer.") But when the result that your opponent is urging would be the result under a different methodological approach, use the alternative approach to demonstrate that your adversary is confusing the methodologies. ("Your Honor, they are using interest analysis—even if they aren't mentioning it by name—but our Supreme Court has adopted the center of gravity approach. The policy behind that statute is not relevant here even though my opponent is trying to sneak it in to influence the outcome.")

Critics of the center of gravity approach emphasize its unpredictability both *ex ante* and *ex post*. With respect to the former, you cannot advise your client with certainty what law will apply under anticipated circumstances. And with respect to the latter, the parties and the court may expend substantial resources resolving the center of gravity of a given transaction or occurrence.

As a policy-maker (or as a litigator) you may be forced one day to defend a particular choice of law approach. Do not allow others to exaggerate its flaws. For example, to be sure, the center of gravity approach gives judges more flexibility to decide the applicable law than a more prescriptive approach. Since Chapter 3 we have been aware of the stock arguments for and against flexibility. But you should ask: more flexible *than what*? Demand a baseline against which the predictability of this or any approach should be measured. Is the baseline some Platonic ideal or an approach that has actually existed?

The professed virtue of the traditional approach was its certainty and predictability. (Cue the stock arguments for uniformity from Chapter 3.) But in Chapter 4, we saw that a public policy exception allowed judges an escape from applying the chosen law.[4] We also learned in that chapter that judges could alter the outcome by re-characterizing the case. In Chapter 2 we saw that the characterization of a matter as procedural allows a court to apply its own procedural law; we will return to that in Chapter 10. And in Chapter 12, we will study renvoi—another device that allowed judges deploying a traditional approach to escape the conclusion demanded by the rigid formula.

A policy maker or advocate might even argue that a center of gravity approach is, in an important sense, as—or maybe even more—predictable than the traditional approach. Jurisdictions that follow the center of gravity consider facts that the traditional approach considered relevant, but not *only* those facts. When the place of contracting (or place of injury) is the center of gravity of the transaction (or occurrence) that jurisdiction's law will be applied—as it would in a traditional jurisdiction. But in circumstances where it would be nonsensical to apply the law of place of contracting (or place of injury), other facts will guide the judge to a sensible selection of the applicable law. By contrast, there is uncertainty in a jurisdiction that follows the traditional approach because the judge might follow a nonsensical result prescribed by the rigid formula or might instead use some escape device to reach the sensible result.

---

4   We will study the public policy exception more closely in Chapter 11.

PODLIN v. GHERMEZIAN

U.S. Court of Appeals for the Second Circuit
601 Fed.Appx. 31 (2nd Cir. 2015)

PER CURIAM.

[Mark Podlin is a Georgia attorney and land developer. In December 2009, Podlin applied to join Triple Five Worldwide ("Triple Five") as Chief Executive Officer of its International Shopping Center Development operations. The defendant Ghermezian family owns Triple Five Worldwide, a multinational conglomerate that is best known for its ownership of two of North America's largest shopping centers: the Mall of America in Minneapolis and the West Edmonton Mall in Canada.

On February 23, 2010, Nader Ghermezian contacted Podlin and asked if Podlin could assist them with acquiring the Meadowlands Xanadu, the original name for a recreation facility owned by the New Jersey Sports and Exposition Authority that is located in the Meadowlands Sports Complex in East Rutherford New Jersey. Nader also asked Podlin if he was still interested in the C.E.O. position. Podlin answered yes to both questions, and Nader invited him to a meeting in New York City the very next day.

The meeting focused on Podlin's ability to help Triple Five get control of the Xanadu property so that Triple Five could (re)develop it. Podlin described his experience redeveloping properties in New Jersey, recounted his contacts with New Jersey officials, and assured Nader that he could get control of Xanadu for Triple Five if he was Triple Five's C.E.O. of International Shopping Center Development operations.

Nader said Triple Five would hire Podlin for the C.E.O. position at a salary of $12,000 per month, plus commissions equal to 10% of the appraised value of all deals he brought in. However, Nader cautioned that before any employment agreement could be finalized, Podlin would need to meet with other members of the Ghermezian family.

Podlin met with other members of the Ghermezian family, and Podlin again emphasized his ability to deliver the Xanadu deal to Triple Five. The family said "Okay, but you have to get it for us first."

On March 2, 2010, Podlin flew to Edmonton, Alberta (Canada) to begin work at Triple Five's headquarters. When Podlin arrived he was issued an ID badge labeled "Consultant." Podlin pointed out the error, but Triple Five security told him to ignore it. Podlin began work on a number of projects but focused primarily on the Xanadu acquisition. He asked for a written employment agreement, but instead received only excuses. He was also told that his arrangement would need to be restructured as a consulting relationship; Podlin objected to that arrangement but continued his work.

On April 2, 2010, Podlin complained that he had received neither a written contract nor his monthly salary. Nader told Podlin that he would not be paid until Triple Five started making money on the projects. Podlin immediately ceased working, flew back to the United States, and had no further contact with Triple Five or the Xanadu project for the rest of the year.

On December 23, 2010, Triple Five acquired an ownership interest in the entertainment and retail component of Xanadu. Four months later, Podlin called Nader and Donald Ghermezian, offering to lead redevelopment of the project. The Ghermezians rejected Podlin's offer.

In May 2013, Triple Five took complete control of Xanadu, now called The American Dream @ Meadowlands. Triple Five is the third successive developer on a project that has been underway since 2002. With a total price tag now approaching approximately $6 billion, American Dream Meadowland may become the most expensive retail project in the world. The American Dream @ Meadowlands promises to be the busiest shopping mall in the country, with an indoor ski slope, an indoor water park, a skating rink, an amusement park, an observation wheel, and high-end shopping.

In June 2013 Podlin sued, claiming that he was a partner on the deal, and that Triple Five promised him a 10% commission. Podlin claimed damages of at least $200 million. The district court dismissed Podlin's suit for failing to state a claim. Podlin appealed.]

. . . "To survive a motion to dismiss, a complaint must contain sufficient factual matter, accepted as true, to state a claim to relief that is plausible on its face." *Ashcroft v. Iqbal*, 556 U.S. 662, 678 (2009) (internal quotation marks omitted). We review *de novo* the dismissal of a complaint under Rule 12(b)(6), accepting all factual allegations in the complaint as true and drawing all reasonable inferences in favor of the plaintiff. *TechnoMarine SA v. Giftports, Inc.*, 758 F.3d 493, 498 (2d Cir. 2014).

A federal court sitting in diversity must apply the choice-of-law rules of the state in which the court is located; the district court thus properly applied New York choice-of-law principles. *See Klaxon Co. v. Stentor Elec. Mfg. Co.*, 313 U.S. 487, 496–97 (1941). In New York, the first inquiry in a choice-of-law analysis is into the existence of an actual conflict of laws. As regards New York and New Jersey, each state requires that real estate brokers working the respective state be licensed in order to bring to bring actions for commissions, but Podlin was licensed in New York only. Consequently . . . the application of each statute will lead to a different result: Under New York law, his claims are not barred, but under New Jersey law, they are. . . . Because there is a conflict, we must resolve the choice-of-law issue, using New York choice-of-law principles. . . .

In contract suits, "the court evaluates the 'center of gravity' or 'grouping of contacts,' with the purpose of establishing which state has the most significant relationship to the transaction and the parties." *Fieger v. Pitney Bowes Credit Corp.*, 251 F.3d 386, 393 (2d Cir. 2001). New York courts consider (1) the place of contracting, (2) the place of negotiation, (3) the place of performance, (4) the location of the subject matter, and (5) the domicile or place of business of the contracting parties. In this case, the place of contracting and place of negotiation are both New York, the place of performance is New Jersey (and Edmonton, insofar as Podlin was physically located in Edmonton while he was calling and emailing people located in New Jersey), the location of the subject matter is also New Jersey, the domicile of Defendants is alleged in the complaint to be New York, and Podlin's domicile is Georgia. "In addition, the policies underlying conflicting laws in a contract dispute may also be considered in instances where they are readily identifiable and reflect strong governmental concerns." *Madison Realty, Inc. v. Neiss*, 676 N.Y.S.2d 672, 673 (1998). In this case, "the interest of New York in seeing that its licensed brokers are compensated," *Rosenberg & Rosenberg, P.C. v. Hoffman*, 600 N.Y.S.2d 228, 229 (1993), and New York's recognition of other states' "strong interest in regulating the activities of real estate brokers who perform services in connection with the sale of [in-state] property," *Madison Realty*, 676 N.Y.S.2d at 674, leave the case in equipoise.

In *Madison Realty*, a plaintiff who was a licensed New York real estate broker informed one of the defendants of the availability of certain real property in Florida and "assisted [that defendant] in negotiating the purchase of the property"; the plaintiffs thereafter sued to recover "a commission for procuring the sale." *Id.* at 673. The Appellate Division, Second Department, held that the plaintiff could not recover because he was not licensed as a real estate broker in Florida, and Florida had the most significant relationship to the case, placing heavy weight on the location of the property that gave rise to the claim.

In *Rosenberg & Rosenberg*, by contrast, the Appellate Division, First Department, held that the New York real estate broker plaintiff was entitled to sue for his commission for securing his client financing to purchase a condominium in New Jersey, even though the plaintiff was not licensed in New Jersey, 600 N.Y.S.2d at 229. The court emphasized that the contract arose "from initial contacts in New York and [was] made in New York," and that "a New York [financing] source was found and the loan commitment issued and the loan agreement closed in New York. *Id.*

Finally, in *TDH-Berkshire, Inc. v. Korff*, 823 N.Y.W.2d 20 (2006), a more recent case, the Appellate Division, First Department, held that the plaintiff could not recover a commission for successfully finding a purchase for a parcel of New Jersey real estate, because he was licensed as a real estate broker in New York, but not New Jersey. Although the client was domiciled in New York, "all information concerning the subject property came through defendants' New York offices, [and] the final sale of the property was closed here," the court stated that "the heaviest weight is given to the location of the property being transferred." *Id.* The court concluded that, "[i]n light of the out-of-state locus of this property, as well as plaintiff's admission that over 100 meetings were held at the property site . . . New Jersey law must apply." *Id.*

Unlike *Rosenberg & Rosenberg*, in which the location of the subject matter realty was really the only connection to New Jersey, this case includes extensive New Jersey involvement beyond the location of the Meadowlands. As far as appears from Podlin's complaint, nearly all of his performance of the contract was directed toward New Jersey and took place (at least partly) in New Jersey, since Podlin was calling and emailing people who were physically located there. Those contacts, in combination with *TDH-Berkshire*'s indication that the locus of the property is entitled to the heaviest weight, albeit not dispositive weight, demonstrate that the district court was correct in holding that New Jersey had the most significant relationship to the facts of this case, and consequently applying New Jersey law.

The New Jersey real estate broker licensing statute, N.J.S.A. 45:15–3, provides that "[n]o person . . . shall bring or maintain any action . . . for the collection of compensation for the performance of any of the acts mentioned in R.S. 45:15–1 *et seq.* without alleging and proving that he was a duly licensed real estate broker at the time the alleged cause of action arose," which Podlin cannot do. The "acts mentioned" are extremely broad: relevant for this appeal, the statute bars suits by a person who "attempts to negotiate a sale, exchange, purchase or rental of real estate or an interest therein . . . or assists or directs in the procuring of prospects or the negotiation or closing of any transaction which does or is contemplated to result in the sale, exchange, leasing, renting or auctioning of any real estate." N.J.S.A. 45:15–3. Podlin's actions in attempting to negotiate a takeover of the Xanadu property by Defendants fall within the ambit of the statute, and Podlin is thus barred from bringing an action to recover any compensation deriving from those actions.

Podlin's argument that he is seeking compensation under an employment contract, not seeking compensation for brokering a real estate transaction, is unavailing. Even drawing all factual inferences in Podlin's favor, it still appears from the allegations in Podlin's complaint that the primary purpose of his agreement with Triple Five was securing and redeveloping the Xanadu project. Defendants may have kept Podlin busy with other projects in between, but Podlin alleges facts that demonstrate that Defendants' only real interest in Podlin was his New Jersey political connections. Podlin himself alleged that the primary focus of his work was the Meadowlands deal, and he also alleges facts indicating that Defendants saw him as a consultant, not an employee, and treated him accordingly. In fact, Podlin quotes a statement from Nader Ghermezian that seems to indicate that the entire contract itself was contingent on Podlin securing the Meadowlands project for Triple Five. And even Podlin admits that his "salary" was "an artificially low figure designed only to meet minimal living costs." Am. Compl. ¶ 76. Ultimately, the work for which Podlin seeks to be compensated through this suit is not whatever work he may have done on Triple Five's projects in Libya or the Congo—he seeks to recover damages with respect to the Meadowlands deal, and nothing else.

Second, Podlin argues that, when a plaintiff brokers a deal that includes the sale or lease of both personalty and realty, the New Jersey real estate broker licensing statute only bars suit as to the recovery of compensation traceable to the realty. Podlin is correct. In *Kazmer-Standish Consultants,*

Inc. v. Schoeffel Instruments Corp., 89 N.J. 286 (1982), the Supreme Court of New Jersey held that, when a broker not licensed as a real estate broker negotiates the sale of an entire business, which includes some realty and some personalty, the broker may "recover a commission on the portion of the sale of an ongoing business attributable to personal property even if the sale includes an interest in real estate." *Id.* at 1152. Podlin's complaint, however, fails to allege that there was any personalty involved in the Xanadu deal. His complaint focuses entirely on the realty involved. We must, of course, draw all reasonable factual inferences in his favor—but we may not read allegations into his complaint that are not there. Thus, the New Jersey real estate broker licensing statute bars Podlin's claim for his commission in its entirety, whether pled in contract, unjust enrichment, or quantum meruit, and the district court properly dismissed those claims. . . .

COMMENTS AND QUESTIONS

1. There are two different phenomena happening in this opinion that should be distinguished. First, Podlin's claim is characterized as (or simply presumed to be) a claim by a real estate broker (instead of a claim for breach of an employment agreement). Second, the court concludes that New Jersey is the center of gravity of Podlin's brokerage activities. The first is peculiar, but beyond the scope of this course—except as a useful lesson about how savvy litigators will use one doctrine (here, choice of law) to frame the case when some other issue (here, the nature of the contract between Podlin and Triple Five) is more essential but less likely to be resolved in your favor.

2. The court lists five facts that New York courts consider when determining the center of gravity of a contract, but only four facts appear in the text that opened this chapter. Each state has the prerogative to chart its own course with respect to choice of law. Many of the facts on the lists have related or sub-parts. For example, does "place of performance" refer to both parties or only the place of performance of the party whose performance is the subject of the dispute? Many of the facts on the lists are also dynamic events. For example, is the "location of property that is the subject matter of the contract" determined as of the date of contracting,

when the dispute arose, when the complaint was filed, or when choosing the applicable law?

3. In *Podlin*, the court grafts some interest analysis into its center of gravity approach. An orthodox center of gravity approach focuses exclusively on *factual* contacts. By including some interest analysis, New York incorporates some consideration also of the *laws*.

4. In this case the choice of law dispute arose on a motion to dismiss for failure to state a claim. On one hand, it makes sense that a dispute about the applicable law should arise at that stage: if the substantive law creates and defines the contours of the *claim*, then we need to know which substantive law we are talking about. But on the other hand, a motion to dismiss for failure to state a claim typically occurs in the earliest stages of litigation. Especially with a methodological approach that requires more factual context (like center of gravity), the factual predicate of the claim may not then be fully known. A motion to dismiss is based on the sufficiency of the plaintiff's complaint, but what does plaintiff know at that preliminary stage about where the Ghermezians were when they telephoned him, where they were when they decided to squeeze him out, which of the various Triple Five corporate affiliates hired him as CEO (and where that entity is incorporated and based)?

    A decision about the applicable law can be preliminary and, therefore, revisited at a later stage of litigation when more facts surface. But that is an option only for plaintiffs and defendants in circumstances when the complaint survives the motion to dismiss. Podlin's claim was dismissed. Knowing when to raise the choice of law issue is yet another strategic opportunity to consider and to leverage.

5. The court recites the familiar standard that, on a motion to dismiss, they must draw all reasonable factual inferences in plaintiff's favor. It then says: "[B]ut we may not read allegations into his complaint that are not there." What, then, is an inference?

6. Podlin represented himself in this litigation. That decision proved quite unwise.

KENDER v. AUTO-OWNERS INS. CO.

Court of Appeals of Wisconsin
329 Wis.2d 378 (2010)

CURLEY, PRESIDING JUDGE.

. . . I. Background

This lawsuit arises out of a motor vehicle accident that occurred in the early morning hours of March 13, 2005, in Oak Creek, Wisconsin and involved vehicles operated by Matt Lucey and Jake Kender.

At the time of the accident, Lucey was driving a vehicle that Strom, his employer, had rented from Enterprise-Rent-A-Car Company, Inc. (Enterprise), which was insured by Empire Fire & Marine Insurance Company (Empire). Lucey was in Wisconsin to work with Strom Engineering Corporation's client CNH at the CNH factory in Racine, Wisconsin. Lucey testified during his deposition that prior to the accident, he and a co-worker had spent time at a club discussing employment over drinks. At the time of his deposition, Lucey was unable to recall where he was going or what time he left the club prior to the accident.

Strom Engineering Corporation (Strom) is a Minnesota company, and at the time of the accident, it had motor vehicle insurance coverage through Auto-Owners Insurance Company (Auto-Owners). The "Minnesota Amendatory Endorsement" in the Auto-Owners policy issued to Strom provides [liability coverage for bodily injury and property damage on behalf of any person using an automobile "with your permission."]

[Kender, who was injured in the accident caused by Lucey, sued Strom, Lucey, Auto-Owners, Enterprise, Empire, and others.]

Strom moved for summary judgment on the basis that Lucey was not acting within the scope of his employment at the time of the accident. The trial court granted the motion and dismissed all claims against Strom. [The dismissal of Strom is not an issue on this appeal.]

[Enterprise, which was liable only if Auto-Owners was *not* liable, filed a motion for a declaratory judgment seeking a ruling that Minnesota law should determine whether Lucey was using the car "with permission" at time of the accident. The trial court granted that motion and] held that Lucey was entitled to coverage under the Auto-Owners policy. Auto-Owners filed a petition for interlocutory appeal, which we granted.

II. Analysis

Auto-Owners argued that the trial court's decision is in error because . . . there is no basis to apply Minnesota law. . . . Auto-Owners asserts that choice of law analysis dictates that Wisconsin law should apply to the facts surrounding the accident, namely, the extent of Lucey's permission to use the vehicle. . . .

When it comes to permissive use, Wisconsin applies the mere deviation rule, which allows insurance coverage only where the deviation from the scope of permission was minor, when determining the scope of permission under an automobile liability policy. In contrast, Minnesota adheres to the initial permission rule, "which provides that when a named insured initially gives another permission to use a vehicle, subsequent use, short of conversion or theft of the vehicle, remains permissive even though the use is outside the initial grant of permission." *Christensen v. Milbank Ins. Co.*, 658 N.W.2d 580, 582 (Minn. 2003).

Thus, the determination of whether Minnesota or Wisconsin law applies to the permissive use issue is pivotal to the outcome of this case. As Auto-Owners points out, if Minnesota's initial permission rule applied, then Lucey is a permissive user under Strom's policy with Auto-Owners; however, if Wisconsin law applies, whether Lucey was driving with Strom's permission at the time of the accident is a question to be resolved by the jury. . . .

To make this determination, we employ a choice-of-law analysis. The choice-of-law rules of the forum state, Wisconsin, control this question.

Case law reveals that "insurance-related issues which arise as part of a personal injury lawsuit are not always readily categorized as sounding in tort or contract." *Drinkwater v. American Family Mut. Ins. Co.*, 290 Wis.2d 642 ¶ 36 (2006). This is evident here where the parties dispute whether contract or tort choice-of-law analysis applies. Auto-Owners submits that because this case arises out of a Wisconsin motor vehicle accident, tort choice-of-law analysis dictates that Wisconsin law should apply to the facts surrounding the accident, including those related to Lucey's permissive use of the vehicle involved in the accident.* In contrast, Enterprise contends that because this appeal arises out of a contract dispute over the interpretation of the term "permission," which is found in the omnibus provision of the Auto-Owners policy, contract choice-of-law analysis is applicable.

Two leading cases discussing choice-of-law analysis are *State Farm Mutual Auto Ins. Co. v. Gillette*, 251 Wis.2d 561 (2002), and *Drinkwater*. Auto-Owners relies on *Drinkwater*, while Enterprise contends that *Gillette* should guide our analysis. We briefly discuss both cases.

Gillette arose out of an action brought by Wisconsin residents to recover underinsured motorist benefits for injuries resulting from an accident that occurred in Manitoba, Canada. *Id.*, 251 Wis.2d 561 ¶ 2. The court applied two separate choice-of-law analyses: At the outset, it employed a contract choice-of-law analysis to determine which jurisdiction's law applied to the contractual dispute, *see id.*, ¶¶ 5, 26–28, and after resolving that issue and construing the policy, it employed a tort choice-of-law analysis to determine which jurisdiction's law controlled the damages the insureds were entitled to recover, *see id.*, ¶¶ 7, 49, 53.

At issue in *Drinkwater* was whether a health plan could enforce its contractual subrogation rights to recover from the proceeds of the plaintiff's tort action. *Id.*, 290 Wis.2d 642 ¶¶ 37–38. The court acknowledged that "contract law applies to the interpretation of the [p]lan's insurance contract with [the plaintiff]'s employer," *id.*, ¶ 37, but that because "[the plaintiff]'s right to recover in tort [was] . . . tightly bound to the plan's subrogation right," the tort choice-of-law analysis set forth in *Gillette* applied, *Drinkwater*, 290 Wis.2d 642 ¶ 39.

The circumstances of this case are unlike those presented in *Drinkwater* and in *Gillette* to the extent that they warranted the application of tort choice-of-law analysis because the injured parties' rights to recover in tort were "tightly bound" to the rights asserted by the health plan and the insurance company, respectively, *see Drinkwater*, 290 Wis.2d 642 ¶ 39; *see also Gillette*, 251 Wis.2d 561 ¶ 49. In our case, Kender's right to recover in

---

*   [Eds.' Note: Remember that the claim at issue is Kender v. Auto-Owners. Kender is not a party to the insurance contract, nor in privity with anyone or anything that is a party to that contract. Hence the argument that this is a tort claim.]

tort is not tightly bound to Auto-Owners' asserted rights under the policy that it issued to Strom.

At issue is whether Auto-Owners has contractual responsibility, under the terms of the policy it provided to Strom, to insure Lacey. Consequently, we apply the "grouping of contacts" rule to determine whether Minnesota or Wisconsin law applies to this contractual dispute. *See Gillette*, 251 Wis.2d 561 ¶ 26.

Pursuant to the "grouping of contacts" rule, contract rights are "determined by the law of the jurisdiction with which the contract has its most significant relationship." *Id.* The contacts to be considered when determining the applicable state law include:

> (a) the place of contracting, (b) the place of negotiation of the contract, (c) the place of performance, (d) the location of the subject matter of the contract, and (e) the domicile, residence, nationality, place of incorporation and place of business of the parties.

Utica Mut. Ins. Co. v. Klein & Son, Inc., 157 Wis.2d 552, 557 (Ct. App. 1990).

After considering the relevant contacts under the grouping of contacts rule, we conclude that Minnesota has the more significant relationship with the Auto-Owners policy. The contract was executed and negotiated in Minnesota given that both Strom and its insurance agent are located there. The contract was performed in Minnesota (along with other states). In addition, the place most relevant to the subject matter of the contract is Minnesota as Strom was located there, and most telling for our purposes, is the fact that the policy incorporated Minnesota-specific endorsements. The parties to the policy were Strom, a Minnesota corporation, and Auto-Owners, a Michigan insurance company. We agree with Enterprise that "it is clear from the parties' inclusion of endorsements specifically adding Minnesota provisions to the insurance contract, that the parties to this contract expected Minnesota law to apply to its interpretation." Consequently, we conclude that the significant contacts in this case strongly favor Minnesota, not Wisconsin. As such Minnesota law controls our interpretation of the term "permission" as used in the omnibus provision of the Auto-Owners policy.

As previously stated, Minnesota utilizes the initial permission rule when determining the scope of coverage created by omnibus clauses. *See Christensen*, 658 N.W.2d at 585. Because Lucey was using the vehicle involved in the accident with Strom's permission, and there is no evidence that he intended to steal or convert the vehicle, Minnesota's initial permission rule obligates Auto-Owners to provide coverage to Lucey. . . . Accordingly, we affirm.

COMMENTS AND QUESTIONS

1. It is difficult to tell the extent to which a court's choice of law is influenced by the *consequences* of choosing that law instead of the other. Do you think the court would have chosen Minnesota law if that was the law that prevented Kender from recovering? If the *consequences* of the choice play even a modest role in this process, why not be explicit about it? Is it "wrong" to err on the side of ensuring that an injured plaintiff is compensated?

2. What law would apply if the forum followed the traditional approach or interest analysis?

3. The center of gravity is a metaphor. The center of a transaction or occurrence is a function of how that transaction or occurrence is presented. Broaden or narrow the transaction or occurrence, and its center may move. Notice how the court's opinion tells us very little about what happened in Wisconsin. What kind of work was Lucey doing in Wisconsin? How long was he there? What do we know about Kender? What do we know about the accident—the injuries, the recovery? Of course Minnesota is the center of a story that includes only Minnesota facts. In whose interest would it be to build out the Wisconsin "side" of this story? Control the narrative and you control the result.

SAMPLE EXAM QUESTIONS

Question 6-4

The activities director of the Natural History Museum in Miami, Florida organized a trip for senior citizens who were interested in an archaeological dig. The group of eight flew to South Dakota, which has the largest known natural aggregation of woolly mammoth fossils in North America.

In advance of their one-week trip, the activities director made all of the flight and lodging arrangements for the group, and obtained permission from the appropriate authorities. He also checked a web site that indicated that the trip was appropriate for people "of all ages." Although there is an information center near the dig area that indeed is appropriate for persons of all ages, the actual dig site requires one to traverse rocky terrain that can be dangerous, especially when it is wet.

When the tour group encountered the rocks, only a few were able to scramble to the site; the rest turned around and spent the week swimming at the hotel and visiting accessible tourist sites like Mount Rushmore. The few who were able to reach the site and dig for fossils enjoyed the trip, until the penultimate day of the trip when Sherman fell as he was leaving the site. When he fell, he broke the tibia, fibula, and femur on his right leg. His injuries are severe and the expenses associated with those injuries are significant.

You represent the Natural History Museum. The museum's insurance policy does not extend to sponsored events outside the state of Florida. The museum is a charity, and Florida is one of the few jurisdictions that still recognize the doctrine of charitable immunity for museums. That doctrine does not extend to claims for gross negligence or willful and wanton conduct, but Sherman's claim would likely be for ordinary negligence. The issue, though, is whether Florida law will apply. South Dakota abolished the doctrine of charitable immunity many years ago.

If Sherman files his action in a jurisdiction that follows the center of gravity approach, what law should it apply?

Question 6-5

Rapid Check Cashing Corporation (RCC), incorporated in Nevada and based in Las Vegas, operates a number of check cashing stores across the southwestern United States. Some time before noon on a recent Friday,

Sparks, an RCC employee in Los Angeles, received a phone call from a woman claiming to be the wife of RCC's owner. Over the course of a wide-ranging chat, the caller told Sparks that RCC was opening a new check-cashing store that same day in another part of Los Angeles. During this call, Sparks received a second call from another woman who identified herself as the manager of the new store. The second caller said that a government official had arrived at the new store to collect a tax bill, but because the store had just opened, it had insufficient cash on hand to pay the bill. Sparks relayed this information to the original caller, who told Sparks that a man named Stedman would come to Sparks' store to collect $120,000.

A man who identified himself as Stedman came into the store. Sparks buzzed him into the store's offices and gave him $120,000 cash. Sparks never felt threatened by Stedman, and at the time, did not believe that Stedman was dangerous or was a thief.

Over the course of the afternoon, Sparks did not hear anything further from the owner or his wife. She gradually grew suspicious and eventually called the police that evening. In fact, this was a ruse. The police never caught the perpetrators nor recovered the money.

After the loss, RCC made a claim under a crime insurance policy that it purchased from Mattos Insurance Co. in Las Vegas. RCC asserted that the crime was covered under the policy's definition of "robbery," but Mattos Insurance denied the claim. The facts are undisputed and both parties have moved for summary judgment. The damages are $112,500. (The $120,000 loss minus the $7,500 deductible.) The policy contains no choice of law clause.

The policy defines robbery as "the unlawful taking of insured property by violence, threat of violence, or other aggressive felonious act." California law respects the maxim of contra proferentem in insurance cases: where the plain language of a policy permits more than one reasonable reading, a court must adopt the reading upholding coverage. Nevada law has no such preference in favor of coverage.

If an action against the insurer is filed in a jurisdiction that follows the center of gravity approach, what law should it apply?

Question 6-6

Tana Lerner, a lifelong resident of southern Maine, was diagnosed with cancer. Her oncologist at Massachusetts Global Hospital (MGH, in Boston) prescribed the drug Zometa to treat some of her symptoms. She took the drug for sixteen months. During the time that she was taking Zometa, her local dentist (in Maine) extracted two of Lerner's teeth. Complications arose and Lerner then consulted an oral surgeon at MGH, who diagnosed Lerner as having osteonecrosis of the jaw (ONJ). The oral surgeon contacted the oncologist who, in turn, immediately discontinued Lerner's prescription for Zometa.

Lerner filed a lawsuit, alleging that the manufacturer of the drug, Vonartis, failed to provide adequate warnings of the risk of developing ONJ. It is uncontroverted that the risk of ONJ was not mentioned in the package inserts. Vonartis is a Tennessee company that has its principal place of business in Knoxville.

Lerner suffered a slow and painful decline because of the cancer, and the ONJ caused her to suffer a great deal of pain in her jaw during the last year of her life in Maine. Shortly after filing suit against Vonartis, Lerner died. Lerner's only child, her daughter, a New Yorker, was substituted as plaintiff on behalf of her mother.

The elements of Lerner's failure-to-warn claim are constant across jurisdictions, but the availability of punitive damages varies. Under Tennessee law punitive damages "shall not be awarded when a drug that caused the claimant's harm was approved by the federal Food and Drug Administration (FDA)." It is undisputed that Zometa was approved by the FDA. Neither Maine nor Massachusetts has laws that single out prescription drug cases for special treatment with respect to punitive damages; punitive damages are thus generally available upon the requisite proof.

If the action is pending in a jurisdiction that follows the center of gravity approach, what law should it apply? What is the result in a jurisdiction that follows the traditional approach? Interest analysis?

Question 6-7

Lahav was seriously injured in her New York home by an employee of Renovation LLC who was demolishing part of Lahav's kitchen. Two weeks after the accident, Renovation LLC was insolvent and is now out of business. Lahav attempted to determine whether Renovation was carrying liability insurance, but did not find any such proof or details until about a year after the injury. Lahav then immediately sent a letter to that insurer, Gold Star Insurance Co., informing them of the accident. Gold Star disclaimed coverage of any liability for Lahav's injury, citing Renovation's failure to provide notice of the accident within 30-days thereof, as required by the terms of the policy.

The policy that Gold Star issued to Renovation was negotiated and executed in Texas. Gold Star is a Texas corporation with its principal place of business in Texas. Renovation is (was) a New York corporation with its principal place of business in New York City.

During the period of time when Lahav was unaware of the insurer's identity, she sued Renovation. Renovation never answered, and the court ultimately entered a default judgment in the amount of $275,000.

Lahav then initiated a direct action against Gold Star in New York. A direct action statute enumerates circumstances under which an injured person can sue an insurance company directly when their insured causes an injury. Insolvency of the insured is a classic example of when direct action statutes are useful. In a direct action, however, plaintiffs like Lahav still must establish the liability of the insurance company in order to obtain recovery from the insurer. Gold Star has moved for summary judgment, arguing that it is entitled to disclaim coverage because of National's failure to provide adequate notice of the accident. Lahav concedes that Renovation did not notify Gold Star of the claim.

Under Texas law, a liability insurer may disclaim coverage on the basis of defective notice only if it was prejudiced by the defect. Under New York, a liability insurer may generally disclaim coverage on the basis of defective notice, regardless of whether the insurer was prejudiced by the defect. These are the "prejudice" and "no prejudice" rules, respectively.

Lahav filed this action in New York. If New York uses a "grouping of contacts" theory to resolve choice of law disputes, will the court apply (i) New York law and grant summary judgment; or (ii) apply Texas law, deny summary judgment, and prepare for trial on whether Gold Star suffered prejudice as a result of the delay?

Quick Summary

- The center of gravity of a transaction or occurrence is often contestable

- Effective litigators will often emphasize why certain factors of a multi-factor test deserve more weight than other factors

- A flexible approach to choice of law has both advantages and disadvantages

- All of the choice of law methodologies presented in Chapters 4–8 regard only the applicable substantive law; the court can (and usually will) always apply its own procedural law

7

Better Law

Key Concepts

- Interrogating the "real reasons" that judges apply the law that they do
- Incorporating older choice of law methodologies as elements of a new choice of law methodology
- Multi-factor tests

In the 1960s, Professor Robert Leflar criticized "mechanical rules and circuitously devised approaches" that masked the "true reasons that underlie choice-of-law adjudication."[1] He observed that choice of law methodologies are designed to generate outcomes that approximate our desired results about what law should apply. But why have a methodological substitute for that inquiry, he asked, when you can instead have the real thing? Unnecessary intermediaries spawn doctrinal complexity. The "real reasons" as to why judges apply the law in the manner they do have "been there all along, whether they were stated or not."[2]

Leflar's tentative summarization included five considerations:

1. Predictability of results. The justified expectations of the parties should be protected.

2. Maintenance of interstate and international order. Social and economic commerce is productive and requires mutual recognition and respect for foreign laws.

3. Simplification of the judicial task. Ease of judicial performance, while not of first importance, is important in some choices.

---

1 Robert A. Leflar, *Conflicts Law: More on Choice-Influencing Considerations,* 54 CAL. L. REV. 1584, 1585 (1966).

2 *Id.*

4.   Advancement of the forum's governmental interests. Genuine concerns that motivate a state's public policy are a major choice-influencing consideration.

5.   Application of the better rule of law. A judge should prefer the rule of law that makes good socio-economic sense for the time when the court speaks. "The preference is objective, not subjective. It has to do with preferred law, not preferred parties."[3]

The fifth consideration is the most provocative, and is why this approach is often labeled the better law approach. The approach is also sometimes called "Leflar's Choice-Influencing Considerations." A few states follow this approach, as illustrated in the table in Chapter 3. Some jurisdictions use a better law approach in combination with another approach. (Some jurisdictions may apply the better law approach in practice even if they nominally follow some other approach.)

This approach, like the center of gravity approach, is multivariate without strict guidance as to how it should be applied. Leflar suggested that the third consideration is probably the least significant and the fourth consideration may be the most important. The second and fourth considerations resemble interest analysis. The third consideration may be a built-in preference for forum law; this is a frequent criticism of the better law approach.

The first consideration is new in the sense that other approaches have not explicitly asked what law the parties would expect to apply.[4] That appears to be an important and useful question in determining what law should apply. Indeed, it seems unfair to allow a party to escape the obligations of some law that they expected would have applied.

That argument can be so strong that an advocate needs some good stock arguments ready to counter it. One of those counter-arguments is that people do not really possess such expectations. For example, when someone takes a job to work remotely at home for an employer who is in another state, they tend not to think about what state's law will apply if disputes arise, much less whether the potential dispute would concern a contract, tort, or other kind of issue. Moreover, to the extent that someone has expectations, they may be based on factors having little if anything to do with choice of law rules—*e.g.* where the work is done rather than where the employment contract was entered into. Alternatively, the applicable

---

3   *Id.*

4   Methodologies that purport to be *predictable* try to achieve this indirectly. To say that someone could reliably predict what law would apply under certain circumstances is to say that they could—and should—have foreseen it.

choice of law rules may have created those expectations (rather than vice versa). If the forum always applies forum employment law, then that may become the expectation (to the extent that it is known). But that doesn't mean that the jurisdiction must keep doing so; change the choice of law approach and you could change the expectation. All of this is, of course, premised on the assumption that the parties will even think about what law would govern any dispute they may have. Often they do not—unless, of course, a contract is involved that includes a choice of law clause—and it is not unusual even for attorneys in court to overlook choice of law issues.

The fifth consideration is problematic because it is so subjective. Leflar believed that a judge knows when foreign law is better than forum law, or vice versa. But it is not obvious to what ideology one should consult to make that determination. Where is this superlaw? Finding consensus on the common good is usually elusive. Accordingly, effective advocates tend to use objective measures to argue that one law is better than another: it is more recent or is time-tested; it is mainstream or is a useful experiment; it is a legislative enactment or a judicial decision; it is more specific or is all-encompassing.

As with any multivariate test, litigators will leverage the more favorable considerations while downplaying the others. However, judges cannot similarly rely on advocacy as their guiding star; they must apply the test. A good advocate, therefore, will frame her arguments in a way that assists the judge in writing the order or opinion.

Hypothetical 7-1

Jemma Woods was involved in a two-car automobile accident when she was struck near her home in Newport, Rhode Island by a minivan driven by Nazmun Mazumder. Temporarily blinded by the strong glare of the sun, Mazumder crossed into Woods' lane of travel. The vehicle driven by Mazumder was owned by Alamo, a car rental corporation which is incorporated in Florida, has its principal place of business in Florida, and has branches in many parts of the United States. The automobile was rented by Mazumder from an Alamo office at the Newark International Airport in New Jersey. Mazumder is a British domiciliary. She has no liability insurance and is judgment-proof.

As part of the rental agreement between Mazumder and Alamo, liability coverage was extended to Mazumder, covering bodily injury, death, or property damage, up to the minimum required by state law in any state in which the car was driven and an accident occurred. When Mazumder returned the car, the odometer indicated that the vehicle had been driven 1,976 miles during the one-week rental. At the time of the rental agreement Alamo had no office in Rhode Island. The vehicle was registered in New Jersey.

Ten years ago, the Rhode Island Supreme Court refused to impose vicarious liability on the owner of a rental vehicle. Many state legislatures, including Florida and New Jersey, have recently passed legislation imposing joint and several liability on auto rental companies.

You represent Woods. If you file this action in a jurisdiction that follows the better law approach, what law is the court likely to apply? You also have a summer associate to whom you can assign research tasks. With respect to the choice of law question, what *exactly* would you ask him to research?

Hypothetical 7-2

Two years ago representatives of Moran Airline Repair Corp. (Moran) attended several meetings in Minnesota concerning proposals for undertaking work to refurbish aircraft which Northwest Airlines, Inc., had purchased from another carrier. These meetings included a preliminary meeting attended by several potential bidders for the refurbishment contracts, as well as meetings where Moran submitted proposals and negotiated the refurbishment contracts. In addition, Moran made numerous telephone calls to Northwest's offices in Minnesota during this time.

Over the course of the following year several contracts resulted. The first refurbishment contract was executed by the parties in Minnesota. A second contract, executed by email, provided that Moran would refurbish additional planes. Eventually the parties also entered into a maintenance contract, also by email, under which Moran was to provide routine maintenance for a substantial portion of Northwest's fleet of airplanes.

Pursuant to the terms of the contracts, Northwest delivered planes to Moran's facility in Dallas, Texas. Northwest sent voluminous amounts of information (manuals, specifications, etc.) to Dallas and also stationed some of its employees there to oversee Moran's work. Representatives from Moran also traveled to Minnesota on three occasions to discuss issues that arose under the contracts.

Disputes arose about the quality of Moran's work. Aware of these rumors, a local Minneapolis, Minnesota newspaper reporter contacted Northwest. A Northwest employee told the reporter that the company had concerns about the quality of Moran's work, including defective parts, a leaky fuel line, and an undetected tail crack on one of the aircraft. Those statements were included in an article in the newspaper, which also appeared online. A Texas newspaper reprinted the article. A Northwest employee also distributed copies of the article to other customers of Moran. Meanwhile the contracts expired with neither party seeking to extend their relationship further.

Still suffering injury to its reputation, Moran is contemplating pursuing defamation and libel claims against Northwest. Minnesota law considers a corporation a public figure and thus requires a plaintiff to show that the defendant's statements were made with actual malice—meaning that the statement was made with knowledge that it was false. Texas law does not require proof of actual malice. Plaintiff may recover under Texas law with proof that a reasonably prudent person would have investigated the statement before publishing it. The refurbishment and service contracts between the companies contained choice of law clauses directing the application of Minnesota law. But the parties concede that the narrow scope of those clauses does not include Moran's tort claims.

If a complaint is filed in a jurisdiction that follows the better law approach which law is the court likely to apply? You represent Moran. Should the action instead be filed in a jurisdiction that follows the traditional approach? Interest analysis? Center of gravity?

Hypothetical 7-3

David Numberman hosted a popular late-night talk show on a national television network for more than three decades. Numberman was closely associated with New York City, where the show was filmed before a live studio audience five nights per week. Numberman retired from television more than a year ago. Just a few months after retiring to the city in Indiana where he was born and raised, Numberman died.

Darden Motors is a chain of automotive retailers that is popular in eastern New York. Around the time of Numberman's retirement, Darden offered him a lucrative sum to lend his distinctive voice to radio advertisements that Darden was planning to run across the State. Numberman declined. After Numberman died, Darden hired a voice actor whose voice is similar to the vocal timbre and styling of Numberman. Darden has been running these ads on the radio for several weeks.

A statute in Indiana recognizes a right of publicity, which allows a person to control the commercial use of a person's name or likeness. The thinking behind the statute is that it is unfair for a business to profit from a person's celebrity status without compensating that celebrity.

Generally speaking, the right of publicity is an evolving and complex right. Many states (like Indiana) have codified a right of publicity. Some states have recognized a right of publicity through case law. Some states have rejected a right of publicity. In states that recognize a right of publicity, the scope varies considerably; indeed there is so much variance that there routinely are calls for national legislation to codify and standardize the right (as with trademark law). To date, however, that national legislation has not passed.

New York has a statute that is textually similar to Indiana's. In New York, however, there is case law holding that a deceased person has no right of publicity.

You represent the beneficiaries of Numberman's estate, who would benefit from the application of Indiana's law, rather than New York's. Assuming that the case is filed in Indiana, that Darden Motors would be subject to personal jurisdiction in Indiana, and that Indiana follows the better law approach, how likely is the court to apply Indiana law? If New York law follows interest analysis, should we instead file there—an approach that would have the additional benefit of avoiding a fight about obtaining personal jurisdiction over Darden in Indiana?

FROM THE COURTS

KUEHN v. CHILDRENS HOSPITAL, LOS ANGELES

U.S. Court of Appeals for the Seventh Circuit
119 F.3d 1296 (7th Cir. 1997)

Posner, Chief Judge.

The parents of Andrew Kuehn brought this diversity suit in a federal district court in Wisconsin both on his behalf and on their own behalf against a Los Angeles hospital. . . . The district judge granted summary judgment for the defendants on the ground that under Wisconsin's conflict of law rules, which are applicable to this diversity suit because Wisconsin is the state in which the suit was brought, the law governing the plaintiffs' tort claims is California law, under which the plaintiffs have no right to relief. So he dismissed the suit, and the plaintiffs appeal, arguing that Wisconsin's conflict of law rules make Wisconsin law, not California law, applicable to the substantive issues in the suit.

The facts are gruesome. In 1994, Andrew, aged 2, was diagnosed as having neuroblastoma, an often fatal children's cancer. His parents enrolled him in an experimental treatment program offered by Childrens Hospital of Los Angeles in cooperation with the hospital of the University of Wisconsin. The treatment required Andrew to go to Childrens Hospital to have bone marrow removed from him, the marrow to be cleansed of cancer cells by the hospital and shipped back in a vacuum-sealed container to the University of Wisconsin hospital, where the marrow would be reinserted in him. His parents flew with him to Los Angeles and the bone marrow was removed without incident at Childrens Hospital. The removal of bone marrow is a painful process that requires drilling many holes in the patient's hips. After removal the marrow was duly treated and then sent back to the University of Wisconsin hospital via Federal Express. The container in which Childrens Hospital shipped the boy's marrow was defective, however; and in addition Childrens Hospital turned the container wrong side up, which made it more likely to tip over in transit, and also took no special measures, as it could easily have done, to ensure prompt delivery. Delivery was in fact delayed; and the delay, in combination with the container's having been shipped upside down, caused the marrow to arrive in a "thawed" state in which it was unusable. The parents were told they would have to take their son back to Childrens Hospital for more of his bone marrow to be removed. They flew him back and he underwent the painful procedure a second time. Andrew's father carried the newly "harvested" marrow back to Wisconsin personally, and it was reinserted into Andrew there.

The treatment was unsuccessful and Andrew died eight months later, but no evidence has been presented that the botch of the first marrow treatment and resulting delay in the reinsertion of the cleansed marrow hastened his death. As the case comes to us, shorn of some of its original claims, it is a suit not for wrongful death or for the expenses of the treatment but only for the pain and suffering that Andrew underwent in the second extraction of marrow, which would have been unnecessary had Childrens Hospital not been negligent. . . . There is not even a claim that the hospital's negligence, while it cannot be shown to have hastened Andrew's death, deprived him of a *chance* of a longer life, viewed as a legally protected interest separate from life itself. *See, e.g., Doll v. Brown*, 75 F.3d 1200, 1205–06 (7th Cir. 1996). . . . Although California does not recognize the loss of a chance doctrine, *Dumas v. Cooney*, 235 Cal.App.3d 1593 (1991), Wisconsin recognizes a variant of it. *See Ehlinger v. Sipes*, 155 Wis.2d 1 (1990). . . .

[T]here is an undeniable conflict between California and Wisconsin law with regard to the plaintiffs' . . . claim for damages for the pain and suffering that the second extraction inflicted on Andrew. In California, a claim for such damages does not survive the death of the victim. Cal. Civ. Proc. Code § 377.34. . . . In Wisconsin it does. Wis. Stat. § 895.01(1). . . . So we must decide whether . . . the state court would have applied the California or the Wisconsin rule on the survivability of claims for damages for pain and suffering. Answering this question is complicated by the fact that Wisconsin uses a laundry-list approach to conflicts questions. The list has five items: predictability of results, maintenance of interstate order (that is, not applying the law of a state that lacks a significant interest in how the case is decided), simplification of the court's task, advancement of the forum state's interests, and which state's law is better. *Heath v. Zellmer*, 35 Wis.2d 578 (1967). . . . The items are not weighted, but the presumption is in favor of the forum state's, that is, Wisconsin's law.

In choosing California law, the district judge emphasized the first and the last two items on Wisconsin's list. He thought that since the negligent act and injury had occurred (or at least had occurred mainly) in California, the parties would have expected California law to apply. And he thought that since Wisconsin's residents have a big stake in cancer research, and imposing tort liability on Childrens Hospital would retard such research, California's nonsurvival rule was both the better law and the one that actually served Wisconsin's interests better. The defendant adds that subjecting Childrens Hospital to the different tort rules of all 50 states (for the hospital draws its patients from all over the country) would make the hospital's legal obligations highly uncertain and therefore costly, and that California's rule on the nonsurvival of claims for pain and suffering is the better rule because it denies Andrew's parents a windfall, since it was his pain and suffering and he is dead.

Which state's law applies under the applicable conflict of law rules is a pure question of law. We therefore cannot give any deference to the answer given by the district judge; the Supreme Court has held that a federal court of appeals is not to give weight to a determination of state law by a district judge even if he is sitting in that state and so is presumed to be especially familiar with its laws. *Salve Regina College v. Russell,* 499 U.S. 225 (1991). . . . We must give our independent view and it is that Wisconsin's method of resolving conflicts points to Wisconsin, not California, law to govern this case. Because both states have substantial interests at stake—Wisconsin because it is the home of the tort victim, California because it is both the home of the defendant and the place where the defendant's careless acts occurred—the "interstate order" criterion drops out. *Heath v. Zellmer, supra,* 151 N.W.2d at 674. As for simplifying the judicial task, all that comes to mind is that of course if California law applies, barring the plaintiffs' only remaining claim and thus requiring the dismissal of their suit, the judicial task will be simplified, because it is easier to dismiss a case at the outset than to proceed to the summary judgment stage and perhaps to trial. We cannot imagine that such a consideration, systematically favoring defendants, is entitled to significant weight. . . .

That leaves us with three criteria to consider. The first criterion, predictability, might seem to point unerringly to California, because that's where the medical procedure that caused the child's pain and suffering was performed. Closer consideration shows the compass wobbling. The defendant is arguing in effect for *lex loci delicti*—the law of the place of the tort should govern. That was the reigning rule in the early part of this century, . . . and had the virtue of relative certainty, and therefore predictability. It persists in attenuated form in some states. . . , but not, so far as we can find, in Wisconsin—and even if it did, this would not help the defendant. The place of the tort, for conflicts and other purposes, is not where the negligent act occurs but where the injury is felt. . . . The negligent *act* occurred not at the time of the second extraction, which was conducted without negligence, but when the first extraction of marrow was shipped. The *injury* to Andrew occurred when that marrow arrived in unusable form; for at that point he had been deprived of cells that he needed in order to have a chance of extending his life. And he was in Wisconsin then. The return to California for the second procedure amounted to an effort by the tortfeasor to mitigate the harm by replacing the product that it had damaged in shipment. The pain and suffering from the second procedure occurred in California (where the marrow was extracted) and Wisconsin (where it was reinserted), but was not inflicted tortuously; the tortious injury had occurred in Wisconsin, earlier, when the botched shipment deprived Andrew of the marrow and thus necessitated the second extraction and reinsertion.

Suppose you broke your leg in Illinois but were sent across the state line to Wisconsin to have it set. If the setting of the bone though done without any negligence was painful, the pain would be deemed an incident of the injury in Illinois, and Illinois would be the *locus delicti* even if the only damages you were seeking were for the pain and suffering of the setting. It would be like a case in which the plaintiff, injured in one state, is treated in his state of domicile; the state of injury would still, we take it, be the *locus delicti*, though we cannot find a case on the question.

Since the tort occurred in Wisconsin rather than in California, the defendant cannot get any mileage out of the doctrine of *lex loci delicti* even if it retains some force in Wisconsin, of which we cannot find any evidence. This does not resolve the issue of predictability. But that issue can be resolved by noting that if Childrens Hospital, a sophisticated enterprise, had wanted predictability of outcome it would undoubtedly have included in its contract with the Kuehns pursuant to which Andrew was enrolled in the experimental bone marrow extraction and reinsertion program a clause specifying California as the state whose law would apply in the event of a suit growing out of the experimental treatment. Ever since informed consent became the rage, hospitals have been expert at including elaborate disclaimers in their contracts with patients. Choice of law clauses are common and when reasonable are enforced. . . .

A defendant's failure to negotiate a choice of law provision when as in this case the defendant has a written contract with the potential plaintiff makes the claim that applying the law of another state would unsettle the defendant's legal obligations ring hollow. It may indeed unsettle them but evidently the defendant does not much care. It is not as if Childrens Hospital could not have foreseen that it might be sued in another state—specifically Wisconsin. Its cooperative arrangement with the University of Wisconsin in the treatment program in which Andrew was enrolled clearly made it suable there. There is no suggestion, moreover, that exposing Childrens Hospital to the different tort laws of the different states would subject it to conflicting obligations. The only difference between California and Wisconsin tort law, so far as bears on this case at any rate, is in the scope of liability for negligence, not in the standard of care. It is not as if California had required one method of packing and shipping bone marrow and Wisconsin another.

So considerations of predictability do not strongly favor California law in this case, and the other considerations strongly favor Wisconsin law. Even if one thought that imposing slightly greater liability for negligence on Childrens Hospital would have a perceptible effect on the vigor of cancer research in the United States, which is exceedingly unlikely even apart from the fact that the negligence was in the shipping of a good rather than in the course of medical research, the injury to Wisconsin's residents from this imperceptible diminution in research would be outweighed by the state's interest in obtaining for its residents the measure of relief that the state believes appropriate in tort cases. Or so the Wisconsin courts would probably think. . . . This means that the application of Wisconsin law will advance the forum state's interests. . . .

California's rule (nonsurvival) is not the better rule, moreover, but the worse rule or at least the more archaic one. The needs of cancer research cannot logically have *any* weight in the choice. That would imply that whether the Wisconsin courts applied California law rather than their own would depend on whether the defendant was thought to be engaged in work of peculiar merit—an approach that would eliminate all predictability and greatly complicate the judicial task. It would also put the Wisconsin courts and their federal surrogates in the role of selectively reviving the tort immunity of charitable institutions, even though the immunity has been rejected in Wisconsin as elsewhere. . . .

The defendant is correct that if the victim is dead the award of damages for his pain and suffering constitutes a windfall—the award is to someone other than the victim. But that logic is too powerful; it implies that *all* tort suits should abate with the death of the victim, not just suits seeking damages for pain and suffering. That *was* the common law rule, but it was changed in the nineteenth century . . . and its survival (the survival of nonsurvival) in California with respect to pain and suffering is quaintly vestigial, rather than its being the better law and the law of the future. A few states retain this vestige . . . but we cannot find any articulated justification for it. Although the California legislature did in 1961 reject a recommendation by the state's law review commission to abolish it . . . we do not know why the legislature rejected the recommendation. So it is not as if what we are describing as a vestige is actually the first stage in a new wave of tort reform.

The objection to making a tort suit abate with the death of the victim is that it gives the injurer an incentive to make a clean kill and reduces the deterrent effect of tort law by eliminating any tort sanction for inflicting fatal injuries. The objection is diminished when the rule of abatement is limited as California has done to one item of damages. But it reappears in that situation as an objection to drawing arbitrary distinctions with less cause than in the case of negligent infliction of emotional distress with which we began. So strongly do the other considerations besides predictability favor Wisconsin law in this case that the application of that law was predictable—thus completing the sweep. . . . [T]he dismissal of the pain and suffering claim is reversed and the case remanded for further proceedings consistent with this opinion.

COMMENTS AND QUESTIONS

1. The court's discussion of the first criterion—predictability—begins with consideration of whether California or Wisconsin is the place of Andrew's injury. Why would the traditional approach define the expectation of the parties?

    What do we mean when we talk about the expectation of the parties? We could present the facts of *Kuehn* as a hypo to our non-lawyer friends and ask them whether they think California or Wisconsin law should apply; is their collective intuition what we mean by reasonable expectations? Do you include or exclude from the hypo, when stating it to those friends, the fact that Wisconsin has the pro-recovery rule and California has the anti-recovery rule?

2. Why does Judge Posner conclude that Wisconsin is the place of injury? Imagine the case had been filed in a third state, neither Wisconsin nor California. And imagine that that third state followed the traditional approach. What law do you think they would have applied (as *lex loci delicti*)?

3. Judge Posner is unsympathetic to Childrens Hospital's argument about predictability because they could have but did not include a choice of law clause. We will study choice of law clauses in Chapter 9. Choice of law clauses are especially useful techniques to resolve uncertainty about what law will apply in the event a dispute arises.

How much uncertainty was present here? The patient came to the hospital for treatment.

4. The court is dismissive of the third criterion—simplification of the judicial task. When should the complexity of foreign law be an excuse for not applying it? The answer to that question is surely not by celebrating slothfulness—one of the so-called deadly sins, after all. Instead, you would cast it as an expression of humility and skepticism about our ability to apply another jurisdiction's substantive law. To be sure, one person's humility and skepticism will be another's "chauvinism" or "provincialism" when thoughtful restraint leads to the application of forum law rather than foreign law. But the argument is that we cannot faithfully apply it—perhaps because of its complexity, or maybe because it is intertwined with foreign procedure (and we will instead be applying forum procedure). The argument is that we cannot apply that law with fidelity to its mandate. We will address proof of foreign law in Chapter 18.

5. With respect to the fifth criterion—the better law—the court suggests not that the California law is inferior (a subjective assessment), but rather that it is archaic and out-of-step with modern developments (an objective assessment). Childrens Hospital similarly tied its preferred law to an objective good: the promotion of cancer research. Skillful advocates will argue that a law is *better* by appealing to some objective benchmark.

    Judge Posner discusses how the common law's nonsurvival of tort actions has been abandoned by most jurisdictions because nonsurvival has perverse incentives. And he observes that "we cannot find any articulated justification" for California's nonsurvival rule with respect to pain and suffering. Was this case lost because of a failure of proof on the part of Childrens Hospital's counsel?

FROM THE COURTS

HAGUE v. ALLSTATE INS. CO.

Supreme Court of Minnesota
289 N.W.2d (Minn. 1978)*

YETKA, JUSTICE.

Appeal by defendant Allstate Insurance Co., from an order of the district court granting plaintiff's motion for summary judgment and denying defendant's motion to dismiss. We affirm. . . .

The facts are not in dispute. The cause of action upon which this case is based arises out of an automobile and motorcycle accident which occurred on July 1, 1974, in Pierce County, Wisconsin, which is immediately adjacent to the border near Red Wing, Minnesota. Ralph A. Hague was a passenger on a motorcycle owned and operated by his son, Ronald Hague.

The Hagues were traveling west on State Highway No. 35, and they intended to turn left (to the south) onto a road that led to Elderwood Heights, Wisconsin. They slowed to an eventual stop and signaled their intention to make a left turn. While waiting for an eastbound car to pass in the oncoming lane, the motorcycle was struck from behind by an automobile owned and operated by Richard R. Borst, a resident of Ellsworth, Wisconsin. Ralph Hague died as a result of injuries sustained in this accident.

At the time of the accident, Ralph Hague resided with his wife, Lavinia Hague, in Hager City, Wisconsin, which is located just 1½ miles from Red Wing, Minnesota. Although Ralph Hague resided in Wisconsin, he was employed in Red Wing, Minnesota, and he had been employed in Red Wing for 15 years immediately preceding his death. After the accident, and prior to the initiation of the above entitled matter, Lavinia Hague moved her residence to Red Wing, Minnesota. On June 19, 1976, almost concurrently with the initiation of this action, Lavinia Hague was married to a Minnesota resident who operated an automobile service station in Bloomington, and established residence with her husband in Savage, Minnesota.

---

* [Eds.' Note: This case was appealed to the United States Supreme Court, and you will read about that opinion in Chapter 14. The U.S. Supreme Court opinion focuses on a different issue, however.]

The motorcycle which Ralph Hague was riding was owned by Ronald for about 1 year prior to the accident.

Ronald Hague owned other vehicles that were insured by Allstate, but his motorcycle was not insured. Richard Borst was without valid insurance coverage at the time of the accident.

Ralph Hague was insured at the time of the accident by Allstate, which had issued one policy to decedent that extended coverage to three automobiles Ralph Hague owned. A separate premium was paid for each automobile. The policy was effective as of June 8, 1974, and it provided for uninsured motorist coverage to a limit of $15,000 for each automobile.

On May 28, 1976, the Registrar of Probate for the County of Goodhue, State of Minnesota, appointed Lavinia Hague personal representative of the estate of her deceased husband, Ralph Hague. Subsequent to her appointment as personal representative, Lavinia Hague initiated the above-entitled action against Allstate.

Plaintiff is suing for declaratory relief construing the above indicated policy so as to "stack" the separate $15,000 uninsured motorist coverages on each automobile and therefore afford coverage in the total amount of $45,000. Questions of liability and amount of damages are not at issue in this proceeding, only the amount of coverage available. . . .

[The parties agreed that Minnesota law allowed "stacking" of the uninsured motorist benefits in the insurance policy. Wisconsin law was less clear, but the court concluded that stacking would not be permitted if Wisconsin law applied. Defendant argued that Wisconsin law applied. Plaintiff argued for the application of Minnesota law.]

In *Milkovich v. Saari*, 295 Minn. 155 (1973), this court adopted a methodology of analysis for resolving conflicts of laws questions.[4] This analysis involves the following "choice-influencing considerations" 295 Minn. 161: (1) predictability of result, (2) maintenance of interstate and international order, (3) simplification of the judicial task, (4) advancement of the forum's governmental interest, (5) application of the better rule of law. . . .

---

4   The approach adopted was taken from the proposal made by Professor Robert Leflar in *Choice-Influencing Considerations in Conflict Law*, 41 N.Y.U. L. Rev. 267.

Defendant argues that application of the five tests mandate application of Wisconsin law. It argues that predictability of result, interstate order, and advancement of the forum's governmental interest mandate this result. Plaintiff argues, and the trial court agreed, that the *Milkovich* line of cases involving foreign torts makes the advancement of the forum's governmental interest and better rule of law the only relevant considerations. The discussion of interests is based on the peculiar hybrid nature of the problems involved in automobile liability insurance cases. The analysis should determine the choice of laws by examining both tort and contract considerations.

(1) Predictability of Results

Defendant argues that this factor favors application of Wisconsin law because the insurer of a vehicle is concerned with setting of standard rates. Plaintiff argues that this analysis is mistaken insofar as defendant was reasonably to be presumed to travel in Minnesota and insofar as Minnesota law would clearly apply if the accident had occurred in Minnesota. This consideration weighs slightly in defendant's favor, but the fact that one cannot predict automobile accidents because they are unplanned makes predictability of results less important in automobile liability insurance cases than in other contract cases.

(2) Maintenance of Interstate Order

This concept requires that the state whose laws are ultimately applied have sufficient contacts with the facts in issue. ["Minnesota's contacts . . . begin with plaintiff's residence at the time of suit, defendant's license to do business, and defendant's conduct of business in the state. . . . Minnesota contacts . . . are, however, more extensive because the contract involved is one concerning automobile liability insurance. Insofar as the contract is one of indemnity for tort recovery, the kinds of contacts relevant to tort cases may be considered. The facts show that plaintiff's decedent traveled to work in Minnesota for 15 years. Thus, the risk which was covered by the policy was located in Minnesota as well as Wisconsin. One additional interest, not addressed by the parties, is Minnesota's interest in the administration of estates. According to the stipulated facts, plaintiff was appointed personal representative of her husband's estate by a Minnesota court. The plaintiff as an heir resides in Minnesota."]. . . . Leflar points out that retaliation by one state for mere forum preference of another state may also be considered in a decision to apply non-forum law where forum contacts are minimal. . . .

In the present case, if the contacts with Minnesota were less substantial, this would be a stronger consideration. Under this heading the court may also consider whether or not application of Minnesota law will encourage forum shopping. This would also be a strong consideration in the present case if there was any evidence that plaintiff had moved to this state for the purpose of bringing suit. This consideration thus does not require application of Wisconsin law.

(3) Simplification of the Judicial Task

The parties appear to agree that this issue is irrelevant because there is an applicable Wisconsin statute which this court is capable of interpreting.

(4) Advancement of the Forum's Governmental Interest

Minnesota's governmental interest will most clearly be advanced by application of Minnesota law. The state's interest in fully compensating resident accident victims and thus keeping them off welfare rolls and enabling them to meet financial obligations will be met most adequately by allowing stacking. The advancement of Minnesota's interest is only partially inconsistent with the advancement of Wisconsin's in that Wisconsin is interested in giving the plaintiff some recovery, but at minimum limits.

The factual contacts with this state are more limited than the contacts which mandated application of Minnesota law in *Schwartz v. Consolidated Freight-ways Corp.,* 221 N.W.2d 665 (1974). In *Schwartz,* the plaintiff, injured in Indiana, was a lifelong Minnesota resident and employed by a Minnesota corporation at the time of the accident. Because the present case involves a third-party insurance beneficiary rather than a plaintiff personally injured in an accident, we are not convinced that the Minnesota contacts are, in themselves, sufficient to mandate application of our law. Thus, we must consider the remaining factor.

(5) The Better Rule of Law

This consideration clearly mandates application of Minnesota law. Minnesota follows a majority of jurisdictions in allowing stacking and this fact has been recognized by the Wisconsin Supreme Court. *Nelson v. Employers Mut. Cas. Co.,* 63 Wis.2d 558. Although majority status is not by itself sufficient to make a rule "better," the decisions on stacking are fairly recent and well considered in light of current uses of automobiles. Additionally, the line of decisions in Minnesota which favors stacking is impliedly based on the premise that the rule allowing stacking is the better rule of law. We believe that it is preferable to compensate victims of accidents to the full extent of their injuries, and we believe that is the policy adopted by the legislature. The Minnesota rule is better because it requires the cost of accidents with uninsured motorists to be spread more broadly through insurance premiums than does the Wisconsin rule. . . .

COMMENTS AND QUESTIONS

1. A case where the party who never should have won, wins, is an opportunity to examine expert advocacy (by the winner) and/or lousy advocacy (by the loser). Expert advocacy requires mastery of the doctrine (law), extraordinary attention to detail (facts), and control of the narrative (rhetoric).

    Judges read and listen to the advocates' arguments, and a judge's opinion reflects what s/he heard or read. For example, although Justice Yetka does not include much factual detail about the insurance policy, he does note that: "A separate premium was paid for each automobile." He also observed that Ralph Hague lived "just 1½ miles" from Minnesota, and that he commuted to Minnesota "for 15 years." These facts were important to the Justice because plaintiff-appellee's counsel emphasized them.

2. The first criterion of the better law approach—predictability of results—"weighs slightly" in favor of the application of Wisconsin law. Is the predictability of where an automobile accident might occur the relevant question here?

3. The policy did not include a choice of law clause. As Judge Posner observed in *Kuehn*, a company that wants certainty can include a choice of law clause in their contract. Does it follow that if a company does not include a choice of law clause, the court can (or should) err on the side of choosing the law that is less favorable to that party?

4. Notice the court's effort to determine the "better law" by appealing to an objective benchmark: a majority of jurisdictions allow stacking (—and these decisions are "fairly recent.") The court also observes

that stacking is better social policy. But where does one find the list of these better social policies? Might one fairly have thought that avoiding windfalls and keeping insurance premiums low so that more people can afford insurance is a good—maybe even better—policy?

FROM THE COURTS

LAPLANTE v. AMERICAN HONDA MOTOR CO., INC.

U.S. Court of Appeals for the First Circuit
27 F.3d 731 (1st Cir. 1994)

Bownes, Senior Circuit Judge.

. . . On Saturday, March 11, 1989, the course of Arthur LaPlante's life was dramatically and irreversibly altered. On that morning plaintiff, a twenty-four-year-old army mechanic stationed at Fort Carson, Colorado, and three friends, Kelly Kallhoff, Randy Leib, and Mike Mohawk, ventured to nearby Pikes Peak in order to ride Kallhoff's three-wheel ATV, a 1982 Honda ATC200. This ATV is a three-wheeled motorized vehicle intended for off-road use. The vehicle has handlebar steering and large low-pressure tires, two in the rear, and one in front.

Plaintiff, who had never before ridden an ATV, was the third to ride after Kallhoff and Leib. After climbing to the top of a knoll, plaintiff began to descend at a speed of 5–10 miles per hour. When plaintiff was unable to negotiate a left-hand turn onto a twelve foot wide dirt road, he fell over a steep embankment and broke his neck, resulting in permanent paralysis from the neck down.

On January 11, 1991, plaintiff, who lived in Rhode Island before enlisting in the Army in 1983 and returned there after the accident, commenced this diversity action in the U.S. District Court for the District of Rhode Island. . . .

A twenty-three day trial on liability and compensatory damages began in July 1993. At the close of plaintiff's case Honda moved for judgment as a matter of law. Only the claims for negligent failure to warn and strict liability design defect survived the motion. Ultimately the jury found Honda liable on these two claims, and awarded plaintiff $2,652,000 for medical expenses and lost wages, and $6,000,000 for physical injuries and pain and suffering. The jury also found that plaintiff was comparatively negligent, and reduced his award by fifteen percent. . . .

The punitive damages phase of this action commenced on September 16, 1993. On the same day, at the close of plaintiff's evidence, the district court granted Honda's motion for judgment as a matter of law. These cross-appeals ensued. . . .

Honda argues that the district court's decision to apply Rhode Island, rather than Colorado law, to the issue of compensatory damages was erroneous.[5] We disagree.

. . . A federal court sitting in diversity must apply the conflict of law rules of the state in which it sits. *Klaxon Co. v. Stentor Elec. Manuf. Co.,* 313 U.S. 487 (1941). . . .

Under [the state of Rhode Island's] approach various interests are weighed in order to decide which jurisdiction has the most significant relationship with reference to a particular substantive issue. *Pardey v. Boulevard Billiard Club,* 518 A.2d 1349, 1351 (R.I. 1986). . . . The first set of factors to be taken into account are (1) the place where the injury occurred; (2) the place where the conduct causing the injury occurred; (3) the place that the parties call home (*e.g.,* their domicile, residence, place of incorporation or place of business). *See Brown v. Church of the Holy Name,* 105 R.I. 322 (1969). . . .

The resolution of choice-of-law problems may not always turn on the number of contacts, but rather, the qualitative nature of those contacts affected by the following factors: (1) predictability of results; (2) maintenance of interstate order; (3) simplification of the judicial task; (4) advancement of the forum's governmental interest; and (5) application of the better rule of law. . . .

Our review of the district court's ruling is plenary. . . .

---

5   The difference between the two is substantial. While neither state limits a plaintiff's recovery of "economic" damages, or damages for physical impairment and disfigurement, Colorado sets a $250,000 cap on damages for noneconomic loss or injury." (i.e., pain and suffering), Colo. Rev. Stat. § 13–21–102.5 (1987 & 1993 Supp.). Rhode Island has no such limit.

Regarding the number of contacts, we can discern no material difference between Rhode Island and Colorado. Although the injury occurred in Colorado, none of the defendants are domiciliaries of Colorado.[6] Furthermore, the tortious conduct allegedly giving rise to plaintiff's injuries occurred in Japan, where the subject ATV was designed and its warnings devised. *See Price v. Litton Sys., Inc.*, 784 F.2d 600, 604 (5th Cir. 1986) (conduct occurred at place of design in design defect case). Finally, there being no "relationship" between the parties in the ordinary sense of the word, this factor is unhelpful in making a choice-of-law determination. . . . Consequently, Colorado, as the place of injury, has a single material contact with the present action.

Rhode Island too has one contact with this litigation because, at the time of the accident, plaintiff was a domiciliary of Rhode Island. . . . [The plaintiff returned to Rhode Island immediately after the accident.] That plaintiff was stationed at an army base in Colorado at the time of the accident was a matter of pure chance. In fact, in his six years of service, plaintiff had been stationed in Hawaii, Maryland, Kentucky and Korea prior to arriving in Colorado.

Because the number of contacts claimed by each state is equivalent, we examine the additional factors enumerated by the Rhode Island courts, beginning with "predictability of results." This factor militates against the application of Colorado law. Honda, a large multi-national corporation, cannot argue convincingly that it expected Colorado law to apply to a case arising from a product manufactured in Japan and involving a Rhode Island citizen simply because the product was originally sold in Colorado. It would be difficult for Honda to persuade us that it molded its behavior in reliance on Colorado's damages law, particularly where that law was not enacted until four years after the subject ATV was thrust into the stream of commerce. . . . Honda certainly did not purchase liability insurance based on its potential exposure under a nonexistent Colorado law. Honda can neither claim nor rely on a vested right to limited exposure for non-economic damages under Colorado law. Consequently, Honda's justified expectations would not be upset by the application of Rhode Island law.

We turn to the next factor: maintenance of interstate order. "Interstate order is served when application of one state's law offends no law or policy

---

6   [There are three defendants collectively referred to as Honda in the opinion.] American Honda is a California corporation with its principal place of business in that state. Honda Motor Co. and Honda R&D Co. are both Japanese corporations and have their principal place of business in that country.

of the other state." *Roy v. Star Chopper Co.*, 584 F.2d 1124, 1129 (1st Cir. 1978), *cert. denied*, 440 U.S. 916 (1979). . . . To perform this analysis, we must identify the purposes or policies which underlie each state's rule of law, and the degree to which the purposes underlying each rule would be furthered by the rule's application. Inevitably, this analysis subsumes the fourth factor delineated by the Rhode Island courts: "advancement of the forum's governmental interests."

Colorado has little governmental interest in limiting the amount of damages for pain and suffering available to plaintiff in the present litigation. The Colorado statute limiting the amount of damages for pain and suffering in civil actions, Colo. Rev. Stat. § 13–21–102.5, reflects an economic policy consideration. According to the Colorado Supreme Court, "[i]t is clear from the legislative history of section 13–21–102.5 . . . that the primary goal of the legislature was to increase the affordability and availability of insurance by making the risk of insured entities more predictable." *General Elec. Co. v. Niemet*, 866 P.2d 1361, 1364 (Colo. 1994). Thus, the goal of Colorado's legislature was:

> to improve the predictability of risks faced by insurance companies. If an insurance company can predict risks with reasonable accuracy, then it can also predict its losses and profits. The concern of an insurance company is the risk associated with insuring each individual insured, not with denying an injured person damages that may be paid by another insurance company or person.

Id. at 1365. The crucial question, then, is whether, on the facts of this particular case, Colorado's policy will be advanced by the application of its damages cap.

We can see no reason why the Colorado legislature would be concerned with the affordability of insurance to a multinational Japanese corporation or its wholly-owned subsidiary, a California corporation. Honda sells its cars, motorcycles and recreational vehicles in all fifty states, and Colorado's damages law plays, at best, an insignificant role in setting Honda's insurance rates. In fact, there is no evidence in the record that Honda has ceased doing business in any state because of a failure by that state to limit the amount of damages a plaintiff may recover in a civil action.

Rhode Island courts, on the other hand, have repeatedly stressed that a plaintiff should be fully compensated for his personal injuries, including pain and suffering. *See, e.g., Hayhurst v. LaFlamme*, 441 A.2d 544, 548–59 (R.I. 1982). . . . Domiciliary states have a strong interest in the welfare of their plaintiffs, and in seeing that their plaintiffs are adequately compensated for their injuries. *See In re Air Crash Disaster Near Chicago*, 644 F.2d 594, 612–13 (7th Cir.), *cert. denied,* 454 U.S. 878 (1981). . . .

The interests of simplification of the judicial task and application of the better rule of law do not weigh heavily in either state's direction. As to the former, we cannot see how the judicial task would be more or less simplified by application of one rule as opposed to the other. As for the latter, the Rhode Island Supreme Court would undoubtedly favor a compensatory damage standard without limits. We are confident that a Rhode Island court faced with this choice-of-law dilemma would apply its own law. The district court, it follows, acted properly in applying Rhode Island law. . . .

COMMENTS AND QUESTIONS

1. Rhode Island generally follows the better law approach, but with its own twist. What role does the "set of [three] factors" play in this analysis? Approximately $5.75 million turns on the answer to the choice of law question. (For the contingent fee lawyer, this means that about $1.9 million in fees hangs in the balance.)

2. The court says that the first criterion—predictability of results—"militates against the application of Colorado law." But what law would one expect to apply in a case where someone who was living in Colorado, was riding an ATV that was purchased in Colorado, was injured in Colorado, and then treated in Colorado? Instead the court applied Rhode Island law—the state where plaintiff lived 6 years before the accident (when he left to enlist in the Army) and lives now, but has no other connection to the case, the ATV, or the defendants.

    The court says that Honda could not have "rel[ied] on Colorado's . . . law" and that Honda's "justified expectations would not be upset by the application of Rhode Island law." Scolding Honda, the court also says that Honda could not "rely on a vested right" under Colorado law. Why is the court referring to a requirement of reliance, and invoking vested rights? Is the court simply selecting what it views as the 'better law" without saying so? If so, is Rhode Island law "better" because it provides a greater recovery to a plaintiff who was horribly injured?

Did the plaintiff rely on the remedies available under Rhode Island law when he got on the ATV?

3. Is a (strong) preference for forum law a legitimate approach to choice of law? Does forum law systematically favor plaintiffs? Defendants? Residents? You will recall from Chapters 2 and 3 that *lex fori* is a methodological option. *See also* Albert A. Ehrenzweig, *The Lex Fori—Basic Rule in the Conflict of Laws*, 58 Mich. L. Rev. 637 (1959); Albert A. Ehrenzweig, *A Proper Law in a Proper Forum: A 'Restatement' of the* Lex Fori *Approach*, 18 Okla. L. Rev. 340 (1965).

4. Keenly aware of the utility of an orthodox application of interest analysis to these facts, plaintiff's counsel, a small personal injury law firm in Providence, Rhode Island, appears to have used interest analysis to clarify the otherwise murky waters of the second and fourth factors of the better law approach. This was brilliantly deployed. Honda was represented by Mayer Brown, one of the largest firms in the United States.

5. Each of the choice of law approaches that we study has variations. Some of those variations prevail as hybrid or unique approaches in jurisdictions today. Other variations are purely academic. One example of the latter is Professor Juenger's alternative version of a better law approach. He proposed a "substantive law approach" where judges would cobble the competing laws into an ad hoc hybrid or compromise that also reflects modern standards. *See* Friedrich K. Juenger, *Choice of Law and Multistate Justice* 172 (1993).

Professor McDougal has suggested that the law that is applied in multistate situations need not be restricted to the law of the states that are involved in the conflict. Courts would apply best practices—the "best law." *See* Luther L. McDougal III, *Toward Application of the Best Rule of Law in Choice of Law Cases*, 35 Mercer L. Rev. 483 (1984). Would this amount to judicial legislation? (Moreso than the creative application of choice of law rules?)

These scholars interject some imagination into the otherwise binary choice of applying the law of State *x* or State *y*. What about a *midpoint* between the two conflicting laws? Especially when the conflict regards damages, something that can be divided, a midpoint seems feasible. But is there something wrong (or at least intellectually flimsy) about applying *law* that is not really the *law* anywhere? Of course you might wonder whether federal law might provide the appropriate mandate for torts and contracts disputes that transcend state boundaries. We will revisit (but ultimately reject) this notion of a federal common law in Chapter 19.

SAMPLE EXAM QUESTIONS

Question 7-4

Gakh Bus Lines, Inc. (Gakh) operates several bus routes servicing cities and towns in Massachusetts and New Hampshire. It maintains a ticket counter in the main bus terminal in Boston, Massachusetts as well as at the main airport there. Gakh is incorporated in New Hampshire and its principal place of business is in Salem, New Hampshire.

Nussbaum is a resident of Massachusetts. She purchased a round-trip ticket from Boston to New Hampshire. For her return trip to Boston, she boarded a bus in Manchester, New Hampshire. The bus driver was licensed in New Hampshire and the bus was registered in New Hampshire. When traveling through Salem, New Hampshire, an unidentified car, traveling at a slow speed, allegedly pulled in front of the bus from an access road marked for "authorized vehicles only," requiring the bus driver to forcefully apply the brakes. As a result of this action, Nussbaum fell on the bus and broke her leg in two places.

Nussbaum has filed a personal injury action against Gakh in Massachusetts. The laws of both Massachusetts and New Hampshire provide compensation to individuals who sustain personal injuries in a motor vehicle accident. And the elements of the relevant causes of actions are fundamentally the same under these states' laws. However, New Hampshire case law permits the apportionment of liability for damages to unknown third parties, including those who are not parties to the litigation. Here, this would be the driver of the unidentified vehicle that allegedly pulled into traffic in front of the bus. Under New Hampshire law, if a jury found that the unknown third party was more than fifty percent at fault, liability would be several, not joint. Massachusetts, on the other hand, does not permit the jury to apportion damages to anyone other than the parties to the litigation.

If Massachusetts follows the better law approach should the judge give an instruction to the jury allowing them to apportion a percentage of fault to unknown third parties?

Question 7-5

Vera Stark, a resident of Tennessee was injured when the tractor trailer she was driving through Missouri collided with another vehicle driven by an uninsured resident of Missouri. Stark suffered a broken arm, broken ribs, and serious injuries to her face; she is unable to return to her chosen occupation of truck driving. At the time of her accident she was employed by Chemical Inc. (Chemical). Chemical carried liability insurance with Home Insurance Inc. (Home).

Stark was the sole driver assigned to the truck which she drove regularly on interstate trips across the country. When she was home in Tennessee, she parked the rig at her house or at Chemical's depot in nearby Memphis, Tennessee. The trailer was licensed and registered in Tennessee, but the truck (which was owned by Chemical) was licensed and registered in Texas. Chemical is a Texas corporation and its principal place of business is in Houston, Texas.

Stark filed a workers' compensation claim against Chemical and its workers' compensation carrier, CIGNA Property & Casualty Company; she ultimately received $150,000 in a settlement. She also filed a claim for uninsured motorist benefits with Home to recover under Chemical's liability policy. Although there is no dispute that the policy was in effect on the day of the accident, according to the policy, benefits for uninsured motorist coverage must be offset by any amounts paid or payable as workers' compensation benefits.

Home denied any benefits under the uninisured motorist provision because that coverage, which was capped at $100,000, was subject to the offset for money that Stark had already received.

Texas law invalidates clauses that limit uninsured motorist coverage based on the applicability of other insurance, including workers' compensation. Under Tennessee law clauses reducing damages payable under uninsured motorist coverage by the amount paid or payable under any workers' compensation law are valid.

Your firm represents Stark. We—and she—would prefer to file a lawsuit against Home in her home state of Tennessee. But if Tennessee follows the better law approach will the courts apply Texas law? Also, should you suggest that someone research Missouri law?

Question 7-6

A helicopter piloted by Bob Juengels crashed in Arkansas, killing Juengels. The helicopter involved in the accident was designed and manufactured by Firenze Copter Co. (Firenze), a Delaware corporation with its principal place of business in New Jersey. Juengels was an Arkansas domiciliary.

Juengels' family sued Firenze in an Arkansas court for negligence, failure to warn, breach of warranty, and strict product liability. The plaintiffs allege that the causes of the crash were defects in flight control components that Firenze designed and manufactured.

Defendants moved for summary judgment arguing, inter alia, that plaintiffs have failed to produce evidence of a safer alternative design. New Jersey law requires plaintiffs to prove a practical and technologically-feasible alternative as an element of the prima facie case. Arkansas law does not require a plaintiff alleging defective design to show that a safer alternative design actually exists.

If Arkansas follows the better law approach what law should it apply to resolve the pending summary judgment motion with respect to the product liability claim? What if Arkansas instead follows interest analysis?

Quick Summary

- The justified expectation of the parties is introduced as a relevant criterion for determining the applicable law

- Effective litigators will often emphasize why certain factors of a multi-factor test deserve more weight than other factors

- A flexible approach to choice of law has both advantages and disadvantages

- For one law to be "better" than another, there must be a set of values against which laws can be measured

8

Most Significant Relationship

Key Concepts

- The simplicity/rigidity of the traditional approach combined with the complexity/flexibility of the contemporary methodologies

- Terminology of the Second Restatement: rebuttable presumptions, policy factors, and subject-specific factual contacts

- Choice of law analysis proceeds on an issue-by-issue basis

- Incorporating older choice of law methodologies as elements of a new choice of law methodology

- Multi-factor tests

Between the mid-1960s and the mid-1980s, a substantial majority of states abandoned the jurisdiction-selecting rules of the traditional approach. These jurisdictions adopted interest analysis, center of gravity, better law, or some combination thereof. Because the traditional approach was the methodology presented in the (First) Restatement of Conflicts, that publication became increasingly anachronous, offering a *restatement* only of what the law once was.

During this same period, the American Law Institute, the body that writes the Restatements, started work on a Second Restatement of Conflicts. But unlike the First Restatement, and unlike the Restatements in other areas of the law, the Second Restatement of Conflicts was more than an attempt to restate the law—the drafters explicitly wanted to reshape it.[1] And they did. The approach of the Second Restatement is by far the most popular choice of law methodology in the United States. (*See* the chart in Chapter 3.)

---

1   *See* Reese, *Choice of Law: Rules or Approach*, 57 Cornell L. Rev. 315 (1972).

The Second Restatement combines elements of *all* other choice of law approaches. An expertly calibrated combination of best practices, the Second Restatement may be the "best of all worlds": it preserves the essential virtue of the traditional approach while also incorporating the insights of each of the modern methodologies. But whenever you hear someone suggest that anything is the "best of both worlds," know that there is often a "worst of both worlds" counter-narrative; in this vein, the Second Restatement is a clumsy aggregation of the worst traits of its predecessor techniques. In truth, the Second Restatement, like the approaches before it, has its merits and demerits.

The Second Restatement prescribes a two-stage process. In one stage, a set of subject-specific provisions establish what some courts call "rebuttable presumptions" about which state's law should apply. In a second stage, a combination of general policy factors plus subject-specific factual contacts identify the state with the most significant relationship. We will discuss the uneasy relationship between these two stages after we've described each of them.

The Second Restatement contemplates choice of law analysis on an issue by issue basis. This could mean that, in the case *A* v. *B* & *C*, different laws may apply to the *A* v. *B* claims and the *A* v. *C* claims. It could also mean that different laws might apply to Count 1 and Count 2 in the *A* v. *B* claims. It could even mean that different laws apply to *A*'s claim and *B*'s affirmative defense to that claim. This is the doctrine of *dépeçage* that was introduced in Chapter 4 (and that we will revisit in Chapter 15). Although the Second Restatement prescribes a choice of law analysis on an issue-by-issue basis, as a practical matter courts almost always apply only one jurisdiction's law in a given case.

Because the Second Restatement is the most popular methodology and because it is the approach tested on the Uniform Bar Exam, we quote extensively from the Second Restatement, describe it thoroughly, offer many hypotheticals, and include more case law. The overarching objective of the Second Restatement approach is to identify the statute has the *most significant relationship* to the parties and the occurrence.

Stage One: Rebuttable Presumption

This first stage resembles the First Restatement because it assigns consequences to specific triggering facts. This first stage of analysis establishes rebuttable presumptions about what law will apply to a given circumstance or issue.

The rules are divided by subject matter. Accordingly, there is a process of characterization that precedes the selection of the rebuttable presumption. (Remember the discussion of characterization in Chapter 4.) You will notice that there are presumptions for causes of action and also for specific issues. Each of the following sections sets forth a place whose law will presumptively apply.

Restatement (Second) of Conflict of Laws

<u>Particular Torts</u>

§ 146. In an action for a personal injury, the local law of the state where the injury occurred determines the rights and liabilities of the parties, unless, with respect to the particular issue, some other state has a more significant relationship under the principles stated in § 6 to the occurrence and the parties, in which event the local law of the other state will be applies.

§ 147. In an action for an injury to land or other tangible thing, . . . where the injury occurred. . . .

§ 148. [In an action for fraud or misrepresentation,] . . . where the false representations were made and received [, provided the plaintiff's action in reliance also took place in that state]. When the plaintiff's action in reliance took place in whole or in part in a state other than that where the false representations were made, the forum will consider [many enumerated factual contacts to determine which state] has the most significant relationship. . .

§ 149. In an action for defamation, . . . where the publication occurs . . . except as stated in § 150 [multistate defamation]. . . .

§ 152. In an action for an invasion of a right of privacy, where the invasion occurred . . . except as stated in § 153 [multistate invasion of privacy]

§ 154. [In an action for interference with a marriage relationship,] . . . where the conduct complained of principally occurred. . . .

§ 155. [In an action for malicious prosecution and abuse of process,] . . . where the proceeding complained of occurred. . . .

<u>Important [Torts] Issues</u>

§ 156. [W]hether the actor's conduct was tortious, . . . where the injury occurred.

§ 157. [T]he standard of care by which the actor's conduct shall be judged, . . . where the injury occurred.

§ 163. [W]hether a person is excused from liability by reason of the fact that his action was required or privileged, . . . where he acted.

§ 164. [W]hether contributory fault on the part of the plaintiff precludes his recovery, . . . where the injury occurred.

§ 169. [W]hether one member of a family is immune from tort liability to another member of the family, . . . the state of the parties' domicil.

§ 175. [A right of action for wrongful death,] where the injury occurred. . . .

Particular Contracts

§ 189. [The validity of and rights created by contracts for the transfer of interest in land, if there is no choice of law clause in the contract,] where the land is situated. . . .

§ 191. [The validity of and rights created by contracts to sell interests in chattel, if there is no choice of law clause in the contract,] where under the terms of the contract the seller is to deliver the chattel. . . .

§ 192. [The validity of a life insurance contract,] where the insured was domiciled at the time the policy was applied for. . . .

§ 193. [The validity of and rights created by contracts for fire, surety, or casualty insurance, if there is no choice of law clause in the contract, where the insured risk was principally located] during the term of the policy. . . .

§ 195. [The validity of and rights created by contracts for the repayment of money lent, if there is no choice of law in the contract,] where the contract requires that repayment to be made. . . .

§ 196. [The validity of and rights created by contracts for the rendition of services, if there is no choice of law in the contract,] where the contract requires that the service . . . be rendered. . . .

§ 197. [The validity of and rights created by contracts of transportation, if there is no choice of law in the contract, where] the passenger departs or the goods are dispatched. . . .

Particular [Contracts] Issues

§ 198. The capacity of a party to contract, . . . the state of his domicil.

§ 199. The formalities required to make a valid contract, . . . where the parties execute the contract. . . .

§ 202. The effect of illegality upon a contract, . . . the place of performance. . . .

§ 206. Issues relating to details of performance, . . . the place of performance.

Property: Immovables

§ 223. [The validity and effect of conveyance of interest in land,] the law that would be applied by the courts of the situs [of the land].

§ 227. Whether there has been a transfer of an interest in land by adverse possession or by prescription, . . . the situs.

§ 228. Whether a mortgage creates an interest in land, . . . the law that would be applied by the courts of the situs.

§ 235. The existence and extent of an equitable interest in land, . . . the law that would be applied by the courts of the situs.

Property: Movables

§ 244. The validity and effect of a conveyance of an interest in a chattel, [if there is no choice of law clause,] the location of the chattel . . . at the time of the conveyance. . . .

§ 251. The validity and effect of a security interest in a chattel, [if there is no choice of law clause,] the location of the chattel at the time that the security interest attached. . . .

Status

§ 283. The validity of a marriage, . . . where the marriage was contracted. . . .

§ 287. Whether a child is legitimate, . . . where either (a) the parent was domiciled when the child's status of legitimacy is claimed to have been created or (b) the child was domiciled when the parent acknowledged the child as his own.

The Second Restatement contains dozens more presumptions. Moreover, for each section of black-letter text (parts of which are quoted above), there are numerous *comments* and *illustrations* that provide additional context for litigators and judges.

These presumptions are generally rebuttable. They are rebutted when some other state has a "more significant relationship." (*See e.g.*, Second Restatement § 146, *supra*). Determination of the state with the most significant relationship is the second stage of the Second Restatement's process.

Stage Two: Most Significant Relationship

This second stage is a multivariate analysis designed to identify the jurisdiction that has the most significant relationship to the issue. This second stage has two components: (1) Section 6 policy factors; and (2) subject-specific factual contacts.

First, the centerpiece of the Second Restatement's approach is Section 6, which outlines the general policy considerations.

Restatement (Second) of Conflict of Laws

§ 6. Choice-of-Law Principles

(1) A court, subject to constitutional restrictions, will follow a statutory directive of its own state on choice of law.

(2) When there is no such directive, the factors relevant to the choice of the applicable rule of law include

   (a) the needs of the interstate and international systems;

   (b) the relevant policies of the forum;

(c)   the relevant polices of other interested states and the relative interests of those states in the determination of the particular issue;

(d)   the protection of justified expectations;

(e)   the basic policies underlying the particular field of law;

(f)   certainty, predictability and uniformity of result; and

(g)   ease in the determination and application of the law to be applied.

Paragraph (1) observes that courts are obliged to follow the directions of their legislature. This is an important point that we have not yet covered in the course. It is something of a detour to address it here, but it is a critical one—and it is not limited to jurisdictions that follow the Second Restatement. Conflict of laws approaches are designed to resolve *uncertainty* about whether a court should apply forum law or some other state's law. However, there is no uncertainty—and thus no need for any choice of law methodology—when the legislature intended that their statute be applied to the multistate factual situation before the court. The statute may have this intended range stated explicitly in the text (*E.g.,* "This statute applies even if the employee was injured in another state. . . .") or its broad reach may be construed from the text or may be apparent from legislative history. If the forum's legislature has prescribed the applicable law for the circumstances presented, then the court should apply that law. Additionally, because there is no choice of law uncertainty or question, the court should apply that forum law regardless of the text of the other jurisdiction's law. (We will study this again in Chapter 16.) The only exception to this principle is that the court should not apply forum law if that application would be unconstitutional; this restriction also appears in the text of paragraph (1) above. We will study constitutional restrictions in Chapter 14.

When there is uncertainty about whether forum law or some other jurisdiction's law should apply, we have a choice of law problem. Paragraph (2) enumerates the policy factors that are relevant to that inquiry.[2] The Section 6(2) factors should look familiar, as they resemble a combination of interest analysis (subparagraphs (b) and (c)) and the better law approach (subparagraphs (a), (d), (f), and (g)).

Only subparagraph 2(e) arguably adds something new. The policies underlying a field of law are surely debatable, but according to the drafters' commentary, their intention with this subparagraph (e) was to encourage results that, for example, "sustain the validity of a contract" or "valid[ate] a trust of movables against the charge that it violates Rule Against Perpetuities."[3] The notion that it is a better outcome for a court to apply the law that would validate a contract rather than to apply the law that would invalidate a contract is sometimes referred to as the "rule

---

2   The list is not exhaustive. Other factors could be relevant.

3   Restatement (Second) of Conflict of Laws § 6 cmt. h.

of validation." In fact, it is more of an empirical policy preference than a "rule." It also reveals something profound (about *all* choice of law methodologies), because it may capture some of the intuition that guides us toward certain conclusions. On one hand, it makes sense to assume that contracting parties intended to enter into a valid and enforceable contract; surely parties enter into a contract in good faith and for a purpose. But on the other hand, it is not obvious why refusing to enforce a contract shows less fidelity to the policies underlying contract law. Query whether some principles of contracts are more important than others.

The Section 6 factors must be combined with a second component (of this second stage) to determine which jurisdiction has the most significant relationship. Specifically, the Section 6 policy factors must be combined with the subject-specific factual contacts. In particular, the significance of the factual contacts must be evaluated in light of the policy factors in Section 6. For each subject matter there are contacts that courts are expected to consider.[4]

Restatement (Second) of Conflict of Laws

Torts

§ 145. The General Principle

(1) The rights and liabilities of the parties with respect to an issue in tort are determined by the local law of the state which, with respect to that issue, has the most significant relationship to the occurrence and the parties under the principles stated in § 6

(2) Contacts to be taken into account in applying the principles of § 6 to determine the law applicable to an issue include:

   (a) the place where the injury occurred,

   (b) the place where the conduct causing the injury occurred,

   (c) the domicil, residence, nationality, place of incorporation and place of business of the parties, and

   (d) the place where the relationship, if any, between the parties is centered.

   These contacts are to be evaluated according to their relative importance with respect to the particular issue.

Contracts

§ 188. Law Governing in Absence of Effective Choice by the Parties[5]

(1) The rights and liabilities of the parties with respect to an issue in contract are determined by the local law of the state which, with respect to that issue,

---

4   Again, the lists are not exhaustive.

5   Contracts with choice of law clauses are addressed in Chapter 9.

has the most significant relationship to the occurrence and the parties under the principles stated in § 6.

(2) In the absence of an effective choice of law by the parties (see § 187), the contacts to be taken into account in applying the principles of § 6 to determine the law applicable to an issue include:

(a) the place of contracting,

(b) the place of the negotiation of the contract,

(c) the place of performance,

(d) the location of the subject matter of the contract, and

(e) the domicil, residence, nationality, place of incorporation and place of business of the parties.

These contacts are to be evaluated according to their relative importance with respect to the particular issue.

(3) If the place of negotiating the contract and the place of performance are in the same state, the local law of this state will usually be applied, except as otherwise provided in §§ 189–199 and 203.

These lists of contacts should also look familiar to you. These lists match the contacts emphasized by the center of gravity approach in Chapter 6.

Stages One and Two in Action

The significance of the factual contacts must be evaluated using the policy factors set forth in § 6. In other words, the two sets of items must be *combined*. Further, they are combined to determine which state has the most significant relationship *to the issue* for which there is a conflict of laws. Whether the disputed *issue* regards the availability of a cause of action, a cap on a remedy, or the viability of an affirmative defense, will influence which of the factual contacts and which of the policy factors deserve more attention in the combined inquiry.

So let us now combine the rebuttable presumption of stage one with the most significant relationship test of stage two. In a typical personal injury case the first column would be populated by § 146, the rebuttable presumption for personal injury claims. (If instead the dispute was about the elements of a cause of action for defamation, the rebuttable presumption would be drawn from § 149. If the dispute was about intra-familial immunity, then you would consult § 169.) The second column is constant for all inquiries. The court would evaluate the significance of the factual contacts populated by the subject-specific contacts in the third column in light of the policy factors in Section 6 (the second column).

Stage One: Rebuttable Presumption	Stage Two: Most Significant Relationship	
	Section 6 Policy Factors	Subject-Specific Factual Contacts
§ 146. In an action for a personal injury, the local law of the state where the injury occurred determines the rights and liabilities of the parties unless, with respect to the particular issue, some other state has a more significant relationship under the principles stated in § 6 to the occurrence and the parties, in which event the local law of the other sate will be applied.	§ 6. . . . factors relevant to the choice of the applicable rule of law include: (a) the needs of the interstate and international systems; (b) the relevant policies of the forum; (c) the relevant polices of other interested states and the relative interests of those states in the determination of the particular issue; (d) the protection of justified expectations; (e) the basic policies underlying the particular field of law; (f) certainty, predictability and uniformity of result; and (g) ease in the determination and application of the law to be applied.	§ 145(2) Contacts to be taken into account in applying the principles of § 6 to determine the law [of the state which, with respect to that issue, has the most significant relationship] include: (a) the place where the injury occurred, (b) the place where the conduct causing the injury occurred, (c) the domicil, residence, nationality, place of incorporation and place of business of the parties, and (d) the place where the relationship, if any, between the parties is centered.

In a typical dispute involving a contract for services, the framework would be as follows.

Stage One: Rebuttable Presumption	Stage Two: Most Significant Relationship	
	Section 6 Policy Factors	Subject-Specific Factual Contacts
§ 196. The validity of a contract for the rendition of services and the rights created thereby are determined, in the absence of an effective choice of law by the parties, by the local law of the state where the contract requires that the services, or a major portion of the services, be rendered, unless, with respect to the particular issue, some other state has a more significant relationship under the principles stated in § 6 to the transaction and the parties, in which event the local law of the other state will be applied.	§ 6. . . . factors relevant to the choice of the applicable rule of law include: (a) the needs of the interstate and international systems; (b) the relevant policies of the forum; (c) the relevant polices of other interested states and the relative interests of those states in the determination of the particular issue; (d) the protection of justified expectations; (e) the basic policies underlying the particular field of law; (f) certainty, predictability and uniformity of result; and (g) ease in the determination and application of the law to be applied.	§ 188(2) [C]ontacts to be taken into account in applying the principles of § 6 to determine the law [of the state which, with respect to that issue, has the most significant relationship] include: (a) the place of contracting, (b) the place of the negotiation of the contract, (c) the place of performance, (d) the location of the subject matter of the contract, and (e) the domicil, residence, nationality, place of incorporation and place of business of the parties.

The *second* stage of the analysis identifies which state's law has the most significant relationship to the disputed issue. This leaves a dubious role for the *first* stage because the presumption is rebutted if some other state has a more significant relationship. So either the rebuttable presumption of the first stage is confirmed in the second stage (i.e., the presumptively-selected state is also the state with the most significant relationship), in which case the rebuttable presumption served little or no purpose. Or the presumption of the first stage is rebutted by the second stage (i.e., the presumptively-selected state is not the state with the most significant relationship), again, leaving no meaningful role for the presumption. For this reason some Second Restatement jurisdictions practically ignore the presumptions. Other Second Restatement jurisdictions, however, take the presumptions more seriously; a presumption can be easier or harder to rebut depending upon how aggressively one undertakes the task of rebuttal. This leaves a role for advocacy.

Litigators who master choice of law seize the many opportunities that are available to affect the outcome of these inquiries. This variability in outcome is discomfiting or disconcerting to some judges. Especially for that contingent, your mastery of the process will give them confidence in you and in your argument; but mastery requires practice.

Hypothetical 8-1

Martin and Shelley Criminale relocated from California to Massachusetts about a decade ago. They purchased an elegant home in the suburbs of Boston. In 2016, they also bought an historic mansion in Newport, Rhode Island. Recently, the Criminales retained Rich Piatt, an interior designer based in California, to decorate these homes. Shelley directed Piatt to travel around the U.S. and Europe to locate "outrageous" antiques for purchase.

In 2015 and 2016, Piatt visited the Roll Gallery in New York City. Piatt told Roll that he was a decorator, but did not tell Roll that he represented the Criminales. Piatt identified the antiques that he was interested in purchasing and received written and oral descriptions of the items. Piatt then asked Roll to send the "tear sheets" (descriptions and pictures) for the antiques to his (Piatt's) office in California.

In 2015, Roll sent Piatt tear sheets for two vases, and in 2016, Roll sent Piatt tear sheets for a grandfather clock and two commodes. Both times, after receiving these documents, Piatt traveled to Massachusetts to discuss the items with the Criminales. Piatt and the Criminales called Roll and told him that they wanted to purchase the items; Roll gave the Criminales wiring instructions, and the payment was made.

Piatt arranged to have the items shipped to Massachusetts for storage. Eventually, the vases were displayed in the Criminales' Boston home, and the clock and commodes were displayed at the Rhode Island mansion.

The Criminales have since learned that the antiques were not what they were represented to be. The tear sheet for the clock described it as an "exceptionally rare Regence grandfather's clock with superb vernis Martin decoration depicting Peace and Justice above a panel showing cupid and psyche . . . French, 18th century." According to the Criminales' experts, the clock was in fact an amalgam of parts and pieces from the late 18th and 19th centuries and originated in Italy. This antique is worth at least $500,000 less than what they paid for it.

The tear sheets for the commodes described them as a "fine transitional marquetry commode . . . French 18th century," and the other as a "transitional Louis XV/XVI marquetry commode with pictoral marquetry depicting ruins . . . French 18th century." According to the Criminales' experts, these antiques are, in fact, 19th or 20th century pieces of furniture art that are worth at least $1,200,000 less than what they paid for them.

The Criminales have filed a lawsuit that includes a number of causes of action against Roll. The immediate focus is on the defendant's motion for partial summary judgment on the plaintiff's claim for breach of express warranty. New York has a "fine arts statute" that governs express warranty claims; this fine arts statute supplants both the U.C.C. and any common law warranty claims. Under this statute, Roll's statements to Piatt attributing the antiques to specific time periods are *opinions* rather than facts. Opinions do not create express warranties. Under the law of every other state, the representations on the tear sheets could constitute warranties.

Assume that the action was filed in a jurisdiction that follows the Second Restatement. Will the court apply New York law and grant the defendant's motion for partial summary judgment?

One attribute of an experienced litigator is knowing certain unwritten, even unstated "rules." Consider again, for example, the rule of validation. The rule, which is no rule at all, establishes a preference for selection of the law that validates a contract rather than the law that would invalidate a contract. In a typical application, the selection of State *X*'s law would validate an agreement but the selection of State *Y*'s law would invalidate it. This preference for State *X*'s law could be stronger or weaker and thereby do more or less work in the decisional calculus. One way to have the rule of validity do more work is to use it in more than one of the factors. In fact, a preference for validating a contract could appear in any or all of the Section 6 factors. Validating a contract will

- advance the "needs of the interstate and international systems" which rely on the enforceability of contracts to encourage travel and commerce. § 6(2)(a);

- further "the relevant policies of the forum" and is never wholly antagonistic to the "the relevant policies of other interested states" since every jurisdiction has case law extolling the virtues of certainty in contract. § 6(2)(b) & (c);

- protect the "justified expectations" of the parties who entered into the contract to achieve something. § 6(2)(d);

- advance "the basic policies underlying the [field of contracts]"—something specifically mentioned by the drafters in Section 6 cmt. h. § 6(2)(e);

- ensure "certainty, predictability and uniformity" by minimizing traps for the unwary that otherwise can frustrate expectations and commerce. § 6(2)(f); and

- assist in the "determination and application of the law to be applied" because courts can use the contract to determine the parties' rights and responsibilities rather than resort to quasi contract and restitutionary remedies to deal with the consequences of behavior attendant to an invalidated contract. § 6(2)(g).

The rule of validity is relevant also in the other choice of law methodologies.

In its strongest version, the rule of validity—*lex validitatis*—stands for the proposition that the court should apply whatever law the parties can reasonably be assumed to have taken into account that validates the contract. Validity is a norm or preference that may be stronger or weaker, and it may be stated or unstated.

Hypothetical 8-2

Ralph Albertson and Vita Gardner were married in Phoenix, Arizona. Ms. Gardner was employed by Toll Brothers, Inc., in Phoenix both before and after the couple married. Ms. Gardner was covered by a group life insurance policy issued by Cabot Mutual Life Insurance Company (Cabot). Under the terms of the policy, a death benefit of $500,000 was payable upon the death of Ms. Gardner, and an additional $250,000 was payable if her death was an "accident." Mr. Albertson was designated as the primary beneficiary and Annette Mann, Gardner's daughter from a previous marriage, was designated as the secondary beneficiary; Ms. Mann lives in Reno, Nevada.

About two and a half years into their marriage, the couple's relationship was strained and they physically separated. Ms. Gardner accepted an indefinite but temporary work assignment in Dallas, Texas with Toll Brothers; she took the dog and moved some of her belongings there. Mr. Albertson continued to live in Nevada, but he visited Ms. Gardner a few times while she was in Dallas, and the couple sought counseling there.

On the third anniversary of their wedding, Ms. Gardner died as the result of multiple gunshot wounds inflicted by Mr. Albertson at Ms. Gardner's Dallas condo. Last month, about eleven months after the shooting Mr. Albertson was found guilty of manslaughter and was sentenced to seven years in prison.

Mr. Albertson has contacted your law office, seeking assistance in obtaining the death benefit proceeds from his wife's life insurance policy. Your call to Cabot confirmed that the proceeds have not been paid to anyone.

Recovery of the proceeds by Mr. Albertson may be barred by a so-called "slayer statute"—a statute that generally prohibits a person from acquiring or receiving any property of the individual that s/he killed. *See, e.g.,* Unif. Probate Code § 2–803. Slayer statutes are not uniform, however, and in fact, vary considerably from state to state.

Five years ago the Arizona legislature broadened the scope of its slayer statute to include manslaughter as a defense that disqualifies a person from recovering. Before the amendment it included only persons convicted of first- or second-degree murder. The stated purpose of the new legislation was to subject more killers to civil disinheritance.

Texas does not have a slayer statute. However, there is a recent decision of an intermediate appeals court holding, for the first time, that the beneficiary of a life insurance policy who committed murder forfeited the right to the proceeds of the policy.

No lawsuit has yet been filed. Ms. Mann might file suit. Cabot might file an interpleader. Or we could file suit on behalf of Mr. Albertson. If we file a suit in Texas, and if Texas follows the Second Restatement, can we expect the court to apply Texas law?

Hypothetical 8-3

McHale Metalweld Corp. (McHale) is an Ohio welding company that specializes in railroad track repairs. Trammel Railway Co. hired McHale to repair various welds on several Trammel railroad tracks in southern Missouri and northern Arkansas. Trammel is an Illinois corporation with its principal place of business in Chicago. The contract was negotiated and signed there. It does not contain a choice of law clause.

Three days after McHale began its repair work, a Trammel train derailed near Poplar Bluff, Missouri where McHale was working. Trammel directed McHale to stop its repair work and sued McHale for breach of contract in an Illinois court, seeking $750,000 in contract damages. Trammel's evidence suggests that McHale's failure to smooth out bumps on its welds was a direct cause of the derailment. McHale's evidence tends to show that its welds were not defective and that there were other defects in the track unrelated to their repair work that caused the accident.

As this case moves toward trial, a dispute has arisen about whether McHale will be able to argue comparative fault. Only a few states, including Missouri, allow a plaintiff's comparative fault as a basis for apportioning contract damages. All other states, including Illinois and Arkansas, do not allow comparative fault to reduce contract damages.

If the Illinois court follows the Second Restatement approach, should it allow defendant to raise the issue of comparative fault?

Hypothetical 8-4

A motion to a certify a class action is pending in a case filed by 750 truck drivers against their employer, Westeros Trucking, a company that is incorporated in Arizona and has its principal place of business there. The truck drivers claim breach of an implied covenant of good faith and fair dealing, charging that the company systematically underpaid them.

The truck drivers live in 10 states throughout the western United States, and drive to, from, and through all 22 of the continental United States west of the Mississippi River. Not all states imply a duty of good faith into every contract. In fact, only 3 of the 10 states where the truckers live, and 9 of the 22 states where they work find an implied duty of good faith in every contract (including employment agreements). Arizona is one of those states.

You clerk for the Arizona judge before whom the motion to certify the class action is pending. One of the factors that a judge must consider when deciding whether to certify a class like this one is how *similar* the 750 plaintiffs' claims are, and how *manageable* a class action would be. A key component of those inquiries is whether the same substantive law would apply to these claims *if each of the 750 claims were filed separately* in this court. The judge has asked you to focus exclusively on that choice of law question. Arizona follows the Second Restatement approach. What is your answer?

Hypothetical 8-5

Emma Scott is a network administrator at Massachusetts Life Care Co. (MLCC). MLCC is a Massachusetts corporation with its only place of business in Woburn, Massachusetts. Scott is a Massachusetts domiciliary.

One of MLCC's vendors is Quora Software Development (Quora). Quora is a Virginia corporation with its only place of business in Arlington, Virginia.

A Quora employee, Ryan Hislop, was dispatched from the Virginia office to Massachusetts for three days to install software upgrades on MLCC's networks. Hislop met Scott during his visit to MLCC and grew fond of her; Scott did not feel the same way about Hislop.

When Hislop returned to Virginia he called Scott on numerous occasions. Hislop recorded those brief phone calls without Scott's permission or knowledge. Hislop has used parts of those recorded messages (including Scott's voice) in rap songs that he produced, uploaded to the internet, and are now attracting the public's attention.

Scott has filed a lawsuit in Massachusetts, and one of her claims alleges a violation of the Massachusetts Wiretap Act.

The Massachusetts Wiretap Act requires that "all parties to a conversation" be notified that a call is being recorded. This act provides that: "An aggrieved person whose oral or wire communications were secretly recorded shall have a civil cause of action against any person who so intercepts, discloses or uses such communications . . . and shall be entitled to recover actual damages, punitive damages, and reasonable attorney's fees from such person."

On the other hand, Virginia law permits one party to record a telephone conversation, even without the other party's knowledge. According to a recent decision of the Virginia Supreme Court, "It shall not be a criminal or civil offense for a person to intercept a wire, electronic, or oral communication, where such person is a party to the communication."

If Massachusetts follows the Second Restatement, what law should it apply?

Hypothetical 8-6

Corrine Downey lives in Opelika, Alabama. The nearest city to her is Columbus, Georgia, which is across the border and about 30 miles away. Downey was 37 weeks pregnant when she went for a routine prenatal examination at her obstetrician-gynecologist's office in Columbus, Georgia.

During the examination Downey learned that her unborn baby did not have a heartbeat.

The following day, Downey was admitted to Columbus (Georgia) Hospital where labor was induced and she delivered a stillborn baby girl. After the delivery, the hospital's bereavement coordinator spoke with Downey and her husband. This conversation led to a decision that the remains of the baby would be released to a funeral home in Opelika. The bereavement coordinator completed the permit and supporting documents, and gave these documents to the hospital.

The stillborn baby was taken to the hospital morgue. A tragic mix-up in the morgue involving two different stillborn babies, led Downey's stillborn child to receive the wrong identification tag. Because of the wrong tag, the hospital mistakenly released the wrong baby to the Opelika funeral home.

Downey, her family members, and other mourners attended a funeral at an Opelika cemetery for a deceased stillborn baby that they believed was Downey's. Downey and her family members did not view the baby's remains before or during the funeral service because the funeral director advised against it, given the condition of the remains. The costs of transporting the baby from the hospital to the funeral home were paid by Downey's husband through the military, and Downey's pastor paid for the funeral service and donated the burial plot.

Eleven days after the funeral, Columbus Hospital discovered that it had released the wrong baby to the Opelika funeral home. The hospital informed Downey of their mistake. The hospital paid to have the baby exhumed from the Opelika cemetery and for the subsequent burial of the proper remains. Downey did not attend the second burial because she "could not handle having to go through that all over again. It's devastating."

Downey sued the hospital for the emotional distress she suffered as a result of the mishandling of her stillborn child's remains. After discovery, the hospital moved for summary judgment. Under the law of Georgia, an essential element of a claim for emotional distress is physical injury or pecuniary loss. Under Georgia law, Downey has suffered neither. But under Alabama law, she is not required to prove physical injury or pecuniary loss to support an emotional distress claim.

If she files suit in Georgia, where her lawyer is licensed to practice, and if Georgia follows the Second Restatement, what is the likelihood that it will apply Alabama substantive law?

While the Second Restatement approach is the most popular choice of law methodology in one sense of the word, it is the least popular in another. Some of the most elegant hand-wringing about it comes from courts struggling with the question whether to follow it or some alternative choice of law approach. The following excerpt is from a decision of the Indiana Supreme Court:

> The Second Restatement has been an inviting target for critics who assert that it supplies little real guidance to courts (much less to actors). As Professor Shreve observed, "The Second Restatement has attracted many judges (if fewer commentators), but it has not prevented the subject of choice of law from reaching what many believe is a state of crisis." Gene R. Shreve, *Introduction, Symposium: Preparing for the Next Century—A New Restatement of Conflicts?*, 75 IND. L.J. 399, 399 (2000). Another commentator noted:
>
>> The second Restatement thus was a hodgepodge of all theories. A court was to compare apples, oranges, umbrellas, and pandas, and determine which state's law to apply by the relative importance assigned to these factors. The supposed virtue of the second Restatement was the freedom it provided courts to weigh all conceivably relevant factors and then tailor the choice of law to the circumstances of the case. That very flexibility was, however, equally its vice: courts could arrive at any outcome applying its factors, and no one could predict in advance what state's law governed their actions. The problem was not merely that courts were afforded the opportunity to be manipulative; the problem was that even a court without such desire could find in the second Restatement no guidance as to how it was to decide a case after identifying the factors in play.
>
> Michael H. Gottesman, *Draining the Dismal Swamp: The Case for Federal Choice of Law Statutes*, 80 GEO. L.J. 1, 8 (footnote omitted).[6]

Simon v. U.S., 805 N.E.2d 798 (Ind. 2004).

---

[6]   *See also*, Douglas Laycock, *Equal Citizens of Equal and Territorial States: The Constitutional Foundations of Choice-of-Law*, 92 COLUM. L. REV. 249, 253 (1992) ("Trying to be all things to all people, it produced mush."); Friedrich K. Juenger, *A Third Conflicts Restatement?*, 75 IND. L.J. 403, 405 (2000) ("Many courts seem to like the 'mishmash,' or 'kitchen-sink,' concoction the restaters produced; after all, it enables judges to decide conflicts cases any which way they wish. To be sure, the Second Restatement's unprincipled eclecticism has done little to strengthen the intellectual underpinnings of our discipline."); Symeon C. Symeonides, *The Judicial Acceptance of the Second Conflicts Restatement: A Mixed Blessing*, 56 MD. L. REV. 1248, 1281 (1997) ("The Restatement (Second) was intended to be and was 'a transitional work.' ").

HOILES v. ALIOTO

U.S. Court of Appeals for the Tenth Circuit
461 F.3d 1224 (10th Cir. 2006)

MURPHY, CIRCUIT JUDGE.

I. Introduction

This appeal arises out of a contingent fee agreement (the "Fee Agreement") entered into by Plaintiff-Appellee Timothy Hoiles, a resident of Colorado, and Defendant-Appellant Joseph Alioto, an attorney licensed to practice law in California.*

II. Background

In 2001, Freedom was a closely held media conglomerate owning various newspapers, magazines, and broadcast television stations throughout the country. Timothy Hoiles, the grandson of Freedom's founder, owned 511,221 shares in the company. Hoiles' ex-wife and two daughters (the "Davidson Defendants") owned a total of 155,740.5 shares. Hoiles' and the Davidson Defendants' shares represented approximately 8.6% of the outstanding shares of Freedom; the remaining shares were owned by other descendants of Hoiles' grandfather. Hoiles believed mismanagement of the company and family shareholder disputes were damaging the value of Freedom's stock. Thereafter, he hired a consultant, Joseph Barletta, to develop a plan to improve Freedom's operations so Hoiles could sell his shares at a fair price and exit the company. Hoiles' relatives, however, were unwilling to pay what Hoiles considered a fair price and outside buyers were reluctant to purchase a minority interest in a family-owned company.

At Hoiles' direction, Barletta contacted Joseph Alioto, an attorney licensed to practice law in California, about the possibility of providing legal representation on a contingent fee basis. Hoiles subsequently traveled from his home in Colorado to meet with Alioto in California. The parties dispute the substance of their conversation. According to Hoiles, the parties discussed

---

* [Eds.' Note: Joseph Alioto is a very well-known antitrust lawyer. His law office is in San Francisco. He is the son of the former mayor of San Francisco.]

pursuing a lawsuit against Freedom shareholders to force the purchase of Hoiles' stock. Alioto claims Hoiles wanted him to take any action that was necessary, including but not limited to filing a lawsuit to force the purchase of Hoiles' and the Davidson Defendants' interest in Freedom. At the end of the meeting, the parties reached an oral agreement whereby Alioto would represent Hoiles on a contingent fee basis. Hoiles paid a $500,000 retainer and advanced Alioto $100,000 for expenses and costs.

Several weeks after the meeting, Alioto faxed a letter to Hoiles in Colorado, memorializing the terms of the legal representation. The letter indicated Alioto's firm would represent Hoiles in the "Freedom Communications matter." It provided Alioto was to receive "[f]ifteen percent (15%) of anything recovered before the filing of a complaint; 20% of anything recovered after the filing of a complaint but before the commencement of the trial; and 25% of anything recovered after the commencement of the trial." If Hoiles withdrew from or dismissed the case, or refused to settle against Alioto's recommendation, he was obligated to pay a reasonable hourly rate of $1,000 for Alioto's time and $500 for co-counsel's time. The Fee Agreement also required Hoiles to pay all out-of-pocket and litigation expenses. Hoiles signed the Fee Agreement in Colorado approximately six months after receiving it.

Two years later, Freedom entered into a recapitalization agreement with Blackstone/Providence Merger Corporation. The cause of the recapitalization is disputed. Alioto contends the recapitalization of Freedom was instigated by the following actions on his part: (1) his drafting of, and threatening to file, a complaint against Freedom shareholders; and (2) his hiring of Christopher Shaw, an English newspaper broker, to generate market interest in the sale of Freedom. Hoiles, on the other hand, claims Alioto's contribution to the recapitalization was minimal. Instead, he contends the recapitalization was the result of an independent effort by shareholders to restructure the ownership of Freedom. Whatever its cause the recapitalization enabled all Freedom shareholders to exchange their shares for cash or shares in a newly formed corporation. Hoiles and the Davidson Defendants elected the cash option and received $212.71 per share, a total of $141,869,380.67.

After the recapitalization, Hoiles asked Alioto to submit a billing statement for his services at $1,000 per hour in accordance with the Fee Agreement. Alioto responded by demanding a $28.4 million contingent fee. Hoiles subsequently filed suit in Colorado . . . seeking, *inter alia* a declaration that Alioto was not entitled to a contingent fee. . . . Alioto subsequently filed counterclaims . . . [alleging that] Hoiles and the Davidson Defendants breached the Fee Agreement [and/or engaged in tortious conduct.]. . . .

Applying Colorado's conflict of laws rules, the district court determined Colorado law governed all issues in the case. The district court further determined, as a matter of law, that the Fee Agreement did not substantially comply with Colorado's rules governing contingent fee agreements. *See* Colo. R. Governing Contingent Fees ch. 23.3. Thus the Fee Agreement was deemed unenforceable, and Alioto's breach of contract claim was dismissed. The district court also dismissed Alioto's fraud and negligent misrepresentation claims stating, "[t]his is not going to be a tort case." The case proceeded to trial on whether Alioto was entitled to quantum meruit. The jury returned a verdict in favor of Alioto for $1,150,000 which the district court reduced by the $500,000 retainer Hoiles had previously paid.

III. Discussion

Alioto argues the district court erred in applying Colorado law to determine whether the Fee Agreement was enforceable; he contends California law should govern the issue. We review choice of law determinations *de novo*. The underlying factual determinations of the district court, however, are reviewed for clear error. *Id.*

Because the Fee Agreement does not contain a choice of law provision, the district court was required to apply the choice of law principles of the state in which it sits, *i.e.*, Colorado. Colorado has adopted the "most significant relationship" approach of the Restatement (Second) of Conflict of Laws ("Restatement") for resolving conflict of laws questions in contract cases. This approach requires courts to apply the law of the state which, with respect to the particular issue in dispute, has the most significant relationship to the transaction and the parties. Restatement (Second) of Conflict of Laws § 188(1) (1971). The state with the most significant relationship is determined by considering the following factors.

(a) the needs of the interstate and international systems,

(b) the relevant policies of the forum,

(c) the relevant policies of other interested states and the relevant interests of those states in the determination of the particular issue,

(d) the protection of justified expectations,

(e) the basic policies underlying the particular field of law

(f) certainty, predictability and uniformity of result, and

(g) ease in the determination and application of the law to be applied.

Id. §§ 6(2), 188(1). In evaluating these factors, courts take into account the place of contracting; the place of negotiation of the contract; the place of performance; the location of the subject matter of the contract; and the domicile, residence, nationality, place of incorporation, and place of business of the parties. *Id.* § 188(2).

The first factor—the needs of the interstate and international systems—seeks "to further harmonious relations between states and to facilitate commercial intercourse between them." *Id.* § 6 cmt. d. This factor favors the application of California law in this case. Alioto did not solicit business in Colorado. Instead, Hoiles traveled to California to retain a lawyer licensed to practice law in California. The majority of the legal services rendered pursuant to the Fee Agreement was performed in California. Strategy meetings and telephone conferences took place or were arranged from California. Part of Alioto's representation entailed consideration of a possible lawsuit against Freedom shareholders. Although suit was never filed, Alioto drafted a complaint to be filed in California state court that alleged violations of a California antitrust statute. The majority of shareholders named in the complaint were California residents.

Hoiles nevertheless contends a significant portion of services were also performed in Colorado. He argues Alioto's representation strategy required everything to come out of Hoiles' office in Colorado to ensure the interface was between Hoiles and Freedom, not Hoiles' attorneys and Freedom. To this end, Alioto regularly dictated letters to Hoiles' staff in Colorado for them to prepare and mail. Hoiles notes he also performed substantial background research and gathered documents in Colorado. Although Hoiles and his staff did substantial work in Colorado, the Fee Agreement at issue here was a contract for the rendition of Alioto's legal services. Therefore, performance of the Fee Agreement occurred largely in California where Alioto dictated the letter to Hoiles' staff and provided other legal advice. Legal services were rendered in Colorado on only one occasion: a member of Alioto's legal team traveled to Hoiles' office in Colorado for one day to review documents. Alioto himself never went to Colorado. Thus, significant services were not performed in Colorado.[3]

Applying Colorado law under these circumstances would likely impede the interstate practice of law thereby creating discordant relations between states. An attorney who is licensed to practice law only in California, does not travel outside California to solicit business, and performs legal services mainly in California is not likely to enter into attorney-client relationships with citizens from other states if he is required to conform to each state's unique contingent fee agreement requirements merely because his client is a resident of another state. The needs of the interstate system therefore favor the application of California law here.

The second and third factors consider and compare the policies of states having an interest in the dispute. Restatement (Second) of Conflict of Laws § 6 cmts. e, f. Here, both Colorado and California have some interest in the validity of the Fee Agreement because the agreement was negotiated in California and executed in Colorado by citizens of each state.[4] Hoiles contends that Colorado's interest is more compelling than California's because of Colorado's need to protect its citizens who enter into contingent fee agreements. Colorado's interest in protecting its citizens is attenuated in this case, however, because Hoiles traveled outside of Colorado to solicit representation by an attorney who resides in, and is licensed to practice law in, California. Colorado's interest is further diluted because California also has enacted statutes to protect clients, regardless of their state of residence, who enter into contingent fee agreements with attorneys licensed to

---

3   Although the majority of services were performed in California, the Fee Agreement did not explicitly require services to be performed in California. We therefore decline to rely on § 196 of the Restatement to resolve this dispute. Section 196 applies to contracts for the rendition of services; it creates a rebuttable presumption requiring application of the law of the state where the contract requires the services to be rendered unless some other state has a more significant relationship to the transaction and the parties. Restatement (Second) of Conflict of Laws § 196 (1971). The presumption only applies, however, when the contract expressly states where services are to be performed or the place of performance can be inferred from the contract's terms, the nature of the services involved, or other circumstances. *Id.* § 196 cmt. a. The Fee Agreement does not indicate where Alioto's services were to be rendered. Moreover, the district court did not determine whether the anticipated place of performance could be inferred from the contract's terms or other circumstances. Because it is not necessary for us to decide this question of fact in the first instance to resolve this case, we decline to do so.

4   The terms of the Fee Agreement were negotiated in California during Hoiles' and Alioto's initial meeting. At this meeting, the parties reached an oral agreement that Alioto subsequently reduced to writing. Because the written agreement was executed by Hoiles in Colorado, the place of contracting for purposes of applying the Restatement is Colorado. *See* Restatement (Second) of Conflict of Laws § 188 cmt. e (indicating the place of contracting is the place where, under the forum's rules of offer and acceptance, the last act necessary to give the contract binding effect occurred).

practice law in California. Cal. Bus. & Prof. Code § 6147. . . . Moreover, California has an interest in enforcing these rules against attorneys licensed to practice law in California. California's interest is especially compelling where, as here, the attorney does not leave the state to solicit business and performs the majority of the services required by the agreement in California. Colorado, on the other hand, has no significant interest in enforcing its rules regulating contingent fee agreements against attorneys who are not licensed to practice law in Colorado, do not solicit business in Colorado, and do not perform legal services in Colorado. *See Goldfarb v. Va. State Bar*, 421 U.S. 773, 792 (1975) (noting "States have a compelling interest in the practice of professions *within their boundaries*.") (emphasis added); *Int'l Tele-Marine Corp. v. Malone & Assocs., Inc.*, 845 F. Supp. 1427, 1431 (D. Colo. 1994) (concluding Colorado's interest in regulating attorneys licensed and practicing in Colorado is greater than Florida's interest when no legal services were performed in Florida). Because California's interests are more deeply affected by this dispute, factors two and three also favor the application of California law.

The fourth factor seeks to protect the parties' justified expectations. Restatement (Second) of Conflict of Laws § 6(2)(d). Although the parties here contest the meaning of the Fee Agreement, neither party disputes that he intended to enter into a contingent fee agreement. Hoiles traveled to California specifically to locate an attorney willing to represent him on a contingent fee basis. The parties subsequently entered into an agreement that explicitly provided for a fee based on a percentage of "anything recovered." Protecting the parties' expectations therefore requires application of whichever state's law will uphold the validity of the Fee Agreement. Alioto concedes the Fee Agreement is not enforceable under Colorado law. The parties contest the agreement's validity under California law. Therefore, only the application of California law will preserve the possibility of protecting the parties' justified expectations that they executed a valid contingent free agreement. *See id.* § 6 cmt. g.

The fifth factor requires consideration of which state's law "will best achieve the basic policy, or policies, underlying the particular field of law involved" in the dispute. Restatement (Second) of Conflict of Laws § 6 cmt. h. The parties disagree as to the particular field of law at issue here. Hoiles claims that the appropriate field of law is attorney-client contingent fee agreements. He contends the policies underlying this field of law include protection of the client by full, written disclosure; assumption by the attorney of the risk of no recovery; and compensation for the attorney only upon the occurrence of an agreed-upon contingency. Alioto contends the appropriate field of law is contracts. He urges us to achieve the fundamental goal of contract law—giving effect to the intent of the parties—by applying California law to uphold the validity of the Fee Agreement. The law of contingent fee agreements is merely a subset of contract law. The Fee Agreement is both a contract and, more specifically, a contingent fee agreement. Therefore, the policies underlying both fields of law are relevant in determining the validity of the Fee Agreement.

The law governing contingent fee agreements in Colorado and California is similar. Both states require contingent fee agreements to be in writing and contain specific information to ensure full disclosure to the client. Cal. Bus. & Prof. Code § 6147; Colo. R. Governing Contingent Fees ch. 23.3. Once a contingent fee agreement is deemed valid, both states interpret the agreement by looking to its express language to ascertain the intent of the parties. Cal. Civ. Code § 1638. . . . Both Colorado and California also construe any ambiguous language in the agreement in favor of the client. Nevertheless, the description of information that must be disclosed in a contingent fee agreement under Colorado law is more exacting than that which must be disclosed under California law. Colorado law therefore arguably better ensures full disclosure of all pertinent information to the client. As a result, the policies underlying the law of contingent fee agreements arguably favor the application of Colorado law. We need not definitively decide this issue, however, because the policies underlying the law of contracts favor the application of California law in this case. Contract law strives to "[protect] the justified expectations of the parties." Restatement (Second) of Conflict of Laws § 188 cmt. b. As discussed above, the application of California law might fulfill the parties' expectation that they executed a valid contingent fee agreement whereas the application of Colorado law will clearly defeat the parties' expectation. Thus, even if the policies underlying the law of contingent fee agreements favor the application of Colorado law, this fifth factor does not favor the application of Colorado law because the policies underlying the law of contracts, which are equally relevant, favor California law. At most, this factor is neutral.

The sixth factor—certainty, predictability, and uniformity of result—favors the application of California law. Restatement (Second) of Conflict of Laws § 6(2)(f). In this case, a citizen traveled from his residence in Colorado to California to solicit representation from an attorney licensed to practice law only in California. The majority of legal services performed pursuant to the contingent fee agreement the parties subsequently entered into were performed in California. Under these circumstances, it is predictable that California law would govern the Fee Agreement. Application of Colorado law, on the other hand, is less predictable. The relevant contacts with Colorado are limited. Although Hoiles is a Colorado resident and the Fee Agreement was signed by Hoiles in Colorado, these two contacts do not make the application of Colorado law predictable when compared to the numerous contacts with California present in this case.[5] *See id.* § 188(2) (listing contacts to be taken into account in determining state with most significant relationship).

The application of California law in this case would also create certainty and uniformity of result. Alioto is licensed to practice law only in California. He did not leave California to solicit business in another state. The legal services he rendered pursuant to the Fee Agreement were performed largely in California. In particular, he drafted a complaint asserting claims under a California antitrust statute for filing in California state court. Alioto is entitled, under these circumstances, to anticipate that California law will govern and draft his contingent fee agreement accordingly. Requiring an attorney to conform to the law of whichever state a client happens to reside in when the attorney is not licensed to practice in that state, does not solicit business in that state, and does not perform legal services in that state would create unnecessary uncertainty.

The seventh and final factor does not favor the application of either Colorado or California law. This factor evaluates the ease in determining and applying each interested state's law. Restatement (Second) of Conflict of Laws § 6(2). Both Colorado and California have statutes explicitly enumerating the requirements for a valid and enforceable contingent fee agreement. Cal.

---

5   Hoiles contends other relevant contacts with Colorado include the following: Hoiles paid all expenses incurred by Alioto under the Fee Agreement from Colorado; if Hoiles breached the Fee Agreement by not paying the contingent fee, the breach occurred in Colorado; and the subject matter of the Fee Agreement, Hoiles' Freedom shares, were located in Colorado. These contacts are not persuasive. First, the origin of payments under a contract and the location of the breach are not relevant contacts under § 188 of the Restatement. Second, although the location of the subject matter of the contract is relevant, it does not carry great weight in this case. *See* Restatement (Second) of Conflict of Laws § 188(2) (noting "contacts are to be evaluated according to their relative importance with respect to the particular issue" in dispute). Alioto and Hoiles entered into a contingent fee agreement whereby Alioto would perform legal services with the aim of enabling Hoiles to sell his Freedom shares. The majority of the legal services rendered pursuant to the Fee Agreement were performed in California. Freedom, the company whose stock Hoiles owned, is incorporated in California and has its [principal] place of business in California. Under these circumstances, the fact that Hoiles' stock certificates were located in Colorado is of limited relevance.

Bus. & Prof. Code § 6147; Colo. R. Governing Contingent Fees ch. 23.3. Therefore, neither state's law would be difficult to determine or apply in assessing the validity of the Fee Agreement.

Five of the seven factors for ascertaining the state with the most significant relationship under § 6 of the Restatement weigh in favor of applying California law in this case. The remaining two factors are neutral. Accordingly, California has the most significant relationship to the transaction and the parties, and its law should have been applied in determining the validity of the Fee Agreement. . . . We therefore reverse the district court's determination that the Fee Agreement is unenforceable, and remand. . . .

COMMENTS AND QUESTIONS

1. The stakes of this choice of law inquiry are stark: a $1.1 million recovery if Colorado law applies, and a $28.4 million recovery if California law applies.

2. What was the applicable rebuttable presumption in this case?

3. Notice that some courts frame their analysis primarily around the Section 6 factors while others march methodically through Section 145 (in torts cases) or Section 188 (in contract cases). Judges may not write enough choice of law opinions to have strong feelings one way or the other about the proper framework. Accordingly, either you or your opponent will likely supply the judge with the best way to approach a case. Do you think it matters which framework she uses? And if it matters, how will you get her to follow your approach rather than your adversary's?

4. Why wouldn't Colorado have an interest in regulating conduct by out-of-state attorneys giving legal advice to its citizens? How could factors (2) *and* (3) favor the application of California law?

5. It is probably obvious *why* Hoiles filed in Colorado, but *how* could he do so? What was his cause of action against Alioto?

CALLIES v. UNITED HERITAGE PROP. & CAS. INS. CO.

Court of Appeals of Arizona
2014 WL 1048846 (Ariz. Ct. App. Mar. 18, 2014)

JONES, JUDGE.

Kenneth and Dorene Callies, husband and wife (collectively, Callies), appeal the trial court's dismissal of their insurance bad faith cause of action against United Heritage Property and Casualty Insurance (United). . . .

Facts and Procedural History

The Callies maintained a homeowner's insurance policy with United. At the time they purchased the policy, the Callies were Oregon residents, while United was domiciled in Idaho and conducted business in multiple states, including Idaho, Oregon, Arizona, and Utah. The relevant policy covered the Callies' home in Eugene, Oregon, as well as their personal property "while it was anywhere in the world."

In June 2011, the Callies moved from Oregon to Arizona. To this end, the Callies rented a moving truck and drove to Surprise, Arizona. As the Callies had not yet secured permanent living arrangements in Arizona, they rented a room from The Lodge at Sun Ridge for the nights of June 10 through June 14. The Callies were allowed to park their moving truck in The Lodge's parking lot during their stay.

On the morning of June 11, the Callies discovered their truck, containing all of their personal property, had been stolen during the night. The Callies notified both the Surprise Police Department and United of the theft that same day. On June 28, the truck was discovered by the Glendale Police Department, but the Callies' personal property had been removed.

Toward the administration of the Callies' insurance claim, United directed an Arizona adjustor to contact the Callies in Arizona and take their statements. The Callies also provided complete inventory lists of the property taken, per United's request. With that, United advised the Callies that payment on their claim would be forthcoming, and that the only remaining issue was to determine the exact amount due. Acting on such assurance, the Callies proceeded to purchase a house in Arizona.

However, rather than make the promised payment, United instead decided to initiate a fraud investigation into the Callies' claim. United informed them of this decision by telephone in August. Following the phone call, Kenneth began displaying behavioral issues, suffering from emotional and mental agitation and confusion.

Later in August, the Callies received another phone call, this time from an attorney representing United, in which they were told to have no direct contact with any person at United and were asked to agree to be questioned under oath. When Dorene explained she did not believe Kenneth would be able to handle the examination, the attorney concluded the phone call. The Callies heard nothing further from United for several months. During that intervening time period, Kenneth continued to suffer emotional and psychological problems, and on October 28, he was civilly committed to a mental health facility [back] in Oregon.

On April 23, 2012, the Callies initiated suit [in an Arizona state court] against United and the Lodge at Sun Ridge and its owners (collectively, The Lodge). Within their complaint, the Callies alleged two claims: (1) insurance bad faith against United, and (2) negligence (premises liability) against The Lodge. [The Lodge did not join United's motion to dismiss, and is not party to this appeal.]

United responded by filing a motion to dismiss for failure to state a claim. *See* Ariz. R. Civ. P. 12(b)(6). In its motion, United argued Oregon law, rather than Arizona law, should be applied, and that Oregon did not recognize a cause of action for first-party insurance bad faith. . . . To its motion, United appended a certified copy of the Callies' insurance policy, as well as a partial transcript of Dorene's examination under oath. Within their response, the Callies argued to the contrary, asserting Arizona law should be applied. . . .

Following oral argument on United's motion to dismiss, the trial court, applying the principles delineated within the Restatement (Second) Conflict of Laws §§ 6 and 145 (1971), found Oregon law should apply, and granted United's motion to dismiss for failure to state a claim. In so finding, the trial court noted: (1) the Callies suffered the initial injury in Arizona but "the effects of [United's] conducts are continuing to be felt in Oregon, where [the Callies] reside;" (2) United's bad faith actions were centered in

Oregon; (3) the Callies "were and are Oregon residents, but briefly lived in Arizona;" (4) United was an Idaho corporation that conducted business nationwide; (5) the parties' relationship was centered in Oregon; and (6) "Oregon's interests stand out—it has an interest in ensuring that its citizens are treated appropriately by insurers." While recognizing Arizona and Oregon differ in their treatment of insureds, the trial court did not find Oregon's treatment unfair. . . .

Discussion

On appeal, the Callies argue the trial court erred by granting United's motion to dismiss because it found Oregon law, rather than Arizona law applied to this action. We agree.

I. Choice of Law

The parties agree the choice of law determination is dispositive of this matter. Oregon courts do not recognize a separate tort cause of action for an insurance bad faith claim that stems from an insurer's refusal to pay benefits, instead holding that such an action sounds in contract. *See Emp'rs' Fire Ins. Co. v. Love It Ice Cream Co.*, 670 P.2d 160, 165 (Or. Ct. App. 1983). Arizona does allow such a tort action. *See Zilisch v. State Farm Mut. Auto Ins. Co.*, 196 Ariz. 234, 237. . . .[4] Therefore, if Oregon law applies to this dispute, the Callies will have failed to state a claim upon which relief may be granted; the converse being true if Arizona law applies.[5]

As the forum state, Arizona law will govern the choice of law determination. . . . Arizona courts follow the Restatement (Second) of Conflict of Laws (1971) (Restatement) in determining the controlling law for multistate torts. . . .

A. Restatement § 146

Restatement § 146 entitled "Personal Injuries," has been found applicable to insurance bad faith claims when sufficient mental distress or physical harm has been alleged, as in the immediate case. *See Bates*, 156 Ariz. at 49 ("We

---

[4] Idaho, United's place of incorporation, similarly recognizes first party insurance bad faith as independently actionable in tort. *See Weinstein v. Prudential Prop. & Cas. Ins. Co.*, 233 P.3d 1221, 1240 (*Id.* 2010). . . .

[5] Neither party argues that Idaho law should be applied to this action, but rather focuses their arguments entirely on Oregon and Arizona law. As such, we discuss the Restatement contacts in Arizona or Oregon, and mention Idaho's contacts only when it would support an Arizona or Oregon contact. . . .

conclude that § 146 is pertinent because plaintiff claims that the alleged bad faith acts [of the defendant] caused her to suffer personal injury, mental and physical harm.").[7] Section 146 provides:

> [T]he local law of the state where the injury occurred determines the rights and liabilities of the parties, unless, with respect to the particular issue, some other state has a more significant relationship under the principles stated in § 6 to the occurrence and the parties, in which event the local law of the other state will be applied.

The "place of the injury," in the context of § 146, equates to the place where "the last event necessary for liability occurs." *Pounders v. Enserch E & C, Inc.*, 232 Ariz. 352, 356 (2013). Here, Kenneth began suffering emotional and psychological problems in Arizona immediately following United's informing the Callies their claim was being investigated. Further, the Callies allege having experienced extreme stress during the months they remained in Arizona due to United's decision to withhold payment on the Callies' claim during its investigation.

The Callies argue the place of the injury is determined at the time of the commission of the tort, leading to the conclusion that Arizona is the place of the injury. United argues that, in this instance, "the place of injury is, at best, transitory," and therefore cannot be said to be Arizona, because bad faith is a continuing tort and the Callies have alleged they are continuing to suffer the effects of United's alleged bad faith in Oregon, where they now reside. . . . We agree with the Callies that the place of injury is Arizona, as it was the state where they were located when the allege having initially suffered damage by virtue of United's actions. . . .

B. Restatement § 145

Having found that § 146 initially suggests the application of Arizona law, we still must consider whether Oregon has a more significant relationship to the parties and the issue than does Arizona. In doing so, we consider and analyze the factors outlined in Restatement § 145(2):

---

7   United invites us to resolve the choice of law issue under Restatement § 193. We decline to do so, as Restatement § 193 applies to "[t]he validity of a contract of fire, surety or casualty insurance and the rights created thereby," which are not at issue in this case. Further, *Bates* illustrates that choice of law cases regarding multistate insurance bad faith claims are analyzed under Restatement §§ 6, 145 and 146. *Bates*, 156 Ariz. at 48–51.

(a) The place where the injury happened,

(b) The place where the conduct causing the injury occurred,

(c) The domicil, residence, nationality, place of incorporation and place of business of the parties, and

(d) The place where the relationship, if any, between the parties is centered.

Bates, 156 Ariz. at 49.

The first factor, as previously established, weighs in favor of applying Arizona law. United consistently argues that the weight given this factor should be diminished because the injury occurring in Arizona was "merely fortuitous." *See Pounders,* 232 Ariz. at 357 (quoting Restatement § 145 cmt. e ("Situations do arise, however, where the place of injury will not play an important role in the selection of the state of the applicable law. . . . [W]hen the place of injury can be said to be fortuitous. . .")). In support of this assertion, United notes that the theft and events giving rise to the Callies' insurance claim occurred on the first night in Arizona.

First, United's focus upon the theft occurring on the Callies' first night in Arizona as the basis for its assertion the injury is fortuitous is misplaced, as it is not the theft that gives rise to the allegation of tortious conduct, but rather United's actions, thereafter. The Callies' bad faith allegation is that they suffered injury as a result of United's unreasonable decision to launch an insurance fraud investigation. The theft of the rental truck, itself, was no more than the triggering event that lead to the Callies' insurance claim. It was United's handling of the claim in August, two months after the theft, which resulted in the Callies' complaint of injury.

Second, we determine that Arizona was not a fortuitous place of injury. An injury is only fortuitous when it "just happens to occur" in a particular state. *See id.* (finding manifestation of mesothelioma in Arizona was fortuitous as the injured could have moved anywhere following his exposure to asbestos in New Mexico); *Garcia v. Gen'l Motors Corp.,* 195 Ariz. 510 (1999) (finding Idaho was a fortuitous place of injury because the injured passengers of an automobile accident that occurred in Idaho were Arizona residents that were taking a trip to Washington with the intent to return to Arizona). . .

The Callies had not only moved to Arizona, but proceeded with the purchase of a home by the time United determined to further investigate their claim.

Further, the Callies had filed their insurance claim with United from Arizona. Unlike the cited cases where the injury was deemed fortuitous because the mere happening of the event in the state was considered random (such as a car accident or the manifestation of an injury stemming from prior toxic exposure), in this case the Callies' location at the time of their injury was not a random event as they had not only decided to reside in Arizona but had relocated to this State, with United subsequently directing its actions toward the Callies with full knowledge they, by then, resided in Arizona. *See* Restatement § 146 cmt. e ("The local law of the state where the personal injury occurred is most likely to be applied when the injured person has a settled relationship to that state, either because he is domiciled or resides there or because he does business there.").

The second factor, given this case's procedural posture, is unclear. The complaint merely alleges that United informed the Callies their claim was to be investigated by a United adjustor, without specifying which office they would be in contact with or where the adjustor was located. Naturally, both parties argue the conduct occurred in the locale that supports their position, with the Callies arguing the decision was made in Idaho and United arguing the conduct occurred in Oregon.[9] However, it is unlikely, based upon the facts alleged in the complaint and contained within the associated papers, the complained of conduct—United's decision to undertake an investigation of the Callies' claim—occurred in either Oregon or Arizona. *See Bates*, 156 Ariz. at 50 (noting the place where the injury-causing conduct occurred was found where the decision to terminate plaintiff's medical benefits was made, at Nationwide's headquarters); *See, e.g., Baroldy v. Ortho Pharm. Corp.*, 157 Ariz. 574, 579 (Ct.App. 1988) (finding that in failure to warn cases "the 'place of conduct' is where the [tortious] decision is made"). As the trial court found, United's place of incorporation is Idaho. Further, Idaho appears to also be United's principal place of business, as the address given for United in the Callies' policy is in Meridian, Idaho. . . .

When reviewing a dismissal pursuant to Rule 12(b)(6), we assume the truth of the well-plead allegations contained within the complaint, as well as all reasonable inferences arising from those facts. In this instance, where the facts alleged the Callies were told by a United adjustor, rather than the insurance agent (Gambill Insurance Agency) from whom the Callies

---

9   This is common when conducting choice of law determinations at the motion to dismiss stage, as the choice of law inquiry is necessarily fact intensive, and at this stage discovery has yet to take place and the factual record has not been developed. . . .

purchased their policy in Oregon, that an investigation of their claim was going to commence, it is reasonable to infer that the decision to investigate their claim was made at United's principal place of business—Idaho—rather than in another State where it simply conducts business. Therefore, this factor does not particularly weigh in favor of either state's law being applied. However, as Idaho recognizes a tort action for insurance bad faith we may consider this factor as weighing in favor of the application of Arizona law. *See Baroldy,* 157 Ariz. at 579 (noting that "when the law of two states does not conflict, the contacts from those two states should be considered as if they were from the state involved in the choice of law question") (citing Restatement § 145 cmt. i).

The third factor favors the application of Arizona law. The Callies were domiciled in Arizona at the time of the alleged bad faith. They had moved themselves and their belongings to Arizona and purchased a home with the intent to remain. *Arizona Bd of Regents v. Harper,* 108 Ariz. 223, 228 (1972) ("Domicile is primarily a state of mind combined with actual physical presence in the state.") Although they have now returned to Oregon, such bears little significance to this factor. *See Summers v. Interstate Tractor & Equip. Co.,* 466 F.2d 42, 48 n.3 (9th Cir. 1972) (noting that the change of domicile to another state should carry no weight in deciding which law applies, as granting weight to it would encourage forum shopping). . . ; *see also Pounders,* 232 Ariz. at 358 (stating the place of the plaintiff's current domicile was entitled to little weight as he could have relocated to anywhere following his asbestos exposure); *See, e.g.,* Restatement Intro Note, ch. 7 (although not taking a specific stance, noting that a party's change in domicile following the commission of the tort but prior to the commencement of litigation should "[p]resumably [ ] . . . have no effect upon the law governing most of the issues involving the [tort]"). United, on the other hand, is incorporated and maintains its principal place of business in Idaho, while licensed to conduct business in several states, including both Arizona and Oregon. In a personal injury case, "we give greater weight to the residence of the alleged tort victim." *Bates,* 156 Ariz. at 50 (citing Restatement § 145 cmt. e).

The fourth factor, similar to the second, is unclear based upon the record. The Callies were Oregon residents when they purchased their United insurance policy from an Oregon insurance agent toward insuring their Oregon home and personal possessions. Nevertheless, at the time of the alleged bad faith, the Callies had relocated to Arizona, wherefrom their insurance claim to United was submitted and adjusted Because insureds possess greater mobility than insurers we generally assume the relationship is centered at the insurer's headquarters. *Id.* In the immediate case that is Idaho. Again, as Idaho and Arizona law is harmonious, we may consider this factor to weigh in favor of applying Arizona law. . . . Restatement § 145 cmt. i. . . .

In total, the first and third factors weigh in favor of Arizona law, while factors two and four arguably weigh toward either Idaho or Arizona law. However, this is a qualitative, rather than quantitative analysis. *Bates,* 156 Ariz. at 51; *see* Restatement § 145. Under § 146, "the law of the state 'where the injury occurred' is determinative unless some other state has a more significant relationship." *Bates*, 156 Ariz. at 51 (citing Restatement § 146).

C. Restatement § 6

Having determined the factors from § 145 illustrate Arizona has greater concerns relevant to the dispute, we still may only apply Arizona law if doing so would be consistent with the principles stated in Restatement § 6. Section 6(2) sets forth general principles to be applied in every choice of law determination:

(a) the needs of the interstate and international systems,

(b) the relevant policies of the forum,

(c) the relevant policies of other interested states and the relevant interests of those states in the determination of the particular issue,

(d) the protection of justified expectations,

(e) the basic policies underlying the particular field of law

(f) certainty, predictability and uniformity of result, and

(g) ease in the determination and application of the law to be applied.

In this case, the first, fifth, and seventh factors are insignificant. The needs of the interstate and international systems are not implicated or affected by the application of either Oregon or Arizona law. Likewise, both states would be easily able to determine and apply either state's law.

United argues that the fourth factor, the protection of justified expectations, weighs in favor of Oregon having a more significant relationship to this dispute because the contract originated in Oregon and none of the parties could have expected the Callies to gain greater contractual rights by moving to Arizona. United's assertion creates a misnomer, as the claim alleged sounds in tort, and in no way expands the Callies' "contractual benefits." Further, however, we simply disagree with the argument as the very language of United's insurance contract specifically asserted the contracted-for coverage for personal property applied anywhere in the world. United could not have believed that no matter where the Callies moved and regardless of the circumstances giving rise to a claim or subsequent actions following a claim being filed, throughout the world, Oregon law would apply.

Additionally, the claim is not one arising "from breach of some express covenant inserted by [United] as a matter unique to its [Oregon] business. [It instead] arises, rather, from breach of a good faith covenant implied in law" *Bates*, 156 Ariz. at 50. *Bates* rejected the argument that the law of the state where the contract was entered into (here, Oregon) necessarily is applied to a bad faith claim arising from conduct and resulting injury occurring in another state (here, Idaho and Arizona respectively). *Id.* at 51. Any expectations that would be the case are unjustified. *Id.* at 50. Further, "the protection of the justified expectations of the parties . . . is of lesser importance in the field of torts." Restatement § 145 cmt. b. The underlying purpose of this policy is to avoid penalizing a person for conforming to the law of one state "when he had justifiably molded his conduct to conform to the requirements of another state," which is less of a concern in the area of torts. Restatement § 6 cmt. g. Even assuming this policy carried great relevance to the tort of bad faith, this factor does not weigh in favor of Oregon law, as United did not justifiably mold its conduct to conform to the law of Oregon. Oregon does not excuse liability for insurer's bad faith actions, but rather limits any cause of action to contract claims. *Emp'rs' Fire Ins. Co.*, 670 P.2d at 165.

United also argues the application of Oregon law would best serve the policies, provided in factors six and seven, of "certainty, predictability, and ease of determination." Specifically, it argues Oregon law would provide greater ease because the tort is not recognized, therefore the trial court would not have to go through the task of "consider[ing] a vast array and detailed analysis of the handling of the claim under the bad faith tort." Succinctly stated, if this Court, on appeal, were to decide in favor of United, any bad faith claim would be eliminated. However, this policy bears no weight in our analysis as this principle is concerned with "choice-of-law rules [being] simple and easy to apply," and both Oregon and Arizona follow the Restatement's choice of law approach. Moreover, the principle of certainty and predictability of result is more significant in areas where "the parties are likely to give advance thought to the legal consequences of their transactions," such as the effect and validity of a contract or will. . . . Restatement §§ 6 cmt. j, 145 cmt. b. In the immediate matter, the parties gave no such advance thought to the legal consequences of the alleged bad faith actions.

The remaining principles require consideration of the policies and interests of the forum state and other interested states. Restatement § 6(2)(b)-(c). These two principles gain greater significance due to the limited importance of the other § 6 principles in tort cases. *Pounders*, 2323 Ariz. at 359; Restatement § 145 cmt. b (noting that the relevant policies in tort cases usually are the policies of the forum and other interested states). These policies are compared with particular weight being given to the Arizona's policy, as it is the dominant state. *See Pounders*, 232 Ariz. at 359 (citing Restatement § 145 cmt. b).

Oregon and Arizona's policies regarding insurance bad faith are drastically different. Arizona recognizes that conduct constituting insurance bad faith may cause a person to suffer more than mere economic injuries, and thus recognizes it as a tort. Oregon, however, limits bad faith causes of action to contract, thus making emotional distress or physical damages unrecoverable.

As the policies of the states are substantially different, we turn to the interests of the respective states. Arizona has a strong interest in ensuring its residents are made whole for injuries sustained while in Arizona. Toward that end, it allows recovery for plaintiffs injured by insurance bad faith practices to recover all damages caused by an insurer's conduct, including economic and emotional damages.[11] It also has a strong interest in deterring wrongful conduct directed against its citizens. Oregon's interests, on the other hand, are limited here, where the insureds were Arizona residents at the time of the complained of conduct, the conduct occurred outside Oregon, and the tortfeasor is incorporated in Idaho. Although United conducts business in Oregon, this creates no greater interest in Oregon as United equally conducts business in Arizona. After weighing the relevant principles of §§ 6, 145, and 146, we find Arizona has the more substantial interest to this occurrence, and, therefore, Arizona law is appropriately applied, even though neither party is currently a domiciliary of the State. . . .

---

11   Punitive damages, however, are not automatically recoverable, but may only be recovered if the plaintiff can demonstrate the insurer's wrongful conduct was done with an intent to injure the plaintiff or done with knowledge that the conduct created a substantial risk of harm.

COMMENTS AND QUESTIONS

1. Why did the plaintiffs file this case in Arizona if they live in Oregon? One reason might be that they wanted to name The Lodge as a defendant and The Lodge may not be subject to personal jurisdiction in Oregon. A second reason is that an Arizona court is more likely (than an Oregon court) to apply Arizona law. Remember the "homeward trend" discussed in Chapter 2: all else being equal, a judge will usually prefer to apply familiar law—not only because it is easier, but also because they are less likely to make a mistake.

2. Naming The Lodge as a party defendant in this case could have been a strategic move that has nothing to do with proving that The Lodge was negligent in allowing the Callies' truck to be stolen. Think of it this way: there is no doubt that Arizona law applies in the Callies' action against The Lodge. (Everything about that claim is Arizona-based.) Including the claim against The Lodge can create some litigation momentum for the application of Arizona law to the other claims in the suit. To be sure, the Second Restatement embraces depecage: the law that applies to the claim against United requires separate, independent analysis. (We will study depecage in Chapter 15.) Yet there can be a subtle, unstated, even subconscious momentum that favors the application of Arizona law to United if the court is already applying Arizona law to the claims against The Lodge.

3. When is a contact fortuitous? Need it be fortuitous to only one party or to both parties?

4. Notice that the court makes effective use of the transitive property to count all of Idaho's contacts as Arizona contacts. Comment i to Section 145 provides that

> When certain contacts involving a tort are located in two or more states with identical local law rules on the issue in question, the case will be treated for choice-of-law purposes as if these contacts were grouped in a single state.

Illustration: . . . By conduct in state X, A injures B in state Y. X and Y have the same local law rules with respect to liability in tort for causing personal injuries. The case will be treated for the purposes of this Section as if conduct and injury had taken place in one state.

This is especially effective when deployed here. Before we assign Idaho's contacts to Arizona, the breakdown of the Section 145 factors looked like this:

F1 (place of injury): AZ

F2 (place of wrongful conduct): ID/OR/AZ

F3 (domicile of the parties): AZ/OR/ID

F4 (place where relationship formed): OR/AZ/ID

But if, by the transitive property, Idaho's contacts can be treated as Arizona contacts, this becomes an easier case:

F1: AZ

F2: AZ/OR/AZ

F3: AZ/OR/AZ

F4: OR/AZ/AZ

It is important, then, for defense counsel to resist this grouping. What is your argument that Comment i to Section 145 does not apply here?

5. Reread the last sentence of the opinion. Is the fact that "Arizona has the most substantial interest to this occurrence" the same thing as it being the state with the *most significant relationship* to the disputed issue?

TOWNSEND v. SEARS, ROEBUCK & CO.

Supreme Court of Illinois
227 Ill.2d 147 (2007)

JUSTICE FREEMAN.

Plaintiffs, Michelle Townsend, individually and on behalf of her minor son, Jacob, brought a personal injury action in the circuit court of Cook County [Illinois] against defendants Sears, Roebuck and Company (Sears). A question arose as to whether Illinois or Michigan law would govern the liability and damages issues presented in the case. The circuit court ruled that Illinois law governs these substantive issues, but certified the following question of law for interlocutory appeal pursuant to Supreme Court Rule 308 (155 Ill.2d R. 308):

> Whether Illinois or Michigan law applies to a products liability and negligence action where the plaintiff is a resident of Michigan and the injury occurs in Michigan, the product was manufactured in South Carolina, the defendant is a New York corporation domiciled in Illinois, and the conduct complained of, including certain design decisions, investigations of prior similar occurrences, product testing and the decision to distribute nationally in its retail stores occurred in Illinois.

In its answer, the appellate court reached the same conclusion as did the circuit court.

We allowed Sears' petition for leave to appeal (210 Ill.2d R. 315). We disagree with the appellate and circuit courts, and hold that Michigan law governs the liability and damages issues presented in this case.

I. Background

Michelle and James Townsend, and their son, Jacob, reside on North Begole Road in Alma, Michigan. Sears is a New York corporation with its principal place of business and corporate headquarters in Cook County, Illinois. In the spring of 2000, James purchased a Sears Craftsman brand riding lawn tractor from a Sears store in Michigan. The lawn tractor was manufactured by Electrolux Home Products, Inc. (EHP), in South Carolina. James bought the 20-horsepower, 42-inch-wide lawn tractor for use around his home. This particular lawn tractor developed a faulty engine. In early 2001, James received an identical riding lawn tractor as a warranty replacement. Through early May 2001, James had operated the tractor three or four times to mow the Townsends' 1.8-acre property.

On the afternoon of May 11, 2001, James returned home from work and began to mow his lawn. At this time, his four children, including 3½-year-old Jacob, were inside their home. As James was mowing, he encountered the 16- by 14-foot rectangular railroad-tie-edged planting plot in his front yard. He attempted to mow around the plot by positioning the left edge of the mower deck as close to the ties as possible. However, the tractor became stuck against one of the ties. James shifted the tractor into reverse, looked over his right shoulder, and released the brake. The tractor struggled to move rearward, taking approximately 20 seconds to move approximately six feet. While backing up, he heard a noise, looked to his right, and saw Jacob's sandal on the lawn. He stopped the tractor, turned around, and saw Jacob behind and under the tractor's rear wheels. James overturned the tractor picked up Jacob, and rushed him to Gratiot Community Hospital in Alma. Jacob was subsequently treated at Sparrow Hospital in Lansing, Michigan. Jacob's right foot was amputated and his lower right leg was severely injured.

Michelle, individually and on behalf of Jacob, filed a complaint against Sears pleading strict product liability and negligence, premised on defective design and failure to warn. Plaintiffs alleged that Sears "designed, marketed, manufactured, inspected, test, and sold a Sears Craftsman Law Tractor"; that the tractor "was defectively designed, defectively marketed and unreasonably dangerous"; and that the design created such a risk of injury to small children that a reasonably prudent designer and marketer of riding lawn tractors, being fully aware of the risk, would not have put the lawn tractor on the market. Plaintiffs specifically alleged that the tractor lacked a "no-mow-in-reverse" (NMIR) safety feature to prevent back-over injuries. Plaintiff further alleged that Sears had actual knowledge of this specific unreasonably dangerous condition. . . .

Plaintiffs filed a motion to apply Illinois law to the issues of liability and damages. Plaintiffs also filed a petition for leave to amend the complaint to add a prayer for relief seeking punitive damages. . . . The circuit court identified conflicts between Illinois and Michigan law pertaining to liability and damages. The court employed the choice-of-law analysis of the Restatement (Second) of Conflict of Laws. The circuit court ruled that Illinois law should govern these substantive issues. . . . [T]he court certified the choice-of-law question for interlocutory appeal.

The appellate court allowed Sears' application for leave to appeal. . . . [A]s did the circuit court, the appellate court concluded that Illinois law should govern the issues of liability and damages presented in the case. This court allowed Sears' petition for leave to appeal. . . .

II. Analysis
. . . [A.] Identifying the Conflict

. . . In 1970, this court adopted, for tort cases, the choice-of-law methodology of what would become the Second Restatement of Conflict of Laws. *See Ingersoll v. Klein*, 46 Ill.2d 42 (1970) (citing preliminary draft of Restatement (Second) of Conflict of Laws). During the subsequent 37 years, this court has had only a relatively few occasions to address choice-of-law issues arising from the Second Restatement. . . In the present case, the appellate court's analysis and the arguments of counsel before this court indicate that a thorough discussion of choice-of-law principles and methodology is necessary.

For example, we take this opportunity to stress that a choice-of-law analysis begins by isolating the issue and defining the conflict. A choice-of-law determination is required only when a difference in law will make a difference in the outcome. . . . In the present case the parties agree that three conflicts exist between Illinois and Michigan law. The first conflict involves liability. Illinois has adopted a rule of strict liability in tort for product design defects. *See, e.g., Lamkin v. Towner*, 138 Ill.2d 510, 528–29 (1990). In contrast, Michigan has refused to adopt the doctrine of strict liability, instead imposing a pure negligence standard for product liability actions based on defective design. *Prentis v. Yale Manuf. Co.*, 421 Mich. 670, 690–91 (1984). The difference between the two theories lies in the concept of fault. A real conflict exists because, in a strict liability action, the inability of the defendant to know or prevent the risk is not a defense. However, such a finding would preclude a finding of negligence because the standard of care is established by other manufacturers in the industry. . . .

The second conflict concerns compensatory damages. Illinois currently does not have a statutory cap on compensatory damages for noneconomic injuries. *See Best v. Taylor Machine Works*, 179 Ill.2d 367, 384–416 (1997) (declaring statutory cap unconstitutional). In contrast, Michigan currently imposes caps on noneconomic damages in product liability actions. *See* Mich. Comp. Laws Ann. § 600.2946a (West 2000). . . .

The third conflict concerns punitive damages. Illinois does not prohibit the recovery of punitive damages in product liability cases when appropriate. *See Kelsay v. Motorola, Inc.*, 74 Ill.2d 172, 186 (1978). . . . Subject to specific statutory exceptions, "it is well established that generally only compensatory damages are available in Michigan and that punitive damages may not be imposed." *McAuley v. General Motors Corp.*, 457 Mich. 513, 519–20.

[B.] Overview: The Second Restatement of Conflicts

. . . One scholar has described the Second Restatement as "a document that could not—and cannot—be fairly called a 'restatement' of anything. Instead, it is an amalgamation of different conflict approaches, producing a document of a distinctly normative character." P. Borchers, *Courts and the Second Conflicts Restatement—Some Observations and an Empirical Note*, 56 Md. L. Rev. 1232, 1237 (1997). Indeed, "the Second Restatement is by far the most popular among the modern methodologies, being followed [as of 2004] in 22 states in torts conflicts." E. Scoles, P. Hay, P. Borchers & S. Symeonides, Conflict of Laws § 2.23, at 98 (4th ed. 2004). . . .

Section 6 is the cornerstone of the entire Restatement. . . . Section 6 provides as follows:

(1) A court, subject to constitutional restrictions, will follow a statutory directive of its own state on choice of law.

(2) When there is no such directive, the factors relevant to the choice of the applicable rule of law include

(a) the needs of the interstate and international systems,

(b) the relevant policies of the forum,

(c) the relevant policies of other interested states and the relevant interests of those states in the determination of the particular issue,

(d) the protection of justified expectations,

(e) the basic policies underlying the particular field of law

(f) certainty, predictability and uniformity of result, and

(g) ease in the determination and application of the law to be applied.

Restatement (Second) of Conflict of Laws § 6, at 10 (1971).

These multiple and diverse principles are not listed in any order of priority, and some of them point in different directions. . . . In some ways, § 6 was the logical response to the perceived flaws of the traditional rules. Critics had identified a variety of concerns that these rules failed to take into account, and § 6 offers a kind of laundry list response that enables the court to consider all of them when appropriate. . . .

Another fundamental concept of the Second Restatement's methodology is the concept of the "most significant relationship." While section 6 enunciates the guiding principles of the choice-of-law process, the most-significant-relationship formula describes the *objective* of that process: to apply the law of the state that, with regard to the particular issue, has the most significant relationship with the parties and the dispute. For example, in a tort case, the general principle that a court applies is: "The rights and liabilities of the parties with respect to an issue in tort are determined by the local law of the state which, with respect to that issue has the most significant relationship to the occurrence and the parties under the principles stated in § 6." Restatement (Second) of Conflict of Laws § 145(1), at 414 (1971). . . .

Lastly, the Second Restatement provides a list of the factual contacts or connecting factors that the forum court should consider in choosing the applicable law. In a tort case, for example, section 145(2) provides as follows:

(2) Contacts to be taken into account in applying the principles of § 6 to determine the law applicable to an issue include:

(a) The place where the injury happened,

(b) The place where the conduct causing the injury occurred,

(c) The domicil, residence, nationality, place of incorporation and place of business of the parties, and

(d) The place where the relationship, if any, between the parties is centered.

These contacts are to be evaluated according to their relative importance with respect to the particular issue.

Restatement (Second) of Conflict of Laws § 145(2), at 414 (1971).

. . . Thus, section 145 is no more definite than section 6, and perhaps even less so. On top of the "factors" listed in section 6, section 145 adds a generous dollop of territorial and personal contacts. . . .

[C.] The Presumption: The Law of the State Where the Injury Occurred

The parties disagree as to the nature and effect of a choice-of-law presumptive rule applicable in this case. The Second Restatement of Conflict of Laws does not abandon the rules entirely. "Separate rules are stated for different torts and for different issues in tort. In other words, the identity of the state of the most significant relationship is said to depend upon the nature of the tort and upon the particular issue." Restatement (Second) of Conflict of Laws, ch. 7, Topic 1, Introductory Note 2, at 413 (1971). . . .

[T]he Second Restatement of Conflict of Laws has been described as "schizophrenic," in that one portion of its split personality consists of general sections such as sections 6 and 145, while the other portion is a set of reasonably definite rules and a preference for territorial solutions, including the injury-state rule for tort cases, endorsed by its predecessor. The general sections embody a free-form approach to choice of law, while the specific sections are quite close to the territorial system embodied by the First Restatement.

We agree with the concern that the bench and bar have overemphasized the general sections of the Second Restatement of Conflict of Laws and have undervalued the specific presumptive rules. . . . [A] presumption exists, which may be overcome only by showing a *more* or *greater* significant relationship to another state. . . .

Generally speaking, then, the Second Restatement contemplates a two-step process in which the court (1) chooses a presumptively applicable law under the appropriate jurisdiction-selecting rule, and (2) tests this choice against the principles of § 6 in light of relevant contacts identified by general provisions like § 145 (torts) and § 188 (contracts). . . .

In this personal injury action, the appellate court was correct to cite section 146 of the Second Restatement of Conflict of Laws in holding that under

Illinois choice-of-law rules, the law of the place of injury controls unless another state has a more significant relationship with the occurrence and with the parties with respect to the particular issue. . . . One court has explained this presumption as follows:

> Often, however, the simple old rules can be glimpsed through modernity's fog, though spectrally thinned to presumptions—in the latest lingo, "default rules." For in the absence of unusual circumstances, the highest scorer on the "most significant relationship" test is—the place where the tort occurred. For that is the place that has the greatest interest in striking a reasonable balance among safety, cost, and other factors pertinent to the design and administration of a system of tort law. . . .

Spinozzi v. ITT Sheraton Corp., 174 F.3d 842, 844–45 (7th Cir. 1999)

We now apply section 146 to the record before us.

Plaintiffs are domiciled and reside in Michigan, and James works in Michigan. Plaintiffs allege that Sears' tortious conduct occurred in Illinois. Comment *e* of section 146, entitled "When conduct and injury occur in different states," addresses this specific situation. "The local law of the state where the personal injury occurred is most likely to be applied when the injured person has a settled relationship to that state, either because he is domiciled or resides there or because he does business there." Restatement (Second) of Conflict of Laws § 146, Comment *e*, at 432 (1971). In contrast:

> The state where the conduct occurred is even more likely to be the state of most significant relationship . . . when, in addition to the injured person's being domiciled or residing or doing business in the state, the injury occurred in the course of an activity or of a relationship which was centered there.

Restatement (Second) of Conflict of Laws § 146, Comment *e*, at 432 (1971).

If this guidance were not enough, the comments to section 146 further advise: "The likelihood that some state other than that where the injury occurred is the state of most significant relationship is greater in those *relatively rare* situations where, with respect to the particular issue, the state of injury bears little relation to the occurrence and the parties." (Emphasis added.) Restatement (Second) of Conflict of Laws § 146, Comment *c*, at 430–31 (1971).

In this case, Jacob was injured while James was operating the tractor mower in the front yard of their home in Michigan. This activity was centered in plaintiffs' Michigan community. Based on the record before us, a *strong* presumption exists that the law of the place of injury, Michigan, governs the substantive issues herein, unless plaintiff can demonstrate that Michigan bears little relation to the occurrence and the parties, or put another way, that Illinois has a more significant relationship to the occurrence and the parties with respect to a particular issue.

[D.] Another State With a More Significant Relationship

We now test this presumptive choice against the principles of section 6 in light of the contacts identified in section 145(2). . . .

First, the injury occurred in Michigan. As previously discussed, in a personal injury action, this raises a presumption in favor of Michigan law. Restatement (Second) of Conflict of Laws § 146 (1971). . . . [S]ituations exist where the place of the injury will not be an important contact, for example, where the place of the injury is fortuitous. Restatement (Second) of Conflict of Laws § 145, Comment *e*, at 419 (1971). In this case, however, Michigan has a strong relationship to the occurrence and the parties. Michigan is the place where James purchased the lawn tractor, the place where he used the lawn tractor, and the place where he and the named plaintiffs, his wife Michelle and his son Jacob, are domiciled and reside.

The second contact in section 145 is the place where the conduct causing the injury occurred. According to plaintiffs' theories of the case, Sears committed the allegedly culpable acts in Illinois. The appellate court excluded from its analysis James' alleged conduct contributing to the injury, reasoning that he was not a party. However, Sears pled affirmative defenses alleging contributory negligence on the part of James *and Michelle*. A court's consideration of injury-causing conduct in a section 145 analysis includes all conduct from any source contributing to the injury. . . . We view this contact as a wash.

The third contact is the domicile, residence, place of incorporation, and place of business of the parties. Here, plaintiffs reside in Michigan and Sears is headquartered in Illinois. We view this contact as a wash. The fourth contact is the place where the relationship, if any, between the parties is centered. In this case, the relationship between plaintiffs and Sears arose from James' purchase of the lawn tractor at a local Sears store doing business in Michigan.

In sum, the first contact favors Michigan; we consider the second and third contacts each a wash; and the fourth conduct favors Michigan. Considered alone, these contacts certainly do not override our presumption that Michigan law governs the substantive issues presented in this case. However, we must not merely "count contacts," but, rather, consider them in light of the general principles embodied in section 6.

A detailed analysis of all seven of the section 6 general principles is unnecessary. The commentary to section 145 explains that, in a personal injury action, section 6(2)(d), the protection of justified expectations, and section 6(2)(f), certainty, predictability, and uniformity of result, are implicated only minimally in a personal injury action arising from an accident. Restatement (Second) of Conflict of Laws § 145, Comment *b*, at 415–16 (1971).* Similarly, section 6(2)(a), the needs of the interstate system, is only minimally implicated in personal injury actions. It cannot be said that harmonious relations between states will be advanced by applying either Michigan or Illinois law. Further, section 6(2)(g), the ease in the determination and application of the law to be applied, yields no discernible advantage to Illinois law over Michigan law in this case.

Thus we are left to consider the following general principles embodied in section 6(2) with respect to each of the three identified conflicts: (b) the relevant policies of the forum; (c) the relevant policies of other interested states and the relative interests of those states in the determination of the particular issue; and (e) the basic policies underlying the particular field of law. . . .

Considering the policies and interests of Michigan and Illinois, and of the field of tort law, we are unable to conclude that Illinois' relationship to this case is so pivotal as to overcome the presumption that Michigan, as the state where the injury occurred, is the state with the most significant relationship.

---

* [Eds.' Note: Comment b includes the following text: "The factors listed in Subsection (2) of the rule of § 6 vary somewhat in importance from field to field. Thus, the protection of the justified expectations of the parties, which is of extreme importance in such fields as contracts, property, wills and trusts, is of lesser importance in the field of torts. This is because persons who cause injury on nonprivileged occasions, particularly when the injury is unintentionally caused, usually act without giving thought to the law that may be applied to determine the legal consequences of this conduct. Such persons have few, if any, justified expectations in the area of choice of law to protect, and as to them the protection of justified expectations can play little or no part in the decision of a choice of law question."]

1. Liability

The first conflict is between Illinois' strict liability standard and Michigan's negligence standard for product liability actions based on defective design. . . .

Every state has an interest in compensating domiciliaries for their injuries. But tort rules which limit liability are entitled to the same consideration when determining choice-of-law issues as rules that impose liability.

2. Compensatory Damages for Noneconomic Injuries

The next conflict is between the absence of a statutory cap on compensatory damages for noneconomic injuries in Illinois, and the existence of such a cap in Michigan. The appellate court, observing that this court declared a statutory cap unconstitutional . . . reasoned as follows:

> We recognize that plaintiffs, as Michigan residents, are not subject to Illinois's constitutional protections and, therefore, Illinois would have little or no interest in protecting plaintiffs from caps on noneconomic damages. Nevertheless, we must also consider that Illinois, as the forum state where the case will be tried, has a very strong interest in its constitutional protection of separation of powers within its borders and, therefore, has a strong interest in protecting against another state's legislative encroachment on the inherent power of its judiciary to determine whether a jury verdict is excessive. Thus, Illinois has a compelling public policy interest in applying Illinois law with respect to caps on noneconomic damages.

368 Ill.App.3d at 912.

We cannot accept this reasoning. We agree with Sears that enforcement by an Illinois court of the Michigan cap on noneconomic damages does not constitute an encroachment of separation of powers in Illinois. Rather, such enforcement simply applies a Michigan statute against a Michigan resident that has been upheld as constitutional in Michigan.

3. Punitive Damages

The last conflict is between the availability of punitive damages in product liability cases when appropriate, in Illinois, and the general unavailability of punitive damages in Michigan. . . .

Illinois certainly has a legitimate interest in the liability to be imposed on Illinois-based defendants under strict liability or negligence principles. However, Michigan has an equally legitimate interest in the remedies to be afforded its residents who suffer such tort injuries. And if the substantive law of these two states looks in different directions, each state would seem to have an equal interest in having its tort rule applied in the determination of the conflicting issues presented in the case. . . . We conclude that a section 145 analysis does not override our strong presumption that the law of Michigan, as the state where plaintiffs reside and where the injury occurred, governs the conflicting issues presented in this case. . . .

COMMENTS AND QUESTIONS

1. This case is an excellent example of a jurisdiction (or at least a judge) taking the presumption seriously. Does Justice Freeman give the presumption even more weight than the text of the Second Restatement assigns it? Remember that the Restatements are not law; a jurisdiction can adopt a Restatement wholesale, adopt it with modifications, or reject it completely. As an advocate you may be urging or resisting a deviation from a model approach. What are the advantages (and disadvantages) of a state remaining in lockstep with a model approach like the Second Restatement?

2. The court, when discussing the second contact of section 145 (the place where the conduct causing the injury occurred), said that this conduct was a wash because the allegedly wrongful conduct occurred in both Illinois and in Michigan. The only allegedly wrongful conduct in Michigan was James' and Michelle's alleged contributory negligence. Notice, then, that the fact that Sears asserted those affirmative defenses had some effect on the calculus of what law would apply to the Townsends' claim against Sears. Is that consistent with the Second Restatement's approach?

3. With respect to Section 6(e), what are "the basic policies underlying [tort] law" in a personal injury case? Why doesn't the court talk about these?

4. With respect to Section 6(b), how does the court describe Michigan's interest in frustrating its residents' attempt to recover compensation for their injuries? Is this (orthodox) interest analysis or something else?

From the Courts

ORTEGA v. YOKOHAMA CORP. OF NORTH AMERICA

Superior Court of Delaware
2010 WL 1534044 (Del. Super. Ct. Mar. 31, 2010)

Jurden, Judge.

I. Introduction

Before this Court is Yokohama Corporation of North American (hereinafter "YCNA") and Yokohama Tire Corporation's (hereinafter "YTC") Choice of Law Motion. Defendant's Motion is filed pursuant to Superior Court Civil Rule 44.1.[2]

Defendants argue that the substantive law of [the Mexican State of Michoacán] should apply to all of Plaintiffs' claims. In the alternative, they argue that California law should apply to all of Plaintiffs' claims. . . .

II. Background

The Parties

Plaintiffs are residents of [Estado de] Mexico, a state within the Republic of Mexico. YCNA is a Delaware corporation with its principal place of business in California. YTG is incorporated in California with its principal place of business in California.

The Accident

The suit stems from a motor vehicle accident that occurred on June 8, 2005 in the Mexican State of Michoacán [which neighbors Estado de Mexico]. Nelson Flores Hernandez (hereinafter "Decedent") was driving his 1998 Ford Explorer. Marcelino Valdez was his passenger. Plaintiffs claim the right rear tire of the Explorer suffered a sudden catastrophic tread separation

---

2   Superior Court Civil Rule 44.1 provides: "A party who intends to raise an issue concerning the law of a foreign country shall give notice in the party's pleadings or other reasonable written notice. The Court, in determining foreign law, may consider any relevant material or source, including testimony, whether or not submitted by a party or admissible under the Delaware Rules of Evidence. The Court's determination shall be treated as a ruling on a question of law."

which caused the Explorer to lose control and roll over. Decedent suffered fatal injuries.

Plaintiffs filed suit on June 7, 2007 alleging, *inter alia*, (1) strict liability, (2) breach of warranty, and (3) that Defendants negligently designed, tested, manufactured, and marketed an unsafe tire.

The Product

The tire is identified as a Yokohama Prodigy Radial A/T, DOT CCD6U-SH1902 (hereinafter "the Tire"). It is undisputed that the Tire was designed and manufactured in Virginia and tested in Ohio. No other information about the Tire is known by the parties.

III. Discussion

Delaware courts apply the "most significant relationship" test of the Restatement (Second) of Conflict of Laws in order to determine choice of law. The significant relationship test is a flexible one and requires each case to be decided on its own facts. Pursuant to Section 145 of the Second Restatement, the local law of the state which "has the most significant relationship to the occurrence and the parties under the principles stated in § 6" will govern the rights of litigants in a tort suit.

Section 145 lists contacts which should be considered when determining the law applicable to an issue. These contacts include:

(a) The place where the injury happened,

(b) The place where the conduct causing the injury occurred,

(c) The domicil, residence, nationality, place of incorporation and place of business of the parties, and

(d) The place where the relationship, if any, between the parties is centered.

Each of the aforementioned contacts must be weighed in light of § 6 of the Restatement (Second) of Conflict of Laws, which requires consideration of the following:

(1) the needs of the interstate and international systems,

(2) the relevant policies of the forum,

(3) the relevant policies of other interested states and the relevant interests of those states in the determination of the particular issue,

(4) the protection of justified expectations,

(5) the basic policies underlying the particular field of law,

(6) certainty, predictability and uniformity of result, and

(7) ease in the determination and application of the law to be applied.

Section 146 of the Restatement (Second) of Conflict of Laws directs the Court to apply the law of the state where the injury occurred in an action for a personal injury unless "some other state has a more significant relationship under the principles stated in § 6 to the occurrence and the parties, in which event the local law of the other state will be applied." A place of injury does not play an important role in the selection of the applicable law "when the place of injury can be said to be fortuitous or when for other reasons it bears little relation to the occurrence and the parties with respect to the particular issue." *Rasmussen v. Uniroyal Goodrich Tire Co.,* 1995 WL 945556, at *2 (Del. Super. Aug. 18, 1995) (quoting Restatement (Second) of Conflict of Laws § 145 cmt. e).

Place of Injury

The place of injury in this case is fortuitous. The motor vehicle accident occurred in the Mexican State of Michoacán. However, neither of the parties has significant ties with that state. Neither Plaintiffs nor Defendants are residents of Michoacan. Because Michoacán has no connection to the claim other than the fact that it was the location of the accident, it is considered fortuitous and, thus, accorded less weight than the other factors.

Place Where Conduct That Caused the Injury Occurred

The wrongful conduct alleged by Plaintiffs in their lawsuit occurred within the United States. Although there are many facts unknown about the Tire, it is undisputed that it was designed and manufactured in Virginia, and tested in Ohio.

*Domicile, Residence, Nationality, Place of Incorporation
and Place of Business of the Parties*

[A]t all relevant times Plaintiffs were residents of the State of Mexico. YTC is incorporated in California and YCNA is incorporated in Delaware. Both YTC and YNCA have principal places of business in California.

Defendants argue that California has the most significant contacts over any other United States jurisdiction because it is where YTC is incorporated and where YTC and YNCA have principal places of business.[31] However, the most significant relationship test does not allow a court to simply add up all of the contacts as listed in Section 145 and § 6 and apply the law of the state with the most contacts. The Court must weigh and consider the significance of each of the contacts.

The Place Where the Relationship Between the Parties is Centered

The relationship between the parties in this case is centered in the State of Virginia, the place where the Tire was designed and manufactured. Although the State of California has several contacts, and quantitatively more contacts perhaps than Virginia, Section 145 has a qualitative element. Section 145 clearly states that the "contacts are to be evaluated according to their relative importance with respect to the particular issue."

Because much is unknown about the Tire, the choice of law determination is a bit more challenging in this case. First, it is not known when or where the Tire was placed into the stream of commerce. It is also not known how the Tire arrived in Mexico or when or how Decedent obtained the Tire. Finally, and perhaps more importantly, it is not known where the Tire was marketed. "Modern choice of law considerations suggest that the jurisdiction where a product is marketed has a greater interest than a jurisdiction where a product is manufactured, developed, or tested. *Rasmussen*, 1995 WL 945556, at *2.

If the Court rejects the application of Mexican law, Defendants argue in the alternative that California is "the place where all corporate decisions pertaining to the subject tires marketing, advertising, instructions, labeling, warnings, warranties, distribution, and sales are made[,]" and thus, California law should apply to marketing claims. While Defendants' "marketing

---

31 Defendants further suggest that California is where the tire was marketed because California is the location of Yokohama's marketing headquarters.

headquarters" may very well be located in California, *"the jurisdiction where a product is marketed"* is to be considered, not the location of a company's marketing headquarters or the state in which marketing decisions take place. Plaintiffs argue that Virginia law should apply to the warranty, marketing and consumer claims because Virginia is the place where the Tire was designed, manufactured, and placed into the stream of commerce. In making this argument, Plaintiffs offer no support for their assertion that the Tire was placed in the stream of commerce in Virginia. Here, there is no way to ascertain where the Tire was marketed or where it was placed into the stream of commerce.[41]

Based on what is known about the Tire, the Court concludes the state where the relationship between the parties is centered is Virginia. Virginia is where the Tire came into existence, where it was both designed and made.

Factors—Section 6 Restatement (Second) Conflict of Laws

After weighing each of the aforementioned contacts in light of the factors set forth in § 6 of the Restatement, the Court finds that Virginia law shall apply to all claims and damages in this case.

The laws of Mexico severely limit the amount of damages a plaintiff can recover in a wrongful death action and do not provide for a survival cause of action. The purpose of those laws would seem to be to protect resident defendants from being accountable for large monetary damages associated with such actions. Because Defendants in this case are from the United States, neither the Country of Mexico nor any Mexican State has a strong policy interest in the application of its laws. Here, the State of Virginia has a stronger interest because, presumably, it would want to protect the public from any wrongful and/or harmful conduct allegedly caused by product designers and/or product manufacturers which conduct business within the state.

In addition, although the accident occurred in Michoacán, "a foreign plaintiff has come to the U.S. . . . in order to hold defendants accountable for alleged wrongful conduct which occurred solely in the U.S." [*Cervantes v. Bridgestone/Firestone North Amer. Tire Co.*, 2008 WL 3522373, at *3 (Del. Super. Aug. 14, 2008), *amended by* 2010 WL 4311788 (Del. Super. Feb. 8, 2010).] It therefore does not offend fundamental fairness to allow for the suit to proceed under United States law. Furthermore, it seems fair to hold

41   It is also known that Yokohama does not sell tires in the Country of Mexico.

Defendants to the laws of the country in which they are incorporated and the country in which they conduct extensive business, rather than have Defendants comply with the laws of a foreign country.

Although the States of Delaware and California may have some interest in the application of their respective laws, these interests are not as significant as those of Virginia. As discussed *supra*, Defendants are incorporated in Delaware and California and have principal places of business in California. But today, it is common for businesses to incorporate in one state, have a principal place of business in another, and conduct business both nationally or internationally. All contacts must be considered and weighed in terms of significance to the issues of the particular case. And Defendants should reasonably expect to be held accountable under the laws of a state in which they conduct business.

Finally, application of Virginia law will foster certainty, predictability, uniformity and ease in determination in this case. The application of Mexican law could be more costly and complicated for both the parties and the Court. . . .

COMMENTS AND QUESTIONS

1. The court says that place of injury is of little or no significance in its decisional calculus because the place of injury was fortuitous. Was it fortuitous only because the accident happened to occur in the State of Michoacán rather than in the plaintiff's home state of Estado de Mexico (Edomex)? Put another way, why isn't the place of injury and also the residence of the plaintiff "Mexico" (the country)? Does it matter whether the laws of those two Mexican states are similar or different with respect to the amount of damages a plaintiff can recover in a wrongful death action?

2. The Second Restatement downplays the significance of the place of injury when that place is "fortuitous." However, the drafters make those comments in the context of a Section 6 and Section 145 analysis. Here the court uses the fortuity of the place of injury as an excuse to ignore the rebuttable presumption of Section 146. What would the result be in this case if the court had followed the approach of the court in *Townsend, supra*?

Remember also Section 175 of the Second Restatement (quoted at the outset of this chapter). What does the court say about that rebuttable presumption?

3. Imagine that, in *Townsend*, the lawn mower accident had occurred in a different small town in Michigan where, say, the family had traveled to engaged in a service project to help clean up a neighborhood park. Would the Michigan place of injury then have been *fortuitous*?

4. Why was Virginia the place where the relationship between the parties was centered? Is there any evidence that plaintiffs or the decedent had any contact with Virginia?

5. There is little hard evidence about where key events regarding this tire occurred. The absence of evidence to determine the applicable law should prejudice which party? The absence of evidence also presents an opportunity to think more deeply about what facts drive the analysis. If we knew that the tire was first sold retail in Virginia (or Texas or Edomex or Michoacán), does that alone change the result in this case? If we knew that a car with this tire was sold to Ortega in Virginia (or Texas or Edomex or Michoacán), does that change the result?

6. Which party is arguing for the application of Mexican law here? What is at stake in the choice of applicable law?

7. Why does Virginia have the most significant relationship if it is not the place of injury, not the residence of the plaintiffs, not the state of incorporation, nor the principal place of business of the defendants? If you asked a non-lawyer which state had the "most significant relationship" to the facts in this case, what would you expect them to say?

8. In its consideration of the Section 6 factors, the court analyzes the interests of Mexico and Virginia, respectively. Is this orthodox interest analysis or something else?

9. The last sentence of the excerpt from the court's opinion reminds us of the difficulty of applying a foreign country's law. We will revisit the topic of proving foreign law in Chapter 18.

10. Five years after *Ortega* the Delaware Supreme Court heard a very similar case involving a helicopter crash in Mexico. The Court applied Mexican law. *See Bell Helicopter Textron, Inc. v. Arteaga*, 113 A.3d 1045 (2015).

FROM THE COURTS

DAY v. AMOR MINISTRIES

Court of Appeals of Arizona
2013 WL 709660 (Ariz. Ct. App. Feb. 26, 2013)

SWANN, JUDGE.

Defendant/Appellant/Cross-appellee Central Christian Church of the East Valley ("Central") appeals a jury verdict in favor of Plaintiffs/Appellees/Cross-appellants Ron and Heather Day and the superior court's denial of its motion for new trial. . . .

Facts and Procedural History

In November 2006, Ron and Heather Day, members of Central, travelled to Mexico with other church members on a volunteer mission to build wood-framed structures. Central partially coordinated the trip to Mexico, organized and assigned the volunteers, and supervised the work at the construction sites. Amor Ministries ("Amor"), an organization that arranges mission construction projects in impoverished areas, also partially coordinated and facilitated the trip. Amor designed the buildings and delivered the materials to the construction sites.

During the trip, a sub-group of volunteers, including the Days, built a church. On November 12, 2006, while constructing the roof of the church, Ron stepped on an unsheathed rafter that broke under his weight. He fell through the unfinished roof and sustained multiple injuries to his head, neck, and back.

The Days sued Central and Amor for negligence and loss of consortium. They claimed that Central breached the duty of care it owed Ron because it did not properly train or warn him about the safety risks associated with stepping on an unsheathed rafter. Central argued that the rafter was an open and obvious hazardous condition and noted Amor's construction manual did not contain any safety warnings or instructions for rooftop workers. Amor asserted that Central was in charge of the construction site and building process. Central and Amor both argued that the Days failed to mitigate their damages, and identified the supplier of the construction materials, Mat Materiales, as a non-party at fault.

On June 7, 2011, the jury returned a verdict awarding Ron $4,695,000 in damages and allocating 5% fault to Ron, 15% to Amor, 80% to Central, and 0% to nonparty Mat Meriales. The jury awarded Heather Day $1,250,000 for her loss of consortium claim. . . .

Discussion

Central . . . contends the superior court erred when it determined that Arizona law, and not the law of Mexico, applied in this case. ["The parties recognize that there is a conflict between the law of Arizona and the law of Mexico. Arizona has adopted a pure comparative negligence standard, whereas Central offered evidence that Mexico follows a negligence system, which limits damages to direct out-of-pocket expenses and bars relief to a plaintiff who is found to have contributed to his injuries."] We review de novo the court's choice of law determination.

Arizona has adopted the "most significant relationship" test set forth in the Restatement (Second) Conflict of Laws (1971) ("Restatement") to determine the controlling law for multistate torts. *Bates v. Super. Ct.*, 156 Ariz. 46, 48–49 (1988). Three sections of the Restatement apply. First, the Court must examine the "general principles of [Restatement] § 145 to determine the number of contacts and the weight of each state's contacts with the parties and the occurrence." *Baroldy v. Ortho Pharm. Corp.*, 157 Ariz. 574, 578 (1988). Second, those contacts must be considered under the principles of Restatement § 6 to determine which state has the most significant relationship to the parties and the occurrence. *Id.* Third, the Court must also apply the specific principles of Restatement § 146.

1. Restatement § 145

In deciding which jurisdiction has the most significant relationship, a court should first consider: "(a) the place where the injury occurred, (b) the place where the conduct causing the injury occurred, (c) the domicile, residence, nationality, place of incorporation and place of business of the parties, and

(d) the place where the relationship, if any, between the parties is centered." Restatement § 145(2).

There is no dispute Ron was injured in Mexico and Central's negligence took place in Mexico. And while we acknowledge the Days' argument that Central's negligence began in Arizona when it failed to properly train and instruct Ron and that the effect of Ron's injury will be predominantly felt here, we nonetheless determine the first two factors favor Mexico as the jurisdiction with the most significant relationship.

However, the Days are Arizona residents and Central is an Arizona corporation. "In § 145 analyses, the domicile of the plaintiff often carries the greatest weight . . ." because "[c]ompensation of an injured plaintiff is primarily a concern of the state in which plaintiff is domiciled." *Baroldy*, 157 Ariz. at 579. Therefore, this factor weighs heavily in favor of Arizona as the jurisdiction with the most significant relationship.

Central contends the final factor—the place where the parties' relationship is centered—should favor Mexico because Central's volunteers were subject to Mexican building codes and safety labor restrictions during the construction project. Those matters, however, are not pertinent to the question where the parties' relationship is centered. The Days attended Central's church services in Arizona for years, volunteered and registered in Arizona for the mission project, and travelled from Arizona in a Central vehicle to the construction site. The parties established their relationship in Arizona, and it is centered here. Therefore, this factor weighs in favor of Arizona.

Two factors from Restatement § 145 favor Mexico and two favor Arizona. Because "the determination of which state has the most significant contacts is primarily qualitative, not quantitative," we next evaluate the parties' contacts with Arizona and Mexico in light of the principles of Restatement § 6 to determine which law should apply. *Wendelken v. Super. Ct.*, 137 Ariz. 455, 458 (1983).

2. Restatement § 6

Restatement § 6 provides that in the absence of a statute that prescribes how broadly a state's law is to be applied, courts should consider: (a) the needs of the interstate system, (b) the relevant policies of the forum, (c) the relevant policies of other interested states, (d) the protection of justified expectations,

(3) the policies underlying the field of law, (f) uniformity of result, and (g) ease in determination of application of the law to be applied.

As the Arizona Supreme Court recognized in *Wendelken*, our choice of law determination in this matter "should have little effect on the harmonious relationship or on the commercial interaction between Arizona and Mexico." 137 Ariz. at 458. This is a private dispute between an Arizona citizen and an Arizona corporation whose relationship is centered in Arizona. It does not implicate Mexican tourism or commerce.[9]

"Arizona, in addition to being the forum state and the place of the trial, has considerable interest in this matter." *Wendelken*, 137 Ariz. at 458. Arizona has an interest in both Central and the Days because they are domiciliaries of the state and has a particular interest in ensuring the Days are appropriately compensated for their injuries. *Id.* Mexico does not have a comparable interest in the liability that an Arizona corporation has to an Arizona citizen.

Further, the protection of justified expectations is not a consideration in this case because neither party anticipated the negligent act and therefore could not have formed an expectation as to which law would apply in the event of negligence. Similarly "[p]redictability and uniformity of result" are irrelevant in this case because these considerations "are of greatest importance in cases where the parties are likely to give advance thought to the legal consequences of their transactions, i.e., contracts or will validity, not where negligence is at issue." *Id.* at 460.

Having fully considered the Restatement § 6 factors and the interests of Arizona and Mexico in this action, we conclude that the trial court properly determined that Arizona has the most significant relationship to this occurrence and these parties.

3. Restatement § 146

In a personal injury action, the law of the state where the injury occurred should be applied unless another state has a more significant relationship.

---

9   Central's argument that the application of Arizona law in this case would serve as a significant disincentive for charitable organizations to conduct similar missions in foreign countries is based solely on speculation. Absent evidence, we have no reason to conclude that Arizona charitable organizations are incentivized to conduct missions in other countries in hopes of securing the advantages of their more defense-friendly negligence laws.

Restatement § 146. Here, although Ron's injury occurred in Mexico, Arizona has a more significant relationship to the parties and occurrence. We hold that the superior court properly ruled Arizona law applies in this case. . . .

COMMENTS AND QUESTIONS

1. One way that skilled litigators counter a good policy (or common sense) argument is to demand hard evidence that the proposition is true. If someone proposes that the speed limit on a street in front of a school be lowered because the speed of the cars poses a risk, a stock response is: "But what evidence do you have that posting a sign with a lower speed limit will change anyone's behavior?" And even if the person proposing the policy change has evidence that lowering speed limits works, the stock response is "But that study is from another state, did not involve a school zone, did not take into account the unique circumstances of why people are speeding here, etc." Now reread note 9 of the court's opinion. Is it especially speculative to imagine that a church might be disinclined to engage in charitable activity if it has to replicate in the foreign country all of the safety precautions that would be undertaken in its home state?

2. The court analyzes the governmental interests of Mexico and Arizona. Is this orthodox interest analysis? Why isn't Mexico's interest in encouraging tourism and charitable ventures valid?

3. Does the court's decision also mean that any violation of Arizona building codes might be negligence *per se*?

4. If Ron Day had been asked on the day before he was injured what law he thought would apply in the event he were injured, what would he have said? The court discounts the role of the justified expectations of the parties in tort cases, as many courts do. But why not contemplate what law he would reasonably have expected to apply?

5. Most of Ron's $4.7 million damages award and all of Heather's $1.25 million award would be vacated if Mexico law applied. If you represented the plaintiff, about $2 million of your fees turns on the outcome of this choice of law question on appeal. If you represented the defendant, an

award of this magnitude could cripple a client like this, a church in Gilbert, Arizona.

6. Why isn't the court moved by the presumption in Section 146? (Or Section 156 or 157?) Is it because this is another case where the place of injury was *fortuitous*?

FROM THE COURTS

ENTERPRISE PRODS. PARTNERS, L.P. v. MITCHELL

Court of Appeals of Texas
340 S.W.3d 476 (2011)*

EVELYN V. KEYES, JUSTICE.

. . . Background

On the morning of November 1, 2007, a liquid propane pipeline operated by Dixie Pipeline Company ("Dixie") ruptured in a rural area near Carmichael, Mississippi. Upon its release into the air, the liquid propane changed to gas and formed a cloud that rose over a nearby neighborhood and ignited into a large fireball that could be seen and heard for miles around. The resulting fire killed two people, injured seven others, and resulted in the evacuation of approximately 60 families from their homes. Four homes were destroyed, several others were damaged, and more than 70 acres of the woods and grassland surrounding the site of the explosion were burned. The National Transportation Safety Board (NTSB) reported that approximately 10,253 barrels, or 430,000 gallons, of propane were released.

Appellees, Catherine Mitchell, O'Neal Pacley, Linda Mitchell, and Johnny Jones, as wrongful death beneficiaries of the two decedents, Mattie L. Mitchell and Nacquandrea Mitchell, along with Catherine Mitchell, Catherine Pacley, and Samida Mitchell as personal injury claimants and other plaintiffs who suffered property damage (collectively, plaintiffs) sued Dixie and Enterprise Products Partners, L.P. ("Enterprise'), Dixie's managing partner, in Harris County, Texas. Dixie and Enterprise moved the trial court to apply Missis-

---

*   Review granted (Aug. 17, 2012), case abated (May 17, 2013), cause dismissed (Sept. 20, 2013).

sippi law to the issue of the amount of recoverable compensatory damages, arguing that the Restatement (Second) of Conflict of Law's balancing test favors application of Mississippi's $1 million cap on noneconomic damages in civil actions.[2] Dixie and Enterprise argued that, as the domiciliary state of the plaintiffs, Mississippi has the greatest interest in determining the amount of compensation to be awarded to its residents and in protecting defendants doing business in its state. The plaintiffs argued that Texas law should apply because both Enterprise and Dixie have their principal place of business in Texas, the pipeline was manufactured in Texas, and Enterprise and Dixie control the pipeline's multi-state operation from Texas.

The trial court issued an order ruling that "the issue of recoverable compensatory damages with regard to all wrongful death and personal injury claims is to be governed by Texas law" and certifying the order for interlocutory appeal pursuant to Texas Civil Practice and Remedies Code section 51.014(d). This interlocutory appeal was filed. . . .

It is undisputed that Dixie and Enterprise are both Delaware corporations whose principal place of business is Houston, Texas. All of the wrongful death and personal injury plaintiffs are Mississippi residents and domiciliaries. It is likewise undisputed that the failed segment of pipeline was manufactured in 1961 in Texas, that it was subsequently installed in Mississippi, and that the explosion occurred in the state of Mississippi. Furthermore, the portion of the pipeline that exploded was part of a 1,300 mile pipeline in a 35,000 mile pipeline system and spanned from Texas through Louisiana, Mississippi, Alabama, Georgia, South Carolina, and North Carolina.

Decisions about Enterprise and Dixie's operations were made in Texas. Dixie's corporate representative indicated that its policies, procedures, and manuals all come from the Houston, Texas office, that the pressure, flow, and operation of valves and pumps are monitored and conducted from Houston via a computer system whose control system is likewise in Houston, and that the Houston employees are generally responsible for the operation of the pipeline. Furthermore, key employees such as the manager of pipeline integrity, the pipeline integrity engineer for this particular pipeline, and the pipeline controller responsible for monitoring this pipeline on the day of the explosion are all located in Houston, Texas. None of the pump sta-

---

2   *See* Miss. Code Ann. § 11–1–60 (2004) (providing limit of $1 million in awarding non-economic damages against any civil defendant other than health care liability defendant, providing limit of $500,000 in awarding non-economic damages in medical liability actions, and defining noneconomic damages as "subjective, nonpecuniary damages" arising from an injury).

tions or other facilities along the pipeline's route through Mississippi are manned on a routine basis, although Dixie does have about five employees who work in Mississippi.

Choice of Law

Which state's law governs an issue is a question of law for the court to decide. Therefore, we review the trial court's decision to apply Texas law de novo.

We decide choice of law issues by applying the "most significant relationship" test found in the Restatement (Second) of Conflict of Laws. Section 6 of the Restatement sets out general factors relevant to the choice of law:

(a) the needs of the interstate and international systems,

(b) the relevant policies of the forum,

(c) the relevant policies of other interested states and the relevant interests of those states in the determination of the particular issue,

(d) the protection of justified expectations,

(e) the basic policies underlying the particular field of law

(f) certainty, predictability and uniformity of result, and

(g) ease in the determination and application of the law to be applied.

Torrington Co. v. Stutzman, 46 S.W.3d 829, 848 (Tex. 2000) (quoting Restatement (Second) of Conflict of Laws § 6(2) (1971)).

Section 145 of the Restatement provides specific considerations relevant when applying the general conflict of laws principles to a tort case:

(a) the place where the injury happened,

(b) the place where the conduct causing the injury occurred,

(c) the domicil, residence, nationality, place of incorporation and place of business of the parties, and

(d) the place where the relationship, if any, between the parties is centered.

Torrington Co., 46 S.W.3d at 848 (citing Restatement (Second) of Conflict of Laws § 145(2) (1971)).

Section 145 also provides, "The rights and liabilities of the parties with respect to an issue in tort are determined by the local law of the state which, with respect to that issue, has the most significant relationship to the occurrence and the parties under the principles stated in [section] 6." Restatement (Second) of Conflict of Laws § 145(1) (1971). . . . The Restatement's "most significant relationship test" includes a presumption in favor of applying the law of the place of the injury. Section 146, governing personal injuries, and section 175, governing wrongful death, create a presumption that

> the law of the state where the injury occurred determines the rights
> and liabilities of the parties, unless, with respect to the particular
> issue, some other state has a more significant relationship under
> the principles stated in section 6 to the occurrence and the par-
> ties, in which event the local law of the other state will be applied.

Restatement (Second) of Conflict of Laws §§ 146, 175.

Using this presumption in favor of the law of the state where the injury occurred as the starting point for our analysis, we consider the various factors listed in the Restatement to determine if Texas has a greater interest in the determination of the particular issue than Mississippi, the state where the injury occurred. *See id.* § 175 cmt. d (also providing that courts should examine "the purpose sought to be achieved by their relevant local law rules and the particular issue involved"). The number of contacts with a state is not determinative; rather, we evaluate the contacts in light of the state policies underlying the particular substantive issue. . . .

In *Torrington*, the supreme court analyzed which state's law should apply to compensatory damages in a helicopter crash that killed two marines. *Id.* at 833. The marines were North Carolina residents whose domiciles were in Nebraska and Michigan, and at least two of the defendant corporations, Bell and Textron, had their principal place of business in Texas. In holding that the trial court correctly applied Texas law, the court stated,

> We have noted that a plaintiff's domiciliary state usually has a
> strong interest in seeing its compensatory damages law applied.
> But Texas, as the forum state, also has a significant interest in
> protecting resident defendants, such as Bell and Textron. And
> other Restatement factors weigh in favor of applying Texas law.
> For example much of the conduct that allegedly caused the injury
> occurred in Texas. The helicopter that was involved in the crash

was manufactured and delivered in Texas, several communications about the bearing failure . . . were issued from Texas, and Torrington sent communications about the investigation to Bell in Texas. Moreover, Texas is the forum state and the parties acquiesced to the trial court's application of Texas laws to the liability issue. "Ease in the determination and application of the law to be applied" is one of the factors to be considered in resolving the choice-of-law questions under the Restatement.

Id. at 850 (internal citations omitted).

Here, Mississippi's contact with the tort arises from the fact that all of the wrongful death and personal injury plaintiffs were residents and domiciliaries of Mississippi at the time of the explosion. Mississippi has an interest in ensuring that its citizens receive adequate compensation so that the costs of injured residents are not borne by the public, but Mississippi's damages cap does not further that interest. Moreover, while the explosion and its resulting injuries occurred in Mississippi, we note that the pipeline could have exploded at any point along its 1,300 mile span. *See id.* at 849; *Duncan v. Cessna Aircraft Co.*, 665 S.W.2d 414, 421 (Tex. 1984) (rejecting using location of incident alone as method for determining which state's law should govern).

The policy behind Mississippi's Tort Reform Act of 2004, including the compensatory damages cap, was essentially "to end the state's 'hell-hole' reputation and attract more business and insurers to Mississippi." *See generally* Miss. Code Ann. § 11–1–60 (2004) (providing limit of $1 million in awarding non-economic damages against any civil defendant other than health care liability defendant, providing limit of $500,000 in awarding non-economic damages in medical liability actions, and defining noneconomic damages as "subjective, nonpecuniary damages" arising from an injury); H.B. 13, 2004 Leg., 2d Ex. Sess. (Miss. 2004) (amending section 11–1–60 and others); Mark Behrens & Cary Silverman, *Now Open for Business: The Transformation of Mississippi's Legal Climate*, 24 Miss. C.L. Rev. 393, 415–16 (2005) (discussing "comprehensive civil justice reform bill, H.B. 13" that, among other provisions, amended section 11–1–60 to limit non-economic damages). These policy concerns are not implicated here. Mississippi's interest in applying its damages cap to lawsuits in that state has little applicability to a lawsuit brought in a different state against defendants domiciled in that different state where the tortious conduct also occurred in that other state.

When the incident occurred, Enterprise and Dixie has only limited business activity in the state of Mississippi, and the pipeline, which was built through the state of Mississippi in the 1960s, was not built in reliance on this reform, as the Tort Reform Act was passed in 2004.

Texas, however, is the forum state with a significant interest in protecting resident defendants. . . . Both of the defendants, Enterprise and Dixie, are corporations with their principal place of business in Texas, and the decisions regarding maintenance and operation of the pipeline—i.e., the conduct causing the injury—occurred in Texas. Additionally, Texas's compensatory damages law is at least equally capable of serving the interest of fairly compensating injured plaintiffs.

Enterprise and Dixie argue in their brief that *Torrington* is distinguishable from the present case because *Torrington* involved 'the unique setting of an aviation crash" while this case does not, because "the unique background of the Mississippi legislation limiting compensatory damages" creates a stronger policy interest in favor of applying Mississippi law than was present in *Torrington*, and because all of the plaintiffs here are residents and domiciliaries of Mississippi, unlike the claimants in *Torrington*, whose residences and domiciles implicated three different states. We disagree. As we have already discussed, the "unique background" of the Mississippi damages cap is not implicated by these facts, as neither Enterprise nor Dixie maintained any significant business presence in Mississippi. *See id.* at § 849; *Duncan*, 665 S.W.2d at 421. Furthermore, even considering that all of the wrongful death and personal injury plaintiffs in this case share the same state residence and domicile, that one factor does not overwhelm the other considerations. *See Torrington Co.*, 46 S.W.3d at 848–49; *Hughes Wood Prods.*, 18 S.W.3d at 205; Restatement (Second) of Conflict of Laws § 145(1).

We conclude that Texas law should be applied to the issue of compensatory damages available to the wrongful death and personal injury plaintiffs in this case. Thus, the trial court's interlocutory order was proper.

We overrule Enterprise and Dixie's sole issue.

COMMENTS AND QUESTIONS

1. What role does the section 146 presumption play in the court's analysis? Is the place of injury less significant here because it is *fortuitous*?

2. Are these plaintiffs forum-shopping for more favorable law by filing in Texas rather than in Mississippi? It seems quite unlikely that plaintiffs, after suffering these terrible injuries, called a *Texas* lawyer for assistance. But on the other hand, are they forum-shopping in Texas if both Mississippi and Texas follow the Second Restatement to determine the applicable law? The basic personal jurisdiction rule in the Civil Law tradition is *actor sequitur forum rei*—the plaintiff sues at the defendant's domicile. Viewed this way, does plaintiffs' suing in Texas smack of forum-shopping?

3. One way to spot forum-shopping (and to shame those who do it) is to observe that the forum probably would not have personal jurisdiction over these litigants if they were defendants instead of plaintiffs.

4. Does the Second Restatement's approach to choice of law discourage forum-shopping or discriminate against those who forum-shop? How?

5. Notice the deployment of interest analysis to minimize the significance of Mississippi laws that would cap the plaintiffs' recovery. Mississippi's tort reform laws are typical of tort reform measures across the country. What does the court mean when it labels them "unique"? Is this orthodox interest analysis? What did the defendants do wrong here?

GRUPO TELEVISA, S.A. v. TELEMUNDO COMMUNICATIONS GROUP, INC.

U.S. Court of Appeals for the Eleventh Circuit
485 F.3d 1233 (11th Cir. 2011)

FAY, CIRCUIT JUDGE.

This appeal challenges a decision to apply Mexican law in a suit alleging tortious interference with a contract for the services of a Mexican soap opera star. The appellants (collectively "Televisa") are a trio of Mexican corporations that produce radio and television programs for Spanish-speaking audiences in Mexico and abroad. They license an American broadcaster, Univision, to carry their "telenovelas" or soap opera programs in the United States. The appellees (collectively "Telemundo") are rival Spanish-language television producers and broadcasters that are head-quartered in Florida. After an actor who was under exclusive contract to Televisa accepted a role in a Telemundo soap opera, Televisa sued its American rival in federal district court in Miami, claiming tortious interference under Florida law.

Telemundo moved to dismiss the claim pursuant to Rule 12(b)(6), arguing that Mexican law, which does not recognize a cause of action for tortious interference, governed the dispute. Televisa urged the court to apply Florida law since the acts leading to the allegedly offensive conduct occurred in Florida. The district court denied Telemundo's motion to dismiss and ordered the motion converted to a motion for summary judgment. The court followed the choice of law rules of the forum state, which dictate that the court apply the law of the state with the "most significant relationship" to the occurrence and the parties. Although the court declined to make a finding as to where the conduct causing the injury occurred, it found that other contacts favored the application of Mexican law, which would bar the claim. Accordingly, the court awarded Telemundo summary judgment, and Televisa filed an immediate appeal, challenging the court's "most significant relationship" calculus. For the reasons stated below, we vacate the district court's summary judgment decision and remand the case for trial under Florida's law of tortious interference.

I. Background

[Grupo Televisa S.A., Televisa S.A., and Televisa Talento S.A. de C.V. (collectively, "Televisa"), are three closely affiliated Mexican corporations which produce Spanish-language television and radio programs for broadcast both in Mexico and abroad. Televisa maintains its international sales office in Florida, but it does not broadcast its telenovelas to the states directly. Instead, it licenses Univision Communications Group, Inc., a large Spanish-language broadcasting corporation, to carry its television programming in the U.S. on its networks, Univision and Telefutura.

Univision's chief rival for the attention of Spanish television audiences in the U.S. is the Telemundo Network, which is headquartered in Florida, also produces telenovelas.

In 2000, a Mexican actor named Juan Mauricio Islas Ilescas ("Islas") entered into an agreement with Televisa to provide various services, including "artistic interpretation" in certain productions, "artistic interpretation" in certain productions, "personal presentations" for promotional purposes, "voice interpretations in respect to any production" and "use of image" to Televisa on an exclusive basis for seven years. Televisa had been grooming Islas as an actor since 1990 and had sent him to its acting school and cast him in a number of telenovelas.

The agreement contained a Mexican choice of law provision, and it contained a penalty provision that stated Islas would owe Televisa P$840,000 in Mexican pesos in the event that he breached the terms of the agreement, and a separate penalty of P$5,880,000 in Mexican pesos should he breach his exclusiveness obligations under the agreement.

Additionally, Islas pledged that he would not render his services to any third party in Mexico or abroad for at least six months following early termination of the agreement by Televisa for breach. The Agreement also contained a first right of refusal provision that gave Televisa the right to match any third party offer that Islas might receive within six months of the termination of the Agreement.

On November 7, 2003, Mr. Islas, who was still under contract to Televisa, signed an exclusive production agreement with Telemundo at its offices in Hialeah, Florida. The Agreement with Telemundo contained an exclusivity provision in which Islas pledged that he "would not commence or participate in any negotiations for his services with, or render services for any third parties without Telemundo's prior written consent" during the term of the agreement.

On December 17, 2003, Islas issued a press release in which he stated that he planned to leave Televisa. Televisa sent Telemundo a letter on January 5, 2004, informing them that Islas had an exclusivity contract which would run through January 2007. Televisa also notified Islas on January 6, 2004 that it planned to film a new telenovela beginning January 8th, and expected him to report for the taping. Islas did not report to Mexico for taping of Televisa's project on January 8th.

On the day that Telemundo began filming the first project in which it planned to cast Mr. Islas, Televisa filed suit against Telemundo in federal district court in Miami, alleging tortious interference with contract. Televisa also requested a preliminary injunction to prevent Telemundo from using Islas's services through the duration of the Televisa-Islas contract. Televisa filed a separate motion for a temporary restraining order to keep TCG from moving forward with its plans for the Islas project, a telenovela which was billed as "La Prisionera." The requests for interlocutory relief were denied.

The district court ultimately granted summary judgment to Telemundo on the ground that Mexican law governed the dispute and that Mexican law did not recognize a cause of action for tortious interference. This appeal followed.

The defendants held one meeting with Islas's agent in Mexico and four meeting s with Islas and/or his representatives in Miami, including the meeting at which Islas and the defendants executed their agreement. Most of the written communications between the defendants and Islas originated from the Telemundo offices in Miami.]

[II.] Discussion

A. Choice of Law Rules for Federal Courts Sitting in Diversity

A federal court sitting in diversity will apply the conflict-of-laws rules of the forum state. *Klaxon Co. v. Stentor Elec. Mfg. Co.,* 313 U.S. 487, 496 (1941). As a preliminary matter, the court must characterize the legal issue and determine whether it sounds in torts, contracts, property law, etc. Once it has characterized the legal issue, it determines the choice of law rule that the forum state applies to that particular type of issue. *Acme Circus Operating Co., Inc. v. Kuperstock,* 711 F.2d 1538, 1540 (11th Cir. 1983).

Florida resolves conflict-of-laws questions according to the "most significant relationship" test outlined in the Restatement (Second) of Conflict of Laws. *Bishop v. Florida Specialty Paint Co.,* 389 So.2d 999, 1001 (Fla. 1980). The Restatement (Second) of Conflict of Laws provides a "General [Tort] Principle" in section 145 that is intended to inform courts as they apply the more specific "Choice of Law Principles" outlined in section 6. The more specific "Choice of Law Principles" apply to all areas of law which determine choice of law through a most significant relationship test, not just to issues of tort.

B. § 145 of the Restatement (Second) of Conflict—The General Tort Principle

Section 145(1) lays out the basic principle for tort actions and section 145(2) lists four "contacts" that courts should consider in the course of applying the specific Choice of Law Principles under section 6. Section 145 of the Restatement (Second) of Conflict of Laws provides:

(1) The rights and liabilities of the parties with respect to an issue in tort are determined by the local law of the state which, with respect to that issue, has the most significant relationship to the occurrence and the parties under the principles stated in § 6.

(2) Contacts to be taken into account in applying the principles of § 6 to determine the law applicable to an issue include:

(a) the place where the injury occurred,

(b) the place where the conduct causing the injury occurred,

(c) the domicil, residence, nationality, place of incorporation and place of business of the parties, and

(d) the place where the relationship, if any, between the parties is centered.

Section 145 advises that "[t]hese contacts are to be evaluated according to their relative importance with respect to the particular issue." *Id.*

In this case, the court characterized the nature of the alleged tort as "the misappropriation of trade values." In keeping with the commentary to section 145, the court concluded that the "place of injury" should not play an important role in a case of this type as the plaintiffs would normally feel the loss most acutely at his headquarters. *See* § 145(2) cmt. f. However, the district court largely ignored the remaining commentary under this section, which states that the "principal location of the defendant's conduct" is the single most important contact in cases involving misappropriation of trade values. *Id.*

Although it noted that the alleged tortious conduct occurred in both Florida and Mexico, the court declined to make a finding as to the principal location of the defendant's conduct. While the facts do indicate that the defendants held one meeting with Islas' agent in Mexico, they held four such meetings with Islas and/or his representatives in Miami. The Florida meetings included: the initial contact between representatives of both parties; the first meeting between the parties that Islas attended directly, which defendants' in-house counsel and its CEO also attended; a second meeting between Islas and the defendants; and the meeting where Islas and the defendants entered into an exclusivity agreement, thereby breaching Islas' pre-existing exclusivity agreement with the plaintiffs. The defendants also generated most of the written communications regarding Islas from their home offices in Florida.

Thus, the Florida contacts are both numerically and qualitatively more significant when it comes to determining the "principal location of the defendant's conduct." The record simply doesn't support the district court's decision to dismiss the significance of this point of contact or its failure to recognize that this contact pointed conclusively to Florida. Moreover, comment "e" to section 145(2) notes that "when the primary purpose of the tort rule involves is to deter or punish misconduct, the place where the conduct occurred has peculiar significance (see Comment c)." *Id.* Although, Televisa argued that this was the primary purpose of Florida's tortious interference rule, the court rejected this argument. The district court concluded that the primary purpose of the alleged tort was to protect property rights in contract, not to regulate conduct, as the plaintiffs asserted.

However, as comment "c" in section 145(1) of the Restatement (Second) of Conflict of Laws notes, "[t]o some extent, at least, every tort rule is designed both to deter other wrongdoers and to compensate the injured person." Florida's law of tortious interference is clearly conduct-regulating on some level since the law allows for punitive damages, which are meant to punish wrongdoers. *See HGI Assocs. v. Wetmore Printing Co.,* 427 F.3d 867, 876–77 (11th Cir. 2005).

And, although Florida does not generally recognize punitive damages for breach of contract claims, it may recognize them "where the acts constituting a breach of contract also amount to a cause of action in tort." *Id.* . . .

In such cases, the underlying tort must be based on "an intentional wrong, willful or wanton misconduct, or culpable negligence, the extent of which amounts to an independent tort. . . ." *S. Bell Tel. & Tel. Co. v. Hanft*, 436 So.2d 40, 42 (Fla. 1983).

This is clearly the case with respect to Televisa's complaint, which alleges an intentional tort. Persons who commit tortious interference with a contract desire, or at the very least anticipate, certain consequences such as breach. By refusing to recognize that Florida's tortious interference rule is intended to regulate conduct, the district court undervalued the importance of the contacts relating to the place where the conduct causing the injury occurred.

With respect to the other contacts listed under section 145(2), the court found, quite correctly, that they were inconclusive for the purpose of determining choice of law in this case. Those contacts include "the domicil, residence, nationality, place of incorporation and place of business of the parties," § 145(2)(c), and the "place where the relationship between the parties, if any, is centered," § 145(2)(d). Certainly, Televisa and Telemundo do not share any contacts in terms of domicil, nationality, [or] place of incorporation. Moreover, the parties agreed that they share no relationship.[23]

C. § 6 of the Restatement (Second) of Conflicts—Specific Choice of Law Principles

Having concluded that the section 145(2) contacts did not point conclusively to either Florida or Mexico for choice of law purposes, the district court examined the section 6 factors to "resolve the standoff." Section 6 of the Restatement (Second) of Conflict of Laws provides that, absent a statutory directive on a choice of law, a state will consider the following factors for their relevance to the issue:

(a) the needs of the interstate and international systems,

(b) the relevant policies of the forum,

(c) the relevant policies of other interested states and the relative interests of those states in the determinations of the particular issue,

(d) the protection of justified expectations,

---

23   The . . . two parties share in a business rivalry since their Spanish television programs are broadcast on competing stations in the United States. Although Televisa does not broadcast its productions in the U.S. directly, it does license them for broadcast through Univision, a corporation in which Televisa holds an unconsolidated equity interest. . . .

(e) the basic policies underlying the particular field of law,

(f) certainty, predictability and uniformity of result, and

(g) ease in the determination and application of the law to be applied.

Restatement (Second) of Conflict of Laws § 6(2)(a)–(g) (1971).

The commentary to this section cautions that the factors are not listed in order of relative importance and that varying weight will be given to particular factors in different areas of law. Id. § 6(2) cmt. c. Unfortunately, the district court weighed the various factors as though Televisa's tortious interference claim sounded in contract law. Yet, as comment "v" under section 766 of the Restatement (Second) of Torts explains, a plaintiff may maintain an action against a third party for tortious interference and a separate action against another party for breach of contract. Both the breaching party and the party who induced that party to breach his contract are wrongdoers and are liable to the plaintiff for harm. Restatement (Second) of Torts § 766 cmt. v. (1979).

Moreover, under Florida law, a plaintiff can maintain a cause of action against a third party for tortious interference in a contract even though he might not be able to enforce the underlying contract. *Border Collie Rescue, Inc. v. Ryan*, 418 F.Supp.2d 1330, 1344 (D. Fla. 2006) . . . . This fact suggests that the terms of the underlying contract and the parties' expectations should have little bearing on the law that governs third party interference in that contract.

Nevertheless, the district court found that the "needs of the interstate and international forums," "the relevant policies of other interested states," "the protection of justified expectations," and "certainty, predictability and uniformity of result" all weighed heavily in favor of Mexico because the underlying contract was based there. It also found that application of Florida law would do nothing to advance the "relevant policies of the forum" because Florida's primary purpose in allowing tortious interference claims was to protect rights to performance of a contract. When rights to the performance of a contract exist in another forum, Florida has no interest in protecting such outside property rights, the court reasoned. Accordingly, the court concluded that Mexico represented the state with the most significant relationship to the parties and the occurrence.

We believe that the court overstated the extent to which the "needs of the interstate and international systems" favor the application of Mexican law in this case. Indeed, the court stated that those needs could only be met through the application of Mexican law since the contracting parties were both Mexican, the contract was to be performed in Mexico and Mexican law governed any contractual disputes. Applying Florida law in this case, the court reasoned, would undermine the international commercial system. In such a case, the parties would be exporting Florida law to control the rights and liabilities of a Mexican contract, the court concluded.

Televisa is not seeking to enforce its contract rights against Islas under Florida contract law, however. And, the Florida law that Televisa is seeking to impose will do nothing to effect its rights and liabilities under the Islas contract. Televisa is seeking to apply Florida tort law that will compensate it for the losses caused by a third party's interference in the Islas contract. That third party is a corporate domiciliary of Florida and it allegedly used Florida as the venue for its tortious acts.

Denying Mexican businesses the right to sue Florida domiciliaries for tortious interference in their contracts would do little to "facilitate commercial intercourse" between Mexico and Florida. *See* Restatement (Second) of Conflict of Laws § 6 cmt. d (1971). The record indicates, for example, that Televisa maintains its international sales office in Florida. As the "Association of Producers and Distributors of Mexican Films" and the "National Chamber of Commerce for the Radio and Television Industries (of Mexico)" indicated in their amicus curiae brief, the district court's ruling would hinder the ability of Mexican companies to compete in the international marketplace. They argue that if the ruling were affirmed, it would be tantamount to granting Florida domiciliaries a safe haven from which to interfere in foreign contracts. Clearly, this would not serve the needs of the international systems.

The district court also appears to have accorded too much weight to what the "justified expectations of the parties" were, concluding that they weighed heavily in favor of Mexico. Granted, Televisa and Islas stipulated that Mexico's Federal Copyright law would govern interpretation of the exclusivity contract and all disputes arising out of that contract. However, their agreement did not anticipate tortious interference by a third party. As the Florida Supreme Court pointed out when it contrasted contract actions and tort actions in *Sturiano v. Brooks*, 523 So.2d 1126, 1130 (Fla. 1988), "[w]ith tort law, there is no agreement, no foreseen set of rules and statutes which the parties had recognized would control the litigation."

We also note that intentional torts are not like negligent torts. When parties commit a negligent act, they give no thought to the legal consequences of their conduct or to the particular law that may apply. *See* Restatement (Second) of Conflict of Laws § 6(2) cmt. g (1971). Intentional torts, however, presuppose a certain level of awareness, a recognition of potential consequences. As the facts demonstrate, Telemundo was aware that its actions were likely to induce Islas to breach his contract with Televisa and move to Florida where Telemundo films its productions. That was the objective.

Indeed, Telemundo had its legal counsel research the question of whether Televisa might be able to pursue a claim against it under Florida tort law. Although the parties' justified expectations may not be as pivotal a factor for determining choice of law in torts issues as it is for contracts issues, to the extent that it figures in this case at all, we find that it points to Florida.

The district court also concluded that it could best assure "certainty, predictability and uniformity of result" by applying Mexican law. In doing so, it focused once again on the nature of the underlying contract as opposed to the nature of the alleged tort. Given that the plaintiffs are Mexican, and that they stipulated Mexican law should govern the underlying contract, the court opined "if the law were equal in both states, [p]laintiffs would have filed in Mexico."

This assumes that the plaintiffs could have filed an action against the defendants in Mexico and simply want to avail themselves of more liberal recovery laws in a different forum. In such a case, a court could simply deny jurisdiction on the grounds of *forum non conveniens*. But there is nothing in the record to suggest that the plaintiffs could have filed this suit in Mexico. Mexican jurisdiction does not have the extra-territorial reach that the individual states enjoy in the U.S. Mexican law applies to all persons within the country and to all events that occur there. Federal Civil Code, Preliminary Provisions, Article 12 in: Mexican Civil Code Annotated. Bilingual Edition. Translated by Professor Jorge A. Vargas. Thomson/West Publishing Co. 2005 at 3. The defendants committed their allegedly tortious acts outside Mexico, and neither one of the defendants are Mexican corporations. . . .

Finally, the district court found that the application of Mexican law could, conceivably, advance a Mexican policy interest relating to contracts, whereas the application of Florida law would do nothing to advance the policy interests of the forum. (Contrast Restatement (Second) of Conflict of Laws § 6(2) (c) with § 6(2)(b).) This finding relies upon pure conjecture. The district court speculated that Mexico might have a policy of facilitating "efficient breach" of contracts, but did not cite a single legal authority in support of this proposition. Indeed, this Court refused to accept a "foreign investment interest" theory which one of the parties in *Cortes v. American Airlines, Inc.*, 177 F.3d 1272, 1301 (11th Cir. 1999), advanced under a choice of law analysis because the party did not present any evidence in support of the theory.

Although it was plausible that such a scheme could be designed to encourage non-domiciliary corporations to transact business within a jurisdiction, this Court observed in *Cortes*, "a party invoking the theory must adduce evidence to support the assumptions underlying the theory. . . . In the absence of such evidence, the assumptions underlying this theory are 'too strained to merit serious weight under section 6(2)(c),' " Id. . . .

Assuming, arguendo, that Mexico has a policy of facilitating "efficient breach," the crucial question is whether that policy would be advanced by application of its rule regarding tortious interference claims. It is difficult to see how a hypothetical Mexican policy favoring "efficient breach" would be advanced by denying Televisa the right to obtain redress in Florida when a third party commits tortious acts in Florida that interfere with Televisa's Mexican contract.

Although Mexico might not have a policy that would be advanced by applying its law in this situation, Florida does. . . .

The final factor to be considered for determining the "most significant relationship" under section 6(2) is the "ease in the determination and application of the law to be applied." *See* Restatement (Second) of Conflict of Laws § 6(2)(g) (1971). The court concluded that this factor favored Mexico because a "Mexican plaintiff should look to Mexican law to remedy an interference with a Mexican contract." But such a comment ignores the difference between an action for breach of contract and one based upon the tort of deliberate interference with a contract. Nothing could be easier than for a court in Florida to apply Florida law to tortious conduct which took place in Florida.

IV. Conclusion

We find that the factors to be considered in determining whether Mexico or Florida has the "most significant relationship" to the parties and the conduct alleged in this case tip the scales decidedly in favor of Florida. . . . The summary judgment entered by the district court is vacated and the matter remanded for proceedings consistent with this opinion.

COMMENTS AND QUESTIONS

1. Although transactional lawyers do not engage in litigation, they conduct their work in anticipation of—and avoidance of—litigation. Where should the in-house lawyers at Telemundo have insisted that their business folks meet with Islas?

2. Would the court have applied Florida law if the policies were reversed and it was Mexico that recognized tortious interference with contractual relations (and Florida did not)? Put another way, what is driving the court's analysis and conclusions? If the principal driver of the analysis is that Telemundo engaged in deviant behavior that should be punished, why doesn't the court say (only) that?

3. This opinion is an exquisite example of a Second Restatement approach. Lawyers for both sides were likely exceedingly competent in briefing these issues for the court.

4. The Second Restatement is an aggregation of all of the choice of law methodologies. The complexity of the approach combined with its flexibility make it difficult to predict what law will apply. One way to impose some order is to evaluate empirically whether one of the approaches that is embedded in the Second Restatement is doing most of the work. We can do that by looking at the seven cases reprinted in this chapter. The first column of data in the chart below indicates what law would apply in a *lex fori* regime—the law of the forum. The last column of data reveals that in 4 of 7 instances, the court, applying a Second Restatement approach, applied the law of the forum. (What about the homeward trend?) Complete the chart to see which of the other methods is the best predictor

of a Second Restatement analysis? (*E.g.,* What law would have applied in *Hoiles* if the court followed a traditional approach and applied the law of the place of contracting?)

	Fori	Trad	IntA	CoG	BtrL	2dR
Hoiles	CO					CA
Callies	AZ					AZ
Townsend	IL					MI
Ortega	DE					VA
Day	AZ					AZ
Enterprise	TX					TX
Televisa	FL					FL

SAMPLE EXAM QUESTIONS

Question 8-7

Knutsen, a resident of Thunder Bay, Ontario, purchased a miter saw from a local Sears Canada, Inc., retail outlet. Shortly after she purchased the saw, she removed the upper and lower guards on the saw and reattached the blade so that she could make deeper cuts with the saw. When she turned the saw on, the rotating blade disengaged at a very high speed and struck her arm just below the shoulder. Her arm, which was nearly severed, was surgically reattached, but as a result of the accident, she now has only limited use of it.

This saw was sold by Sears Canada Inc., a Canadian corporation that is now defunct and judgment proof. The saw was designed and tested by Devereaux Electric Co., a Delaware corporation that has its principal place of business in Kansas City, Missouri. Devereaux sold its saws to Sears Canada Inc. and to other retailers. Devereaux outsourced the manufacturing of these saws to Nylund Inc., a Taiwanese corporation. The saw that Knutsen purchased from Sears Canada, Inc., was part of a larger shipment that Devereaux instructed Nylund to send there.

Canadian law does not recognize strict products liability. Nor does its tort law allow plaintiffs to establish negligence on a theory of res ipsa loquitur. If the action is filed in a Missouri court that follows the Second Restatement approach to choice of law, will Canadian law apply?

Question 8-8

Durand & Hamilton is a small law firm that is located in Washington D.C. Over the course of ten years the law firm provided services to McClure Chemicals, Co., a Nebraska corporation with its principal place of business in Omaha. The law firm represented McClure on a number of federal and state regulatory matters regarding gasoline contracts and petroleum futures.

About two years ago, catastrophe struck when about 100,000 gallons of petroleum leaked out of McClure's holding tanks that were located in Colorado. A number of regulatory actions followed, and McClure called the law firm for help. The firm represented McClure in regulatory proceedings and litigation in Colorado, and counseled McClure on other regulatory issues, including notifying agencies in other states about the spill.

McClure fell behind on paying its bill for legal services and then ultimately quit paying altogether. The law firm filed a law suit against McClure in Washington, D.C. to collect $500,000 of fees owed. McClure asserted various defenses that excused payment. The suit went to trial, and the law firm was awarded $170,000.

Pursuant to the terms of the retention agreement, the law firm is entitled to recover the "costs of collecting any fees due and owing, including reasonable attorneys fees and expenses." According to the law firm its collection costs were $275,000.

McClure does not challenge the enforceability of the attorneys fee provision in the retention agreement, but it challenges the $275,000 amount of those fees, because the law firm represented itself in the litigation. It argues that the law firm cannot recover as "costs" or "fees" the retail value of services that it provided to itself. McClure's position is correct under Nebraska and Colorado law: law firms may not recover attorney fees incurred while representing itself. However, under the law of the District of Columbia, the law firm is entitled to recover the reasonable value of its services.

If D.C. courts follow the Second Restatement, which law is it likely to apply?

Question 8-9

Antonio Gidi is a resident of Philadelphia, Pennsylvania. He was working as a delivery person for Queen's Quality Foods Inc. (Queen's) which delivered items to all of Derner's Warehouse Grocery Markets (Derner's) in Pennsylvania, Delaware, and Maryland. In a typical week Gidi delivers to 24 Derner's locations in Pennsylvania, 8 in Delaware, and 1 in Maryland. Queen's and Derner's are Pennsylvania corporations with their principal place of business in Philadelphia.

Approximately one year ago, Gidi drove to the Derner's market in Elkton, Maryland for a regular delivery. Gidi entered the store to notify them of his arrival, and returned to his truck. He then walked up the ramp into the store pulling a handcart behind him that was loaded with approximately 100 pounds of boxes. He held the door with one hand and pulled the cart through the doorway with the other, so his body was twisting as he walked. He looked straight ahead as he walked into the warehouse, not at the ground. As he took two steps inside the warehouse he tripped over the forks of a pallet jack. As the forks of the pallet jack were low to the ground and a similar color to that of the warehouse floor, he did not see them before he tripped. Gidi fell to the ground and permanently injured his knee.

Pennsylvania has a comparative negligence statute that allows plaintiffs with a right to partial recovery when they are found 50% or less negligent. In contrast, Maryland still utilizes the common law doctrine of contributory negligence, which insulates defendants from tort claims if the plaintiff is negligent to any degree.

If Gidi files suit against Derner's in Pennsylvania, and if Pennsylvania follows the Second Restatement, is this a comparative negligence (per Pennsylvania law) or a contributory negligence (per Maryland law) case?

Question 8-10

Lane LaVine drove a garbage truck for the defendants, Waste Disposal of Mississippi, Inc. (Waste), a Mississippi corporation. A resident of Tennessee, Mr. LaVine reported to work daily in Corinth, Mississippi. Corinth is about two miles from the state line. The route that LaVine covered for Waste included parts of both Tennessee and Mississippi.

Mr. LaVine injured his back while on the job in Tennessee. He sought and received benefits under Tennessee's workers' compensation law. When he was cleared to return to work, Mr. LaVine was told that he was no longer needed on the truck route in Tennessee but could work instead as a truck washer for Waste, a position that was located in Tupelo, Mississippi. According to Waste, when LaVine was injured the company realized that four drivers could complete the work that five had previously covered; hence the downsizing that led to LaVine's reassignment.

After about three months of washing trucks, LaVine quit the new job. In a lawsuit that he filed in Tennessee, LaVine alleged that the humiliation, lower pay, and the additional commute time was a constructive discharge. LaVine believes that the reassignment was in retaliation for his pursuit of workers' compensation benefits.

Waste moved for summary judgment on the ground that the parties' dispute was governed by Mississippi law, which does not recognize a cause of action for retaliatory discharge. The district court granted the motion. LaVine filed a timely appeal. Tennessee follows the Second Restatement. The Tennessee Supreme Court has recognized a cause of action for retaliatory discharge actions arising from an employee's exercise of statutory rights. What are LaVine's prospects on appeal?

Quick Summary

- The Second Restatement determines the applicable law by considering the rebuttable presumption, which may be displaced if some other state has a more significant relationship

- The role of the presumption in determining the applicable law can be emphasized or de-emphasized by courts and parties

- When determining which state has the most significant relationship, the relevance of certain policy factors may vary depending upon the nature of the cause of action

- This methodology is a combination of all of the choice of law methodologies that preceded it

- As Second Restatement § 6(1) observes, a statute that localizes a cause of action within the forum will usually be applied without recourse to any choice of law methodology; this applies to all of the choice of law methodologies presented in Chapters 4–8

- The characterization of a claim (e.g., tort, contract) is often debatable

- Every issue in a case requires an independent choice of law analysis

9

Choice of Law Clauses

Key Concepts

- The tension between party autonomy and legislative authority
- The enforceability vel non of choice of law clauses
- The scope of (enforceable) choice of law clauses
- Default rules and mandatory rules
- Non-sovereign laws

Contracting parties often include choice of law clauses in their agreements. These clauses memorialize an understanding between the parties about what jurisdiction's law will govern their rights and responsibilities as their relationship unfolds (or unravels, as the case may be). If a party knew what disputes were likely to arise over the term of the agreement, a choice of law clause would present an extraordinary opportunity to choose the most favorable law. It is more likely, however, that the parties are choosing a law that will apply to presently unknown disputes that will arise for presently unknown reasons and will be heard by presently unknown judges at some presently unknown time. Even amid these unknowns—or perhaps especially amid these unknowns—choice of law clauses create some certainty: they allow the parties to revert to a specific corpus of laws in order to (i) perform their legal obligations and avoid disputes; or (ii) invoke their rights and resolve disputes once they arise.

But choice of law clauses will not generate certainty or predictability unless courts consistently enforce them. In the vast majority of cases, courts do enforce them. Yet some judges and courts are less enthusiastic than others about enforcement, and all courts have some reservations. After all, why should private parties have the ability to compel one of our most important public institutions—the courts—to apply a particular law? If the dispute were in arbitration, perhaps one might feel comfortable allowing a private dispute resolution provider to apply the law of the parties' choosing. But when the parties invoke the majesty of the dispute resolution system established by the state, for which they pay very little and of which they do not have the same expectations of control over the process, why should their opinion as to what law should govern the case carry any weight? We might imagine that a court would say to the parties, "You might have ideas about what law you would like to apply, but I am the ultimate authority, and I will decide what law applies to this case."

In this chapter we will explore the issue of party autonomy concerning the applicable law, and the line that separates enforceable from unenforceable choice of law clauses. But more important than memorizing the paths of those lines in various jurisdictions is understanding the set of considerations that leads courts to introduce—and to revisit—those lines, or in fact to pay any attention at all to the parties' choice of law. This area of the law is in transition. Indeed, you can expect this line to move in practice. By mastering these materials you may even may be the litigator who moves it in your jurisdiction.

Choice of law clauses present two topics for you to master. The first is the threshold issue of *enforceability*: when courts enforce clauses and when they refuse to do so. Enforceable choice of law clauses present a second issue: *scope*. Just because the parties agreed to a choice of law clause does not necessarily mean that all or any of their claims fall within the scope of that clause.

Enforceability

In an empirical survey of 700 cases decided prior to 2003, two law professors found that courts enforced choice of law clauses about 80 percent of the time.[1] That data is consistent with the notion that courts routinely enforce choice of law clauses. But it also suggests that advocates—especially good advocates—get around them. Let us begin with a hypothetical.

 ### Hypothetical 9-1

Earthworm is a large manufacturer of front-end loaders, bulldozers, graders, drills, and other construction equipment. Earthworm sells its products through a network of dealers. Each dealer purchases a franchise from Earthworm, and Earthworm provides that investor with products that have a recognizable trade name and, thus, an established customer base.

---

1   ERIN A. O'HARA & LARRY E. RIBSTEIN, THE LAW MARKET 83 (2009).

Investors pay an initial franchise fee of $500,000, and enter into a franchise agreement with Earthworm. The franchise agreement controls every aspect of the formation and operation of the dealership: from the wholesale and retail prices of the products, to advertising and store design, to the brand of soap that must be used in the store bathrooms. The franchise agreement provides for an initial term of ten years and can be renewed upon agreement of the parties. The franchise agreement also contains the following termination clause:

> After the completion of the fifth (5th) full year of the term, Earthworm may terminate this agreement at any time without cause by written notice of termination delivered to Investor, such termination to be effective not less than sixty (60) days after receipt by Investor of such notice.

Another clause in the contract reads:

> This agreement and the rights and responsibilities of the parties hereunder shall be governed by the laws of the State of Florida.

Earthworm is a Delaware corporation with a principal place of business in Milwaukee, Wisconsin. Six years ago, Pingree (the aforementioned "Investor") opened an Earthworm franchise in Walnut Creek, California. Pingree has complied with all of the terms of the franchise agreement, and the franchise has performed well by all measures. However, management at Earthworm recently set new strategic initiatives for the company. The new initiatives led Earthworm to issue Pingree a written notice of termination of the franchise agreement.

The choice of law clause in this hypothetical contemplates the application of a *state*'s law. A modest amount of legal research would reveal that the regulation of franchise agreements is almost entirely a matter of state (as opposed to federal) law. Of course if the contract were between parties from different countries, the law selected might be that of Germany or Morocco.

Importantly, states vary considerably on the extent to which their statutes and case law accord franchisees special protection against the opportunistic conduct of franchisors. Some states extend special protection to franchisees because those states' lawmakers are concerned that franchisors have an informational (to say nothing of an economic) advantage upon entry into the agreement; after all, franchisors are repeat-players who know this business far better than their inexperienced franchisee counterparts. Further, by the terms of the franchise agreements, the franchisees necessarily surrender much of the operational control of the business to the franchisor; the one-sided nature of these contracts can make franchisees vulnerable to unreasonable and even extortionate demands of the franchisor. As one court described it,

> Don't do exactly everything the franchisor demands and the franchisee risks declaration of a material breach backed up by the whip of a giant lost future profits award. . . . Franchisors . . . seldom have to apply that whip, of course. It would be enough to crack it now and then to keep their franchisees in line. This is nearly the definition of oppression.[2]

Assume, then, that there exists a continuum of approaches. At one end of that continuum one finds the state that is most skeptical of franchise agreements, and this state has laws that err on the side of giving franchisees too much protection. Yet at the other end of the continuum is that state that is most sanguine about franchise agreements and/or most desirous of attracting large franchisors; this state has laws that treat such agreements like all other contracts; this state errs on the side of giving franchisees too little protection. The other 48 states are scattered at various points along the continuum, offering more protection than some, but less than others. The net result, of course, is that the laws of different states would provide subtly or even dramatically different answers to questions about the enforceability of the termination clause in the Earthworm/Pingree franchise agreement.

Should contracting parties be allowed to determine *for themselves* the law that governs the enforceability of their agreement as well as their rights and responsibilities thereunder? If the answer to that question is yes, we should consider whether there should be any limits on the parties' capacity to make that choice. But first one must consider the possibility that the determination of what law applies is not the parties' choice to make.

The fundamental objection to enforcing choice of law clauses is that it gives "permission to the parties to do a legislative act. It practically makes a legislative body of any two persons who choose to get together and contract."[3] Imagine, for example, that seven years ago the State of California passed a set of strict laws to protect Pingree and other franchisees in its state from oppressive franchisors; one of those laws might, for example, refuse to enforce a termination clause in a franchisor-franchisee agreement that is asymmetrical or one-sided. Should the parties be able to trump this mandate of California law with a choice of law clause selecting some other state's law?

2   *Postal Instant Press, Inc. v. Sealy*, 51 Cal. Rptr. 2d 365, 375 (Ct. App. 1996).

3   Joseph H. Beale, *What Law Governs the Validity of a Contract?*, 23 Harv. L. Rev. 260, 260 (1910).

Leading commentators in the field of Conflicts were once deeply troubled with the notion that parties could be vested with such authority.

> The adoption of a rule to determine which of several systems of law shall govern a given transaction is in itself an act of the law. . . . If [the authority to choose the applicable law is] left to the will of the parties to determine, that gives to the parties what is in truth the power of legislation so far as their agreement is concerned. . . . [They would be able to] free themselves from the power of the law which would otherwise apply to their acts.[4]

The author of that passage was Joseph Beale, the father of the First Restatement and the vested rights theory of choice of law. It should not surprise you, then, to learn that the First Restatement did not incorporate a role for choice of law clauses; in fact, it ignored them altogether, and implied that courts should do the same.

The word *ouster* is often used to describe the displacement of one law in order to apply some other law, as well as to dispossess courts of jurisdiction to determine the applicable law. In this sense of the word, then, enforcement of a Florida choice of law clause *ousts* the state of California of its authority to regulate conduct and protect its citizens. This would seem to give great public power to private parties.

Yet "[o]ne of the few non-controversial maxims of conflicts is that the autonomy of the parties should be given great weight."[5] This principle, which has deep roots in English law and elsewhere, is attractive.

> Prime objectives of contract law are to protect the justified expectations of the parties and to make it possible for them to foretell with accuracy what will be their rights and liabilities under the contract. These objectives may best be attained in multistate transactions by letting the parties choose the law to govern the validity of the contract and the rights created thereby. In this way, certainty and predictability of result are most likely to be secured. Giving parties this power of choice is also consistent with the fact that, in contrast to other areas of the law, persons are free within broad limits to determine the nature of their contractual obligations.

Restatement (Second) of Conflict of Laws § 187 cmt. e. The allure of some "certainty and predictability" is easier to appreciate now that you have studied the

---

4   *Id.* at 260–261.

5   Phaedon John Kozyris, *Choice of Law in the American Courts in 1987: An Overview*, 36 Am. J. Comp. L. 547, 560 (1988).

modern choice of law methodologies—even if you have developed a higher tolerance for uncertainty and lack of predictability.

So we have two competing values when it comes to enforcing choice of law clauses. On one hand, we would like to respect a jurisdiction's authority to regulate conduct within its borders. Yet on the other hand, respect for party autonomy is also an admirable objective. A jurisdiction could choose one extreme position and enforce all choice of law clauses; or it could choose the other extreme position and enforce none of them. Most jurisdictions instead try to locate an ideal, intermediate position—one that delivers the best of both worlds, to-wit, certainty where it is needed and flexibility where it is not. Query whether, in fact, an intermediate solution is instead the worst of both worlds.

When states embrace an intermediate position between the extremes of enforcing all and rejecting all choice of law clauses, one challenge is to identify the principles that sort one group of clauses from the other. Thereafter, a second challenge is to articulate a policy that informs those principles.

In this Chapter we focus primarily on the approach of the Restatement (Second) of Conflict of Laws because of its wide adoption. But before we turn to the Restatement's approach to enforcing choice of law clauses, it may be useful to survey other approaches. All are compromise approaches between the extremes of enforcing all and rejecting all choice of law clauses.

The Uniform Commercial Code (UCC) is model legislation available for adoption by state legislatures that is intended to harmonize state laws that apply to the sale of goods and some other commercial transactions. All 50 states have adopted it, albeit with some variations from state to state. The UCC includes a provision that addresses the enforceability of choice of law clauses. Section 1–301 orders the enforcement of a covered choice of law clause provided the underlying transaction "bears a reasonable relation" to the state of the chosen law. This relatedness test is a compromise approach that, on the one hand, gives parties the autonomy to choose the law of any of those states that have some meaningful connection to the transaction. Yet on the other hand, at least one of the states with a legitimate claim to legislative authority over that transaction will not have its laws applied. And why require a "reasonable relation"? In fact, what *is* a "reasonable relation"? Can the parties select the law of a third state that has nothing to do with them or the transaction, perhaps on the sole ground that that third state's set of laws is neutral? Does the fact of neutrality give the state a "reasonable relation" to the underlying transaction?

The drafters of the UCC have flirted with other approaches. In a short-lived experiment between 2001 and 2008 their model legislation proposed the following with respect to choice of law clauses:

- sharply differential treatment of "consumer" and non-consumer contracts; and

- abandoning the "reasonable relation" test for non-consumer contracts; but also

- adding safeguards to preclude enforcement where a choice of law would be contrary to a "fundamental policy" in the ousted jurisdiction.

The drafters included these changes as part of a much larger package of reforms called "Revised Article 1." Most states adopted the new Revised Article 1, but only the Virgin Islands incorporated the proposed change in approach to choice of law clauses. All of the other states rejected the proposed, quoted changes and retained the old "reasonable relation" test. In 2008 the drafters of the UCC put the old "reasonable relation" test back into their model law.

Although they were not accepted by most states and were ultimately abandoned by the drafters of the UCC, the proposed changes still offer interesting reference points. Indeed, we see the possibility of other intermediate positions between the extremes of enforcing all or rejecting all choice of law clauses. Most importantly, the proposal demonstrates the idea that certain *types* of contract (i.e., consumer contracts) might require a different balance between party autonomy and legislative authority.

A look at the European Union's approach is also enlightening. The Regulation on the Law Applicable to Contractual Obligations, Reg (EC) No 593/2008 (often referred to as the "Rome I Regulation") enshrines party autonomy as a fundamental virtue, yet enumerates categories of contracts that "cannot be derogated from by agreement." The categories of cases that are immune to choice of law clauses include (1) contracts in which "all other elements" other than the parties' choice are "located in a country other than the country whose law has been chosen"; and (2) consumer, employment, and some insurance contracts. Why do you suppose the European Union imposed these restrictions on party choice? Is it self-evident that they should apply?

Let us now look at the Second Restatement of Conflicts which, in Section 187, addresses the enforcement of choice of law clauses. Section 187 is among the most widely adopted provisions in the Second Restatement. Even states that do not generally follow the Second Restatement approach to choose the applicable law follow—whether more or less explicitly—Section 187. This includes even those jurisdictions that follow the traditional or First Restatement approach. Accordingly, it is fair to say that Section 187 generally describes contemporary practice throughout the United States with respect to choice of law clauses.

Restatement (Second) of Conflict of Laws

§ 187. Law of the State Chosen by the Parties

(1) The law of the state chosen by the parties to govern their contractual rights and duties will be applied if the particular issue is one which the parties could have resolved by an explicit provision in their agreement directed to that issue.

(2) The law of the state chosen by the parties to govern their contractual rights and duties will be applied, even if the particular issue is one which the parties could not have resolved by an explicit provision in their agreement directed to that issue, unless either

    (a) the chosen state has no substantial relationship to the parties or the transaction and there is no other reasonable basis for the parties' choice, or

    (b) application of the law of the chosen state would be contrary to a fundamental policy of a state which has a materially greater interest than the chosen state in the determination of the particular issue and which, under the rule of § 188, would be the state of the applicable law in the absence of an effective choice of law by the parties.

(3) In the absence of a contrary indication of intention, the reference is to the local law of the state of the chosen law.

Appreciate the significance of determining whether "the particular issue is one which the parties could have resolved by an explicit provision in their agreement." When that condition is satisfied, there are no constraints on judicial enforcement of the choice of law clause. When that condition is not satisfied, the clause is enforced, upon confirmation that (i) the chosen law has a substantial relationship to the parties or there is some other reasonable basis for the parties' choice; *and* (ii) application of the chosen law would not violate a fundamental policy of a state that has a materially greater interest in the resolution of the disputed issue. We will consider each of these stages separately.

The first step of analysis under the Second Restatement is to determine whether "the particular issue is one which the parties could have resolved by an explicit provision in their agreement." § 187(1). Consider the following hypothetical.

Hypothetical 9-2

In a vending agreement to supply services, the supplier, a call center, waived its right to invoke impossibility as a defense. The customer is in California and the supplier is in Wisconsin. Case law in the states of California and Wisconsin have long recognized impossibility as an affirmative defense to contract claims. The state of Florida does not recognize this defense. A dispute between the parties has arisen. The vending agreement contains a Florida choice of law clause. The parties dispute the availability of the defense. Neither party does any business is Florida.

The scope of § 187(1) invokes a concept that you may remember from your study of contract law. Any jurisdiction's law of contracts includes "default rules" and "mandatory rules." Some rules of contract law are intended only to fill whatever gaps the contract fails to address directly; these rules ensure that contracts are not incomplete. However, these directives (which may be codified in statutes or embedded in the common law) are only defaults or gap-fillers; the parties may contract around them by providing otherwise in their agreement. By contrast, mandatory rules are just that: the parties are not at liberty to contract around them.

To figure out whether some law is a default rule or a mandatory rule, the key to framing your research question is to ignore the contacts with multiple states. Assume that everything that is relevant to the case happened within the forum state. Then ask or research: Would forum law allow the parties (in that entirely domestic setting) to opt out of the law? For example, most jurisdictions have a warranty of merchantability in their laws; but in most of those jurisdictions, that warranty can be waived by contract. In those jurisdictions, then, the warranty of merchantability is but a default rule. The idea of default rules is not limited to contract law. The rules of intestate succession, for example, are "default rules;" individuals can opt of those default rules by having a will. Similarly, in the law of business associations there is a corpus of mandates that operate as defaults to fill whatever gaps the organizational documents fail to address.

Section 187(1) of the Restatement (Second) of Conflicts applies only to issues that are default rules. Accordingly, choice of law clauses should be enforced to the extent that the chosen law is merely filling gaps. After all, by choosing that law the parties are simply adopting a corpus of rules, rather than spelling out the prescription for every possible contingency. These choice of law clauses are enforced no matter the connection, if any, between the transaction and the chosen law.

In the standard parlance of contract law, mandatory rules differ from default rules in that mandatory rules apply no matter the parties' intention or agreement. (Again, hypothesize an entirely domestic fact pattern. Then ask: Can the parties opt out of that obligation?) For example, the UCC imposes a duty to act in good faith. In virtually all jurisdictions, this is a mandatory rule that cannot be waived: a provision in a contract waiving any duty to act in good faith is simply unenforceable.

The Restatement maps this distinction between default rules and mandatory rules. If the chosen law would supply a mandatory rule, then Section 187(1) does not apply. Examples of issues that typically cannot be resolved by choice of law clauses include capacity, enforceability, formalities, and validity.[6] Accordingly, if someone lacks the capacity to enter into a contract in a jurisdiction, a choice of law clause cannot, through § 187(1), create that capacity.

The issue in Hypothetical 9–2 falls within the scope of §187(1) if and only if that issue is a "default rule" in the jurisdiction as opposed to a "mandatory rule." Legal research would determine whether the availability of the defense is a default rule. If it is a default rule, then pursuant to the choice of law clause, Florida law would be dispositive under § 187(1).

Judge Frank Easterbrook of the U.S. Court of Appeals for the Seventh Circuit offered a description of a mandatory rule that may be generally useful. In *Secretary of Labor v. Lauritzen*, 835 F.2d 1529, 1545 (7th Cir. 1989), he described a particular statute as one that was "designed to defeat rather than implement contractual arrangements." The compulsoriness and paternalism of such a command would be indicative of a mandatory rule. Of course even a mandatory rule could still be displaced by a choice of law clause under the Restatement, but the clause would need to satisfy § 187(2), to which we now turn.

Section 187(2) prohibits the enforcement of choice of law clauses in two circumstances. The first of these, outlined in subparagraph (a) of this section of the Restatement, asks whether there is a "substantial relationship" with the state of the chosen law or some "reasonable basis" for choosing that law. In Hypothetical 9–1 the parties and the transaction have a substantial relationship with the state of California, where the retail store is located, and with the state of Wisconsin, where the franchisor has its principal place of business. But since the clause chose Florida law, what is the relationship of the parties or the transaction with *that* state?

---

6   *See* Restatement (Second) of Conflict of Laws § 187, cmt. d (*"Issues the parties could not have determined by explicit agreement directed to particular issue*. . . . Examples of such questions are those involving capacity, formalities and substantial validity. A person cannot vest himself with contractual capacity by stating in the contract that he has such capacity. He cannot dispense with formal requirements, such as that of a writing, by agreeing with the other party that the contract shall be binding without them. Nor can he by a similar device avoid issues of substantial validity, such as whether the contract is illegal.").

Consider the putative additional facts in the chart below. If it were in your client's interest to argue that there is/was a *substantial relationship* per § 187(2)(a) with the state of Florida, and if you could choose any two of these additional facts to be true, *which two* would you choose?

The franchise agreement was negotiated in FL.	The franchise agreement was signed in FL.	Earthworm has more retail stores in FL than in any other state.	Earthworm's largest manufacturing facility is in FL.
Pingree insisted on the FL choice of law clause.	Earthworm's outside counsel is located in FL.	Pingree's counsel is located in FL.	Pingree is domiciled in CA but owns a condo in FL.
The franchise agreement requires Pingree to send royalty payments to a FL bank.	Pingree made his first inquiry to Earthworm while vacationing in FL.	All of Earthworm's intellectual property is owned by a FL affiliate of the company.	The franchise agreement requires all franchisees to attend an annual conference that is in FL.

The purpose of the chart is to emphasize the importance of facts to litigators. All lawyers see and use the obvious facts. Excellent lawyers, however, appreciate that cases are often decided on the basis of facts that are harder-to-find, subtle, concealed, or inconspicuous.

Section 187(2)(a) also contemplates that some "other reasonable basis" for choosing FL will suffice (in lieu of a "substantial relationship"). Some of the putative additional facts in the table above might (help) establish such a basis for choosing Florida law. Consider also whether any of the following putative additional facts would likely establish a *reasonable basis* that is sufficient to satisfy § 187(2)(a).

The courts of FL have developed some expertise because they hear more franchisor-franchisee litigation than any other state.	Earthworm wanted a FL choice of law clause because FL law is especially favorable to franchisors.	The applicable law was the subject of much negotiation. Pingree received a price concession by agreeing to the FL choice of law clause.	Earthworm is a member of a consortium of franchisors. The consortium is headquartered in FL.
Earthworm puts FL choice of law clauses in all of its franchise agreements.	Earthworm is presently litigating a nearly identical case with another franchisee in FL.	Pingree owns a frozen yogurt franchise in FL.	The complaint was filed in FL.

Of course § 187(2)(b) is a second hurdle. Even if the choice of law clause chooses a state that has a substantial relationship to the parties (or if that state's law was chosen for some other reasonable basis), the chosen state's law must also not be inconsistent with "a fundamental policy" of an ousted state that has a materially greater interest in the application of its law.

With every meaningful application of § 187(2)(b) the chosen law and the ousted law have different *policies*. Indeed, if there were no difference, there would be no reason to litigate the question. So when does that difference regard a matter of *fundamental* policy? Unfortunately, this term lacks a clear definition. Indeed, the Restatement confesses that "[n]o detailed statement can be made of the situations where a 'fundamental' policy of the state of the otherwise applicable law will be found to exist." § 187, cmt. g.

> To be "fundamental," a policy must in any event be a substantial one. Except perhaps in the case of contracts relating to wills, a policy of this sort will rarely be found in a requirement, such as the statute of frauds, that relates to formalities. . . . Nor is such policy likely to be represented by a rule tending to become obsolete, such as a rule concerned with the capacity of married women, or by general rules of contract law, such as those concerned with the need for consideration. On the other hand, a fundamental policy may be embodied in a statute which makes one or more kinds of contracts illegal or which is designed to protect a person against the oppressive use of superior bargaining power.

Restatement § 187 cmt. g.

Hypothetical 9-3

Armanda, a California domiciliary, purchased an office complex in Davis, California. 100% of the financing for the purchase was provided by Rohwer Savings & Loan (Rohwer), a California bank. The promissory note included a choice of law provision adopting Wyoming law. The bank routinely includes a choice of law clause, whenever possible, to avoid the application of California law. Armanda is a part-year resident of Wyoming, so the bank suggested a Wyoming choice of law clause and Armanda agreed.

Armanda defaulted on the loan and the bank foreclosed on the building. After the bank collected the proceeds of the foreclosure sale and applied them to Armanda's balance, there was still $210,000 owed to the bank.

Rohwer sought a deficiency judgment from a California court so that it could collect the money from Armanda's other assets.

California law bars a deficiency judgment following foreclosure of a purchase-money security interest like this transaction. Wyoming law would allow Rohwer to obtain a deficiency judgment. The issue, then, is whether allowing a deficiency judgment would be contrary to a fundamental policy of California? What do you think? And what else do you need to know (about the California law, about the Wyoming law, about the transaction, or about something else) in order to resolve this issue?

The question is whether the policy of the ousted jurisdiction is a *fundamental* policy. Naturally, the meaning of the word fundamental is paramount. As an advocate it is often useful to probe the meaning of a word by identifying its antonym. What is the opposite of fundamental? By placing the word *fundamental* against its antonym, that binary choice between a word and its antonym can make it easier to see (and to argue) that a certain policy is or is not fundamental. For advocates this exercise can be illuminating because there are usually several antonyms from which to choose. The opposites of *fundamental*, for example, would include *trivial* and *extrinsic* and *inessential*. Do any of these help you think differently about how you might argue to the court that the policies in the above scenarios either are or are not fundamental?

Further still, the state with the fundamental policy that Section 187(2)(b) allows to trump the choice of law clause must also be a state with a "materially greater interest" than the interest of the state of the chosen law. The Restatement provides that "[t]he more closely the state of the chosen law is related to the contract and the parties, the more fundamental must be the policy of the state of the otherwise applicable law to justify denying effect to the choice of law provision." § 187, cmt. g. In other words, if all of the key events and relationships in the transaction point to one state while the choice of law clause points to another state, it might be easier for the court to find the former's policy "fundamental." And conversely, when a choice of law clause points to a state, and that state is also where important events happened or where relationships are located, it may be more difficult for the court to displace the choice of law clause upon a finding that some other jurisdiction's policy is "fundamental."

Litigators arguing in favor of enforcing a choice of law clause should emphasize that the very purpose of a choice of law clause is to select one body of governing law even though more than one state's law could apply. Indeed, there is no need for a choice of law clause in circumstances where everything occurs in—and everyone is from—one state. Nor should it surprise that the chosen law will favor one party. Even if one of the parties advocated for the state's law in anticipation of this type of dispute (itself an unlikely proposition), the choice of law clause was part of the exchange of rights and obligations under the agreement.

Some courts are simply more likely than others to impose forum policy at the expense of the law selected by the parties. For example, recently, in *Rincon EV Realty LLC v. CP III Rincon Towers, Inc.*,[7] a California court refused to apply a New York choice of law clause in a contract dispute between a New York lender and a New York borrower. In the contract, the borrower specifically waived its right to a jury trial and also its right to invoke the law of any jurisdiction other than New York. (Somewhat inexplicably, there was no forum selection clause.) The borrower sued in a California state court, and under California law, contractual waivers of the right to a jury trial are unenforceable. To be sure, the contract had a connection to California—the contract between the parties involved a $110 million loan to finance the purchase of a luxury apartment building in San Francisco. But this was a commercial transaction between sophisticated parties who were both New Yorkers. Nevertheless, the court found that jury waivers were a "fundamental" policy of California, and the forum had "a materially greater interest than New York in determining the enforceability of the jury waivers at issue here. . . . [The policy] is not focused solely on the protection of California *residents* [;]. . . it protects the rights of California *litigants*, and is a core aspect of how California has chosen to adjudicate cases within its civil justice system as a whole."[8]

In summary, Section 187(2) requires judges to apply the meaning of such terms as "substantial relationship," "reasonable basis," and "fundamental policy" to an infinite array of fact patterns. These inquiries are highly fact-contingent. Hence the importance of finding and leveraging all of the possibly relevant facts. Query also whether an enforcement regime that turns on such fact-contingent inquiries is compatible with the goals of certainty and predictability—which was the primary catalyst for enforcing choice of law clauses in the first place.

Hypothetical 9-4

Pat Moore owns a marine salvage repair and resale business in South Carolina. Two years ago, Moore purchased for his company a 61-foot Hatteras yacht at an auction in Newark, New Jersey for $65,000. He renamed the yacht the M/V GOAT. The GOAT was at auction because it had been de-

---

7   8 Cal. App. 5th 1 (2017).

8   8 Cal. App. 5th at 16.

clared a total loss by the insurance company that was selling it. This means that the cost to repair the boat was greater than the market value that the insurer believed it would ultimately fetch.

After making some preliminary repairs to improve the boat's seaworthiness Moore piloted the vessel from New Jersey to South Carolina. In South Carolina, Moore systematically overhauled the boat using first class material and craftsmanship, ultimately restoring the GOAT to excellent condition.

Moore financed his original purchase and, after restoring the GOAT, wanted to refinance the loan. The bank required insurance for the vessel. Moore purchased an insurance policy from Hols Marine Insurance Co. (Hols Marine). The insurance application included spaces for "Market Value" and for "Purchase Price," both of which Moore filled in with "$300,000." Hols Marine is a U.K. insurance company that maintains its primary American savings account in New York. Although it has no physical presence in the United States, Hols Marine issues policy to insureds throughout the United States.

About ten months later, the GOAT caught fire while in dry dock at a boatyard in South Carolina. The boat was completely destroyed. After an investigation of the claim, Hols Marine rejected Moore's claim because the policy application contained a misrepresentation about the boat's purchase price.

The insurance policy contained a choice of law clause providing that it "shall be governed by and construed in accordance with the laws of the State of New York." New York is one of a few states (and is the only coastal state) the follows the uberrimae fidei ("utmost good faith") doctrine under which a material misrepresentation voids a policy without an inquiry into an insured's intent. In the law of almost all other states (including South Carolina) the policy can be invalidated retroactively only upon proof that the insured intended to deceive the insurer. That is a fact question that can be difficult to prove.

If Moore sues Hols Marine in a South Carolina court and South Carolina follows § 187, should we expect the court to enforce the choice of law clause?

———————————

We have now worked through all of the language of Section 187 of the Restatement except for paragraph (3). That paragraph simply clarifies that when a choice of law clause requires the court to apply the law of, say, Florida, the court should apply the substantive law of Florida. Without this clarification one might argue that the court should apply the conflicts principles of the state of Florida, meaning that the choice of law clause would lead, in turn, to an inquiry of what law the Florida courts would apply. If such were the case, conflicts questions could ricochet about like a pinball. Although paragraph (3) precludes such pinball action, the formal name of such a phenomenon is called *renvoi* and we will study that doctrine in Chapter 12.

Even when a court is directed, whether by a choice of law clause or as the result of a choice of law analysis, to apply some other jurisdiction's law, a court will always apply forum *procedure*. Only the foreign *substantive* law will be applied. We saw this introduced in Chapter 2 and will revisit it in Chapter 10. As you can imagine, battles are sometimes fought over whether a given law is substantive or procedural in character.

Scope

A second battleground for litigators involves the scope of a choice of law clause. The choice of law clause might be enforceable for all of the reasons that we have surveyed above, yet the clause may not include within its scope the particular dispute between the parties. The referral to a state's law is limited to the scope of the referring language. The scope of a choice of law clause is essentially a matter of contract interpretation.

Reread the choice of law clause in Hypothetical 9–1 above. Consider the extent to which each of the following alternative variations would narrow or expand the scope of the clause. The scope of the clause could matter if, for example, Pingree defamed Earthworm in a television interview; would the choice of law clause dictate which state's defamation law applied?

(1) This agreement and any dispute or claim arising out of or in connection with it or its subject matter or formation (including non-contractual disputes or claims) shall be governed by and construed in accordance with the laws of the State of Florida.

(2) This agreement shall be governed by the laws of the State of Florida.

(3) This agreement shall be governed by and construed in accordance with the laws of the State of Florida.

(4) This agreement and its enforcement shall be governed by and construed in accordance with the laws of the State of Florida.

(5) This agreement, and all claims or causes of action (whether in contract or tort) that may be based upon, arise out of or relate to this agreement, or the negotiation, execution or performance of this agreement (including any claim or cause of action based upon, arising out of or related to any representation or warranty made in or in connection with this agreement or as an inducement to enter into this agreement), shall be governed by the internal laws of the State of Florida.

(6) This agreement and any and all claims arising hereunder shall be governed by and construed in accordance with the laws of the State of Florida.

Naturally, issues about scope become more relevant if the dispute is only tangentially related—or even unrelated—to the subject matter of the contract. And the narrower the scope of the clause, the more likely a party will escape its clutches.

Section 187 of the Restatement appears to peremptorily limit the scope of choice of law clauses to *contract* claims. Indeed, paragraph (1) refers to "[t]he law of the state chosen by the parties to govern their *contractual* rights and duties." Yet most courts instead allow the scope of a clause to extend to the reach of its text.

As Professor Symeonides has observed: under this logic, a clause that explicitly encompasses "any and all disputes between the parties" is deemed to include tort claims, while a generic, less categorical clause is not. At the same time, however, courts tend to scrutinize clauses that purport to encompass tort-like issues much more closely than clauses confined to purely contractual issues.[9]

Hypothetical 9-5

Michele Hunter suffered a severe leg fracture when another vehicle struck her motorcycle in Arkansas. The driver of the other vehicle was at fault, and when Hunter filed a lawsuit, the other driver's insurer paid its policy limit of $250,000.

Meanwhile Chase Health Plan (the Plan) paid Hunter's medical expenses which were approximately $105,000. The Plan paid those expenses pursuant to a group health insurance contract that it had issued to Hunter's em-

---

9   Symeon C. Symeonides, *Oregon's Choice-of-Law Codification for Contract Conflicts: An Exegesis*, 44 Willamette L. Rev. 205, 225 (2007).

ployer. The Plan is an Iowa nonprofit corporation and its principal place of business is in Iowa. Hunter is an Arkansas resident but was employed by an Iowa employer to perform work in Iowa.

The health plan contained a subrogation clause that enables the Plan to recover its $105,000 outlay from Hunter's $250,000 tort recovery. The health insurance plan also included a choice of law clause stating that "the agreement shall be governed by and interpreted in accordance with the laws of Iowa."

The laws of Arkansas have, for 75 years, recognized a "made whole" doctrine that requires injured plaintiffs to be fully compensated before the subrogated party is entitled to receive payment. Under Arkansas law, the made-whole doctrine can trump express language in an (Arkansas) insurance contract. Under Iowa case law, the Plan is entitled to "first dollar" reimbursement and payment in full for all of its subrogated expenses without deduction or offset.

Your firm represents Hunter. You have filed a lawsuit on her behalf in Arkansas seeking a declaration of her rights. What are your arguments that the Iowa choice of law clause is inapplicable?

The "foreign" law selected in a choice of law clause might be another state's law or another country's law. (*See* Chapter 18.) But consider also the possibility that a choice of law clause would choose a corpus of laws that is not grounded in any sovereign at all. If the principle of party autonomy is what we advance by enforcing choice of law clauses, why limit the universe of available options to substantive laws that have been endorsed by sovereigns? For example, imagine a choice of law clause that identifies "lex mercatoria" as the applicable law[10]—or, instead, "the customary and best practices of commerce." Does the Second Restatement address this?

From the parties' perspective, one downside of such an approach could be insecurity about the precise content of the applicable "law." But compared to a clause choosing the law of, say, Georgia (whether the foreign country or the state), the non-Georgian party entering into the contract would not have to worry about some peculiar trap for the unwary that is buried deep in Georgia law.

---

10   Friedrich Juenger, *American Conflicts Scholarship and the New Law Merchant*, 28 VAND. J. TRANSNAT'L L. 487 (1995).

Imagine that your professor or your law school produced a commercial code that was elegantly drafted with fair and balanced mandates that both channeled tradition and fueled innovation. Should parties be able to choose this "law" to govern their relationship? Imagine yourself as a policy maker, and prepare a list of the arguments against allowing the selection of non-state law. How many of the items on that list would also apply when we allow parties to choose the law of some obscure (*i.e.,* distant, unfamiliar) state or country yet expect some other court to enforce it?

FROM THE COURTS

EXXON MOBIL CORP. v. DRENNEN

Supreme Court of Texas
452 S.W.3d 319 (Tex. 2014)

JUSTICE GREEN.

. . . I. Factual and Procedural Background

[William Drennen, III, worked as a geologist with Exxon Mobil Corporation (ExxonMobil) in Houston for over thirty-one years, from 1976 through May of 2007, culminating his career with the title of Exploration Vice President of the Americas. During his employment, he received several forms of incentive compensation, including company stock that delayed delivery for several years (to ensure retention). The employment agreement and program documents (Incentive Program) contained termination provisions that allowed ExxonMobil to terminate the delivery of the shares if Drennen engaged in "detrimental activity," which was defined as "acceptance of duties to a third party under circumstances that create a material conflict of interest." Material conflict of interest was defined to include being employed "by an entity that regulates, deals with, or competes with the Corporation or an affiliate."

Until 2006, Drennen consistently ranked in the top 20% of ExxonMobil employees in his annual review. However, Drennen received a very unfavorable annual performance review in 2006; he was told that he would be replaced but that the company was trying to find him a new position there. When Drennen told his supervisor (Cejka) that he would rather resign, Cejka said that Drennen would still receive his unvested options so long as he did not go to work for one of the other four "majors" (Shell, BP, ChevronTexaco, or ConocoPhilips). Drennen informed Cejka that he was considering taking a position at Hess Corporation (another large energy company), and Cejka warned him that if he accepted the position, "it would be highly likely that [Drennen] would lose all [of his] incentives." Despite this warning, Drennen accepted the position and began working at Hess as Senior Vice President for Global Exploration and New Ventures in July 2007. Invoking the "detrimental activity" provision of the agreement, ExxonMobil canceled the outstanding stock, which was worth about $5 million.

ExxonMobil is headquartered in Texas and is incorporated in New Jersey. All of the documents were executed in Houston, Texas. The program documents contained a New York choice of law clause.

Drennen sued and the case ultimately went to a jury trial. The jury found for ExxonMobil on Drennen's various breach of contract, oral modification, and waiver/estoppel theories. The plaintiff then moved for judgment by the court on the theory that the "detrimental activity" provisions ExxonMobil relied upon were, as a matter of law, a form of unenforceable noncompete agreement under Texas law. The trial court disagreed and found he was not entitled to the shares. On appeal, however, the intermediate appellate court agreed with Drennen and ruled that Texas law applied, and that under Texas law, the provision was unenforceable. ExxonMobil then petitioned the Texas Supreme Court for review, arguing primarily that the New York choice-of-law provisions were enforceable and that the detrimental-activity provisions should, therefore, be enforced under New York law.]

II. Discussion

We begin our analysis by determining whether the choice-of-law provisions, electing to apply New York law for all disputes arising out of the Incentive Programs, are enforceable.

A. Enforceability of the Choice-of-Law Provisions

ExxonMobil argues that New York law should govern because the choice-of-law provisions are enforceable under the Restatement. *See* Restatement (Second) of Conflict of Laws § 187. We first note that Texas law recognizes the "party autonomy rule" that parties can agree to be governed by the law of another state. . . . While we recognize that parties "cannot require that their contract be governed by the law of a jurisdiction which has *no relation whatever* to them or their agreement," *DeSantis v. Wackenhut Corp.*,

793 S.W.2d 670, 677 (Tex. 1990) (emphasis added), both Texas and New York bear some relation to the parties and the agreements at issue in this case. ExxonMobil is now headquartered in Texas, and Drennen worked in Houston when he executed both Incentive Program agreements. But Drennen spent three years of his career working for ExxonMobil in its New York City office in the mid-1980s. Additionally, ExxonMobil's outside counsel is a New York law firm. Finally, the subject-matter of the transaction—XOM shares—are traded on the New York Stock Exchange and are valued based on the average of the high and low price of the shares as reported on the consolidated tape at the New York Stock Exchange in New York City.

In *DeSantis v. Wackenhut Corp.,* we adopted Restatement section 187, which provides the framework for determining whether the parties' agreement as to choice of law is enforceable. Section 187(2) provides:

> The law of the state chosen by the parties to govern their contractual rights and duties will be applied, even if the particular issue is one which the parties could not have resolved by an explicit provision in their agreement directed to that issue, unless either
>
> (a) the chosen state has no substantial relationship to the parties or the transaction and there is no other reasonable basis for the parties' choice, or
>
> (b) application of the law of the chosen state would be contrary to a fundamental policy of a state which has a materially greater interest than the chosen state in the determination of the particular issue and which, under the rule of § 188, would be the state of applicable law in the absence of an effective choice of law by the parties.

We have already explained that some relationship exists between the parties and agreements in this case and their chosen jurisdiction. Nowhere does the Restatement define "substantial relationship," nor have we defined the term. The comments to the Restatement do indicate, however, that parties will be held to their choice when "the state of the chosen law [has] a sufficiently close relationship to the parties and the contract to make the parties' choice reasonable." *Id.* § 187 cmt. f. Even when a relationship is not substantial, the parties may be held to the chosen state's law when they had a reasonable basis for their choice, such as choosing law they know well or that is well developed. *Id.* Here, ExxonMobil claims that the choice of New York law was reasonable because it assures uniformity, certainty, and predictability in the application of its Incentive Programs. ExxonMobil provided affidavit testimony that New York law was chosen to govern its incentive agreements for three reasons: (1) ExxonMobil provides incentive awards to large numbers of employees in many states and countries, many of whom move throughout their careers, so consistency is required to administer the Incentive Programs; (2) New York has a well-developed and clearly defined body of law regarding employee stock and incentive programs; and (3) ExxonMobil's stock is listed on the New York Stock Exchange, and New York—as home of the Stock Exchange—has a well-developed and predictable body of law regarding a wide variety of financial transactions, securities, and securities-related transactions, making it a routine choice of law for parties to stock-related transactions and agreements. Indeed, the Restatement recognizes that the prime objectives of contract law—protecting parties' expectations and enabling parties to predict accurately what their rights and liabilities will be—are best furthered, and certainty and predictability of result most likely to occur, when parties to multistate transactions can choose the governing law. *Id.* § 187 cmt. e. Further, "[c]ontracts are entered into for serious purposes and rarely, if ever, will the parties choose a law without good reason for doing so." *Id.* § 187 cmt. f. Under the circumstances of this case, we conclude that section 187(2)(a) of the Restatement does not preclude application of New York law.

We must next determine, in accordance with the three-step approach set forth in *DeSantis*, 793 S.W.2d at 678, whether Drennen and ExxonMobil's choice of New York law is enforceable under section 187(2)(b) of the Restatement.

1. Most Significant Relationship

The first determination of Restatement section 187(2)(b) is "whether there is a state the law of which would apply under section 188 of the Restatement absent an effective choice of law by the parties." *DeSantis*, 793 S.W.d2d at 678. [The court concluded that Texas law would apply if the choice of law clause were unenforceable.]

2. Materially Greater Interest

Under the Restatement, if Texas does not have a materially greater interest than New York in the determination of this particular issue, it is immaterial whether the application of New York law here would be contrary to a fundamental policy of Texas. The next step in the analysis, then, is determining whether Texas has a materially greater interest in the determination of whether the detrimental-activity provisions are enforceable. [The court concluded that Texas had a materially greater interest than New York.]

3. Contrary to Fundamental Policy

The final step in the analysis is determining whether the application of New York law would be contrary to a fundamental policy of Texas. In *DeSantis,* we recognized that neither this Court nor the Restatement has adopted a general definition of "fundamental policy," and we declined to define it then. 793 S.W.2d at 680. We determined that applying the Florida choice-of-law provision would contravene fundamental policy in Texas because the law governing enforcement of non-competes is fundamental policy in Texas, and that "to apply the law of another state to determine the enforceability of such an agreement *in the circumstances of a case like this* would be contrary to that policy." *Id.* at 681 (emphasis added). . . .

Looking at the facts in our prior non-compete cases, it is clear that the agreement here does not fit the mold. . . . There is a difference, although a narrow one, between an employer's desire to protect an investment and an employer's desire to reward loyalty. Non-competes protect the investment an employer has made in an employee, ensuring that the costs incurred to develop human capital are protected against competitors who, having not made such expenditures, might appropriate the employer's investment. Forfeiture provisions conditioned on loyalty, however, do not restrict or prohibit the employees' future employment opportunities. Instead, they reward employees for continued employment and loyalty. . . .

Accordingly, we hold that, under Texas law, this provision is not a covenant not to compete. . . .

Turning back to our analysis under Restatement section 187(2)(b), . . . [t]he drafters of the Restatement explained the rationale for section 187 by stating that "[p]rime objectives of contract law are to protect the justified expectations of the parties and to make it possible for them to foretell with accuracy what will be their rights and liabilities." Restatement (Second) of Conflict of Laws § 187 cmt. e. In multistate transactions, these prime objectives "may best be attained . . . by letting the parties choose the law to govern the validity of the contract." *Id.* Our fear in *DeSantis* that "[e]mployers would be encouraged to attempt to invoke the most favorable state law available to govern their relationship with their employees in Texas or other states," 793 S.W.2d at 680, is directly addressed by the drafters of the Restatement:

It may . . . be objected that, if given this power of choice, the parties will be enabled to escape prohibitions prevailing in the state which would otherwise be the state of the applicable law. Nevertheless, the demands of certainty, predictability and convenience dictate that, subject to some limitations, the parties should have power to choose the applicable law.

Restatement (Second) of Conflict of Laws § 187 cmt. e. As the court of appeals noted, ExxonMobil's argument, in essence, is that, "as a large, multi-national corporation, ExxonMobil has a strong interest in uniform application of its employment agreements." 367 S.W.3d at 297. Uniformity is a frequent goal of contracting, as recognized in the comments to Restatement section 187, and parties should be able to achieve that goal by choosing the applicable law. . . . Because enforcement of New York law does not contravene any fundamental public policy of Texas, we are bound to enforce the parties' choice-of-law provisions and apply New York law.

B. Application of New York Law

[In this section the court concluded that "under New York law, ExxonMobil lawfully terminated the outstanding awards upon Drennen's breach of the Incentive Programs and voluntary resignation from ExxonMobil."]

COMMENTS AND QUESTIONS

1. When applying § 187 of the Restatement to these facts, the judge started with § 187(2) rather than § 187(1). This is because the issue of whether a non-compete agreement is enforceable is not a question the parties could have resolved by an explicit provision in the agreement. Put another way, the law on this point is a mandatory rule. If the law on this point were instead a default rule, the choice of law clause would have been enforceable under § 187(1), and the § 187(2) analysis would have been unnecessary and irrelevant.

2. What specific facts did the court invoke to establish that there was (i) a "substantial relationship" between the state of New York and the parties or the transaction, and/or (ii) some other "reasonable basis for the parties' choice" of New York law? As you think about the importance of facts,

remember the charts from Hypothetical 9-1 that contemplated possible additional facts that might satisfy the two inquiries of § 187(2)(a).

3. Section 187(2) of the Second Restatement imposes constraints on party autonomy. In their masterful book titled *The Law Market*, Professors O'Hara and Ribstein argue for the expansion of party autonomy. Through careful analysis of the full range of choice of law problems, they argue that the broad enforcement of choice of law clauses promotes individual welfare and prompts legislatures to enact efficient laws. Other scholars are much more cautious. For example, Professor Joe Singer has observed: "From reading conflicts scholarship, one would have no idea that . . . the goal of contract law in the twentieth century has moved steadily away from freedom of contract to the regulation of contract as a means of protecting the weaker party against unequal bargaining power and promoting social justice." Joseph W. Singer, *Real Conflicts*, 69 B.U. L. Rev. 1, 75–76 (1989).

From the Courts

TAYLOR v. EASTERN CONNECTION OPERATING, INC.

Supreme Judicial Court of Massachusetts
465 Mass. 191 (2013)

Lenk, Justice.

. . . 1. Background

. . . The plaintiffs, Judith Ann Taylor, Gardner Taylor, and Donald Wellington, are individuals who live in New York and work there as couriers for the defendant, Eastern Connection Operating, Inc., a corporation headquartered in Woburn, Massachusetts. The defendant is in the business of delivering packages in various States along the East Coast, including Massachusetts and New York.

The plaintiffs entered into identical contracts (collectively, the contract) with the defendant to perform package pickup and delivery services exclusively in New York. Under the language of the contract, the plaintiffs are classified as "independent contractors" and the defendant is classified as a "broker" arranging transportation services. The contract also includes the following clause:

> This Contract and all rights and obligations of the parties shall be construed in accordance with the laws where the Broker is headquartered and any action shall be commenced in that jurisdiction in the closest [S]tate court.

In 2010, the plaintiffs brought this action in the Superior Court [of Massachusetts] on behalf of themselves and other similarly situated individuals. They alleged that the defendant had misclassified them as independent contractors rather than as employees, in violation of G.L. c. 149 § 148B, the Massachusetts independent contractor statute. They also alleged that the defendant failed to pay them wages and overtime in violation of G.L. c. 149 § 148, the Massachusetts wage statute, and G.L. c. 151 § 1A, the Massachusetts overtime statute (collectively, the Massachusetts wage statutes). [The trial court refused to apply the Massachusetts choice of law clause. Applying the narrower definition of employee under New York law, the trial court dismissed the complaint. Appeal followed.]

2. Discussion

. . . The plaintiffs' first claim, on which their other claims are predicated, is that the defendant misclassified them as independent contractors when they are, in fact, employees. Specifically, the plaintiffs invoke the protections of the Massachusetts independent contractor statute. They argue that the choice-of-law clause in the contract requires the application of Massachusetts law to their claims. The defendant contends that the Massachusetts independent contractor statute does not apply to the plaintiffs, who live and work exclusively in New York. We must consider whether, in the circumstances, the parties' express choice of Massachusetts law is controlling. . . .

Where, as here, the parties have expressed a specific intent as to the governing law, . . . Massachusetts courts generally uphold the parties' choice.[8]

---

8   A choice-of-law clause should not be upheld where the party resisting it did not have a meaningful choice at the time of negotiation—i.e., where the parties had unequal bargaining power, and the party now attempting to enforce the choice-of-law clause essentially forced the clause upon the weaker party. *See* Restatement (Second) of Conflict of Laws § 187 comment b (1971) ("A factor which the forum may consider is whether the choice of law provision is contained in an 'adhesion' contract, namely one that is drafted unilaterally by the dominant party and then presented on a 'take-it-or-leave-it' basis to the weaker party who has no real opportunity to bargain about its terms"); L.L. McDougal, III, R.L. Felix, & R.U. Whitten, American Conflicts Law § 137 (5th ed. 2001) ("A court should disregard [the parties'] stated intent when it is contained in an adhesion contract"). . . .

Under the Restatement, if the particular issue to which the choice-of-law clause is being applied is "one which the parties could have resolved by an explicit provision in [the contract] directed to that issue," Restatement, *supra* at § 187(1), the parties' choice of law should be upheld, on the theory that, where permissible, the parties "may incorporate into the contract by reference extrinsic material which may, among other things, be the provisions of some foreign law." *Id.* at § 187 comment c. . . .

If, however, the particular issue to which the choice-of-law clause is being applied is "one which the parties could not have resolved by an explicit provision" in the contract, the parties' choice of law should be upheld, unless (1) "the chosen [S]tate has no substantial relationship to the parties or the transaction and there is no other reasonable basis for the parties' choice," or (2) "application of the law of the chosen [S]tate would be contrary to a fundamental policy of a [S]tate which has a materially greater interest than the chosen [S]tate in the determination of the particular issue and which . . . would be the state of the applicable law in the absence of an effective choice by the parties." Restatement, *supra* at § 187(2). . . .

Here, the parties expressed a specific intent that the contract be construed in accordance with Massachusetts law. The particular issue—whether the plaintiffs were independent contractors or employees—is not one the parties could resolve with an explicit provision in the contract, as, under either New York or Massachusetts law, a court could conclude that the plaintiffs were employees regardless of their classification under the language of the contract. Therefore, we apply the "two-tiered analysis" of § 187(2).

[handwritten margin note: not fixed by provision in K]

First, because the defendant is headquartered in Massachusetts, we readily conclude that Massachusetts has a "substantial relationship" to the transaction.

Second, even if we were to assume that New York has a greater interest in the determination of the issue, and that New York law would apply in the absence of an effective choice by the parties, application of Massachusetts law would not in any event contravene a fundamental policy of New York. Under both Massachusetts and New York law, a purported independent contractor who does not enjoy sufficient independence from the hiring party is deemed an employee. . . . Although the Massachusetts independent

---

Here, there is no concern that the choice-of-law clause was forced upon the party now resisting it, as the defendant, the party that drafted the choice-of-law clause, is now attempting to disclaim it, rather than to enforce it. . . . Any concern over unequal bargaining power in the underlying negotiation would suggest that the clause should be enforced, rather than discarded. . . .

contractor statute features a more expansive definition of "employee" than the New York common-law test, "[t]he fact . . . that a different result might be achieved if the law of the chosen forum is applied does not suffice to show that the [forum] law is repugnant to a fundamental policy" of the State whose law would otherwise apply. *Johnson v. Ventra Group, Inc.,* 191 F.3d 732, 740 (6th Cir. 1999). . . . *See* Restatement, *supra* at § 187 comment g ("To be 'fundamental,' a policy must . . . be a substantial one"). . . .

The defendant points to no authority, and we are aware of none, indicating that it is a fundamental policy of New York that employees be defined only in accordance with the New York common-law test for employment. Rather, we view the fundamental policy of New York in this area as being roughly equivalent to that of Massachusetts; both States seek to protect workers by classifying them as employees, and thereby grant them the benefits and rights of employment, where the circumstances indicate that they are, in fact, employees. New York simply uses a different mechanism to effectuate this aim than does Massachusetts. Accordingly, under the two-tiered analysis of the Restatement, we discern no reason not to uphold the parties' express choice of law. . . .

COMMENTS AND QUESTIONS

1. The Massachusetts independent contractor statute was silent as to its effect outside the state. If the statute stated that it applied to persons who live and work outside the state for in-state employers, the court would have applied that statute without even conducting a choice of law inquiry. Reread Restatement (Second) of Conflicts § 6(1). A substantive law that contemplates a multistate factual situation is called a localizing statute or a localizing rule. Only if the localizing statute were unconstitutional in its reach (a topic we will tackle in Chapter 14) would the statute not apply. This paragraph is very important. Reread it if necessary. You will also see localizing statutes in Chapter 16.

2. The court in *Taylor* states that there is no ouster of a "fundamental policy" of New York law even if a different definition of the word *employee* under Massachusetts law would lead to a different outcome in this case for these litigants. The difference in policy, then, must be fundamental to *whom?*

3. Earlier in this chapter we talked about litigators using antonyms of the word *fundamental* to explore whether a court should or would oust that policy. We can also use synonyms of the word *fundamental* to find better arguments. These synonyms include the words *major, principal, necessary, basic, theoretical,* and *elemental.* Some (but not all) meanings of the word *fundamental* might lead one to require a policy difference that is dramatic and profound. And in *Taylor* the court downplays the policy difference between New York and Massachusetts laws by highlighting their similar purpose or intent. But couldn't even subtle differences be *fundamental* if that difference was the product of an especially thoughtful, deliberate, careful choice? What might you seek to find in the legislative history of New York's laws that would support an argument that the difference between that state's and Massachusetts' definitions of what constitutes an "employee" is a matter of fundamental policy?

4. The clause in *Taylor* was drafted by Eastern, who is now the party trying to escape its clutches. How much does that explain this court's decision? Does this fact make it less likely that Eastern will get any benefit of the doubt on its argument that the policy difference is fundamental?

FROM THE COURTS

WILLIAMSON POUNDERS ARCHITECTS, P.C. v. TUNICA CTY., MISSISSIPPI

U.S. District Court for the Northern District of Mississippi
681 F.Supp.2d 766 (N.D. Miss. 2008)*

MICHAEL P. MILLS, CHIEF DISTRICT JUDGE.

[Tunica County entered into a standard American Institute of Architects contract with Williamson Pounders Architects, P.C. ("WPA") to design and supervise construction of a river front park. Approximately one year later, some Tunica County personnel met with WPA to increase the size of the project from $18 million to $24 million. At that time, the County Administrator orally approved the changes. Yet when WPA ultimately submitted its bill for the extra work done, the Tunica County Board of Supervisors refused to pay. Tunica argued that the Board never approved

---

* Affirmed, 597 F.3d 292 (5th Cir. 2010).

the additional expenses. The Board's position was substantiated by the absence of any mention of the additional expense in the minutes of their meetings. WPA filed suit.]

. . . Mississippi has adopted a "general rule . . . that courts will give effect to an express agreement that the laws of a specified jurisdiction shall govern, particularly where some material element of the contract has a real relation to, or connection with, such jurisdiction." *Miller v. Fannin*, 481 So.2d 261, 262 (Miss. 1985). However, that principle is tempered where a choice of law provision would violate the forum state's public policy.*

Article 9.1 of the contract between Tunica County and WPA contains a choice of law provision designating that Tennessee law will apply to the agreement. Additionally, there is no dispute that WPA's principal place of business is in Tennessee and thus the choice of law provision clearly has some "real relation" to the state law chosen to govern the contract. The Mississippi Supreme Court has held that "no foreign state's substantive law will be enforced in courts of this state where to do so would be offensive to the deeply ingrained or strongly felt public policy of the state." *Boardman v. United Services Auto. Ass'n*, 470 So.2d at 1038. The court in that matter found that all Mississippi laws, whether statutory or part of the common law, reflected the public policy of the state. The court, however, recognized some public policies "are more fundamental and more inviolable than others . . . reflect[ing] public policies which are more strongly felt and more deeply ingrained than others." *Id.* at 1038–39. The court then states public policy will only override the enforcement of general conflict of laws principles when justice requires those fundamental principles preclude enforcement of the laws of another state. *Id.* at 1039. . . .

Tennessee law allows for oral contracts to be enforced against governmental entities. [citations omitted] Mississippi has explicitly held that oral contracts can not be formed by or enforced against county boards of supervisors. [citation omitted]

---

* Tunica County asserts this represents Mississippi adopting Restatement (Second) of Conflict of Laws § 187. The rule put forth by the Mississippi Supreme Court, however, differs from § 187. The Mississippi rule takes into account the public policy of the forum state. Section 187 takes into account "the policy of a state which has a materially greater interest than the chosen state in the determination of the particular issue." Restatement (Second) of Conflict of Laws § 187. This difference may not affect the choice of public policy to use in the present matter, but it does call into question Mississippi's adoption of § 187. *But see Newman v. Newman*, 558 So.2d 821, 823 (Miss. 1990) ("[I]n 1968 this Court embraced the choice of law principles now generally advanced in Restatement (Second) of Conflict of Laws (1971).") . . . .

The Mississippi Supreme Court has dealt with this issue for more that 125 years. Their rulings have consistently held that a board of supervisors can "act only as a body, and its act[s] must be evidenced by an entry on its minutes." *Nichols v. Patterson*, 678 So.2d 673, 677 (Miss. 1996). Further they have stood by the principle that "a county board of supervisors can contract only by an order on its minutes" finding that rule to be "well established." *Butler v. Board of Sup'rs for Hinds County*, 659 So.2d 578, 581 (Miss. 1995) [more citations omitted] This rule applies not only to contract formation, but also to the alteration of a contract. *Warren County Port Comm'n v. Farrell Const. Co.*, 395 F.2d 901, 903–04 (5th Cir. 1968).

This difference reflects a public policy conflict between Tennessee and Mississippi law. The question of enforcement then becomes whether the Mississippi public policy is so fundamental that justice requires the rejection of Tennessee law as it deals with implied contracts made by boards of supervisors.

Mississippi courts have addressed the minutes requirement's place in the public policy. The state Supreme Court has held that the minutes requirement is "an important public policy," writing that the "public interest requires adherence thereto, notwithstanding the fact that in some instances the rules may work an apparent injustice." *Butler*, 659 So.2d at 579. The court went on to state that even its extension to contract modification . . . in *Warren County* was based on "a long history of adherence by the . . . Court to the public policy involved." *Id.* at 581. The reasoning behind this rule is three-fold: (1) to protect a board from being bound by the acts of its individual members or agents; (2) because the public is entitled to the judgment of the board after examination of a proposal, a discussion of it among the board members, and a result representing the wisdom of the majority rather than the opinion or preference of some individual member; and (3) so "that the decision or order when made shall not be subject to the uncertainties of the recollection of individual witnesses . . . , but that the action taken will be evidenced by a written memorial entered upon the minutes at the time, and to which all the public may have access." *Id.* . . .

This well established history coupled with the rule's importance in providing for open governance of Mississippi's counties makes this an important public policy. As a fundamental and inviolable policy of the state, no contract provision violating it may be brought in a Mississippi court. In the instant matter, the choice of law provision is ineffective in requiring the application of Tennessee law as it relates to enforcing any oral modification of the contract. Mississippi law will apply to any claim seeking to enforce a contract modification not recorded in Tunica County's minutes. This does not invalidate the choice of law provision in its entirety, but simply renders it unenforceable on this issue.

WPA is thus unable to proceed under the theory of implied contract and [their] request to be allowed to recover because of a course of dealing between the parties is denied. . . .

COMMENTS AND QUESTIONS

1. In *Williamson Pounders*, the "well-established history" of the policy substantiates its *fundamental* nature. Are policies with well-established histories more important than those that are not as well chronicled? Can an advocate help create a history after-the-fact—or must it be a contemporaneous account?

2. Why did the plaintiffs sue in Mississippi?

3. Notice how the relevant public policy is framed as a matter of "open governance." Why is open governance a more compelling policy than "whether oral agreements are enforceable against a county"?

4. The Second Restatement is only a model law. States can adopt it or ignore it. Or states can adopt some but not all of it. How has the state of Mississippi put its own gloss on Restatement § 187(2)(b)? Reread the judge's footnote.

NEDLLOYD LINES B.V. v. SUPERIOR COURT

Supreme Court of California
3 Cal.4th 459 (1992)

Baxter, Associate Justice.

We granted review to consider the effect of a choice-of-law clause in a contract between commercial entities to finance and operate an international shipping business. In our order granting review, we limited our consideration to the question whether and to what extent the law of Hong Kong, chosen in the parties' agreement, should be applied in ruling on defendant's demurrer to plaintiff's complaint. . . .

Statement of Facts and Proceedings Below

Plaintiff and real party in interest Seawinds Limited (Seawinds) is a shipping company, currently undergoing reorganization under chapter 11 of the United States Bankruptcy Code, whose business consists of the operation of three container ships. Seawinds was incorporated in Hong Kong in late 1982 and has its principal place of business in Redwood City, California. Defendants and petitioners Nedlloyd Lines B.V., Royal Nedlloyd Group N.V., and KNSM Lines B.V. (collectively referred to as Nedlloyd) are interrelated shipping companies incorporated in the Netherlands with their principal place of business in Rotterdam.

In March 1983, Nedlloyd and other parties (including an Oregon corporation, a Hong Kong corporation, a British corporation, three individual residents of California, and a resident of Singapore) entered into a contract with Seawinds to purchase shares of Seawinds's stock. The contract, which was entitled "Shareholders' Agreement in Respect of Seawinds Limited," stated that its purpose was "to establish [Seawinds] as a joint venture company to carry on a transportation operation." The agreement also provided that Seawinds would carry on the business of the transportation company and that the parties to the agreement would use "means reasonably available" to ensure the business was a success.

The shareholders' agreement between the parties contained the following choice-of-law and forum selection provision: "This agreement shall be governed by and construed in accordance with Hong Kong law and each party hereby irrevocably submits to the non-exclusive jurisdiction and service of process of the Hong Kong courts."

In January 1989, Seawinds sued Nedlloyd, alleging in essence that Nedlloyd breached express and implied obligations under the shareholders' agreement by: "(1) engaging in activities that led to the cancellation of charter hires that were essential to Seawinds' business; (2) attempting to interfere with a proposed joint service agreement between Seawinds and the East Asiatic Company, and delaying its implementation; (3) making and then reneging on commitments to contribute additional capital, thereby dissuading others from dealing with Seawinds, and (4) making false and disparaging statements about Seawinds' business operations and financial condition." Seawinds's original and first amended complaint included causes of action for breach of contract, breach of the implied covenant of good faith and fair dealing (in both contract and tort), and breach of fiduciary duty. This matter comes before us after trial court rulings on demurrers to Seawinds's complaints.

Nedlloyd demurred to Seawinds's original complaint on the grounds that it failed to state causes of action for breach of the implied covenant of good faith and fair dealing (either in contract or in tort) and breach of fiduciary duty. In support of its demurrer, Nedlloyd contended the shareholders' agreement required the application of Hong Kong law to Seawinds's claims. In opposition to the demurrer, Seawinds argued that California law should be applied to its causes of action.

In ruling on Nedlloyd's demurrer, the trial court expressly determined that California law applied to all of Seawinds' causes of action. It sustained the demurrers with leave to amend as to all causes of action, relying on grounds not pertinent to the issues before us. Nedlloyd sought a writ of mandate from the Court of Appeal directing the application of Hong Kong law. After the Court of Appeal summarily denied Nedlloyd's initial writ petition, we granted Nedlloyd's petition for review and transferred the case back to the Court of Appeal with instructions to issue an alternative writ.

After complying with our direction, the Court of Appeal denied Nedlloyd's first writ petition and discharged the alternative writ. In a published opinion, the Court of Appeal upheld the application of California law to Seawinds's claims. We granted Nedlloyd's petition for review.

In the meantime, the trial court overruled Nedlloyd's demurrer to Seawinds's first amended complaint, again applying California law to Seawinds's causes of action. The Court of Appeal summarily denied Nedlloyd's second writ petition challenging the order overruling the latter demurrer; we also granted review of that order and consolidated proceedings on the two writ matters so as to preserve the choice-of-law issue for review. As noted above, we have limited review in both proceedings to the choice-of-law issue.

Discussion

I. The proper test

. . . In determining the enforceability of arm's-length contractual choice-of-law provisions, California courts shall apply the principles set forth in Restatement section 187, which reflect a strong policy favoring enforcement of such provisions. . . .[3]

Briefly restated, the proper approach under Restatement section 187, subdivision (2) is for the court first to determine either: (1) whether the chosen state has a substantial relationship to the parties or their transaction, or (2) whether there is any other reasonable basis for the parties' choice of law. If neither of these tests is met, that is the end of the inquiry, and the court need not enforce the parties' choice of law. If, however, either test is met, the court must next determine whether the chosen state's law is contrary to a *fundamental* policy of California. If there is no such conflict, the court shall enforce the parties' choice of law. If, however, there is a fundamental conflict with California law, the court must then determine whether California has a "materially greater interest than the chosen state in the determination of the particular issue. . . ." Rest., § 187, subd. (2). If California has a materially greater interest than the chosen state, the choice of law shall not be enforced, for the obvious reason that in such circumstance we will decline to enforce a law contrary to this state's fundamental policy. We now apply the Restatement test to the facts of this case.

---

3 Subdivision (1) of section 187 . . . is not at issue, and we need not and do not further consider its potential application or scope.

II. Application of the test in this case

[A.] . . . Implied covenant of good faith and fair dealing

1. Substantial relationship or reasonable basis

As to the first required determination, Hong Kong—"the chosen state"—clearly has a "substantial relationship to the parties." Rest., § 187, subd. (2)(a). The shareholders' agreement, which is incorporated by reference in Seawinds' first amended complaint, shows that Seawinds is incorporated by reference in Seawinds' first amended complaint, shows that Seawinds is incorporated under the laws of Hong Kong and has a registered office there. The same is true of one of the shareholder parties to the agreement—Red Coconut Trading Co. The incorporation of these parties in Hong Kong provides the required "substantial relationship." *Id.* com. f (substantial relationship present when "one of the parties is domiciled" in the chosen state); *Carlock v. Pillsbury Co.*, 719 F.Supp. 791, 807 (D. Minn. 1989) ("A party's incorporation in a state is a contact sufficient to allow the parties to choose that state's law to govern their contract.). . .

Moreover, the presence of two Hong Kong corporations as parties also provides a "reasonable basis" for a contractual provision requiring application of Hong Kong law. "If one of the parties resides in the chosen state, the parties have a reasonable basis for their choice." *Consul Ltd. v. Solide Enterprises, Inc., supra*, 802 F.2d 1143, 1147. The reasonableness of choosing Hong Kong becomes manifest when the nature of the agreement before us is considered. A state of incorporation is certainly at least one government entity with a keen and intimate interest in internal corporate affairs, including the purchase and sale of its shares, as well as corporate management and operations. . . .

2. Existence of fundamental public policy

We next consider whether application of the law chosen by the parties would be contrary to "a fundamental policy" of California. We perceive no fundamental policy of California requiring the application of California law to Seawinds's claims based on the implied covenant of good faith and fair dealing. The covenant is not a government regulatory policy designed to restrict freedom of contract, but an implied promise inserted in an agreement to carry out the presumed intentions of contracting parties. *Foley v. Interactive Data Corp.*, 47 Cal.3d 654, 689–90 (1988) ("When a court enforces the implied covenant it is in essence acting to protect 'the interest in having promises performed'—the traditional realm of a contract action—rather than to protect some general duty to society which the law places on an employer without regard to the substance of its contractual obligations to its employee.")

Seawinds directs us to no authority exalting the *implied* covenant of good faith and fair dealing over the *express* covenant of these parties that Hong Kong law shall govern their agreement. We have located none. Because Seawinds has identified no fundamental policy of our state at issue in its essentially contractual dispute with Nedlloyd, the second exception to the rule of section 187 of the Restatement does not apply.

[B.] Fiduciary duty cause of action

1. Scope of the choice-of-law clause

Seawinds contends that, whether or not the choice-of-law clause governs Seawinds's implied covenant claim, Seawinds's fiduciary duty claim is some-how independent of the shareholders' agreement and therefore outside the intended scope of the clause. Seawinds thus concludes California law must be applied to this claim. We disagree.

When two sophisticated, commercial entities agree to a choice-of-law clause like the one in this case, the most reasonable interpretation of their actions is that they intended for the clause to apply to all causes of action arising from or related to their contract. Initially, such an interpretation is supported by the plain meaning of the language used by the parties. The choice-of-law clause in the shareholders' agreement provides: "This agreement shall be *governed by* and construed in accordance with Hong Kong law and each party hereby irrevocably submits to the non-exclusive jurisdiction and service of process of the Hong Kong courts." (Italics added.)[7]

The phrase "governed by" is a broad one signifying a relationship of absolute direction, control, and restraint. Thus, the clause reflects the parties' clear contemplation that "the agreement" is to be completely and absolutely con-

---

7   . . . [T]he question of whether that clause is ambiguous as to its scope (i.e., whether it includes the fi-duciary duty claim) is a question of contract interpretation that in the normal course should be determined pursuant to Hong Kong law. . . . The parties in this case, however, did not request judicial notice of Hong Kong law on this question of interpretation, Evid. Code § 452, subd. (f), or supply us with evidence of the relevant aspects of that law, Evid. Code § 453, subd. (b). The question therefore becomes one of California law. . . .

trolled by Hong Kong law. No exceptions are provided. In the context of this case, the agreement to be controlled by Hong Kong law is a shareholders' agreement that expressly provides for the purchase of shares in Seawinds by Nedlloyd and creates the relationship between shareholder and corporation that gives rise to Seawinds's cause of action. Nedlloyd's fiduciary duties, if any, arise from—and can exist only because of—the shareholders' agreement pursuant to which Seawinds's stock was purchased by Nedlloyd.

In order to control completely the agreement of the parties, Hong Kong law must also govern the stock purchase portion of that agreement and the legal duties created by or emanating from the stock purchase, including any fiduciary duties. If Hong Kong law were not applied to these duties, it would effectively control only part of the agreement, not all of it. Such an interpretation would be inconsistent with the unrestricted character of the choice-of-law clause.

Our conclusion in this regard comports with common sense and commercial reality. When a rational businessperson enters into an agreement establishing a transaction or relationship and provides that disputes arising from the agreement shall be governed by the law of an identified jurisdiction, the logical conclusion is that he or she intended that law to apply to *all* disputes arising out of the transaction or relationship. We seriously doubt that any rational businessperson, attempting to provide by contract for an efficient and businesslike resolution of possible future disputes, would intend that the laws of multiple jurisdictions would apply to a single controversy having its origin in a single, contract-based relationship. Nor do we believe such a person would reasonably desire a protracted litigation battle concerning only the threshold question of what law was to be applied to which asserted claims or issues. Indeed, the manifest purpose of a choice-of-law clause is precisely to avoid such a battle.

Seawinds's view of the problem—which would require extensive litigation of the parties' supposed intentions regarding the choice-of-law clause to the end that the laws of multiple states might be applied to their dispute—is more likely the product of postdispute litigation strategy, not predispute contractual intent. If commercially sophisticated parties (such as those now before us) truly intend the result advocated by Seawinds, they should, in fairness to one another and in the interest of economy in dispute resolution, negotiate and obtain the assent of their fellow parties to explicit contract language specifying what jurisdiction's law applies to what issues.

Justice Mosk long ago cogently observed that "Given two experienced businessmen dealing at arm's length, both represented by competent counsel, it has become virtually impossible under recently evolving rules of evidence to draft a written contract that will produce predictable results in court. The written word, heretofore deemed immutable, is now at all times subject to alteration by self-serving recitals based upon fading memories of antecedent events. This, I submit, is a serious impediment to the certainty required in commercial transactions." *Delta Dynamics, Inc. v. Arioto*, 69 Cal.2d 525, 532 (1968) (dis. opn. of Mosk, J.).

With due acknowledgement of Justice Mosk's prescience, other courts have more recently reiterated that, "While [the] rule [of easily pleaded ambiguity] creates much business for lawyers and an occasional windfall to some clients, it leads only to frustration and delay for most litigants and clogs already overburdened courts." *Trident Center v. Connecticut General Life Ins.*, 847 F.2d 564, 569 (9th Cir. 1988). . . . We need not envelop choice-of-law clauses in this fog of uncertainty and ambiguity.

For the reasons stated above, we hold a valid choice-of-law clause, which provides that a specified body of law "governs" the "agreement" between the parties, encompasses all causes of action arising from or related to that agreement, regardless of how they are characterized, including tortious breaches of duties emanating from the agreement or the legal relationships it creates.

2. Enforceability of chosen law as to fiduciary duty claim

Applying the test we have adopted, we find no reason not to apply the parties' choice of law to Seawinds's cause of action for breach of fiduciary duty. As we have explained, Hong Kong, the chosen state, has a "substantial relationship to the parties" because two of those parties are incorporated there. Moreover, their incorporation in that state affords a "reasonable basis" for choosing Hong Kong law.

Seawinds identifies no fundamental public policy of this state that would be offended by application of Hong Kong law to a claim by a Hong Kong corporation against its allegedly controlling shareholder. We are directed to no California statute or constitutional provision designed to preclude freedom of contract in this context. Indeed, even in the absence of a choice-of-law clause, Hong Kong's overriding interest in the internal affairs of corporations domiciled there would in most cases require application of its law. *See* Rest., § 306 (obligations owed by majority shareholder to corporation determined by the law of the state of incorporation except in unusual circumstances not present here); *McDermott Inc. v. Lewis*, 531 A.2d 206, 214–16 (Del. Super. Ct. 1987) (corporate voting rights dispute governed by law of state of incorporation); *Matter of Reading Co.*, 711 F.2d 509, 517 (3d Cir. 1983) (minority shareholder fiduciary duty claim governed by law of state of incorporation).

For strategic reasons related to its current dispute with Nedlloyd, Seawinds seeks to create a fiduciary relationship by disregarding the law Seawinds voluntarily agreed to accept as binding—the law of a state that also happens to be Seawinds's own corporate domicile. To allow Seawinds to use California law in this fashion would further no ascertainable fundamental policy of California; indeed, it would undermine California's policy of respecting the choices made by parties to voluntarily negotiated agreements.

Disposition

By a choice-of-law clause in a fully negotiated commercial contract, the parties have chosen Hong Kong law to apply to their dispute in this case, including each of the causes of action asserted by Seawinds. . . .["We conclude the choice-of-law clause, which requires that the contract be "governed by" the law of Hong Kong, a jurisdiction having a substantial connection with the parties, is fully enforceable and applicable to claims for breach of the implied covenant of good faith and fair dealing and for breach of fiduciary duties allegedly arising out of the contract. Our conclusion rests on the choice-of-law rules derived from California decisions and the Restatement Second of Conflict of Laws, which reflect strong policy considerations favoring the enforcement of freely negotiated choice-of-law clauses. Based on our conclusion, we will reverse the judgments of the Court of Appeal and remand for further proceedings."]

[Justice Kennard wrote a separate opinion, concurring in part and dissenting in part, to express the view that the chosen law should not apply to the breach of fiduciary duty claims that were only indirectly related to the contract. She observed that there was no extrinsic evidence of the parties' intent regarding these non-contractual claims.]

COMMENTS AND QUESTIONS

1. What happened to § 187(1)? Couldn't the court have simply stopped there?

2. Although a choice of law clause can *expressly exclude* some claim(s) from its scope, lawyers very rarely do so. Yet the Court uses the fact that this clause contained no exceptions as part of its justification for reading it broadly. Is that justifiable?

    The notion of excluding some claim(s) from the scope of a choice of law clause may seem odd, but is a choice of law clause with a narrow scope *impliedly* excluding some claim(s) from its scope? Does the difference between express and implied exclusions lend any interpretive insight?

3. Would a clause that said only "The choice of law of the parties is the law of the State of California" be interpreted by the California Supreme Court as broad enough to cover tort claims arising between the parties? This hypothetical clause does not include the magic words "agreement" and "governed by." But isn't the general rationale of *Nedlloyd* that any sane businessperson would, *ex ante*, want this clause (or any clause) to apply broadly?

4. Does *Nedlloyd* apply all of Section 187(2)(b) of the Second Restatement?

5. Footnote 7 reflects the inclination of courts to apply forum law unless one of the parties initiates a choice of law inquiry. Litigators who do not see (and leverage) the opportunity to have foreign law applied should not expect the judge to raise the issue *sua sponte*.

FROM THE COURTS

MAXIM CRANE WORKS, L.P. v. TILBURY CONSTRUCTORS

California Court of Appeal, Third District
208 Cal. App. 4th 286 (2012)

DUARTE, JUSTICE.

[Maxim Crane Works (Maxim) signed a contract with Tilbury Constructors (Tilbury) to provide Tilbury with a crane and an operator at a construction site in Stockton, California. Maxim drafted a contract that required Tilbury to indemnify Maxim for any claims related to the agreement. The contract provided that Pennsylvania law "shall govern" the contract. A Tilbury employee, Steven Gorski, was injured while working on the construction site. Although a worker injured on a job is generally limited to workers compensation remedies against the employer, that worker may file suit against a third party. Accordingly, Gorski sued Maxim, alleging its crane was negligently operated. Maxim cross-complained against Tilbury seeking indemnity and asserting other claims. Maxim settled with Gorski for $900,000 and proceeded to trial on its cross-complaint against Tilbury. The Maxim-Tilbury contract was signed the same day that Gorski was injured.]

Maxim initially contended that Pennsylvania law applied. Tilbury's counsel then unearthed a Pennsylvania statute providing that an injured worker's employer has no liability to a third party tortfeasor, unless such liability is provided by a written contract entered into *prior to the date* of the worker's injury. Tilbury argued that because it signed Maxim's contract the day Gorski was injured, not the *prior* day, the indemnity contract was unenforceable.[16] Maxim then argued the choice-of-law provision was unenforceable on the facts of this case.

The trial court rejected Maxim's position, as follows:

> "While the result might appear on first blush to be harsh in application . . . reflection on the facts that MAXIM (not TILBURY) drafted the contract, MAXIM (not TILBURY) chose to make Penn-

---

16 The parties do not dispute the interpretation of Pennsylvania law that holds there is no liability to a third party unless the contract is signed "prior to the date" of the injury. Under California law, a similar indemnity agreement is effective if signed "prior to the injury."

sylvania law applicable, and certainly MAXIM could have insisted on getting a signed contract in place the day before the work began, all weigh against the Court finding that California public policy considerations should be . . . a reason to deny the application of Pennsylvania law to . . . MAXIM's Cross–Complaint."

Tilbury later moved for attorney fees as the prevailing party, predicated on Maxim's contract, which contained a fee agreement. *See* Civ. Code, § 1717. . . .

Discussion

. . .Touting California's strong public policy to ensure California workers are compensated for injuries occurring in California, Maxim asserts the trial court should have rejected the choice of law provision in the contract. We disagree.

Generally speaking:

> The basic policy in the field of contracts is protection of the justified expectations of the parties. Parties will generally enter into a contract with the expectation that the provisions of the contract will be binding on them. These expectations "should not be disappointed by application of the local law rule of a state which would strike down the contract or a provision thereof unless the value of protecting the expectations of the parties is substantially outweighed in the particular case by the interest of the state with the invalidating rule in having this rule applied."

1 Witkin, *Summary of Cal. Law* (10th ed. 2005) Contracts, § 65, p. 109.

Indemnity agreements are common in construction work, and "subject to public policy and established rules of contract interpretation, the parties have great freedom to allocate such responsibilities as they see fit." *Crawford v. Weather Shield Mfg., Inc.,* 44 Cal.4th 541, 551 (2008). They may require a promisor to indemnify and defend the promisee whether or not the promisor was negligent.

We agree with Maxim that a choice of law provision, although generally enforceable, may be unenforceable if it violates a strong public policy in California, the forum state. . . .

Maxim is a Pennsylvania company. That fact makes Pennsylvania law initially reasonable under the *Nedlloyd* [*Lines B.V. v. Superior Court*, 3 Cal.4th 459, 465 (1992)] (and Restatement) test, and Maxim concedes the point.

The burden thus shifts to Maxim to demonstrate that some California public policy would be impaired by application of Pennsylvania law to this case. . . . Maxim rests its case on the policy behind the workers' compensation system. We agree California has a strong policy ensuring that injured California workers are fairly compensated. As stated by the California Supreme Court:

> California maintains a stronger interest in applying its own law to an issue involving the right of an injured Californian to benefits under California's compulsory [worker]s' compensation act than to an issue involving torts or contracts in which the parties' rights and liabilities are not governed by a protective legislative scheme that imposes obligations on the basis of a statutorily defined status. Its interest devolves both from the possibility of economic burden upon the state resulting from non-coverage of the [worker] during the period of incapacitation, as well as from the contingency that the family of the [worker] might require relief in the absence of compensation. The California statute, fashioned by the Legislature in its knowledge of the needs of its constituency, structures the appropriate measures to avoid these possibilities. Even if the employee may be able to obtain benefits under another state's compensation laws, California retains its interest in insuring the maximum application of this protection afforded by the California Legislature.

Travelers Ins. Co. v. Workmen's Comp. Appeals Bd., 68 Cal.2d 7, 12–13 (1967).

But, as the trial court stated, such public policy has *nothing* to do with this case. Gorski has been compensated. Maxim has cited no authority showing that California has a fundamental policy regarding which of two purses must be opened to compensate an injured Californian. Gorski's suit against Maxim was not governed by the California workers compensation scheme. [However, Gorski *also* filed a workers' compensation claim and received a substantial award, leading Tilbury's insurance carrier to file a lien on his tort recovery.] *Maxim* cannot rely on that scheme's protections. . . .

[N]o California public policy is offended by the fact that Maxim's contract gave Maxim *less* protection, by virtue of Maxim's choice of Pennsylvania law and Maxim's choice to deliver the crane the same day the contract was signed.

As the trial court found, Maxim, the drafter, was in the best position to avoid this result. As a Pennsylvania company, Maxim is presumed to know Pennsylvania law. (*See* 31A C.J.S. Evidence (2008) § 228, p. 282 [parties "presumed to know the general public laws of the state or country where they reside, and the legal effect of their acts"].) The relevant Pennsylvania statute and cases interpreting it long predated the contract.

Maxim could have avoided its plight by including a provision making the indemnity agreement valid immediately, notwithstanding Pennsylvania law. (*See* 11 Williston on Contracts (4th ed. 1999) Interpretation and Construction, § 30:19, pp. 202–203 ["parties to a contract who are not otherwise subject to a statute may choose to incorporate parts of the statute to define their relationship without bringing the full force of the statute to bear"].) Alternatively, Maxim could have insisted that Tilbury sign the contract the day before Maxim delivered or began operation of Maxim's crane.

In short, like the trial court, we cannot see how the result—denying Maxim recovery based on Maxim's contract and conduct—implicates any fundamental California public policy. . . . The judgment is affirmed.

COMMENTS AND QUESTIONS

1. Although we summarized rather than reprinted the first paragraphs of the *Maxim Crane* opinion, the very first line of the court's opinion reads as follows: "Appellant Maxim Crane Works (Maxim) was hoist by its own petard when the trial court enforced an unfavorable choice-of-law provision in a form contract written by Maxim." The tone and placement suggests that the court may find something furtive about this Pennsylvania company including a Pennsylvania choice of law clause in its form contract. What is troubling the court here? Is this something that transactional lawyers who draft choice-of-law clauses need to worry about? How can we know in advance whether we will be the party arguing for or arguing against enforcement of the clause? If you knew, how would that influence your drafting?

2. Maxim Crane did not challenge the court's assumption that, if applicable, Pennsylvania law foreclosed the possibility of recovery. Presumably there is at least an argument that this interpretation of Pennsylvania law is nonsensical; surely the Pennsylvania legislature's intent was the same as California's. If there was an open question as to what Pennsylvania law required, then isn't it possible that the court might have been less reluctant to find Pennsylvania law applicable? Yet Maxim removed any uncertainty that the judge might have harbored about misapplying Pennsylvania law. What did Maxim Crane hope to achieve by conceding this particular interpretation of Pennsylvania law?

3. The court alludes to burdens of proof. Who *should* bear the responsibility of proving that a choice of law clause should be enforced: the party seeking to enforce it or the party resisting its enforcement? Assigning the burden of proof is especially important in contexts where the legal standard is imprecise; whether something is "substantial," "reasonable," or "fundamental," is very subjective.

4. In the penultimate paragraph of Judge Duarte's opinion she observes that "Maxim could have avoided its plight by including a provision making the indemnity agreement valid immediately." This would be another way of stating that the effective date/time of a contract is a default rule (rather than a mandatory rule). And if that is the case here, then wouldn't § 187(1) of the Second Restatement urge enforcement of the Pennsylvania choice of law clause without any further inquiry at all?

FLORIDA STATE BD. OF ADMIN. v. LAW ENG. & ENV. SERVS., INC.

U.S. District Court for the District of Minnesota
262 F.Supp.2d 1004 (D. Minn. 2003)

DOTY, DISTRICT JUDGE.

. . . Background

Plaintiff [Florida State Board of Administration (FSBA)] is an agency of the State of Florida responsible for managing and investing the assets of various trust funds. In the summer of 1997, plaintiff expressed interest in purchasing commercially developed property in Eden Prairie, Minnesota. The property, known as the One Southwest Crossing Office Building ("One Southwest Crossing"), consists of a five-story, Class A office building and an attached three-level parking structure.

Before purchasing One Southwest Crossing, plaintiff hired defendant [Law Engineering and Environmental Services, Inc.] to assess its structural soundness. The parties executed a building assessment agreement. Pursuant to this agreement, defendant inspected One Southwest Crossing and issued a building condition assessment report. According to the report, "the structure did not exhibit signs of structural distress or excessive movement or distortion. With adequate and continued future maintenance, the parking structure should perform as designed well beyond the 10–year evaluation period." The report also estimated that maintenance costs for the parking structure would not exceed $487,600 over the ten-year evaluation period, with only $34,600 of this amount needed for immediate repair.

Plaintiff purchased One Southwest Crossing . . . for $34,100,000. As plaintiff began to implement the maintenance program that defendant recommended, the parking structure experienced concrete failures including corroded reinforcing steel, concrete delaminations, spalling in the structural slabs, water intrusion, and distress on the structure's protective traffic coating. Plaintiff began repairs and it is estimated that the total cost of repairs and associated expenses will exceed $1.8 million. Plaintiff contends that if it had known that it would be required to spend at least $1.8 million to repair and maintain the parking structure, it would not have purchased One Southwest Crossing or would have negotiated a much lower price.

Plaintiff filed this action against defendant [asserting breach of contract claims as well as tort causes of action for negligence, breach of fiduciary duty, and negligent misrepresentation.] Defendant raise[d] several affirmative defenses, including . . . the economic loss rule. . . . [The parties filed cross-motions for summary judgment. Plaintiff moved for partial summary judgment seeking a ruling that the economic loss doctrine did not prevent recovery. Defendant moved for summary judgment on the theory that the economic loss doctrine was an obstacle to any recovery in tort. The economic loss doctrine provides that a party who suffers only economic harm may recover damages for that harm only under theories of contract, not tort.]

Discussion

. . . Plaintiff . . . asserts that Minnesota law applies and that Minnesota does not apply the economic loss doctrine to claims against engineers for negligence. In opposing plaintiff's motion, defendant responds that the choice of law clause governs plaintiff's tort claims. [Article XIV of Paragraph E of the contract between the parties provides: "This Agreement shall be governed by and construed in accordance with the laws of the State of Florida."]

As a threshold matter, the court must determine whether the choice of law clause governs plaintiff's tort claims and thus defendant's economic loss doctrine defense. In determining whether a choice of law provision in the parties' agreement will be given effect, a federal court sitting in diversity looks to the choice of law principles of the forum state, in this case Minnesota. Minnesota courts honor choice of law clauses. *Northwest Airlines, Inc. v. Astraea Aviation Servs., Inc.*, 111 F.3d 1386, 1392 (8th Cir. 1997); *Milliken and Co. v. Eagle Packaging Co.*, 295 N.W.2d 377, 380 n. 1 (Minn. 1980).

Many courts, though not applying Minnesota law, have distinguished between broad and narrow choice of law provisions in order to determine whether a choice of law agreement includes tort claims. [citing cases] Those courts have found that narrow choice of law provisions which provide that the contract will be "governed by" or "construed" under the laws of a particular state do not govern tort claims between contracting parties. . . .

However, in *Northwest Airlines, Inc. v. Astraea Aviation Servs., Inc.*, 111 F.3d at 1392, the Eighth Circuit Court of Appeals, applying Minnesota law, recognized that a choice of law provision in a contract will govern non-contract claims if the those claims "are closely related to the interpretation of the contract[ ] and fall within the ambit of the express agreement" that the contract will be interpreted under the laws of a particular state. . . . In that case, [the] contract between the parties stated: "This Agreement shall be deemed entered into within and shall be governed by and interpreted in accordance with the laws of the State of Minnesota. . . . "

Astraea claimed that the choice of law provisions did not govern the tort claims of negligent performance, misrepresentation, deceptive trade practices and unjust enrichment because they were not contract claims. Despite the seemingly narrow language of the choice of the law provision, the court disagreed, [and found the plaintiff's tort claims to be sufficiently] related to the parties' contractual relationship.

[In this case,] plaintiff's breach of fiduciary duty claim is related to contract performance. In the introduction of the complaint, plaintiff alleges that defendant "breached the express fiduciary duties it undertook pursuant to [its] agreement" with plaintiff. (Compl. at 1.) Plaintiff further alleges that "[i]n the Building Assessment Agreement, Law Engineering explicitly undertook to act as a fiduciary for FSBA in its performance of the agreement. . . ." (Compl. § 14.) Plaintiff's allegation is based upon Section XIII.B of the contract, which provides, in part: "Consultant accepts the relationship of trust and confidence established between Consultant and the Board by this Agreement and acknowledges that the Board may rely on Consultant's advice and counsel." Plaintiff further emphasizes the connection between the breach of fiduciary duty claim and contract performance throughout count two of the complaint. (Compl. at ¶ 35–41.) Thus the court finds that plaintiff's fiduciary duty claim arises from the contract between the parties and is closely related to defendant's performance under the contract.

Plaintiff's negligence claim also is closely related to defendant's performance under the contract. In count three of the complaint, plaintiff alleges: "Law Engineering agreed to perform its assessment services 'with sufficient detail and scope to meet the standards of practice exercised by a responsible engineering professional in performing such services for an institutional investor of real estate in the current marketplace.' " Plaintiff then cites Section XIII.B of the contract. The issues raised in the negligence claim essentially concern whether defendant's assessment sufficiently met the contract's requirements and whether defendant failed to sufficiently perform its obligation under Section XIII.B. While the complaint also alleges that defendant has a duty to exercise reasonable care, that duty is largely the same as defendant's duty under the contract, as plaintiff conceded in oral argument. Thus, plaintiff's negligence claim is closely intertwined with defendant's performance under the contract.

Further, plaintiff's claim of negligent misrepresentation closely relates to defendant's performance of the contract because that allegation is premised upon plaintiff's allegation that the report defendant delivered pursuant to the contract did not accurately reflect the condition of the structure, the extent of project repair or the total cost of maintenance.

[T]his case involves the application of Minnesota law, the law of the forum, to determine whether a seemingly narrow choice of law clause includes tort claims that . . . are closely related to contract performance. . . . [T]he court finds that the tort claims involved in this case are closely intertwined with the interpretation of the contract and "fall within the ambit of the express agreement that the contract would be governed by [Florida] law." *Astraea,* 111 F.3d at 1392.

[P]laintiff nevertheless relies on the Eighth Circuit case *Inacom Corp. v. Sears, Roebuck and Co.,* 254 F.3d 683, 687 (8th Cir. 2001), and argues that Minnesota law applies to the tort claims in this case. In *Inacom,* Inacom filed an action against Sears alleging breach of contract, fraudulent misrepresentation and fraudulent concealment, and Sears counterclaimed for breach of contract. *Inacom,* 254 F.3d at 686. The agreement between the parties stated that the "[a]greement shall be governed by and construed in accordance with the law of the State of Illinois." The court instructed the jury to evaluate Inacom's breach of contract claim under Illinois law and its fraudulent concealment claim under Nebraska law. *Id.* In its motion for a new trial, Sears argued that the court erred in instructing the jury on choice of law because, according to Sears, the fraudulent concealment claim was intertwined with the contract claim and because it therefore fell within the ambit of the choice of law provision stating that Illinois law governs all contract claims. *Id.* The Eighth Circuit Court of Appeals, applying Nebraska law, disagreed, explaining:

> While this provision adequately covers disputes concerning how to construe the [agreement], the language is not broad enough to govern the choice of law for the fraudulent concealment claim, which sounds in tort. Although the claim arose out of the circumstances surrounding the formation of the contract, there is no indication in the [agreement] that the parties intended to elect Illinois law as the forum for every contract-related claim.

Id.

While plaintiff argues that the court should follow *Inacom, Inacom* is clearly distinguishable from this case for three reasons. The court in *Inacom* applied Nebraska law rather than Minnesota law, the law of the forum in this case. The tort claims involved in *Inacom* did not relate to contractual performance, as they do in this case, but instead related to allegations that arose from contract formation. And, the choice of law provision in *Inacom* was narrower than the provision in this case, providing that "the Agreement shall be governed by and construed in accordance with the law of the State of Illinois, *as applied to contracts." Id.* at 687 (emphasis added). Thus, because the court concludes that *Astraea* rather than *Inacom Corp.* governs this case, the court finds that the choice of law provision in the contract between the parties incorporates plaintiff's tort claims alleged in counts two, three and four of the complaint and the court applies Florida law to those claims.

[Applying Florida law, the court concluded that the economic loss doctrine barred plaintiff's breach of fiduciary duty and negligence causes of action, but not the claim for negligent misrepresentation.]

COMMENTS AND QUESTIONS

1. The quote from *Inacom* introduces the idea of "contract-related" tort claims. The court went on to say that not all contract-related tort claims fell within the scope of that particular choice of law clause. But the idea of tort claims that are "contract-related" may be a useful category. This descriptor might distinguish tort claims for negligent performance, misrepresentation, deceptive trade practices, and unjust enrichment from, say, tort claims for slander, defamation, and libel. Is there a better way of describing tort claims that (arguably should) fall within the ambit of a generic choice of law clause?

2. Who should bear the responsibility of proving that a choice of law clause includes a cause of action (or affirmative defense) within its scope: the party seeking to enforce it or the party resisting its enforcement? This question seems especially problematic in light of the fact that the parties may not have thought much about the scope of their choice of law clause. Indeed, if the parties had wanted the scope to include or to exclude a particular type of dispute they could have written the clause to resolve any ambiguity.

3. Choice of law clauses are frequently described as "boilerplate." What is the point of assigning a provision such a label? Should "boilerplate" provisions never have a significant effect on the outcome of a case? Do contracts include a hierarchy of provisions, wherein some provisions are more serious and deserving of enforcement than others?

SAMPLE EXAM QUESTIONS

Question 9-6

Agribusiness, Inc., a Virginia corporation with a principal place of business in Newport News, Virginia, entered into a contract with Brandname Cereals, Co., a Georgia corporation with a principal place of business in Savannah, Georgia. The vending agreement provided for the purchase and sale of a large quantity of corn, but did not specifically address which of them bore the risk that the contents would be damaged in shipment. The agreement contained a clause, which provided that "The resolution of all claims and controversies arising hereunder or otherwise related to this agreement shall be governed by the laws of the state of Florida." Under Florida law, the seller bears the risk of loss during shipment. Under the laws of most other jurisdictions, including Virginia and Georgia, the buyer bears this risk. The bulk of the shipment was destroyed because of a recent hurricane, and the parties dispute which of them bore the risk of loss during shipment.

The Georgia buyer has sued the Virginia vendor in a Georgia court. Assuming that Georgia follows the Second Restatement with respect to the enforcement of choice of law clauses in contracts, who will bear the risk of loss? If you need additional information, be specific about what information you need and state exactly how that information would affect your answer.

Question 9-7

Maxwell was a sales representative in Maryland for Bard, Inc. She worked there for several years before she was terminated without cause. Bard refuses to pay her for unvested shares earned through the company's long-term profit sharing plan. Bard is a New Jersey corporation, and their employment agreements contain a New Jersey choice of law clause. Maxwell has filed suit in Maryland. Maryland's Wage Payment and Collection Law would allow Maxwell to recover some of the value of the unvested shares; after all, she deferred salary in exchange for shares in the profit sharing plan. In contrast, New Jersey's Wage Payment and Collection Law ensures only the recovery of unpaid wages, and not incentives or bonuses. The issue, then, is whether the inability to recover some of the value of the unvested shares, a consequence of enforcing the New Jersey choice of law clause, would be contrary to a fundamental policy of Maryland. What do you think? And what else do you need to know (about the New Jersey law, about the Maryland law, about the employment relationship, or about something else) in order to resolve this issue?

Question 9-8

Last year the dean of the law school at the University of Alaska visited Robin Ebinger at Ebinger's home in Missoula, Montana. Ebinger is an alum of the school, and the dean persuaded Ebinger to commit $2.5 million to the school for the construction of a new building. Ebinger and the dean executed a Gift Agreement while they sat, watching the sun set, on

Ebinger's porch in Montana. The agreement included the following provision: "This agreement shall be construed in accordance with the laws of the state of Alaska, as such laws are applied to contracts entered into and performed in such state."

Ebinger recently reneged on the commitment. Under the law of Alaska and of most other states, the gift agreement is probably unenforceable for lack of consideration. However, because the law school began construction shortly after Ebinger promised the money (a fact of which Ebinger was aware), the law school may (depending on what law applies) have a claim against Ebinger for promissory estoppel. Preliminary research suggests that Alaska law is a dead-end with respect to such a claim, but Montana law looks promising. What is the argument for the application of Montana law, and how strong is that argument?

Question 9-9

Albany Brothers of Reno, Nevada, entered into a construction agreement with Royer, a Californian, to build her a house in Truckee, California. The agreement includes a choice of law clause that provided "This Agreement is entered into under the laws of the State of Nevada and shall be construed and interpreted thereunder." Dissatisfied with Albany Brothers' work, Royer filed a lawsuit in California. Royer asserted two causes of action—the first for breach of contract, and a second for deceptive business practices based upon false statements of material facts in advertisements. The deceptive business practices claim relies on a California consumer protection statute; the state of Nevada has no such statutory tort. If the choice of law clause included this deceptive business practice claim within its scope, then Nevada law applies and Royer's second cause of action should be dismissed. What is the best argument(s) that the claim falls within the scope of the clause? What is the best argument(s) that the claim falls outside the scope of the clause? What is the percentage of likelihood that a California court would dismiss the second count?

Question 9-10

Emms enters into an employment agreement with Larkey Enterprises Inc. Larkey Enterprises, a Massachusetts company, entered into the relationship with Emms while Emms was living in Syracuse, New York. Emms worked from New York for the first ten months of her employment, but she eventually relocated to Massachusetts, as contemplated by the parties. A choice of law clause provides: "All questions concerning the construction, validity, enforcement, and performance of these shall be governed by the internal law, and not the law of conflicts, of the Commonwealth of Massachusetts."

You are an employment lawyer in Massachusetts who has been retained by Emms. Emms has explained to you that, when she was hired, she understood that she would receive overtime pay when she worked more than forty hours per week. Although the employment agreement is silent on this point, email correspondence between Emms and Larkey Enterprises confirms Emms' understanding—and Emms, in fact, has twice received overtime pay. Emms claims, however, that she is entitled to much more overtime pay than she has received. Larkey Enterprises claims that when Emms was promoted after her first five months of the job she became a salaried employee who was no longer entitled to overtime.

Both New York and Massachusetts have wage acts that allow employees like Emms to sue employers like Larkey Enterprises for unpaid wages. But New York's law is much more employee-friendly—with lower thresholds of proof required for recovery, presumptive exemplary damages, and the near-automatic recovery of attorney's fees. What is your recommended course of action for Emms?

Quick Summary

- Choice of law clauses were once viewed with suspicion as parties did not have the authority to do a legislative act—that is, to determine the legal standard by which their conduct would be judged

- Today there is a very strong preference in favor of enforcing choice of law clauses

- With respect to default rules (i.e., legislative mandates that courts would allow even domestic parties to bypass by contract), courts will enforce a choice of law clause regardless of whether there is any connection between the selected law and the parties or events

- With respect to mandatory rules (i.e., legislative mandates that are intended to thwart contractual agreements), courts will enforce a choice of law clause unless either (1) the selected law has no substantial relationship to the parties or the transaction and there is no other reasonable basis for the parties' choice; or (2) the selected law contravenes a fundamental policy of the state that has the most significant relationship

- Basic principles of contract interpretation determine the scope of a choice of law clause; courts generally interpret the scope as broadly as the text allows

10

Substance and Procedure

Key Concepts

- Substantive and procedural law are treated differently
- The substance/procedure dichotomy is situation-specific

In Chapter 2 we observed that courts will apply forum procedural law even when they apply foreign substantive law. But what qualifies as *substantive* and what as *procedural*? In this chapter we focus more intently on this characterization problem. Courts apply forum procedural law, no matter whether the parties have chosen another state's law in a contract or what choice of law methodology they use to determine the applicable substantive law. Because the characterization of an issue as *procedural* allows a court to apply forum law, it is a classic escape device[1]— a device that can be used to allow the court to escape from the clutches of a rule requiring the application of foreign law.

Choice of law is one of several diverse legal contexts that rely on a substance/procedure dichotomy. For example, whenever a new *criminal* law is passed, a common question is whether that law applies retroactively; generally speaking, a substantive law cannot apply retroactively (because it would be an invalid *ex post facto* law), but a procedural law can be applied retroactively. The substance/procedure dichotomy also surfaces when the power of a court or legislature to make (procedural) rules is in issue. The dichotomy also plays an important role in applications of the *Erie* Doctrine, which concerns whether state or federal law applies when cases involving state law are, by virtue of diversity jurisdiction, in federal court. (*See* Chapter 19.)

---

1   The pantheon of escape devices also includes the public policy exception (*see* Chapter 11), renvoi (*see* Chapter 12), and characterization by subject matter (*see* Chapters 4 and 17). Depecage (*see* Chapter 15) and proof of foreign law (*see* Chapter 18) can also operate as escape devices. The substance/procedure escape device that is the subject of this chapter appears in a similar context in Chapter 19. The use of escape devices flourished during the heyday of the traditional approach because of its straightjacket-like quality.

On one hand, the substance/procedure dichotomy is quite similar in all the various doctrinal contexts in which it arises: once you appreciate the dichotomy in any one of these areas you have the gist in the other contexts as well. Yet, on the other hand, it is *not* true that what is substantive for, say, purposes of the *Erie* Doctrine, is also substantive in the choice of law context. Accordingly, while you might be able to transplant some of the *techniques* for distinguishing substance and procedure from one context to another, you cannot transplant the *label* itself. A law that is substantive in one context may be procedural in another. In this chapter, we will focus exclusively on the choice of law context.

The substance/procedure dichotomy is only about 250 years old. These categories emerged during the Enlightenment, when scientists and philosophers sought to understand all of the world around them by categorizing it. The capacity to distinguish between and among things became an integral part of intelligibility. Enlightenment epistemology produced particularly binary thinking, such as subject/object, culture/nature, mind/matter, and rational/irrational. A substance/procedure dichotomy likewise resonated, especially for William Blackstone, a law professor at Oxford who wrote his famous Commentaries on the Laws of England for instructional purposes.[2]

In the instructional context, the dichotomy was useful. The dichotomy introduced a nuanced and sophisticated appreciation for laws' multiple intentions and meanings—substantive mandates, on one hand, and the procedural mechanics of implementation, on the other. The dichotomy revealed the diverse purposes and functions that for centuries had been seamlessly integrated (in concept and in nomenclature) in a corpus of laws. Substance and procedure were conceptual opposites even if the two terms were open-ended and not necessarily mutually exclusive nor cumulatively exhaustive.

But rather than remaining in the ivory tower for maturation and refinement, the categories of substance and procedure were put to immediate use as foundational legal infrastructure. The nascent United States of America was forming new systems and courts and methodologies. This apparent distinction between matters substantive and procedural offered a tempting and accessible conceptual structure for a system of jurisprudence that was, in significant part, being built from scratch. The First Congress, for example, passed a statute providing that the new federal courts would, in cases at law, generally follow the "modes of process" of the state in which the court sat. The Second Congress prescribed a distinctive court procedure

---

2   Jeremy Bentham, Blackstone's former student, is also frequently credited for introducing the distinction between **substance** and "**adjective**" law. *See generally* Jeremy Bentham, *Of Laws in General* (1782).

for equity cases. Other statutes recognizing a substance/procedure distinction soon followed.

So the substance/procedure dichotomy quickly transitioned from a theoretical paradigm to formal, legal architecture. Most importantly, lost in this transition was the conceptual possibility for laws that belonged in both categories or in neither category.

The substance/procedure dichotomy might then have appeared more mature and developed than it was. The dichotomy was probably confused with (or perceived as equivalent to) the "right-remedy distinction," which is a concept that has historical roots that are traceable to the thirteenth century. In private international law (the international counterpart of domestic conflict of laws), the right-remedy distinction separates the underlying substantive right from the range of available remedies for its breach. And the right-remedy distinction had defined "right" so narrowly that there was very little subtlety or nuance to that traditional test; most laws fell on the "remedy" side of the divide.

But the substance/procedure dichotomy was importantly different than the right-remedy distinction. In the vernacular of the substance/procedure dichotomy, both the right and the remedy are generally part of the substantive law. Necessarily, then, procedure includes neither right nor remedy, but is instead something else. To this day, some of the confusion about the substance/procedure dichotomy is traceable to its blending with the right-remedy distinction. Some of the classic categorizations of the substance/procedure dichotomy are traceable, too. (Statutes of limitations are one example, and we discuss this below.)

Most of the contemporary confusion about the substance/procedure dichotomy is attributable to the fact that the categories *substance* and *procedure* are not inherently mutually exclusive nor cumulatively exhaustive. It is quite obvious that certain procedural rules, such as burdens of proof and the class action device, also have a substantive orientation. Likewise, certain substantive statutes, such as the statute of frauds and strict liability, also have something procedural at their core.

Some have suggested that organized confusion is the official doctrine for this dichotomy. The line between substance and procedure is routinely described as vague, unpredictable, imprecise, amorphous, unresolvable, unclear, chameleon-like, murky, blurry, hazy, and fuzzy. Professor Herbert Goodrich's *Handbook on the Conflict of Laws* (1927) advised only "that the distinction is made by courts, and the lawyer must figure it out as best he can."

Of course good litigators will help the judge make that distinction. An advocate's argument must be in the form that the judge can adopt for her order or opinion. She will not write an opinion that says: "The substance/procedure dichotomy is a mess. The cases are confused. Because there is no controlling law I can do what I want. Accordingly, I will label this law as [substantive/procedural]." Instead our argument as advocates to the court will incorporate doctrine, case law, and policy arguments in a fashion that makes a coherent argument for one label or the other. Our conclusion will also resonate with the judge's intuition (or will create the intuition) that this label is a good result.

In the choice of law context, there is an enormous number of laws that trigger the need for characterization. The following is a list of some of the most frequent battleground areas. These are the frequent battlegrounds because states vary considerably in their approaches in these areas, giving rise to "conflicts" between their laws. Also, the stakes of characterization can be very high in these areas. A common misperception of law students and young lawyers is that there will typically be recent, relevant, and binding case law on point. Yet for litigators, case precedent is surprisingly unhelpful—first, because there usually is very little of it; and second, because each case is different. Even when there is case law in your jurisdiction suggesting that the law on [issue x] was procedural, an effective litigator will have reasons—good and persuasive reasons, not trivial ones—that the [issue x] laws in the two cases warrant different results. As you read each of these, identify their "substantive" and "procedural" characteristics.

• **Prefiling requirements.** In some jurisdictions, prior to filing suit a plaintiff must perform acts x and y. These prerequisites could be part of a medical malpractice reform statute, a general tort reform statute, or a generalized effort to reduce litigation.	• **Expert affidavit requirements.** Some jurisdictions require medical malpractice (or other) plaintiffs to file with their complaint (or within x days thereof) an affidavit from a doctor attesting to the viability of the plaintiff's claim.
• **Mandatory mediation.** Some jurisdictions require one or more forms of alternative dispute resolution.	• **Heightened pleading requirements.** Statutes or procedural rules may require certain causes of action to be pled with particularity.
• **Accord and satisfaction of claims.** The conditions for release from a debt obligation vary by jurisdiction.	• **Factfinder.** Whether a cause of action is triable by a jury or a judge.

• **Claim preclusive effect of a prior judgment.** The scope of what is precluded may or may not include causes of action that were not asserted in the earlier suit.	• **Issue preclusive effect of a prior judgment.** Jurisdictions have different approaches as to prior adjudications of fact, e.g., with respect to determining whether a party's interests were adequately represented in the earlier suit.
• **Allowance of set-offs and counterclaims.** Liability rules in one jurisdiction may be inconsistent with another jurisdiction's rules for the joinder of claims.	• **Joinder of Parties.** Liability rules in one jurisdiction may be inconsistent with another jurisdiction's mandatory or permissive joinder rules.
• **Availability of interlocutory relief.** A preliminary injunction may be presumptively available in one jurisdiction for certain causes of action yet unavailable in another jurisdiction.	• **Contempt sanctions.** The authority of a judge to impose a jail term, impose fines, order shaming punishments, or require compensation to the other party can vary by jurisdiction.
• **Prejudgment interest.** Rates vary by jurisdiction.	• **Postjudgment interest.** Rates vary by jurisdiction.
• **Statute of frauds.** These statutes vary in scope, applicability, and consequences.	• **Parol evidence rule.** These vary by state, especially with respect to fraud in the inducement claims.
• **Statutes of limitations.** Lengths vary by jurisdiction.	• **Statutes of repose.** Lengths vary by jurisdiction.
• **Notice and proof of foreign law.** Requirements about proving the contents of the substantive law and the effect of failure to do so vary.	• **Burdens of proof.** A cause of action may have a tailored burden of proof. Or a jurisdiction might treat burdens of proof differently for different causes of action.
• **Competency of witnesses.** Some states are much stricter than others with respect to allowing lay and expert witness testimony.	• **Scope of privileged communications.** The scope and even the existence of privileges varies by jurisdiction.

To tackle this analysis in practice (or on exams), we need tools to help us with the characterization. A good place for you to start your brainstorming is by focusing on the underlying justification for the dichotomy. The following excerpt from the Second Restatement is a good place to start.

Restatement (Second) of Conflict of Laws

The General Principle

§ 122. Issues Relating to Judicial Administration. A court usually applies its own local law rules prescribing how litigation shall be conducted even when it applies the local law rules of another state to resolve other issues in the case.

Comment:

a. Rationale. . . . The forum is more concerned with how its judicial machinery functions and how its court processes are administered than is any other state. Also, in matters of judicial administration, it would often be disruptive or difficult for the forum to apply the local law rules of another state. The difficulties involved in doing so would not be repaid by furtherance of the values that the application of another state's local law is designed to promote.

Parties do not usually give thought to matters of judicial administration before they enter into legal transactions. They do not usually place reliance on the applicability of the rules of a particular state to issues that would arise only if litigation should become necessary. Accordingly, the parties have no expectation as to such eventualities, and there is no danger of unfairly disappointing their hopes by applying the forum's rules in such matters.

Enormous burdens are avoided when a court applies its own rules, rather than the rules of another state, to issues relating to judicial administration, such as the proper form of action, service of process, pleading, rules of discovery, mode of trial and execution and costs. Furthermore, the burdens the court spares itself would have been wasted effort in most instances, because usually the decision in the case would not be altered by applying the other state's rules of judicial administration. Even if the outcome would be altered, however, the forum will usually apply its own rule if the issue primarily concerns judicial administration. The statute of limitations is a striking example of such an issue (see § 142*). . . .

According to this excerpt, the purpose of applying forum procedural law is (1) to respect the forum's interest in matters of judicial administration; and (2) to avoid the difficulties of applying the foreign law. Further, (3) procedure is something to which the parties are not likely to have given thought in the course of the underlying transaction or occurrence. And finally, (4) procedures tend not to be outcome determinative.

---

* [Eds.' Note: Section 142 of the Second Restatement then prescribed the application of the forum state's statute of limitations even when the claim would be barred by the statute of limitations of the state whose substantive law applies. That language was adopted in 1971—an era when statutes of limitation were *ipso facto* procedural (the choice of law context). Since that time, however, several states have shifted away from that characterization; only a slim majority of states continue the follow the traditional approach. Seven states have adopted the Uniform Conflict of Laws—Limitations Act, which essentially treats statutes of limitations as substantive. Many other states have passed borrowing statutes (see Chapter 16) which achieve results that are akin to recharacterizing statutes of limitations as substantive. In 1988, the American Law Institute revised Section 142 to reflect the different approaches of states with respect to the characterization of statutes of limitations.]

An advocate arguing for the characterization of a particular issue as procedural should, if (1) and/or (2) is implicated, emphasize alignment with the justification for having the substance/procedure dichotomy. And all the better if (3) and/or (4) can confirm that characterization. If the particular issue does not align well with items (1) through (4), then emphasizing the justifications underlying the dichotomy may not be helpful. Naturally, for the advocate who is arguing for the characterization of that same issue as substantive, the roles are reversed.

Your toolkit for characterization should also include the use of prototypes. What is a prototypical *procedural* law? Imagine a law (rule, regulation, tradition, mandate) that everyone would surely agree is procedure, not substance; then examine that law's qualities. Consider, for example, a law that requires a signature on all filings with the court. What makes such a law *procedural*? It applies generically and broadly. It is unambiguous. It is a straightforward and objective mandate. It serves an administrative purpose. It does not create a right or a remedy. It is something that no one would think or care about until there is dispute. It is probably included in something labeled the rules of procedure. And so on. Although none of these descriptors is dispositive, a prototype offers a template for you to evaluate the procedural characteristics of any law.

In Practice

A strategy that you may find helpful for arguing that something is procedural (or is substantive) is to avoid using that word until you complete your analysis. A young lawyer arguing that something is procedural will often say little more than: "The law is procedural because it is about the processing of things that are procedural." A conclusory argument does not help the judge write the order resolving the dispute. Rather, argue the qualities and characteristics of the law at issue.

If all laws are either substantive or procedural, then another way to argue that something is procedural is to establish that it is *not substantive*. What is the prototypical *substantive* law? Consider, for example, the elements of a cause of action. The elements of a cause of action are substantive because they defines the scope of the parties' rights and responsibilities. It is something to which one might conform his or her behavior. Again the list would continue, and although none may be dispositive, the prototype can help you evaluate a law.

Hypothetical 10-1

Stockholders of North American Railroad Inc. (NARI) recently filed a shareholder derivative suit in a Tennessee state court. The plaintiff shareholders sued the defendant Utah corporation and its board of directors and officers, claiming that the defendants' unlawful labor violations caused hundreds of millions of dollars of financial damage to the corporation.[4]

Approximately seven years ago, when NARI employees attempted to unionize, the defendants committed egregious and pervasive violations of the National Labor Relations Act. As a result of the directors' and officers' actions, NARI was fined tens of millions of dollars by the federal government, reached settlements with employees for millions more, incurred enormous legal fees and costs, and caused a public relations disaster that devalued the company by more than $200 million.

Shareholder derivative suits typically have a number of requirements that are unique to shareholder derivative suits. In particular, pre-suit demands (from the shareholder to the officers and directors) are a standard prerequisite for shareholder derivative suits. The purpose of the pre-suit demand is to give the officers and directors the opportunity to determine whether the shareholders' claim is valid and to take corrective action. The directors have a fiduciary obligation to act reasonably and in good faith when considering and responding to the demand. If the board accepts the shareholders' demand, the corporation itself will file the suit (against the officers and directors). But if, after the expiration of a prescribed period of time, the demand is rejected or not acted upon, the shareholders may file suit.

The defendants moved to dismiss this derivative suit because of the plaintiffs' failure to make a pre-suit demand on the corporation. That motion to dismiss is pending before the Tennessee state trial court judge.

The parties agree that, because NARI is a Utah corporation, Utah law defines the parties' substantive rights and responsibilities with respect to

---

4   In a shareholder derivative suit, a shareholder sues, on behalf of the corporation, against the officers or directors of the corporation for malfeasance. The device is useful because often the officers or directors who engaged in the malfeasance still (directly or indirectly) control the corporation. Because these individuals control the corporation, that corporation is not going to sue the individuals to recoup the losses suffered by the corporation. A shareholder derivative suit allows a shareholder to sue on behalf of the corporation. To make the corporation a party to the suit, the plaintiff must name the corporation as a party defendant.

corporate internal affairs. Even though most of the officers' and directors' anti-unionization efforts were targeted at job sites in Tennessee, Utah substantive law will be applied in this case. But the parties disagree about the characterization of the pre-suit demand requirement. The defendant officers and directors argue that the requirement is bound up with—and therefore part of—the substantive law. The most important difference between the two laws regards the futility exception.

Utah's Revised Business Corporation Acts provides:

16–10a–740. Procedure in derivative proceedings.

. . .

(3) (a) A shareholder may not commence a derivative proceeding until:

(i) a written demand has been made upon the corporation to take suitable action; and

(ii) 90 days have expired from the date the demand described in Subsection (3)(a)(i) is made. . .

(c) A derivative proceeding shall comply with the procedures of Utah Rules of Civil Procedure, Rule 23.1.

Within the statutory code of Tennessee governing corporate law, the following statutory requirements appear:

48–17–401. Procedure in derivative proceedings.

(a) A person may not commence a proceeding in the right of a domestic or foreign corporation unless the person was a shareholder of the corporation when the transaction complained of occurred or unless the person became a shareholder through transfer by operation of law from one who was a shareholder at that time.

(b) A complaint in a proceeding brought in the right of a corporation must be verified and allege with particularity the demand made, if any, to obtain action by the board of directors and either that the demand was refused or ignored or why the person did not make the demand.

Tennessee courts recognize that paragraph (b) establishes a "futility exception" to the pre-suit demand requirement. The defendants concede that the plaintiff shareholders' complaint complies with the requirements of Tennessee law. The plaintiff shareholders concede that their complaint does not comply with the requirements of Utah law.

The stakes of the choice of law are significant. The failure to comply with pre-suit requirements typically leads to a dismissal with prejudice (at least with respect to the named plaintiff shareholders—and sometimes even as to all shareholders and putative plaintiffs). Moreover, because the statute of limitations has run, finding other shareholders to name as plaintiffs in another lawsuit is not an option. Is the court more likely to apply Utah's or Tennessee's pre-suit demand requirements?

This hypothetical includes many subtle details for you to leverage. These mandates appear in statutes, not rules or case law. Notice the titles of the statutes. The requirements pertain to pre-filing requirements; in other words, they prescribe conduct before there is any pending litigation. The statutory requirements are virtually identical (even if the small difference is enormously consequential on these facts); which way does that cut? What is Tennessee's interest in applying Tennessee law? Would it be cumbersome for Tennessee to apply Utah's law?

Hypothetical 10-2

Eight years ago an airplane crash occurred in Kalispell, Montana. The accident was caused by the failure of one of the two engines on the aircraft. The accident resulted in the deaths of the pilot and all four passengers aboard the flight. Two years later, litigation by all of the decedents' estates and representatives was filed in Alabama ("the primary litigation"). All of the deceased were from Alabama, and the fated plane trip departed from Tuscaloosa, Alabama.

The Alabama suit named as defendants Cessna Aircraft Company (Cessna), Bowen Aero, Inc. (Bowen), Lorris-Fassel Inc. (LFI), and Exact Gear Co. (Exact). The central allegation in the primary litigation was that the crankshaft gear in the right engine was defective and that this defect caused the accident. Cessna manufactured the aircraft. Bowen installed the engine that failed. LFI manufactured the engine. Exact manufactured the crankshaft gear and related parts. Alabama follows the traditional method for its choice of law determinations and, thus, throughout the litigation the judge applied Montana law—the place of injury. LFI went out of business and, once judgment-proof, was dismissed from the suit. On the eve of trial, the other three defendants settled the claims that were asserted against them by the plaintiffs in the primary litigation.

Recently, now four years after the primary litigation ended, Bowen filed a suit against Exact for indemnification. Bowen contends that the crankshaft gear failed to meet the applicable specifications that Bowen had provided for the fabrication of the gear. Bowen also contends that, because the engine was delivered fully assembled, disassembly to inspect for potential defects was neither required nor prudent. Bowen seeks indemnification from Exact for the $4.5 million Bowen paid to settle the primary litigation and the $474,036 it incurred in litigation costs (in the primary litigation). Because there was no privity between Bowen and Exact, this indemnification claim arises under the Montana common law, which recognizes a right of indemnity when one, who was only constructively liable to the injured party and was in no manner responsible for the harm, is compelled to pay damages because of the tortious act of another.

The parties agree that statutes of limitation are ordinarily procedural, and therefore, that the Alabama court should apply the forum state's statute of limitations.

However, the parties contest which of Alabama's statutes of limitation applies. Exact argues that Bowen's indemnification claims are time-barred by Alabama's two-year statute of limitation for tort claims. Bowen contends that his indemnity claims are quasi-contractual and, therefore, that Alabama's six-year statute of limitation for contract claims governs.

Montana and Alabama characterize Bowen's claim differently. Alabama case law characterizes this action for noncontractual indemnity as a tort. Montana case law characterizes an action for indemnity as a contract implied in law. Which state's law should be invoked to characterize the nature of Bowen's claim?

Statutes of limitation are a useful case study for the substance/procedure dichotomy. First their traditional label as *procedural* is a vestige of the right-remedy distinction; it is much easier to see how statutes of limitation fall on the remedy side of the right-remedy distinction than why they fall on the procedure side of the substance/procedure dichotomy. Second, the characterization varies on a case-by-case basis. A statute of limitation that is tailored for a particular cause of action (as opposed to a generically applicable term, that is) may be labeled *substantive* even in jurisdictions that generally treat statutes of limitation as procedural. This is sometimes explained as the right being limited by the statute that creates it. Third, the characterization varies across contexts. In the context of the *Erie* Doctrine (*see* Chapter 19), statutes of limitation are famously *substantive*, meaning that the federal court will apply the statute of limitation of state law to claims arising under state law. Fourth, the characterization of statutes of limitation as procedural for choice of law purposes is not uniform across jurisdictions: for example, eight states have adopted the Uniform Conflict of Laws—Limitations Act, which treats statutes of limitation as substantive. And finally, fifth, the characterization of a statute of limitation must be considered in the context of other doctrines in this course. Specifically, in Chapter 16, you will learn how borrowing statutes lead a court to apply the foreign statute of limitation even when statutes of limitation are nominally procedural.

Hypothetical 10-3

Bat Aldisert was driving on a highway in Jacksonville Beach, Florida when the tread on the left rear tire of his late-model minivan separated. The tire separation caused the vehicle to swerve and, ultimately, overturn. Aldisert, who was not wearing a seat belt, was ejected from the vehicle. He suffered serious injuries, including paraplegia.

The minivan was registered in Florida. Aldisert is a domiciliary of Connecticut and has been since 1976. For many years prior to the accident, Aldisert spent several months of each winter in Florida. After the accident and his immediate hospitalization in Florida, Aldisert was flown to Connecticut where he remains.

The tire on the minivan was a Noll Steel 6, manufactured by Cowher Tire, Inc. in Albany, New York. Nine days prior to the accident, Aldisert's vehicle was serviced at a Wal-Mart store in Jacksonville Beach, Florida.

In a Connecticut state court, Aldisert filed a product liability action against Cowher Tire, Inc., Wal-Mart, Inc., and CT InsPect Co. Cowher Tire, Inc. is a Delaware corporation with a principal place of business in Albany, New York. Wal-Mart, Inc., is a Delaware corporation with a principal place of business in Bentonville, Arkansas. CT InsPect Co. is a company that Cowher Tire uses for some of its product testing. CT InsPect Co. is a Delaware corporation with a principal place of business in West Hartford, Connecticut.

Connecticut follows the Second Restatement for its choice of law methodology. Early in the case, the trial judge issued a tentative ruling that the State of Florida had the most significant relationship to the parties and events, and therefore, that the parties should reference Florida substantive law. But with respect to procedural matters, of course, *lex fori* applies.

Connecticut law would preclude any evidence of Aldisert's nonuse of an available seat belt. With certain exceptions not applicable here, Section 14–100a(c)(1) of the Connecticut General Statute requires the operator and any front seat passenger to wear a seat belt while the motor vehicle is being operated on the highway. Section 14–100a(c)(3), in turn, provides "Failure to wear a seat safety belt shall not be considered as contributory negligence nor shall such failure be admissible evidence in any civil action." Aldisert's lawyer argues that Connecticut's seat belt statute is a procedural rule of evidence that the Connecticut court must apply. The legislative history behind this 1985 legislation emphasizes the legislature's desire to "abolish the seat belt defense."

> Since 1984, Florida law has provided for a seat belt defense in the context of comparative negligence. The Florida Supreme Court recently described the defense and its elements as follows: "Defendant has the burden of pleading and proving that the plaintiff did not use an available and operational seat belt, that the plaintiff's failure to use the seat belt was unreasonable under the circumstances, and that there was a causal relationship between the injuries sustained by the plaintiff and plaintiff's failure to buckle up."

How should the court handle Aldisert's nonuse of a seat belt with respect to his negligence suit?

FROM THE COURTS

BOSWELL v. RFD-TV THE THEATER, LLC

Court of Appeals of Tennessee
498 S.W.3d 550 (Tenn. Ct. App. 2016)

BRANDON O. GIBSON, JUDGE.

. . . I. Facts & Procedural History

Plaintiff Troy L. Boswell is a musical performer and a resident of Goodlettsville, Tennessee. He is professionally known as "Leroy Troy." Defendant RFD-TV The Theater, LLC (the "Theater") owns and operates a musical venue in Branson, Missouri. On February 5, 2007, the Theater entered into an entertainment services agreement (the "Contract") with Boswell.

Pursuant to the Contract, the Theater agreed to purchase from Boswell "[m]usical performances for the 2007 season," with a starting date of March 1, 2007, and an ending date of October 31, 2007. The Contract listed 21 days during that period when Boswell would be unavailable, due to previous bookings, and the parties agreed that a pro-rata amount of $715 per day would be deducted from Boswell's weekly fee for those absences. The Contract provided that Boswell's shows would last no more than 45 minutes, and he would perform no more than ten shows per week. However, the specific show dates and times were "[t]o be determined and mutually agreed upon by both parties."

The Contract provided that from March 1 until the opening date of the venue, the Theater would pay Boswell $2,500 per week for rehearsals. Once the venue opened to the public, the Theater would pay Boswell $5,000 per week for the services provided. The Theater agreed to pay a $5,000 deposit to Boswell upon execution of the agreement, which would be applied to the payment for the final week of the contract term. The Contract also contained the following provisions:

> BREACH OF CONTRACT. In the event of any action, suit or proceeding arising from or based on this agreement brought by either party hereto against the other, the prevailing party shall be entitled to recover from the other its reasonable attorney's fees in connection therewith in addition to the costs of that action, suit or proceeding.

> GOVERNING LAW. This Agreement shall be governed by and construed in accordance with the laws of the State of Nebraska.

The parties agree that the Theater paid Boswell the $5,000 deposit as an advance payment for his final week of performances, and it also paid him $2,500 per week for rehearsals from March 1 until March 29, 2007, when the Theater opened to the public. Thereafter, Boswell performed a total of 60 shows at the Theater from its public opening on March 29 through June 28, 2007. The Theater paid Boswell $5,000 per week during that time. However, on July 1, 2007, the president of the Theater called a meeting with all staff and crew and announced that the show was cancelled.

On July 9, 2007, Boswell's attorney sent a letter to the Theater advising it that Boswell was ready, willing, and able to perform pursuant to the parties' Contract. The letter suggested that the Theater was "in material breach" of the Contract by terminating Boswell's weekly payments of $5,000 and indicating that it would no longer honor the Contract. The letter stated that Boswell was making every effort to mitigate his damages, but due to such late notice, he had not been successful in his efforts. Boswell claimed that he was entitled to $5,000 for the previous week's missed payment and "approximately $80,000 in additional compensation." He requested that the Theater contact his attorney "to work out payment of damages," but the Theater never responded to the letter or made payment to Boswell as requested in the letter.

On October 11, 2007, Boswell filed this lawsuit in Davidson County Circuit Court. He named as defendants the Theater and other separate but related entities. The complaint sought recovery based on breach of contract and/or promissory estoppel. The complaint alleged that the term of the Contract was from March 1, 2007, until October 31, 2007, and therefore, the Theater breached the Contract by cancelling the show on July 1, 2007, and discontinuing payments to Boswell. Boswell alleged that he was ready, willing, and able to perform under the Contract but was not allowed to do so. He sought damages for breach of contract in the amount of $82,140. Specifically, he sought $5,000 for each of the remaining weeks of the contract (equaling $90,000), minus the $5,000 deposit already paid, minus the pro rata fee of $715 for four days he would have missed during the remainder of the contract term, totaling $2,860. He also sought an award of prejudgment interest and an award of attorney's fees as provided in the parties' Contract.

The case remained pending for several years. Throughout the proceedings, the parties agreed that Nebraska law applied to the substantive issues in the case, while Tennessee law governed procedural issues. The parties stipulated that the Theater had already paid Boswell a total of $77,500 pursuant to the Contract. However, the Theater asserted that it had no further obligation to pay Boswell after it cancelled the show on July 1, 2007, because the Contract provided that show dates and times were "[t]o be determined and mutually agreed upon by both parties." The Theater claimed that this constituted an unenforceable "agreement to agree."

The trial court held a bench trial from November 17 to November 19, 2014. On March 4, 2015, the court entered a final order entering a judgment in favor of Boswell. The trial court found the contract enforceable, valid, and unambiguous. The court concluded that the Contract was for a specific term—from March 1 through October 31, 2007. The court concluded that

Boswell was obligated to be available to perform during that time, with specific dates and times to be determined on an ongoing basis, and it found that his payment was not conditioned on the number of performances. The court found that the Theater materially breached the Contract by cancelling the show on July 1, 2007, due to no fault of Boswell, and by failing to pay him the weekly sum due under the Contract.

The trial court looked to the Contract to calculate Boswell's damages. It found that he was entitled to be paid $2,500 per week for the four-week period between March 1 and the opening of the Theater on March 30, 2007, for a total of $10,000, in addition to $5,000 per week for the remaining thirty-one weeks of the Contract term, for a total of $155,000. In sum, he was to be paid $165,000 during the term of the Contract. As noted above, the Theater paid Boswell $77,500 prior to the cancellation of the show. The trial court found that the Theater was entitled to deduct from the amount owed the pro rata allowance for the 21 dates specified in the Contract for previously booked performances, at the rate of $715 per day, for a total deduction of $15,015. Finally, the trial court found that Boswell had a duty to mitigate his damages and did so by making reasonable attempts to find other work. The trial court found that he earned $1,741 from performances and merchandise sales, which the trial court deducted from the amount owed by the Theater. In sum, the trial court calculated Boswell's damages for breach of contract at $70,744.

The trial court granted Plaintiff's request for prejudgment interest pursuant to Nebraska Revised Statutes section 45–104. Applying the statutory rate of 12%, and calculating the amount owed from October 31, 2007, through November 19, 2014, the trial court awarded Boswell $59,864.18 in prejudgment interest.

The trial court also awarded Boswell $90,000 in attorney's fees pursuant to the attorney's fee provision in the parties' Contract. The trial court acknowledged the parties' choice of law provision specifying that the law of Nebraska would apply to the Contract. Under Nebraska law, "[i]n the absence of a uniform course of procedure or authorization by statute, contractual agreements for attorney fees are against public policy and will not be judicially enforced." *Stewart v. Bennett*, 727 N.W.2d 424, 426 (Neb. 2007). However, the trial court predicted that a Tennessee appellate court would hold that attorney's fees are a matter of procedural law. Because the law of the forum state governs procedural issues, the trial court applied Tennessee law and found the parties' contract attorneys' fees provision enforceable.

The Theater timely filed a notice of appeal to this Court and now challenges the trial court's awards of . . . attorney's fees under Nebraska law. . . .

[II.] Discussion

When deciding which state's law to apply to a particular dispute, courts undertake a choice of law analysis using the rules applicable in the forum state. As a general rule, the first step is to decide whether a conflict actually exists between the relevant laws of the different jurisdictions. . . .

A conflict clearly exists in the case at bar. In the context of contract interpretation, Tennessee allows an exception to the American rule, which would otherwise prohibit an award of attorney's fees, when a contract specifically or expressly provides for the recovery of attorney's fees. *Cracker Barrel Old Country Store, Inc. v. Epperson*, 284 S.W.3d 303, 309 (Tenn. 2009). . . . To the contrary, the Nebraska Supreme Court "has repeatedly held that in the absence of a uniform course of procedure or authorization by statute, contractual agreements for attorney fees are against public policy and will not be judicially enforced." *Stewart*, 727 N.W.2d at 429. Because an actual conflict exists between Tennessee law and Nebraska law, we will proceed with the choice of law analysis.

"Tennessee will honor a choice of law clause if the state whose law is chosen bears a reasonable relation to the transaction and absent a violation of the forum state's public policy." *Bourland, Heflin, Alvarez, Minor & Matthews, PLC v. Heaton*, 393 S.W.3d 671, 674 (Tenn. Ct. App. 2012). Here, the parties chose the law of Nebraska, where the Theater is headquartered, to govern the Contract, and both parties agree that the choice of law clause is valid and enforceable.

Despite the parties' choice of law, however, Tennessee law governs matters of procedure under our conflict of laws principles. *In re Healthways, Inc. Derivative Litig.*, 2011 WL 882448, at *3 (Tenn. Ct. App. Mar. 14, 2011). Matters of procedure are governed by the law of the forum. *State ex rel. Smith v. Early*, 934 S.W.2d 655, 658 (Tenn. Ct. App. 1996). In other words, we apply our own procedural rules even if the law of another state governs the substantive issues. . . . However, the line is not always clear regarding which matters are substantive and which are procedural.

In Tennessee, substantive law has been described as "that part of the law which creates, defines, and regulates rights; that which creates duties, rights, and obligations; the law which relates to rights and duties which give rise to a cause of action." *Solomon v. FloWarr Mgmt., Inc.*, 777 S.W.2d 701, 705 (Tenn. Ct. App. 1989). We also consider whether the law is "substantive in effect" even if it would initially appear to be "procedural in form." *Gordon's Transports, Inc. v. Bailey*, 294 S.W.2d 313, 324 (1956). Where a rule from another state

> is such that it goes to the very existence of the contract or the right
> of the plaintiff to recover, or of the defendant to resist recovery,
> whether that rule is to be denominated as one of remedy or of sub-
> stance, the fact is that it affects the substantive rights of the parties
> and should therefore be applied, notwithstanding a contrary rule
> of the forum.

Id. (citing 11 Am.Jur pages 523–24, Conflict of Laws, Sec. 203).

The first issue we address on appeal is whether the trial court erred in awarding Boswell attorney's fees on the basis that the issue is procedural and governed by Tennessee law. . . . [W]e review *de novo* the trial court's decision regarding which state's law applies to the issue of attorney's fees.

Tennessee appellate courts have not explicitly addressed whether attorney's fees are a substantive or procedural matter for purposes of conflicts of law. This Court considered the issue on one occasion but found it unnecessary to resolve under the particular circumstances of the case before us. *See McRedmond v. Estate of Marianelli*, 2006 WL 2805158, at *20 (Tenn. Ct. App. Sept. 29, 2006) *overruled by House v. Estate of Edmonson*, 245 S.W.3d 372 (Tenn. 2008) ("we find it unnecessary to address the question of whether an award of attorney's fees is governed by procedural or substantive law"). In another case, we interpreted a contract according to Texas law but then cited Tennessee law when it came to the issue of attorney's fees. *See Cagle v. Hybner*, 2008 WL 2649643, at *21 (Tenn. Ct. App. July 3, 2008). However, we did not discuss whether attorney's fees are a substantive or procedural matter, or otherwise explain why we cited Tennessee law rather than Texas law, probably because the opposing parties conceded that the prevailing party was entitled to recover his attorney's fees. Accordingly, we find no guidance on this issue in the *Cagle* opinion.

Courts in several other jurisdictions have expressly considered whether awards of attorney's fees are governed by substantive or procedural law for purposes of conflicts of law.[3] However, those decisions have produced mixed results. Some courts have held that issues involving attorney's fees are procedural and governed by the law of the forum. *See, e.g., Alaska Rent-A-Car, Inc. v. Avis Budget Grp., Inc.*, 738 F.3d 960, 974 (9th Cir. 2013) (predicting that the Alaska Supreme Court would hold, for choice of law purposes, that its attorney's fee rule is procedural); *Sentinel Indus. Contracting Corp. v. Kimmins Indus. Serv. Corp*, 743 So.2d 954, 960 (Miss. 1999) ("In Mississippi, the law of the forum applies to all procedural and remedial issues. That includes attorneys' fees[.]"); *Neb. Nutrients, Inc. v. Shepherd*, 626 N.W.2d 472, 518 (Neb. 2001) ("Nebraska law deems the recovery of attorney fees in the action in which they are incurred to be a procedural issue governed by the law of the forum");[4] *N. Bergen Rex Transp., Inc. v. Trailer Leasing Co.*, 730 A.2d 843, 848 (N.J. 1999) ("attorneys' fees are a matter of practice and procedure, rather than of substantive law"); *GB Auctions, Inc. v. Private Ledger, Inc.*, 2014 WL 4627773, at *5 (Wash. Sept. 16, 2014) (finding contractual attorney's fees to be a procedural issue governed by the law of the forum); *Smithco Eng'g, Inc. v. Int'l Fabricators, Inc.*, 775 P.2d 1011, 1017 n.4 (Wyo. 1989) (finding a statute that authorized awards of attorney's fees to a prevailing party, "to be taxed and collected as costs," was procedural).

Other courts have held that attorney's fees are substantive issues. *See, e.g., PVI, Inc. v. Ratiopharm GmbH*, 253 F.3d 320, 329 (8th Cir. 2001) (explaining that Missouri law regards a contractual right to attorney's fees as a substantive right created by the contract and governed by the substantive law applicable to the contract generally); *Boyd Rosene & Assocs., Inc. v. Kan. Mun. Gas Agency*, 174 F.3d 1115, 1125 (10th Cir. 1999) (predicting under Oklahoma choice-of-law principles that attorney's fees would be considered a substantive issue in a contractual dispute); *Aries v. Palmer Johnson, Inc.*,

---

3   We limit our discussion to cases deciding the issue in the choice-of-law context. Many courts have addressed whether attorney's fees are a matter of substantive or procedural law for other purposes, such as arbitration proceedings, retroactivity issues, and situations where federal courts apply substantive state law. However, "[t]he line between 'substance' and 'procedure' shifts as the legal context changes." *Hanna v. Plumer*, 380 U.S. 460, 471 (1965). The Restatement comment cautions against "unthinking adherence to precedents that have classified a given issue as 'procedural' or 'substantive,' regardless of what purposes were involved in the earlier classifications." Restatement (Second) of Conflict of Laws § 122, cmt. b (1971). It warns that a decision classifying a matter as "procedural" for one purpose might mistakenly be held controlling on the question of whether the same matter is "procedural" for choice-of-law purposes. *Id.*

4   To be clear, when we apply the substantive law of another state, we do not also apply the other state's choice of law principles. Nebraska's view regarding whether attorney's fees are substantive or procedural does not control our analysis of the issue.

735 P.2d 1373, 1381 (Ariz. Ct. App. 1987) (holding that the recovery of contractual attorney's fees as authorized by statute was a substantive issue); *Seattle-First Nat'l Bank v. Schriber*, 625 P.2d 1370, 1373 (1981) (concluding that a statute authorizing contractual attorney's fee awards involved a matter of substantive right).

Some courts recognize a distinction between different types of claims for attorney's fees, such as those awarded to a party for prevailing on its claim versus those assessed against a party as sanctions for bad faith litigation practices. . . . [W]e emphasize that the precise issue presented in this case is narrow—is a claim for attorney's fees *pursuant to a contract* a substantive issue governed by a choice of law provision in that contract, or is such a claim governed by the procedural law of the forum? It is not necessary for purposes of this appeal to broadly classify all types of claims for attorney's fees and we do not purport to do so.

The Texas Court of Appeals has reasoned that a contractual claim for attorney's fees is "part of [the] substantive claim for breach of contract." *Midwest Med. Supply Co. v. Wingert*, 317 S.W.3d 530, 537 (Tex. Ct. App. 2010). The court found the issue of attorney's fees "inextricably intertwined with the substantive issue of contractual liability—an issue that is undisputably [sic] governed by the choice-of-law provision." *Id.* (quoting *Fairmont Supply Co. v. Hooks Indus., Inc.*, 177 S.W.3d 529, 535–36 (Tex. Ct. App. 2005)). Accordingly, the Texas court viewed the attorney's fee claim as a substantive contractual issue governed by the law chosen by the parties. *Id.* In reaching the same conclusion, the Oregon Court of Appeals considered that attorney's fees based on a contract must be plead and proved and "are not merely costs incidental to judicial administration," therefore, awarding them is a matter of substantive right. *Schriber*, 625 P.2d at 1373. In contrast, the Nebraska Supreme court considers attorney's fees to be elements of court costs that affect only the remedy, rather than damages. *Neb. Nutrients*, 626 N.W.2d at 518. The Nebraska Court considers an attorney's fee provision to be "a stipulation for costs" that "is not a substantive part of the contract itself and cannot be enforced in another jurisdiction." *Id.*

Tennessee's view of contractual attorney's fees is more in line with the courts of Texas and Oregon. "In Tennessee, attorney's fees are not part of costs." *Barrett v. Town of Nolensville*, 2011 WL 856923, at *2 (Tenn. Ct. App. Mar. 10, 2011); *see also Cracker Barrel Old Country Store, Inc.*, 284 S.W.3d at 310 ("The term 'costs' has not generally been construed to encompass attorney fees."). Furthermore, as noted above, Tennessee courts have described "substantive law" as "that part of the law which creates, defines, and regulates rights; that which creates duties, rights, and obligations; the law which relates to rights and duties which give rise to a cause of action." *Solomon*, 777 S.W.2d at 705 (quoting *Spencer Kellogg & Sons, Inc.*, 315 S.W.2d at 518). Contracts providing for attorney's fees impose a contractual liability that one enforces as a matter of substantive right. Rules regarding the recovery of contractual attorney's fees define the parties' rights and obligations. Accordingly, we conclude that a state's rules regarding the recovery of contractual attorney's fees are substantive rules governing the substantive rights of the parties.

In the case at bar, Boswell's claim for attorney's fees pursuant to the attorney's fee provision in the contract is part and parcel of his substantive claim for breach of contract. Accordingly, it should be governed by the choice-of-law provision in that same Contract. The choice-of-law provision states that the Contract is to be governed by and construed in accordance with the laws of the State of Nebraska, and therefore, Nebraska law applies to the provision providing for the recovery of attorney's fees for breach of the contract. We decline to apply Tennessee caselaw regarding contractual attorney's fees provisions to the parties' Contract otherwise governed by the substantive law of Nebraska.

Under the governing Nebraska law, "a contractual provision for attorney fees, where such fees are not provided by statute or uniform course of procedure, is against public policy and will not be judicially enforced." *Stewart*, 727 N.W.2d at 427–28. Consequently, the attorney's fee provision in the parties' Contract is unenforceable pursuant to Nebraska law. . . .

In sum, we conclude that the choice-of-law provision in the parties' Contract determines the law applicable to the attorney's fee provision in the Contract. Thus, Nebraska law governs the issue. Under Nebraska law, Boswell is not entitled to recover his attorney's fees in connection with his claim for breach of contract. We reverse the trial court's ruling to the contrary and vacate its award of attorney's fees. . . .

COMMENTS AND QUESTIONS

1. The court's holding worked a detriment to a local citizen and, instead, benefitted the foreign defendant. (What does this say about the embedded preference for local citizens?) The court applied foreign law. (What does this say about the homeward trend?) The court invalidated a fee-shifting clause in an otherwise enforceable contract. (What does this say about the rule of validation?) The court invalidated a clause that was, in all likelihood, drafted by the Theater. (What does this say about *contra proferentem*, the canon of contractual interpretation that construes unclear provisions against the drafter?)

2. The plaintiffs were awarded a significant amount of prejudgment interest. Prejudgment interest rates vary significantly among jurisdictions. Is the prejudgment interest rate a matter of substantive or procedural law?

3. Plaintiff's counsel needed to provide the court with an argument about the forum state's *interest* in applying forum law with respect to attorney's fee. Is that interest *procedural* or *substantive*?

FROM THE COURTS

MIDDLETON v. CATERPILLAR INDUSTRIAL, INC.

Supreme Court of Alabama
979 So.2d 53 (Ala. 2007)

COBB, CHIEF JUSTICE.

Daniel A. Middleton, Jr., the plaintiff in a personal-injury action in the Mobile Circuit Court appeals from a summary judgment in favor of the sole remaining defendant, Caterpillar Industrial, Inc. We reverse and remand.

I. Background

Middleton was employed as a maintenance mechanic by Ryan-Walsh, Inc., now known as Stevedoring Services of America Gulf Terminals, Inc. (hereinafter "SSA"), at its facility in Charleston, South Carolina. On December 21,

2000, Middleton drove a Caterpillar Model T50D industrial lift truck into a parking lot, raised the mast and carriage of the lift truck approximately 11 to 13 feet, and, while the lift truck was still running, stood in front of the lift truck—and under the raised mast and carriage—to troubleshoot a reported leak in the hydraulics of the lift truck. He did not attempt to support the carriage in any manner. As Middleton searched for the leak, a loss of hydraulic pressure occurred, causing the mast and carriage to fall, crushing Middleton's right arm near his shoulder. The injury required surgical amputation of his right arm.

Shortly before his injury, on September 28, 2000, Middleton had filed for Chapter 13 bankruptcy protection in the United States Bankruptcy Court for the District of South Carolina. As part of his Schedule B, which requires the debtor to list personal property, Middleton was obligated to disclose "[o]ther contingent and unliquidated claims of every nature, including tax refunds, counterclaims of the debtor, and rights to setoff claims." Middleton never amended his Schedule B after he was injured to show his potential claim against Caterpillar, and on March 1, 2001, the bankruptcy court approved Middleton's proposed bankruptcy plan without disclosure of that claim. However, the bankruptcy proceeding was dismissed on June 8, 2001, because of Middleton's failure to comply with the orders of the bankruptcy court.

Middleton again filed for Chapter 13 bankruptcy protection in the Bankruptcy Court for the District of South Carolina on June 28, 2001. Middleton did not disclose in his Schedule B filed in the second bankruptcy proceeding his potential claim against Caterpillar. The bankruptcy court approved Middleton's bankruptcy plan on August 27, 2001. The plan allowed Middleton to avoid certain nonpossessory, non-purchase-money security interests as well as to pay his general unsecured creditors only 5 percent of their allowed claims over a 54-month period.

Middleton's bankruptcy counsel filed a motion with the bankruptcy court on February 3, 2005, seeking a three-month moratorium on Middleton's payments under the bankruptcy plan. As grounds for his motion, Middleton's bankruptcy counsel stated that Middleton "has had substantial difficulty making his required payments due to his short term disability ending and having no income while he awaits to be put on long-term disability." The bankruptcy court granted the motion on February 28, 2005.

As a result of his injury, Middleton filed a worker's compensation claim against his employer, SSA, under the Longshore and Harbor Workers' Compensation Act, 33 U.S.C. § 901 et seq. On April 28, 2005, the United States Department of Labor's Office of Workers' Compensation Programs approved a settlement between SSA and Middleton pursuant to which Middleton received $69,900. At no time did Middleton submit an amended Schedule B notifying the bankruptcy court and his creditors of his worker's compensation claim, either after the claim was filed or after the settlement was approved.

On December 20, 2002, Middleton filed the underlying personal-injury action in the Mobile Circuit Court, asserting that one of the named defendants, Ryan-Walsh, Inc., now known as SSA, was an Alabama corporation whose principal place of business was Mobile County. Even after the personal-injury action was filed, Middleton did not amend his Schedule B to notify the bankruptcy court of his potential claim against Caterpillar. Among the interrogatories propounded upon Middleton by Caterpillar was the following:

> State whether you have ever been involved in any other legal action in any country or jurisdiction (including any bankruptcy matter), and, if so, identify the date, place nature of and disposition of each such action, giving the name of the court, the name of the other party or parties involved, the number of such action, and the names of the attorneys representing each party.

On August 18, 2005, Middleton submitted to Caterpillar the following sworn amended answer in response to the above-quoted interrogatory: "Plaintiff filed a worker's compensation claim as a result of this accident." Middleton never did disclose in his responses to interrogatories that he had filed a petition in bankruptcy.

On October 26, 2005, Caterpillar moved the trial court for a summary judgment in its favor based on the doctrine of judicial estoppel, asserting that Middleton had never disclosed his claim against Caterpillar as an asset in the bankruptcy proceeding. Only after Caterpillar filed its motion for a summary judgment did Middleton amend his Schedule B to include his claim against Caterpillar, as well as his worker's compensation settlement. In response to Caterpillar's summary-judgment motion, Middleton stated that he was unaware that he should have amended his Schedule B and that his failure to do so "was inadvertent at most." The trial court, however, agreed with Caterpillar that Middleton was judicially estopped from pursuing his action against Caterpillar, and it granted Caterpillar's summary-judgment motion. . . .

[II.] Judicial Estoppel and Lex Loci Delicti

Our review of the summary judgment in this case is based upon the principle of *lex loci delicti*, under which the courts of this state "will determine the substantive rights of an injured party according to the law of the state where the injury occurred." *Fitts v. Minnesota Mining & Mfg. Co.*, 581 So.2d 819, 829 (Ala. 1991). For 115 years, the principle of *lex loci delicti* has governed cases such as this one in Alabama courts. *Fitts*, 581 So.2d 819 (reaffirming the doctrine of *lex loci delicti* and declining to adopt the "most significant relationship" approach of the Restatement (Second) of Conflict of Laws (1971)). . . . Although *lex loci delicti* governs substantive law, *lex fori*—the law of the forum—governs procedural matters.

"The distinction between 'substance' and 'procedure' has medieval origins: a court will apply foreign law only to the extent it deals with the substance of the case, i.e., affects the outcome of the litigation, but will rely on the forum law to deal with the 'procedural' aspects of the litigation." *Etheredge v. Genie Indus., Inc.*, 632 So.2d 1324, 1326–27 (Ala. 1994). In its order granting Caterpillar's summary-judgment motion, the trial court determined that the doctrine of judicial estoppel is procedural in nature and, thus, Alabama law applies in this case. On appeal, Middleton argues that the doctrine of judicial estoppel is substantive in nature and that the trial court therefore should have applied the laws of South Carolina relating to the doctrine of judicial estoppel.

"The court before which the question arises is the one that has to decide whether any rule of law, domestic or foreign, will be characterized as substantive or as procedural for choice-of-law purposes." *Etheredge*, 632 So.2d at 1326. The question of whether the doctrine of judicial estoppel sounds in substantive or procedural law is one of first impression for this Court.

This Court has defined judicial estoppel in the following manner:

> The doctrine of judicial estoppel "applies to preclude a party from assuming a position in a legal proceeding inconsistent with one previously asserted. Judicial estoppel looks to the connection between the litigant and the judicial system[,] while equitable estop-

pel focuses on the relationship between the parties to the prior litigation." *Jinright v. Paulk,* 758 So.2d 553, 555 (Ala. 2000).

Ex parte First Alabama Bank, 883 So.2d 1236, 1241 (Ala. 2003). The United States Court of Appeals for the Seventh Circuit has described the doctrine of judicial estoppel as "a hybrid between substance and procedure that on occasion affects the outcome." *Astor Chauffeured Limousine Co. v. Runnfeldt Inv. Corp.*, 910 F.2d 1540, 1551 (7th Cir. 1990).

[W]e find the argument that judicial estoppel is procedural in nature to be the more persuasive argument. The purpose of judicial estoppel is "to protect the integrity of the judicial process by prohibiting parties from deliberately changing positions according to the exigencies of the moment." *New Hampshire v. Maine*, 532 U.S. 742, 749–50 (2001). . . . Simply stated, "judicial estoppel prevents parties from playing fast and loose with the courts," *id.* at 750, and prevents "the system from being manipulated by chameleonic litigants." *Blanton v. Inco Alloys Int'l, Inc.*, 108 F.3d 104, 108 (6th Cir. 1997). This Court has observed:

> Judicial estoppel . . . strives to preserve the sanctity of the oath and protect the integrity of the judicial process. Reliance is not a factor because any inconsistent statement violates the sanctity of the oath and injures the integrity of the judicial process, whether or not some party relied on the first statement. The inconsistency itself damages public confidence in the purity . . . of judicial proceedings.

Ex parte First Alabama Bank, 883 So.2d at 1244. Other courts have noted that "[j]udicial estoppel is a *rule of procedure* under which a party is estopped from taking a position contrary to that taken in prior proceedings." *Heller v. Plave*, 743 F. Supp. 1553, 11571 (S.D. Fla. 1990) (emphasis added); *see also Oscar Mayer foods corp. v. ConAgra, Inc.*, No. 94–1247, Dec. 22, 1994) (Fed. Cir. 1994) ("Judicial estoppel is a *procedural matter*, reviewed under the law of the regional circuit in which the court sits." (emphasis added).

Middleton argues that judicial estoppel is substantive in nature because, he says, it affects the outcome of the litigation in that its application would extinguish his right to pursue this litigation. However, this Court has noted:

> [I]t is simplistic to assume that all law is divided neatly between "substance" and "procedure." A rule of procedure may have an impact upon the substantive result and be no less a rule of procedure

> on that account. . . . As said in *Hanna v. Plumer*, 380 U.S. 460, 471 (1965), "The line between 'substance' and 'procedure' shifts as the legal context changes. Each implies different variables depending upon the particular problem for which it is used."

Schoenvogel v. Venator Group Retail, Inc., 895 So.2d 225, 250 (Ala. 2004). Although the doctrine of judicial estoppel had "an impact upon the substantive result" in Middleton's case, it is "no less a rule of procedure on that account." *Schoenvogel*, 895 So.2d at 250. The primary purpose of the doctrine of judicial estoppel is to protect the integrity of our judicial system from those who may play "fast and loose with the courts." *Consolidated Stores, Inc. v. Gargis*, 686 So.2d 268, 276 (Ala. Civ. App. 1996). Therefore, we conclude that judicial estoppel is procedural in nature, and the rule of *lex fori* shall apply. Thus, the trial court was correct to apply Alabama caselaw regarding the doctrine of judicial estoppel. . . .

COMMENTS AND QUESTIONS

1. The court does not outline the stakes of this characterization: we do not learn how South Carolina's law with respect to judicial estoppel differs from Alabama's. The lawyers may not have educated the judge on the significance of the choice of law. Or is it because the stakes are irrelevant to the characterization question?

2. The court quotes an earlier decision that referred to the "medieval origins" of the distinction between substance and procedure. Although the right-remedy distinction has medieval origins, the substance/procedure dichotomy was introduced in the late eighteenth century. It is often in the interest of one of the parties to elide the distinction between right/remedy and substance/procedure. (And of course, conversely, it is in the interest of the other party to prevent the judge from making this mistake.)

3. Imagine that you represented Caterpillar. During oral argument on the summary judgment motion the judge says, "To label judicial estoppel as procedural is to say that Alabama law rather than South Carolina law should determine the consequences of Middleton's conduct in South Carolina courts. This means that Middleton did not—and could not— know the full consequences of his conduct at the time that he engaged in

it. Indeed, the consequences of those actions would not be known until some later litigation when some other jurisdiction applied its law. How can that be the right outcome, counsel?" What would your answer be?

Quick Summary

- Courts will apply forum procedure even when the choice of law methodology prescribes the application of another jurisdiction's substantive law

- The substance/procedure dichotomy requires a species of characterization; yet the categories of substance and procedure are inherently neither mutually exclusive nor cumulatively exhaustive

- The substance/procedure dichotomy varies according to the situation; often it is highly debatable

- The justifications for applying forum procedural law (even when applying foreign substantive law) are feasibility, efficiency, and the forum state's interest in having its procedural law applied

- The application of forum procedural law could lead to over- or under-enforcement of the substantive rights prescribed by foreign law

11

Public Policy Exception

Key Concepts

- Distinguishing strong or fundamental public policy, from merely different public policy
- The public policy exception is an important escape device

This Chapter is about the public policy exception. Talk of the exception arises whenever a court finds that the public policy of the forum would be offended by the content of the foreign law that its choice of law methodology directs it to apply. We first mentioned this topic in Chapter 4. The public policy exception lurked also in Chapters 5, 6, 7, 8, and 9. It can be controversial and is prone to be used to manipulate results. On one hand, the direction to apply foreign law could be independent of the content of that foreign law. After all, isn't the decision to apply foreign law a commitment to apply foreign law, whatever its content? But on the other hand, applying foreign laws that offend local sensibilities or fly in the face of strongly-held forum public policies compromises the integrity and legitimacy of the local judicial system. It is almost as if the court decided to import a dangerous disease. Why put the imprimatur of the judicial process behind bad laws?

The public policy exception tries to reconcile the tension between applying foreign law in the ordinary course, yet sometimes ignoring it and applying forum law instead. All of the choice of law methodologies are sensitive to local public policy, and this chapter brings the commonality of that rhetoric into relief. The terminology may vary among the various methodological approaches, but once you master the public policy exception in any one context you have mastered it for all of them—even if you need to tailor the argument for the specific context.

First, let us highlight how the public policy exception surfaces in each of the choice of law methodologies. You will recall that the jurisdiction-selecting rules of the First Restatement directed the court to apply the law of the place of injury, the place of contracting, or some other definite place. But rigid rules inevitably create "mischief" because mechanical formulas occasionally produce outcomes that are nonsensical, unfair, or inequitable. A principal mechanism for avoiding especially unpleasant outcomes was the public policy exception. It was a hallmark (and pockmark) of the traditional approach, and was codified in the (First) Restatement of Conflicts:

> No action can be maintained upon a cause of action created in another state the enforcement of which is contrary to the strong public policy of the forum.

Restatement of Conflict of Laws § 612 (1934).

This excuse to depart from the jurisdiction-selecting rules undermined the certainty and predictability of the traditional approach which, of course, were its raison d'être. The exception was easy to invoke and its use became one of the reasons for the decline in popularity of the traditional approach. Because it is debatable when a foreign law "is contrary to the strong public policy of the forum," one could scarcely distinguish its principled use from its unprincipled use. When the traditional approach could not deliver on its promise of certainty and predictability, the alternative approaches surfaced.

The methods that replaced the traditional approach were more sophisticated in their methodology, but something resembling a public policy exception is incorporated into all of them. In interest analysis, the "final step" is to determine whether a public policy exception precludes the application of another state's law.[1] Jurisdictions that follow the center-of-gravity approach will not apply foreign law that violates local public policy even when its center of gravity analysis indicates that it should.[2] Finally, the better law approach puts the public policy choice in the center of the choice of law inquiry.[3]

The Second Restatement followed suit.

> No action will be entertained on a foreign cause of action the enforcement of which is contrary to the strong public policy of the forum.

---

1   *Cooney v. Osgood Mach., Inc.*, 81 N.Y.2d 66, 78 (1993).

2   *See, e.g., Zurich American Ins. Co. v. Goodwin*, 920 So.2d 427, 437 (Miss. 2006).

3   The fifth of Leflar's choice-influencing considerations is which of the competing public policies is the "better law." *See, e.g., Schubert v. Target Stores, Inc.*, 360 Ark. 404 (2005).

Restatement (Second) of Conflict of Laws § 90. Further, you will recall that the general policy considerations that inform all choice of law inquiries include as factors:

- the relevant policies of the forum; [and]
- the relevant polices of other interested states and the relative interests of those states in the determination of the particular issue.

Restatement (Second) of Conflict of Laws § 6(b), (c).

And further still, the enforcement of a choice of law clause is unwarranted when, *inter alia*:

> application of the law of the chosen state would be contrary to a fundamental policy of [the forum] state. . .

Restatement (Second) of Conflict of Laws § 187(2)(b).

In all of these contexts, the rhetoric for successfully invoking the public policy exception—or for resisting its invocation, as the case may be—is fundamentally the same. Litigators who are urging the court to invoke the exception must do more than merely emphasize that there is a difference between the competing policies. After all, this will be the case whenever there is a "conflict" of laws. Although the public policy challenges that jurisdictions face may be nearly universal, the methods for addressing them are not. Every public policy challenge requires a balancing of interests, and jurisdictions calibrate those interests differently. In an area of tort law, the promotion of innovation may be in tension with consumer safety. Parts of contract law ensure respect for party autonomy but also protect individuals who lack equal bargaining power. Property law balances the merits and demerits of formalism. But a judge will not invoke the public policy exception merely because the foreign law is different than the forum law. (Accordingly, it behooves the litigator who is resisting the invocation of the public policy exception to characterize her opponent's argument as *merely* emphasizing the difference between the laws.)

The most common standards except application of a foreign law that:

(1) violates some prevalent conception of good morals or natural justice;

(2) is prejudicial to the best interests of the citizens of the forum state;

(3) violates strong public policy of the forum; or

(4) is contrary to a fundamental policy of the forum.

But what exactly does one consult to ascertain the content of "morality" or "natural justice"? Which citizens' "best interests" are relevant? And because policies are not born with the labels "strong" or "fundamental," which policies do those include? Moreover, the proposition that there are strong and fundamental policies suggests that there are also weak and trivial policies, or policies whose strength lies somewhere in between the two extremes. Which legislative committees and judges are crafting laws expressing weak or trivial policies? They would surely be surprised to learn of their supposed insignificance.

Occasionally the public policy at issue implicates issues with a heavy moral component—such as "prohibited marriages, wagers, lotteries, racing, contracts for gaming or the sale of liquors."[4] In such areas it can be easier for judges to reject the heathen foreign law in favor of forum law. But typically the moral component is more subtle.

All of this is to say that, as a litigator, you can try to argue that a foreign law that, say, imposes a regime of comparative negligence instead of contributory negligence, is against the strong public policy of the forum; however, when the legal standard lacks a meaningful target it is hard to take aim. And because it is not clear what the exception entails most litigators lose when they are trying to argue that some foreign law falls within the public policy exception. After all, an *exception* will almost always be narrowly construed, lest the exception swallow the rule. So a judge is almost always unmoved by an argument that says little more than:

(1) We have a regime of contributory negligence here in the forum.

(2) The foreign law would require Your Honor to impose a regime of comparative negligence.

(3) Comparative negligence is a terrible idea (which is why we don't have it here in the forum).

(4) Therefore, application of the foreign law would contravene a strong public policy of the forum.

The conclusion in paragraph (4) does not *necessarily* follow. No matter how terrible the regime of comparative negligence may be, the fact that it is flawed is *not the same thing* as saying that to apply it would "contravene a strong public policy of the forum." Failing to appreciate that the two, though correlated, are *not the same thing*, is a common mistake of lawyers.

---

4   *Nash v. Tindall Corp.*, 375 S.C. 36 (2007), *cert. denied* (2008).

A judge is more likely to invoke the public policy exception when the invocation is (or at least appears to be) principled. Litigators who can perceive the situation through the eyes of the judge will imagine the judge writing an order or an opinion explaining the reasons for her decision. Ideally we will present an argument for her order or opinion that is as crisp as the classic syllogism:

(1) All men are mortal. (The major premise)

(2) Socrates is a man. (The minor premise)

(3) Therefore, Socrates is mortal. (An unassailable conclusion)

The key is the major premise. A skilled litigator will propose a major premise to which the judge can (maybe even must) subscribe. And that major premise will, when combined with the minor premise, lead to an unassailable conclusion that aligns with the client's interests.

Rarely, case precedent will provide that major premise. When there is case law already establishing that applying a foreign law's regime of comparative negligence would violate the strong public policy of the forum, then you have an easy case:

(1) Foreign laws imposing comparative negligence are void because they violate the strong public policy of the forum. (The major premise, furnished by a cite to case law)

(2) This foreign law would impose comparative negligence. (The minor premise)

(3) Therefore, this foreign law violates the strong public policy of the forum. (An unassailable conclusion)

But case law of this sort rarely exists—especially in light of all of the failed efforts of less able litigators who have tried to invoke the public policy exception for all types of laws, and lost.

A skilled litigator will provide the judge with a principle—a major premise, if you will—to frame the analysis. Some stylized examples follow; in each, the first line introduces a principle, the second line applies it to the facts of a (hypothetical) case, and the third line captures the unassailable conclusion.

(1) All forum laws protecting employees reflect strong public policy.	(1) All laws that are more than a century old embody strong public policy.	(1) All rights expressly enumerated in the state constitution reflect strong forum public policy.
(2) The foreign law would diminish the rights of an employee.	(2) The foreign law would preclude assertion of the impossibility defense, which has been around for 125 years.	(2) The foreign law would compromise the right to privacy, a right that is enshrined in the state constitution.
(3) Therefore, the foreign law violates a strong public policy of the forum.	(3) Therefore, the foreign law violates strong public policy.	(3) Therefore, the foreign law violates strong public policy

Principles can be hard to find or formulate, but good litigators will find them. Understand that the principle need not be broad, showy, or ambitious. In fact, narrow, subtle, and unassuming is probably best when you are defining an exception—it's the public policy *exception*. The major premise you proffer might also be a combination of several circumstances tailored for the unique minor premise that is your case. Imagine that you are trying to get the court to invoke the public policy exception so that the court does not apply foreign law, which would deny your clients the possibility of asserting a loss of consortium claim. That argument might look something like this:

(1) Foreign laws violate strong public policy of the forum if (i) the foreign laws deny (rather than merely the alter the amount of) recovery, provided that the forum laws (ii) are legislative enactments (as opposed to case law) and that the forum laws (iii) are routinely enforced by courts.

(2) The foreign law would deny this plaintiff the opportunity to assert any claim of loss of consortium, which is a statutorily-created right that our courts routinely enforce.

(3) Therefore, application of the foreign law would contravene a strong public policy of the forum.

Litigators who are arguing *against* the invocation of the public policy exception will attack the truthfulness of the major premise. Often the attack will be that the major premise is overly broad. If your adversary's position is that *all laws that are more than a century old embody strong public policy*, then you need only propose some forum law that is more than a century old that surely does *not* embody strong public policy (say, a law that prohibits the sale of dental hygiene products on Sundays) to establish the falsity of the premise. If the major premise is false, then the syllogism falls. Although this doesn't mean that the opposite conclusion is true, the absence of a syllogism removes the unassailability of the conclusion.

Litigators who are arguing against the invocation of the public policy exception will also find countervailing "strong public policy." If your adversary's position is that *all rights expressly enumerated in the state constitution are strong public policy*, then there may be a different right in the state constitution that would be advanced by the application of the *foreign* law.

The public policy exception can be a thinly-veiled excuse to apply forum law. That is, it may simply be an "escape device," a tool for evading the straightjacket of the traditional approach. But whether you are invoking the exception or resisting it, there is no substitute for analysis. Most importantly, the exception does not apply simply because there is some difference between the forum and foreign laws or some difference in outcome. Indeed, such a rule would entirely defeat the utility of choice of law clauses and choice of law jurisprudence. To render foreign law void as against the strong public policy of the forum, one must find a way to take aim at that amorphous and moving target.

Hypothetical 11-1

While in Atlantic City, New Jersey, Perry Friedman wrote a check in the amount of $50,000, drawn upon the Maryland National Bank, and payable to Boardwalk Casino, Inc. The check was to cover his gambling losses. The check was ultimately dishonored and Boardwalk Casino sued Friedman in his home state of Maryland.

Maryland follows the traditional approach when determining the applicable law. The parties concede that, if New Jersey law applies, Boardwalk Casino may successfully recover on the gambling debt. The parties also concede that Maryland law would preclude enforcement of this contract or debt if it had been entered into in Maryland (rather than New Jersey).

Maryland will not enforce an out-of-state contract provision that is against Maryland public policy. There is no Maryland case law with respect to the enforceability of out-of-state gambling debts; some states (like Colorado and Georgia) refuse to enforce out-of-state gambling contracts on public policy grounds, while others (like Texas and New York) have enforced them notwithstanding the unenforceability of analogous in-state contracts.

There is Maryland case law invoking the public policy exception as a reason to refuse enforcement of in-state debts incurred in poker games and other forms of illegal gambling, including dice games and roulette. Some forms of gambling are legal in Maryland, including bingo, raffles, paddle wheels and games of skill. Also, in 1972, the Maryland Constitution was amended to allow a lottery to be operated by and for the benefit of the State.

Should we expect the court to invoke the public policy exception to protect Friedman?

Hypothetical 11-2

Theo Gray was riding a tandem bicycle by himself across the United States to raise awareness and money for the National Cancer Society; the empty seat was a tribute to his sister Asha who died of cancer. Theo was then struck and severely injured in Iron, Kansas when Remus Bolton, a Missouran, was texting while driving his delivery truck, and inadvertently veered onto the shoulder. Bolton is an employee of FedEx Corporation, a Delaware corporation with a principal place of business in Memphis, Tennessee.

Gray's past and future medical expenses are approximately $1 million. Gray's inability to work for the foreseeable future supports an additional pecuniary damage award of approximately $500,000. Gray also has a substantial claim for nonpecuniary damages as a result of his permanent disfigurement, constant pain, and the substantial diminution of his quality of life.

Gray is a domiciliary of Virginia. Missouri follows the traditional approach when determining the applicable law. Kansas has a $250,000 cap on recoveries for noneconomic damages in tort. Missouri has no cap for personal injury actions of this sort. Nor does Virginia or Tennessee. If Gray files an action against Bolton and/or FedEx in Missouri (and assuming that Missouri would have personal jurisdiction), would you expect the court to find Kansas's cap to violate the public policy of Missouri?

FROM THE COURTS

MCCARTHY v. YAMAHA MOTOR MANUF. CORP.

U.S. District Court for the Northern District of Georgia
994 F.Supp.2d 1329 (N.D. Ga. 2014)

TIMOTHY C. BATTEN, SR., DISTRICT JUDGE.

This case comes before the Court on Defendant Yamaha Motor Manufacturing Corporation's ("YMMC") motion for leave to file a motion to determine the substantive law of this case.

I. Motion for Leave to File

This is a products-liability action over which the Court has diversity jurisdiction pursuant to 28 U.S.C. § 1332. Plaintiffs Peter and Maureen McCarthy are Australian citizens. On April 5, 2010, Peter was injured while operating a Yamaha WaveRunner personal watercraft in Queensland, Australia. Peter suffered, among other things, severe injuries to his spinal cord. YMMC is a Georgia corporation with its principal place of business in Newnan, Georgia, where the WaveRunner was manufactured. Based on these facts, YMMC contends that the Court should apply Georgia's choice-of-law rules, which require the application of Australia's substantive law since the accident occurred there.. . .

In Georgia, choice-of-law issues in tort cases are "governed by the rule of *lex loci delicti*, which requires application of the substantive law of the place where the tort or wrong occurred." *Carroll Fulmer Logistics Corp. v. Hines*, 309 Ga. App. 695 (2011). . . . "[T]he place of wrong, the *locus delicti*, is the place where the injury sustained was suffered rather than the place where the act was committed, or . . . it is the place where the last event necessary to make an actor liable for an alleged tort takes place." *RisdonEnters., Inc. v. Colemill Enters., Inc.*, 172 Ga. App. 902 (1984).

But Georgia's choice-of-law rules limit the application of another jurisdiction's laws to "statutes and decisions construing those statutes," even for tort claims. *Frank Briscoe Co. v. Ga. Sprinkler Co.*, 713 F.2d 1500, 1503 (11th Cir. 1983). . . . Consequently, "[w]hen no statute is involved, Georgia courts apply the common law as developed in Georgia rather than foreign case law." *Id.* . . .

Also, Georgia's choice-of-law rules are subject to a public-policy exception. Where the application of foreign law (whether another state or country) contravenes Georgia public policy, the court need not apply the foreign law. *Bailey v. Cottrell, Inc.*, 313 Ga. App. 371 (2011). In order for the exception to apply, the foreign law and Georgia law must be "sufficiently dissimilar" such that applying the foreign law would contravene the public policy of Georgia espoused in the law relevant to the case. . . . *See Alexander v. Gen. Motors Corp.*, 267 Ga. 339 (1996) (Virginia's products-liability law contravened Georgia's public policy and did not apply even though underlying events occurred in Virginia, as application of its law put plaintiff in very position Georgia law was intended to protect against).

[II.] Analysis

[T]he parties do not dispute that the accident occurred in Australia, that Georgia's choice of law rules apply, and that under these rules Australia's substantive law would typically govern the case. Thus, YMMC contends that the following is considered substantive Australian law and is applicable to the claims and defenses in this case:

(1) Statutory caps or limits on potential damages;

(2) Statutory limits on when punitive damages are allowed;

(3) Application of the "English Rule" which entitles the prevailing party to attorney's and expert fees and other reasonable expenses; and

(4) Statutory affirmative defenses that could preclude the McCarthy's claims.

The McCarthys do not challenge YMMC's characterization of the above law as substantive (as opposed to procedural) or its characterization of the substance of Australian law on these four issues. Rather, they contend that . . . the public-policy exception . . . require[s] the application of Georgia law.

Since the McCarthy's contend that the public-policy exception applies, they have the burden of establishing it.

Queensland's Civil Liability Act ("CLA") imposes an approximately $230,000 cap on general damages (including emotional distress, pain and suffering, and other non-economic damages) sought in negligence claims, and Australia's Trade Practices Act ("TPA") imposes an approximately $274,000 cap on damages sought in strict-liability claims. Australia also limits damages for lost income to the average earnings of a Queensland resident, which was AUD $1,485.80 for the relevant time period.

The McCarthys contend that Georgia law does not impose similar limits, and as a result of Australia's damages caps contravenes public policy. They rely on *Tyson Foods, Inc. v. Craig*, 266 Ga. App. 443 (2004), and *Carroll Fulmer*, 710 S.E.2d at 890–91, to support their argument.

Tyson Foods was a negligence action filed by a Texas resident in Georgia for injuries sustained in an accident that occurred in that state. The plaintiff settled with the alleged tortfeasors, and his employer moved to enforce its subrogation claim, which was based on the workers' compensation payments it had paid to the plaintiff as a result of the injuries he suffered in the accident at issue in the negligence action. The employer contended that the court had to give full faith and credit to the Texas workers' compensation statute, which allowed it to be paid first from the settlement funds for its payments.

The court held that [the] Georgia workers' compensation statute governed the employer's claim because the injury occurred and the plaintiff was eligible to receive workers' compensation benefits in Georgia. Most importantly, the court did not hold that Georgia law applied as a result of the public-policy exception. Consequently, this case does not support the McCarthy's argument that the public-policy exception applies in this case.

In *Carroll Fulmer*, the plaintiffs brought a wrongful-death action in Georgia for a tort that occurred in Florida. Under Georgia's choice-of-law rules, Florida substantive law applied. However, the court determined that Florida's wrongful-death statute should not apply because it contravened the public policy promoted by Georgia's wrongful-death statute. Dispositive to the court's holding were the facts that the Florida statute measured damages from a different perspective and eliminated the possibility of a separate recovery for pre-death suffering, which is allowed by Georgia law.

The McCarthys have not shown that Australia's cap on damages suffers similar infirmities, i.e., that it calculates damages from a different perspective than and wholly limits one avenue of recovery allowed under Georgia products-liability law. And the McCarthys have not cited to other cases where damages caps were held to contravene the public policy espoused in Georgia's products-liability or analogous statutes.

Thus the exception does not apply to the McCarthy's request for damages, and the Court will apply Australian law when determining any limits thereon.

[Next, r]elying on provisions of the CLA and TPA, YMMC contends that Australian law does not allow an award of punitive damages unless the plaintiff shows a specific intent to harm during the course of an unlawful act. . . . The McCarthys respond that Georgia's punitive-damages statute explicitly provides that "there shall be no limitation regarding the amount which may be awarded as punitive damages." O.C.G.A. § 51–12–5.1(e)(1). . . .

Australian law does not impose a cap on punitive damages; rather, it limits the cases in which punitive damages are allowed. Georgia's statute also limits when punitive damages can be awarded: it requires the plaintiff to show "by clear and convincing evidence that the defendant's actions showed willful misconduct, malice, fraud, wantonness, oppression, or that entire want of care which would raise the presumption of conscious indifference to consequences." *Id.* 51–12–5.1(0). These limitations appear to be similar enough, or not so dissimilar, to the limitation imposed by Australian law, and the McCarthys have not argued otherwise. Thus, the McCarthys have not shown that the public-policy exception applies, and the Court will apply Australian law when evaluating the merits of the punitive-damages claim.

[Next, a]ccording to YMMC, Australia applies the "English Rule," which entitles the prevailing party to recover its fees and reasonable expenses. . . . [However,] YMMC has not provided a statutory basis for the application of the English Rule. . . . As stated earlier, "[w]hen no statute is involved, Georgia courts apply the common law as developed in Georgia rather than foreign case law." *Frank Briscoe*, 713 F.2d at 1503. . . . As a result, the Court will apply Georgia law when evaluating any request for fees on this basis and need not reach the McCarthy's public-policy-exception argument. . . .

[Finally,] YMMC argues that the CLA allows it to assert the defenses of voluntary assumption of an obvious risk and of participation in a danger-ous recreational activity, and that these defenses may bar the McCarthy's recovery. YMMC also asserts that under the TPA, the McCarthy's damages may be reduced to zero as a result of their contributory negligence. . . . [T]he Court finds that the McCarthys have not carried their burden of showing that the public-policy exception precludes YMMC's assertion of these affirmative defenses under Australian law. . . .

COMMENTS AND QUESTIONS

1. Questions about what substantive law will apply can arise at every stage of litigation—from pleading through trial. In this case, defendant has filed "a motion to determine the substantive law of this case." The defendant's motion is filed pursuant to Fed. R. Civ. P. 44.1, which provides that in federal court, "A party who intends to raise an issue about a foreign *country's* law must give notice by a pleading or other writing." (emphasis-added).

2. The opinion does not limit the protection of Georgia's public policies to those that are *fundamental* or *strong*. In that sense, it seems more likely that a foreign law would violate Georgia public policy. Here, Australia's cap on compensatory damages, its limits on punitive damages, and certain statutory affirmative defenses are significantly different than Georgia public policy. Yet the court finds that the application of these Australian laws do not offend Georgia public policy. Why not?

3. Now with the benefit of hindsight, where should the plaintiffs' counsel have filed this action?

4. Imagine that a few months after the court issued this opinion, Yamaha moves for summary judgment, relying, in part, on an Australian law that was not specifically mentioned previously. Can the plaintiffs (again) raise the public policy exception (but only) with respect to that new law, or has this court committed to the application of Australian law whatever its content? The answer to that question affects how litigators handle the first motion: is it in the interests of the McCarthys and/or Yamaha to bring *all* of Australia's laws to the attention of the judge? Consider the ethical implications of your strategic behavior.

MADDEN v. MIDLAND FUNDING, LLC

U.S. District Court for the Southern District of New York
237 F.Supp.3d 130 (S.D.N.Y. 2017)

SEIBEL, DISTRICT JUDGE.

I. Factual Background

. . . Plaintiff in this action, Saliha Madden, opened a credit card account with Bank of America on April 23, 2005. Plaintiff received the Cardholder Agreement applicable to such accounts, and agreed to be bound by it. The Cardholder Agreement provided that it was "governed by applicable Arizona and federal law."

Plaintiff's August 14, 2006 account statement was sent to her address in White Plains, New York, and disclosed a variable daily periodic interest rate of 0.0883, which corresponds to an annual percentage rate of 32.34%. It stated that payment was to be made online or sent to an address in Newark, New Jersey, and that billing disputes were to be sent to an address in Norfolk, Virginia. The August 2006 account statement also contained an "Important Notice" alerting customers that Bank of America was "changing the terms of the Cardholder Agreement that governs [Plaintiff's] credit card Account." Plaintiff received the Change in Terms attached to her August 14, 2006 account statement.

The Change in Terms advised Plaintiff that, beginning on the effective date of October 19, 2006, the Change in Terms would replace the Cardholder Agreement. It also stated that "beginning on October 19, 2006, . . . your Bank of America credit card account will be issued and administered by FIA Card Services, N.A." The Change in Terms provided that "The Agreement is made in Delaware and we extend credit to you from Delaware. This Agreement is governed by the laws of the State of Delaware (without regard to its conflict of laws principles) and by any applicable federal laws." FIA Card Services, N.A. ("FIA") was at all time relevant to this action an active national bank.

On November 10, 2010, FIA sold, transferred, and set over unto Midland Funding, LLC ("Midland") Plaintiff's outstanding debt of $5,291.25, with full authority to perform all acts necessary for collection, settlement, adjustment, compromise, or satisfaction of the claim. This charge-off constituted an assignment of Plaintiff's debt from FIA to Midland. Midland is in the business of purchasing defaulted debts, and Midland Credit Management, Inc. ("MCM") is in the business of collecting those debts. Both are indirect wholly-owned subsidiaries of Encore Capital Group, Inc., and both have their principal places of business in San Diego, California.

Midland sued Plaintiff in the City Court of the City of White Plains, Westchester County on May 2, 2011 to collect on her debt of $5,291.25. In that complaint, Midland alleged that Plaintiff lived in White Plains, New York, and that its action to collect the debt arose out of transactions in Westchester County, New York. That case has since been dismissed.

II. Procedural Background

Plaintiff filed the amended complaint on May 7, 2012, asserting violations of (1) the Fair Debt Collection Practices Act ("FDCPA"), 15 U.S.C. § 1692 *et seq.*, based on Defendants' attempt to collect interest on her debt above the rate permitted by New York's usury laws; (2) New York General Business Law ("GBL") § 349, based on Defendants' representations that they were entitled to collect interest at a usurious rate; and (3) New York's civil and criminal usury laws, entitling Plaintiff to a declaration that her debts are void and to disgorgement.

[On appeals of earlier orders in this case, the Second Circuit held that the federal National Bank Act did not preempt Madden's state law usury claims. The appeals court remanded the action to the district court "to address in the first instance whether the Delaware choice-of-law clause precludes Madden's claims." The Defendants have moved for summary judgment, arguing that Delaware law applies to the Plaintiff's claims and that Delaware imposes no usury cap. There are also pending issues about whether the action may be certified as a class action.]

III. Summary Judgment

. . . Delaware usury law provides no cap on interest rates, but instead allows interest to be charged in an amount pursuant to the agreement governing the debt. *See* Del. Code Ann. tit. 5 § 943; *Kaneff v. Del. Title Loans, Inc.*, 587 F.3d 616, 622 (3d Cir. 2009) ("Delaware has no usury law.") Defendants argue, and Plaintiff does not dispute, that were Delaware law to apply, it would not prohibit Defendants from charging the interest rate in question.

New York's "civil usury cap" forbids charging interest on a "loan or forbearance" at a rate above 16% annually. *See* N.Y. Gen. Oblig. Law § 5–501(1)-(2); N.Y. Banking Law § 14-a(1). . . . The civil usury cap does not apply to defaulted obligations. The parties agree the Plaintiff's debt is in default, so the civil usury cap is inapplicable here.

New York's "criminal usury cap" makes it a felony to knowingly charge or collect interest on a "loan or forbearance" at a rate above 25% annually [even for defaulted debts]. . . . [The criminal usury statute does not, however, create a private right of action. Accordingly, summary judgment was entered on Plaintiff's effort to seek affirmative relief for violations of that statute.]

I next turn to whether New York law governs Plaintiff's FDCPA and GBL claims. "Where, as here, the parties have agreed on the law that will govern their contract, it is the policy of the courts of this State to enforce that choice of law provided that (a) the law of the State has a 'reasonable relation[ship]' to the agreement and (b) the law chosen does not violate a fundamental policy of New York." *Finucane v. Interior Constr. Corp.*, 264 A.D.2d 618 (1st Dep. 1999). . . .

Generally, courts will enforce a choice-of-law clause so long as the chosen law bears a reasonable relationship to the parties or the transaction. In addressing that issue, courts have looked to the location of the following factors: the parties' negotiation of the agreement, performance under the agreement, including where loan payments were received; the parties' places of incorporation; the parties' principal places of business; and the property that is the subject of the transaction. . . . Most of these factors do not appear to support a finding that a reasonable relationship exists between the parties, the transaction, and the Delaware forum. . . . [The fact that one of the parties' principal place of business is in the selected forum is enough to satisfy the reasonable relationship test. FIA may reside in Delaware.] I need not decide whether the principal place of business of an intermediate creditor suffices to establish a reasonable relationship, because even if it does, to apply Delaware law would violate a fundamental public policy of New York, as discussed below. . . .

A number of cases have applied New York law—despite the parties' choice of another forum's law—because New York's usury prohibition constitutes a fundamental public policy. *See Am. Equities Grp.*, 2004 WL 870260, at *8 ("New York has a strong public policy against interest rates which exceed 25%, which policy must be enforced."); *In re McCorhill Publ'g, Inc.*, 86 B.R. 783, 793 (Bankr. S.D.N.Y. 1988) (holding that enforcing New Jersey law would violate New York's "strong public policy against interest rates which exceed 25%, which policy must be enforced"); . . . *N. Am. Bank, Ltd. v. Schulman,* 123 Misc.2d 516 (Cty. Ct. Westchester Cty. 1984) ("[T]he policy underlying our state's usury laws is in fact of a fundamental nature.")

Decisions made in other contexts have also treated the usury prohibition as an important and longstanding public policy of the state of New York. *See United Mizrahi Bank Ltd. v. Sullivan*, No. 97-CV-9282, 1998 WL 575137, at *8 (S.D.N.Y. Sept. 9, 1998) (New York U.C.C. § 1–102(3) is not a fundamental public policy, while usury prohibition is). . . . Indeed, the New York Court of Appeals has recognized that "[t]he purpose of usury laws, *from time immemorial*, has been to protect desperately poor people from the consequences of their own desperation." *Schneider v. Phelps*, 41 N.Y.2d 238 (1977) (emphasis added). New York's usury prohibition is not a creature of recent statute, *see Welsbach Elec. Corp v. MasTec N. Am., Inc.*, 7 N.Y.3d 624 (prohibition of "pay-if-paid" clauses in construction contracts had "checkered history" and was not clarified until 1995, so was not fundamental public policy), but rather one that reflects a "deep-rooted tradition of the common weal." *Cooney v. Osgood Mach., Inc.*, 81 N.Y.2d 66.

Further, New York has chosen to make it a felony to charge more than 25% annual interest. That New York chose to criminalize such conduct is further evidence that its usury prohibition is a fundamental public policy. . . . I will thus apply New York law to Plaintiff's claims. . . .

COMMENTS AND QUESTIONS

1. Does it matter to the court that the Delaware choice of law clause was added to the terms of contract by amendment? (Why mention it?)

2. The opinion provides three touchstones to explain why enforcement of the clause would violate a fundamental public policy of New York: the prohibition is long-standing, the prohibition protects people, and usury is a criminal offense.

3. Invoking the public policy exception is antagonistic to the norm that respects party autonomy. What is the countervailing norm that prevails here?

4. At the end of Chapter 3 you learned about trends that minimize the likelihood of conflicts between state laws. One of those trends is federal preemption—where a federal law trumps all state laws in that field. For example, the National Bank Act preempts many state law usury claims against national banks. Madden's state law claim was viable because Midland Funding (though an assignee of a national bank) was neither a bank nor was acting on behalf of one. Federal preemption of state law usury claims is a controversial and dynamic area of the law.

FROM THE COURTS

DEARBORN v. EVERETT J. PRESCOTT, INC.

U.S. District Court for the Southern District of Indiana
486 F.Supp.2d 802 (S.D. Ind. 2007)

HAMILTON, DISTRICT JUDGE.

. . . I. Dearborn's Employment and Resignation

Plaintiff Christopher J. Dearborn is a citizen of Indiana who lives in Indianapolis. Defendant Everett J. Prescott ("EJP") is a Maine corporation with its principal place of business in Maine. Dearborn filed this action on January 22, 2007 seeking declaratory and injunctive relief barring EJP from enforcing a three-year non-competition agreement, as well as damages for alleged breaches of contract. . . .

EJP sells and distributes water, sewer, and drain pipe. . . . Its principal customers are municipal and private water and sewer systems, and contractors who build water, sewer, and drain systems in public and private construction projects. EJP is based in Gardiner, Maine. It has a total of 32 offices and distribution centers in a total of nine states, six in New England, plus New York, Ohio, and Indiana. . . .

EJP employed plaintiff Dearborn for approximately ten years in several sales and management positions, all in Indiana. . . . During his work in the

Indianapolis office, Dearborn was successful. . . . Dearborn's compensation increased with his sales, but not to the extent he expected or thought he deserved. . . . By the autumn of 2006, he was ripe for recruitment by a competitor. He was contacted by Ferguson Enterprises, Inc., which . . . competes with EJP in some geographic areas, now including Indiana, where Ferguson opened an office in January 2007.

On January 29, 2007, Dearborn resigned from his position with EJP. . . . The parties have stipulated that "Dearborn is employed with Ferguson in a sales capacity substantially similar to the role he held at EJP in the years immediately preceding his resignation from EJP." Dearborn's sales territory for Ferguson includes all or part of his territory with EJP. . . .

II. The Non-Competition Agreement

Prior to 2005, Dearborn had not been subject to any non-competition agreement with EJP. . . . [In late 2004 and early 2005, all EJP sales representatives and managers were required to sign non-competition agreements as a condition of remaining employed with EJP.] All agreements were identical in form and scope, regardless of the employee's duties and regardless of where the employee worked. All provided they would be governed by Maine law. All provided a token payment of $250 to the employee for signing.]

The agreement is titled "Non-Competition and Non-Disclosure Agreement." The Agreement provides that its term is "the entire time that Employee is employed by Company [EJP] and three (3) years after the termination of employment of Employee for any reason with or without cause." The "Covered Geographic Area" is defined broadly in terms of EJP's entire business: "the marketing and sales areas where Company offers services at the time it seeks to enforce the terms of this Agreement, which includes as of the date of this Agreement the geographical area within a one hundred (100) mile radius of each of the offices, distribution centers, and any other place of business of the Company." [Three key covenants are in dispute: a covenant not to compete, a covenant not to disclose, and a covenant not to solicit.]

[A] key document is the cease-and-desist letter that EJP's attorney sent to Dearborn's attorney on February 9, 2007. The terms of the letter are relevant because EJP argues that Maine law should govern the agreement, as the Agreement itself provides. Under Maine law, whether a non-competition covenant is enforceable depends not on the covenant as written, but on the extent to which the employer seeks to enforce it.

EJP's demand letter did not demand that Dearborn comply with the full scope of the covenants, which are so broad that they reach any area where EJP does business and any EJP customer anywhere. The letter instead made [narrower demands].

III. Enforceability of the Covenants Not to Compete and Solicit

. . . To determine whether the covenants are enforceable, the court must first determine whether Maine and Indiana law are actually in conflict. . . . As explained in detail here, Maine law would allow enforcement of those broad covenants to the limited extent that EJP seeks to enforce them. Indiana law does not allow enforcement of such broad covenants as written. Under Indiana law, an employer cannot save such overly broad covenants by retreating from the broad language in court and asking the court to enforce them only to a narrower degree. Because there is a genuine conflict between Maine law and Indiana law, the decisive issue then becomes which law should be applied.

At a high level of generality, Maine law and Indiana law on non-competition covenants are similar, but important differences appear quickly with more detailed scrutiny. In general, both Maine law and Indiana law treat agreements not to compete as agreements that are in restraint of trade and contrary to public policy. . . . Both states recognize that such restraints may be valid if they serve legitimate interests and are reasonable in terms of time, geography, and scope of activity. The two states diverge sharply, however, where an employer has drafted covenants that are far too broad to be enforceable as written.

1. Indiana Law on Overly Broad Covenants

Under Indiana law, the EJP covenant not to compete and covenant not to solicit customers are clearly unreasonable as applied to plaintiff Dearborn. The geographic covenant not to compete by its terms would bar Dearborn from working for a competitor within 100 miles of any EJP office or facility, from Indiana all the way to Maine. Similarly, the covenant not to solicit by its terms would bar Dearborn from soliciting or accepting business from any "customer or known prospective customer" of EJP, regardless of whether Dearborn himself had any relationship with the customer or prospective customer. . . .

[T]he narrower relief that EJP seeks in court probably would be reasonable under Indiana law because the geographic and customer limits would be tied to Dearborn's own duties. . . . Under Indiana law, however, when an employer drafts an overly broad covenant, the price of over-reaching is that the restriction cannot be enforced at all, even if it would have been possible to draft and enforce a narrower, more reasonable restriction. *See, e.g., Dicen v. New Sesco, Inc.*, 839 N.E.2d 684, 689 (Ind. 2005). . . .

2. Maine Law on Overly Broad Covenants

Maine takes a very different approach to overly broad covenants not to compete, like the EJP covenants. The court does not consider the covenant as drafted and agreed by the parties. Instead, the court considers the scope of the covenant *only as the employer seeks to enforce it*.

This unusual, and perhaps unique, rule appears to have been first stated in Maine in *Chapman & Drake v. Harrington*, 545 A.2d 645 (Me. 1988). The court wrote: "Since the reasonableness of the noncompetition agreement depends upon the specific facts of the case . . . we assess that agreement only as Chapman & Drake has sought to apply it and not as it might have been enforced on its plain terms." Thus, under Maine law . . . the overly broad scope of the EJP covenants does not matter. . . .

3. The Choice of Law—Public Policy Considerations

Because there is a genuine conflict between Maine law and Indiana law as applied to this case, the decisive issue becomes the choice of law. Dearborn argues that Indiana courts would apply Indiana law because application of Maine law would conflict with Indiana's public policy on covenants not to compete. . . .

Indiana law generally enforces contractual provisions that specify a choice of law, at least in commercial and other settings (unlike this case) where the parties have comparable bargaining power, and where the chosen state has some connection to the parties' relationship. . . .

But Indiana will not enforce a contractual provision, including a choice of law provision, if enforcement would be contrary to Indiana's public policy. Another state's law is not contrary to Indiana public policy merely because the result would be different. . . .

Our own scheme of legislation may be different. We may even
have no legislation on the subject. That is not enough to show
that public policy forbids us to enforce the foreign right. A right
of action is property. If a foreign statute gives the right, the mere
fact that we do not give a like right is no reason for refusing to
help the plaintiff in getting what belongs to him. We are not so
provincial as to say that every solution of a problem is wrong
because we deal with it otherwise at home.

Loucks v. Standard Oil Co. of New York, 224 N.Y. 99 (N.Y. 1918) (Cardozo, J.).

Indiana law on the public policy exception to choice of law provisions in
contracts appears to be consistent with the more detailed guidance available
from Section 187 of the Restatement (Second) of Conflict of Laws, which
states in full:

(1) The law of the state chosen by the parties to govern their
contractual rights and duties will be applied if the particular
issue is one which the parties could have resolved by an explicit provision in their agreement directed to that issue.

(2) The law of the state chosen by the parties to govern their
contractual rights and duties will be applied, even if the particular issue is one which the parties could not have resolved
by an explicit provision in their agreement directed to that
issue, unless either

(a) The chosen state has no substantial relationship to the
parties or the transaction and there is no other reasonable
basis for the parties' choice, or

(b) application of the law of the chosen state would be contrary to a fundamental policy of a state which has a materially greater interest than the chosen state in the determination of the particular issue and which, under the
rule of § 188, would be the state of the applicable law in
the absence of an effective choice of law by the parties.

(3) In the absence of a contrary indication of intention, the reference is to the local law of the state of the chosen law.

Comment g to Section 187 addresses the public policy exception in more detail. The comment states in relevant part:

> Fulfillment of the parties' expectations is not the only value in contract law; regard must also be had for state interest and for state regulation. The chosen law should not be applied without regard for the interests of the state which would be the state of the applicable law with respect to the particular issue involved in the absence of an effective choice by the parties. The forum will not refrain from applying the chosen law merely because this would lead to a different result than would be obtained under the local law of the state of the otherwise applicable law. Application of the chosen law will be refused only (1) to protect a fundamental policy of the state which, under the rule of § 188, would be the state of the otherwise applicable law, provided (2) that this state has a materially greater than the state of the chosen law in the determination of the particular issue. . . .
>
> To be "fundamental," a policy must in any event be a substantial one. Except perhaps in the case of contracts relating to wills, a policy of this sort will rarely be found in a requirement, such as the statute of frauds, that relates to formalities (see Illustration 6). Nor is such a policy likely to be represented by a rule tending to become obsolete, such as a rule concerned with the capacity of married women (see Illustration 7), or by general rules of contract law, such as those concerned with the need for consideration (see Illustration 8). On the other hand, a fundamental policy may be embodied in a statute which makes one or more kinds of contracts illegal or which is designed to protect a person against the oppressive use of superior bargaining power. Statutes involving the rights of an individual insured as against an insurance company are an example of this sort (see §§ 192–193).

Judge Sharp relied on Indiana public policy to reject a choice-of-law provision in a covenant not to compete in *South Bend Consumers Club v. United Consumers Club*, 572 F. Supp. 209 (N.D. Ind. 1983). The agreement in question gave an Indiana citizen an exclusive franchise territory in Indiana and Michigan around South Bend, Indiana. The agreement included a covenant not to compete after termination that was overly broad in scope. The agreement provided that Illinois law would govern, but Judge Sharp applied Section 187(2)(b) of the Restatement (Second) of Conflict of Laws to hold that Indiana law would apply, rendering the overly broad covenant unenforceable: "Since the preferred policy of this state is unalterably opposed to the enforcement of this covenant in any degree or manner, Restatement 187(2)(b) would apply and, consequently, this cause will be governed by Indiana law." *Id.* at 214. Judge Sharp did not decide definitively that the result would have been different under Illinois law, but he based the choice of law on the grounds that Illinois courts appeared to be more willing than Indiana courts to enforce such covenants. *Id.* at 214 n.2. . . .

When Indiana courts consider arguments that a contract is contrary to public policy, the public policy they consider is not limited to what is stated in statutes. They consider "the surrounding circumstances of a given case," and if the public policy is not explicit, they consider "the overall implications of constitutional and statutory enactments, practices of officials and judicial decisions to disclose the public policy of this State." *Straub v. B.M.T.*, 645 N.E.2d 597, 599 (Ind. 1994). The Indiana courts are also cautious in such cases. They must "always weigh in the balance the parties' freedom to contract." *Allstate Ins. Co. v. Boles*, 481 N.E.2d 1096, 1101 (Ind. 1985). The Indiana courts recognize that the power of courts to declare a contract void under public policy is "a very delicate and undefined power," requiring caution against its "reckless use." *Straub*, 645 N.E. at 599 n.3. Indiana courts look for a clear manifestation of public policy, a tendency to injure the public, or contracts "against the public good" or "inconsistent with sound policy and good morals." *Id.* at 599.

The Indiana Supreme Court has identified the following factors it considers in cases challenging a contract or contract provision on public policy grounds when there is not a statutory prohibition or tendency to injure the public:

> In determining whether a contract not prohibited by statute nor which tends to injure the public contravenes public policy, we look at five factors: (1) the nature of the subject matter of the contract; (2) the strength of the public policy underlying any relevant statute; (3) the likelihood that refusal to enforce the bargain or term will further any such policy; (4) how serious or deserved would be the forfeiture suffered by the party attempting to enforce the bargain; and (5) the parties' relative bargaining power and freedom to contract.

Trimble v. Ameritech Publishing, Inc., 700 N.E.2d 1128, 1129–30 (Ind. 1998). . . .

[First, t]he subject matter of the EJP Agreement weighs in favor the public policy exception here. The central subject matter of the agreement is the restraint of trade. . . . Indiana law in this area can and often does override the ability and freedom of parties to decide the terms of their own contracts, especially in the context of employment contracts. . . .

Second, the public policy at issue here is strong. The specific issue in this case—the consequences of an employer's overly broad restrictions in a covenant not to compete—is a strong and fundamental feature of the public policy reflected in those many reported decisions. Indiana courts have repeatedly required that covenants not to compete be sufficiently specific in scope to allow the employee a clear understanding of what conduct is prohibited. . . . The strict Indiana approach to overly broad covenants thus helps to protect employees from the intimidating, *in terrorem* effects of such covenants. . . . The Indiana legislature has not seen fit to modify by statute this strong and often-repeated policy. . . .

On the third *Trimble* factor relevant to the public policy decision, it is highly likely that refusal to enforce this choice of law on overly broad covenants will further the Indiana public policy. . . . If employers feel they need enforceable covenants, they must write them carefully, specifically, and narrowly. An employer may not deliberately choose to write overly broad covenants that have intimidating, *in terrorem* effects on employees, and then, when an employee challenges the overly broad covenants in court, back off of those broad provisions in the hope that Indiana courts might bail the employer out by writing a new contract for the parties.

[Fourth, t]he refusal to enforce EJP's choice of law provision on public policy grounds will not impose an unfair or undue forfeiture on EJP. EJP imposed this contract as a condition of Dearborn's employment after he had been working there for eight years, and less than two years before he left. EJP has not shown that it acted in detrimental reliance on the covenants in dispute. EJP gave up only the token payment of $250 (and some portions of the Agreement remain valid). The result of a decision declining to enforce the choice of law provision on public policy grounds will leave EJP free to compete with Ferguson and all the other competing distributors.

The fifth *Trimble* factor, the parties' relative bargaining power, weighs heavily in favor of relying on public policy to refuse enforcement of EJP's choice of law provision. These covenants not to compete were not the product of arms-length bargaining between two parties who were equally free to walk away from the table. . . .

On the choice of law issue, Section 187(b) of the Restatement (Second) of Conflict of Laws also requires consideration of whether Indiana has a materially greater interest in the litigation than Maine. The court finds that it does. Dearborn is an Indiana resident, and his ability to work here in his chosen field is at issue. Indiana was the center of gravity of his employment relationship EJP throughout the ten years he worked for EJP. All his positions were in Indiana. He visited Maine only occasionally, perhaps twice. . . .

EJP contends that it should be entitled to application of Maine law because of its interest in uniformity among its employees in different states. EJP suggests that it would be too expensive and too much trouble to prepare different covenants not to compete for each state where it has employees. . . . But those concerns about convenience and consistency do not justify the double-edge contract that EJP imposed on Dearborn and other employees in Indiana. By choosing to invoke Maine law, EJP tried to pursue a strategy that would allow it the full benefit of the intimidating, *in terrorem* effects of the overly broad covenants, without having to pay the price that Indiana requires of an employer who takes that approach—unenforceable covenants. Also, it would not have been difficult to draft a contract enforceable under both Indiana and Maine law applying to a sales representative's own sales territory and customers.

Applying the five factors spelled out in *Trimble v. Ameritech Publishing*, 700 N.E.2d at 1129–30, therefore, the court predicts that Indiana courts would find that the choice of Maine law in the EJP Agreement is unenforceable as contrary to Indiana public policy. This prediction of Indiana law is consistent with Section 187 of the Restatement (Second) of Conflict of Laws. . . .

COMMENTS AND QUESTIONS

1. The *Trimble* case, which produced the five factors that framed this court's analysis, did not involve foreign law. Rather, that case involved an Indiana auto parts store that purchased an ad in the yellow pages telephone directory. When the publisher failed to run the ad, the store sued for lost business; but the contract contained an exculpatory clause that limited the publisher's liability to a refund. The court used the five factor test to evaluate whether the parties' (Indiana) agreement violated Indiana public policy. Does that make the *Trimble* factors any more or less relevant in *Dearborn*?

2. The court observes that the Maine law on restrictive covenants is "unusual, and perhaps unique." How would each side use the uniqueness of Maine's law to its advantage?

SAMPLE EXAM QUESTIONS

Question 11-3

Stephanie Hodge and her two young children, Carla and Chaz, were seriously injured in a single vehicle accident while vacationing in rural New Mexico.

Hodge is a Kentucky domiciliary who had purchased automobile insured coverage from Wildcat Insurance Co. (Wildcat). Wildcat is a Kentucky company that has its principal place of business in Lexington, Kentucky.

The Kentucky policy had uninsured motorist coverage with limits of $100,000 per person and $300,000 per accident. The policy included a step-down clause (also known as an "intra-family exclusionary" clause), which limited the amount of recovery by any member of the insured's family to the minimum limit mandated by the applicable motor vehicle financial responsibility law. The policy contained no choice-of-law clause.

While still recovering in a New Mexico rehabilitation facility in New Mexico, Hodge consulted a lawyer regarding a dispute that has arisen with Wildcat. Wildcat claims that, because of the step-down provision, the maximum benefit for each of the two children is $25,000. The "step-down" (from $100,000 per person) is triggered by the fact that the children are members of the insured's family (a fact Hodge does not dispute). The minimum coverage required by the motor vehicle responsibility laws of both Kentucky and New Mexico is $25,000; hence the cap of that amount.

New Mexico follows a traditional approach to choice of law determinations, and thus, a suit filed there is likely to lead to the application of Kentucky law, where the contract was entered into. When step-down provisions have been challenged in Kentucky courts, the appellate courts have consistently upheld them, observing that step-down clauses help prevent insurance fraud that can result when one family member has a claim against another family member's policy. Further, the Kentucky Insurance Commissioner has stated that liability coverage is designed to protect insured from liability they may incur to third parties, not to protect the insureds for their own injuries.

The courts of New Mexico have refused to enforce step-down provisions in policies entered into in the state of New Mexico, observing that: "A person who is unrelated to the insured, who is injured while riding in the insured's vehicle should not get more coverage than the insured's own family members who also may be injured in the crash."

But no case has yet asked the New Mexico courts to use the public policy exception to resist enforcement of a step-down provision in a contract for insurance coverage that was entered into outside of the state. Should we expect the court to invoke the public policy exception here? What arguments could be made against invoking the exception?

Question 11-4

Rolnick Jewelers, Inc. (Rolnick) is a Connecticut corporation engaged in the business of manufacturing and distributing high quality precious stones. Its principal place of business is in Mystic, Connecticut.

Sara Gordon (Gordon) was hired in Connecticut by Rolnick eight years ago to work as a manager for its diamond-related operations in Venezuela. No written contract was signed. Gordon worked in this capacity continuously for seven years until Rolnick determined that its Venezuelan operation was unprofitable, and terminated Gordon. During her time in Venezuela, Gordon became a Venezuelan citizen. She is, however, presently residing in Rhode Island. Throughout her employment, Gordon received her pay from Rolnick's Connecticut address.

Under Venezuelan labor law, Rolnick was obligated to pay an annual "vacation bonus" consisting of one day's salary for each year of her employment. Since Rolnick has not complied with this provision, despite due demands, Gordon claims that she is owed in excess of $45,000. Pursuant to Venezuelan labor law Rolnick was also obligated to pay her a minimum mandated profit-sharing bonus, based on her salary. Further still, Rolnick is liable for severance pay, including a lump sum representing "seniority compensation," a lump sum representing "unemployment compensation," interest, and attorneys' fees incurred to enforce these rights. The substantive content of these Venezuelan labor laws is not disputed. Rolnick admits that it has not paid any of these disputed amounts, but disputes that they payments are required.

You represent Gordon. Your current thinking is to file an action in either Rhode Island or Connecticut. Rhode Island follows the First Restatement to determine the applicable law. Connecticut follows the Second Restatement. If Connecticut law applies, Gordon has received all monies to which she is entitled. Which jurisdiction is more likely to apply Venezuelan labor laws (*i.e.*, the laws that benefit your client)?

Quick Summary

- In choice of law methodologies that are more rigid, the public policy exception is an escape device to avoid the application of foreign law (and instead apply forum law)

- In choice of law methodologies that are more flexible, the imprudence of the (foreign) public policy is expressly or impliedly incorporated into the analysis

- To invoke the exception, the public policy must be "strong" or "fundamental." Generally, this means it must be substantial, not tending toward obsolescence, a policy that protects a weaker party against oppression, or makes conduct illegal

12

Renvoi

Key Concepts

- Applying the "whole law" versus the "internal law" of another jurisdiction
- Terminology of renvoi: accept, reject, remission, and transmission
- Escape devices
- Leveraging the insight of renvoi even without invoking the doctrine by name

---

Whenever the choice of law methodology directs one jurisdiction to apply another jurisdiction's law, the question arises whether the direction is to apply the "whole law" of the other jurisdiction, including its choice of law rules, or only its "local law." We thus often have the possibility of applying the foreign jurisdiction's *choice of law* rules, rather than its *substantive law*. Assume, for example, that a suit is brought in Alaska. Alaska's choice of law principles may, under a set of circumstances, direct it to apply the law of Hawaii. But what if, under Hawaii's choice of law rules, it (Hawaii) would not have applied Hawaiian substantive law if the case had instead been filed in Hawaii?

The doctrine of renvoi deals with this situation. It is about applying the *whole* law of another jurisdiction rather than only the *internal* law of that jurisdiction. The whole law includes the choice of law principles of the foreign jurisdiction. The internal law means the substantive law of the foreign jurisdiction, and specifically excludes the choice of law principles. Renvoi is generally "disfavored" but it is a tool that a skilled litigator knows when and how to use.

The possibility of renvoi surfaces only because states have different choice of law methodologies which point to different applicable substantive laws.

Hypothetical 12-1

Carpenter is an Alaska domiciliary who was injured during an attempted burglary in Hawaii while he was on a mission trip with his church. Carpenter claims that the church, McClure Ministries, an Alaska limited liability company, was negligent in failing to secure the premises of his camp.

Under the laws of Alaska and many other states, churches are charities that enjoy immunity from injuries caused by simple negligence. In other jurisdictions, like Hawaii, the law does not extend charitable immunity to religious institutions.

Carpenter files an action against McClure Ministries in Alaska. If Alaska follows the traditional approach to determine the applicable law, what law should we expect an Alaska court to apply?

Imagine further that Hawaii follows interest analysis to determine the applicable law. What law should we expect a Hawaii court to apply if the case were filed there?

The policy question that this hypothetical surfaces is whether the Alaska court should apply Hawaii law (as the situs of injury, per the traditional approach) if even Hawaii would not apply Hawaii law (had the case been filed in Hawaii).[1]

Renvoi is frequently described as an "escape device." Renvoi is an escape from applying foreign law, and is a retreat to the familiar confines of forum law. If the Alaska court invoked the doctrine of renvoi in Hypothetical 12-1 and applied forum law, the standard terminology would be that Alaska *accepted the renvoi*. Renvoi is a French word that connotes a return or a sending-back. Accepting the renvoi, then, is to embrace that return, as if saying: "We (Alaska) were prepared to apply your (Hawaii) law, but if you (Hawaii) would apply our (Alaska) law, then, we will *accept* that decision and will apply our (Alaska) law."

If the Alaska court declined to invoke the doctrine of renvoi in Hypothetical 12-1 and applied Hawaii law, the standard terminology would be that Alaska *rejected the renvoi*. This is to say: "We (Alaska) understand that you (Hawaii) would apply our (Alaska) law if the case were filed there, but the case was filed here (Alaska), we (Alaska) follow the traditional approach, and according to that approach we *reject* the renvoi and will apply your (Hawaii) substantive law." Rejecting the renvoi is another way of saying that the court will apply only the internal (not the whole) law of the other jurisdiction.

---

[1]   We are assuming here that a jurisdiction that follows interest analysis would apply Alaska law. Charitable immunity is a loss-allocating (rather than a conduct-regulating) rule, and this is a dispute between parties whose common domicile is Alaska.

There is a certain logic to applying the whole law of the other jurisdiction. A jurisdiction's choice of law rules can fairly be viewed as defining the scope of its substantive laws. Consider Hawaii's position with respect to what type of charities deserve immunity: churches are not immune. But when a situation is presented where Hawaii's choice of law rules would not lead it to hold churches liable, that is essentially saying that the state's policy does not apply to that fact pattern. Accordingly, if Alaska applies the Hawaii policy to this church, it is expanding the scope of Hawaii's substantive law to circumstances that that law was not intended to reach.

The response to that argument is that it proves too much. If Hawaii's choice of law principles define the scope of Hawaii's substantive laws, then Alaska's choice of law principles define the scope of Alaska's substantive laws. This leads to a merry-go-round on which we are stuck, so we lack the ability to get off in either jurisdiction, and apply its substantive law. Applying neither law is not an option for the court, as it must decide whether the church has immunity.

Renvoi is disfavored and is often viewed as a superficial excuse for applying forum law.[2] Some jurisdictions allow it to avoid an absurd result, or find it appropriate when there is a false conflict (as in Hypothetical 12-1). The Second Restatement generally avoids *renvoi*, contemplating instead application of a jurisdiction's "local law," which is to say the internal law (not the whole law).

> The rights and liabilities of the parties with respect to an issue in tort are determined *by the local law* of the state which . . . has the most significant relationship. . . .
>
> The rights and liabilities of the parties with respect to an issue in contract are determined *by the local law* of the state which . . . has the most significant relationship. . . .
>
> The validity of a marriage will be determined *by the local law* of the state which . . . has the most significant relationship. . . .
>
> The rights and duties of a principal and agent toward each other are determined *by the local law* of the state which . . . has the most significant relationship. . . .

---

2   *See, e.g., Maroon v. State*, 411 N.E.2d 404, 413 (Ind. App. 1980) (referring to renvoi as an "ancient, disfavored doctrine); *Clark v. Clark*, 222 A.2d 205, 209 (N.H. 1966) (rejecting renvoi as a "manipulative technique" used to justify forum law); *Rescildo v. R.H. Macy's*, 594 N.Y.S.2d 139, 140, 142 (N.Y. App. Div. 1992) (rejecting renvoi because it is circular and facilitates forum shopping); *In re the Oil Spill by the Amoco Cadiz Off the Coast of France on March 16, 1978*, 954 F.2d 1279, 1336 (7th Cir. 1992) (describing renvoi as "spectre" that results in "infinite loop[s].").

Restatement (Second) of Conflicts §§ 145, 188, 283, 291 (emphases added). The Second Restatement recognizes the possibility of renvoi in extremely limited circumstances, *see id.* § 8(2) and (3),[3] but generally discourages it—especially in tort cases. *See id.* at § 145 cmt. h ("It should be reiterated that in the torts area the forum will not apply the choice-of-law rules of another state.").

The more thoughtful contemporary use of the foreign state's choice of law rules is as an aid *within* the application of the *forum's* choice of law methodology. Comment (k) to Section 8 of the Second Restatement advises that "[a]n indication of the existence of a state interest in a given matter, and of the intensity of that interest, can sometimes be obtained from an examination of that state's choice-of-law decisions." In other words, any choice of law methodology that examines the interests of the *other* state (*i.e.,* interest analysis, better law, Second Restatement) could incorporate foreign choice of law rules when interpreting the scope of the foreign laws and divining the interests of those states.

The term *renvoi* thus may be less helpful than the insights that it brings to the process of interpreting foreign law and interests. Still, there are two more terms native to the *renvoi* doctrine with which you should be familiar. The first, *remission*, is another way of describing the volley of choice of law principles between two jurisdictions as already discussed above; it describes the return or sending-back. But there is another possibility: Alaska's choice of law principles might point to the application of Hawaii's law; and Hawaii's choice of law principles might point to the application of Oregon's law. This reference to the law of a *third* country is called a *transmission*. The term *renvoi* is used to cover both *remission* and *transmission*. The arguments for accepting transmissions are even more suspect than the reasons for accepting the renvoi on a remission.

Hypothetical 12-2

An Austrian who was domiciled in Belgium died while visiting his New York condominium and curating his art collection at a New York gallery. He died intestate and there is a dispute about the proper method of distribution of his assets.

An action is filed in New York, and under New York's choice of law principles, the law of the decedent's domicile (*lex domcilii*) controls.

---

3   In the case of immovable property, for example, the interests of the parties in that property are determined by the whole law of the state which has the most significant relationship to the property. *See* Restatement (Second) of Conflicts §§ 222, 223. Renvoi is also possible in a subset of situations involving movable property. *See, e.g., id.* §§ 245, 253, (issues involving the effect of a transfer of a chattel upon the interests of persons who were not both parties to the transfer); *Id.* §§ 260–266 (issues involving succession to interests in movables).

Under Belgium's choice of law principles, the law of the decedent's citizenship (*lex nationalis*) determines the applicable law.

Under Austria's choice of law principles, courts would apply the law of the situs of the property (*lex loci rei sitae*).

If the New York court accepts the renvoi, what law will it apply?

Hypothetical 12-3

Conley is the legal representative of Constance Gibson who was kidnapped and killed in Wisconsin by an escapee from the Iowa Department of Corrections.

Conley filed a complaint in a Wisconsin court against Twiqbal Construction, Inc., a government contractor who was engaged in construction work at the Iowa prison. A Twiqbal Construction employee, who was either grossly negligent or acting in concert with the prisoner, allowed the prisoner to escape by failing to secure a wall during a construction project at the prison.

Iowa and Wisconsin laws differ with respect to the availability of punitive damages: Iowa law treats governmental contractors like traditional governmental entities and does not allow punitive awards; Wisconsin law authorizes punitive awards against governmental contractors that are engaged in conduct that is not uniquely sovereign in character.

Wisconsin follows the Second Restatement. Iowa follows the traditional approach. How could you use the insights of renvoi within (i.e., as part of, not in lieu of) your Second Restatement analysis?

FROM THE COURTS

LEMONS v. CLOER

Court of Appeals of Tennessee
206 S.W.3d 60 (Tenn. Ct. App. 2006)

CHARLES D. SUSANO, JR., JUDGE.

These appeals find their genesis in a collision between a Georgia school bus and a CSX freight train in Polk County, Tennessee, just north of the Georgia state line. As a result of the collision, three children were killed and four others on the bus were injured. All of the children were minors. Three wrongful death actions and three personal injury actions—as well as other actions not involved in this appeal—were filed in the trial court. The cases before us named as defendants, Rhonda Cloer, the driver of the bus; the Murray County [Georgia] School District ("the School District"); and other entities. . . . As to all of the claims arising out of the collision, the trial court held that the School District's liability could not exceed $300,000, the total amount of the coverage for one incident under the School District's vehicle liability policy. We affirm.

I

This school bus/freight train collision occurred at approximately 6:35 a.m. on March 28, 2000, at a railroad crossing on Liberty Church Road in Polk County [Tennessee]. The school bus was driven by Rhonda Cloer, an employee of the School District. Seven Georgia school children were on the bus.

[The designated bus route started and ended in Georgia but included travel on a road that straddles the Georgia-Tennessee border and on another road that is in Tennessee.]

On the morning of March 28, 2000, the defendant Cloer was operating a school bus for the School District. . . . Ms. Cloer's bus stopped . . . to pick up several Georgia children at Liberty Baptist Church, a bus stop located on the [Georgia] side of Liberty Church Road[, the road that straddles the Georgia-Tennessee border]. After picking up the children, the school bus continued [on the road that took her into Tennessee.] Before Ms. Cloer's route took her back [into Georgia] her bus would have to cross a set of railroad tracks—the impact site of the collision at issue. The intersection was marked by a railroad crossing sign, which was placed there by the Tennessee Department of Transportation. The railroad crossing did not have warning bells, lights, or crossing arms.

While Ms. Cloer was approaching the tracks, the train was heading toward Liberty Church Road at a speed of 51 miles per hour. On the train were two Tennessee residents—an engineer, Roger Farley, and a conductor, Kendrick Perry. . . . The train's lights were on, and, as was the custom, Mr. Farley sounded a horn cadence upon approaching the crossing. The school bus approached the crossing at approximately 15 miles per hour. As the train got closer to the intersection, Mr. Farley saw the school bus and watched for signs indicating that the bus was going to stop before it reached the railroad crossing. A video camera, which was on the school bus for the purpose of monitoring the behavior of the children, captured the fact that the bus did not stop prior to crossing the railroad tracks. Country music is audible on the tape.

When Mr. Farley realized that the bus was not going to stop, he applied the train's emergency braking system and continuously blew the train's horn. The train hit the bus near its rear axle and pushed the body of the bus, which was now separated from the chassis, some 200 feet. The train came to a stop approximately 1,990 feet beyond the crossing. Tennessee emergency vehicles responded to the collision; the injured children were transported to Tennessee hospitals. Three of the seven children on the bus—Amber Pritchett, Kayla Silvers, and Daniel Pack—died as a result of their injuries. The other children on board, including Ms. Cloer's daughter, . . . suffered minor to severe injuries.

II

On March 27, 2001, within one year of the accident on March 28, 2000,[*] Sharon Lemons and Ralph C. Pritchett filed a complaint in the trial court seeking damages for the wrongful death of their daughter, Amber Pritchett. The complaint seeks to recover damages against the School District and others.[5] . . .

The trial court, acting on [a] motion for partial summary judgment filed by the School District, ruled that, pursuant to Georgia law, which the court found to be applicable to these cases under principles of conflict of laws and comity, the School District's liability for all claims arising out of this accident was capped at $300,000, the total coverage afforded by its vehicle liability insurance policy for a single accident. . . .

The material facts with respect to the issues raised on this appeal are not in dispute. Accordingly, our review is *de novo* on the record of the proceed-

---

[*]   [Eds.' Note: The statute of limitations on personal injury claims was one year. In a part of the opinion not reprinted here, the appeals court upheld the lower court's entry of summary judgment against the wrongful death claims that were brought on behalf of Daniel Pack and Kayla Silvers, two of the children on the bus who died in the accident. Those cases were filed more than one year after the date of the accident and were barred by the statute of limitations.]

5   Also named as defendants were the driver of the bus; CSX Transportation, Inc.; the company responsible for trimming the vegetation along the railroad tracks; and State Farm Mutual Automobile Insurance Company. These claims are not before us on this appeal.

ings before the trial court with no presumption of correctness as to the trial court's conclusions of law.

III

[We must decide whether, with respect to this Lemons/Pritchett claim and all other still-pending claims arising out of this accident,] Georgia's sovereign immunity—as it relates to the School District's $300,000 vehicle liability insurance policy—applies to the facts of this case. The plaintiffs contend that the $300,000 limit does not apply for several reasons. They argue that both Georgia and Tennessee choice of law principles dictate that Tennessee—not Georgia—substantive law should be applied. . . .

A

. . . [W]e must determine if there is, in fact, a conflict of laws. . . . Clearly, there is. Under the operative Georgia law, the School District's liability arising out of claims for negligent use of a motor vehicle is limited to the amount of the School District's motor vehicle liability coverage under the policy in effect at the time of the accident. Ga. Code Ann. § 33–24–51(b), (c), (d) (stating that Georgia's sovereign immunity is waived "only to the extent of the limits or the coverage of the insurance policy.") This means that the School District's liability is capped at $300,000, the total amount of the coverage afforded for one accident under the School District's vehicle liability insurance policy. Therefore, if Georgia substantive law applies, the School District is immune from any liability in excess of $300,000. On the other hand, if the substantive law of Tennessee applies, there is no limit.[9]

The School District does not dispute that the procedural law of Tennessee applies to the facts of this case. However, it does not necessarily follow from this that the substantive law of Tennessee is also applicable to this accident in Tennessee. . . . Thus, the issue before us remains: Does the substantive law of the forum state—here, Tennessee—apply or does the substantive law of Georgia determine the rights of these parties? . . . [In *Hataway v. McKinley*, 830 S.W.2d 53, 59 (Tenn. 1992), the Tennessee Supreme Court declined to apply *lex loci delicti*, opting instead to adopt the "most significant

---

9   Tennessee has a similar Code provision, Tenn. Code Ann. § 29–20–311 (2000), capping damages against a governmental entity. However, if Tennessee law applies, the damages would not be capped in this case because the limit in Tenn. Code Ann. § 29–20–311 applies to Tennessee governmental entities. *See* Tenn. Code Ann. § 29–20–102 (Supp. 2005) (defining a "[g]overnmental entity" as "any political subdivision of the state of Tennessee) (emphasis added).

relationship" test embodied in the Restatement. Pertinent provisions here include §§ 6, 145, 146, and 175.]

In the instant case, all of the children on the bus were residents of Georgia. The bus driver was also a resident of Georgia. The School District is a Georgia governmental entity. The School District's relationships with the plaintiffs were clearly centered in Georgia. This was a Georgia bus picking up children living in Georgia and transporting them to a Georgia school. The contacts with Tennessee are the following: the accident occurred in Tennessee; Tennessee emergency and medical personnel responded to the accident; injured parties were taken to Tennessee hospitals; and the train engineer and conductor, who also filed personal injury claims in the trial court, were residents of Tennessee. When all of this is considered, we conclude that Georgia had a "more significant relationship" to the parties and events at issue. *See* Restatement (Second) of Conflict of Laws § 145(2). This is not to say that Tennessee did not have a relationship to the parties and this school bus/freight train collision; but, in our judgment, Tennessee's relationship is less significant than that of Georgia.

As a somewhat alternative argument for the application of Tennessee law over Georgia law, the plaintiffs appear to rely on the fact that Georgia still applies the *lex loci delicti* rule in its resolution of choice of law conflicts. *Dowis v. Mud Slingers, Inc.*, 621 S.E.2d 413 (Ga. 2005). The plaintiffs mentioned the recent decision in *Dowis* at oral argument. Consequently, we requested that the parties file supplemental briefs addressing its impact, if any, on the issues presently before us. The sole issue in *Dowis* was whether the *lex loci delicti* rule should be retained as Georgia's choice of law rule. 621 S.E.2d at 414. The Georgia High Court looked at the "most significant relationship" test, and specifically Tennessee's *Hataway* opinion, for an alternative approach. *Id.* at 415–18. Citing *stare decisis* and the predictability of the *lex loci delicti* rule, the Georgia Supreme Court held that it would continue to utilize the *lex loci delicti* rule. *Id.* at 419.

The plaintiffs in the instant case argue that the decision in *Dowis* somehow establishes (1) that Tennessee law should apply because Tennessee, as the place where the collision occurred, had substantial interests in the wrongs committed within its borders; and (2) that, because of this difference in approach, Tennessee should not recognize Georgia governmental immunity by way of comity. We find these arguments to be without merit and totally unsupported by the decision in *Dowis*. The conflict of laws rule to which relationship" test embodied in the Restatement. Pertinent provisions here include §§ 6, 145, 146, and 175.]

In the instant case, all of the children on the bus were residents of Georgia. The bus driver was also a resident of Georgia. The School District is a Georgia governmental entity. The School District's relationships with the plaintiffs were clearly centered in Georgia. This was a Georgia bus picking up children living in Georgia and transporting them to a Georgia school. The contacts with Tennessee are the following: the accident occurred in Tennessee; Tennessee emergency and medical personnel responded to the accident; injured parties were taken to Tennessee hospitals; and the train engineer and conductor, who also filed personal injury claims in the trial court, were residents of Tennessee. When all of this is considered, we conclude that Georgia had a "more significant relationship" to the parties and events at issue. *See* Restatement (Second) of Conflict of Laws § 145(2). This is not to say that Tennessee did not have a relationship to the parties and this school bus/freight train collision; but, in our judgment, Tennessee's relationship is less significant than that of Georgia.

As a somewhat alternative argument for the application of Tennessee law over Georgia law, the plaintiffs appear to rely on the fact that Georgia still applies the *lex loci delicti* rule in its resolution of choice of law conflicts. *Dowis v. Mud Slingers, Inc.*, 621 S.E.2d 413 (Ga. 2005). The plaintiffs mentioned the recent decision in *Dowis* at oral argument. Consequently, we requested that the parties file supplemental briefs addressing its impact, if any, on the issues presently before us. The sole issue in *Dowis* was whether the *lex loci delicti* rule should be retained as Georgia's choice of law rule. 621 S.E.2d at 414. The Georgia High Court looked at the "most significant relationship" test, and specifically Tennessee's *Hataway* opinion, for an alternative approach. *Id.* at 415–18. Citing *stare decisis* and the predictability of the *lex loci delicti* rule, the Georgia Supreme Court held that it would continue to utilize the *lex loci delicti* rule. *Id.* at 419.

The plaintiffs in the instant case argue that the decision in *Dowis* somehow establishes (1) that Tennessee law should apply because Tennessee, as the place where the collision occurred, had substantial interests in the wrongs committed within its borders; and (2) that, because of this difference in approach, Tennessee should not recognize Georgia governmental immunity by way of comity. We find these arguments to be without merit and totally unsupported by the decision in *Dowis*. The conflict of laws rule to which

Georgia subscribes is not material in this case. This action was brought in a
Tennessee state court; thus, Tennessee's choice of law rule, *i.e.*, the *Hataway*
test, is the controlling relevant choice of law principle.

The plaintiffs contend that, if we determine Georgia substantive law applies,
all of that law, including *lex loci delicti*, is applicable. The plaintiffs extrapolate
from this proposition that Tennessee's substantive law, including a lack of
immunity for this non-Tennessee entity, applies because Tennessee is where
the accident occurred; therefore, Tennessee law is the *lex loci delicti*. This
circular reasoning is commonly known as *renvoi*, a French word meaning
"sending back." To our knowledge, the only court in Tennessee to consider
the application of *renvoi* is a federal district court. In the case of *Hari &
Assocs. v. RNBC, Inc.*, 946 F. Supp. 531 (M.D. Tenn. 1996), the plaintiff, a
motel developer, sued his lender for fraud in a federal district court located
in Tennessee. *Id.* at 533–34. Applying *Hataway*, the district court found
that, although the motel was to be built in Tennessee, Georgia had the "most
significant relationship" to the tort because all of the parties' contracts and
loan agreements were centered and executed in Georgia. *Id.* at 536. The
plaintiff similarly relied on the *renvoi* doctrine in an attempt to convince
the court that Tennessee, not Georgia, substantive law should apply. *Id.*
at 536–37. The district court rejected the plaintiff's *renvoi* argument and
"decline[d] to adopt this disfavored doctrine for the state of Tennessee."
Id. at 537.

We agree with the district court's approach to the *renvoi* argument. Since
the complaints in the instant case were filed in a Tennessee court, Tennessee's choice of law rule, the "most significant relationship" test, applies. As
previously stated, this test, in our judgment, leads, without any doubt to
Georgia substantive law. At this juncture, the plaintiffs would argue that
Georgia substantive law, to which *Hataway* directs us, includes the Georgia
choice of law, *i.e., lex loci delicti*. This means, according to the plaintiffs,
that we are "sen[t] back" to Tennessee as our source of substantive law. The
problem with this approach is that if Georgia substantive law, in the context
under discussion, is viewed as including its choice of law principles, there
is no reason to hold that the Tennessee substantive law does not include
its choice of law principles. The Georgia choice of law doctrine of *lex loci
delicti* would bring us back to Tennessee, whose substantive law, including
its choice of law doctrine of "most significant relationship," would lead
back to Georgia after which the process, arguably, would be repeated *ad
infinitum*. Obviously, this quagmire cannot be the law. . . .

Whatever our approach it needs to be something that the judge can adopt with confidence. The clarity of our arguments and the thoroughness of our documentation supply that confidence. The court's opinion suggests that plaintiffs failed to do that here.

FROM THE COURTS

THE CHARTER OAK FIRE INS. CO. v. AMERICAN CAPITAL, LTD.

U.S. District Court for the District of Maryland
2011 WL 856374 (D. Md. 2011)

DEBORAH K. CHASAN, DISTRICT JUDGE.

Defendant American Capital, Ltd ("American Capital") is a fund that invests in other companies. One of its purported investments, Defendant Scientific Protein Laboratories, LLC ("SPL"), was allegedly involved in the sale and distribution of a tainted drug. Now, American Capital and SPL find themselves embroiled in several lawsuits in several courts. American Capital wants its insurers, Plaintiffs The Charter Oak Fire Insurance Company ("Charter Oak") and Travelers Property Casualty Company of America ("Travelers"), to defend and indemnify those suits. The insurers resisted and filed this action, wherein they seek to rescind or reform the relevant insurance contracts and ask the court to declare that neither insurer is required to defend or indemnify Defendants in the underlying suits.

American Capital and its co-defendants in this case have now filed a partial motion to dismiss. . . .

I. Background

A. Factual Background

[From 2006 to 2009, American Capital purchased commercial liability insurance. Charter Oak issued the primary policies which annually covered $1 million per occurrence and $2 million aggregate. Travelers issued umbrella policies annually which contained limits on liability from between $10 and $20 million. (Collectively, the "Policies"). The Policies listed only American Capital as the Named Insured.

Like most insurance contracts, the Policies included certain limitations and exclusions. Most importantly, there was no coverage for anyone who wasn't a Named Insured. The Policies also imposed certain obligations on American Capital, including notifying the Plaintiffs of any claims arising under the Policies. There was also a "no action" clause that forbade certain types of payments without the Plaintiffs' consent.

American Capital has sought insurance coverage for itself and its purported subsidiaries for a group of more than 100 lawsuits concerning heparin—a drug that is used to prevent the formation of blood clots. In those suits, American Capital and SPL have been forced to defend several claims that stem from deaths and injuries from allegedly tainted heparin. In particular, the lawsuits assert that one or more ingredients of certain heparin, including its active pharmaceutical ingredient, were tainted or contaminated during processing in China. Changzhou SPL Company, Ltd., a joint venture between SPL and Tech-Pool Bio-Pharma Company, oversaw this processing. Once processing in China was complete, the heparin was purportedly shipped to the United States to be finished by Baxter International, Inc. and Baxter Healthcare Corporations ("Baxter"). It was then distributed for patient use.

Plaintiffs aver that neither American Capital nor any of its subsidiaries is entitled to coverage under the Policies because American Capital made certain "material and intentional" false representations, including that it had no subsidiaries, that it had not acquired any operations, that none of its products had been recalled, that it did not use foreign products, and that it was not a party to a joint venture. Plaintiffs allege also that American Capital settled with Baxter, its co-defendant in several of the heparin lawsuits, even though it was prohibited from doing so without the insurers' consents.]

B. Procedural Background

Plaintiffs filed a five-count complaint on January 16, 2009. That complaint sought to rescind the Policies, alternatively asked to reform the Policies based on mutual or unilateral mistake, asserted a claim of unjust enrichment. . . . Defendants filed the presently pending motion to dismiss. . . .

[II.] Analysis

A. Choice of Law

The court must first determine which state's law governs this dispute. The parties raise the dispute only in arguing over whether the Maryland or

Pennsylvania parol evidence rule applies but this question is actually relevant to all the claims. The answer is that Maryland law governs.

1. General Choice of Law Principles

In a federal diversity case such as this one, the court must apply the choice of law rules of the forum state, *i.e.,* Maryland. *See Klaxon Co. v. Stentor Elec. Mfg. Co.*, 313 U.S. 487 (1941). In the first instance, Plaintiffs and Defendants disagree on whether Maryland tort or contract choice of law principles apply.

All the claims relate to the validity of the Policies or the scope of their coverage. . . . This is a dispute over the interpretation and scope of a contract. Thus Maryland contract choice of law principles apply. . . .

In contract actions, Maryland courts "apply the substantive law of the place where the contract was made." *Cont'l Cas. Co. v. Kemper Ins. Co.*, 173 Md. App. 542, 548 (2007). "A contract is made in the place where the last act occurs necessary under the rules of offer and acceptance to give the contract a binding effect." *Id.* When dealing with an insurance policy, the *locus contractus* "is the state in which the policy is delivered and the premiums are paid." *Id.*

Normally the locations of delivery and payment are easy to determine. Here, however, there is disagreement. Defendants argue that delivery occurred in Pennsylvania because (1) Plaintiffs delivered the Policies to McKee Risk Management Inc., the insurance producer for the Policies, in Pennsylvania; and (2) Defendants mailed their premium payments to McKee's Pennsylvania location. Plaintiffs want discovery to determine where delivery and payment happened.

2. Renvoi

The parties disagree over a moot point. Under the doctrine of *renvoi*, Maryland law applies—even assuming that Pennsylvania was the place of delivery and payment under Maryland choice of law principles. Renvoi means that

> . . . when the forum court's choice-of-law rules would apply the substantive law of a foreign jurisdiction to the case before the forum court, the forum court may apply the whole body of the foreign jurisdiction's substantive law including the foreign jurisdiction's choice-of-law rules. If, in applying renvoi principles, the

foreign jurisdiction's conflict of law rules would apply the forum's law, this reference back of the forum to its own laws is called a remission.

Am. Motorists Ins. Co. v. ARTRA Grp., Inc., 338 Md. 560, 574 (1995) (citations omitted). Maryland courts apply a limited renvoi exception to traditional contract choice of law principles and employ Maryland substantive law when two conditions are met:

(1) Maryland has the most significant relationship, or, at least, a substantial relationship with respect to the contract issue presented; and

(2) The state where the contract was entered into would not apply its own substantive law, but instead would apply Maryland substantive law to the issue before the court.

ARTRA Grp., 338 Md. at 579.

Here, Maryland has a substantial interest in the litigation given that American Capital maintains its principal place of business in Bethesda, Maryland. *Cf. Pink v. A.A.A. Highway Express, Inc.*, 314 U.S. 201, 211 (1941) ("The interpretation and legal effect of policies of insurance entered into by the inhabitants of [a state] . . . are peculiarly matters of local concern."). Thus the only question is whether Pennsylvania would in fact apply Maryland law.

At present, under Pennsylvania choice of law principles, the first step "is to determine whether a conflict exists between the laws of the competing states." *Budtel Assocs., LP v. Cont'l Cas. Co.*, 915 A.2d 640, 643 (Pa. Super. 2006). If no conflict exists, Pennsylvania would apply its own law. That is not the case here, particularly in the context of the rescission claim. In Pennsylvania, the parol evidence rule bars "consideration of prior representations concerning matters covered in the written [integrated] contract, even those alleged to have been made fraudulently, unless the representations were fraudulently *omitted from the contract*." *Dayhoff Inc. v. H.J. Heinz Co.*, 86 F.3d 1287, 1300 (3d Cir. 1996) (citing *HCB Contractors v. Liberty Place Hotel Assoc.*, 539 Pa. 395, 398–99 (1995)). Maryland courts take a more permissive approach:

[The parol evidence rule's] name has distracted attention . . . from the real issues that are involved which may be any one or more of

> the following: (1) Have the parties made a contract? (2) Is that contract void or voidable because of illegality, fraud, mistake, or any other reason? (3) Did the parties assent to a particular writing as the complete and accurate integration of that contract? . . . In determining these issues, or any one of them, there is no parol evidence rule to be applied. On these issues, no relevant evidence, whether parol or otherwise is excluded. No written document is sufficient, standing alone, to determine any one of them.

Whitney v. Halibut, Inc., 235 Md. 517, 527 (1964). Even when a contract contains an integration clause, Maryland—in contrast to Pennsylvania—allows a party to use parol evidence contradicting express contractual terms where the other party acted fraudulently. *See Greenfeld v. Heckenbach*, 144 Md. App. 108, 132–35 (2002). Pennsylvania's more restrictive rule clashes with the Maryland approach, which creates a genuine conflict.

Defendants characterize the present situation as a "false conflict" because they believe that only Pennsylvania has an interest in the application of its law. Pennsylvania courts have indeed found a false conflict "exists when only one state has an actual interest in applying its law." *3039 B Assocs., Inc. v. Lexington Ins. Co.*, 740 F.Supp.2d 671 (E.D. Pa. 2010). And admittedly, Pennsylvania has an interest in not allowing contracts created in that state to be sullied by the excessive use of parol evidence. But Maryland has a competing interest in applying its own law because at least one insured, American Capital, has its principal place of business in the state. Maryland may not wish its residents to benefit from the type of misleading or deceitful behavior alleged here. *Cf. Life Partners, Inc. v. Morrison*, 484 F.3d 284, 296 (4th Cir. 2007) (noting that a state has an interest in "ensuring . . . that its residents not defraud insurance companies").

Having established that a genuine conflict exists, a Pennsylvania court would next determine "which state has the greater interest in the application of its law." *Budtel Assocs.*, 915 A.2d at 643. This approach requires the court to "apply the law of the state having the most significant contacts or relationships with the contract and not the underlying tort." *Nationwide Mut. Ins. Co. v. West*, 807 A.2d 916, 921 (Pa. Super. 2002). . . .

Pennsylvania determines the most significant relationship using the approach found in the Second Restatement of Conflict of Laws. *See Specialty Surfaces Int'l Co. v. West*, 609 F.3d 223, 233 (3d Cir. 2010) (applying Pennsylvania choice of law principles); *Hammersmith v. TIG Ins. Co.*, 480 F.3d 220, 232 (3d Cir. 2007) (same). Section 193 of the Restatement applies specifically to insurance policies and provides that "the principal location of the insured risk" should be the chief consideration. *Id.* at 233. That rule is not especially useful, however, "if the policy covers a group of risks that are scattered throughout two or more states." *Id.* (quoting Restatement (Second) Conflict of Laws § 193 cmt. b). Here, the Policies list a Maryland address for the named insured, American Capital. That might indicate that Maryland is the principal location of the insured risk. On the other hand, Plaintiffs provided Commercial General Liability Exposure Schedules reflecting that the Policies covered locations in at least nine different states. Therefore, Section 193 does not resolve the issue.

When the geographic diversity of the covered risk renders Section 193 "generally inapplicable," Pennsylvania courts look next to the Second Restatement provision governing general contracts. Section 188(2). *Hammersmith*, 480 F.3d at 233. That provision lists five relevant contacts: "(1) the place of contracting; (2) the place of negotiation of the contract; (3) the place of performance; (4) the location of the subject matter of the contract; and (5) the domicile, residence, nationality, place of incorporation and place of business of the parties." *Id.* When applying these factors, the court does not undertake "[a] simple tally of the contacts . . . because an undifferentiated application of the formula to all situations would yield unjust results in too many circumstances." *United Brass Works v. Am. Guarantee & Liab. Ins. Co.*, 819 F. Supp. 465, 470 (W.D. Pa. 1992).

Just as in Maryland, "[t]he place of making an insurance contract is the place of delivery, where delivery is the last essential act." *Crawford v. Manhattan Life Ins. Co. of New York*, 208 Pa. Super. 150 (1966). Again, Defendants contend delivery occurred in Pennsylvania because the Policies were delivered to their "producer," McKee, in that state. Yet under Pennsylvania law, if a company sends a policy agent for delivery to the insured, the place of delivery is the place where the *insured* receives the policy, not the agent. *Crawford,* 22 A.2d at 881. Even if this were not the case, a Pennsylvania court might presume delivery occurred at the residence of the insured—in Maryland—given the murky state of the facts concerning delivery at this time. *Hammersmith*, 480 F.3d at 233. Regardless, this factor weighs in favor of Maryland law.

The parties did not submit any evidence concerning the place of negotiation. This factor weighs in favor of neither Maryland nor Pennsylvania law.

The third factor, the place of performance, looks to where the policyholder paid premiums to the insurer. *Specialty Surfaces*, 609 F.3d at 233. In the case of promises to indemnify and defend, a court might also consider where the insurer's duty would arise, *i.e.,* where the underlying litigation is taking place. *Id.* Again, this factor is unhelpful. The best evidence available regarding payment indicates that American Capital made payment from some unspecified location (perhaps Maryland, perhaps Pennsylvania, or perhaps somewhere else entirely), to the producer (in Pennsylvania), who then forwarded payment to Plaintiffs (in Connecticut). As for the underlying litigation, the heparin lawsuits arose all over the country, with many of them currently being handled in a multidistrict litigation proceeding in the U.S. District Court for the Northern District of Ohio. *See In re Heparin Prods. Lia. Litig.*, No. 1:08–hc–60000–JGC (N.D. Ohio filed June 6, 2008). None of these facts point to Pennsylvania or Maryland as the more appropriate forum.

The location of the subject matter looks to the principal place of insured risk. As has already been explained, the risk is spread over a broad geographic area. Therefore, "this factor is neutral." *Hammersmith*, 480 F.3d at 234.

As to the parties' locations, only the producer of the Policies (McKee) and one of the potential additional insureds are located in Pennsylvania. Both Plaintiffs are incorporated in Connecticut and have their principal places of business there. SPL is a Delaware limited liability company with a principal place of business in Wisconsin. American Capital is incorporated in Delaware and has a principal place of business in Maryland. Given that the central parties to the Policies (*i.e.,* the named insured and the insurers) are from Maryland and Connecticut, this factor suggests Maryland law should apply over Pennsylvania law. *See Gen. Star Nat'l Ins. Co. v. Liberty Mut. Ins. Co.*, 960 F.2d 377, 379 (3d Cir. 1992) (applying Pennsylvania choice of law principles and finding that Pennsylvania would have "little interest" in protecting an insured from another state by means of regulating the conduct of an insurer from another state).

Taking all these factors together, a Pennsylvania court would apply Maryland law. Under Pennsylvania choice of law, the place of contracting took place in Maryland. That, combined with the presence in this state of the only named insured listed in the Policies, reflects that Maryland has the more substantial interest in applying its law. The matter would be remitted to Maryland; Maryland law therefore applies. . . .

COMMENTS AND QUESTIONS

1. The state of Maryland has a "limited renvoi exception to traditional contract choice of principles." It is "limited" to the extent that the case law restricts it to contract cases. (Note the characterization issue.) But its two conditions are hardly "limiting": (i) Maryland has the most significant— or at least a substantial—relationship; and (ii) the foreign state would, according to its choice of law principles, apply Maryland law.

    Maryland follows the traditional approach for choice of law. Rather than having a limited renvoi exception, would Maryland essentially reach the same endpoint if, instead, it adopted the Second Restatement as its approach for contract cases?

2. Does a doctrine of renvoi reduce forum-shopping?

3. Every application of renvoi requires one to predict how the foreign state would apply its choice of law rules. That is an unstable premise. Here, for example, a jurisdiction that follows the traditional approach is predicting what a Second Restatement jurisdiction would conclude. What did you think of the Maryland court's prediction of how Pennsylvania would analyze the Section 6 factors?

4. Accepting the renvoi assumes that the foreign state would apply forum law. Imagine Maryland's choice of law principles point to Pennsylvania, but Pennsylvania's choice of law principles point to Maryland. Maryland could accept the renvoi. But who's to say that if this case were filed originally in Pennsylvania that Pennsylvania wouldn't accept the renvoi (from Maryland) and apply Pennsylvania law?

5. The plaintiffs requested additional discovery so that they could locate evidence to bolster their contention that the place of contracting was not Pennsylvania. Even the simplicity of the traditional approach raises a fact question—the place of contracting—that is better answered if the par-

ties can gather and produce evidence. Imagine the number of potential disputed questions of fact in an application of the Second Restatement's approach.

Quick Summary

- In choice of law methodologies that are more rigid, renvoi can be an escape device to avoid the application of foreign law (and instead apply forum law)

- The doctrine of renvoi is generally disfavored, but the fact that the foreign jurisdiction would not apply its own law may still be part of the decisional calculus for determining which state's law should apply

13

Domicile

Key Concepts

- *Domicile* is a term of art that is not necessarily one's residence or home address
- Domicile is important in the choice of law context and can also be the basis for establishing personal jurisdiction

---

The word domicile is derived from the Latin *domus* which means "home" or "dwelling." Although domicile is a particular conception of being at home, it is importantly different than one's residence, citizenship, current address, permanent address, hometown, family homestead, and other non-legal descriptions of relationships that individuals have with a particular locality. Domicile is a term of art that describes a specific legal relationship between an individual and a particular locality.

Domicile is an important concept in conflict of laws. The First Restatement dedicated thirty-three sections to the topic. Under the traditional choice of law method, the domicile of a party is a jurisdiction-selecting fact for certain causes of action. The Second Restatement likewise features domicile as the dispositive fact for certain claims (like which state's law of intestate succession applies) and as a principal fact for nearly all claims. Interest analysis (and by extension the better law approach, too) uses domicile to determine whether a state's policy would be advanced by application of that state's law. Domicile is also a basis for establishing personal jurisdiction.

A key distinguishing characteristic of domicile is that an individual can only have one domicile at a time for any one purpose. Accordingly, unlike residences or homes or addresses or even citizenships, an individual cannot have more than one domicile for a particular purpose.[1] Nor can someone ever be without a domicile:

---

1   For example, the law may assign a person one domicile for voting purposes and another for intestate succession.

every individual always has one, but only one domicile. Individuals start with their parents' domicile, so that is everyone's first domicile.

A person keeps one's domicile until s/he adopts a new one. In order to change domicile, one must be (i) present in the new domicile, and (ii) intend to remain there indefinitely (or "for the time at least," as the Second Restatement defines it). The first condition is a physical fact, but the second is a state of mind.

A common mistake by young lawyers is mishandling evidence of someone's intention to abandon a domicile. Imagine, for example, that an adult proclaims honestly, earnestly, and loudly as she leaves the state of Maine, where she has spent her entire life, "I hereby leave this state never to return." Importantly, it is not the intention to abandon the (Maine) domicile that establishes a new domicile. Only presence and the intent to remain in a new state will establish a new domicile. Accordingly, even if she leaves Maine and never returns to the state, she will be a Maine domiciliary until she establishes a new domicile elsewhere (which could be never—if she spends the rest of her life in the military, in a traveling circus, on a boat sailing around the world, or otherwise never establishes a permanent home elsewhere). If she settles in, say, West Virginia, she is a domiciliary of that state if and only if, while present in West Virginia, she intends to remain there indefinitely. To prove that intention, evidence of her honest, earnest, and loud pronouncement as she left Maine could be useful evidence. But it is her presence and intent to remain indefinitely in West Virginia (not the pronounced departure from Maine) that changed her domicile.

The stakes of an inquiry into someone's domicile can be as consequential as any choice of law inquiry. The physical fact of someone's presence is seldom the battleground. Instead, it is disagreement about the person's state of mind. When the person whose domicile is at issue is alive, she or he can testify about their intention. But even in these cases, courts will examine all the available evidence for positive and satisfactory proof of the establishment of a new domicile as a matter of fact.

Often there is no dispute about someone's domicile. Many people are lifelong residents of a state, and many others are ensconced in one place. But of course there are individuals whose lives are in transition or whose lives are geographically divided, and it is in these cases where one's domicile is debatable, and must be determined.

The rules for determining one's domicile are expressed chronologically: we start with our parents' domicile (the "domicile of origin"); we keep that domicile until we reach the age of maturity and have the legal capacity to adopt a new domicile (a "domicile of choice"); and then we keep that domicile until we adopt a new domicile; and the cycle repeats. As a practical matter, litigators who are interrogating the domicile of someone tend to work in reverse chronological order. We look at, say, a law student and think: "Well you live in this state, so you are present here; but while present have you also formed an intention to stay here indefinitely?" An affirmative answer to that question means that you are also domiciled here. But if the answer to that question is "no," then we tend to work in reverse chronological order to find the last place that you were both present and intending to remain indefinitely. You might be domiciled in the state that you grew up in and a resident of a different state where you are attending law school. The fact that you are present in the second state and not in the state of your domicile is not important once you have established a domicile in the first state. We will reach the same conclusion about someone's domicile whether we work in forward or in reverse chronological order, but ordinarily we do not need the long history of someone's life to determine his or her domicile.

Hypothetical 13-1

Until recently, Jan McGinley and her husband, Jeff, owned a mobile home as semi-retirees in a mobile home park in Daytona Beach, Florida. That mobile home was recently destroyed in a hurricane; Jan and Jeff promptly collected $105,000 on an insurance policy, and that money is sitting in a Florida bank account until they decide to buy again. Their old Subaru Forester was also destroyed in the hurricane; Jan used the insurance proceeds from that loss to purchase another mini-SUV that is registered in Florida.

Jan has worked for 14 years as an assistant trainer of race horses. For the last 7 years she has been employed by Neb Edwards Racing Stable, a horse trainer in Oceanport, New Jersey. Each April, Jan and Jeff leave Florida to spend five months at training grounds near the Monmouth Park Race Track in New Jersey.

In prior years, Jan and Jeff left the mobile home vacant in Florida, and paid the nominal monthly space rental while they were away. They kept their Florida telephone service, and had their mail forwarded to New Jersey. With the destruction of their mobile home, however, the McGinleys no longer pay rent, no longer have a telephone line, do not have a home, and have no personal belongings in Florida. Jan filed a permanent change of address, forwarding mail to their New Jersey address.

As in prior years, Jan (with Jeff) recently made it back to Oceanport, New Jersey in time for the summer meet this year. Each year the McGinleys have rented the same home in Long Branch, New Jersey. When living there they pay $1000 per month in rent. The landlord likes them and holds the apartment vacant during the winter months so that it will be available when the McGinleys return each spring. In turn, McGinley pays the landlord $250 per month during those vacant months as a token of appreciation.

While present in New Jersey, Jan is involved in an employment dispute with Neb Edwards that arises in part out of a telephone conversation between the two that occurred last winter while Jan was in Florida. Jan's counsel would like to argue that Jan is entitled to certain protections of Florida employment law. And it would help her make that argument if Jan is domiciled in Florida. Is Jan a domiciliary of Florida?

The intent to remain somewhere indefinitely is a concept that non-lawyers and clients can understand. Yet it is not a conception that one ordinarily entertains when one moves: typically one moves without making any solemn commitments about the intended duration of that move. Accordingly, the outcomes of these inquiries usually turn on circumstantial evidence regarding the permanence of the move. A brainstormed list of possibly relevant evidence would include details about such things as:

Voter registration; voting	Involvement in civic organizations	Location of family (kids/ schools)	Address used on forms, contests, applications	Location of physician, dentist, lawyers
Professional licensure	Personal property	Real property; owns/rents	Social commitments	Auto registration
Taxes	Work	Church, Clubs	Driver's license	Bank accounts

Aware of the consequences of having one domicile instead of another, motivated reasoning can lead someone unconsciously (or consciously) to shape the relevant information so that it leads to the more favorable result. Judges are attuned to this and thus will not rely solely on someone's attestation of their intent.

Hypothetical 13-2

Cheryl Miller and Don Harris, the parents of Shakira Harris, filed in a Pennsylvania state court a wrongful death action against ABC, Inc., a government contractor who allegedly caused the death of their daughter. Staff Sergeant Shakira Harris (SSG Harris) died on a military base in Iraq when she was electrocuted during what should have been a routine maintenance operation on base equipment. ABC, Inc., a Texas corporation with a principal place of business in Dallas, had operations and maintenance responsibilities under government contracts.

A choice of law issue has arisen about whether the claims and defenses raised by the parties are governed by (i) Iraqi law, (ii) one of the proportional liability systems utilized by Texas or Tennessee which permit the jury to assign fault to immune non-parties, or (iii) Pennsylvania's joint and several liability system which permits the jury to assign fault only between the parties to the case. The choice between options (ii) and (iii) will likely turn on SSG Harris's domicile at the time of her death.

Cheryl and Don are Pennsylvania citizens who, although divorced, both maintain residences in Philadelphia. Their daughter was born and raised in Philadelphia. After graduating from high school SSG Harris enlisted in the U.S. Army. She received service orders that directed her initially to Fort Benning, Georgia for Boot Camp. Over the course of the four years that followed, she received service orders that transferred her from Louisiana, to North Carolina, to Colorado, to Iraq, to California, and then most recently to Fort Campbell, which is located in both Tennessee and Kentucky.

Two weeks after SSG Harris was stationed at Fort Campbell she purchased an off-base home in nearby Clarksville, Tennessee. She obtained a 30-year mortgage on the single-family home which she financed through a Veterans Administration Program. In order to obtain this loan she was obligated to certify that she would move into the home within 60 days of purchase and that she would occupy the home for at least one year absent extenuating circumstances.

SSG Harris lived in the home for four months before she received orders from the Army to return to Iraq for a second tour of duty. SSG Harris had two roommates who lived with her in the Tennessee house and who paid her rent; after SSG Harris's deployment they continued to live in the house and pay rent. Two months after her deployment to Iraq she passed away after being electrocuted while engaged in maintenance work. At the time of her death she had approximately one year remaining on her reenlistment commitment. SSG Harris's remains were returned to Pennsylvania and she is buried in the National Cemetery in Pennsylvania outside of Philadelphia.

On all forms that she completed during her military service, SSG Harris used one of her parents' Pennsylvania addresses when asked for a permanent address. She did not, however, complete any such forms after the date of her purchase of the Tennessee house. According to her parents, SSG Harris purchased the home only because it was considerably cheaper than the rental options in the area. Her parents also note that SSG Harris had a brother and a sister who also served in the military, and both of her siblings returned to Pennsylvania following their service.

Was SSG Harris a Tennessee domiciliary at the time of her death?

Hypothetical 13-3

Approximately three years ago, Milton was involved in a car accident in Louisiana that caused him severe and permanent injuries. After the accident he had an I.Q. of 75 and was unable to work or function as he had prior to the accident. Milton and his then-wife Edwina sued the responsible parties and each recovered substantial sums. Milton and Edwina were then life-long residents of Baton Rouge, Louisiana.

Over the next two years, Milton and Edwina's marriage deteriorated. The parties eventually agreed to the terms of a judgment of separation and the family court issued a divorce. Milton failed to make the payments he promised to pay. Approximately one year ago, Edwina filed an action for breach of that agreement.

Shortly after Edwina filed her action, Milton moved to Mobile, Alabama. As he describes it now, he "was hoping that life would be better in Alabama," primarily because he had family there. Milton leased an apartment in Mobile, opened a bank account, obtained an Alabama driver's license, changed his vehicle registration to Alabama, and transferred his car insurance to Alabama.

Milton returned to Baton Rouge, Louisiana every weekend to visit a girlfriend-now-fiancée, Ann, and his best friend, Wayne. In addition to the weekend visits, Milton occasionally returned to Baton Rouge on weekdays to receive medical care. He also paid for membership to a gym in Baton Rouge (that he never visited), kept his Louisiana voter registration (though he never voted), and kept his East Baton Rouge Parish Library card (though he never checked out books). His cell phone number still has a Baton Rouge area code.

Milton recently filed a Chapter 7 petition in the U.S. Bankruptcy Court for the Middle District of Louisiana. Under certain circumstances, the Bankruptcy Code incorporates state law to determine property that may be exempt from the bankruptcy estate. The domicile of the debtor at the time of filing can be dispositive of the question which state's law applies.

Where is Milton domiciled?

From the Courts

BAIN v. HONEYWELL INT'L, INC.

U.S. District Court for the Eastern District of Texas
257 F.Supp.2d 872 (E.D. Tex. 2002)

Schell, District Judge.

I. Background

. . . Scott Bain ("Bain") was an Australian citizen that lived and worked in Australia until February 2000. In February of 2000, Bain moved to Alberta, Canada and began taking helicopter flight training lessons. When Bain completed his flight training lessons in Alberta, he moved to British Columbia where he was employed by Bailey Helicopter, Ltd. ("Bailey"). On June 1, 2000, Bain was killed in a helicopter accident in Helmet, British Columbia, Canada. His parents, John and Peta Bain, filed this civil action asserting survival and wrongful death claims against Honeywell [International Inc. ("Honeywell")] in . . . Texas. Plaintiffs allege that the helicopter accident was caused by the fracture of defective retaining screws on the fuel control unit, which caused the unit to leak fuel into the engine compartment and the engine to lose power[, causing the helicopter to crash, resulting in Bain's death.].

[The parties dispute whether Texas, Alberta, British Columbia, or Australian Capital Territory ("ACT") law applies.]

II. Analysis

Both parties agree that the court must apply Texas law to resolve any conflict of law issues. Texas has adopted the Restatement's "most significant relationship test" to determine the proper law to apply. Application of the "most significant relationship" test does not turn on "the number of contacts with one state, but more importantly on the qualitative nature of those contacts as affected by the policy factors set out in section 6 of the Restatement." *Crisman v. Cooper Indus.*, 748 S.W.2d 273, 276 (Tex. App.-Dallas 1988, writ denied)...

Section 145 lists the factual matters to be considered when applying the Section 6 principles to a given case:

(1) The rights and liabilities of the parties with respect to an issue in tort are determined by the local law of the state which, with respect to that issue, has the most significant relationship to the occurrence and the parties under the principles stated in § 6.

(2) Contacts to be taken into account in applying the principles of § 6 to determine the law applicable to an issue include:

(a) the place where the injury occurred,

(b) the place where the conduct causing the injury occurred,

(c) the domicile, residence, nationality, place of incorporation and place of business of the parties, and

(d) the place where the relationship, if any, between the parties is centered.

These contacts are to be evaluated according to their relative importance with respect to the particular issue.

Restatement (Second) of Conflict of Laws § 145. . . .

In considering the first contact of the section 145 analysis, it is undisputed that Scott Bain's death occurred in British Columbia.

Concerning the second contact, Plaintiffs contend the conduct allegedly causing the injury is the "install[ation of] the defective and/or unairworthy screw in the helicopter's fuel control unit" at the Defendant's California maintenance facility. . . . [However, the] court can find no definitive evidence pointing to where the allegedly-defective screw entered the stream of commerce. . . . Therefore, the court would engage in pure speculation by concluding, as the Plaintiffs do, that the allegedly-defective screw was installed in California. Because of the lack of definitive evidence, the court finds it difficult to apply this contact under section 145.

The third contact to be taken into account, the domicile, residence and nationality of the parties, is partially in dispute. It is undisputed that John and Peta Bain are domiciled in the ACT and that Honeywell is domiciled in Texas. However, the domicile of Scott Bain is contested. The Plaintiffs argue that Bain's domicile at the time of the accident was Alberta because "[Bain] moved from Australia to Alberta, went to flight school in Alberta, lived in Alberta, and he opened and maintained a bank account in Alberta." Pl's Mot. for Appl. of Tex. and Alberta Law at 4; Pl's Reply to Honeywell's Resp. to Mot. for Appl. of Tex. and Alberta Law, Exhibit A at 1 (Affidavit of John Bain) ("Scott moved to Edmonton and established a home there. . . . [h]e also opened up a bank account in Alberta . . . [Scott] liked Alberta and had no immediate plans to return to Australia"). According to Honeywell, Bain's domicile at the time of his death was British Columbia, or alternatively the ACT. Honeywell points out that at the time of the accident Bain lived and worked in British Columbia. Alternatively, Honeywell contends that Bain's domicile was the ACT because, among other things, (1) he declared himself to be an Australian citizen and British Columbia resident on his application for a commercial pilot's license, (2) he declared ACT his permanent address on his employment records with Bailey in British Columbia, (3) he was still registered to vote in the ACT, and (4) he did not apply for permanent residency in Canada.

Under Texas law, a "domicile" is defined as (1) an actual residence that is (2) intended to be a permanent home. *Snyder v. Pitts*, 150 Tex. 407 (1951). The Texas Supreme Court has construed "home" as meaning a "'true fixed and permanent home and principal establishment, and to which, whenever he is absent, he has the intention of returning.' " *Id.* (citing *Ex Parte Blumer*, 27 Tex. 734 (1865)). In applying this definition, it is clear to the court that Alberta was not Bain's domicile at the time of the accident. At the time of the accident, Bain did not have a residence in Alberta. The affidavit of Scott Bain's father, John Bain, merely states, inter alia, that Scott moved to Alberta to advance his career and that he "liked" Alberta. There is no evidence that Alberta held any special significance to Bain. In fact, according to the Plaintiffs' own affidavit Bain moved to Alberta *only to advance his career*, and it appears to the court that he only lived there one month and once British Columbia offered a better opportunity for career advancement Bain promptly left Alberta. There is no definitive evidence showing that, even though he moved to British Columbia, Bain intended to return to Alberta.[3] John Bain's affidavit, however, does assert that Bain did not intend to return to ACT in the near future, thus, casting doubt on whether ACT remained Scott Bain's domicile at the time of his death. There is evidence to support a conclusion that British Columbia was Bain's domicile because at the time of his death he was employed there, he had a residence there, and, according to Plaintiffs, had no immediate plans to return to ACT. On the other hand, Bain was not a citizen of British Columbia and was not attempting to become a citizen. Therefore, the court finds, based on the limited amount of evidence before it, that either British Columbia or ACT was Bain's domicile at the time of his death. It is unnecessary to decide which jurisdiction, in fact, was Bain's domicile because the court finds such an exercise ultimately unnecessary in its choice of law analysis on the liability issues.

The fourth and final contact of the section 145 analysis concerns "the place where the relationship, if any, between the parties is centered." The court finds this contact inapplicable because there was no direct relationship prior to the accident between any of the Plaintiffs and Honeywell. . . .

In weighing the criteria set forth in sections 6 and 145 of the Restatement, the court finds that both policy considerations[4] and factual considerations compel the conclusion that British Columbia has the most substantial relationship regarding the liability issues in this lawsuit. As stated above, two of the factors set forth in section 145 point to British Columbia. First, British Columbia is the place of the injury. Second, Bain resided in British Columbia at the time of the accident. Moreover, it is clear to this court that British Columbia has the greatest interest in the outcome of the case because

3   John Bain does state that based on conversations with his son he believes that Scott wanted to return to Alberta. Mr. Bain bases this belief on the fact that Scott Bain "established . . . good relationships and friends in Alberta." However, John Bain's belief about his son's future intentions is outweighed by the fact that Scott Bain declared himself to be an Australian citizen and a British Columbia resident on his application for a commercial pilot's license.

4   In the response to Honeywell's motion to apply the law of British Columbia, Plaintiffs' contend that the court should not apply the law of British Columbia "as British Columbia law contravenes Texas public policy." . . . Plaintiffs' argument is unconvincing. Plaintiffs support their argument by citing a Texas Supreme Court case, *Gutierrez v. Collins*, that does in fact hold that "Texas courts will not enforce a foreign law that violates good morals, natural justice or is prejudicial to the general interests of our own citizens." *Gutierrez*, 583 S.W.2d at 321. However, Plaintiffs ignore the rest of the opinion that ultimately allows the application of Mexican law that "differ[s] in several aspects" to the laws of Texas. *Id.* In fact, the *Gutierrez* court held that the fact that Mexican law does not recognize pain and suffering as an element of damages and that the Plaintiff's potential damages will be substantially reduced does not render Mexican law violative of Texas public policy. *Id.* Moreover, plaintiffs have not shown how the laws of British Columbia violate "good morals [or] natural justice." *Id.*

the helicopter was based in British Columbia, the helicopter was registered in British Columbia and the helicopter crashed in British Columbia. . . .

After considering the evidence submitted in light of the contacts enumerated in section 145 of the Restatement, the court finds that British Columbia has the most significant relationship regarding the liability issues in this lawsuit. . . .

COMMENTS AND QUESTIONS

1. Arguments about someone's domicile can be a strategic distraction. Scott Bain had some geographic connection with Alberta, British Columbia, and the ACT. Why not simply evaluate each of these connections for what they are (i.e., connections of different types and with different intensities) rather than trying to identify one domicile?

2. The court observed that there was "no definitive evidence showing that, even though he moved to British Columbia, Bain intended to return to Alberta." Sentences like that suggest that a failure of proof may explain the court's decision. How would you have obtained better evidence?

3. How long was Bain in Alberta? Domicile can be established on the day of arrival in a new place (assuming an intent to remain indefinitely). Nevertheless, would plaintiffs' argument that Bain was domiciled in Alberta seem stronger if he had stayed there longer? The opinion emphasizes that "Bain moved to Alberta *only to advance his career*" (emphasis in original). Why was a move that was motivated by a career change inconsistent with the conclusion that Bain intended to remain there indefinitely? If not for career advancement what, then, is a motivation for a move that would properly constitute an intent to remain somewhere indefinitely (To study law? To enjoy better weather? To live near family? To live in a [blue/red] state?)?

4. Many courts are reluctant to apply a foreign country's law. (See Chapter 18.) Was the argument for applying British Columbia law so strong here that the court really had no choice but to apply it?

5. Approximately one month after the court issued this opinion, Honeywell
    moved for summary judgment. Applying British Columbia law, the court
    granted the defendant's motion because plaintiffs were not entitled to pain
    and suffering, loss of consortium, nor punitive damages.

FROM THE COURTS

MACDONALD v. GENERAL MOTORS CORP.

U.S. Court of Appeals for the Sixth Circuit
110 F.3d 337 (6th Cir. 1997)

BOYCE F. MARTIN, JR., CHIEF JUDGE.

At approximately 10:30 pm on October 29, 1987, six members of the University of Kansas debate team and three of their coaches were driving to a
tournament in Georgia when a deer appeared in front of their van on an
interstate highway near Clarksville, Tennessee. The driver, Philip Voight, a
graduate student and a debate coach at the University of Kansas had received
his driver's license just a few months earlier. When Voight swerved to avoid
the deer, the rear brakes of the van locked up, Voight lost control of the
vehicle, and the van ran off the highway and rolled over several times before
coming to rest. David MacDonald, a student and debate team member, died
as a result of the accident. Another student, Peter Cannistra, was rendered a
paraplegic. Two other passengers, Ofray Hall and Susan Stanfield, suffered
substantial injuries but recovered fully.

Cannistra, Hall, Stanfield, and MacDonald's estate initially sued the University of Kansas and its employees, including Voight, alleging that their
negligence caused the accident. The plaintiffs later added a claim against
General Motors, alleging that it failed to advise the van's purchaser adequately
regarding proper brake maintenance, and that the van was defectively
designed because the rear wheels would lock before the front wheels under
some braking conditions, thus making the vehicle "rear-biased."

Ultimately, the plaintiffs settled their claims against the University of
Kansas and its employees and proceeded to trial against General Motors
alone. On April 10, 1995, the jury returned a verdict in the plaintiffs' favor,
finding General Motors one percent, and the University of Kansas and its

employees ninety-nine percent at fault. The district court entered judgment on the verdict and denied the parties' motions for judgment as a matter of law and for a new trial. . . .

The . . . issue on appeal is the choice of law for the measurement of damages for the MacDonalds' wrongful death claim. The district court applied Kansas law, which limits non-pecuniary damages to $100,000. *See* Kan. Stat. Ann. § 60–1903 (1995). The MacDonalds argue that North Dakota law, which places no cap on damages, was more appropriate. *See* N.D. Cent. Code § 32–03.2–04 (1993). We review a district court's choice of law determination de novo. *Salve Regina College v. Russell*, 499 U.S. 225, 231 (1991).

In a diversity action such as the present one, a federal court applies the conflicts law of the forum state. *Erie R.R. v. Tompkins*, 304 U.S. 64 (1938). Thus, we apply Tennessee law to determine whether the district court properly applied Kansas law to determine damages for the MacDonald's wrongful death claim. Tennessee has adopted the "most significant relationship" approach of the Restatement (Second) of Conflict of Laws (1971).

Section 178 of the Restatement explains that "the law selected by application of the rule of § 175 determines the measure of damages in an action for wrongful death." Restatement (Second) of Conflict of Laws § 178. Section 175, in turn, sets forth the foundation of the "most significant relationship test," and reads as follows:

> § 175. Right of Action for Death
>
> In an action for wrongful death, the local law of the state where the injury occurred determines the rights and liabilities of the parties unless, with respect to the particular issue, some other state has a more significant relationship under the principles stated in § 6 to the occurrence and the parties, in which event the local law of the other state will be applied.

Restatement (Second) of Conflict of Laws § 175.

Other relevant Restatement principles are set forth in sections 6 and 145, which are referenced by section 175 and which address, respectively, general choice of law principles and choice of law principles applicable to tort actions. The full text of these sections is as follows:

§ 6. Choice-of-Law Principles.

(1) A court, subject to constitutional restrictions, will follow a statutory directive of its own state on choice of law.

(2) When there is no such directive, the factors relevant to the choice of the applicable rule of law include:

- (a) the needs of the interstate and international systems,
- (b) the relevant policies of the forum,
- (c) the relevant policies of other interested states and the relative interests of those states in the determination of the particular issue,
- (d) the protection of justified expectations,
- (e) the basic policies underlying the particular field of law,
- (f) certainty, predictability and uniformity of result, and
- (g) ease in the determination and application of the law to be applied.

§ 145. The General Principle.

(1) The rights and liabilities of the parties with respect to an issue in tort are determined by the local law of the state which, with respect to that issue, has the most significant relationship to the occurrence and the parties under the principles stated in § 6.

(2) Contacts to be taken into account in applying the principles of § 6 to determine the law applicable to an issue include:

- (a) the place where the injury occurred,
- (b) the place where the conduct causing the injury occurred,
- (c) the domicil, residence, nationality, place of incorporation and place of business of the parties, and
- (d) the place where the relationship, if any, between the parties is centered.

These contacts are to be evaluated according to their relative importance with respect to the particular issue.

Restatement (Second) of Conflict of Laws §§ 6, 145.

Under the Restatement approach, where wrongful death damages are at issue, the court applies the local law of the state where the injury occurred, unless some other state has a more significant relationship to the issue of damages, the occurrence, and the parties. Restatement (Second) of Conflict of Laws §§ 175, 178 (1971). In the present case, the parties agree that the law of Tennessee, the state where the injury occurred, should not be applied because the location of the accident there was fortuitous. Thus, section 175 of the Restatement requires that we determine, with respect to the issue of damage, which other state has the most significant relationship to occurrence and the parties. We do this by examining the contacts set forth in section 145 of the Restatement [and] are guided in this analysis by general principles governing choice of law [set forth in section 6.] A proper application of these factors shows that the law of North Dakota, not Kansas, should be applied to the measurement of damages for the MacDonalds' claim.

A simple examination of the contacts listed in section 145 is of little importance in the present case, as it points toward several different states. The injury occurred in Tennessee. The conduct causing the injury occurred in Tennessee, the site of the accident, and Michigan, the state where General Motors designed the van. The decedent was domiciled in North Dakota but was a resident of Kansas at the time of his death. The decedent's parents, the plaintiffs in this wrongful death suit, are domiciled and reside in North Dakota. General Motors [is incorporated in Delaware, its principal place of business is in Michigan,] and it conducts business in Kansas, North Dakota, and Tennessee. The center of the relationship is Kansas: all persons in the van were residents of Kansas; the van was purchased, garaged, and maintained in Kansas by a Kansas organization; the passengers boarded the van in Kansas; and the trip was scheduled to terminate there as well. The Restatement contacts point toward no one state in particular, but rather cover Tennessee, Michigan, North Dakota, Kansas, and Delaware.

At trial, General Motors argued, and the district court agreed, that Kansas was the state that had the most significant relationship with all aspects of the MacDonalds' wrongful death claim. General Motors based this assertion on the ground that where the contacts are scattered, the "center of the relationship" is the most important factor in making a choice of law determination. This premise is incorrect. The mere fact that contacts are scattered does not automatically heighten the importance of the "center of the relationship" contact. Here, Kansas may be the center of the relationship, but [MacDonald's] domicile remained in North Dakota. *See* Restatement (Second) of Conflict of Laws § 145 cmt. e (1971) (noting that the center of the relationship may be the most important contact on rare occasions, such as when a plaintiff from state X is injured in a train accident while passing through state Y and other important contacts are also located in that state). Instead, the Restatement makes clear that the court is to evaluate the contacts "according to their relative importance with respect to the particular issue," and that this is to be accomplished by carefully examining the policies behind the laws of the interested states and the interests of those states in the claim. Restatement (Second) of Conflict of Laws §§ 6, 145(2); § 145 cmt. e (1971). In this regard we emphasize that the Restatement specifically discusses the importance of domicile in determining choice of law for the measurement of damages in a wrongful death action. Comment b to section 178 explains, for example, that "[i]n a situation where one state is the state of domicil of the defendant, the decedent and the beneficiaries, it would seem that, ordinarily at least, the wrongful death statute of this state should be applied to determine the measure of damages." Restatement (Second) of Conflict of Laws § 178 cmt. b.

The parties agree that the first two contacts, place of injury and place of conduct (which point toward Tennessee and Michigan), should not be controlling here. Thus, we must examine the last two contacts to determine which state's law to apply to determine damages, giving due consideration to the policy concerns discussed above.

The third set of contacts—domicile, residence, nationality, place of incorporation and place of business of the parties—involves several states, including Delaware, Michigan, Kansas, and North Dakota. A person's "domicile" is his or her permanent and principal home, to which he or she intends to return whenever away. *Snodgrass v. Snodgrass*, 49 Tenn. App. 607 (1961) (defining "domicile" as "the place 'where a person has his principal home and place of enjoyment of his fortunes; which he does not expect to leave, except for a purpose; from which when absent, he seems to himself a wayfarer; to which when he returns, he ceases to travel' ") (citations omitted). *See also Eastman v. Univ. of Michigan*, 30 F.3d 670, 672–73 (6th Cir. 1990) (stating that a person's domicile is his or her "true, fixed, and permanent home and principal establishment" and is "the place to which he [or she] returns whenever . . . absent") (citing Black's Law Dictionary 484 (6th ed. 1990)). . . .

Under these definitions, North Dakota is the domicile of both David MacDonald and his parents. It is his parents' domicile because it is their established and permanent home. Likewise, North Dakota is David Mac-Donald's domicile because it was his domicile prior to college and there is no evidence that he ever intended to abandon it to establish a new domicile in Kansas, which is what he would have had to have done to change his domicile to that state. *See In re Conservatorship of Clayton*, 914 S.W.2d 84, 89 (Tenn. Ct. App. 1995) (stating that to change domicile, a person must actually change his or her residence to a new place, intend to abandon his or her old domicile, and intend to establish a new domicile at the new residence). That David resided in Kansas while in school thus does nothing to diminish the fact that North Dakota was his domicile.

While David MacDonald and his parents were clearly domiciliaries of North Dakota, we note, and General Motors makes much of the fact that David MacDonald, who was attending the University of Kansas, was technically a resident of Kansas at the time of his death. While we acknowledge David's connection to Kansas, we nonetheless find that the third set of Restatement contacts points to the law of North Dakota, where David and his parents were domiciled, rather than to Kansas, where David alone was merely a resident. This conclusion is based on our opinion that although residence is a factor in the third set of contacts, it is not as significant a factor as domicile. Not only is a person's connection to his or her domicile more substantial than any links he or she may have to his or her place, or places, of residence, but a state clearly has more of an interest in preserving the welfare of its domiciliaries—those persons who have made the state their true, fixed, and permanent home—than that of its residents—persons who live in the state without necessarily having any permanent connections there and who are domiciled and may have residences in other states. Indeed, the Restatement itself suggests that domicile is the more important factor in the third set of section 145 contacts. *See* Restatement (Second) of Conflict of Laws § 178 cmt. b (emphasizing the importance of the domicile of the defendant, the decedent, and the beneficiaries in determining which state's wrongful death statute to apply to determine damages), § 145 cmt. d (noting that the state where interested persons are domiciled typically has the greatest interest in having its law applied to resolve a tort action). For these reasons, we find that David MacDonald's domicile—North Dakota—is a more important contact than his residence for purposes of applying the Restatement's most significant relationship test. Given that both David MacDonald and his parents were domiciliaries of North Dakota, we conclude that the third set of section 145 contacts suggests that North Dakota has the most significant relationship to the measure of damages for the MacDonald's wrongful death claim.

[The court observed that the fourth contact—the center of the parties' relationship—pointed to the application of Kansas law. "To determine which of these contacts [wa]s more important," the court then examined the policies behind the laws of the two interested states. It found that North Dakota had a "strong interest in assuring that next of kin are fully compensated for the tortious death of its domiciliaries." Although Kansas had "an interest in ensuring that its residents [we]re adequately compensated for their injuries . . . this interest [wa]s adequately served by applying North Dakota law.]

COMMENTS AND QUESTIONS

1. Once again, a failure of proof may explain the court's decision. Judge Martin writes, "there is no evidence that [John MacDonald] ever intended to abandon [North Dakota] to establish a new domicile in Kansas." What kind of evidence is missing and how would General Motors obtain it? Think about the personal, professional, financial, and educational dimensions of a college student's life.

2. In Chapter 8 we learned that Comment i to Section 145 of the Second Restatement provides that

   When certain contacts involving a tort are located in two or more states with identical local law rules on the issue in question, the case will be treated for choice-of-law purposes as if these contacts were grouped in a single state.

   How could that have been leveraged here?

3. Apparently neither party was invested in having Tennessee law apply. Tennessee is the presumptively applicable law under Section 175, and the place of injury is one of the four Section 145 factors. Under what circumstances would neither party want this law to apply?

Sometimes litigators will concede something inadvertently. For example, a judge might ask in a hearing "Would you agree, counsel, that the place of injury is not dispositive of our inquiry?" You might answer "Yes, Your Honor.", because the place of injury is not *dispositive*, given the complexity of this case. But the judge might think that you have conceded the irrelevance of the place of injury. When asked to concede something, you should clarify exactly what you are conceding.

4.   Judge Martin's opinion contained a sentence that was edited out of the excerpt reprinted above. The sentence was excised because it gets the law wrong. After defining domicile as someone's "true, fixed, and permanent home and principal establishment and . . . the place to which he or she returns whenever absent," the excised sentence reads: "In contrast, residence requires physical presence and an intention to remain some indefinite period of time, but not necessarily permanently." If residence required an intent to remain indefinitely, then we would need a new term to describe the situation where someone intends to remain somewhere for a definite period of time. It would also require us to spend time divining the difference between an intent to remain somewhere indefinitely from an intent to remain somewhere permanently. The confusion is attributable to the fact that occasionally (and unfortunately) domicile is referred to as someone's *legal residence*. A legal residence converts, by operation of law, someone's residence (in the colloquial sense) into their legal residence. The rules for determining one's domicile are an example of such an operation of law.

Notwithstanding the regrettable sentence in his opinion, the judge doesn't actually think that residence requires an intent to remain somewhere indefinitely. If he did, he wouldn't have referred to David as a resident of Kansas.

5.   The difference between residence and domicile surfaced in claims of voter fraud in the 2016 elections. Much attention was given the 5,313 people who voted in New Hampshire in 2016 but did not reside there. (New Hampshire had some very close races. Hillary Clinton won the state by approximately 2,700 votes. In the Senate race, Maggie Hassen won by approximately 1,000 votes.) New Hampshire allows same-day registration, and 6,540 of the same-day registrants used an out-of-state identification. The fact that 5,313 of those registrants did not, in the months after the election, obtain a New Hampshire identification (because New Hampshire law requires new residents to get a drivers' license within 60 days) was presented by some commentators as proof of voter fraud. But New

Hampshire does not require its voters to be residents of New Hampshire; they can be domiciled in the state, and thus a valid voter, even if they are a resident of another state.

KING v. CAR RENTALS, INC.

New York Supreme Court, Appellate Division
29 N.Y.A.D.3d 205 (2nd Dept. 2006)

SPOLZINO, JUSTICE.

[Jody King and Syed Ali were friends and recent graduates of New York University (NYU). King had started work as a teacher at a private school in Hamden, Connecticut. Ali was between jobs, and was staying with his parents in New Jersey. About six months after college graduation, Ali rented a car in New Jersey, picked up King in Connecticut, and drove to Montreal, Canada for the New Year's weekend. On January 3, 1999, during the return drive, they were involved in a one-car accident in the City of St. Pierre De Veronne in Quebec. King, the passenger in the car driven by Ali, was seriously injured.

King sued Ali. King also named as a defendant the rental car company, Car Rentals, Inc. (d/b/a Avis Rent A Car), on a theory of vicarious liability. Car Rentals, Inc. is a New Jersey corporation that does business solely in New Jersey. Under New York law, King would be able to recover damages from Car Rentals, Inc. Under New Jersey law, vicarious liability is viable only if the driver was the employee or agent of the owner—and Ali is neither. Under Quebec law, King would be able to recover only economic damages.

The court observed that the domiciles of the parties would be an important factor in determining the applicable law.]

The plaintiff [King] is unquestionably a domiciliary of the State of New York. His deposition testimony, that he was born in New York and resided there, in his mother's home in Kings Park, until September 2001, was undisputed. At the time of the accident he had a New York driver's license. While it is true that Ali picked him up in Connecticut for the trip and was returning him to Connecticut when the accident occurred, the plaintiff's residence in Hamden, Connecticut, where he had been employed since September 1998 as a teacher, does not require a different conclusion.

Residence means living in a particular place; domicile means "living in that locality with intent to make it a fixed and permanent home," *Matter of Newcomb*, 192 N.Y. 238, 250 (1908), or, as it has more recently been put, "one's principal and permanent place of residence where one always intends to return from wherever one may be temporarily located." *Laufer v. Hauge*, 140 A.D.2d 671, 672 (1988). . . . A party may thus have more than one residence, but only one domicile. *See Kleinrock v. Nantex Mfg.* Co., 201 App. Div. 236, 237 (1922). Measured against this standard, the plaintiff's deposition testimony was sufficient to establish his New York domicile. There is nothing in the record to establish to the contrary that his Connecticut residence had become his domicile.

Determining Ali's domicile is not as simple. Ali grew up in Metuchen, New Jersey, and resided there, in his parents' home, until he left to attend NYU, in Manhattan, in November 1994. There is no dispute that Ali was again living at his parents' New Jersey home at the time of the accident, having moved to that residence some time in December 1998, within a month before the accident. It is also undisputed that at that time Ali had the same New Jersey driver's license that he had had since he was first licensed to drive, which listed his parents' home as his address, and that he was registered to vote at that address, as he had been since he was 18 years of age.

Nevertheless, despite his New Jersey residence at the time of the accident, the facts here establish that Ali was a New York domiciliary at that time. Ali's original domicile was in New Jersey and his residence in New York as a student was not sufficient to change that. *See Matter of Seitelman v. Lavine,* 36 N.Y.2d 165, 171 (1975). . . . Nevertheless, the fact that Ali resided in New York initially as a student does not preclude finding a change of domicile on the basis of other facts. *Matter of Goodman [Bainton]*, 146 N.Y. 284, 287 (1895).

Ali's student residency in New York is not the whole story. Rather than return to New Jersey after graduation, he continued to live and work in New York. Immediately after his graduation from NYU in June 1998, while waiting for his employment with a Manhattan company to commence in January 1999. Ali worked for a temporary employment agency at several locations in Manhattan. During that period, Ali resided with his sister in an apartment on 26th Street in Manhattan, sharing rent and other expenses.

When he did leave New York, moreover, a few weeks before the accident, he did so not with an intent to live permanently in New Jersey, but intending to return to New York to live in a few months, once his training was concluded and his employment had begun in New York. In fact, he planned that upon his return from the employment training in Chicago that he was to commence in January 1999, he would return to Manhattan to find a place to live. In April 1999, three months after the accident, and once month after his employment training had concluded, Ali moved to an apartment in Manhattan. Critically, he testified at his examination before trial that his move to his parents' home was temporary.

The dispositive issue with respect to Ali's domicile is his intent. . . Ali's intent to remain in New York was apparent, both from his testimony and from his action in moving back to New York once he returned from training. . . . It was his move to New Jersey that was temporary. Thus, despite his New Jersey residence at the time of the accident and his other New Jersey connections, Ali was a New York domiciliary at the time of the accident.

[After a lengthy discussion of the interests of New Jersey, New York, and Quebec, the court applied New Jersey law.] In these circumstances, the New Jersey contacts predominate. Moreover, in a situation as closely balanced as this, New York's unique vicarious liability policy cannot be preferred to the more limited policy adopted by New Jersey and most of the rest of the nation "without impairing the smooth working of the multi-state system" *Neumeier v. Kuehner*, 31 N.Y.2d 121, 128 (1972). Thus, despite the strength of New York's policy in favor of protecting New York accident victims, that policy must yield to New Jersey's countervailing interest in protecting its domiciliary, the vehicle owner [Car Rentals, Inc.], from vicarious liability that it deems to be unwarranted. . . .

COMMENTS AND QUESTIONS

1. New York follows a version of interest analysis for its choice of law methodology. You will remember from Chapter 5 that the domiciles of the parties play a key role in determining whether a state is interested.

2. No one disputes the bona fides of King's status as a New York domiciliary. Yet King is a teacher at a school in Hamden, Connecticut. And he is a resident of Connecticut. Does he own that residence? If he signed a lease, what is its term? Is he on the tenure track at the school? Did he opt in to a retirement program that does not vest for a period of x years? Has he prepared any long-range planning documents? Is he networking with Connecticut leaders and educators? If King were a Connecticut domiciliary instead of a New York domiciliary it probably would not have changed this court's decision to apply New Jersey law. But why might Car Rentals have prevailed sooner and more easily if King were a Connecticut domiciliary?

SAMPLE EXAM QUESTION

Question 13-4

Ron Lewhorn was born and raised in Ohio. Intending to retire, he moved to Miami, Florida with his wife, Ami, shortly after each of them turned 65 years old.

Ron, however, has not been a constant fixture in the Florida home. In his words, Ron "flunked retirement." After nine months of living as a retiree in Florida, Ron since has divided his time between Ohio and Florida.

For the past four years, Ron has spent approximately two weeks per month in Ohio, working at a start-up business, Design Application Inc., for which he is the chair of its board and its CEO. Each month Ron leaves Florida around the ninth or tenth of each month, and returns twelve or thirteen days later. When he is in Ohio he spends about twelve hours a day, seven days a week, working at the business.

When Ron and Ami left Ohio for Florida, they deeded a two-thirds interest in the Ohio home (the house where Ron and Ami had lived for

410 • Learning Conflict of Laws •

decades) to their daughter, Boone. Ron and Ami retained the remaining one-third interest. Boone's family moved into the house.

When Ron returns each month he stays in the Ohio house. Although Ron and Ami moved essentially all of their belongings, heirlooms, and personal property to Florida, Ron has a bedroom in the Ohio house that he uses on each visit (and that Boone's family regards as exclusively Ron's). He keeps a car in Ohio that is registered in Ohio. (He has a second car registered in Florida that stays in Florida.)

Ron carefully monitors the number of days that he spends in Ohio so that he can avoid being an Ohio resident for tax purposes. Accordingly, he stays in Ohio fewer than 150 days each year. Ami accompanies him on this trip two or three times each year.

When in Ohio, Ron attends church at his old parish and makes contributions there. His accountant is located in Ohio. The attorneys who handle his estate planning and the legal issues for the business are in Ohio.

Ron has had a Florida driver's license since he moved there nearly five years ago. He is registered to vote in Florida. His family doctor is located in Florida, as is his dentist. He is registered at a Catholic parish in Florida. He maintains checking and savings accounts at a Florida bank. He keeps all of his business records in Florida.

A dispute has arisen between Ron and some of the investors in his business. The parties disagree about what law applies, and one disputed issue is Ron's domicile. What is a court likely to conclude?

Quick Summary

- A person's domicile can be dispositive in certain choice of law contexts; in other contexts, the domicile of the plaintiff and/or defendant may be a relevant factor

- A person's domicile is the last place that she was simultaneously present and intending to remain indefinitely

- Presence is a physical fact

- Intent to remain is a state of mind; this is often debatable

- A person always has one (and only one) domicile for a particular pupose

- A person keeps her domicile until she adopts a new domicile

14

Constitutional Constraints

Key Concepts

- The Due Process Clause and fairness to litigants
- The Full Faith and Credit Clause and respect for sister states

---

The choice of law approaches that we have studied occasionally produce results that may be hard to defend as rational and righteous. The methodology itself can produce the anomaly—such as when the traditional approach applies the law of the place of contracting even when that is a fortuitous location that has absolutely nothing to do with the parties or the transaction. The methodology may enable the anomaly—such as when a judge invokes the public policy exception so that she can apply forum law. The text of a localizing statute (*see* Chapter 16) might produce an anomalous result. Or a court might characterize some law as procedural in order to facilitate the application of forum law. In any circumstance when the law to be applied[1] seems like a dubious choice, one should fairly wonder: What does the U.S. Constitution have to say about choice of law? Put another way, can a state have whatever choice of law methodology it desires?

In fact, there are principally two Constitutional provisions that are on point. First, the Due Process Clause[2] focuses on the relationship between governments and individuals. The state may not deprive persons of life, liberty, or property interests without due process of law. The due process guarantee, in a word, is fairness. In the choice of law context, this means protection against the unfair application of

---

1   Cases that test the protections of the Constitution invariably involve dubious applications of *forum* law. Although a forum state's application of *foreign* law can raise constitutional issues, as a practical matter these cases rarely arise because of the homeward trend (Chapter 2).

2   There are two Due Process Clauses in the Constitution: one restricting the actions of state governments and the other restricting the federal government. *See* U.S. Const. amdmt. XIV, § 1 ("No State shall . . . deprive any person of life, liberty, or property without due process of law."); *id.* amdmt. V ("No person . . . shall be deprived of life, liberty, or property, without due process of law.").

some foreign law. It is not fair to apply a law to the detriment of someone who did not have notice that that law would apply.

Next, the Full Faith and Credit Clause[3] focuses on the relationship between states. Although the Constitution preserves elements of state sovereignty, the creation of a single, unified nation also required states to surrender some of their autonomy. The Full Faith and Credit Clause requires states to give proper regard to the laws of sister states.

The Constitutional tests canvass many of the same facts that are used in choice of law analysis, yet pose different questions. The Due Process Clause asks whether the court *may* apply forum law; the Full Faith and Credit Clause asks whether the court *must* apply foreign law. The Constitutional tests also use some of the same terminology that are used in choice of law analysis. But the Due Process Clause is about fairness to the defendant and avoidance of unfair surprise, while the Full Faith and Credit Clause is about respecting other states and curbing excessive provincialism.

As a practical matter, neither clause plays a significant role in contemporary litigation. Yet there are at least three reasons why you should not be complacent about constitutional limitations on choice of law. First, things change. In fact, things change because some litigator (like you) makes a good argument, and the doctrine shifts. The significance of the Constitution in choice of law doctrine ebbs and flows; be prepared for the inevitable flow. Second, remember that most cases settle and, therefore, the parties' perceptions of the expected value of the case matters. Accordingly, even an argument that has only, say, a 10% chance of winning affects the bargaining positions of the parties. You will want to maximize the value of your case. And third, even if rare, there are circumstances where the Constitution invalidates the choice of law, and you need to know that law.

The relevant histories of both the Due Process Clause and the Full Faith and Credit Clause begin in the 1930s. This chapter first describes the evolution of the Due Process Clause's role in choice of law through its first several decades. We then suspend that chronology and address the parallel history of the role of the Full Faith and Credit Clause in choice of law. These summaries describe some but not all of the key Supreme Court cases from that era. After summarizing the early histories of both clauses, we will study their modern histories and explore their contemporary relevance.

---

3   U.S. Const. art. IV, § 1 ("Full Faith and Credit shall be given in each State to the public Acts, Records, and judicial Proceedings of every other State. And the Congress may by general Laws prescribe the Manner in which such Acts, Records and Proceedings shall be proved, and the Effect thereof.")

The Early History of the Due Process Clause

The Supreme Court's first important due process case in the choice of law context involved a breach of contract claim. In *Home Ins. Co. v. Dick*,[4] a Texas state court invoked its public policy exception and applied Texas law to an unsuspecting party. The underlying dispute was centered in Mexico, and had very little to do with Texas: the contract was not negotiated nor signed in Texas; it was not to be performed in Texas; it did not mention Texas; the subject of the contract was never in Texas; the breach did not occur in Texas; and neither of the original parties to the contract was from Texas.

The only connection to Texas was that the plaintiff was domiciled in Texas.[5] Even this connection was strained by the fact that the plaintiff was not an original party to the contract; he was an assignee (albeit one who was referenced in the original contract). Also, although a domiciliary of Texas, the plaintiff resided in Mexico (and was physically present there) for all of the relevant events that gave rise to this dispute.

The Court announced a standard that, as a general principle, is still good law: the application of forum law violates the Due Process Clause if that state has only an insignificant contact with the parties and the transaction. The Court held that Texas's contacts were insignificant, and therefore Texas lacked the power to affect "the rights of parties beyond its borders having no relation to anything done or to be done within them."[6] The domicile of the plaintiff, without more, was insufficient to justify the application of forum law to a defendant that contracted with a Mexican in Mexico about Mexican property. Invoking the public policy exception may have been consonant with Texas's choice of law methodology, but it violated the Due Process Clause.

In another due process case that the Supreme Court decided twenty-four years later, the forum state whose law was being applied had a few more contacts with the parties and the underlying events than did Texas in *Dick*. In *Watson v. Employers Liability Assurance Corp., Ltd.*,[7] a Louisiana court applied Louisiana law to a case filed by someone who was injured by a defective product in Louisiana. The Louisiana plaintiff was not suing the manufacturer of that product, but was instead suing the manufacturer's insurance company. (Louisiana did not have personal jurisdiction over the manufacturer. Hence the claim against the insurer.) By statute,

---

4   281 U.S. 397 (1930).

5   Texas had quasi in rem personal jurisdiction by attaching the insurer's reinsurers.

6   281 U.S. at 410.

7   348 U.S. 66 (1954).

Louisiana allowed so-called "direct actions" by a personal injury plaintiff against the insurance company. The manufacturer's insurance policy, however, contained a clause which provided that the insurer was not liable unless a judgment was first obtained against the insured. (In other words, the policy prohibited direct actions.) The insurance policy was negotiated and delivered in states that would have enforced that provision and would have dismissed the plaintiff's direct action. The insurance company claimed that the Louisiana court's application of forum law violated the Due Process Clause, but the Supreme Court disagreed.

As in *Dick*, the plaintiff Watson was a domiciliary of the forum state. But that was not the State of Louisiana's only contact with the parties or events. Louisiana was also where Watson suffered injury. Further, the Court emphasized that although the insurance policy was issued in Massachusetts, it insured the manufacturer for losses wherever they might be suffered, including Louisiana. The latter observation reveals the origins of what the Court later characterized as a *reasonable foreseeability* test: the application of Louisiana law was not an *unfair surprise* to an insurance company whose insured was doing business in Louisiana.

The *Watson* Court acknowledged that it was limiting the role that due process would play in choice of law. The Court recognized that if this case had been filed in Massachusetts (instead of Louisiana), then the Massachusetts court would almost certainly have applied Massachusetts law, and would therefore have dismissed Watson's claim. That alternative outcome, the Court observed, also would have satisfied the Due Process Clause.

> More . . . than one [state] may seize hold of local activities which are part of multistate transactions and may regulate to protect interests of its own people, even though other phases of the same transactions might justify regulatory legislation in other states.[8]

Thus, the Court did not envision the Due Process Clause dictating a single right answer when it comes to choosing the applicable law. Instead, the Due Process Clause tolerates multiple right answers and would be invoked only for the occasional wrong answer.

A decade later, in 1964, the Court heard another due process case—this time with factual connections to the forum state that fell somewhere between those of *Dick* (where the application of forum law violated due process) and *Watson* (which survived the due process challenge). In *Clay v. Sun Insurance Office, Ltd.*,[9] an insured

---

8 348 U.S. at 71–72.

9 377 U.S. 179 (1964).

sued his insurance company in Florida for failing to pay covered losses to his personal property. The plaintiff purchased the insurance policy from the defendant in Illinois with a lump-sum payment. Shortly thereafter, the plaintiff moved to Florida; two years later, but during the policy term, the plaintiff's property was destroyed (in Florida).

The insurance policy contained a "suit clause" which provided that no action could be maintained unless commenced within twelve months of the discovery of the loss. That clause was valid under Illinois law, but unenforceable under Florida law. The difference was consequential because Clay did not file his claim within twelve months of the loss. The Florida court applied Florida law, thereby allowing Clay's suit to proceed.

The U.S. Supreme Court held that due process did not forbid the application of Florida law. Again the Court used the template of foreseeability (although still not the word) to reach its conclusion:

> In this . . . case the policy was sold to Clay with knowledge that he could take his property anywhere in the world he saw fit without losing the protection of his insurance. In fact, his contract was described on its face as a "Personal Property Floater Policy (World Wide)." The contract did not even attempt to provide that the law of Illinois would govern when suits were filed anywhere else in the country. Shortly after the contract was made, Clay moved to Florida and there he lived for several years. His insured property was there all that time. The company knew this fact. Par-

TERMINOLOGY

This is another way of describing the Court's reluctance to constitutionalize choice of law. The constitutionalization of choice of law would mean that a state court faced with a question about what law to apply would look to the Court's definition of due process fairness rather than to its choice of law methodology: Why would a jurisdiction that follows the traditional approach bother determining the place of injury (or a jurisdiction that follows the better-law approach engage the five choice influencing considerations) if the Supreme Court's definition of fairness under the Due Process Clause identifies what law must apply? The Supreme Court did not want to develop a jurisprudence of due process for choice of law that would supplant the states' choice of law methodologies.

ticularly since the company was licensed to do business in Florida, it must have known it might be sued there.[10]

Because it was not an *unfair surprise* for the insurance company to be sued in Florida, the application of Florida law did not violate the Due Process Clause.

The three cases summarized here—*Dick*, *Watson*, and *Clay*—prescribe a modest role for the Due Process Clause in the early part of its history. *Dick* suggests that there is an outer bound of tolerance for a state court's application of forum law. But in the other two cases, the Court is forgiving of state courts' inclinations to apply forum law for the benefit of locals suing foreign defendants. Let us turn to the early history of the Full Faith and Credit Clause and choice of law.

The Early History of the Full Faith and Credit Clause

The Full Faith and Credit Clause commands states to give "full faith and credit" to the laws of sister states. This deference is in recognition of the sovereignty of the other state. It is hardly obvious, however, what it means to give "full faith and credit" to the other jurisdiction's law.[11] It cannot mean applying the other state's law in *every* multistate factual situation; surely the Constitution allows the application of forum law in at least some of these circumstances. So again, it was up to the Supreme Court to define the role of this Constitutional mandate. Four cases—all involving workplace injuries—capture the highlights of the first fifty years of case law regarding the Full Faith and Credit Clause and choice of law.

First, in *Bradford Electric Light Co., Inc. v. Clapper*,[12] the Court heard a case involving a Vermonter, Clapper, who was sent on a temporary work assignment by his Vermont employer to New Hampshire, where he (Clapper) was killed during the course of his employment. Clapper's estate sued the employer in New Hampshire and persuaded that court to apply New Hampshire law which allowed a claim for negligence against the employer. Under Vermont law, the state's workers' compensation laws provided the exclusive remedy.

The Supreme Court held that the New Hampshire court's failure to apply Vermont law violated the Full Faith and Credit Clause. Although New Hampshire was the place of injury, New Hampshire was obliged to overlook this "casual" contact lest "the effectiveness of the Vermont act . . . be gravely impaired." The Court was

---

10 377 U.S. at 182.

11 For an examination of the history of the clause, *see* David E. Engdahl, *The Classic Rule of Faith and Credit*, 118 YALE L.J. 1584 (2009).

12 286 U.S. 145 (1932).

sympathetic to Vermont's efforts to regulate an employment relationship between a Vermont employer and a Vermont employee:

> The Federal Constitution prevents the employee or his representative from asserting in New Hampshire rights which would be denied him in the state of his residence and employment. A Vermont court could have enjoined Leon Clapper from suing the company in New Hampshire, to recover damages for an injury suffered there, just as it would have denied him the right to recover such damages in Vermont.[13]

Clapper suggested that the Full Faith and Credit Clause could have a significant role in choice of law analysis. But in fact the Court had only begun its search for a meaningful standard.

Just three years after *Clapper,* the Court took another Full Faith and Credit Clause case. In *Alaska Packers Ass'n v. Industrial Acc. Comm'n,*[14] Juan Palma, a resident of Mexico, was hired by Alaska Packers Association in California to work during the salmon canning season in Alaska. He was promised round-trip transportation between San Francisco and Alaska, and a monthly wage that would be paid upon his return to San Francisco.

After his employment ended and he had returned to California, Palma filed a workers' compensation claim (in California) to recover for an injury that he suffered during the course of his employment in Alaska. The State of California applied California law. After Palma prevailed, the Alaska Packers Association appealed, claiming that California failed to give full faith and credit to Alaska law. Palma's employment contract recited that he was bound by the Alaska Workmen's Compensation Law.

Palma instead sued under the (more generous) California Workmen's Compensation Act, which gave California jurisdiction "over all controversies arising out of injuries suffered without the territorial limits of this state in those cases where the injured employee is a resident of this state at the time of the injury and the contract of hire was made in this state." Case law had already extended the reach of this statute to include non-residents like Palma.

Although not using the word *weigh* (nor *balance*), the Supreme Court did essentially that with respect to the interests of California and Alaska. It recognized that both states had a "legitimate public interest" in the outcome. The Court "apprais[ed]" those interests and concluded that "[t]he interest of Alaska is not

---

13   286 U.S. at 159.

14   294 U.S. 532 (1935).

shown to be superior to that of California. . . [and therefore,] the full faith and credit clause does not require that the statutes of Alaska be given that effect."[15]

Four years later, however, the Court recalibrated its test. In *Pacific Employers Ins. Co. v. Industrial Accident Comm'n*,[16] an employee of a Massachusetts company who had been sent to Oakland, California was injured there while acting as a technical adviser in a factory. The employee, Kenneth Tator, was a chemical engineer who had lived and worked for Dewey & Almy in Cambridge, Massachusetts for five years. When Tator was injured in California, he filed a workers' compensation claim there under California law, and prevailed. The employer challenged the constitutionality of the application of California law (which was more employee-friendly than Massachusetts law).

The Full Faith and Credit Clause envisioned by *Clapper* may have required California to apply Massachusetts law. The application of California law would have undermined "the effectiveness" of a sister state's effort to regulate the relationship between a Massachusetts employer and a Massachusetts employee. As the place of injury, and little more, California's contact was arguably "casual."

The Full Faith and Credit Clause envisioned by *Alaska Packers* would have required California to apply its sister state's law only if Massachusetts had the "superior interest." The interest of the Commonwealth of Massachusetts was quite strong: Tator was hired there; he was a resident of that state; he was employed there; his supervisor was there; and he was paid there. California was the place to which Tator's employer sent him, and it was the place of injury, but little else.

Rather than applying *Clapper* or *Alaska Packers*, the *Pacific Employers* Court held that the Full Faith and Credit Clause required consideration of a different, more modest question: does the forum have a substantial interest in the dispute? According to the Court, California had a sufficient substantial interest because California was the place of the employee's injury; he suffered the injury while performing work that he was sent there to perform. California could apply forum law regardless of the substantiality of the interest of a sister state; no balancing or weighing of interests was required.

The fourth case in the quartet of workers' compensation cases was *Carroll v. Lanza*.[17] An employee and his employer were Missourians. The employee was injured on the job in Arkansas. The plaintiff's employer was a subcontractor of the defen-

15   294 U.S. at 550.

16   306 U.S. 493 (1939).

17   349 U.S. 408 (1955).

dant Lanza. Under Missouri law, claims by an employee against a general contractor (i.e., not the plaintiff's immediate employer) fell within the scope of the state's workers' compensation law. By contrast, Arkansas law allowed Carroll to bring common law claims against the general contractor. Carroll sued in Arkansas, and that court applied forum law.

The Supreme Court held that full faith and credit did not require that Arkansas apply Missouri's law. The Court recognized that Arkansas was allowed to have its own policies "insofar as remedies for acts occurring within her boundaries are concerned. Were it otherwise, the State where the injury occurred would be powerless to provide any remedies or safeguards to nonresident employees working within its borders."[18] The Court bristled at the notion that the Full Faith and Credit Clause demands "subserviency from the State of the injury." Arkansas could apply forum law because the forum state had a substantial interest. Even if Missouri also had an interest—including an interest that was more substantial than Arkansas's interest—the Full Faith and Credit Clause did not require that Arkansas apply its sister state's law. At this point, the observer could be forgiven for concluding that the two clauses had come to require much the same thing.

The Modern History of the Due Process and Full Faith and Credit Clauses

The *modern* history of both the Due Process Clause and the Full Faith and Credit Clause begin in 1981. In *Allstate Ins. Co. v. Hague*, the Supreme Court admitted that the emperor had no clothes, explicitly merging the commands of both constitutional clauses into a single test:

> [F]or a State's substantive law to be selected in a constitutionally permissible manner, that State must have a significant contact [with the parties and the occurrence or transaction] or significant aggregation of contacts, creating state interests, such that choice of its law is neither arbitrary nor fundamentally unfair.[19]

Allstate involved the death of Ralph Hague, who died as a result of injuries he sustained in a motorcycle accident in 1974. Ralph's son was driving the motorcycle, on which Ralph was a passenger, when an automobile struck the motorcycle from behind. Ralph and his son were citizens of Wisconsin, as was the negligent driver. The two vehicles involved in the accident were registered in Wisconsin, and the

---

18 349 U.S. at 414.

19 449 U.S. 302, 308 , 312–313 (1981).

fatal accident occurred in Wisconsin. Both the negligent driver and Ralph's son were uninsured. However, Ralph carried uninsured motorist coverage on each of the three vehicles that he owned. Each of those three policies provided for up to $15,000 of coverage for injuries caused by the negligence of uninsured motorists, regardless of whether the accident involved the insured vehicles. Ralph's cars were registered in Wisconsin and were insured by a policy that Ralph obtained in Wisconsin from a Wisconsin branch of Allstate.

The decedent's personal representative, Ralph's widow, Lavinia Hague, filed a declaratory judgment action in Minnesota. After the accident, she had moved to Minnesota and married a Minnesota resident. In the suit, Lavinia sought a declaration that the uninsured motorist coverage on each of the decedent's automobile policies could be "stacked" or combined. Minnesota law allowed an insured to "stack" the three policies; Wisconsin law did not allow stacking. Pursuant to Minnesota law, her recovery would be $45,000 instead of the $15,000 that Wisconsin law would allow.

Notwithstanding the tenuous connection with Minnesota, the Minnesota trial and appeals courts, using the state's better law approach, applied forum law. (The Minnesota Supreme Court's opinion is excerpted in Chapter 7.) On certiorari, the Supreme Court affirmed. Writing for a plurality of four justices, Justice Brennan stated that Minnesota had a significant aggregation of contacts with the parties and the occurrence such that the choice of law was not arbitrary nor fundamentally unfair.

There were only three facts or contacts that purported to support the application of Minnesota law. First, Allstate did substantial business in Minnesota. This contact was arguably relevant because it minimized any claim by Allstate that they would be unfairly surprised as to the content or relevance of Minnesota law. But as applied here, this contact was dubious because the loss had nothing to do with any of Allstate's Minnesota business. (Could the court have applied Washington law on these facts since Allstate did substantial business there too?)

Second, prior to the accident, Mr. Hague had been a member of Minnesota's work force for fifteen years. He commuted there daily to work from his home in Wisconsin just across the border—1.5 miles from his place of work. According to Justice Brennan, this contact implicated certain "police power responsibilities" of Minnesota owed to non-resident employees. But it is hardly clear why Minnesota's police power responsibilities over non-resident employees extended to insurance policies and automobile accidents unrelated to Mr. Hague's employment status, since he was not commuting to or from work, or otherwise engaged in work-related activity, whether at the time of contracting for insurance or at the time of the accident.

Third, and finally, Lavinia Hague had moved to Minnesota prior to filing the suit. Even Justice Brennan observed that a post-occurrence change in residency could not create an interest in the forum sufficient to justify the application of that law. But he said that such a contact could be included as part of the "aggregation" of contacts that, in combination, satisfied the constitutional test.

Justice Stevens concurred with the plurality's judgment, but emphasized that the Full Faith and Credit and Due Process Clauses were designed to further different policies and required separate analyses. He wrote that the Due Process Clause protected individuals from choice of law determinations that result in unfair surprise; and the Full Faith and Credit Clause protected sovereign interests from encroachment by other states. Justice Stevens concurred with the plurality's outcome because, with regard to the Due Process Clause, Allstate was not unfairly surprised by the application of Minnesota law because of Allstate's Minnesota business. With respect to the Full Faith and Credit Clause, Justice Stevens found no evidence of encroachment upon Wisconsin's sovereign interests: the Full Faith and Credit Clause protected Wisconsin's sovereignty, but allowing stacking posed "no substantial threat to our constitutional system of cooperative federalism."[20]

Justice Powell's dissent, which was joined by two other justices, accepted the plurality's statement that the "significant contacts creating state interests" standard governed state choice of law determinations under both the Due Process and Full Faith and Credit Clauses. However, in applying the test, the dissenters analyzed the case separately under each clause. The dissenters thought the Due Process Clause was satisfied because it was within the reasonable expectation of the parties (before the cause of action accrued) that Minnesota law might apply. But the dissenters did not find any interest Minnesota had in the controversy; the three contacts identified by the plurality were either trivial or illegitimate.

In sum, all eight Justices in *Hague* agreed that the Due Process Clause was satisfied; five agreed that Minnesota's application of forum law was also consistent with the Full Faith and Credit Clause. Because the connection to Minnesota was so tenuous, the question after *Hague* was whether the Constitution would play any meaningful role in choice of law.

---

20   449 U.S. at 323 n.10 (Stevens, J. concurring) (quoting *Nevada v. Hall*, 440 U.S. 410, 424 n.24 (1979)).

The test case came four years later. In *Phillips Petroleum v. Shutts,*[21] the facts were about as extreme a set as one could imagine. The case involved a class action against Phillips, a company that produced and sold natural gas. Phillips extracted some of its gas from leased property in exchange for a payment of royalties to the owners of the land. The plaintiffs were 28,100 class members who owned land in 11 different states. The dispute between the property owners and Phillips regarded interest on delayed royalty payments.

The case was filed in a Kansas state court. However, only 3% of the plaintiffs were Kansans, and only 1% of the leases had any geographic connection to the Kansas. Phillips did business in Kansas, but was a Delaware corporation and its principal place of business was in Oklahoma. Nevertheless, the Kansas court applied forum law to all claims of all 28,100 plaintiffs. To be clear, this means that the Kansas court was using Kansas law to resolve a dispute between, say, an Oklahoma plaintiff-lessor and an Oklahoma defendant regarding payments due on a lease entered into in Oklahoma regarding Oklahoma property and Oklahoma conduct.

This application of Kansas law to transactions and occurrences that had nothing to do with Kansas was at least arguably consistent with Kansas's choice of law methodology: "the law of the forum should be applied unless compelling reasons exist for applying a different law." This methodology is essentially a *lex fori* approach with an escape hatch that allows the application of some other state's law when there is good reason to depart from forum law. The Kansas court saw no reason to depart. In fact, the application of one state's law would ensure that each of the similarly-situated plaintiffs would be treated similarly; it would also make the class action more manageable from an administrative standpoint.

For the first time in decades, the Court struck down as unconstitutional a state court's application of forum law. Justice Rehnquist's opinion observed that Kansas lacked a sufficient interest in claims that were unrelated to the State and, given the difference between Kansas and other states' laws, the application of Kansas law was sufficiently arbitrary and unfair that it exceeded constitutional bounds.

The *Shutts* decision reversing the Kansas Supreme Court may seem like the only conceivable outcome on such extreme facts. After all, how could Kansas law determine the rights and responsibilities of a dispute between an Oklahoma plaintiff-lessor and an Oklahoma defendant regarding payments due on an Oklahoma lease? But on the other hand, how different is that from *Hague*, where the Court allowed Minnesota law to determine the rights and responsibilities of a dispute arising out of a contract that was entered into in Wisconsin by Wisconsin parties regarding an

---

21   472 U.S. 797 (1985).

automobile accident that occurred in Wisconsin involving only Wisconsin parties? (Is it because *Shutts* was a class action with thousands of plaintiffs?)

In any event, the choice of law story in *Shutts* did not end with Justice Rehnquist's opinion. On remand, the Kansas state court applied its own statute of limitations, the longest in the nation, to all of the plaintiffs' claims. That action was bold in light of the fact that almost all of the claims were time-barred under the laws of the other interested states. But this action was not unusual since statutes of limitations are often treated as procedural in the choice of law context and, therefore, are often subject to forum law. (*See* Chapters 2 and 10.)

But the Kansas court, under the guise of applying other states' laws, also concocted a rather extraordinary story about how the other interested states would adopt the same equitable theory of unjust enrichment that Kansas has, and would apply the same interest rates that Kansas did. So the Kansas court, purportedly applying other states' laws (Texas, Ohio, Louisiana), predicted that the application of those states' laws would have led to the same result. Flouting statutory and case law in those other interested states, the Kansas court's prediction was surely erroneous and perhaps disingenuous.

While this *Shutts* litigation was underway, a parallel action in Kansas captioned *Wortman v. Sun Oil Co.* involved nearly identical facts and legal issues. The Kansas court treated the *Wortman* litigation exactly as it had treated *Shutts*. Three years after Justice Rehnquist issued his opinion in *Shutts*, *Sun Oil Co. v. Wortman* came to the Supreme Court.[22] In this appeal, the Supreme Court addressed the Kansas court's characterization of statutes of limitations as procedural and also the highly creative construction of the other interested states' laws.

In an opinion by Justice Scalia, the Supreme Court affirmed. With respect to the traditional characterization of statutes of limitations as procedural in the choice of law context, he wrote:

> If we abandon the currently applied, traditional notions of [substance and procedure] we would embark upon the enterprise of constitutionalizing choice-of-law rules with no compass to guide us beyond our own perceptions of what seems desirable.[23]

With respect to the Kansas court's creative construction of other interested states' laws, Justice Scalia wrote that the petitioners had not offered any case law from the other interested states that clearly indicated that the Kansas court was not applying

---

22   486 U.S. 717 (1988).

23   486 U.S. at 728.

the other states' laws. On this point, Justice O'Connor dissented in an opinion joined by Chief Justice Rehnquist, writing:

> Today's decision discards important parts of our decision in [*Shutts*] and of the Full Faith and Credit Clause. Faced with the constitutional obligation to apply the substantive law of another State, a court that does not like that apparently need take only two steps in order to avoid applying it. First, invent a legal theory so novel or strange that the other State has never had an opportunity to reject it; then, on the basis of nothing but unsupported speculation, "predict" that the other State would adopt that theory if it had the chance. To call this giving full faith and credit to the law of another State ignores the language of the Constitution and leaves it without the capacity to fulfill its purpose.[24]

Justice Scalia did not necessarily disagree with the dissenters' characterization that Kansas got the other states' law wrong. But he said that

> it is not enough that a state court misconstrue the law of another state . . . [I]t must contradict law of the other State that is clearly established and that has been brought to the court's attention.[25]

Appreciate the Supreme Court's predicament. On one hand, the Full Faith and Credit Clause surely demands that the law of the sister-state be applied accurately and with fidelity. But on the other hand, the Supreme Court has neither the expertise nor the capacity to hear appeals from litigants who are aggrieved every time that one state applies some other state's law (and arguably gets it wrong).

We have seen from the foregoing review of the case law that the Due Process and Full Faith and Credit Clauses play a very modest role in contemporary choice of law litigation. It is possible to conclude that, as a general matter, the Constitution will invalidate only the most egregious applications of forum law.

Effective litigators can sometimes breathe life into what appears to be a dead argument by leveraging some unique structural characteristic that distinguishes her case from all of those that came before it. Imagine, for example, a choice of law case where one of the litigants is a state agency of the other state. In *Nevada v. Hall*, for example, an employee of a Nevada state entity caused an automobile accident in California, injuring Hall, a Californian.[26] Hall sued the State of Nevada in a

---

24   486 U.S. at 748 (O'Connor, J., dissenting).

25   486 U.S. at 730–31.

26   440 U.S. 410 (1979).

California court. Under Nevada's Tort Claims Act, Nevada had waived its sovereign immunity but damages were capped at $25,000. California refused to recognize Nevada's law, and the State of Nevada appealed arguing that California failed to give full faith and credit to a sister state's law. The Supreme Court acknowledged that the State of Nevada had a different—and stronger—constitutional argument than an ordinary litigant, but on these facts, the application of California law (refusing Nevada immunity and not capping damages) did not "interfere with Nevada's capacity to fulfill its own sovereign responsibilities"; refusing to apply Nevada law "pose[d] no substantial threat to our constitutional system of cooperative federalism."[27]

This niche area involving states-as-litigants returned in a case that, again, involved the states of Nevada and California, but this time with their roles somewhat reversed. In *Franchise Tax Board of California v. Hyatt*, a former Californian who had moved to Nevada filed a suit in Nevada against the California Franchise Tax Board for harassment, invasion of privacy, and other torts.[28] A California statute immunized California's tax agency from such actions, but Nevada refused to apply the California statute with respect to that state's intentional acts. In doing so, the Nevada court gave California the same immunity that Nevada accorded its own agencies: immunity from negligent acts, but not from intentional acts. California appealed to the Supreme Court, arguing that Nevada's refusal to recognize the California law interfered with its ability to "fulfill its own sovereign responsibilities" regarding tax collection.

Although not citing karma, a unanimous Court found "no principled distinction" between Nevada's interest in *Hall* and California's interest here. The Court further recognized Nevada's "[sensitive application of] principles with a healthy regard for California's sovereign status" because it accorded the California agency the same immunity accorded its own taxing authority. Justice O'Connor's opinion observed that this sensitive application belied a "policy of hostility to the public Acts of a sister State," which would have been unconstitutional.[29]

On remand, the Nevada courts allowed a damages award of $1 million against the Franchise Tax Board for their intentional torts. The liability of a Nevada agency would have been capped at $50,000 under Nevada law. Thus, in allowing an uncapped award, Nevada applied neither Nevada law nor California law.

---

27   440 U.S. at 424 n.24.

28   538 U.S. 488 (2003).

29   538 U.S. at 499.

California again appealed to the Supreme Court. The Court considered two questions: first, whether to overrule *Nevada v. Hall*; and second, whether the damages award constituted a failure to confer full faith and credit to the laws of a sister state.[30] On the first question, the Court was evenly divided. Four justices were prepared to reverse *Nevada v. Hall*'s holding that a state can open the doors of its courts to a private citizen's lawsuit against another state without the other state's consent. But because the court was equally divided, the Court affirmed the Nevada court's exercise of jurisdiction.

On the second question, the Court held that Nevada's "special rule" (*i.e.*, neither the law of Nevada nor the law of California) constituted a "policy of hostility toward California," that threatened cooperative federalism, and that violated the Full Faith and Credit Clause. The Court continued:

> In so holding we need not, and do not, intend to return to a complex balancing-of interests approach to conflicts of law under the Full Faith and Credit Clause. . . . We have since abandoned that approach, and we continue to recognize that a State need not substitute the statutes of other states for its own statutes dealing with a subject matter concerning which it is competent to legislate. But here, we can safely conclude that, in devising a special—and hostile—rule for California, Nevada has not sensitively applied principles of comity with a healthy regard for California's sovereign status.[31]

Chief Justice Roberts, in a dissent that was joined by Justice Thomas, disagreed with the majority's conclusion that Nevada's policy exhibited hostility.

The notion that Nevada is discriminating against Californians invites mention of other clauses of the U.S. Constitution that are peripherally relevant to Conflict of Laws. The Privileges and Immunities Clause[32] and the Equal Protection Clause[33] are designed to prevent acts of discrimination or unequal treatment. These Clauses require that the laws of the forum apply equally to locals and foreigners. Further, the dormant Commerce Clause[34] restricts the extent to which states can interfere with interstate commerce. State laws may not overly discriminate against foreign-

---

30   ___ U.S. ___, 136 S. Ct. 1277 (2016).

31   136 S. Ct. at 1283.

32   U.S. Const. art. IV, § 2 ("The Citizens of each State shall be entitled to all the Privileges and Immunities of Citizens in the several States.").

33   U.S. Const. art. XIV, § 1 ("No State shall . . . deny to any person within its jurisdiction the equal protection of the laws.").

34   U.S. Const. art. I, § 8 ("The Congress shall have the Power . . . To regulate Commerce with foreign Nations, and among the several States, and with the Indian Tribes.").

ers; the laws cannot be anti-competitive; and even facially neutral laws cannot impose a burden on interstate commerce that is "clearly excessive in relation to the putative local benefits."[35] These circumstances are exceedingly rare. The following hypotheticals focus instead on due process and full faith and credit.

Hypothetical 14-1

J.D. Dalton is an Alabamian who worked remotely as a programmer for Thigpen Inc., a restaurant supply company that is incorporated in Pennsylvania and has its principal place of business in Pittsburgh. Thigpen had a pension plan for its employees; upon their retirement, employees would receive a benefit that was the product of a formula that included the number of years worked and the employee's salary at retirement. The accrued amount was payable in a lump sum or in monthly installments. Upon his retirement, Dalton had worked at the company for 15 years and earned a substantial annual salary.

A month before Dalton's retirement, the plan announced that it was inadequately funded and was terminating. The plan had about $150 million in assets to cover approximately $500 million in accrued benefits. In circumstances like this, the Pension Benefit Guarantee Corporation, a government-owned corporation that insures pension plans, will pay Dalton some of what he is owed; and the federal Employee Retirement Income Security Act (ERISA) will provide him with some relief. But his remedies will be limited. And because ERISA expressly preempts all state laws that relate to employer-sponsored health plans, Dalton has no claims against the plan or his employer for breach of contract or breach of fiduciary duty.

Instead, Dalton filed a lawsuit in Alabama against Stevenson Group, Inc. (Stevenson). Stevenson is a Pennsylvania company with its principal place of business in Philadelphia. Stevenson provided actuarial services to Thigpen and other companies around the country (including unrelated business in Alabama). For the last five years of the plan's existence, Stevenson consistently (though incorrectly) determined that the plan was fully funded. As a result, Thigpen made no contributions to the plan in any of those years. Dalton claims that Stevenson breached its professional duty when it certified, year after year, that the plan was adequately funded.

Under Pennsylvania law, professional suppliers of information, such as Stevenson, do not owe a general duty of care to non-clients, such as Dalton. However, Alabama law does not require a plaintiff to be in strict

---

35 *Pike v. Bruce Church, Inc.*, 397 U.S. 137, 142 (1970).

privity with a professional supplier of information in order to bring a professional negligence suit.

Stevenson filed a motion to dismiss for failure to state a claim for which relief may be granted. The court denied the motion, concluding that Alabama law applied. Is that constitutional?

The Alabama court might have applied Alabama law because it follows the *lex fori* approach (because this action was filed in Alabama), the traditional approach (because the injury to Dalton occurred in Alabama), interest analysis (because Alabama is an interested state), the center of gravity approach (because of the concentration of contacts in Alabama), the Second Restatement (because Alabama had the most significant relationship), or some combination of those approaches. The reasoning to support some of those conclusions would be more strained than for others. But for purposes of the Constitutional analysis, it does not matter what methodology led to the court's conclusion that Alabama law applies. The Constitutional issue is not whether Alabama accurately applied its own choice of law methodology, but rather whether Alabama courts *can* apply Alabama law or *must* apply Pennsylvania law.

Hypothetical 14-2

In 2001, Cora Rose was hired by the Joseph Schmaltz Brewing Company (Schmaltz) as an industrial relations manager for its Kansas City, Missouri plant. In 2006, she was promoted to plant manager. And in 2013, Rose accepted a similar position at Schmaltz's largest facility in Winston-Salem, North Carolina.

Two years ago, Rose accepted yet another promotion; she became a vice president at Schmaltz's corporate headquarters in Milwaukee, Wisconsin. Shortly after she had moved and begun that job, she requested the transfer of her office assistant from the Winston-Salem facility to the Milwaukee office. The company refused that request, and tensions grew: Rose threatened to quit if the transfer was not granted; and Schmaltz threatened to fire Rose if she persisted with this demand. Schmaltz asked Rose to resign, but she refused. Schmaltz then terminated her, but issued a press release indicating that she had resigned.

Ready to apply for another job, Rose asked Schmaltz for a service letter, invoking a specific section of Missouri's employment law. "Service letter" laws require employers to provide former employees with letters describing certain aspects of their employment—*e.g.*, dates of employment, salary history, and reason for termination. These laws, which vary substantially from state to state, ensure that former employees can get the information that they need from otherwise reluctant employers, but also protect employers from being sued for defamation for providing truthful information. Missouri's law is the most employee-friendly of all such laws; it provides a right of action and imposes automatic and severe penalties on any employer who makes a false statement in a service letter.

Schmaltz gave Rose a service letter that indicated she had resigned. Rose sued Schmaltz in Missouri, alleging willful and malicious violation of the Missouri service letter statute. The Missouri court applied forum law. A jury awarded her nominal damages of $1.00 and punitive damages of $400,000.

On appeal, Schmaltz challenges the constitutionality of the application of Missouri law, an issue that it timely raised in the trial court without success. Rose requested the service letter while she was residing in North Carolina (the state to which she returned after being terminated by Schmaltz). After she received the service letter, she moved to Missouri before filing this suit, and she still lives there (with her former office assistant). Schmaltz closed its Missouri plant in 2013, and has no manufacturing or processing operations there. Schmaltz, which is incorporated in Delaware, is one of the largest American manufacturers of beer, and its brands are sold by distributors in large numbers in all fifty states. Is the application of Missouri law with respect to service letters constitutional?

Hypothetical 14-3

The village of Weymouth, Nevada hired a local company Samantha Nathan Repair Co. (Nathan) to repair one of the village's water towers. In the course of its repairs, Nathan used a product manufactured by RMH Epoxy Inc. (RMH). RMH's epoxy failed just weeks after the repair, causing property damage to parts of the village property. Nathan compensated the village for $52,000 of property damage that it suffered, and then sought indemnification from RMH. Samantha Nathan claims that Mickey Warren, the technical professional with whom she spoke at RMH, assured her that the epoxy had a 20-year warranty. Unfortunately, the product was inadequate for desert climates—a fact unknown to the employees at RMH, an Iowa corporation with a principal place of business in Marshalltown, Iowa. RMH's customer base was, prior to this unfortunate event, located exclusively in the Midwestern United States.

The contract for the epoxy, with its purchase price of $4,505 was on a pre-printed form that RMH sent to Nathan; a few of the terms, such as the price, were handwritten by RMH onto the form. Samantha Nathan signed and returned that contract. One of the "Terms and Conditions" printed on the form was a choice of law clause that read: "This contract and the relationship between the parties hereunder shall be construed, interpreted, and applied in accordance with the local laws of the State of Iowa."

Nathan sued RMH in Nevada. The contract did not, in fact, include a warranty clause. But rather than arguing for breach of an *implied* warranty (a *contract* claim), Nathan's lawyer would like to bring a *tort* claim, alleging fraudulent misrepresentation (opening the possibility for a higher damage award—maybe even punitive damages). A tort claim under such circumstances is contemplated under the laws of Nevada, but not under the laws of Iowa, where Nathan would, at best, have a contract claim for breach of an implied warranty.

The State of Nevada follows the Second Restatement for choice of law questions, including Section 187 for choice of law clauses. Imagine that the Nevada trial court concluded that "The choice of law clause is unenforceable because this was a contract of adhesion that renders the choice of law clause nugatory. Moreover, a tort claim is *ipso facto* beyond the scope of a choice of a law clause that is contained in a contract. We therefore apply the law of the place of injury, to-wit: Nevada." Is Nevada's application of Nevada law constitutional?

FROM THE COURTS

IN THE MATTER OF THE
ADOPTION OF BABY BOY S.

Court of Appeals of Kansas
22 Kan.App.2d 119 (1996)

RULON, PRESIDING JUDGE.

V.A., the natural father of Baby Boy S., appeals from the district court's order terminating his parental rights and approving the adoption of Baby Boy S.

Essentially, we must decide if Kansas adoption statutes as applied to the natural father violate the Due Process Clause of the United States Constitution. . . . We affirm.

Facts

Baby Boy S. was born on April 26, 1994, in Wichita, Kansas, and his natural mother, R.S., relinquished the newborn infant to the Adoption Centre, Inc., of Kansas, a licensed adoption agency. R.S. left Wichita in May 1994 and moved to North Carolina.

Baby Boy S. was placed with adoptive parents residing in Wichita on April 29, 1994. A petition for adoption was filed on June 8, 1994. Under K.S.A. 59–2133(b), notice of the adoption proceeding was served on V.A. on July 7, 1994. V.A. timely filed objections to the adoption and requested custody of the infant. V.A. at all times was a resident of Ohio.

Later, a petition to terminate V.A.'s parental rights was filed. Ultimately, the district court ordered V.A.'s parental rights terminated under K.S.A. 59–2136(h)(2) and (h)(4).

The findings of the district court can be summarized as follows:

R.S. left her parents' home in Whitehouse, Ohio, in May 1993 when she completed high school. She immediately moved in with V.A. and his parents in Toledo, Ohio. The relationship between R.S. and V.A. was tumultuous from the start due to V.A.'s dislike of R.S.'s parents. R.S. left V.A. following a dispute about her parents.

By early July 1993, R.S. was again living with V.A. and his parents. In early August 1993, a home pregnancy test indicated R.S. was pregnant. V.A.'s parents took R.S. to their doctor, who confirmed the pregnancy and estimated the baby's due date as April 26, 1994. R.S. had three or four doctor visits with V.A.'s family physician. V.A.'s family took her to get a medical card through a state program. Unquestionably, V.A. knew that the baby was due at the end of April 1994.

While living with V.A.'s family, R.S. and V.A. did not pay any living expenses. In late August 1993, V.A. had a fight with his family about R.S. V.A. was so angry that he threw food and furniture and broke holes in the doors at his parents' residence. R.S. and V.A. were then told to move out.

After leaving V.A.'s parents' home in September 1993, R.S. and V.A. lived with several friends but eventually lived in their own apartment. R.S. signed the lease and arranged for the utilities, believing that V.A., who was working, would pay for them. After a fight with V.A., R.S. left on September 18, 1993, and returned to her parents' home.

Eventually, V.A. asked R.S. to resume their relationship. While he promised to be responsible for the baby, there was no offer of money, housing, or maternity clothes, nor did he offer to handle the medical bills associated with prenatal care or delivery. According to R.S., V.A. was only concerned with renewing their relationship and did not inquire about the pregnancy.

About Thanksgiving 1993, R.S. moved out of her parents' house, moved in with a girlfriend, and began considering putting the baby up for adoption. She contacted a lawyer in Toledo who gave her a booklet of couples looking for babies. R.S. chose a couple who happened to live in Wichita, Kansas. She denied knowledge of any difference in the laws of Kansas or Ohio and testified that her lawyer did not suggest a Kansas couple. V.A. knew R.S. had left her parents' home.

Around Christmas 1993, R.S. and V.A. met accidentally at a local shopping mall. He shouted at R.S. and chased her and one of her girlfriends into a store. She and her girlfriend were frightened. The girlfriend told V.A. that R.S. had lost the baby because of a miscarriage. Whether R.S. confirmed the miscarriage to V.A. was disputed. Although he was uncertain if R.S. was still pregnant, V.A. made no effort to follow up to determine the status of the pregnancy.

Eventually, in December 1993, R.S. began living with a new boyfriend, A.T., in his parents' house in Ohio.

In early January 1994, V.A. received correspondence from a Texas adoption agency, indicating that R.S. desired to put her unborn child up for adoption. He called the agency to express his opposition to the adoption. Later, he approved a letter drafted by his father's attorney opposing the adoption, expressing his intention to keep the child and conveying a written acknowledgment of paternity. V.A.'s copy of the letter included a hand-written note from the lawyer to V.A.'s father stating that the response "should take care of the situation *until* the baby is born." V.A. had no direct contact with the lawyer.

V.A. did not tell the Texas agency he would support the mother during her pregnancy. He did not ask for R.S.'s address, nor did he ask the agency to convey any message offering support. He did not contact R.S.'s family or any of her known friends to offer financial support or to express his opposition to the adoption.

A.T. and R.S. moved to Wichita in February 1994. The Adoption Centre helped them find an apartment and paid their bills. R.S. obtained a listed phone number under her name.

After receiving the Texas adoption agency letter, V.A. also contacted a cousin of R.S. In April 1994, R.S.'s cousin told V.A. that R.S. was somewhere in Kansas. Between the end of April (the due date) and June 7, 1994, V.A. did not contact the Texas adoption agency, R.S.'s family, or her friends to determine if the baby had been born.

In June 1994, V.A.'s father learned of an agency called Find People Fast and requested that they locate R.S. Eventually, V.A. learned of R.S.'s location in Wichita. He did not attempt to contact her even though he knew the baby probably had been born in late April. He did not contact an attorney to discuss custody, visitation, or what he needed to do to establish or preserve his relationship with the child.

V.A. first received confirmation of the baby's birth on July 5, 1994, when a private investigator hired by the Adoption Centre contacted him. He was served with notice of the adoption proceeding on July 8, 1994. Prior to that time, he had no knowledge that anyone other than R.S. had custody of the baby.

Based upon the above findings, the district court concluded that V.A. failed to provide support for R.S. during the 6 months prior to the child's birth and did not have reasonable cause for not providing support. The district court relied upon V.A.'s failure to offer any form of financial support to the mother after she moved out of their apartment on September 18, 1993; that V.A. had disposable income which was available to provide support; and that V.A. and/or his parents forwarded unpaid doctor bills and utility bills to R.S.'s parents for payment. The court concluded that V.A. did not pursue all the opportunities and options available to him to carry out his duties.

The district court, in an alternative finding, terminated V.A.'s parental rights on the ground that he was an unfit parent. The court relied upon his failure to make financial arrangements to pay for prenatal care or delivery of the baby. The court found that V.A. was consumed with his personal desire to maintain a relationship with R.S. rather than caring about the unborn child. The court further found that V.A. had a violent temper, evidenced by his damage to property during his fits of anger, to the extent that he was asked to move out of his parents' home. The court further found that V.A. had violated the law by smoking marijuana.

Due Process

We must decide if the provisions of K.S.A. 59–2336(h) can be applied here to terminate the father's parental rights to Baby Boy S.

K.S.A. 59–2136(h) provides:

> [T]he court may order that parental rights be terminated, upon a finding by clear and convincing evidence, of any of the following:
>
> . . .
>
> (4) the father, after having knowledge of the pregnancy, failed without reasonable cause to provide support for the mother during the six months prior to the child's birth;
>
> (5) the father abandoned the mother after having knowledge of the pregnancy.

V.A. argues that due process requires that he be put on fair notice of the actions or inactions that could result in the termination of his parental rights. Because he was not a Kansas resident and could not anticipate the mother moving to Kansas, V.A. argues that application of Kansas law violated his constitutional right to due process. He argues that application of Kansas law impermissibly allows unwed mothers to "forum shop" for jurisdictions with stricter statutes to prevent unwed fathers from opposing an adoption. He claims he was entitled to fair warning of the required or proscribed actions which might have resulted in the loss of his parental rights. . . .

V.A.'s claims essentially raise conflict of law questions, and such issues can implicate due process standards in some circumstances. The United States Supreme Court has long recognized that a certain set of facts giving rise to a cause of action might justify the application of the law of more than one state. *See Watson v. Employers Liability Corp.*, 348 U.S. 66, 72–73 (1954). In analyzing the due process principles in conflicts cases, the Supreme Court has said:

In deciding constitutional choice-of-law questions, whether under the Due Process Clause or the Full Faith and Credit Clause,
this Court has traditionally examined the contacts of the State,
whose law was applied, with the parties and with the occurrence
or transaction giving rise to the litigation. [Citation omitted.] In
order to ensure that the choice of law is neither arbitrary nor fundamentally unfair [citation omitted], the Court has invalidated
the choice of law of a State which has had no significant contact
or significant aggregation of contacts, creating state interests,
with the parties and the occurrence of transaction.

Allstate Ins. Co. v. Hague, 449 U.S. 302, 308 (1981).

The *Hague* Court further noted that when considering conflict of law
questions "for a State's substantive law to be selected in a constitutionally
permissible manner, that State must have a significant contact or significant
aggregation of contacts, creating state interests, such that choice of its law
is neither arbitrary nor fundamentally unfair." 449 U.S. at 312–13.

V.A. does not challenge the Kansas court's jurisdiction over the adoption
proceeding. R.S. had openly been a Kansas resident for at least 60 days
prior to the birth of Baby Boy S. The child was born in Kansas and was
relinquished to a Kansas adoption agency. The child has resided in Kansas
with a Kansas adoptive family throughout the proceeding. Kansas has
an interest in ensuring that children born and residing in this state are
adequately provided for by responsible adults. When parents relinquish or
otherwise ignore their parental obligations to a child living in Kansas, this
state has a compelling interest in ensuring the child's well-being and, when
appropriate, to ensure the children are adopted by responsible and caring
families. Consequently, under the facts of this case, we conclude Kansas has
significant contacts creating state interests in applying its laws.

When considering fairness in the context of a conflicts issue, an important
element is the expectation of the parties. A state "may not abrogate the
rights of parties beyond its borders having no relation to anything done or
to be done within them." *Phillips Petroleum Co. v. Shutts*, 472 U.S. 797,
822 (quoting *Home Ins. Co. v. Dick*, 281 U.S. 397, 410 (1930)). In *Shutts,*
the Court invalidated the Kansas Supreme Court's decision to apply Kansas
law to all gas leases involved in a class action, even though a vast majority
of the leases and property owners had no connection with Kansas.

Applying Kansas law to the facts in this case does not unconstitutionally impair the reasonable expectation of the parties It is not unreasonable for parties to expect that the standards for parental obligations would be determined by the laws of the state where the child resides. This is consistent with Restatement (Second) of Conflict of Laws § 289 (1969) which provides that local law should control in cases of adoption.

Under these facts, it might also be constitutionally permissible to apply Ohio law. However, we believe Ohio's state interests are more tenuous than those of Kansas. R.S. left Ohio prior to the birth of the child and has not returned since. The child was born in Kansas. In our current mobile society, the place of conception of a child carries little weight. However, requiring an unwed father to make substantial efforts to remain in contact with an unwed mother and participate in the pregnancy and birth of the child, wherever it occurs, is not an unreasonable expectation.

Although V.A. likens R.S.'s travels to a helium balloon, he was aware that she was no longer living at her parents' home and knew almost 4 months before the baby's birth that she was considering an out-of-state adoption. However, he made no serious efforts to locate her whereabouts. The district court specifically found that R.S. did not move to conceal herself. Likewise, she testified that she did not choose to put her baby up for adoption through a Kansas agency in order to impose stricter parental obligations on the father.

V.A. relies heavily on the "fundamental" nature of his parental rights to emphasize that the law of his residence should control in this case. . . .

> When an unwed father demonstrates a full commitment to the responsibilities of parenthood by "com[ing] forward to participate in the rearing of his child," [citations omitted] his interest in personal contact with his child acquires substantial protection under the Due Process Clause. At that point it may be said that he "act[s] as a father toward his children." [Citation omitted.] But the mere existence of a biological link does not merit equivalent constitutional protection.

Lehr v. Robertson, 463 U.S. 248, 261 (1983). . . .

For the above reasons we conclude that the application of Kansas law in this case did not deprive V.A. of any substantive or procedural due process rights. . . .

COMMENTS AND QUESTIONS

1. V.A. (the biological father) referred to the "fundamental" nature of the rights at stake in this application of Kansas law. Compare V.A.'s liberty interest with Allstate's property interest in *Hague*. Should the same constitutional standard apply to both situations?

2. The court emphasizes that R.S. (the biological mother) did not choose Kansas for its favorable law regarding the termination of a father's parental rights. What would result, then, if she had? Would her motive change the unfairness of the surprise to V.A. (the due process inquiry) or the offense to Ohio's sovereignty (the full faith and credit inquiry)? If forum-shopping is relevant, should the court accept R.S.'s statements at face value or have an evidentiary inquiry into the matter?

3. If forum-shopping is relevant, but R.S.'s motives are pure, of what relevance are the motives of the Texas adoption agency? Isn't it possible that the agency prefers Kansas adoptions (and funnels their customers toward their Kansas clients) because the process of terminating the absent parent's rights is more streamlined there?

FROM THE COURTS

EARTHCAM, INC. v. OXBLUE CORP.

U.S. District Court for the Northern District of Georgia
2013 WL 11904713 (N.D. Ga. July 18, 2013)

WILLIAM S. DUFFEY, JR., DISTRICT JUDGE.

. . . In this action, Plaintiff EarthCam, Inc. ("Plaintiff" or "EarthCam"), a camera technology company, alleges that its competitor, Defendant OxBlue Corporation ("OxBlue"), engaged in various forms of corporate espionage to misappropriate Plaintiff's technologies and customers. . . . [The complaint also named Richard Hermann as a defendant. Count VI of the complaint alleged that Hermann breached his contract with EarthCam. Hermann is a former EarthCam employee.]

[OxBlue moved to dismiss various claims that it contends were barred by applicable statutes of limitations. Hermann moved to dismiss the breach of contract claim, arguing that the contract was unenforceable under Georgia law. This case focuses primarily on the contract claim against Hermann. Hermann's employment agreement contained covenants not to compete, non-solicitation provisions, and non-disclosure provisions.]

[I.] Relevant Factual Allegations

EarthCam, headquartered in Hackensack, New Jersey, and OxBlue, headquartered in Atlanta, Georgia, compete in the business of selling remote camera products and services. Plaintiff alleges that, after it launched a new "Robotic Megapixel Camera system" in November 2005, the OxBlue Defendants "embarked on . . . a secret mission to appropriate trade secrets behind" the new system. To achieve this goal, Plaintiff alleges, the OxBlue Defendants engaged in a series of unauthorized intrusions into Plaintiff's computer systems for the purpose of accessing and copying proprietary information. The earliest of the alleged intrusions occurred in March and April 2006, when the OxBlue Defendants launched a "brute-force attack" of the EarthCam system from a BellSouth IP address and a Comcast IP address (70.90.75.50), sending 428,494 messages to EarthCam's servers. On numerous other occasions, from February 2008 to May 2011, Plaintiff alleges that the OxBlue Defendants gained unauthorized access to EarthCam's systems by using the login credentials of EarthCam customers.

In response to OxBlue's intrusions, EarthCam "assembled a number of senior engineers and other high-level employees to evaluate damage to EarthCam's systems," which EarthCam claims cost it more than $5,000 in "opportunity costs and actual expense." Also, by May 2011, EarthCam "had created an internal security policy specifically to deny access to anyone attempting to access EarthCam's systems from OxBlue's office's IP address."

In October 2006, Hermann, an EarthCam employee, reached out to McCormack [an OxBlue officer] to discuss possible employment with OxBlue.[1] Over the next three years, Plaintiff alleges that Hermann, at the OxBlue Defendants' request, stayed employed at EarthCam and provided OxBlue

---

1   Hermann, a New Jersey resident, began his employment with EarthCam in September 2005. On July 10, 2006, Hermann and EarthCam entered into an employment contract containing covenants not to compete, non-solicitation provisions, and non-disclosure provisions. The Employment Agreement was entered into in New Jersey and contains a choice-of-law provisions providing that the "Agreement shall be governed by, and construed in accordance with, the laws of the State of New Jersey."

with numerous confidential documents, copyrighted works, and trade secrets. After ending his employment with EarthCam in June 2008, Hermann became an independent contractor of OxBlue, and Plaintiff claims he solicited EarthCam customers in violation of his Employment Agreement with EarthCam.

II. Discussion

. . . [After partially granting OxBlue's motion to dismiss some of the claims against it as time-barred, the court turned to Hermann's motion.]

In his Motion to Dismiss, Hermann argues that . . . Plaintiff's claim for breach of the Employment Agreement is not valid under Georgia law. . . . Plaintiff argues that the Employment Agreement is governed by New Jersey law, under which it is enforceable.

The parties do not dispute that the Employment Agreement is unenforceable under Georgia law and enforceable, or potentially enforceable, under New Jersey law. The question before the Court, therefore, is which state's law applies. The Court applies the law called for by Georgia's choice-of-law rules, so long as the application of that law does not violate the parties' due process rights. *See Phillips Petroleum Co. v. Shutts*, 472 U.S. 797–821–22 (1985). . . .

The Employment Agreement contains a choice-of-law provision calling for the application of New Jersey law to the interpretation and enforcement of the Agreement. Although Georgia courts generally accept choice-of-law provisions contained in contracts, choice-of-law provisions in employment contracts will not be enforced by Georgia courts if restrictive covenants in those contracts violate Georgia public policy.

> The law of the jurisdiction chosen by parties to a contract to govern their contractual rights will not be applied by Georgia courts where application of the chosen law would contravene the policy of, or would be prejudicial to the interests of, this state. Covenants against disclosure, like covenants against competition, affect the interests of this state, namely the flow of information needed for competition among businesses, and hence their validity is determined by the public policy of this state.

See Convergys Corp. v. Keener, 582 S.E.2d 84, 85–86 (Ga. 2003). Because, as the parties agree, the Employment Agreement at issue here is invalid as overbroad under Georgia law, Georgia's choice-of-law rules require the application of Georgia law to prevent the Employment Agreement's enforcement.

Plaintiff argues that, notwithstanding Georgia's choice-of-law rules, the application of Georgia law to the Employment Agreement would violate its due process rights because the contract dispute between Plaintiff and Hermann lacks sufficient contact with the State of Georgia. In a dispute between out-of-state parties, the application of forum law to the dispute satisfies constitutional due process requirements only if the forum state has a "significant contact or significant aggregation of contacts" with the dispute, and the application of the forum state's law would not be "arbitrary or unfair." *See Phillips*, 472 U.S. at 821–22 (quoting *Allstate Ins. Co. v. Hague*, 449 U.S. 302, 312–13 (1981) (plurality opinion)). . . "When considering fairness in this context, an important element is [the] expectation of the parties." *Phillips*, 472 U.S. at 822 (citing *Allstate*, 449 U.S. at 333 (opinion of Powell, J.)).

Plaintiff, a New Jersey-based company, and Hermann, a New Jersey resident, entered into the Employment Agreement in connection with Hermann's employment in New Jersey. The Agreement expressly provides for the application of New Jersey law. The only connection between the parties and the State of Georgia, with respect to the Employment Agreement, is that Hermann allegedly breached the Employment Agreement by supplying certain information to OxBlue, a Georgia-based company, and performed certain work "with or for" OxBlue. These contacts with Georgia, unilateral on the part of Hermann, are not "significant" and do not show that either party ever had an expectation that Georgia law would govern their Employment Agreement. *See Phillips*, 472 U.S. at 822 (holding that the application of Kansas law to contracts entered into between out-of-state parties did not satisfy due process because "[t]here is no indication that when the [contracts] were executed, the parties had any idea that Kansas law would control"). . . . When EarthCam and Hermann entered into the Employment Agreement, they expected and agreed that New Jersey law would govern any claimed violation of it. It is not reasonable to conclude that either EarthCam or Hermann expected or intended one or more of the other forty-nine states' laws would apply because one party's breach of the Agreement might be directed toward one or more other states. The Court concludes that the application of Georgia law to the Employment Agreement here would not satisfy the requirements of due process, and Hermann's motion to dismiss the breach of contract claim is required to be denied. . . .

COMMENTS AND QUESTIONS

1. Why did the plaintiff sue in Georgia?

2. Imagine that OxBlue and EarthCam are the only manufacturers in a niche market for camera technology. Would that strengthen or weaken Hermann's argument in support of his motion to dismiss?

3. Imagine that, while EarthCam was in the process of hiring Hermann, the general counsel of EarthCam scribbled on a first draft of his employment agreement: "Need a New Jersey choice of law clause! Some states like Georgia won't enforce the non-competes, etc." Would that strengthen or weaken Hermann's argument in support of his motion to dismiss?

4. If EarthCam does business nationally, is the choice of law clause the only reason that it would be an unfair surprise for Georgia law to be applied?

FROM THE COURTS

GLOBE COMMUNICATIONS CORP. v. R.C.S. RIZZOLI PERIODICI, S.P.A.

U.S. District Court for the Southern District of New York
729 F. Supp. 973 (S.D.N.Y. 1990)

SAND, DISTRICT JUDGE.

Defendant R.C.S. Rizzoli Periodici, S.p.A. ("Rizzoli") moves this Court pursuant to Fed. R. Civ. P. 12(b)(6) to dismiss the complaint for failure to state a claim. We deny Rizzoli's motion.

Plaintiff Globe Communications Corp. ("Globe") publishes the weekly magazine *Globe,* which is sold throughout the United States and Canada. In May 1984, Rizzoli, a large international publisher based in Italy, published an article in its Italian language magazine *Novella 2000* entitled *"Cat Stevens: Enough of Music, Now I Just Want to Be an Ayatollah!"* (translated from the original Italian) (the "Rizzoli Article"). The Rizzoli Article reported that the singer and entertainer Cat Stevens had converted to the Islamic religion and adopted the Islamic name Yusuf Islam, described his life in Teheran and dedication to Islamic religious principles, and suggested that the new convert was developing a close relationship with the Ayatollah Khomeini.

That month, a reporter for Globe, Len Stone, purchased a copy of the *Novella 2000* issue containing the Cat Stevens article. Globe then published in its June 19, 1984, edition of *Globe* (Volume 31, No. 25) an article entitled *"Pop Superstar's Startling Conversion"* ("Globe Article") which repeated the substance of the Rizzoli Article, attributing statements of European reporters as its source.

Mr. Islam sued Globe alleging that the Globe Article was false and defamatory and placed him in a false light. After Globe determined through discovery that many of the facts contained first in the Rizzoli Article and then in the Globe Article were false, it agreed to settle the suit brought by Mr. Islam. Globe now seeks to recover from Rizzoli the settlement costs and attorney fees it incurred in the defamation suit and punitive damages. Globe's complaint asserts three causes of action against Rizzoli for intentional misrepresentation, contribution, and equitable subrogation.

A threshold issue which must be resolved is whether the law of Florida, New York, or Italy controls in determining whether the complaint alleges viable causes of action. . . .

New York courts choose the substantive tort law of the state that has the most significant relationship with the occurrence and with the parties. *Babcock v. Jackson*, 12 N.Y.2d 473, 482 (1963). *But see Lund's Inc. v. Chemical Bank*, 870 F.2d 840, 845 (2d Cir. 1989) (*lex loci delicti* "remains the general rule in tort cases to be displaced only in extraordinary circumstances"), citing *Cousins v. Instrument Flyers, Inc.*, 44 N.Y.2d 698, 699 (1978) (per curiam). Although New York has not adopted the *Restatement (Second) of Conflict of Laws* (1969), the *Restatement* advocates a similar approach to choice of law questions and lists the relevant factors to be considered by courts. *See Restatement (Second) of Conflict of Laws* §§ 6, 145(2), 148.

The first cause of action in the complaint alleges intentional misrepresentation. Rizzoli argues that either Italy or New York has the most significant relationship to the alleged tort; Globe urged this Court to apply Florida law. Not surprisingly, Rizzoli also argues that Italian law does not impose liability for the acts alleged in the complaint. Globe, on the other hand, submits an affidavit from its Italian law expert that reaches the opposite conclusion. We do not resolve this conflict concerning Italian law because

New York's choice of law principles require the application of Florida law in this case. . . .

[T]he wrongful conduct took place in Italy where the *Novella 2000* article was first published. While the site of the injury was clearly in the United States where the article was read and relied upon, the parties disagree over where the most significant acts in reliance occurred. Rizzoli argues that since Len Stone, the *Globe* reporter purchased and read the article in New York, the reliance, and therefore the injury, occurred in New York. Globe, on the other hand, argues that reliance occurred in Florida since its employees and agents there authored and decided to publish the *Globe* article. . . .

[T]he place of the wrong is considered to be the place where the last event necessary to make the actor liable occurred. . . . Whether the last event necessary to the cause of action against Rizzoli is the decision by Globe to publish, the publication of the Globe article or the imposition of damages, all three occurred in Florida where Globe has its [principal] place of business and defended the lawsuit brought by Mr. Islam. Florida is the place where the great majority of the acts giving rise to liability took place. . . .

Rizzoli argues that the application of Florida law would violate its constitutional right to due process. The Supreme Court held in *Allstate Ins. Co. v. Hague,* 449 U.S. 302 (1981), that "for a State's substantive law to be selected in a constitutionally permissible manner, the State must have a significant contact or significant aggregation of contacts, creating state interests, such that choice of its law is neither arbitrary nor fundamentally unfair." *Id.* at 312–13. Florida has a significant relation to this litigation. Rizzoli's computerized subscription list indicates direct subscription sales to subscribers in 38 states and includes 60 subscribers residing in Florida. Rizzoli also has repeatedly contracted with an exclusive United States distributor for the sale of its periodicals throughout the United States. While the number of issues sold in Florida comprise only a small percentage of Rizzoli's total sales, Rizzoli has regularly sold issues of *Novella 2000* throughout the United States and in Florida. It is unreasonable for Rizzoli to claim unfair surprise at the application of Florida law.

COMMENTS AND QUESTIONS

1. How can an Italian corporation like Rizzoli invoke the protections of the Due Process Clause of the U.S. Constitution? Is Italy's law deserving of Full Faith and Credit?

2. The court says that because Rizzoli has sixty subscribers (and other indirect sales) in Florida it is unreasonable for Rizzoli to claim that it is unfairly surprised by the application of Florida law. Is the court asking what Rizzoli actually knew or what Rizzoli should have known?

3. With respect to the element of unfair surprise (to Rizzoli), one might expect that the publication of defamatory statements about Yusuf Islam (Cat Stevens) could lead to a suit by Yusuf Islam (Cat Stevens). But how foreseeable is it (to Rizzoli) that its publication would be republished by the Globe, that Yusuf Islam (Cat Stevens) would sue the Globe, and that the Globe would then sue Rizzoli (and invoke Florida law)?

SAMPLE EXAM QUESTIONS

Question 14-4

Melissa Farrell was a North Dakota high schooler who was offered a scholarship to play hockey at the University of North Dakota, one of the country's premier hockey programs. After two seasons, she was named captain and was also a conference all-star.

In pre-season conditioning during her junior year, she was advised by the team's coach to run a local 10-mile charity road race that was sponsored by the University of North Dakota. During the race, she was struck by a car and suffered serious injuries. The segment of the road race where she was injured was poorly marked, and there was no security to protect the runners. As this was a hit-and-run, the driver of the car is unknown.

If Farrell sues to recover damages for her medical expenses, lost wages, and pain and suffering, the likely defendant is the University of North Dakota. The University is a public university that is an extension of the state of North Dakota. Historically, all states were immune from negligence suits like Farrell's. However, most states have enacted statutes that waive sovereign immunity for suits like Farrell's—or waive immunity but limit damages to a specific amount. North Dakota very recently passed a statute that waives its immunity to suits like this, but that statute applies only prospectively (i.e., to state conduct that occurs after the statute's enactment date).

Because North Dakota's statute was passed after Farrell's injury, the University will have immunity if North Dakota law applies. Farrell's counsel is contemplating filing suit against the University in Minnesota. Minnesota waived its sovereign immunity decades ago. Minnesota uses the better law approach to determine the applicable law, and plaintiff's counsel may be able to persuade the Minnesota court that Minnesota's law is the better law.

But even if the Minnesota judge can be persuaded to deny North Dakota sovereign immunity, would it be constitutional for the Minnesota court to apply Minnesota law? Plaintiff's counsel has asked for your strategic assistance on the constitutional question(s).

Question 14-5

Jeremy Wallace is a popular science writer who lives in Cleveland, Ohio. Wallace suffered permanent eye damage caused by a virtual reality headset. Wallace used the headset intermittently for about eighteen months before his headaches, dizziness, and blurred vision could be traced to his use of the headset. Even after he quit using the headset, the medical conditions would return for a few days and then dissipate before returning again a week or two later. Wallace assumed that the symptoms would fade over time. Now a full three years after he quit using the headset, Wallace has been diagnosed with permanent eye damage in both eyes.

You represent Wallace. Because of the time that has passed since he first suffered injury, Wallace's tort claims are barred by the statute of limitations in every state. Statutes of limitations for contract claims are always longer than the statutes of limitations for tort claims, but filing suit on a breach of warranty claim in a products case is usually useless where, as here, the manufacturer included the standard warranty disclaimers, thereby limiting the purchaser's remedy to the $1,200 paid for the headset.

However, Wallace's sister, a law professor at the University of Mississippi, told him that the Mississippi version of the Uniform Commercial Code, unlike other states' codes, provides that recovery for physical injuries is available under a warranty theory notwithstanding the presence of a warranty disclaimer. Moreover, Section 1–105 of Mississippi's commercial code explicitly provides that Mississippi law must apply to all warranty claims.

The law of the State of Mississippi shall always govern the rights and duties of the parties in regard to disclaimers of implied warranties of merchantability or fitness, limitations of remedies for breaches of implied warranties of merchantability or fitness, or the necessity for privity of contract to maintain a civil action for breach of implied warranties of merchantability or fitness. . . .

This statute requiring the application of Mississippi law to warranty claims has been embraced by the Mississippi Supreme Court as a legitimate expression of the strong public policy of the state.

Without revealing where he was domiciled or where he purchased the headset, Wallace filed a complaint in Mississippi against Realz Co., the manufacturer of the headset. Realz Co. is a California corporation that has its principal place of business in California. Wallace purchased the headset in Ohio. The headset was designed and manufactured in California. Realz Co. has a worldwide presence and is registered to do and is presently doing business in Mississippi.

The complaint alleges breach of warranty by Realz Co. and seeks recovery for Wallace's personal injuries. Realz Co. answered the complaint and submitted to the jurisdiction of Mississippi. Does the Constitution offer Realz any escape from the application of Mississippi's warranty law?

Question 14-6

MxMatch is a dating website. MxMatch is owned by Hartland Production Co., a Kansas corporation with its principal place of business in Oklahoma City, Oklahoma.

A putative class of plaintiffs claim that MxMatch is a vast, fraudulent scheme that uses fake user profiles to deceive customers into paying to join and continue using the site. According to the plaintiffs, people (mostly men) are attracted to the websites via spam, popup ads, or social networking scams. Potential users see fraudulent signage and fake testimonials, and are offered a free trial membership. Participants then receive pre-written messages that appear to be coming from women who promise romance. Reading the full messages requires a paid membership; subsequent waves of messages entice members to ever higher levels of payment and membership. MxMatch has nearly one million paid members.

The Terms and Conditions for the site disclose that messages containing the nearly imperceptible insignia "OC" are generated electronically by an "online cupid." However, plaintiffs claim that many of the fake profiles do not contain the "OC." Further, the site also employs a handful of individuals who manage hundreds of fictitious profiles—all designed to cultivate and retain paid members.

The nationwide class of plaintiffs claim that the defendant is liable in tort for fraud and negligent misrepresentation. The case was filed in Kansas. As the court ponders certifying the class, questions about choice of law have arisen. Kansas courts generally apply the law of the forum unless compelling reasons exist to apply a different law. Plaintiffs insist that Kansas law can be applied to all plaintiffs. Would that be constitutional?

Quick Summary

- The Due Process Clause prohibits a court from applying a law that would unfairly surprise a litigant

- The Full Faith and Credit Clause prohibits a state from applying forum law (and thereby refusing to apply a sister state's law) unless the forum state has an interest in applying its law

- The application of forum procedural law does not violate the Constitution

15

Dépeçage

Key Concepts

- Choice of law analysis may proceed on an issue-by-issue basis
- Depecage as synergistic success and as synergistic malfunction

---

The scholars who launched the choice of law revolution in the 1950s and 1960s refined the theory and practice of choice of law by focusing on *issues* rather than *claims*.[1] The narrower focus is a tailored and more sophisticated approach to choice of law. But issue-by-issue analysis also creates the possibility of depecage—a French word (*dépeçage*) that means carving up.

Issue-by-issue analysis is especially revelatory when the difference between the laws of the involved states is narrow. Imagine, for example, a simple negligence case that involves the states of New Mexico and West Virginia. The relevant tort law in the two states may be identical except that, say, one state has capped the amount of nonpecuniary damages. The following table depicts the elements of the cause of action in the two jurisdictions.

	New Mexico	West Virginia
Duty of Care	Same	Same
Breach	Same	Same
Causation	Same	Same
Damages	Different	Different

---

1 Issue-by-issue analysis is consistent with interest analysis, center of gravity, better law, and the Second Restatement.

Rather than viewing the choice of law as selecting the "tort law" of one jurisdiction instead of the other, issue-by-issue analysis reveals that only the issue of capping damages actually requires a choice. The narrower focus on the *issue* "is more conducive to a nuanced, individualized, and thus more rational, resolution of conflicts problems."[2]

The price of that more sophisticated, issue-by-issue analysis, however, is depecage. Imagine that the laws of New Mexico and West Virginia differ as to each element of the plaintiff's cause of action:

	New Mexico	**West Virginia**
Duty of Care	Different	Different
Breach	Different	Different
Causation	Different	Different
Damages	Different	Different

An issue-by-issue (i.e., row-by-row) analysis under these circumstances could lead to New Mexico law for some elements of the cause of action and West Virginia law for others. This result is famously characterized as a synthetic hybrid that is half donkey and half camel.

On one hand, an integration of New Mexico's and West Virginia's law could be an enlightened solution that transcends the limitations of a binary choice. The laws of exclusively New Mexico or exclusively West Virginia may not provide the best answer to the choice of law question. But a combination of the two might. Although that synthetic hybrid law exists nowhere in fact, that combination might be eminently fair to the parties and faithful to the respective states' interests. After all, an animal that is half donkey and half camel could be an elegant combination that leverages the strengths of both species.

But a combination of the two states' laws could also be grossly unfair to the parties, an offense to the involved states, and an unwieldy mess for the court. Problems can result because the elements of a cause of action are often interconnected and complementary. For example, whether an act constitutes a breach of duty or the

---

2   Symeon C. Symeonides, *Issue-By-Issue Analysis and Depecage in Choice of Law: Cause and Effect*, 45 U. Tol. L. Rev. 751, 754 (2014).

proximate cause of the injury depends upon the scope of the duty imposed. And the type or amount of recoverable damages may be calibrated to correspond with the difficulty or ease of proving the other elements of the claim. A combination of different states' regimes could frustrate the expectation of the parties and undermine the policies of the involved states.

Issue-by-issue analysis does not always mean combining the elements of more than one jurisdiction's laws into a single cause of action. Issue-by-issue analysis could lead to the application of one state's law for one cause of action and another state's law for a second cause of action. Thus, a plaintiff with both a contract and a tort claim might have her contract claim resolved pursuant to New Mexico law and her tort claim resolved pursuant to West Virginia law. Such a combination *could* be ideal: applying the different laws may elegantly accommodate the respective interests of the two states and fairly reflect the factual connections of each state to the parties and the events. Alternatively, those two causes of action might be interdependent: the boundary between torts and contracts, for example, is a shared boundary. Accordingly, mixing the tort law and contract law of different jurisdictions could create overlaps (over-recovery) or gaps (under-recovery).

Issue-by-issue analysis could mean that in a case where two plaintiffs are suing a single defendant, the claims of one plaintiff may arise under one state's law while the claims of the other plaintiff arise under some other state's law. Alternatively, in a case involving one plaintiff and two defendants, different laws may apply to the claims against each defendant. Issue-by-issue analysis can refer to counterclaims, affirmative defenses, third-party claims, or any other *issue*. When issue-by-issue analysis leads to the application of more than one state's law, this is labeled depecage. Depecage can be worthwhile and appropriate—and sometimes even uncontroversial. Or depecage can be unfair, unjust, or unworkable. Naturally, the latter is generally avoided.

The modern choice of law methodologies encourage or require issue-by-issue analysis. Yet for practical reasons depecage is more of an exception rather than the norm:[3] applying one set of laws to all issues is easier for lawyers and judges.

---

3   Situations where depecage is, in fact, common are seldom referred to as depecage. In every choice of law situation where State *X* applies the substantive law of State *Y*, the court will still apply the *procedural* law of State *X*. (*See* Chapters 2 and 10. *See also* Chapter 19.) Also, even in circumstances that do not involve a multistate factual situation, both federal and state courts routinely apply both state and federal law. That these situations are *not* referred to as depecage is an interesting datum. The creative litigator (the type who carefully reads footnotes!) would think about bringing the insights and arguments of depecage to bear in those areas. And conversely, to the extent that those other areas are not thought of as depecage is an invitation to analogize to those other areas here—arguing, essentially, "This isn't (dangerous) depecage, Your Honor. This is functionally the same thing as applying forum procedural law to foreign substantive law, and we don't worry about *that* as depecage."

A stock argument against depecage is that the pertinent issues are inextricably intertwined, and therefore should not be separated. All laws of a jurisdiction are complementary and their application as a corpus is assumed, even if that assumption is unexpressed or even subconscious. Every law is enacted on a platform that includes all other laws. To separate any law from its platform and allow it to be applied on some other platform introduces a *mismatch* that undermines the integrity of both legal systems.

Another stock argument against depecage invokes the reasonable expectations of the parties. In order for any application of law to be fair, the parties must have notice of that mandate so that they can govern their conduct accordingly. Often, depecage creates a combination of laws that the parties could not reasonably have expected would apply. It is *unfair*, then, to allow it.

Yet another stock argument against depecage is that choosing the applicable law for an issue in isolation increases the likelihood that its purpose and importance will be misconstrued. This could be an argument that depecage is *unworkable*. It could be an argument that depecage *undermines the policies* of the involved states and contravenes legislative intent. Or it could be an argument that depecage does not further the policy of any state.

The argument in favor of depecage is more straightforward: the modern methodologies prescribe it.

Hypothetical 15-1

Dorsett is a domiciliary of Rhode Island who drove his car to a comic-con show in Hartford, Connecticut. The windows on his car were tinted much darker than the State of Connecticut allows. Under Connecticut law, the front windows must allow at least 40% of the light in. Illegal tinting constitutes negligence per se. Rhode Island imposes no restriction on window tinting.

In the parking lot at the show, Dorsett's car struck Staubach when he (Staubach) ran out from between two parked cars. Staubach, coincidentally also a domiciliary of Rhode Island, though a resident of Connecticut, died as a result of his injuries.

Staubach's estate sued Dorsett in Connecticut. Connecticut follows the Second Restatement for its choice of law methodology. Both Rhode Island and Connecticut have similar wrongful death statutes, except that Connecticut restricts damages recoveries to $250,000. You represent the plaintiff. Can you persuade the court to hold Dorsett liable under Connecticut's negligence *per se* rule yet permit unlimited recovery under Rhode Island law?

Hypothetical 15-2

Melanie Hincapie was walking her dog near her home in Pendleton, South Carolina, when a speeding car careened onto the sidewalk and struck her, causing serious injury. The speeding car was driven by nineteen-year-old Kalyn Barber. Barber is a Georgia resident who was visiting friends at Clemson University (in Clemson, South Carolina). Kalyn was driving her friend's car; that car, which was registered in Mississippi, was owned by a friend who is uninsured and judgment-proof.

In an action filed in a South Carolina court, Hincapie sued Barber and Barber's parents. The complaint asserts a negligence claim against Kalyn Barber; that claim is strong on the merits, but Kalyn Barber has very little insurance coverage and no other assets. The complaint asserts a claim against Kalyn Barber's parents for vicarious liability; the plaintiff claims that the parents are liable for the negligent acts of their child.

The parents have moved to dismiss the complaint for failure to state a claim. They have cited a recent case of the Georgia Supreme Court which unequivocally holds that parents are not responsible for the negligent acts of their children.

South Carolina follows the traditional method for choice of law. Under South Carolina common law, parents are liable for "damages from driving accidents caused by the negligent acts of their minor children." Pursuant to a general provision of the South Carolina Code, the age of majority is eighteen years old.

A general provision of the Georgia Laws provides that the age of majority is twenty-one years old.

Should the court grant the parents' motion to dismiss?

FROM THE COURTS

SCHOEBERLE v. U.S.

U.S. District Court for the Northern District of Illinois
2000 WL 1868130 (N.D. Ill. Dec. 18, 2000)

SCHENKIER, MAGISTRATE JUDGE.

These three related cases arise from an air crash that killed a pilot and his two passengers on April 29, 1996. The plaintiffs are: Mary Leiske, personally and representing the estate of her deceased husband, the pilot, Roy Lesike, and Kevin Leiske ("the Leiske plaintiffs"); and Mary C. Schoeberle, individually and representing the estate of her deceased husband, Andrew P. Schoeberle ("the Schoeberle plaintiffs"). . . . All plaintiffs have sued (1) the United States of America ("United States") under the Federal Tort Claims Act ("FTCA"), 28 U.S.C. § 2671 et seq., based on alleged conduct by air traffic controllers employed by the Federal Aviation Administration ("FAA"), and (2) Signature Flight Support Corporation ("Signature Flight") under state common law, based on its alleged conduct as an aircraft maintenance facility. In addition, the Schoeberle plaintiffs have asserted state common law claims against (1) Monarch Aviation Services ("Monarch"), which owned the aircraft, and (2) the Leiske Estate, based on the alleged conduct of the deceased pilot.

Plaintiffs in all three cases have moved for a choice of law determination on liability and damage issues. . .

I

The relevant facts for purposes of this motion are as follows. On April 29, 1996, a Cessna 421 aircraft, en route from Cedar Rapids, Iowa, to Milwaukee, Wisconsin, crashed on a farm near Bernard, Iowa. The airplane was owned and operated by Monarch, a Wisconsin corporation. Roy Leiske was Monarch's principal stockholder and sole employee. The pilot of the airplane, Mr. Leiske, and [two passengers, including] Andrew Schoeberle, died in the accident. [Everyone aboard the plane] lived in Wisconsin.

On the day of the accident, Mr. Leiske had been experiencing problems with the airplane. Mr. Leiske reported fluctuating oil pressure during the last ten minutes of the inbound flight to Cedar Rapids, Iowa. Upon arrival, the plane was losing significant amounts of oil, and oil was covering the left engine and flap. After landing at Cedar Rapids, the plane initially would not start again. Maintenance work was performed on the aircraft at the Cedar Rapids airport by Signature Flight, which has its principal place of business in Florida but which also conducts substantial business in Iowa and Wisconsin. After the maintenance was completed, Signature Flights employees and Mr. Leiske determined that the aircraft was airworthy; the aircraft then departed from Cedar Rapids for the return flight to Milwaukee, Wisconsin.

The aircraft never made it to the planned destination. After take-off from Cedar Rapids, Mr. Leiske continued to have problems. While the aircraft was flying through airspace controlled by the Chicago Air Route Traffic Control Center ("CARTCC"), located in Aurora, Illinois, Mr. Leiske contacted Federal Aviation Administration ("FAA") Air Traffic Controllers. According to the allegations in this case, air traffic control advised Mr. Leiske that although the plane was only 6.5 miles from the Monticello airport in Iowa, Monticello was a non-"IFR" ("Instrument Flying Rules") airport: that is, an airport without instrumentation for pilots to use in making approaches and landings when visibility is obscured due to poor weather conditions. Plaintiffs allege that, in fact, Monticello was an IFR airport. Plaintiffs further allege that because of poor weather, based on this erroneous information Mr. Leiske re-routed the plane to Dubuque Municipal Airport in Iowa, an IFR airport that was approximately 18 miles away. The aircraft then traveled at least 7.5 additional miles—a distance that would have been sufficient to reach Monticello but was short of the Dubuque airport—before crashing on a farm in Jackson County, Iowa, near the town of Bernard.

II

Because the parties' domiciles, events, injuries and places of business in this case touch three different states—Illinois, Iowa, and Wisconsin—there is (not surprisingly) some disagreement concerning which state's law applies to the various liability and damage claims. Despite this disagreement, there is much that the parties agree upon concerning the rules to apply to decide the choice of law questions.

First, the parties agree that Illinois choice of law rules govern. In FTCA cases, the whole law, including the choice-of-law rules, of the state where the alleged negligent act or omission occurred governs the rights and liabilities of the parties. *Richards v. U.S.*, 369 U.S. 1, 6–11 (1962). The parties agree that the alleged governmental negligence by the FAA air traffic controllers occurred solely in Illinois, and that Illinois choice of law rules govern the FTCA claims made against the United States. The parties also agree that a district court sitting in diversity in the Northern District of Illinois is obligated to apply the choice-of-law rules for the State of Illinois. *Klaxon Co. v. Stentor Elec. Mfg. Co.*, 313 U.S. 487, 496 (1996). Thus, the law governing plaintiffs' state law claims likewise must be determined by reference to Illinois choice of law rules.

Second, the parties agree that "[t]he Illinois Supreme Court uses the 'most significant relationship' test for choosing the appropriate law in tort cases." *Frederick v. Simmons Airlines, Inc.*, 144 F.3d 500, 503 (7th Cir. 1998); Restatement (Second) of Conflict of Laws (1971) ("Restatement"). The Restatement (Second) § 145 provides:

> (1) The rights and liabilities of the parties with respect to an issue in tort are determined by the local law of the state which, with respect to that issue, has the most significant relationship to the occurrence and the parties under the principles stated in § 6.
>
> (2) Contacts to be taken into account in applying the principles of § 6 to determine the law applicable to an issue include:
>
> > (a) the place where the injury occurred,
> >
> > (b) the place where the conduct causing the injury occurred,
> >
> > (c) the domicile, residence, nationality, place of incorporation and place of business of the parties, and
> >
> > (d) the place where the relationship, if any, between the parties is centered.

These contacts are to be evaluated according to their relative importance with respect to the particular issue.

The principles set forth in the Restatement (Second) § 6 (Choice-of-Law Principles) are as follows:

> (1) A court, subject to constitutional restrictions, will follow a statutory directive of its own state on choice of law.
>
> (2) When there is no such directive, the factors relevant to the choice of the applicable rule of law include

(a) the needs of the interstate and international systems,

(b) the relevant policies of the forum,

(c) the relevant policies of other interested states and the relative interests of those states in the determination of the particular issue,

(d) the protection of justified expectations,

(e) the basic policies underlying the particular field of law,

(f) certainty, predictability and uniformity of result, and

(g) ease in the determination and application of the law to be applied.

The comments to Section 145 further observe that "courts have long recognized that they are not bound to decide all issues under the local law of a single state," but instead "[e]ach issue is to receive separate consideration if it is one which would be resolved differently under the local law rule of two or more of the potentially interested states." Restatement (Second) § 145, cmt. d. And, indeed, the Seventh Circuit cases applying Illinois choice of law rules endorse this concept of "depecage": that is, "the process of applying rules of different states on the basis of the precise issue involved." *In re Air Crash Disaster Near Chicago, Illinois on May 25, 1979*, 644 F.2d 594, 610–11 (7th Cir. 1981). One court has explained the rationale for using depecage as follows:

> Thus, it is important to understand that the search for the applicable law is not a general one, but rather it is one that takes proper notice of the fact that the significance of a state's relationship to a particular aviation disaster may vary as a function of the particular issue presented. Consequently, under the doctrine of depecage, it is not uncommon for courts to apply the substantive law of several different states in resolving air crash cases.

In re Air Crash Disaster Near Roselawn, Indiana on October 31, 1994, 926 F. Supp. 736, 740 (N.D. Ill. 1996) ("*Roselawn III*") (citing cases). Thus, the Court must examine separately the interests involved as they relate to the separate questions of liability, compensatory damages and punitive damages.

A

In addition to the general choice of law principles set forth in Section 145, the Restatement (Second) speaks to the choice of law decision with respect to specific types of liability issues. Restatement (Second) § 175 covers wrongful death actions, and provides as follows:

> In an action for wrongful death the local law of the state where the injury occurred determines the rights and liabilities of the parties unless, with respect to the particular issue, some other state has a more significant relationship under the principles stated in § 6 to the occurrence and the parties, in which event the local law of the other state will be applied.

Restatement (Second) § 146 covers actions for personal injury, and provides as follows:

> In an action for a personal injury, the local law of the state where the injury occurred determines the rights and liabilities of the parties unless, with respect to the particular issue, some other state has a more significant relationship under the principles stated in § 6 to the occurrence and the parties, in which event the local law of the other state will be applied.

Finally, Restatement (Second) § 164 addresses the question of contributory fault, and provides as follows

(1) The law selected by application of the rule of § 145 determines whether contributory fault on the part of the plaintiff precludes his recovery in whole or in part.

(2) The applicable law will usually be the local law of the state where the injury occurred.

Thus the Restatement (Second) "incorporates a presumption that the local law of the state where the injury occurred should govern, unless another state has a 'more significant relationship' to the occurrence or to the parties," *In re Air Crash Disaster Near Chicago, Illinois on May 25, 1979*, 644 F.2d at 611. And so does Illinois law. *Ingersoll v. Klein*, 46 Ill.2d 42, 48 (1970).

The reason for this presumption in liability cases is that liability is concerned primarily with assigning fault in wrongful death cases, and thus it is fair to presume that the place of injury is usually the place with the most significant relationship to the issues involved. Where the place of injury and misconduct are the same, there are even stronger reasons to choose the law of the place where the injury occurred to determine liability. Restatement (Second) § 175 cmt. e: "In the majority of instances, the actor's conduct, which may consist either of action or nonaction and the resulting injury will occur in the same state. In such instances, the local law of this state will usually be applied to determine most issues involving the tort" (citing Restatement (Second) § 145, cmts. d–e).

B

Different considerations apply when the issue concerns damages rather than liability. The Restatement (Second) § 178 (Damages) states that "[t]he law selected by application of the rule of § 175 determines the measure of damages in an action for wrongful death." Since Section 175 creates a presumption that the law of the place of injury will govern liability, it might appear at first blush that Section 178 applies that presumption to damages as well. However, the Restatement's "Rationale" for Section 178 demonstrates otherwise:

> The choice of law principles stated in § 6 should be applied in determining the state whose local law will be applied to determine the measure of damages in a wrongful death action. In general, this should be the state which has the dominant interest in the determination of this issue. *The state of conduct and injury will not, by reason of these contacts alone, be the state which is primarily concerned with the measure of damages in a wrongful death action.* The local law of this state will, however, be applied unless some other state has a greater interest in the determination of this issue. *In a situation where one state is the domicile of the defendant, the decedent and the beneficiaries, it would seem that, ordinarily at least, the wrongful death statute of this state should be applied to determine the measure of damages.*

In light of these considerations, "[i]n the area of compensatory damages," the case law "supports the application of the law of the injured person's domicile, on the ground that the state has the greatest interest in ensuring that its residents are approximately compensated for their injuries." *See In re Air Crash Disaster Near Roselawn, Indiana on October 31, 1994*, 948 F. Supp. 747, 756 (N.D. Ill. 1996) ("*Roselawn IV*") (citing cases). By contrast, the state where the injury occurred has "relatively little interest in the relief afforded to non-residents." *Id.* at 757.

However, the domiciliary state may not have the greatest interest when punitive damages are the issue. In the area of punitive damages, "many authorities suggest that the place of the misconduct and the defendants' domiciles have the greatest interest in balancing the deterrence of wrongdoing with the costs of imposing high damages upon resident business defendants." *Roselawn IV*, 948 F. Supp. at 756 (citing cases). The Restatement (Second) speaks generally to this balancing question:

> the interest of a state in having its tort rule applied in the determination of a particular issue will depend upon the purpose sought to be achieved by that rule and by the relation of the state to the occurrence and the parties. *If the primary purpose of the tort rule involved is to deter or punish misconduct, . . . the state where the conduct took place may be the state of dominant interest and thus that of most significant relationship* (see § 154, cmt. c). . . .

Restatement (Second) § 145 cmt. c (Purpose of tort rule) (emphasis added).

III

With these legal principles in mind, we turn to the choice of law issues raised by the parties. All relevant parties agree that the law of Iowa controls the liability issues raised by the plaintiffs against Signature Flight, thus rendering unnecessary any choice of law determination on that liability issue.[6] However, disagreements do exist concerning: (1) the law governing the alleged liability of defendants Monarch and the Leiske Estate in the case brought by the Schoeberle plaintiffs; (2) the law governing the alleged liability of the United States under the FTCA in the cases brought by the Leiske plaintiffs;[7] and (3) the law governing the plaintiffs' compensatory and punitive damages claims. We address the liability issues first, proceeding then to a discussion of the choice of law regarding compensatory and punitive damages.

---

6   Indeed, a straightforward application of the Restatement would not support another result. Signature Flight employees allegedly committed negligent acts only in Iowa; the accident occurred in Iowa; and Signature Flight alleges that Mr. Leiske committed substantial acts of negligence and other fault in Iowa.

7   We also note that as of the time the choice of law motions were filed, the United States has settled the claims brought by the . . . Schoeberle plaintiffs, so the only claim pending against the United States is that brought by the Leiske plaintiffs.

A

1. The Schoeberle Plaintiffs' Liability Claims
Against Monarch and the Leiske Estate

With respect to Monarch and the Leiske Estate, the Schoeberle plaintiffs argue that the law of Iowa should be applied to determine questions of liability. The Schoeberle plaintiffs argue that Iowa law should apply because (1) the accident giving rise to the plaintiffs' claims occurred in Iowa; (2) the decedents were in Iowa on business and departed on a flight from that state, making it foreseeable that Iowa law would govern any injury to them there; (3) the relationship of the parties is centered in Iowa because Mr. Leiske's alleged negligence in maintaining and flying the plane occurred there, not Wisconsin, and the parties were injured and died in Iowa; and (4) Iowa has an interest in preventing airplane crashes from occurring within its borders.

Under the Restatement and Illinois law, the place where the injury occurred presumptively applies, *e.g. In re Air Crash Disaster Near Chicago*, 644 F.2d at 611—and that is Iowa. Indeed, that presumption is particularly strong here, because the injury and the alleged misconduct by Monarch and the Leiske Estate occurred principally in Iowa. *See* Restatement (Second) § 175, cmt. e. Other than their bare allegation that Wisconsin law should apply, Monarch and the Leiske Estate do not make any arguments to counteract the presumptive applicability of Iowa law. Because we find no considerations under the Restatement (Second) or Illinois law that suggest Wisconsin has an interest superior to that of Iowa in the liability question as between these parties, the Court agrees that Iowa law should control the issues of liability against Monarch and the Leiske Estate.

2. The Leiske Plaintiffs' Liability Claim
Against the United States

. . . [A]lthough both Iowa and Illinois law provide for limited joint and several liability, those laws contain different substantive provisions. . . . In Iowa, a defendant who bears fifty percent or more of the total fault is jointly and severally liable for economic damages only. By contrast, in Illinois a defendant who is found to bear more than twenty-five percent of the total fault is jointly and severally liable not only for medical expenses (which all defendants held liable must pay regardless of the percentage of their fault), but for all other damages as well. . . .

The plaintiffs argue that Illinois law should apply to its claims against the United States because "the focus of the plaintiffs' claims is on the actions or inactions of the air traffic controllers located in Illinois." Because the place of the FAA's alleged negligence is Illinois, the plaintiffs further argue that the parties' relationship is centered in Illinois. Indeed, plaintiffs claim that "[t]he subject aircraft flown by pilot Leiske was flying through airspace controlled by the [CARTCC] in Illinois" while the FAA traffic controllers were providing assistance to the plane. Consequently, argue plaintiffs, Illinois has a strong interest in deterring tortious conduct within its borders, while Iowa has "little or no interest in deterring such out-of-state conduct."

The United States disagrees, arguing that "a conflicts analysis under the Restatement (Second) would lead to the application of Iowa's liability law, rather than the law of Illinois." . . . The United States asserts that there is no more significant contact than the place of injury (or accident), and the acts of negligence committed by Mr. Leiske that led up to or arguably caused the plane to malfunction and crash. . . .

The Court rejects the United States position for several reasons. First, the Court finds that, although there is an apparent dispute about whether the aircraft was located in Illinois or Iowa airspace when it radioed air traffic control for guidance, there is no dispute that it was CARTCC in Aurora, Illinois that answered the call, and that it was the FAA traffic controllers in Illinois who gave the allegedly erroneous answer that the Monticello airport was a non-IFR landing site. . . .

Second, it is not merely "fortuitous" that the aircraft was communicating with air traffic control in Illinois. The plan for the flight from Des Moines to Milwaukee plainly took the aircraft through airspace controlled by the Illinois air traffic controllers. . . .

Third, the place of injury in this case cannot be determined simply by locating the site where the aircraft ultimately crashed and the occupants died. The Restatement (Second) § 175, cmt. b. defines the place of injury as "the place where the force set in motion by the actor first takes effect on the person. This place is not necessarily that where the death occurs." In this case, several forces allegedly contributed to the tragic accident, and they did not all occur at one time, or in one state. . .

Fourth, we find that Iowa's relationship to the crash itself is outweighed by Illinois' interest on this specific question. With respect to liability, the principle [sic] interest of the state where the accident occurs is in "ensuring that persons who cause injury do not escape liability." *Roselawn IV*, 948 F. Supp. at 758. In this case, that interest is served by application of either Iowa or Illinois law. . . .

Accordingly, given that both the alleged negligent misconduct and the alleged fault attributable to the United States occurred in Illinois, the Court finds that Illinois law, not Iowa law, controls the liability aspects of the Leiske plaintiffs' claims against the United States under the FTCA.

B

A true conflict also exists with respect to both the compensatory and punitive damage claims in this case, which requires the Court to determine the law that will apply to those claims. We address the compensatory damages issues first.

1. Compensatory Damages

Under Iowa law, there is no limit on the amount of compensatory damages recoverable for loss of society and companionship, but in Wisconsin there is a limit—which recently has become more stringent.

When the accident in this case occurred on April 29, 1996, Wisconsin law provided for a cap of $150,000 for non-economic damages in adult wrongful death actions. Wis. Stat. § 895.04(4) (1995–96). . . .

Not surprisingly, the plaintiffs seek application of Iowa law (which would not limit their potential damages for loss of society), while defendants urge the application of Wisconsin law (which would place a ceiling of $150,000 on that element of the plaintiff's potential recovery in each case). In particular, plaintiffs allege that Iowa law controls because the accident and the injury took place in Iowa, and the alleged negligence giving rise to the accident and injury took place in Iowa. Plaintiffs argue that under the Restatement, it is presumed that the law of the place of injury applies to the question of damages where the place of injury is not fortuitous. The plaintiffs argue that Iowa was not a fortuitous location for the accident and the injury because it was the state where the flight originated, and it was the state where all three decedents regularly traveled for business. Plaintiffs claim that in cases where these factors are present, courts have rejected the fortuity rational and applied the presumption. [citations omitted]

The defendants counter that although there is a "presumption" under the Restatement (Second) to apply the law of the state where the injury occurred, this presumption virtually disappears when the issue to be determined involves damages in a wrongful death case. [citations omitted] Moreover, the defendants argue that the presumption should not apply in this case because the place of injury, Iowa, was fortuitous given that the plane was scheduled to travel through three states during the intended flight (*i.e.*, it originated in Iowa on takeoff; flew through airspace controlled by an FAA facility in Illinois; and was to land in Milwaukee, Wisconsin) before Mr. Leiske attempted to re-route the plane to the Dubuque, Iowa airport. The defendants claim that Wisconsin law should be used to determine the compensatory damage issue because Wisconsin is the domiciliary state of each of the decedent and his survivors, and Monarch is (or was) a Wisconsin corporation. The defendants argue that the holding in *Roselawn IV* supports their position that the domiciliary state's law should be applied in cases such as this because the place of injury is fortuitous. *See Roselawn IV*, 948 F. Supp. at 756 (law of decedents' domicile chosen over place of injury on grounds that domiciliary states had "greatest interest in ensuring that its residents [were] appropriately compensated for their injuries" because place of injury was fortuitous).

The Court finds that Wisconsin rather than Iowa law applies to the compensatory damage claims. In making this determination the Court recognizes that it cannot simply add up the factors delineated in Section 145(2) and then apply the law of the sovereign with the greatest numerical total. Instead, the Court must make a qualitative analysis of the strength of each state's interest in having its law govern compensatory damages in this case, an analysis guided by the factors delineated in Section 6 to determine which sovereign has the most significant contact. While the importance of the seven factors listed in Section 6 varies depending on the nature of the issue that underlies the conflict of laws, the factors most important in wrongful death cases are the relevant policies of the forum where the case was filed and the other interested states. In this case, those policy interests lead to the choice of Wisconsin law for several reasons.

First, although the Restatement (Second) provides that the place of injury usually determines the rights and liabilities of the parties, any preference for applying the law of the state in which the injury occurred "all but disappears when the conflict of laws involves the issue of damages in wrongful death actions." *Cortes v. American Airlines, Inc.*, 177 F.3d 1272, 1297 (11th Cir. 1999), *cert. denied*, 120 S. Ct. 980 (2000). . . .

Second, we believe that Wisconsin has a stronger interest than Iowa in applying its law of compensatory damages in this case. A state's law regarding compensatory damages reflects a balance of the desire to fairly compensate its citizens for injuries they suffer, and the goal of creating a climate conducive to business by protecting "resident defendants from excessive claims." *Roselawn IV,* 948 F. Supp. at 757. . . . In this case, Wisconsin has an interest superior to that of Iowa on the question of ensuring appropriate compensation, as all decedents and their survivors are Wisconsin residents. Indeed, the case can be made that the place of injury has relatively little interest in the relief afforded non-residents. In any event it is hard to see how any interest that Iowa possesses in fair compensation to Wisconsin residents injured within Iowa borders is undermined by applying Wisconsin law, which reflects Wisconsin's judgment as to what maximum level of compensation for loss of society is fair for Wisconsin residents.

Moreover, two of the defendants—the Leiske Estate and Monarch—are Wisconsin residents; the remaining two defendants—Signature and the United States, through the FAA—also have a presence in Wisconsin. The presence (although not residence) of all defendants in Wisconsin, along with the decedents and their survivors, also augers in favor of applying Wisconsin law. *Cf.* Restatement (Second) § 178 (Damages), Rationale ("[i]n a situation where one state is the state of the domicile of the defendant, the decedent and the beneficiaries, it would seem that, ordinarily at least, the wrongful death statute of this state should be applied to determine the measure of damages").

Since none of the four defendants is an Iowa resident, Iowa has no greater interest than Wisconsin in seeing to it that the level of compensation available to injured parties does not deter people from doing business in the state. Indeed, Iowa's interest on this score is weaker than Wisconsin's interest, as two of the defendants are Wisconsin residents. And Iowa's interest in protecting businesses from "excessive claims" certainly is not compensated by applying Wisconsin law, which provides a ceiling on recoverable damages for loss of society.

Third, it was not entirely fortuitous that the injury occurred in Iowa, since the flight departed from Iowa. But the place of the accident was fortuitous in the sense that the accident could have occurred in any of three states that the aircraft planned to cross on the trip from Des Moines to Milwaukee. The fortuity of the place of the accident is underscored by the fact that the accident occurred as the aircraft was headed for the Dubuque airport, which was not the planned destination. In these circumstances, the rationale of the *Roselawn* case is persuasive. The law of the state of injury should give way where the place of the accident was somewhat fortuitous, and the domiciliary state is the state of all the decedents and their survivors. . . .

Fourth, application of the law of the decedents' domicile for compensatory damages purposes serves the policies articulated in Restatement (Second) § 6 in other respects. Applying Wisconsin law promotes the needs of the interstate commerce system, because it minimizes forum shopping (for a state that gives larger compensatory damage awards), and it promotes certainty.

In sum, we find the application of the law of the decedents' domicile on the issue of compensatory damages, which is concerned with compensation rather than conduct, best supports the policies underlying the Restatement (Second's) approach. We thus hold that Wisconsin law applies to the issue of compensatory damages recoverable in these cases.

2. Punitive Damages

There is only one set of plaintiffs making a claim for punitive damages: the Schoeberle plaintiffs seek punitive damages from Signature Flight, Monarch and the Leiske Estate under Iowa law. Those defendants argue that any liability for punitive damages should be governed instead by Wisconsin law. There is a true conflict regarding this issue because in Wisconsin, punitive damages are recoverable in a survival action for the period of time that the decedent experienced pain and suffering prior to death, but are not recoverable in a wrongful death action. In Iowa, punitive damages are recoverable against a corporation for the acts of a negligent employee in both survival and wrongful death actions. Thus, in this wrongful death action, the Schoeberle plaintiffs may seek punitive damages only if Iowa law applies.

As with all other conflicts, the Court must apply the law of the state with the most significant interest. Both sides recognize that choice of law determinations with respect to punitive damages are governed by the purpose of such damages. Both sides also recognize that two of the primary purposes underlying the allowance of punitive damages are punishment of the defendant and deterrence of future wrongdoing. The purpose of disallowing such damages is protection of defendants from excess financial liability.

When a balance between punishment and deterrence on the one hand, and protection from excessive liability on the other, must be struck, it is fitting that the state whose interests are most deeply affected should have its local law apply. In this case, the Court finds that the state with the most significant interest on this question is Iowa. Iowa was not only the place of injury, but it was also the place of most of the alleged misconduct by these defendants. Iowa has an obvious interest in having its law govern whether to punish those responsible for any such misconduct. Iowa also has an obvious interest in deterring such misconduct and occurrences in the future, since it was Iowa, not Wisconsin, which was called upon to respond to the crash and to deal with its tragic aftermath.

These interests, in the Court's view, weigh more heavily in the balance than Wisconsin's interests in the parties and the flight. The fact that the decedents resided in Wisconsin is entitled to little weight, as the goal of punitive damages is not to compensate victims but to punish and deter misconduct. . . . Signature Flight and Mr. Leiske engaged in some conduct in Wisconsin, [but] the most serious alleged misconduct by these defendants occurred in Iowa. And, while Monarch and Signature did business in Wisconsin, they also did business in Iowa.

On these facts, Wisconsin's interest in protecting its resident corporate defendant (Monarch) from excessive liability is outweighed by Iowa's interest in applying its punitive damage law to conduct within its borders. The application of Iowa law is consistent with the Restatement (Second) § 145 cmt. c., which indicates that where deterrence or punishment of misconduct is the purpose to be served, "the state where the conduct took place may be the state" with the "dominant interest" and the "most significant relationship."

Conclusion

For the reasons discussed in this opinion, . . . the Court holds that:

1. Illinois law of liability applies to the Leiske plaintiffs' liability claim against United States;

2. Iowa law of liability applies to plaintiffs' claims against Signature Flight, Monarch, and the Leiske Estate;

3. Wisconsin law applies to plaintiffs' compensatory damages claims against the United States, Signature Flight, Monarch and the Leiske Estate; and

4. Iowa law applies to the Schoeberle plaintiffs' punitive damages claims against Signature Flight, Monarch and the Leiske Estate.

COMMENTS AND QUESTIONS

1. The court relies on the purpose of a legal rule to reveal the most relevant contact. Complete the missing cells in the table:

Legal Rule	Purpose	Most Relevant Contact
Compensatory Damages	To compensate plaintiff	Plaintiff's domicile
Punitive Damages	To deter wrongful conduct	Place of wrongful conduct
Liability		

2. The court prescribes different liability rules for the non-governmental defendants, on one hand, and the United States government, on the other. Defend this exercise of depecage by (i) acknowledging the risk that attends the combination of liability rules in a single case, and (ii) explaining why this exercise of depecage does not implicate that danger.

3. The court prescribes different damages rules for compensatory damages and punitive damages. Defend this exercise of depecage by (i) acknowledging the risk that attends the combination of damages rules, and (ii) explaining why this exercise of depecage does not implicate that danger.

4. When the contact of a state to an occurrence is *fortuitous*, the relevance of that state's law is heavily discounted. In this case, the court says that the place of the accident was "somewhat fortuitous"; yet it was "not merely 'fortuitous' that the aircraft was communicating with air traffic control in Illinois." We observed in earlier chapters that the word *fortuitous* has special traction in debates about choice of law. What does it mean here?

5. In footnote 7 the court acknowledges that some of the claims were settled while others remained. Appreciate the connection, generally, between joinder of claims/parties and choice of law. This is a matter of litigation strategy. More causes of action or more parties increases the likelihood of depecage. But resistance to depecage also means that the inclusion of peripheral claims or parties might push the court toward application of the law of state *x* rather than the law of state *y*. Plaintiffs' lawyers get the chance to wield strategy in framing the complaint. Defendants' lawyers get the chance to wield strategy by, *inter alia*, settling certain claims— perhaps before the choice of law decision is made.

6. In this case depecage leads to a combination of laws that is something of a compromise between legal rules that favor the plaintiffs and legal rules that favor the defendants. To the extent that depecage is a vehicle for "splitting the baby," is that an achievement or a failure?

7. What law would the court have applied if depecage were not an option? Put another way, depecage benefitted which party(ies)?

ERIE INS. EXCH. v. HEFFERNAN

Court of Appeals of Maryland
399 Md. 598 (Ct. App. 2007)

GREENE, JUDGE.

Facts

. . . On April 18, 2003 at about 6:30 a.m. Mallory Heffernan, a minor, was fatally injured in an automobile accident that occurred on Route 301 in the State of Delaware. Ms. Heffernan (hereinafter "Decedent") was transported from the scene and taken to a Delaware hospital where she subsequently died. The Decedent and another minor, Curtis Jones, had been passengers in a vehicle driven by John McMahon, Jr., also a minor, and owned by his mother, Angela McMahon. The accident occurred when John McMahon, Jr. apparently fell asleep at the wheel and collided with a tractor-trailer. At the time of the accident, the Decedent resided with her parents, Edmund and Diane Heffernan, in Queenstown, Maryland. The driver, John McMahon, Jr. and the other passenger, Curtis Jones, were step-brothers who resided with Mr. McMahon's father and Mr. Jones's mother in Ingleside, Maryland.

The group of teenagers, all Maryland residents, had driven from Maryland to Pennsylvania after school on April 17, 2003 in order to attend a concert in Allentown, Pennsylvania that night. After the concert, they began to make their way back to Maryland. The group first drove a friend home to Kutztown, Pennsylvania. After doing so, they became lost and called the Heffernans to help them get directions back to the highway. The group then drove another friend home to Swedesboro, New Jersey. The occupants of the McMahon vehicle were on their way back to Maryland, driving through Delaware, when the accident occurred at approximately 6:30 a.m. As planned prior to the trip, John McMahon, Jr. was the only individual in the group who drove the car throughout the entire trip to or from the concert.

At trial, Erie Insurance Exchange ("Erie") believes that it will introduce evidence that the Decedent called her parents at home in Maryland at least twice between midnight and 4:40 a.m., during their drive back to Maryland. Further, Erie's evidence would show that, during these calls, the Decedent informed her parents that they were too tired to continue and requested her parents' permission to stop traveling for the night and sleep at the home of friends in either Kutztown, Pennsylvania, or, later, in Swedesboro, New Jersey. Erie believes that it will present evidence showing that her parents refused these requests and demanded that the group continue the drive home.

At trial, the Heffernans believe that they will introduce evidence that there were telephone contacts between them and Mallory. Further, the Heffernans believe that they would present evidence that at no point during the entire evening were any requests made to them for permission to stop nor at any point were the Heffernans advised that the driver or any of the other persons in the vehicle being driven by John McMahon were suffering from fatigue.

At the time of the accident, the Decedent's parents, Edmund and Diane Heffernan, carried a Pioneer Family Auto Policy (#Q01 080493 M) and a Personal Catastrophe Policy (#Q31 2350156 M) with Erie. These are Maryland policies, designed to comply with Maryland mandatory insurance requirements, which were issued, sold and delivered in Maryland to Maryland residents, Edmund and Diane Heffernan. Their auto policy included underinsured motorists coverage in the amount of $300,000 per person/$300,000 per accident; the catastrophe policy provided $1,000,000 in underinsured motorists coverage. It is agreed that the vehicle driven by Mr. McMahon was an underinsured motor vehicle with respect to the Erie policy.

The Heffernans and Erie were unable to come to an agreement on issues of liability and the amount of benefits to be paid, and the Heffernans filed suit . . . seeking damages pursuant to the underinsured motorists coverage. . . . The underinsured motorists coverage in the Erie policies provided, in part, that Erie would pay damages (up to the applicable limits) "that the law entitles you" to recover from the owner or operator of an underinsured motor vehicle. The Heffernans have asserted that Maryland's non-economic damages cap, Md. Code Ann., Cts. & Jud. Proc. § 11–108, does not limit the damages available to them. Erie contends that § 11–108 applies to limit the damages available. [The Maryland statute would cap the plaintiff's recovery for noneconomic damages at approximately $620,000.] In addition, the Heffernans assert that Delaware's tort law, including the comparative negligence doctrine should be applied to determine whether, and to what extent, they are entitled to recover from the uninsured motorist. Erie contends that Maryland law, including the doctrines of contributory negligence and assumption of risk, should be applied. [Application of these doctrines could prove fatal to the Heffernans' claim.]

Discussion

What is ultimately at issue in this case is whether, in determining what the law, and therefore the policies, entitle the insureds to recover, [Maryland or Delaware law applies.] Erie contends that to determine an insurer's liability (what the Heffernans are "entitled to recover") amounts to an interpretation of the contract and that it was contemplated by both parties that the policies would be interpreted by referencing Maryland law only, despite the fact that the automobile collision occurred in Delaware. The issue, Erie asserts, is properly decided under Maryland contract law. In Erie's view, the interpretation of "entitled to recover" requires reference to "general principles of tort law" only and is not a mixed question of contract and tort law. Erie argues that because only the law of Maryland is implicated, it is not a choice of law issue. . . .

Conversely, the Heffernans contend that "contract and tort law converge in uninsured motorist coverage" and, as a result, contract principles should apply to certain portions of an action for uninsured motorist benefits and tort principles to other aspects. In the Heffernans' view, our interpretation of the phrase, "that the law entitles you," as it appears in the insurance policies (or "entitled to recover" as used in Md. Code (1997, 2006 Rep. 1. Vol), § 19–509(c) of the Insurance Article) is a question of mixed law, contract and tort. The Heffernans take the position that because tort law varies from state to state, specifically the tort law of Delaware, the *situs* of the collision, is different from that of Maryland, the place where the contract was performed; hence, a conflict of law exists. The Heffernans urge that this Court would apply the principle of *lex loci delicti* to resolve the conflict of laws, and, in doing so, apply the substantive tort law of Delaware to determine what they are "entitled to recover.". . .

[The court concluded that, in this case, contract and tort law converged, and that the forum was obliged to apply contract principles to the certain portions of the underinsured motorist claim and tort principles to other aspects. It thus undertook to make two choice of law analysis: one for contracts issues and one for torts. Because Maryland is a *lex loci* state, this was fairly straightforward: the contract would be governed by Maryland law (because Maryland was the place of contracting), and the torts issues would be governed by Delaware law (because Delaware was the place of injury).]

Our decision in this case embraces the concept of "depecage." Discussing depecage the Supreme Court of Virginia noted that "it has always been understood . . . that different substantive issues could be properly decided under the laws of different states, when the choice-influencing considerations differ as they apply to different issues." *Buchanan v. Doe*, 246 Va. 67 (1993). Erie warns against this Court's adoption of depecage. According to Erie, the depecage framework is inappropriate in this case because it would act to "legitimize a smorgasbord approach which inures only to the benefit" of the Heffernans. To the contrary, our holding today presents a clear framework for resolving choice of law issues such as the one presented in the instant case. This determination will allow insurers and insureds to predict with reasonable certainty the law that will apply in a breach of contract action against the insurer on the basis of an uninsured/underinsured motorist claim. Specifically, all parties to a contract which provides uninsured/underinsured motorist benefits can anticipate that, absent a contractual choice of law provision, any dispute as to the validity of the policy or the meaning of its terms will be resolved based on the law of where the contract was made, but that the substantive tort law of the place where the automobile collision occurred will control what the claimants are "entitled to recover." . . .

COMMENTS AND QUESTIONS

1. The court's decision provides *ex post* certainty to the insurer, the insured, *and the court*. What about *ex ante* predictability for an insurer that needs to price a policy? What about *ex ante* predictability for an insured that needs to know how much actual coverage they have purchased?

2. The court's decision promises *ex post* certainty and predictability. But would it have applied Delaware law in this case if Delaware law capped the recovery of noneconomic damages at, say, $100,000 (or might it invoke the public policy exception and refuse to enforce such a law)?

3. Why wouldn't Erie include choice of law clauses in their policies?

4. Why is the court working so hard to *escape* the application of forum law? The court would not have had to work so hard if it were not committed to the traditional approach to choice of law. Erie used this case to argue that the court should abandon the lex loci approach and adopt the Second Restatement as its choice of law methodology. In a portion of the opinion not reprinted here, the court responded: "We disagree. The rule of lex loci delicti is well established in Maryland. When its rationale has been put into question, this Court has consistently followed the rule. . . . A virtue of the rule, for the courts and all parties concerned, is the predictability and certainty as to which state's tort law will govern."

FROM THE COURTS

CERTAIN UNDERWRITERS AT LLOYDS, LONDON v. CHEMTURA CORP.

Supreme Court of Delaware
160 A.3d 457 (2017)

STRINE, CHIEF JUSTICE.

This is an insurance coverage dispute between a chemical company and a group of insurers over whether the insurers must compensate the company for expenses and fines associated with environmental claims against the company in Ohio and Arkansas. The policies in question were part of a comprehensive insurance program that covered the chemical company's operations around the world. . . .

I

A. Uniroyal's Operations

A chemical company—doing business from at least the early 1940s as the United States Rubber Company, then as variants on the Uniroyal name until it was purchased by Chemtura Corporation in 2005—purchased a complex set of insurance policies from Lloyd's Underwriters [and various other insurers]. . . which covered personal injury liability and property damage liability for its global operations beginning in the early 1950s. . . .

At the outset of this insurance program, United States Rubber Company was the named insured and New York was its principal place of business.

After United States Rubber Company changed its name to Uniroyal, [its corporate headquarters were in New York or Connecticut.]

B. Environmental Liability

Over time, the environment around many facilities producing and using Uniroyal's chemicals was damaged. . . . After a settlement covering thirty-three sites in fifteen states and two Canadian provinces, Chemtura is seeking coverage [in the instant suit] for losses related to a site in Arkansas and a site in Ohio, specifically a judgment that Lloyd's "breached their contracts by refusing to cover past and future defense costs and damages." . . .

C. The Superior Court Litigation

Although extensive litigation from 1984 to 2005 resolved many of the environmental claims for which Chemtura sought compensation from Lloyd's, claims related to the Arkansas and Ohio sites remained. . . . Their dispute hinges on which, if any, of the relevant insurance contracts provide coverage for these costs, and, specifically, on what approach to allocation applies. If the all sums approach applies,[28] each insurer is liable for the entire risk, within policy limits. If the pro-rata approach applies, each insurer is liable only for its proportionate share of the risk.[30]

[Delaware follows the Second Restatement as its choice of law methodology. The policies did not include choice of law clauses, so the Superior Court, using the "most significant relationship" framework, concluded that the "site-of-the-risk" should determine which state's law applies. In other words, the underlying contract law of the states where the claims arose would govern on a claim-by-claim basis. The Superior Court concluded that the claims arose in Arkansas and Ohio, respectively, and that New York did not have any current contacts.]

II.

The Second Restatement Framework

This Court reviews questions of law . . . de novo. . . . Here, the Superior Court correctly observed that the insurance policies did not specify a par-

---

28   Lloyd's and Chemtura do not dispute that this is the approach used by Ohio law. The Superior Court found that Arkansas also uses the all sums approach, which Chemtura disputes, but that is an issue that we do not reach.

30   . . . The parties do not dispute that New York uses the pro-rata approach.

ticular state law. . . . Thus, the [relevant question is] which state has the most significant relationship to the contract and parties to the contract. . . .

The Superior Court placed great weight on § 193 to find that the law of Ohio would apply to the Ohio site and the law of Arkansas would apply to the Arkansas site. [Section 193 provides: "The validity of a contract of fire, surety or casualty insurance and the rights created thereby are determined by the local law of the state which the parties understood was to be the principal location of the insured risk during the term of the policy, unless with respect to the particular issue, some other state has a more significant relationship under the principles stated in § 6 to the transaction and the parties, in which event the local law of the other state will be applied."]

Significantly, § 193's language uses the past tense but is prospective. The state with the most significant relationship is "the state which the parties *understood was to be* the principal location of the insured risk." In other words, the presumptive most significant relationship is based on the parties' expectations at an earlier point in time. Section 193 also does not read "were to be the principal locations," plural, but instead focuses on identifying a single state to supply the contract law to govern the interpretation of the contract's terms.

The most sensible earlier point to assess the parties' expectations in the contract context is at the beginning of their relationship. . . . [Thus] § 193's language would identify New York as the singular principal location of the insured risk and thus support a decision that New York's law applies. . . .

Because § 193's presumption is, at best, directionally helpful but arguably not conclusive, our analysis returns to § 188's factors. . . .

[The Court then surveyed the Section 188 factors, but with an eye toward identifying one state as having the most significant relationship.]

Applying one law to interpret these contracts, based on the contacts among the parties at the outset of the insurance program, advances several important policy goals this Court recognizes in both contracts and choice of law. The *Second Restatement* emphasizes the importance of "the protection of justified expectations" and "certainty, predictability and uniformity of result,"[82] both of which can be best achieved by applying a single state's law.

---

82   Restatement (Second) of Conflict of Laws § 188 cmt. b.

The alternative would result in a court being forced to inconsistently apply the same contract language based on the happenstance of remaining sites with liability and the meaning of certain terms varying only on that happenstance. Indeed, under the approach Chemtura urges, insurers would be subject to a choice-of-law roadtrip any time an insured changed the location of its headquarters or opened a facility in a different state. That would be "a bizarre result whereby later activities . . . could change the parties' bargain with no evidence of any intent to do so."[83] Such a roadtrip wouldn't just involve environmental claims, but because of the breadth of the policies making up this program, would involve all the variation of different states' tort and insurance law.

Insurance programs like this one are intended to work together to provide overall protection to the insured. That result would be frustrated if identical policy language, granting identical coverage, was interpreted in different ways based on the happenstance of the geographic location of a particular incident of environmental damage. Indeed, if a court were to "conduct a different choice of laws analysis for each policy, then there would be a risk of a court inconsistently applying identical policy language within a single integrated insurance scheme."[84] Accepting Chemtura's preferred approach would result in difficult-to-predict results that would be inconsistent for no reason relevant to the expectations of the parties. Thus, this Court finds that New York has the most significant relationship with the parties and subject matter of the dispute and so New York law applies. The Superior Court's decision of April 27, 2016 is therefore reversed and this case is remanded for further proceedings. . . .

---

83   Viking Pump, Inc. v. Century Indem. Co., 2 A.3d 76, 90 (Del Ch. 2009).

84   Id. at 88–89.

COMMENTS AND QUESTIONS

1. If the parties wanted the uniformity and certainty of having one state's law apply to the "insurance program," they could have included a choice of law clause. Why is the Court giving the insurer the benefit of this clause retroactively? What does this say about *contra proferentem*, the canon of contractual interpretation that construes unclear provisions against the drafter?

2. The Second Restatement repeatedly emphasizes that choice of law is *issue*-specific—not *claim*-specific nor *contract*-specific nor *transaction*-specific nor *party*-specific. Does this opinion show fidelity to that approach? Only twice in the court's lengthy opinion, and both times only in footnotes, does the court even use the word *issue* in the sense that it is used in the Second Restatement.

3. The court never uses the word *depecage*. Why not? What does the court mean when it uses the word *roadtrip*?

4. Does the rebuttable presumption of Section 193 presume that there will be one law applied to an insurance program?

5. The Delaware Court of Chancery that decided *Viking Pump* is a court that is structurally inferior to the Delaware Supreme Court. The decisions of lower courts can be persuasive.

SAMPLE EXAM QUESTIONS

Question 15-3

Piper and Douglas were a married couple in the process of separating, but not yet divorced when the husband, Douglas, caused an automobile accident that seriously injured his wife. The couple were domiciliaries of New Jersey (residents of Newark, NJ) and the accident occurred in New York City.

The state of New Jersey has retained the ancient common law rule that precludes a married person from suing their spouse for ordinary negligence.

Two years ago, the state of New York passed a statute finally abandoning the discredited common law rule of spousal immunity. When the New York legislature passed that bill, insurance companies successfully lobbied the legislature for a companion measure to address their additional liability for suits against their insureds filed by their spouses. The amendment to the insurance law provided that no insurance policy shall be deemed to insure against liability to a spouse unless an express provision to that effect is included in the policy.

Douglas is insured by Chambers Insurance Co., a New Jersey insurance company that issued the policy in New Jersey. The insurance policy does not mention liability to a spouse. The couple has no significant assets.

New York follows the center of gravity approach to determine the applicable law. New Jersey follows the Second Restatement. You represent Piper. Where should you file the case against Douglas? (Anticipate the depecage argument. When do we expect that issue to arise? How do we want it to be resolved?)

Question 15-4

A small bus carrying members of the University of Toronto Glee Club crashed into a tractor-trailer parked on the side of the highway near Detroit, Michigan. Three bus passengers were killed and several others were seriously injured; all were Canadian citizens and domiciliaries. The driver of the bus and his employer (Cooling Transport, Inc.) are citizens and domiciliaries of Toronto (Ontario, Canada). The driver of the tractor-trailer and his employer (D4 Trucking, Inc.) are citizens of Michigan.

The bus driver was operating at a very unsafe speed, and the driver of the tractor trailer was negligently parked on the side of the highway. In an action filed in Michigan by the families of the three bus passengers killed in the accident, a jury has found for the plaintiffs, assigning 90% of the fault for the accident to Cooling Transport, Inc., and 10% of the fault to D4 Trucking, Inc. The family of each of plaintiff was awarded $5,000,000 for a total jury award of $15,000,000.

In post-trial motions, a dispute has arisen about the applicable law. Michigan follows the Second Restatement. The wrongful death laws of Ontario and Michigan are substantially similar except that Ontario has an absolute cap of (US) $500,000 of damages per plaintiff in wrongful death cases. Michigan law has no cap. In anticipation of the trial, the defendants raised the damages cap, but the judge postponed consideration of the issue, promising to deal with it "if and when it mattered."

You are a clerk to the judge. How much does each of Cooling Transport, Inc. and D4 Trucking, Inc. owe each of the plaintiff's families?

Quick Summary

- Depecage is inherently neither constructive nor destructive; each application must be evaluated on its own merits

- The application of forum procedural law and foreign substantive law is a species of depecage

16

Statutes and Choice of Law

Key Concepts

- Localizing statutes
- Borrowing statutes

In this Chapter we emphasize the significance of forum statutes in the context of choice of law determinations.

Statutes can play a role in choice of law determinations because the choice of law methodology in a state may be codified, rather than developed through decisional law. In the United States, both Oregon and Louisiana have codified their general choice of law rules. Likewise, in the European Union, regulations codify choice of law. States that have formally adopted the First or Second Restatement of Conflicts have not literally codified their choice of law methodology, but they have embraced an approach that resembles a statutory framework. The fact of codification does not necessarily make an approach more or less complex, nor any more or less rigid. (Remember the modeling of choice of law methodologies in Chapter 3.) Even with codification, the case law interpreting those mandates will draw the litigators' attention.

Even jurisdictions that have not codified their general choice of law methodology may nevertheless have statutes that, in particular cases, will be consequential with respect to determining the applicable law. We will focus on two types here: localizing statutes and borrowing statutes.

Localizing Statutes

A localizing statute requires a local court to apply forum law. In these circumstances, a court does not resort to its native choice of law methodology to determine what law applies, because there is no choice of law question presented. A localizing statute (also sometimes called a spatially-conditioned substantive rule) either explicitly or implicitly contemplates application in multistate factual situations. Imagine, for example, a workers' compensation statute in West Virginia that specifically contemplates its application to employees who, while working for a West Virginia employer, are injured outside the state of West Virginia. In litigation brought in West Virginia, that workers' compensation statute must be applied by the West Virginia court; there is no choice of law question to be asked, much less answered.[1] The only exception would be if application of the localizing statute violated the Constitution. (Chapter 14.)

Localizing statutes are more common than many litigators may realize.

> [L]ocalizing rules exist in other statutes dealing with franchises, consumer protection, construction contracts, and especially insurance contracts. For example, ... [a]n Alabama statute provides that "[a]ll contracts of insurance, the application for which is taken within this state, shall be deemed to have been made within this state and subject to the laws thereof." . . . Some of these localizing statutes take the further step of expressly prohibiting the contractual choice of another state's law.[2]

Localizing statutes would not bind a court in some other state. If, in the previous example, the West Virginia employer's employee was injured in Georgia and she brought suit in Georgia, a Georgia court may or may not apply West Virginia law.

Hypothetical 16-1

> Octavian Inc. was formed by a small group of businesspersons to operate three Little Caesars franchises in Waterloo, Iowa. The franchisor, Little Caesar Enterprises, Inc., is a Michigan corporation that has its principal place of business in Detroit.

---

1   You will recall that Section 6 of the Second Restatement lists the seven factors that inform the choice of law. But subparagraph (1) of that Section reminds that there is no choice of law inquiry when there is a statutory directive.

  § 6. Choice of Law Principles

   (1) A court, subject to constitutional restrictions, will follow a statutory directive of its own state on choice of law.

   (2) When there is no such directive, the factors relevant to the choice of the applicable rule of law include

     (a)   the needs of the interstate and international systems,

     (b)   the relevant policies of the forum. . .

  Restatement (Second) of Conflict of Laws § 6.

2   Symeon C. Symeonides, *Choice of Law in the American Courts in 2017: Thirtieth Annual Survey*, 66 Am. J. Comp. L. 1 (2018).

The franchise agreement includes the following provision:

> The law regarding franchise registration, employment, covenants not to compete, and other matters of local concern will be governed by the laws of the State of Iowa; but as to contractual and all other matters, this agreement and all provisions of this instrument will be and remain subject to the application, construction, enforcement, and interpretation under the governing law of Michigan.

Octavian Inc. is frustrated by several changes announced by the franchisor, namely (1) new suppliers that charge higher rates; (2) a new product line that requires the purchase of equipment and the remodeling of its restaurants; and (3) a new computer system that requires extensive employee training. The franchise agreement gives the franchisor "unfettered discretion" with respect to "any and all matters" regarding "suppliers," "products," and "information processing systems." Michigan case law suggests that the franchise agreement would be strictly enforced absent bad faith on the part of the franchisor.

The Iowa Franchisee Protection Act provides that "Any provision in a franchise agreement requiring the application of the laws of another state is void with respect to a claim otherwise enforceable under this chapter." The Iowa Franchisee Protection Act requires franchisors to "consult and coordinate" with their franchisees prior to the implementation of any significant unfunded mandate. The Act also allows franchisees to terminate a franchise agreement upon terms favorable to the franchisee.

If the franchisee files a case in Iowa, will the Iowa court apply Michigan law or Iowa law?

Borrowing Statutes

Borrowing statutes are, in certain limited respects, the opposite of localizing statutes. A borrowing statute is a deliberate effort on the part of a state to fulfill the intentions of foreign law at the expense of forum law. The forum *borrows* the mandate of some other jurisdiction to extinguish a claim that would otherwise be valid in the forum state.

Statutes of limitation (and statutes of repose)[3] can be classified as either substantive or procedural for purposes of choice of law. When a statute of limitations is labeled

---

3   Statutes of limitation require that a claim be filed within a certain time period from the time that the cause of action accrues. For example, in many jurisdictions the statute of limitations for contract claims is five or six years.

substantive, then the forum will apply the statute of limitations of the jurisdiction whose substantive law it is applying and, in these circumstances, there is no need for a borrowing statute. But if a statute of limitations is labeled procedural in a given jurisdiction, we know that the court will apply forum procedural law even if it applies foreign substantive law. (*See* Chapters 2 and 10.) The forum's statute of limitations may be longer than the statute of limitations in the state whose substantive law applies, and naturally, plaintiffs will take advantage of this.

A borrowing statute provides that a cause of action that would be barred in the jurisdiction whose (substantive) law applies will also be barred in the forum. Borrowing statutes typically borrow not only the term of the foreign jurisdiction's statute of limitations but also the accompanying tolling provisions. Borrowing statutes also typically work in only one direction: the forum borrows the foreign statute of limitations when the foreign statute is shorter than the forum's, but not when it is longer. The foreign right is thus limited temporally by the state that created it.

Hypothetical 16-2

On August 23, 2016, Sally Morris and Maureen Powers, a married couple domiciled in Massachusetts, were occupants of a helicopter flying from Plymouth, Massachusetts to Wellfleet, Massachusetts. Powers was piloting the helicopter and Morris was the only passenger. The helicopter lost control and power, and crashed into Cape Cod Bay. Powers, who could not swim, drowned. Morris suffered only minor injuries and survived.

The helicopter Powers was piloting was manufactured in California by Randolph Helicopter Company, Inc. (Randolph). Starland LLC (Starland) purchased the helicopter in 2008, and owned it at the time of the crash; Powers was the president of Starland.

The statute of limitations for unintentional torts is usually two or three years, and just one year for intentional torts. The cause of action accrues when the last element constituting the cause of action occurs—usually the moment that the plaintiff suffered injury or damage.

Statutes of repose require that a claim be filed within a certain time period from the time of some statutorily-designated event. That event could be the wrongful act that ultimately gave rise to the suit—e.g., the breach, the decision, the conduct. Or the statute might prescribe some other triggering event. For example, many states have statutes that provide that products liability actions may not be commenced after ten years from the date the product was first purchased. Some jurisdictions that characterize statutes of limitations as procedural nevertheless label statutes of repose as substantive: statutes of limitations limit the time within which a party who has a cause of action may assert that cause of action (i.e., a procedural limit); statutes of repose limits the time within which a party can acquire a cause of action (i.e., a substantive limit).

The policy behind both statutes of limitations and statutes of repose is the same: to avoid litigating stale claims.

On August 22, 2018, Morris filed a wrongful death action against Randolph in a California state court. The complaint alleged that the helicopter was defectively designed and defectively manufactured. The complaint also alleges, in detail, that Randolph was aware of problems with its Model 10/61 helicopter (the model that Powers was flying) beginning in 2001 and that, among other acts of negligence, Randolph failed to warn purchasers and pilots of these problems.

Under Massachusetts law,

> When death is caused by the wrongful act or omission of any person or corporation, the decedent's representative may maintain an action therefor if the decedent might have maintained an action, had the decedent lived, for an injury caused by the wrongful act or omission. An action to recover damages for a death caused by an intentional act constituting murder may be commenced at any time after the death of the decedent. Any other action under this section may be commenced within three years after the date of death provided that the action must be commenced within six years after the defendant's act or omission that forms the theory of liability.

Under California law, the analogous statute provides:

> The period prescribed for the commencement of an action for assault, battery, or injury to, or for the death of, an individual caused by the wrongful act or neglect of another is two years.

As a general rule, courts in California apply the governmental interest analysis to resolve choice of law questions. Section 361 of the California Code of Civil Procedure also provides:

> When a cause of action has arisen in another State, or in a foreign country, and by the laws thereof cannot there be maintained against a person by reason of the lapse of time, an action thereon shall not be maintained against him in this State, except in favor of one who has been a citizen of this State, and who has held the cause of action from the time it accrued.

Was Morris's claim filed timely?

GRIFFIN v. SIRVA, INC.

Court of Appeals of New York
29 N.Y.3d 174 (2017)

CHIEF JUDGE DIFIORE.

The United States Court of Appeals for the Second Circuit has posed three questions regarding who may be liable under the New York State Human Rights Law. Two questions concern Executive Law (Human Rights Law) § 296(15), which prohibits discrimination against individuals with prior criminal convictions. A third question concerns section 296(6), which prohibits aiding and abetting discriminatory conduct.

Plaintiffs [Trathony Griffin and Michael Godwin] are two former employees of Astro Moving and Storage Co., Inc., a New York company. Astro hired plaintiffs as laborers in August 2008 and May 2010, respectively. Both have prior criminal convictions for sexual offenses against young children.

In June 2010, Astro entered into a contract with Allied Van Lines, Inc., pursuant to which Astro performed moving services for Allied. Allied, a nationwide moving company based in Illinois, is a subsidiary of Sirva, Inc. Thereafter, approximately 70% to 80% of Astro's work was performed for Allied. The contract precluded Astro from working for other motor carriers, with limited exceptions.

The contract required Astro to adhere to Allied's Certified Labor Program guidelines, which required that employees who "conduct the business of Allied at customer's home or place of business . . . must have successfully passed a criminal background screen . . . as specifically approved by Allied." If Astro violated the guidelines by using unscreened labor, it was subject to escalating monetary penalties. Under these guidelines, employees automatically failed the criminal background screen if they had ever been convicted of a sexual offense.

In 2011, plaintiffs consented to have Sirva and/or its agents investigate their criminal records, which identified their convictions for sexual offenses against young children. Soon thereafter, Astro fired plaintiffs.

Plaintiffs . . . sued Astro, Sirva, and Allied in the United States District Court for the Eastern District of New York. The complaint alleges violations of the New York State Human Rights Law § 296(15) and (6) [and other statutes not relevant here].

Plaintiffs moved for partial summary judgment against all defendants on liability for their section 296(15) claim, which alleged discrimination on the basis of their prior criminal convictions. Defendants Allied and Sirva cross-moved for summary judgment. The district court denied plaintiffs' motion and granted Allied and Sirva's motion. The district court held that section 296(15) applies only to employers; that neither Sirva nor Allied was plaintiffs' employer; and that neither Sirva nor Allied was liable under section 296(6), which imposes aiding and abetting liability, because neither participated in firing plaintiffs.

Plaintiffs appealed to the Second Circuit. Recognizing that the appeal presented unresolved questions under New York law, the Second Circuit certified three questions to this Court regarding who is liable under the New York State Human Rights Law.

Certified Question No. 1

The first certified question asks: "Does Section 296(15) of the New York State Human Rights Law, prohibiting discrimination in employment on the basis of a criminal conviction limit liability to an aggrieved party's 'employer'?" We answer this question in the affirmative.

Human Rights Law § 296(15) provides that

> [i]t shall be an unlawful discriminatory practice for any person, agency, bureau, corporation or association, including the state and any political subdivision thereof, to deny any license or employment to any individual by reason of his or her having been convicted of one or more criminal offenses . . . when such denial is in violation of the provisions of article twenty-three-A of the correction law. Further, there shall be a rebuttable presumption in favor of excluding from evidence the prior incarceration or conviction of any person, in a case alleging [negligent hiring claims], if after learning about an applicant or employee's past criminal conviction history, such employer has evaluated the factors set forth in [Correction Law § 752], and made a reasonable, good

faith determination that such factors militate in favor of hire or retention of that applicant or employee.

Plaintiffs argue that, by its plain language, the law extends liability beyond employers to "any person," in contrast to other Human Rights Law prohibitions, which expressly limit liability to employers or related entities such as licensing or employment agencies.

[After reviewing the legislative history, the court concluded that the] language of the state was intended to apply [only] to private employers and public agencies. . . . Accordingly, we answer the first certified question in the affirmative.

Certified Question No. 2

Because we answered the first certified question in the affirmative, we turn to the second question, which asks:

> If Section [296](15) is limited to an aggrieved party's "employer," what is the scope of the term "employer" for these purposes, i.e., does it include an employer who is not the aggrieved party's "direct employer," but who, through an agency relationship or other means, exercises a significant level of control over the discrimination policies and practices of the aggrieved party's "direct employer"?

The question presumes that "a significant level of control" over "discrimination policies," standing alone, might confer employer status on an entity that is not the aggrieved party's direct employer. However, other factors are relevant to that determination. We therefore reformulate this question to reflect what the Second Circuit described in its ruling as an open question of New York law for this Court: "if Section 296(15) is limited [to an employer], how should courts determine whether an entity is the aggrieved party's "employer" for the purposes of a claim under Section 296(15)?" *Griffin v. Silva*, 835 F.2d 283, 285 (2nd Cir. 2016).

[After reviewing case law, the court concluded that, when determining who may be liable as an employer under section 296(15) of the Human Rights Law emphasis should be] placed on the alleged employer's power "to order and control" the employee in his or her performance of work.

Certified Question No. 3

The third certified question asks:

> Does Section 296(6) of the New York State Human Rights Law,
> providing for aiding and abetting liability, apply to § 296(15)
> such that an out-of-state principal corporation that requires its
> New York State agent to discriminate in employment on the basis
> of a criminal conviction may be held liable for the employer's
> violation of § 296(15)?

In our view, this question does not concern whether there was discrimination in this particular case, but rather seeks clarification as to who may be liable under section 296(6)—similar to the two prior questions regarding section 296(15). Therefore, we reformulate the question to ask "whether section 296(6) extends liability to an out-of-state nonemployer who aids or abets employment discrimination against individuals with a prior criminal conviction." To this reformulated question, we answer in the affirmative.

Section 296(6) states: "It shall be an unlawful discriminatory practice for any person to aid, abet, incite, compel or coerce the doing of any of the acts forbidden under this article, or to attempt to do so." . . . Section 296(6) extends liability to persons and entities beyond joint employers, and this provision should be construed broadly. . . . Indeed, the purpose of subdivision (6) was "to bring within the orbit of the bill all persons, no matter what their status, who aid or abet any of the forbidden practices of discrimination or who attempt to do so". . . (Rep. of N.Y. St. Temp. Comm'n Against Discrimination, 1945 N.Y. Legis. Doc. No. 6 at 31). . . .

Section 296(6) also applies to out-of-state defendants. The Human Rights Law contains an extraterritoriality provision, which provides: "The provisions of this article shall apply as hereinafter provided to an act committed outside this state against a resident of this state . . . if such act would constitute an unlawful discriminatory practice if committed within this state." Executive Law § 298–a [1]. We have held that "[t]he obvious intent of the State Human Rights Law is to protect 'inhabitants' and persons 'within' the state, meaning that those who work in New York fall within the class of persons who may bring discrimination claims in New York." *Hoffman v. Parade Publs.*, 15 N.Y.3d 285, 291 (2010). In particular, the extraterritoriality provision "protects New York residents . . . from discriminatory acts committed outside the state." *Id.* at 292. To prevail, the injured party "must plead and prove that the alleged discriminatory conduct had an impact in New York." *Id.* at 291. . . .

COMMENTS AND QUESTIONS

1. Does Section 298 reach foreign corporations when the act of discrimination against a New York employee occurs outside of New York?

2. Imagine that Allied and Sirva filed a declaratory judgment action against Griffin and Godwin in Illinois. Would Section 298 bind the Illinois court? (But would an Illinois court have personal jurisdiction over Griffin and Godwin?)

FROM THE COURTS

PORTFOLIO RECOVERY ASSOCIATES LLC v. KING

Court of Appeals of New York
14 N.Y.3d 410 (2010)

PIGOTT, JUDGE.

In April 1989, defendant Jared King, then a resident of Connecticut, opened a credit card account with Greenwood Trust Company, a Delaware corporation with a principal place of business in Greenwood, Delaware. The agreement contained a standard choice of law clause stating that it would be governed by the laws of Delaware. Greenwood subsequently changed its name to Discover Bank.

It is undisputed that, on January 27, 1999, King sent a letter to Discover cancelling his credit card, which he had cut in half and enclosed with the letter. King demanded that Discover advise him on how to proceed in paying the card's outstanding balance, but concededly made no payment on the account after December 1998. In August 2000, Discover transferred to plaintiff Portfolio Recovery Associates, LLC, "all right, title and interest in and to" King's outstanding account.

On April 1, 2005, nearly five years after the assignment and more than six years after the account was canceled, Portfolio commenced this action against King, now a resident of New York, asserting causes of action for breach of contract and account stated. King asserts in his answer, among other things, that upon application of CPLR 202—this State's "borrowing statute"—Portfolio's claims are time-barred. Specifically, King claims that Delaware's three-year statute of limitations for breach of a credit card contract (*see* Del. Code. Ann., tit. 10, § 8106) applies and, alternatively, Portfolio's claims are untimely under this State's six-year breach of contract limitations period (*see* CPLR 213[2]).

Portfolio obtained summary judgment on its complaint. The Supreme Court directed that judgment be entered in Portfolio's favor and the Appellate Division affirmed. We now reverse.

The Appellate Division properly concluded that the Delaware choice of law clause did not require the application of the Delaware three-year statute of limitations to bar Portfolio's claims. Choice of law provisions typically apply to only substantive issues, and statutes of limitations are considered "procedural" because they are deemed as pertaining to the remedy rather than the right. There being no express intention in the agreement that Delaware's statute of limitations was to apply to this dispute, the choice of law provision cannot be read to encompass that limitations period. We conclude, however, that the Appellate Division should have applied CPLR 202 to Portfolio's claims to determine whether they were timely brought.

CPLR 202 provides, in relevant part, that "[a]n action based upon a cause of action accruing without the state cannot be commenced after the expiration of the time limited by the laws of either the state or the place without the state where the cause of action accrued." Therefore, when a nonresident sues on a cause of action accruing outside New York, CPLR 202 requires the cause of action to be timely under the limitation periods of both New York and the jurisdiction where the cause of action accrued. If the claimed injury is an economic one, the cause of action typically accrues where the plaintiff resides and sustains the economic impact of the loss.

Portfolio, as the assignee of Discover, is not entitled to stand in a better position than that of its assignor. We must therefore first ascertain where the cause of action accrued in favor of Discover. Here, it is evident that the contract causes of action accrued in Delaware, the place where Discover sustained the economic injury in 1999 when King allegedly breached the contract. Discover is incorporated in Delaware and is not a New York resident. Therefore, the borrowing statute applies and the Delaware three-year statute of limitations governs.

That does not end the inquiry, however, because in determining whether Portfolio's action would be barred in Delaware, this Court must "borrow" Delaware's tolling statute to determine whether under Delaware law Portfolio would have had the benefit of additional time to bring the action. Delaware's tolling statute—Delaware Code Annotated, title 10, § 8117—provides that

> [i]f at the time when a cause of action accrues against any person, such person is out of the State, the action may be commenced, within the time limited therefor in this chapter, after such person comes into the State in such manner that by reasonable diligence, such person may be served with process. If, after a cause of action shall have accrued against any person, such person departs from and resides or remains out of the State, the time of such person's absence until such person shall have returned into the State in the manner provided in this section, shall not be taken as any part of the time limited for the commencement of the action.

Section 8117 was meant to apply only in a circumstance where the defendant had a prior connection to Delaware, meaning that the tolling provision envisioned that there would be some point where the defendant would return to that state or where the plaintiff could effect service on the defendant to obtain jurisdiction. Indeed, Delaware's highest court has held that the literal application of its tolling provision "would result in the abolition of the defense of statutes of limitations in actions involving nonresidents" (*Hurwitch v. Adams*, 52 Del. 247, 252 [1959]).

There is no indication that King ever resided in Delaware, nor is there any indication from the case law that Delaware intended for its tolling provision to apply to a nonresident like King. Therefore, we conclude that Delaware's tolling provision does not extend the three-year statute of limitations. Moreover, contrary to Portfolio's contention, it is of no moment that Portfolio was unable to obtain personal jurisdiction over King in Delaware; this Court has held that it is not inconsistent to apply CPLR 202 in such a situation (*see Insurance Co. of N. Am. v. ABB Power Generation*, 91 N.Y.2d 180, 187–188 [1997]).

Applying Delaware's three-year statute of limitations, the instant action should been commenced not later than 2002. Because the contract claims were not brought until 2005, they are time-barred in Delaware, where the causes of action accrued, and therefore they are likewise time-barred in New York upon application of the borrowing statute. This holding is consistent with one of the key policies underlying CPLR 202, namely, to prevent forum shopping by nonresidents attempting to take advantage of a more favorable statute of limitations in this state (*see Antone v. General Motors Corp. Buick Motor Div.*, 64 N.Y.2d 20, 27–28 [1984]). . . .

COMMENTS AND QUESTIONS

1. The trope of forum-shopping is often a useful rhetorical device. Portfolio is a Delaware corporation with a principal place of business in Virginia. Yet there is a good argument that King is essentially the forum-shopper. What is that argument? (Is the word *fortuitous* also helpful?)

2. A borrowing statute is the functional equivalent of (re)labeling statutes of limitations as substantive (instead of procedural). What are the relative advantages of borrowing statutes, on one hand, and characterization, on the other?

3. Borrowing statutes (or the relabeling of statutes of limitations as substantive) avoid depecage. Is applying the cause of action from one jurisdiction with the statute of limitations of another jurisdiction a problematic combination?

Quick Summary

- Localizing statutes eliminate the need for a choice of law inquiry, because localizing statutes eliminate uncertainty regarding the applicable law

- Borrowing statutes instruct courts, when applying foreign law, to borrow the shorter statute of limitations of the foreign law; borrowing statutes are important because statutes of limitations are often treated as procedural (rather than substantive) law

- Borrowing statutes can apply to statutes of limitations and also to statutes of repose

17

Corporate Internal Affairs

Key Concepts

- Internal corporate affairs
- External corporate affairs

This Chapter reveals a distinction between the *external* and *internal* affairs of a corporation. The terms are not self-defining, yet the characterization is important. Internal affairs are subject to a special choice of law rule.

The external affairs of a corporation include acts where the corporation interacts with someone outside the corporation. Corporations enter into contracts with lenders, vendors, or landlords. Corporations sell products to consumers. And corporations trespass, spill toxic waste, and compete in markets. Choice of law with respect to these external affairs of a corporation is no different than choice of law with respect the acts of individuals. Indeed, the external affairs of a corporation are sometimes defined as acts of a sort that can also be done by natural persons. Chapters 4 through 9 included many cases that involved corporations, and all of those cases involved external affairs.

The *internal affairs* of a corporation are defined to include governance and fiduciary issues that are peculiar to corporate entities. These include the rights of stockholders, the duties and obligations of the officers and directors, election and appointment of directors, issuances of shares, meetings, inspection rights, acquisition procedures, dividend regulation, and dissolution procedures. Natural persons do not have officers, directors, and shareholders. The *internal affairs rule* is a choice of law rule dictating that the law of the jurisdiction where the corporation is incorporated (or organized) furnishes the governing law.

The internal affairs rule is a mainstay of corporate law. In the seminal case *McDermott Inc. v. Lewis*, the Delaware Supreme Court applied foreign law—not just foreign to Delaware, but foreign even to the United States—to determine a shareholder's voting rights. Delaware law prohibited a subsidiary corporation from voting any shares held by the subsidiary's parent in favor of the parent in a given transaction, but Panamanian law allowed it. The court held that it was inappropriate for the state law of Delaware to interfere with the Panamanian corporation's voting rights because the corporation was incorporated in Panama, not Delaware.[1]

> ### TERMINOLOGY
>
> Unfortunately, the word *external* can be misleading. A contract between a corporation and its employee (or labor union), for example, is usually characterized as an external act of a corporation even though it is superficially internal.

The act of incorporation thus also involves establishing the body of law that will apply to resolve disputes that arise about the corporation's internal affairs. The internal affairs rule is universally recognized and now applies also to other U.S. business associations that are formed under a particular state's law.[2] But it is not uniformly applied. New York and California, for example, have a limited set of corporate provisions that apply to some (private) corporations that are incorporated outside their states, but have a certain percentage of stockholders or taxable income in their states. Some states also accord stockholders and directors of foreign corporations inspection rights regardless of the rights of inspection available under the law of the state of incorporation.

The Second Restatement of Conflict of Laws establishes this framework with respect to corporate powers and liabilities. Section 301 captures what is described above as the external affairs. Section 302 captures the internal affairs, invoking the Section 6 principles that we saw in Chapter 8 and relying upon a rebuttable presumption that the state of incorporation will provide the governing law.

Restatement (Second) of Conflict of Laws

§ 301. Rights Against and Liabilities to Third Person

The rights and liabilities of a corporation with respect to a third person that arise from a corporate act of a sort that can likewise be done by an individual are determined by the same choice-of-law principles as are applicable to non-corporate parties.

§ 302. Other Issues with Respect to Powers and Liabilities of a Corporation

(1) Issues involving the rights and liabilities of a corporation, other than those dealt with in § 301, are determined by the local law of the state which, with

---

1   531 A.2d 206 (Del. 1987).

2   *See* Unif. Ltd. Part. Act § 901, 6A U.L.A. 254 (stating that the law of the state where the limited partnership is organized governs the partnership's internal affairs).

respect to the particular issue, has the most significant relationship to the occurrence and the parties under the principles stated in § 6.

(2) The local law of the state of incorporation will be applied to determine such issues, except in the unusual case where, with respect to the particular issue, some other state has a more significant relationship to the occurrence and the parties, in which event the local of the other state will be applied.

The internal affairs rule provides "certainty and predictability of result," and protects "the justified expectations of parties with interests in [the business organization]."[3] The rule also reduces the possibility of inconsistent regulation of governance issues, and thus, at least arguably, has some constitutional dimensions. It would be anomalous to permit one group of stockholders to be covered by a different set of rules than another set of stockholders who acquired their shares in different markets.

Hypothetical 17-1

The shareholders of a company ordinarily have the power to make big corporate decisions, including who sits on the board of directors. Typically, each share of stock confers one vote. Thus, if a shareholder, Sharon, owns 100 shares of stock, she would have 100 votes. If there were an election for three seats on the board of directors, Sharon would receive 100 votes for each race—for a total of 300 votes.

In a voting system called statutory or straight voting, Sharon the shareholder would have to divide her 300 votes evenly between each of three races. She would allocate 100 of her votes for her preferred candidate for each seat on the board. Statutory voting generally protects the interests of majority shareholders. Imagine that Sharon is one of only two shareholders in the company: Sharon has 100 shares and the other owner has 101 shares. Even though Sharon owns 49.75% of the company, the other owner would choose all three of the directors in a statutory voting system: for each slot, Sharon's nominee would receive 100 votes and the other shareholder's nominee would receive 101 votes.

To protect the interests of minority shareholders in non-publicly traded companies, California long ago passed a corporate law establishing cumulative voting as a statutory right. Cumulative voting allows voting shareholders to allocate their votes among the candidates or to cast them all in favor of one candidate. In other words, Sharon could cast all 300 of her votes for her preferred candidate for one of the board seats (and not vote

---

3   *First Nat. City Bank v. Banco Para El Comercio Exterior de Cuba*, 462 U.S. 611, 621 (1983).

in the other two contests); or allocate 200 of her votes for her candidate in race number one, 75 of her votes for her candidate in race number two, and the remaining 25 of her votes for her candidate in race number three. Under these voting rules (plus a little game theory), Sharon is essentially guaranteed that one of her preferred candidates will be elected. Cumulative voting strengthens the likelihood of minority representation in corporate governance.

Starlight Amusement Park Co. (Starlight) is incorporated in Utah, and has its only place of business in California. The company's assets and employees are in California. All of the company's business is in California. All of the company's shareholders are in California. The meetings of its shareholders and directors are in California.

The corporate law of Utah provides for straight voting in an election of directors, but permits cumulative voting if the articles of incorporation so provide. Neither the articles of incorporation nor the bylaws of Starlight provide for cumulative voting.

A minority shareholder of Starlight approaches you for advice about how she might challenge the upcoming election in which Starlight plans to fill three open board seats. What is your advice?

FROM THE COURTS

JOHNSON v. JOHNSON

Supreme Court of Nebraska
272 Neb. 263 (2006)

GERRARD, JUSTICE.

The question presented in this case is whether the substantive law of Nebraska or Delaware applies to a complaint alleging oppression of a shareholder of a Delaware corporation, the sole asset of which is all the stock of a Nebraska corporation. . . .

The plaintiff, Michael R. Johnson is a shareholder of Western Securities, a Delaware corporation. Michael is an employee of Modern Equipment Company, Inc. (Modern Equipment), a Nebraska corporation. The principal place of business for both Western Securities and Modern Equipment is

Omaha, Nebraska. Western Securities owns all the stock of Modern Equipment, but no other property.

Richard W. ("Dick") Johnson incorporated and was originally the sole shareholder and director of Western Securities. In 1975, Western Securities acquired Modern Equipment, and Dick became the sole director of that business as well.

In 1990, Michael moved to Omaha and began working full time for Modern Equipment. He worked full time until 1992, when he began to work both full and part time while he completed a college degree. He completed his degree in 1996 and became a vice president of Modern Equipment, responsible for quality management. Michael's duties later expanded to include corporate development. He received regular salary increases and excellent performance reviews on an annual basis.

In 1998, Dick transferred shares of stock in Western Securities to his five children. . . . After the transfers, Dick owned 75 percent of Western Securities stock, Richard 10 percent, Michael 6 percent, William 3.5 percent, Nancy 3.5 percent, and Thomas 2 percent. Dick's stated intent was that Richard would succeed Dick as president and chief executive officer of Modern Equipment and that Michael would in turn succeed Richard. Dick promised Michael and Richard that Dick's Western Securities stock would be devised to them in equal shares. After October 3, 2000, Western Securities and Modern Equipment each had three-member boards, composed of Michael, Richard, and Dick.

Dick became ill in March 2001 and resigned as president of Modern Equipment in October. Richard was elected by Dick, Richard, and Michael to succeed Dick as president. Dick died on November 6, and his will provided that Michael and Richard were each to receive one-half of Dick's shares of Western Securities stock. Richard was appointed personal representative of Dick's estate.

After Dick's death, Richard appointed Modern Equipment's vice president of manufacturing to fill vacancies on the boards of Western Securities and Modern Equipment, without notice to, meeting of, or the knowledge or consent of the other shareholders. On August 28, 2002, Richard fired Michael and barred him from the premises of Modern Equipment. Since then, Michael has been denied any participation in the operation of Modern Equipment and has not shared in its earnings.

Modern Equipment's before-tax profits have declined from $374,745 in the fiscal year ending August 31, 2001, to $5,367 in the following fiscal year. Richard's 2002 salary was $187,000, which was a 22 percent raise from the previous year. Western Securities has never paid dividends, and between Dick's death and February 28, 2003, no shareholders' meetings for Western Securities or Modern Equipment were held.

On February 28, 2003, Michael notified counsel for Western Securities and Modern Equipment of Richard's conduct. Shortly thereafter, Michael was notified that meetings of the shareholders and boards of directors of Western Securities and Modern Equipment would be held on April 15. At those meetings, Richard, in his capacity as personal representative of Dick's estate, voted all the shares of stock then still held in the estate to ratify his prior conduct.

Dick's Western Securities stock was finally distributed by his estate in 2004, after which time, Richard held 48.083 percent of the stock, Michael held 44.083 percent, William and Nancy held 3.5 percent each, and Thomas held five-sixths of 1 percent.

Procedural History

Michael filed suit in the district court on May 22, 2003, against Richard, Western Securities, and Modern Equipment (collectively the defendants). According to Michael, Richard had oppressed Michael and misapplied the corporate assets of Western Securities and Modern Equipment by depriving him of his legitimate expectation of full-time employment; depriving him of his right to meaningfully participate in the operation, management, and control of Modern Equipment; operating Modern Equipment for his own benefit to the detriment of Michael; eliminating financial benefits to which Michael had a reasonable expectancy; removing Michael from his employment and denying him the opportunity to serve as president; and failing to keep him fully and fairly informed of the operation of Modern Equipment. Michael alleged that these practices were oppressive because they violated the reasonable expectations of Michael as established by the intentions of Dick and years of past practice, and were also in breach of the fiduciary duties owed to Michael.

Michael prayed that the court require an accounting from Richard and require him to return to Modern Equipment any amounts received by him in excess of the proportionate share of earnings and profits, as well as any amounts attributable to a misapplication of misappropriation of company assets. Michael prayed that the court require Modern Equipment to pay Michael the funds to which he would have been entitled had he not been excluded from employment and participation in Modern Equipment's earnings and profits.

Michael also prayed that the court enter an order requiring Western Securities to cease carrying on business in Nebraska, appointing a receiver to take charge of the corporate assets of Western Securities and Modern Equipment and supervise the sale of those assets, and distributing the proceeds of the sale of Western Securities and Modern Equipment to Michael and the other shareholders of Western Securities. In the alternative, Michael prayed that the court enter an order finding Western Securities to be the corporate alter ego of Modern Equipment and/or imposing a constructive trust on the shares of Modern Equipment for the benefit of Michael, dissolving Modern Equipment, appointing a receiver to supervise the sale of Modern Equipment's assets, and distributing the proceeds of the sale directly to Western Securities' shareholders in proportion to their ownership interests. Alternatively, Michael prayed for an order finding Western Securities to be the alter ego of Modern Equipment and directing Western Securities or its remaining shareholders to redeem Michael's interests for fair market value.

Richard, Western Securities, and Modern Equipment filed motions to dismiss Michael's complaint. . . . [T]he court . . . concluded that the case dealt with the internal affairs of the corporation and that under the applicable choice-of-law principles, the need for uniformity regarding internal affairs dictated that Delaware law control the case. Because Delaware law did not permit the dissolution of Western Securities or appointment of a receiver under the facts alleged, the court dismissed Michael's complaint.

Assignments of Error

Michael assigns that the district court erred (1) in concluding that Delaware law applied to the facts of this case and in granting the defendants' motions to dismiss on that basis, thus (a) holding that the internal affairs doctrine prohibited the application of Nebraska law in this case, (b) holding that considerations of uniformity and predictability prohibited the application of Nebraska law in this case, and (c) concluding that Nebraska public policy does not mandate the application of Nebraska law in this case; (2) in concluding that Michael sought dissolution of a foreign corporation and in concluding that the inclusion of a proposed remedy relating to the appointment of a receiver and the winding up of Western Securities' business in Nebraska required dismissal; and (3) in refusing to address the viability of Michael's remaining proposed remedies and in thereby concluding that the court could not fashion a remedy for Michael in the exercise of its equitable powers. . . .

Analysis

. . . The internal affairs doctrine is a conflict of laws principle which recognizes that only one state should have the authority to regulate a corporation's internal affairs—matters peculiar to the relationships among or between the corporation and its current officers, directors, and shareholders—because otherwise, a corporation could be faced with conflicting demands. *Edgar v. MITE Corp.*, 457 U.S. 624 (1982). The internal affairs doctrine is codified in Nebraska law pursuant to Neb. Rev. Stat. § 21–20,172 (Reissue 1997), which provides

> (1) A certificate of authority shall authorize the foreign corporation to which it is issued to transact business in this state subject, however, to the right of the state to revoke the certificate as provided in the Business Corporation Act.

> (2) A foreign corporation with a valid certificate of authority shall have the same but no greater rights and shall have the same but no greater privileges as, and except as otherwise provided by the act, shall be subject to the same duties, restrictions, penalties, and liabilities now or later imposed on, a domestic corporation of like character.

> (3) *The act shall not be construed to authorize this state to regulate the organization of internal affairs of a foreign corporation authorized to transact business in this state.*

(Emphasis supplied.) Section 21–20,172(3) was intended to preserve "the judicially developed doctrine that internal corporate affairs are governed by the state of incorporation even when the corporation's business and assets are located primarily in other states." 4 Model Business Corporation Act Ann. § 15.05(c), official comment at 15–71 (3d ed. 2002). *See* Restatement (Second) of Conflict of Laws § 302 (1971).

The internal affairs doctrine was developed on the premise that in order to prevent corporations from being subjected to inconsistent legal standards the authority to regulate a corporation's internal affairs should not rest with multiple jurisdictions. By providing certainty and predictability, the internal affairs doctrine protects the justified expectations of the parties with interests in the corporation. *Vantagepoint v. Examen, Inc.*, 871 A.2d 1108 (Del. 2005). *See, e.g., Harrison v. NetCentric Corp.*, 433 Mass. 465 (2001). It has also been held that pursuant to the Due Process Clause, directors and officers of a corporation have a significant right to know what law will be applied to their actions and stockholders have a right to know by what standards of accountability they may hold those managing the corporation's business and affairs. *Vantagepoint, supra.* Furthermore, under the Commerce Clause, a state has no interest in regulating the internal affairs of foreign corporations. Therefore, application of the internal affairs doctrine may be mandated by constitutional principles, except in the rare situation when the law of the state of incorporation is inconsistent with a national policy on foreign or interstate commerce. *Vantagepoint, supra.* . . .

[T]he defendants' argument is based on their claims that since Western Securities' assets consist of Modern Equipment stock, disposing of those assets would effectively dissolve Western Securities. But while the general rule is that a court of equity cannot appoint a *general* receiver for a foreign corporation, there is an important distinction between the appointment of a general receiver and the appointment of a receiver merely of the corporation's assets and property within the state. *See generally* 17A William Meade Fletcher et al., Fletcher Cyclopedia of the Law of Private Corporations § 8555 (perm. ed. Rev. vol. 1998 & Cum. Supp. 2005). It is well established, in Nebraska and elsewhere, that equity has jurisdiction to appoint a receiver for the instate assets of a foreign corporation. *See Starr v. Bankers Union of the World*, 81 Neb. 377 (1908); 17 Fletcher et al., *supra.* . . .

Furthermore, Michael's complaint suggested several alternative forms of relief beyond the appointment of a receiver. Among other things, Michael asked for an accounting, an order directing Richard to return money received by him to Modern Equipment, damages in the amount Michael would have received had he not been excluded from Modern Equipment, or an order directing Western Securities to redeem his interest. . . . If Michael stated a cause of action for which relief could be granted, a Nebraska court would have the power to grant at least some of the relief sought by Michael's complaint, including the appointment of a receiver. . . Therefore, we turn to the dispositive question whether Michael can obtain *any* relief from Nebraska law, or whether Delaware law controls this case and precludes his recovery.

Michael does not dispute that his action involves the internal affairs of Western Enterprises and that the internal affairs doctrine is applicable. Rather, Michael contends that under exceptions to that doctrine, Nebraska law should apply here. The Restatement (Second) of Conflict of Laws § 302 (1971) recognizes that the local law of the state of incorporation applies to internal affairs, except in the unusual case where, with respect to the particular issue, some other state has a more significant relationship to the occurrence and the parties, in which case, the local law of the other state will be applied. Where "internal affairs" are concerned—the relations among the corporation, its shareholders, directors, officers, or agents—the local law of the state of incorporation will be applied unless application of the local law of some other state is required by reason of the overriding interest of that other state in the issue to be decided. *See id.*, comments *a.* and *b.* As previously noted, the rule of § 302 has been adopted in Nebraska by statute. *See* § 21–20,172(3).

The factors applicable to such a choice of law include (1) the needs of the interstate and international systems; (2) the relevant policies of the forum; (3) the relevant policies of other interested states and the relative interests of those states in the determination of the particular issue; (4) the protection of justified expectations; (5) the basic policies underlying the particular field of law; (6) certainty, predictability, and uniformity of result; and (7) ease in the determination and application of the law to be applied. Restatement, *supra*, § 6.

Michael is focused on Nebraska's public policy and Nebraska's relative interest as the location of the alleged events giving rise to the action. But this overlooks the weight of factors that bear against interference with the internal affairs of a foreign corporation. A single rule for each corporation's internal affairs reduces uncertainty and the prospect of inconsistent obligations; it also enables the corporate venturers to adjust the many variables of the corporate life, confident that they can predict the legal effect of these choices.

> Large corporations that are listed on national exchanges, or even regional exchanges, will have shareholders in many States and shares that are traded frequently. The markets that facilitate this national and international participation in ownership of corporations are essential for providing capital not only for new enterprises but also for established companies that need to expand

their businesses. This beneficial free market system depends at its core upon the fact that a corporation—except in the rarest situations—is organized under, and governed by, the law of a single jurisdiction, traditionally the corporate law of the State of its incorporation.

CTS Corp. v. Dynamics Corp. of America, 481 U.S. 69, 90 (1987). As the Restatement explains:

> Application of the local law of the state of incorporation will usually be supported by those choice-of-law factors favoring the needs of the interstate and international systems, certainty, predictability and uniformity of result, protection of the justified expectations of the parties and ease in the application of the law to be applied. Usually, application of this law will also be supported by the factor looking toward implementation of the relevant policies of the state with the dominant interest in the decision of the particular issue.
>
> Uniform treatment of directors, officers, and shareholders is an important objective which can only be attained by having the rights and liabilities of those persons with respect to the corporation governed by a single law. To the extent that they think about the matter, these persons would usually expect that their rights and duties with respect to the corporation would be determined by the local law of the state of incorporation. This state is also easy to identify, and thus the value of ease of application is attained when the local law of this state is applied.

Restatement (Second) of Conflict of Laws § 302, comment *e*. at 309 (1971).

Here, Nebraska certainly has an interest in the dispute by virtue of Modern Equipment's location in the state. Nebraska has a declared public policy, pursuant to the Business Corporation Act, *see* Nev. Rev. Stat. § 21–2001 et seq. (Reissue 1997 & Cum. Supp. 2004), of affording relief upon some of the allegations made by Michael. But Nebraska also has a stated public policy, enacted as part of the same statutory scheme, of not interfering in the internal affairs of foreign corporations, and the conflict of laws principles stated in § 6 of the Restatement generally weigh in favor of applying Delaware law to this dispute. Admittedly, the reasons for applying the local law of the state of incorporation carry less weight when the corporation has little or no contact with the state other than the fact that it was incorporated there. Restatement, *supra*, § 302, comment *g*. But, application of the local law of the state of incorporation also furthers certainty, predictability, and uniformity of result, ease in the application of the law to be applied, and perhaps most important, protection of the justified expectations of the parties. *See id.* Simply stated, stockholders in a foreign corporation should not be surprised—and under Nebraska statutes have a right to expect—that issues involving the internal affairs of a corporation will be decided pursuant to the law of the state of incorporation. This is simply not the extraordinary case in which the internal affairs doctrine is to be set aside.

Michael also argues that Western Securities and Modern Equipment are alter egos and that Western Securities' corporate veil can be pierced. To the extent that Michael's alter ego theory is intended to address the internal affairs doctrine, however, it is without merit. It is well established that when determining whether to pierce a corporate veil, the local law of the state of incorporation is applied. *See Kellers Systems v. Transport Intern. Pool*, 172 F.Supp.2d 992 (N.D. Ill. 2001). Stated another way, whether Western Securities and Modern Equipment are alter egos, and the legal effect of such a finding, is determined by Delaware law. While Delaware law permits a corporate veil to be pierced, this is simply a remedy available when a cause of action has been alleged, and as previously noted, Michael does not contest the district court's conclusion that the facts he alleged do not state a cause of action recognized by Delaware law. In other words, even if Delaware law would regard Western Securities and Modern Equipment to be one and the same, Michael has not stated a cause of action against either corporation.

For the foregoing reasons, the judgment of the district court dismissing Michael's complaint is affirmed.

COMMENTS AND QUESTIONS

1. The internal affairs doctrine essentially embeds a choice of law clause into every transaction or occurrence regarding the internal affairs of the corporation. Should the law that governs those relationship be determined solely by reference to the law of the state of incorporation even if none of the company's operations occur there? (What are the constraints on choice of law clauses? *See* Chapter 9.)

2. In *Johnson*, Judge Gerrard hails the virtues of consistency and predictability as justifications for the internal affairs doctrine. Occasionally in conflict of laws (and in law more generally), inconsistency, unpredictability, and disuniformity are evils to be avoided. While in other instances, inconsistency, unpredictability, and disuniformity are mere inconveniences—necessary byproducts of giving every person their day in court. When is inconsistency a monster and when is it merely a bogeyman?

3. The court emphasizes that the directors of a corporation "have a right to expect . . . that issues involving the internal affairs of a corporation will be decided pursuant to the law of the state of incorporation." How should the court handle a situation where, as a matter of undisputed fact, the directors did not expect the law of the state of incorporation to apply and did not know the content of the law of the state of incorporation?

4. Hypothesize the facts of the "extraordinary case" for which the internal affairs doctrine should be set aside. Would the facts in Hypothetical 17-1 reach that standard?

SAMPLE EXAM QUESTION

Question 17-2

Italian Petroleum S.p.A. (IP) , an Italian corporation, owns and operates an oil pipeline system in the Gulf of Mexico southeast of Houston, Texas. Three years ago, repeated spills and two fatal explosions led to scrutiny by the Environmental Protection Agency which, in turn, fined the corporation $3 million, ordered extensive cleanup that cost $7 million more, and temporarily shuttered part of the oil field which reduced net revenues by at least $5 million.

Shareholders of IP recently filed a "Shareholders Derivative Suit" in a Texas state court against directors of the company. They allege that the defendants' failure to maintain and update a pipeline system that had been decaying for years constituted a breach of their fiduciary duties. All of the relevant actions and inactions of the company's directors took place in or just off the coast of Texas.

Texas follows the Second Restatement for its choice of law methodology.

Shareholder derivative suits are not permitted under Italian law unless the claims fall under any of three limited exceptions that, plaintiffs concede, do not apply here. Although Italy recently passed a law that will broadly allow shareholder derivative suits (like the instant one) that law will not take effect until December 31st and the statute explicitly does not apply retroactively.

Texas has a rule for shareholder derivative suits that is modeled on the federal rule. Defendants concede that the plaintiff shareholders have complied with the rule's prerequisites for filing a derivative suit.

The defendants, who were served with a summons and a copy of the complaint yesterday, have hired you to represent them. What is your *advice* to the clients, your *research* agenda for the next few days, and your tentative *forecast* for the outcome of this law suit?

Quick Summary

- The act of incorporation establishes the body of law that will apply to resolve disputes regarding a corporation's internal affairs

- The internal affairs of a corporation include governance and fiduciary issues that arise because of the unique status of corporations

- The corporate internal affairs doctrine is justified by concerns about certainty and predictability of results and about uniform treatment of similarly situated persons

18

Proving Foreign Law

Key Concepts

- Question of law (as opposed to a question of fact)
- Interpreting and translating foreign law
- Role of expert testimony
- Homeward trend and forum non conveniens dismissals

Most of this course is about the application *vel non* of foreign law. A law is foreign if it is not native to the forum state. To a court in Texas, even Missouri law is foreign. Of course the law of Mexico, a foreign country, would also be foreign to a court in Texas. In this Chapter we focus on the task of proving the content of foreign law. That task might be triggered by any of the choice of law methodologies that we studied in Chapters 3–8. The enforcement of a choice of law clause might require the application of foreign law. (*See* Chapter 9.) Or something like the corporate internal affairs doctrine may trigger the application of foreign law. (*See* Chapter 17.) Federal legislation also incorporates foreign law.[1] And in addition to those situations where courts are expected or required to *apply* foreign law, other doctrines expect or require courts to *consider* foreign law as part of the calculus for some other decision. (*See* Chapters 20, 21, 22, and 23.)

Proving foreign law can be difficult. First, it bears emphasis that applying the native law of a jurisdiction is seldom simple and uncontestable. Indeed, lawyers will often disagree about the content and meaning of the law in a jurisdiction in which they have practiced for decades. Similarly, judges can struggle to discern the mandates of their own state's laws. The task of proving foreign law gets progressively more difficult as one contemplates applying the law of other states. Of course the

---

1   Tax, intellectual property, and immigration matters routinely implicate state laws and the laws of foreign countries. Several domestic laws, such as the Foreign Corrupt Practices Act, *see* 15 U.S.C. §§ 78dd–1(c), 78dd–2(a)(1)A), 78dd–2(c) (2006), also incorporate foreign law by reference.

law of some states may be easier to apply—perhaps a neighboring state that shares a metropolitan area, or a nearby state with a shared history. But literal and figurative distance might make it harder for, say, a Massachusetts court to appreciate the nuances of Wyoming law. Of course the task grows ever more complicated as one anticipates the application of a foreign *country's* law.

Understanding a foreign country's law is notoriously difficult. As a threshold matter, simply accessing the foreign law can be challenging. To be sure, technology and enthusiasm for globalization has led to a proliferation of materials about foreigners, foreign legal systems, and foreign laws. However, this information is still difficult to digest, explain, adapt, and apply elsewhere. Indeed, information is not the same thing as knowledge.

In Practice

In most respects, proving the law of a sister state differs only in degree from proving the law of a foreign country. Accordingly, some of the issues discussed in this chapter are generally applicable. In one important respect, however, the two situations differ in kind: when a court applies state (or federal) law, the court does not permit expert testimony.

"There are very few points [of foreign law] which lend themselves to . . . simple treatment."[2] The inherently inconstant character of laws aggravates the interpretation of the laws of a foreign system, as the effect of any law may differ from time to time. One must contemplate questions of constitutional validity and other threshold matters. The law may vary depending upon whether one adopts the interpretive lens of intentionalism, purposivism, textualism, or some other theory. The foreign law may be unsettled and controversial. As the instruments of lawmaking are as malleable as words and laws themselves, one may encounter such phenomena as deliberately ambiguous laws.

Further, to apply or evaluate *foreign* law begs the jurisprudential question: What is *law?* Trawling the depths of that question, legal pluralism literature explores the characteristics and consequences of the relationship between and among the overlapping, semiautonomous layers of formal and informal law. The uninitiated often presume the applicable foreign law to be some state code, but there may be

---

2 William B. Stern, *Foreign Law in the Courts: Judicial Notice and Proof,* 45 CALIF. L. REV. 23, 40 (1957).

other formal codifications that amplify or qualify that code provision, or scholarly commentaries that interpret code provisions in a quasi-authoritative way. Surely we should consider foreign law *on its own terms*. Some legal systems are formally pluralistic, recognizing various other family, religious, business, or customary legal systems. Further, various influential, even if formally non-binding forms of "soft law" complicate the foreign law inquiry.

Part of the challenge to understanding foreign law can be explained as a matter of cognitive science. "[S]peakers produce the minimum linguistic information sufficient to achieve the speaker's communicational needs."[3] The natural audience for a law is a domestic audience; effective communication with an outsider is not the purpose of such a test. Thus, the foreign law will not express all of the cues, assumptions, presumptions, exceptions, canons, common sense, and peripheral knowledge essential to a comprehensive understanding. An apt analogy to the task of understanding foreign law is that of trying to learn the law on a complex, unfamiliar, specialized subject solely from bar review outlines: reading about, say, the elements of a strict products liability claim assumes lots of other knowledge. Others have said that when judges apply the laws of their own legal systems they act as architects; but when dealing with foreign law, judges act merely as photographers.[4]

Translation of foreign laws from another language presents a related but additional obstacle. Legal translation is almost always difficult, and sometimes may (by virtue of the limitations of language) be impossible to accomplish. Translations can be difficult to comprehend because the laws are often merely translated into the target language rather than placed within context. However, even if capturing that context were possible, there are other dangers in contextualizing because, when translating, "people tend to find what they seek."[5] Manipulation can occur because translation necessarily requires a certain amount of creativity and interpretation; there is no sense of equivalence in the abstract that can guide the practice of translation. Indeed, elementary hermeneutics teaches us that every interpretation or translation, no matter how conscientious, will involve actual participation by the translator. Even if fidelity to the original language were possible, there are always interlinguistic gaps, as some words may be untranslatable.

---

3   Brian G. Slocum, *Linguistics and "Ordinary Meaning" Determinations*, 33 Statute L. Rev. 39, 47 (2012).

4   1 Albert A. Ehrenzweig, Private International Law 193 (1967); Friedrich K. Juenger, Choice of Law and Multistate Justice 85–86 (1993).

5   Andrew N. Adler, *Translating & Interpreting Foreign Statutes*, 19 Mich. J. Int'l L. 37, 54 (1998). "The courts' inquiries . . . very often (implicitly or explicitly) conclude that alien and forum rules correlate quite closely." *Id.* at 63. Maybe this is because they are more comparable than they appear—a benign explanation. "The general methodological problem of 'wish-fulfillment' mars the universality thesis." *Id.*

Ascertaining foreign law suggests great expectations of the judiciary. In most American courts, judges must decide the content of foreign law as a matter of law.[6] Accordingly, judges must resolve these questions of law on the record and with an explanation of the ruling. The high expectation of and attention forced upon the judiciary resurfaces anew on appeal since the content of federal law must be decided by appellate judges de novo.

When determining the content of foreign law, courts "may consider any relevant material or source, including testimony, whether or not submitted by a party or admissible under the Federal Rules of Evidence."[7] It often behooves the litigating parties to present expert testimony to assist the court on issues regarding the content of foreign law, and this is the ordinary course. Although the absence of a qualified expert witness can be a problem for courts, the problem is more commonly the opposite. In many cases, each party will have a foreign law expert who contradicts the other.

A battle-of-the-experts can be expensive and inefficient. Experts can become partisans and substance can be perverted. Hosting a battle-of-the-experts can be embarrassing to the judge who has to determine between the two adversaries. Learned Hand's query is an abiding articulation of the problem facing judges: "[How should one choose] between two statements each founded upon an experience confessedly foreign in kind to their own? It is just because they are incompetent for such a task that the expert is necessary at all."[8]

Unfortunately, the classic instruments of assuring veracity—oaths and cross examination—are not effective tools to obtain the truth about foreign law. Indeed, the question may not be whether the expert on foreign law is credible or reliable. Rather, it is possible that legal experts arrive at different conclusions on the law of a foreign legal system in the best of faith; such is certainly the case when reasonable minds disagree about the applicability or meaning of some domestic law.

To resolve conflicting expert testimony, then, the court may believe one expert over the other because of their respective qualifications. But judging the messenger rather than the message is notoriously flawed. "Credentials . . . are an imperfect proxy for knowledge under the best of circumstances, and far worse in court where they become yet another factor for lawyers to manipulate."[9] Moreover, there is

---

6   When the content of foreign law is a question of fact, the burden of proving it rests with the parties. We address this again below.

7   Fed. R. Civ. P. 44.1.

8   Learned Hand, *Historical and Practical Considerations Regarding Expert Testimony*, 15 Harv. L. Rev. 40, 54 (1902).

9   Samuel R. Gross, *Expert Evidence*, 1991 Wis. L. Rev. 1113, 1182–83 (1991).

randomness and unpredictability since it is not clear exactly what qualifications are preferred. Occasionally judges prefer an expert who practices in the foreign legal system; others suggest that an *American* lawyer who is learned in the law of a foreign country may be better situated to locate the foreign law within the context of the pending litigation. Even with this latter approach, which expert should you call: the mid-career practitioner from a U.S. office of an international law firm who has considerable first-hand experience in the foreign country or the senior comparative law professor from the University of North Carolina who has studied that foreign legal system in depth? Experience and expertise can be difficult to compare; for the same reason, these measures can be inadequate criteria for finding one foreign law expert more credible than another.

The Federal Rule empowers the court to ascertain the foreign law itself. In fact, Rule 44.1's invitation to consider "any relevant material" suggests that the court can (or perhaps even should) play an active role in the process of ascertaining foreign law. After all, the court has the ultimate responsibility for arriving at a correct decision on the content of foreign law. Yet an independent investigation into the content of foreign law—and all of that law's attendant context—is unappealing to "[m]ost judges [who] do not have the time, the knowledge, or scholarly predilection to undertake their own research."[10] As one judge expressed, "We have quite a few things to do besides decoding the *Código Civil*."[11]

"Most judges strive mightily to avoid even having to glance at foreign laws."[12] The artful dodge of foreign law comes in many forms. The most popular is the *forum non conveniens* dismissal. In federal courts and in most state courts, judges have the authority to dismiss a case on grounds of *forum non conveniens*. (*See* Chapter 21.) The difficulty in applying foreign law is one of more than a dozen factors that courts are instructed to consider when deciding *forum non conveniens* motions. (Ironically, however, a threshold determination that courts are instructed to address on *forum non conveniens* motions is the *adequacy* of the foreign forum—an inquiry that requires some engagement with the foreign law and the foreign legal system.)

Another way for judges (or parties) to avoid the application of foreign law is to leverage the discretion that inheres in most of the choice of law methodologies. (*See* Chapters 3–8.) Some of the methodologies even include the difficulty of applying foreign law as a formal consideration. (*See* Chapters 7 and 8.) Of course the escape devices—characterization, renvoi, the distinction between substance and proce-

---

10   Symeon C. Symeonides, *Choice of Law in the American Courts in 2010: Twenty-Fourth Annual Survey*, 59 Am. J. Comp. L. 303, 393 (2011).

11   Milton Pollack, *Proof of Foreign Law*, 26 Am. J. Comp. L. 470, 471 (1978).

12   Adler, *supra*, 19 Mich. J. Int'l L. at 171.

dure, and the public policy exception—also facilitate the application of forum law even when foreign law otherwise applies. (*See* Chapters 2, 4, 10, 11, and 12.)

Further still, on occasions where judges purport to be applying foreign law, a host of implausible presumptions and remarkable fictions invade the judicial process. A presumption of similarity, for example, enables courts to conclude that, absent compelling evidence to the contrary, foreign law is the same as forum law.[13] And of course the more difficult it is to ascertain foreign law, the more difficult it is to overcome this presumption. Hence a court may presume (absent proof to the contrary) that Mexico and Arizona have the same property laws, or that Illinois and Germany have the same commercial law.[14] For decades, courts presumed that, absent contrary proof, all so-called "civilized" countries had essentially the same laws.[15]

Much like adopting a presumption, some courts assign a burden to prove foreign law. First, most judges will not consider foreign law until one of the parties invokes it. And, prior to 1966, in federal court, the content of foreign law was a question of fact that the parties had to prove. (In many state courts, it still is a question of fact.) Accordingly, if the issue of foreign law was not raised, or if the content of foreign law was not proven to the satisfaction of the judge, the party's failure of proof would lead either the application of forum (or perhaps some other state's) law or to dismissal of the case. The harshness of a dismissal is what led to many of the presumptions and fictions described above.

In 1966, Rule 44.1 of the Federal Rules of Civil Procedure was promulgated "to make the process of determining alien law identical with the method of ascertaining domestic law to the extent possible to do so."[16] Importantly, this makes the

---

13 1 Ehrenzweig, *supra* at 187 (suggesting that the presumption is "nothing but a crude fiction" and *manifestamente priva di senso*). *See also* Gregory S. Alexander, *The Application and Avoidance of Foreign Law in the Law of Conflicts*, 70 Nw. U. L. Rev. 602, 610, 613 (1976) (discussing the "sophistry of presumptions," which are 'little more than a thin disguise for the application of the forum's law. . . .").

14 *See, e.g., Butler v. IMA Regiomontana S.A. de C.V.*, 210 F.3d 381 (9th Cir. 2000); *In re Griffin Trading Co.*, 399 F.R. 862, 865 (Bankr. N.D. Ill. 2009). *See also Tidewater Oil Co. v. Waller*, 302 F.2d 638 (10th Cir. 1962) (regarding Turkish and Oklahoma tort and workers' compensation laws).

15 *See E. Gerli & Co. v. Cunard S.S. Co.*, 48 F.2d 115 (2nd Cir. 1931) ("The extent of our right to make any assumptions about the law of another country depends upon the country and the question involved; in common-law countries we may go further than in civil law; in civilized, than in backward or barbarous. We can say more in the case of France or Italy, than of Abyssinia, or Afghanistan. . . ; less, than in the in the case of England or Australia. No doubt, when there is no evidence, we are always much limited in cases where the common law does not prevail; but we are not quite without power in commercial matters arising in one of the great commercial countries of Western Europe. . . . We can assume that in Italy an agreement of carriage creates obligations, generally measured by the language used. . . . We may not, however, assume anything as to how far a carrier by contract is allowed to set a value upon the goods he carries; as to that we know nothing.")

16 9 CHARLES ALAN WRIGHT & ARTHUR R. MILLER, FEDERAL PRACTICE AND PROCEDURE § 2444 (1971).

application of foreign law (in *federal* courts) a question of law. Yet it is not entirely clear whether this relieves the parties of the task of proving the law of a foreign country. On one hand, Rule 44.1 authorizes but does not require the judge to do independent research. On the other hand, because foreign law is a question of law, it may be incumbent upon the court to find and apply foreign law once it becomes apparent that it governs. As a practical matter, most federal judges leave it up to the lawyers to raise and to describe the foreign law; often, courts then avoid the question of foreign law by blaming the parties for failures of proof.

Finally, we want to return to an issue that we first raised in Chapter 9 with respect to choice of law clauses. Respect for party autonomy and enthusiasm for the enforcement of choice of law clauses could lead to more applications of foreign law (as legal systems compete for parties' attention in choice of law clauses through substantive legal regimes) and to more applications of non-sovereign laws. With respect to the latter, a choice of law clause could identify as the applicable law "the customary and best practices of commerce." Or that clause could choose a law prepared by an institution like a chamber of commerce, industry guild, or law school. Proving the content of non-sovereign law raises interesting questions that future litigators will surely engage.

FROM THE COURTS

PENGBO FU v. YONGXIAO FU

Appellate Court of Illinois
2017 IL App (1st) 162958-U (June 29, 2017)

JUSTICE HOWSE.

Plaintiff, Pengbo Fu, brought suit for breach of a gift agreement against his son, defendant Yongxiao Fu. Both parties are citizens of the People's Republic of China (PRC), though defendant is currently a resident of Massachusetts. The parties entered into the gift agreement in the PRC, and the agreement specifies PRC law governs its terms. Plaintiff brought suit in Cook County because the money at issue in the litigation was being held by the International Bank of Chicago. The trial court found plaintiff's complaint deficient on its face for failure to establish the fact of the foreign law supporting the basis of plaintiff's claim, and found that plaintiff's interpretation of PRC law was immoral and against public policy. For the reasons that follow we affirm the judgment of the trial court.

Background

On February 27, 2012, in China, the parties entered into a gift agreement where plaintiff agreed to "make a free and unconditional gift" of $590,000 to defendant so that defendant could pursue an EB-5 Visa to immigrate to the United States. The gift agreement is written in Chinese and an English translation is provided in the record. The immigration and Nationality Act provides for the allocation of visas granting immigrant status to foreign nationals entering the United States for the purpose of engaging in a commercial enterprise through capital investment in a U.S. business. 8 U.S.C. § 1153 (2006). Title 8 of the Code of Federal Regulations governs the procedure for employment creation aliens to apply for an EB-5 Visa. 8 C.F.R. § 204.6 (2016). Under the Code, an alien must invest at least $500,000 "in a targeted employment area within the United States" to be considered for an EB-5 Visa. *Id.* Additionally, the alien must "show that he has invested his own capital obtained through lawful means." *Matter of Ho*, 22 I&N Dec. 206, 210 (AAO 1998). In May 2012, defendant attempted to obtain an EB-5 visa by investing $500,000 in a project to finance construction of a hotel and conference center near O'Hare Airport. In May 2013, the SEC found the project was fraudulent and defendant was able to recover his money. Defendant then informed plaintiff of his failure to obtain an EB-5 visa and that defendant would find another project to invest in. Plaintiff did not seek the return of his gift at that time.

In July 2013, defendant invested $500,000 in an entity known as Lake 1 LLC for the construction of a garment manufacturing and retail facility in Melrose Park, Illinois. Defendant transferred the funds to the Lake 1 LLC EB-5 Escrow Account at the International Bank of Chicago. On February 3, 2016, the United States denied EB-5 approval for the Lake 1 LLC project. Lake 1 LLC made no claim on defendant's investment held in the escrow account.

On March 10, 2016, defendant signed an agreement to invest $500,000 in an EB-5 project for development of an apartment complex in New York. On March 21, 2016, and again on March 23, plaintiff's attorneys wrote to the International Bank of Chicago to inform them of a dispute over the funds being held in the Lake 1 LLC EB5 Escrow Account and claimed that the funds belonged to plaintiff. Defendant sought to withdraw the money from the escrow account to invest in the New York project, but the International

Bank of Chicago refused to release the funds to defendant because of the dispute with plaintiff.

On May 17, 2016, plaintiff filed a petition in a Shanghai court in the PRC to revoke the gift agreement. On May 20, 2016, plaintiff filed the current suit to revoke the gift agreement and recover $500,000 from the escrow account. On May 31, 2016, the PRC court entered an order freezing the funds in the escrow account.

Plaintiff's complaint in the Cook County circuit court claimed that "plaintiff has never relinquished rights over the EB-5 Money pursuant to the laws of the [PRC]." Plaintiff argued defendant breached the "contract" of the gift agreement where defendant was to use the gift to obtain an EB-5 visa, but defendant failed to do so. Plaintiff attached to the complaint a translation of the gift agreement as well as translations of his claim in the Shanghai court. Plaintiff's litigation in the Shanghai court claimed two grounds for his revocation of the gift agreement under Article 192 of the Contract Law of the PRC: (1) under paragraph 2 of Article 192, a donee "has the obligation to support the donor but does not fulfill it"; and, (2) under paragraph 3 of Article 192, a donee "does not fulfill the obligations as stipulated in the gift agreement." Plaintiff claimed defendant did not fulfill his obligations because defendant is not supporting his parents and refused to talk with them. Plaintiff also claimed defendant was not fulfilling his obligations under the gift agreement because plaintiff did not obtain an EB-5 visa, and his current pursuits of an EB-5 visa include his spouse, arguing that the third party beneficiary violates the gift agreement.

On August 4, 2016, defendant filed a motion to dismiss plaintiff's complaint. . . . Defendant argued plaintiff's complaint failed to adequately plead PRC law, failed to state a claim under Illinois law, and the defendant was complying with the terms of the gift agreement. Plaintiff replied to the motion by arguing PRC law governed the terms of the gift agreement and PRC law allowed for the revocation of gifts. Plaintiff argued that under the Contract Law of the PRC, a gift agreement is a contract that may be revoked under Article 192 if "(1) the donee seriously harms or infringes the rights or interests of the donor or the donor's close relatives; (2) the donee has an obligation to provide for the donor but fails to fulfill this obligation; or (3) the donee does not perform obligations agreed upon in the gift contract." Plaintiff did not provide citation to how "a free and unconditional gift" could be revoked. Plaintiff claimed defendant violated the Contract Law of the PRC by harming plaintiff through defendant's perceived "inconsiderate behavior towards plaintiff" because defendant had become estranged from plaintiff. Plaintiff also claimed that whether defendant was in pursuit of another EB-5 visa was immaterial due to plaintiff's other claim and possible political exigencies. Plaintiff further argued defendant violated the Marriage Law of the PRC by not fulfilling his duty to support plaintiff. Plaintiff included an affidavit from his attorney in the PRC. The attorney wrote that she filed plaintiff's claim in a Shanghai court and included references to two PRC cases with only a sparse description of both. The trial court noted for one case, "[n]o factual details were given," and that the other dealt with a failed marriage agreement. Plaintiff also attached English translations of the Contract Law of the PRC and the Marriage Law of the PRC.

On October 11, 2016, the trial court dismissed plaintiff's complaint with prejudice, finding "[p]laintiff has not provided any evidence" for his interpretation of PRC law. The trial court noted it "cannot take judicial notice of a foreign country's law," that "[p]laintiff is required to plead and prove the law like any other fact," and that "[p]laintiff has not provided an iota of evidence to support his interpretation of Article 192 of the Contract Law and Article 21 of the Marriage Law." The trial court then decided plaintiff's "complaint must therefore be dismissed under Section 2–619." The court noted it "would have no problem enforcing the express language contained in Article 192 of the Contract Law and Article 21 of the Marriage Law, even though the language differs considerably from Illinois law on the subject. The strained interpretation of that language urged by plaintiff is another matter." The trial court went on to explain plaintiff's improperly pled interpretation of PRC law was "oppressive, immoral, and impolitic" and dismissed plaintiff's claims with prejudice as unenforceable under Illinois law. This appeal followed.

Analysis

. . . Plaintiff argues that he should be able to revoke his unconditional gift to his son because his son has become estranged from him. The trial court dismissed under 2–619, 735 ILCS 5/2–619 (West 2016), plaintiff's complaint for failure to state a claim for which he could obtain relief because plaintiff failed to adequately plead PRC law. However, on appeal, we review the judgment of the court, not its reasoning, so we may affirm for any reason found in the record.

The gift was delivered and accepted, so plaintiff made a valid gift to defendant. A valid *inter vivos* gift requires "delivery of the property by the donor to the donee, with the intent to pass the title to the donee absolutely and irrevocably, and the donor must relinquish all present and future dominion and power over the subject matter of the gift." *Pocius v. Fleck*, 13 Ill.2d 420, 427 (1958). Here, plaintiff transferred ownership of the money to defendant. Plaintiff clearly wrote that he wanted to "make a free and unconditional gift" of $590,000 to defendant so that defendant could pursue an EB-5 Visa to immigrate to the United States. Based on the language of the gift agreement, plaintiff intended to, and did, transfer ownership of $590,000 to defendant. Strictly enforcing the terms of the gift agreement, based on the agreed upon translation of the gift agreement, still results in dismissal of plaintiff's case because plaintiff made the gift free of any conditions. He cannot promise that he will give a gift unconditionally and only after he is unhappy with his son apply a condition on the gift so that he can revoke it. The gift was made with intent to permanently transfer the property, plaintiff delivered the property to defendant, and defendant accepted.

Plaintiff argues PRC law controls the gift agreement, and that PRC law gifts may be revocable. However, plaintiff never established this interpretation of PRC law in any of the pleadings. "The general rule is that a foreign law must be pleaded." *Christiansen v. William Graver Tank Works*, 223 Ill. 142, 151 (1906). In plaintiff's reply to defendant's motion to dismiss, plaintiff attached exhibits but didn't explain how they supported his argument that he has a claim against defendant under PRC law simply for defendant's allegedly "inconsiderate behavior towards plaintiff." "When an exhibit is attached to a complaint it becomes part of the complaint [citation], and when the allegations in the complaint differ from those shown in the exhibit attached to the complaint, the exhibit controls. [Citation.]" *Bianchi v. Savino Del Bene Int'l Freight Forwarders, Inc.*, 329 Ill. App. 3d 908, 921 (2002). However, in this case plaintiff only attached translations of PRC law without explaining why defendant's conduct constituted an actionable claim under that law. Plaintiff simply asserted PRC law governed the gift agreement, that gift agreements are contracts under PRC law, and that PRC law allows for revocation of gifts when the donee seriously harms the donor. This fails to explain how defendant's conduct could be characterized as seriously harming plaintiff under PRC law. . . . "[I]n Illinois, the laws of foreign countries must be pled and proven as any other fact. [Citation.]" *Id.* at 922. Plaintiff failed to do so here.

Plaintiff cannot revoke a "free and unconditional gift" under Illinois law and plaintiff failed to plead PRC law. Therefore, the complaint may be properly dismissed . . . because it failed to state a claim for which plaintiff could receive relief. . . .

[The court went on to hold that, even if PRC law allowed the plaintiff to revoke the gift, the court would refuse to enforce that law because it would violate the public policy of Illinois.]

COMMENTS AND QUESTIONS

1. The state of Illinois does not have a "proof of foreign law" rule analogue to Fed. R. Civ. P. 44.1. The state's common law, cited above, treats the content of foreign law as a question of fact (rather than a question of law). If the plaintiff's lawyer had anticipated this hurdle, s/he might have filed elsewhere. The Commonwealth of Massachusetts, for example, where the defendant resides, has a rule that resembles the federal rule. Would that have made a difference?

2. Even when a plaintiff carries the burden of proof on an issue, *when* that burden must be satisfied is a separate question. Justice Howse observed that "plaintiff never established this interpretation of PRC law in any of the pleadings." Which other questions of fact must be "established" in the pleadings? If Justice Howse was referring to the *pleading* burden, rather than the burden of *proof*, did the plaintiff satisfy that burden by referencing the relevant law and attaching the affidavit and cases?

3. The court was moved by the parties' characterization of the gift as "free and unconditional." But even under basic principles of American property law a gift can be impeached for fraud, duress, or mistake. Is that relevant here?

4. What significance does the court give to the fact that a "PRC court had entered an order freezing the funds in the escrow account"?

5. Imagine that the court were informed by an expert that, under Chinese law, the *son* had the burden of proving that he had *not* breached the contract. Should this shift in the ultimate burden of proof also shift the burden of proof with respect to the content of the foreign law itself?

6. The court criticized the plaintiffs for not explaining the content of their submissions with respect to Chinese law. If the trial judge had these questions, why not have oral argument on the motion and ask the questions (rather than dismiss the case)? What is the lesson for litigators here?

7. The United States Supreme Court recently decided a case regarding the extent to which a federal court should (or must) defer to a foreign government's testimony about the content of its law. *Animal Science Prods., Inc. v. Hebei Welcome Pharm. Co. Ltd.*, __ U.S. __, 138 S. Ct. 1865 (2018). The Court concluded that such testimony would be credible and important evidence though not dispositive. Would the attorney general (or governor or secretary of state or chief justice of the courts) of, say, Iowa be an authoritative source for the content of Iowa law?

FROM THE COURTS

PANAM MANAGEMENT GROUP, INC. v. PEÑA

U.S. District Court for the Eastern District of New York
2011 WL 3423338 (E.D.N.Y. August 4, 2011)

BIANCO, DISTRICT JUDGE.

Plaintiff Panam Management Group ("Panam") brings this diversity action alleging breach of contract and unjust enrichment. The defendants are Raymond Peña, Doris Peña, Eladio Sanchez, Juan Carlos Lopez (collectively the "individual defendants"), Yuma Bay Development Corporation ("Yuma Bay"), Brigid Lenderborg, and Lenderborg Lending Service.

The individual defendants, who are sued in their official capacity as officers of Yuma Bay, have renewed their motion to dismiss the Second Amended Complaint pursuant to Fed. R. Civ. P. 12(b), arguing that Yuma Bay's corporate veil cannot be pierced under either Dominican or Panamanian law. Plaintiff opposes, relying on New York law. . . .

I. Background

[Panam is a real estate marketing company with offices in New York and the Dominican Republic. On January 20, 2006, Panam executed a predevelopment marketing contract with defendant Yuma Bay for the promotion and sale of residential units at a resort called the "Yuma Bay Resort Village" in the Dominican Republic. Pursuant to this contract, Panam was to be the defendants' exclusive real estate marketing agent and marketing firm until December 31, 2009. The agreement had a choice of law clause selecting Dominican law.

Panam alleges that it performed its obligations pursuant to this agreement, which included brokering the sale of approximately 59 pre-construction residential sales contracts between Yuma Bay and real estate investors between January 2006 and August 2006.

According to the complaint, Yuma Bay failed to perform. Plaintiffs allege that the Yuma Bay Resort Village did not exist, that defendants failed to disclose to the investors that they were unable to obtain necessary government approval to develop the land, and that defendants were not registered to do business in the Dominican Republic.

The defendants named in the Second Amended Complaint (SAC) include Yuma Bay, the aforementioned individual defendants (various directors and officers of Yuma Bay), and financial affiliates. Panam asserts claims of its own and on behalf of 27 of the investors who have assigned to Panama their claims against Yuma Bay. Prior iterations of the complaint included causes of action for fraud and misrepresentation, conversion, unjust enrichment and others; the SAC, however, pursues claims only for breach of contract and unjust enrichment. Damages include the investors' $192,744 in down payments, 8% commission on total sales owed Panam under the marketing contract, and $500,000 in liquidated damages.

Panam's claims against the individual defendants rely on a theory of piercing the corporate veil. Ordinarily, the people who own and run corporations (like Yuma Bay) cannot be held personally responsible for the debts of the business. Exceptions to that general principle are referred to as piercing the corporate veil. When the veil is pierced, courts ignore the limited liability of a corporation and hold its officers, directors, and shareholders personally liable for its debts.

Yuma Bay is incorporated in Panama.

The individual defendants moved to dismiss Panam's complaint on the ground that, because the corporate veil could not be pierced, the complaint failed to state a claim against the individual defendants. Plaintiffs argued that New York law applied and that the standard for piercing the corporate veil was met.]

[II.] Discussion

For the reasons set forth below, plaintiff's claims against the individual defendants must be dismissed. As an initial matter Panamanian law applies to the issue of veil-piercing. However, in an abundance of caution, the Court concludes that Yuma Bay's corporate veil cannot be pierced under Panamanian, Dominican, or New York law.

A. Choice-of-Law

The individual defendants argue that Dominican law should apply to the issue of veil-piercing based on the choice-of-law clause in the January 2006 Agreement. In the alternative, they argue that Panamanian law should apply. Plaintiff, on the other hand, asserts that New York law should apply because: (1) all the transactions under the January 2006 Agreement took place in New York; [and] (2) the individual defendants cannot rely on Panamanian law "for protection" because Yuma Bay did not renew its corporate registration in Panama. . . .

As an initial matter, the Court finds unpersuasive plaintiff's argument that the individual defendants cannot rely on Panamanian law because Yuma Bay did not renew its corporate registration in Panama. Plaintiff does not point to any statutes or caselaw in support of its argument. The individual defendants admit that Yuma Bay did not pay its annual corporate registration fee in Panama in 2008, 2009, and 2010. However, as the individual defendants point out, under Panamanian Law No. 49 of September 17, 2009, a company is not automatically dissolved under Panamanian law until it fails to pay the annual registration fee for ten consecutive years.[2] Thus, Yuma Bay remains a corporation registered under the laws of Panama and can therefore rely on Panamanian law to the extent it is applicable. . . .

The Court concludes that Panamanian law must apply to the issue of veil-piercing based on New York's choice-of-law rules. "Federal courts exercising diversity jurisdiction apply the choice-of-law rules of the forum state, here New York, to decide which state's substantive law governs." *Celle v. Filipino Reporter Enterprises, Inc.*, 209 F.3d 163, 175 (2d Cir. 2000). New

---

2   This Court can rely on the individual defendants to provide the relevant excerpts of Panamanian law even without reliance on expert testimony. . . .

York's choice-of-law doctrine dictates that "the law of the state of incorporation determines when the corporate form will be disregarded." *Fletcher v. Atex, Inc.*, 68 F.3d 1451, 1456 (2d Cir. 1995). This is so because "the state of incorporation has the greater interest in determining when and if that insulation is to be stripped away." *Kalb, Voorhis & Co. v. Am. Fin. Corp.*, 8 F.3d 130, 132 (2d Cir. 1993). The law of the state of incorporation applies to the veil-piercing analysis even if there is a choice-of-law provision in a contract that governs the relationship between the parties. *Id.* ("The choice of law provision in the debentures are irrelevant. The issue is the limited liability of shareholders of a corporation—not Circle K's obligations under the debentures. The law of the state of incorporation determines when the corporate form will be disregarded. . . .").

In this case, it is apparent that Yuma Bay is incorporated in the Republic of Panama. Thus, Panama's veil-piercing doctrine is controlling in this case. . . .

B. Piercing the Corporate Veil

Under Fed. R. Civ. P. 44.1, which "controls determinations of foreign law in federal court[,] . . . the court may consider any relevant material or source, including testimony, whether or not submitted by a party or admissible under the Federal Rules of Evidence" in determining foreign law. Courts may conduct "their own independent research to determine foreign law[,] . . . [but] the party claiming foreign law applies carries . . . the burden of proving foreign law to enable the district court to apply it in a particular case." *Bigio v. Coca-Cola Co.*, 2010 WL 3377503, at *4 (S.D.N.Y. Aug. 23, 2010). Either oral or written testimony from expert witnesses who are "not required to meet any special qualifications" is the "basic mode of proving foreign law" *Bigio*, 2010 WL 3377503, at *4, though such reports "are not necessary . . . to carry the [ ] burden of establishing aspects of foreign law." *In re Alstom SA Sec. Litig.*, 253 F.R.D. 266, 291 (S.D.N.Y. 2008). However, "[t]he purpose of expert testimony . . . is to aid the Court in determining the content of the applicable foreign law—not to apply it to the facts of the case. Furthermore, the Court is not obliged to credit the parties' partisan application of the governing law." *Bigio*, 2010 WL 3377503, at *4. The Court may also rely on the decisions of other courts in its analysis of foreign law. *See In re Alston SA Sec. Litig.*, 253 F.R.D. at 291.[4]

---

4   The Court notes that plaintiff has failed to provide any evidence regarding Panamanian or Dominican law on veil-piercing, whether in the form of expert reports or otherwise.

1. Panamanian Law

The individual defendants have satisfied their burden of demonstrating that veil-piercing is not available in this case under Panamanian law. Under Law No. 32 of February 26, 1927 (which relates to shareholder liability), in conjunction with Section 444 of the commercial Code of the Republic of Panama, "shareholders, directors, and officers, are not liable to pay with their personal assets for their rights and obligations acquired by the corporation, regardless of whether they acted on behalf of the corporation." (Defs.' Mem. Ex. E at 4. (Legal Opinion from Cedabo Cedeño Abogados).) Specifically, Section 444 states:

> Directors shall not assume any personal liability for the corporation's obligations, but they shall be liable personally or jointly and severally, as the case may be, to the corporation and to third parties: for the validity of the payments made by the shareholders, for the real existence of the dividends decided, for the good management of the accounting and, in general for the good or bad performance of their mandate and any violation of any law, the Articles of Incorporation, the Bylaws or any resolution by the General Meeting. . . . Liability may only be demanded based on a resolution by the Shareholders' General Meeting.

According to the expert opinion provided by the individual defendants,

> Panamanian legislation does not provide for mechanisms to pierce the Corporate Veil . . . . [U]nder exceptional circumstances [Panama's] Supreme Court of Justice has allowed it . . . [where] a corporation has been used for the sole purpose of defrauding third parties or violating the law, thus resulting in a case of abuse of the legal personality. . . . The criterion used by [the courts] to pierce the corporate veil always has, as a common denominator, the fact that the [shareholders or directors] have not respected the legal entity, as well as the breach of the principle of the separation of personalities, in order to thus punish those hiding behind it.

Legal Opinion from Cedabo Cedeño Abogados at 6–7. According to the Supreme Court of Justice, piercing of the corporate veil "is an exceptional measure that is only admissible on a provisional basis for purposes of interim relief. . . ." (*Id.* at 7.) In sum, the corporate veil may be pierced under Panamanian law where it is demonstrated that directors or shareholders controlled and used the corporation for the sole purpose of perpetrating fraud or "violating the law," thereby abusing the corporate form and hiding behind it to avoid liability.

Plaintiff has failed to allege conduct that rises to the level of abuse of the corporate form as required under Panamanian law to pierce the corporate veil. In the SAC plaintiff does not make any allegations of fraud against the individual defendants or Yuma Bay. Nor does plaintiff allege in the SAC that Yuma Bay was a corporation solely created for the purpose of perpetrating fraud or otherwise violating the law. In its opposition papers, plaintiff asserts that Yuma Bay misrepresented: (1) that it was a "corporation legitimately registered to do business in any jurisdiction"; (2) that it had the "corporate formalities including legal status and corporate capacity and capitaliza-tion" (where allegedly Yuma Bay' bank account, address, email and phone number belonged to the individual defendants and corporate funds were funneled "through to Defendants' trade company"); and (3) that it actually owned land in the Dominican Republic, which belonged to the individual defendants. Plaintiff attaches various documents to its opposition papers that allegedly support plaintiff's assertions. As an initial matter, the court cannot consider allegations and documents clearly outside of the pleadings on a motion to dismiss. However, even if these allegations are true, they are insufficient to pierce the corporate veil under Panamanian law.

First, these alleged misrepresentations do not suggest that the individual defendants "have not respected the legal entity" and breached the "principle of the separation of personalities" to perpetrate fraud. In fact, the allega-tions in plaintiff's opposition largely focus on misrepresentations by Yuma Bay without explaining how the individual defendants were involved in the alleged misrepresentations.[6] Second, plaintiff does not allege in its opposi-tion papers that Yuma Bay was created for the sole purpose of perpetrating fraud.[7] In sum, the Court concludes that Yuma Bay's corporate veil cannot be pierced under Panamanian law because plaintiff has failed to either allege

---

6   Plaintiff's sole allegation against the individual defendants is that they "did not disclose to Plaintiff that [Yuma Bay] was not legally able to do business in the State of Florida, New York, nor the Dominican Republic." First, this statement is entirely conclusory. Second, it is at least partially incorrect because Yuma Bay was able to do business in the Dominican Republic. In any event, it does not suggest that Yuma Bay was created for the sole purpose of perpetrating fraud.

7   The individual defendants assert that all of the allegations made by plaintiff in its opposition are false, citing to and attaching documents outside of the SAC. As noted above, the Court cannot consider matters outside of the pleadings on a motion to dismiss. However, even if plaintiff's allegations were true, they are insufficient to pierce the corporate veil for the reasons stated above.

that Yuma Bay was created for the purpose of perpetrating fraud or that the individual defendants abused the corporate form to perpetrate that fraud. . . .

2. Dominican Law

Yuma Bay's corporate veil also cannot be pierced under Dominican law. The individual defendants provided two reports from Dominican attorneys explaining Dominican law on veil-piercing. According to both reports, this Court has to look to the Commercial Code of the Dominican Republic of 2006, the year the January 2006 Agreement was executed. (Defs.' Mem. Ex. C at 2 (Legal Opinion of José Gregori Cabrera Cuello), Ex. D at 2 (Legal Opinion from E&M International Consulting, S.A.).) Under Section 32 of the Commercial Code of 2006, Board Members "do not assume, by reason of management, any personal or joint-and-several obligation related to the company's commitments" so that they "may not be deemed to be personally liable, whether for their management of or jointly and severally, for the contractual and/or financial commitments of the company, even if such board members have acted as the[ ] company's attorneys-in-fact or legal representatives." (*Id.* Ex. C at 2; *see also* Ex. D at 2.)[8] While Law No. 479–08 enacted on December 12, 2008 provides for piercing the corporate veil in cases of fraud, among others, the law is not retroactive and is "only applicable to any legal relationship formed or situation that in fact took place" after the enactment of the new veil-piercing law. (*Id.* Ex. D at 2; Defs.' Mem. at 5; Defs.' Reply Ex. C at 1.) Since the conduct complained of, along with the signing of the January 2006 Agreement, took place prior to the enactment of Law No. 479–08, that law is inapplicable to this case. Nor did plaintiff argue in its opposition papers that the 2008 law should apply here. In fact, plaintiff did not discuss Dominican law at all. Thus, it is apparent that the corporate veil cannot be pierced in this case under Dominican law.

3. New York Law

Finally, plaintiff cannot pierce Yuma Bay's corporate veil under New York law. "Generally . . . piercing the corporate veil requires a showing that: (1) the owners exercised complete domination of the corporation in respect to the transaction attacked; and (2) that such domination was used to commit a fraud or wrong against the plaintiff which resulted in the plaintiff's injury." *Morris v. N.Y. State Dep't of Taxation and Fin.*, 623 N.E.2d 1157,

---

8   Additionally, under Section 33 of the Commercial Code of 2006, shareholders "are only liable for the loss of the capital they hold in the company." (*Id.* Ex. C at 2; *see also id.* Ex. D at 2.)

1160–61 (N.Y. 1993). . . . To satisfy the second prong set out in *Morris*, plaintiff must demonstrate "(1) the existence of a wrongful or unjust act toward that party, and (2) that the act caused that party's harm." *JSC Foreign Econ. Ass'n Technostroyexport v. Int'l Dev. & Trade Services, Inc.*, 386 F.Supp.2d 461, 465 (S.D.N.Y. 2005).

Plaintiff cannot satisfy those requirements based upon plaintiff's allegations in the Second Amended Complaint. As noted above, plaintiff does not allege fraud or domination by the individual defendants in the SAC. Plaintiff's allegations relating to fraud and domination are entirely in its opposition papers, and cannot be considered on a motion to dismiss. In any event, even if the Court considers them and assumes them to be true, plaintiff's reliance on New York's corporate veil-piercing doctrine is misplaced for the same reasons as discussed *supra* with respect to Panamanian law. In particular, plaintiff has failed to allege "complete domination" with respect to the "transaction attacked." In fact, it is not clear what "transaction" plaintiff is actually taking issue with. On the one hand, plaintiff's SAC and opposition focus on breach of contract but, on the other hand plaintiff's opposition also alleges fraudulent conduct on the part of Yuma Bay. To the extent plaintiff is suggesting that it was fraudulently induced to enter into the January 2006 Agreement, there are no specific allegations that the individual defendants were somehow involved in the contract negotiations. With respect to claims of fraud, once again there are no allegations that the individual defendants were somehow involved in misrepresenting certain information to plaintiff. . . .

[III.] Conclusion

For the reasons set forth above, the Court grants the individual defendants' motion to dismiss. The remaining parties shall proceed with discovery at the direction of Magistrate Judge Lindsay.

COMMENTS AND QUESTIONS

1. Remember the paramount concern regarding the "reasonable expectation of the parties" with respect to choice of law clauses. (*See* Chapter 9.) Why an "exception," then, for corporate internal affairs? (*See* Chapter 17.)

2. In footnote 4 the court observed that the plaintiff offered no proof of the content of the potentially applicable foreign laws. Why might it be a strategic decision for a lawyer to offer no proof?

3. Why didn't the Second Amended Complaint include allegations of fraud to satisfy the prima facie requirements of the Panamanian law with respect to piercing the corporate veil?

4. Oddities about this case prompted the casebook authors to find the rest of the story. The plaintiff's lawyer, a New York lawyer named Edward Robert Adams, was himself a fraudster. The plaintiff in this case, Panam Management Group, was part of the larger scam administered by Adams and a former New York Police Department sergeant. Adams was later indicted, sent to prison, and disbarred. *See generally* New York Attorney Pleads Guilty to Participating in Multi-Million Dollar Real Estate Fraud Scheme, https://www.justice.gov/usao-sdny/pr/new-york-attorney-pleads-guilty-participating-multi-million-dollar-real-estate-fraud (June 10, 2013) (with links to the indictment).

FROM THE COURTS

BODUM USA, INC. v. LA CAFETIERE, INC.

U.S. Court of Appeals for the Seventh Circuit
621 F.3d 624 (7th Cir. 2010)

EASTERBROOK, CHIEF JUDGE.

From the mid-1950s through 1991, Société de Anciens Etablissements Martin S.A. ("Martin") distributed a successful French-press coffee maker known as the Chambord. A French-press coffee maker (called a cafetière à piston in France) is a carafe in which hot water is mixed with coffee grounds.

When the brewing is complete, a mesh screen attached to a rod drives the grounds to the bottom of the carafe. Clear coffee then can be poured from the top. In 1991 Bodum Holding purchased all of Martin's stock. Today subsidiaries of Bodum Holding sell throughout the world coffee makers that use the Chambord design and name.

Martin's principal investor and manager was Louis-James de Viel Castel, who had other businesses. One of these, the British firm Household Articles Ltd., sold a French-press coffee maker that it called La Cafetière, which closely resembles the Chambord design. Viel Castel wanted to continue Household's business after Bodum bought Martin. So Viel Castel and Jørgen Jepsen Bodum, the main investor in Bodum Holding, negotiated. An early draft agreement provided that Household could sell the Chambord design in the United Kingdom, but nowhere else. After several rounds of revisions, however, the agreement provided that Household would never sell a French-press coffee maker in France, that it would not use the trade names Chambord or Melior, and that for four years it would not distribute through the importers, distributors, or agents that Martin employed during 1990–91. The agreement was signed, and Bodum Holding acquired Martin.

La Cafetière, Inc., was incorporated in Illinois in 2006 to serve as the distributor of Household's products in the United States. One of these is the La Cafetière model, which carries the name "Classic" in this country. To avoid confusion between the corporation (which since 2008 has been one of Household's subsidiaries) and the product, we refer to the distributor as "Household." Household has itself been renamed The Greenfield Group, but we stick with the original name for simplicity. Bodum Holding's U.S. distributor (Bodum USA, Inc.) filed this suit under federal and state law, contending that the sale of any coffee maker similar to the Chambord design violates Bodum's common-law trade dress. Trade dress, a distinctive appearance that enables consumers to identify a product's maker, is a form of trademark. The Chambord design is not registered as Bodum's trademark, but common-law marks may be enforced under both 15 U.S.C. § 1125(a), a part of the Lanham Act, and 815 ILCS 510/2(a). Household contends that the 1991 agreement permits it to sell the La Cafetière design anywhere in the world, except France, provided that it does not use the words Chambord or Melior—and Household has never used either of those marks. The district court agreed with this contention and granted summary judgment in Household's favor.

The Chambord design and the La Cafetière design are indeed similar, and although they are not identical a casual coffee drinker (or purchaser) would have trouble telling them apart. . . .

Bodum assumes that the proprietor of any distinctive design has an intellectual-property right in this design, which it alone can sell. That assumption is unwarranted. The Chambord design is distinctive—so much so that Martin received a design patent for it—but the patent expired many years ago. After a patent expires, other firms are free to copy the design to the last detail in order to increase competition and drive down the price that consumers pay. A distinctive design may be protected as a trademark only if it has acquired secondary meaning—that is, if consumers associate the design with a particular manufacturer—and the design's identifying aspects are not functional. Bodum has not produced evidence that the Chambord design has secondary meaning, so that purchasers of a La Cafetière coffee maker think that they are getting one of Bodum's products. But because Household has not asked us to affirm the district court on this ground we move on to the contract.

Here is the critical language, from Article 4 of the contract:

> In consideration of the compensation paid to Stockholder [Viel Castel] for the stocks of [Martin,] Stockholder guarantees, limited to the agreed compensation, see Article 2, that he shall not—for a period of four (4) years—be engaged directly or indirectly in any commercial business related to manufacturing or distributing [Martin's] products. . . .

> Notwithstanding Article 4 [Bodum Holding] agrees that Stockholder through Household . . . can manufacture and distribute any products similar to [Martin's] products outside of France. It is expressly understood that Household [ ] is not entitled, directly or indirectly, to any such activity in France, and that Household [ ] furthermore is not entitled, directly or indirectly, globally to manufacture and/or distribute coffeepots under the trade marks and/ or brand names of "Melior" and "Chambord," held by [Martin]. Stockholder agrees that Household [ ] is not entitled to use for a period of four (4) years the importers, distributors, and agents which [Martin] uses and/or has used the last year. Any violation of these obligations will constitute a breach of Stockholder's obligation according to Article 4.

The parties agree that this is an accurate translation of the French original, and that French substantive law governs its interpretation. The district judge thought that the contract is clear and that Household can sell its La Cafetière outside of France, if it does not use the Chambord or Melior names. Even if the La Cafetière or Classic model is identical to the Chambord model (which it is not . . .), a thing identical to something else also is "similar" to it.

Bodum contends that, under French law, the parties' intent prevails over the written word. Article 1156 of the French Civil Code provides: "One must in agreements seek what the common intention of the contracting parties was, rather than pay attention to the literal meaning of the terms." (Again this is an agreed translation, as are all other translations in this opinion.) Jørgen Bodum has submitted an affidavit declaring that he understood the contract to limit Household's sales of the La Cafetière model to the United Kingdom and Australia. This means, Bodum Holding insists, that there must be a trial to determine the parties' intent. It supports this position with the declaration of Pierre-Yves Gautier, a Professor of Law at Université Panthéon-Assas Paris II, who Bodum tenders as an expert on French law. Household has replied with declarations from two experts of its own.

Although Fed. R. Civ. P. 44.1 provides that courts may consider expert testimony when deciding questions of foreign law, it does not compel them to do so—for the Rule says that judges "may" rather than "must" receive expert testimony and adds that courts may consider "any relevant material or source." Judges should use the best of the available sources. The Committee Note in 1966, when Rule 44.1 was adopted, explains that a court "may engage in its own research and consider any relevant material thus found. The court may have at its disposal better foreign law materials than counsel have presented, or may wish to reexamine and amplify material that has been presented by counsel in partisan fashion or in insufficient detail."

Sometimes federal courts must interpret foreign statutes or decisions that have not been translated into English or glossed in treaties or other sources. Then experts' declarations and testimony may be essential. But French law, and the law of most other nations that engage in extensive international commerce, is widely available in English. Judges can use not only accepted (sometimes official) translations of statutes and decisions but also ample secondary literature, such as treatises and scholarly commentary. It is no more necessary to resort to expert declarations about the law of France than about the law of Louisiana, which had its origins in the French civil code, or the law of Puerto Rico, whose origins are in the Spanish civil code. No federal judge would admit "expert" declarations about the meaning of Louisiana law in a commercial case.

Trying to establish foreign law through experts' declarations not only is expensive (experts must be located and paid) but also adds an adversary's spin, which the court then must discount. Published sources such as treatises do not have the slant that characterizes the warring declarations presented in this case. Because objective, English-language descriptions of French law are readily available, we prefer them to the parties' declarations.

Article 1156 says that courts must seek the parties' "common intention"— which means their *joint* intent, not one side's unilateral version. Jørgen Bodum tells us what he understood by the contract, but Bodum Holding does not offer any evidence of statements by Viel Castel that would tend to demonstrate that this view is mutual. For its part, Household offers the contract's negotiating history, which French law takes to be a more reliable indicator of intent than the litigants' self-serving declarations. *See* Alberto Luis Zuppi, *The Parol Evidence Rule: A Comparative Study of the Common Law, the Civil Law Tradition, and Lex Mercatoria*, 35 Ga. J. Int'l & Comp. L. 233, 258–60 (2007).

Article 1341 of the Civil Code forbids evidence about what negotiators said to one another—often called parol evidence in the United States. . . . This constraint illustrates the proposition that although

> as a general rule, French and German law do not limit the admissibility of relevant external materials in the process of interpretation . . . this does not mean that it is easy for a party to induce a court to rely on extrinsic evidence in order to "add to, vary or contradict a deed or other written instrument." On the contrary, civilian systems are acutely aware of the need to strike a balance between the desire to achieve a materially "right" outcome on the one hand, and the struggle for legal certainty on the other. As a consequence, they are extremely reluctant to admit that the wording of a contract concluded in writing might be overridden by other factors. . . . Extrinsic evidence can, however, be used for the purposes of interpreting a written document that contains internal contradictions or is otherwise unclear. . . .

Stefan Voganauer, *Interpretation of Contracts: Concluding Comparative Observations, in* Contract Terms 123, 135–36 (Andrew Burrows & Edwin Peel eds. 2007).

Article 110–3 of the Commercial Code is more tolerant of oral parol evidence, but it is not clear whether the Commercial Code governs the sale to Bodum Holding of Viel Castel's stock in Martin. The Commercial Code applies to "all obligations between dealers, merchants, and bankers." Art. 110–2. The contract by which Viel Castel sold his stock was a hybrid, affecting the business of Household as a merchant at the same time as it affected Viel Castel as an investor. It is unnecessary to decide whether Art. 110–3 applies, however, because Bodum Holding does not offer any parol evidence that would tend to show Viel Castel's oral agreement with Jørgen Bodum's beliefs. This leaves the written record.

The negotiating history is straightforward. Bodum's lawyers submitted an initial draft for Viel Castel's consideration. The relevant provision said this:

> In consideration of the compensation paid to Stockholder [Viel Castel] for the stock of [Martin,] Stockholder guarantees that he shall not—for an indefinite period of time—be engaged directly or indirectly in any commercial business related to manufacturing and/or distributing [Martin's] products. . . .
>
> Notwithstanding article 4 [Bodum Holding] agrees that Stockholder through Household . . . can manufacture and distribute any products within the United Kingdom. It is expressly understood that Household [ ] is not entitled, directly or indirectly, to distribute products outside the United Kingdom.

Viel Castel rejected this proposal and negotiated to allow Household the right to sell the La Cafetière design outside the United Kingdom. The next draft said this:

> Notwithstanding Article 4 [Bodum Holding] agrees that Stockholder [Viel Castel] through Household .. can manufacture and distribute any products within the United Kingdom. It is expressly understood that Household [ ] is not entitled, directly or indirectly, globally to manufacture and/or distribute coffeeposts under the trade marks and/or brand names of "Melior" and "Chambord." [Bodum Holding] agrees that Household [ ] with the limitation mentioned in the previous sentence outside of the

United Kingdom on markets where Household [ ] prior to signing of this Agreement has proved to [Bodum Holding] that he is
already manufacturing/distributing products can manufacture and
distribute products which, directly or indirectly, do not compete
with the business of the Company as run today.

This too was unacceptable to Viel Castel. Eventually the parties signed the
final version that we quoted several pages ago. The lesson is easy to grasp.
The initial draft placed on Household the sort of restriction that Jørgen
Bodum imputes to the final version. But the final version allows Household
to sell the La Cafetière design anywhere except France—provided that it
does not use the Chambord or Melior names (which Household has never
done) and does not use Martin's supply channels for four years (a promise
Household kept).

The Cour de Cassation (France's highest civil court) has concluded that a
clear and precise contract must not be "denatured" by resort to one party's
declaration of intent. *See* Jacques H. Herbots, "Interpretation of Contracts"
in *The Elgar Encyclopedia of Comparative Law* 334–35 (2006); Cass. 2e
civ., March 8, 2006, Bull. Civ. II, No. 66. Article 4 of this contract is clear
and precise as it stands; the negotiating history shows that it means what
it says. And we are not the first court to reach this conclusion. Bodum and
another of Household's subsidiaries litigated in Denmark. Relying heavily
on the negotiating history, the Court of Randers concluded, in a judgment
dated February 8, 2008 (Case FS 40–6066/2007), that Article 4 means
exactly what the district judge held in this litigation. The Court of Randers reached its judgment under French law (which a choice-of-law clause in
the contract requires). The judgment was affirmed by the Western Danish
High Court on Mary 12, 2009 (Appeal No. V.L. B-0329–08, Ref. No.
138212). It would not be sensible to create an international conflict about
the interpretation of this contract. Denmark is a civil-law nation, and a
Danish court's understanding and application of the civil-law tradition
is more likely to be accurate than are the warring declarations of the paid
experts in this litigation.

When the facts are undisputed, interpretation of contractual language is a
question of law for the judge. Bodum contends that the French preference
for intent over text means that interpretation must be a question of fact.
But in the United States, too, contractual interpretation seeks to find the
parties' shared intent. And in the United States, as in France, this is done

by objective means (through devices such as the negotiating history) rather than attempting to read the parties' minds.

If this dispute were proceeding in France, it would not be submitted to lay jurors (which France does not use) or even to a judge. It would be submitted to an arbitral panel of business executives, the International Court of Commerce in Paris, as Article 18 of the contract provides. Bodum has not asked that this dispute be arbitrated, in Chicago or Paris, although that might have been preferable. That the suit depends on a mixture of U.S. trademark law and French contract law would not prevent arbitration. Having chosen to litigate in Chicago rather than arbitrate in Paris, however, Bodum must abide by the forum's procedural doctrines, such as the allocation of tasks between judge and jury. *See Mauyer v. Gary Partners & Co.*, 29 F.3d 330 (7th Cir. 1994). . . .The judgment is affirmed.

POSNER, CIRCUIT JUDGE, concurring.

I join the majority opinion, and write separately merely to express emphatic support for, and modestly to amplify, the court's criticism of a common and authorized but unsound judicial practice. That is the practice of trying to establish the meaning of law of a foreign country by testimony or affidavits of expert witnesses, usually lawyers or law professors, often from the country in question. . . .

The contract in this case is in writing and unambiguously entitles the defendant to continue to sell its "Classic" coffee maker in the United States, because, although it is a product "similar" to the plaintiff's coffee maker, only in France is the defendant forbidden to sell products "similar" to the plaintiff's products. The plaintiff argues that nevertheless it is entitled to a trial at which Jørgen Bodum, its principal, would testify that part of the deal the parties *thought* they were making, although it is not reflected in the written contract, was that the defendant would be barred from selling its "Classic" coffee maker in the United States because it is identical rather than merely "similar" to the plaintiff's "Chambord" coffee maker. (Yet the plaintiff concedes in its reply brief that "it may certainly be true that all identical products are similar.") The issue of contractual interpretation is governed by French law.

Rule 44.1 of the Federal Rules of Civil Procedure provides that a federal court, "in determining foreign law, . . . may consider any relevant material or source, including testimony, whether or not submitted by a party or admissible under the Federal Rules of Evidence." The committee note explains that the court

> may engage in its own research and consider any relevant material thus found. The court may have at its disposal better foreign law materials than the counsel have presented, or may wish to reexamine and amplify material that has been presented by counsel in partisan fashion or in insufficient detail.

Thus the court doesn't *have* to rely on testimony; and in only a few cases, I believe, is it justified in doing so. This case is not one of them.

The only evidence of the meaning of French law that was presented to the district court or is found in the appellate record is an English translation of brief excerpts from the French Civil Code and affidavits by three French law professors (Pierre-Yves Guatier for the plaintiff and Christophe Caron and Jérôme Huet for the defendant, with Huet's affidavit adding little to Caron's). The district court did no research of its own, but relied on the parties' submissions. . . .

Lawyers who testify to the meaning of foreign law, whether they are practitioners or professors, are paid for their testimony and selected on the basis of the convergence of their views with the litigating position of the client, or their willingness to fall in with the views urged upon them by the client. These are the banes of expert testimony. When the testimony concerns a scientific or other technical issue, it may be unreasonable to expect a judge to resolve the issue without the aid of such testimony. But judges are experts on law, and there is an abundance of published materials, in the form of treatises, law review articles, statutes, and cases, all in English (if English is the foreign country's official language), to provide neutral illumination of issues of foreign law. I cannot fathom why in dealing with the meaning of laws of English-speaking countries that share our legal origins judges should prefer paid affidavits and testimony to published materials.

It is only a little less perverse for judges to rely on testimony to ascertain the law of a country whose official language is not English, at least if it is a major country and has a modern legal system. Although most Americans are monolingual, including most judges, there are both official translations of French statutes into English, . . . and abundant secondary material on French law, including French contract and procedural law, published in English. [Citations to 1986, 1992, 1997, 2007, 2008 books, book chapters, and articles] Neither party cited *any* such material, except translations of statutory provisions; beyond that they relied on the affidavits of their expert witnesses.

Because English has become the *lingua franca*, it is unsurprising that most Americans, even when otherwise educated, make little investment in acquiring even a reading knowledge of a foreign language. But our linguistic provincialism does not excuse intellectual provincialism. It does not justify our judges in relying on paid witnesses to spoon feed them foreign law that can be found well explained in English-language treatises and articles. I do not criticize the district judge in this case, because he was following the common practice. But it is a bad practice, followed like so many legal practices out of habit rather than reflection. It is excusable only when the foreign law is the law of a country with such an obscure or poorly developed legal system that there are no secondary materials to which the judge could turn. The French legal system is obviously not of that character. The district court could—as this court did in *Abad v. Bayer Corp.*, 563 F.3d 663, 670–71 (7th Cir. 2009), with respect to the law of Argentina—have based his interpretation of French contract law on published writings as distinct from paid testimony. . . .

The parties' reliance on affidavits to establish the standard for interpreting their contract has produced only confusion. They should have relied on published analyses of French commercial law.

WOOD, CIRCUIT JUDGE, concurring.

While I endorse without reservation the majority's reading of the 1991 contract that is at the heart of this case, I write separately to note my disagreement with the discussion of Fed. R. Civ. P. 44.1 in both the majority opinion and in Judge Posner's concurring opinion. Rule 44.1 itself establishes no hierarchy for sources of foreign law, and I am unpersuaded by my colleagues' assertions that expert testimony is categorically inferior to published, English-language materials. Exercises in comparative law are notoriously difficult, because the U.S. reader is likely to miss nuances in the foreign law, to fail to appreciate the way in which one branch of the other country's law interacts with another, or to assume erroneously that the foreign law mirrors U.S. law when it does not. As the French might put it more generally, apparently similar phrases might be *faux amis*. A simple example illustrates why two words might be "false friends." A speaker of

American English will be familiar with the word "actual," which is defined in Webster's Third New International Dictionary as "existing in act, . . . existing in fact or reality; really acted or acting or carried out—contrasted with *ideal* and *hypothetical*. . . ." So, one might say, "This is the actual chair used by George Washington." But the word *actuel* in French means "present" or right now. Le Robert & Collins, Compact Plus Dictionnaire 7 (5th ed. 2003). A French person would thus use the term *les événements actuels* or *actualité* to refer to current events, not to describe something that really happened either now or in the past.

There will be many times when testimony from an acknowledged expert in foreign law will be helpful, or even necessary, to ensure that the U.S. judge is not confronted with a "false friend" or that the U.S. judge understands the full context of the foreign provision. Some published articles or treatises, written particularly for a U.S. audience, might perform the same service, but many will not, even if they are written in English, and especially if they are translated into English from another language. It will often be most efficient and useful for the judge to have before her an expert who can provide the need precision on the spot, rather than have the judge wade through a number of secondary sources. In practice, the experts produced by the parties are often the authors of the leading treatises and scholarly articles in the foreign country anyway. In those cases, it is hard to see why the person's views cannot be tested in court, to guard against the possibility that he or she is just a mouthpiece for one party. Prominent lawyers from the country in question also sometimes serve as experts. That too is perfectly acceptable in principle, especially if the question requires an understanding of court procedure in the foreign country. In many places, the academic branch of the legal profession is entirely separate from the bar. Academic writings in such places tend to be highly theoretical and removed from the day-to-day realities of the practice of law.

To be clear, I have no objection to the use of written sources of foreign law. Rule 44.1 permits the court to consider "any relevant material or source, including testimony, whether or not submitted by a party or admissible under the Federal Rules of Evidence." The written sources cited by both of my colleagues throw useful light on the problem before us in this case, and both were well within their rights to conduct independent research and to rely on those sources. There is no need, however, to disparage oral testimony from experts in the foreign law. That kind of testimony has been used by responsible lawyers for years, and there will be many instances in which it is adequate by itself or it provides a helpful gloss on the literature. The tried and true methods set forth in Fed. R. Evid. 702 for testing the depth of the witness's expertise, the facts and other relevant information on which the witness has relied, and the quality of the witness's application of those principles to the problem at hand, suffice to protect the court against self-serving experts in foreign law, just as they suffice to protect the process for any other kind of expert. . .

COMMENTS AND QUESTIONS

1. Judge Easterbrook quotes the pertinent language from the contract. Is the manifestation of the parties' intent clear and unambiguous (to you)?

2. Judge Easterbrook and Judge Posner have little tolerance for expert testimony on the content of foreign law. Is there reason to believe that expert testimony about foreign law is more problematic than expert testimony about other subjects?

3. Federal Rule 44.1 is limited to inquiries into a foreign *country*'s law. If expert testimony about the content of unfamiliar law is helpful, why not allow it also in cases involving complicated matters regarding the laws of a sister *state*?

4. Do Judges Easterbrook and Posner actually expect a federal district judge to apply the law of a foreign country after reading translations of the relevant documents, consulting an encyclopedia of comparative law, and reading a few articles about the law of the foreign country? Is this demystification of foreign law alarming or refreshing?

5. The judges who sat on this panel are three of the most distinguished federal appellate judges of recent generations. If Supreme Court appointments tracked merit, all three would be on the United States Supreme Court. (Judge Posner retired from the bench in 2017.)

Quick Summary

- In federal court, the content of foreign law is a question of law that may impose a burden on the court, not only the parties

- In many state courts, the content of foreign law is a question of fact that the parties must prove

- Applying foreign law requires a certain amount of confidence in one's ability to understand other cultures and systems

- Expert testimony about the content of foreign law is common if problematic

- The complexity of understanding and applying foreign law can cause parties and courts to avoid it altogether

- Applying forum law (i.e., the homeward trend) or dismissing the case pursuant to the common law doctrine of forum non conveniens are alternatives to applying foreign law

19

Federal Law and Federal Courts

Key Concepts

- Extraterritoriality
- Federal law incorporating state law
- The *Erie* doctrine

In a federal system, state and federal governments coexist. In this Chapter we examine choice of law questions that are unique to cases that arise under *federal* law or are litigated in *federal* courts. We address each of these categories in turn.

A. Claims Arising Under Federal Law

The vast majority of claims that arise under federal law do not raise any choice of law issues. Instead, in the typical case, a plaintiff has a cause of action pursuant to some federal statute that prohibits, say, employment discrimination, infringement of intellectual property rights, or unfair competition. Litigation of these claims— whether in federal or state court—involves the interpretation and construction of the federal mandate, and there often is no choice of law issue; the federal law is applied. The Supremacy Clause, after all, provides that the "Constitution and the laws of the United States which shall be made in pursuance thereof . . . shall be the supreme law of the land."[1]

There are two circumstances, however, when a plaintiff asserting a claim that arises under federal law triggers our attention in this course. The first involves the geographic reach of federal laws, and the second involves the substantive content of some federal laws.

---

1   U.S. Const. art. VI.

1. Extraterritoriality

The question of *extraterritoriality* asks: to what extent do the mandates and protections of federal laws (or the U.S. Constitution) extend beyond our national borders? Consider, for example, the protections of Title VII against sexual harassment in the workplace.[2] When the employer, the employee, and the relevant facts are all within the United States—even if they are scattered across different states of the United States—Title VII undoubtedly applies. Title VII has one mandate and that same mandate applies across all of the United States. But what if the executive of a Pennsylvania employer harasses a Pennsylvania employee while the two of them are on a business trip in Germany? Does the mandate of Title VII still apply?

In certain respects, this question resembles the choice of law questions that we considered in Chapters 3 through 8. Yet, rather than framing the question as whether U.S. or German law applies (and then invoking the preferred choice of law methodology to answer that question), federal courts instead tend to frame the question as whether Title VII *applies extraterritorially*? Put differently, the content and reach of the German law, and the interest and intention of the German lawmakers is irrelevant; only the extraterritoriality *vel non* of the American law matters.

Some federal statutes include text that expressly provides that they apply extraterritorially—to foreign events and/or persons. Some federal statutes—especially criminal statutes—proscribe certain conduct by Americans even if they engage in that conduct in some other country.[3] Other federal statutes give Americans remedies for injuries that occurred while that American was in some other country.[4] In theory, a federal statute could give foreigners remedies against other foreigners for conduct that occurred in some other country.[5] In all of these instances where the statute *expressly* purports to apply extraterritorially with respect to (foreign) persons and/or (foreign) events, courts apply the statute as written.[6] These are the easy cases.

---

2   Title VII of the Civil Rights Act of 1964 is a federal law that prohibits most workplace harassment and discrimination. 42 U.S.C. § 2000e et seq.

3   *See, e.g.,* The Prosecutorial Remedies and Other Tools to End the Exploitation of Children Today Act of 2003, 18 U.S.C. § 2423(c) ("Any United States citizen . . . who travels [to] . . . a foreign country . . . and engages in any illicit sexual conduct with another person. . . .").

4   *See, e.g.,* The Antiterrorist and Effective Death Penalty Act of 1996, 18 U.S.C. § 32 (amending the Foreign Sovereign Immunities Act by eliminating the sovereign immunity of states that sponsor terrorism in actions by filed by or on behalf of U.S. citizens who are killed or injured by acts of terrorism sponsored or aided by those states).

5   *See, e.g.,* The Alien Tort Claims Act, 28 U.S.C. § 1350 (conferring original jurisdiction and a limited private right of action over "a civil action for a tort . . . committed in violation of the law of nations"). *But see Kiobel v. Royal Dutch Petroleum Co.*, 569 U.S. 108, 124–25 (2013) (limiting the reach of the Alien Tort Statute).

6   Imposition of the statutory mandate must be constitutional *See* Chapter 14.

Many statutes, however, are silent or ambiguous with respect to Congressional intent about territorial reach. But as it turns out, these cases are fairly easy too, because the Supreme Court has embraced a presumption against extraterritoriality.

> It is a basic premise of our legal system that, in general, "United States law governs domestically but does not rule the world." *Microsoft Corp. v. AT&T Corp.*, 550 U.S. 437, 454 (2007). This principle finds expression in a canon of statutory construction known as the presumption against territoriality: Absent clearly expressed congressional intent to the contrary, federal laws will be construed to have only domestic application. *Morrison v. Nat'l Australia Bank Ltd.*, 561 U.S. 247, 255 (2010). The question is not whether we think "Congress would have wanted" a statute to apply to foreign conduct "if it had thought of the situation before the court," but whether Congress has affirmatively and unmistakably instructed that the statute will do so. *Id.* at 261. When a statute gives no clear indication of an extraterritorial application, it has none." *Id.* at 255.
>
> There are several reasons for this presumption. Most notably, it serves to avoid the international discord that can result when U.S. law is applied to conduct in foreign countries. *See, e.g., Kiobel v. Royal Dutch Petroleum Co.*, 569 U.S. 108, 114–15 (2013). . . . But it also reflects the more prosaic "commonsense notion that Congress generally legislates with domestic concerns in mind." *Smith v. U.S.*, 507 U.S. 197, 204, n.5 (1993).

RJR Nabisco, Inc. v. European Community, ___ U.S. ___, 136 S. Ct. 2090, 2100 (2016).

Statutes that *could* be interpreted as applying extraterritorially will seldom overcome the presumption against extraterritoriality. Accordingly, a statute that uses terms like "any plaintiff" or "any act" will not alone suffice—even though the word "any" would plausibly include foreign plaintiffs or foreign acts. Rather, an express statement of extraterritoriality or unmistakable context is necessary.

Occasionally it is the facts, rather than the law, that create the controversy. For example, imagine a situation where some of the conduct giving rise to a suit occurred outside the country, while some occurred within the United States. If the plaintiff's claim arises under a federal statute that has extraterritorial effect, then there is no complexity here. But if the statute does *not* have extraterritorial effect, we can expect the lawyers for each side to describe this case very differently.

Typically, it is the plaintiff's lawyer who is invoking the statutory right; she will focus on the conduct or effect that occurred within the United States, and will argue that this is a domestic application of the statute.[7] Meanwhile the defendant's lawyer will characterize the plaintiff as trying to circumvent the fact that the statute does not have extraterritorial reach.

The Supreme Court has said that "[i]f the conduct relevant to the *statute's focus* occurred in the United States, then the case involves a permissible domestic application even if other conduct occurred abroad; but if the conduct relevant to the focus occurred in a foreign country, then the case involves an impermissible extraterritorial application regardless of any other conduct that occurred in U.S. territory."[8] These cases turn, then, on where the conduct that is the focus of the statute occurred. A defendant cannot use extraterritoriality as an escape device just because some tangential conduct occurred outside the country. And conversely, a plaintiff cannot escape the presumption against extraterritoriality just because some tangential conduct occurred within the United States.

Hypothetical 19-1

Nohemi Gonzalez, an American, was a 26-year-old California State University student studying abroad in Paris France when she was killed with others in a terrorist attack at a Paris bistro. The Islamic State of Iraq and Syria (ISIS) claimed responsibility for the attack in video messages posted on YouTube, a free online video platform owned and operated by Google, Inc.

Gonzalez's estate filed a lawsuit against Google in a California federal district court. In the suit, plaintiff alleged that YouTube played an essential role in the rise of ISIS becoming the most feared terrorist organization in the world. Specifically, YouTube provided ISIS with a unique and powerful tool of communication that enabled it to plan the Paris attack in particular, and more generally, to achieve its program of terrorism that included motivating others to carry out more terrorist attacks. Google, in turn, earned revenue from the YouTube videos because Google posted advertisements that were matched to the viewer.

---

7   She is *not* arguing that the statute has extraterritorial effect; that is a losing argument. Instead, she is arguing that, even though some of the relevant conduct is extraterritorial, the federal statute was violated within the United States.

8   *RJR Nabisco, Inc.*, 136 S. Ct. at 2101 (emphasis added).

Plaintiff's cause of action arises under The Anti-Terrorist Act of 1991, 18 U.S.C. § 2333(a) and (d). Section (a) provides that:

> Any national of the United States injured in his or her person, property, or business by reason of an act of international terrorism, or his or her estate, survivors, or heirs, may sue therefor in any appropriate district court of the United States and shall recover threefold the damages he or she sustains and the cost of the suit, including attorney's fees.

"International terrorism" is defined as an act that is dangerous to human life, that would be a criminal violation if committed within the jurisdiction of the United States, and that is intended to intimidate or coerce a civilian population or the policy of a government.

Section 2333(d) provides that liability attaches to those who aid or abet an act of international terrorism by knowingly providing substantial assistance.

Defense counsel argues that the conduct alleged by plaintiff occurred outside the United States and that the statute does not apply extra-territorially.

Defense counsel also argues that, in the Communications Decency Act of 1996, Congress immunized providers of interactive computer services from liability arising from content created by third parties. Indeed, under 47 U.S.C. § 230(c)(1), "No provider or user of an interactive computer service shall be treated as the publisher or speaker of any information provided by another information content provider." Plaintiff's counsel argues that the immunity statute does not apply extra-territorially.

How is the court likely to resolve these two questions regarding extraterritoriality?

ADHIKARI v. KBR, INC.

U.S. District Court for the Southern District of Texas
2017 WL 4237923 (S.D. Tex. 2017)

Ellison, District Judge.

Pending before the Court is Defendants' Motion to Dismiss. After considering the Motion, the responses thereto, and all applicable law, the Court determines that the Motion should be granted in part and denied in part.

I. Background

The plaintiffs in this case, five Nepali men, allege that they were promised work in Jordan but were instead trafficked to work for KBR [Kellogg Brown & Root], a U.S. defense contractor, on a U.S. military base in Iraq. Plaintiffs brought claims against KBR and various KBR subsidiaries under the Trafficking Victims Protection Reauthorization Act (TVPRA), the Alien Tort Claims Act (known more commonly as the Alien Tort Statute or ATS), and Iraqi law, as well as claims of false imprisonment, negligence, negligent hiring, negligent supervision, and intentional infliction of emotional distress. Defendants have moved to dismiss all claims.

The claims in this case (*"Adhikari II"*) are similar, though not identical, to the claims brought in *Adhikari v. Daoud & Partners*, Civil Action No. 4:09–CV–1237 (*"Adhikari I"*). As in the instant case, the *Adhikari I* complaint alleged that different Nepali men had also been trafficked to work on a U.S. military base in Iraq after being promised work in Jordan. In *Adhikari I*, summary judgment was granted to Defendants on all claims. *Adhikari v. Kellogg, Brown & Root, Inc.*, 845 F.3d 184, 191 (5th Cir. 2017)[, *cert. denied*, ___ U.S. ___, 138 S. Ct. 134 (2017)]. The Fifth Circuit affirmed. *Id.*

II. Legal Standard

A court may dismiss a complaint for a "failure to state a claim upon which relief can be granted." Fed. R. Civ. P. 12(b)(6). "To survive a Rule 12(b)(6) motion to dismiss, a complaint 'does not need detailed factual allegations' but must provide the plaintiff's grounds for entitlement to relief—including factual allegations that when assumed to be true 'raise a right to relief above the speculative level.' " *Cuvillier v. Taylor*, 503 F.3d 397, 401 (5th Cir. 2007) (quoting *Bell Atl. Corp. v. Twombly*, 550 U.S. 544, 555 (2007)). . . .

III. Analysis

A. Trafficking Victims Protection Reauthorization Act

Defendants argue that Plaintiffs cannot state a claim under the TVPRA because (1) the alleged trafficking took place prior to 2008; (2) the TVPRA did not apply extraterritorially before 2008; and (3) the 2008 amendment to the TVPRA is not retroactive. This argument reiterates the conclusions that the Fifth Circuit reached on the TVPRA claims in *Adhikari I*, 845 F.3d at 200–06. In response, Plaintiffs argue that extraterritoriality is beside the point. According to plaintiffs' allegations "KBR violated the TVPRA *inside of the United States* through its actions to aid and abet the trafficking of Plaintiffs." Plaintiffs point to allegations in the Complaint that U.S.-based KBR personnel: analyzed staffing patterns in Iraq to detect labor shortfalls; exercised control over Daoud & Partners' recruitment and supply of workers [hereafter "Daoud"; Daoud was KBR's Jordanian subcontractor]; supervised medical clearances for workers; determined the workers' pay rates; set policy for the workers' equipment use; transmitted payments comprising all of Daoud's revenue; intervened to ensure that Daoud maintained liability insurance to comply with U.S. law; conducted legal reviews of Daoud's subcontracts; assigned staff and designated a hotline, email, and postal address to process trafficking complaint; received reports from media, the U.S. military, and other sources about trafficking; brought reports about trafficking to the attention of KBR's U.S.-based Board of Directors; developed responses to trafficking allegations; and provided direction once the U.S. military imposed requirements on labor brokers. Plaintiffs further allege that U.S.-based KBR personnel failed to take steps to eliminate trafficking and that they profited from the alleged scheme. As such, Plaintiffs argue that KBR's domestic activity is sufficient to create liability under the TVPRA.

Statutes are presumed not to have extraterritorial application absent congressional intent to the contrary. *Morrison v. Nat'l Austl. Bank Ltd.*, 561 U.S. 247, 255 (2010). In applying the presumption against extraterritoriality to a particular statute, courts use a two-step inquiry. *RJR Nabisco, Inc. v. European Comty.*, 136 S. Ct. 2090, 2101 (2016). First, the court must determine whether the statute gives a clear, affirmative indication that it applies extraterritorially. *Id.* In *Adhikari I*, the Fifth Circuit ruled that the

TVPRA did not give such an indication prior to the 2008 amendment. 845 F.3d at 191. Second, the court must determine whether the case involves a domestic or extraterritorial application of the statute. *RJR Nabisco*, 136 S. Ct. at 2101. In cases involving both conduct in the United States and conduct abroad, the court looks to the "focus of Congressional concern" in enacting the statute. *Morrison v. Nat'l Austl. Bank Ltd.*, 561 U.S. 247, 266–70 (2010) ("For it is a rare case of prohibited extraterritorial application that lacks *all* contact with the territory of the United States" (emphasis in original)). "If the conduct relevant to the statute's focus occurred in the United States, then the case involves a permissible domestic application even if other conduct occurred abroad." *RJR Nabisco*, 136 S. Ct. at 2101. On the other hand, if the conduct relevant to the statute's focus occurred in a foreign country, then the case involves an extraterritorial application. *Id.*[14] As the Supreme Court made clear in *RJR Nabisco*, this analysis must be done separately for each statutory provision at issue. *Id.* at 2106–10.

Few courts have examined the TVPRA's focus for the purposes of the extraterritoriality analysis. Contrary to Defendants' argument, the Fifth Circuit did not do so in *Adhikari I*. Two district courts have said that the focus of the TVPRA is "where the forced labor occurred and to where . . . victims were trafficked." *Samuel v. Signal Int'l L.L.C.*, 2015 WL 12765986, at *3 (E.D. Tex. Jan. 26, 2015) (quoting *Tanedo v. E. Baton Rouge Parish Sch. Bd.*, 2012 WL 5378742, at *6 (C.D. Cal. Aug. 27, 2012)). These cases examined trafficking schemes that brought workers into the U.S. after employing some deception or coercion in the workers' countries of origin. *Samuel*, 2015 WL 12765986, at *1 (describing false promises made and debts incurred prior to arrival in the U.S.); *Tanedo*, 2012 WL 5378742, at *11–2 (describing advertisements, misleading job offers, and financial coercion experienced prior to U.S. arrival). Tasked with deciding whether trafficking that began elsewhere and ended in the U.S. entailed a domestic or extraterritorial application of the TVPRA, those courts sensibly selected the former. Interpreting the law otherwise would leave it with little force or effect.

---

14 For example, in *Morrison*, the Supreme Court considered whether § 10(b) of the Securities Exchange Act of 1934 was being applied domestically or extraterritorially. 561 U.S. 247 (2010). The alleged misrepresentations that formed the basis of the claim were made in the United States and were about an American company, but the securities that were affected were only traded on a foreign stock exchange. *Id.* at 251–53. The Supreme court found that the focus of § 10(b) was "transactions in securities listed on domestic exchanges, and domestic transactions in other securities." *Id.* at 267. The Court therefore focused on where the securities were traded rather than where the misrepresentations occurred. *Id.* Because the securities were only traded on a foreign exchange, imposing liability would require an extraterritorial application of the statute.

The allegations in the present case are different. Plaintiffs' allegations detail a transnational human trafficking scheme that moved workers through various foreign countries but never brought them to the U.S. Viewed in the most favorable light, as they must be, Plaintiffs' allegations also indicate that actors in the U.S. instigated, directed, funded, protected, and perpetuated the exploitation of those workers. These domestic actors' activities entailed close collaboration with partners on the ground that interacted directly with the trafficking victims. The direct trafficking activities clearly are within the focus of the TVPRA. The present question is whether the activities of the domestic participant in the scheme, without which the trafficking would not have occurred, are also within the focus of Congressional concern.

The Trafficking Victims Protection Act of 2000 has been amended several times since its enactment. Plaintiffs allege violations of the law occurring after the United States' invasion of Iraq in 2003 and ending in 2007. The version of the law in effect for that period has three relevant provisions: Section 1589, prohibiting forced labor; Section 1590, prohibiting trafficking; and Section 1595, a civil remedy. Section 1589 subjected to fine or imprisonment anyone who

> knowingly provides or obtains the labor or services of a person—
>
> (1) by threats of serious harm to, or physical restraint against, that person or another person;
>
> (2) by means of any scheme, plan, or pattern intended to cause the person to believe that, if the person did not perform such labor or services, that person or another person would suffer serious harm or physical restraint; or
>
> (3) by means of the abuse or threatened abuse of law or the legal process.

Trafficking Victims Protection Act of 2000, Pub. L. 106–386, § 112(a)(2) (2000). Section 1590 subjected to fine or imprisonment anyone who "knowingly recruits, harbors, transports, provides, or obtains by any means, any person for labor or services in violation of this chapter. . . ." *Id.* Section 1595 allowed "an individual who is a victim of a violation of section 1589, 1590, or 1591 of this chapter [to] bring a civil action against the perpetrator in an appropriate district court of the United States and [to] recover damages and reasonable attorneys fees." Trafficking Victims Protection Reauthorization Act of 2003, Pub. L. 108–193, § 4(a)(4)(A) (2003). Not until 2008 did the law gain the provision that confers extraterritorial jurisdiction on the federal courts. William Wilberforce Trafficking Victims Protection Reauthorization Act of 2008, Pub. L. 110–457, § 223(a) (2008) (codified at 18 U.S.C. § 1596[*]).

The focus of the TVPRA identified in *Samuel* and *Tanedo*—"where the forced labor occurred and to where . . . victims were trafficked"—is a plausible interpretation of Section 1589. That statute's text speaks specifically of the means and mechanisms of coercion used to extract forced labor. It is reasonable, therefore, to conclude that Congress's focus was on the location where the forced labor occurred, given that the prohibited techniques of coercion are likely to be employed at the same site. In the present case, the forms of coercion listed in Section 1589 all occurred entirely in foreign countries. As such, applying Section 1589 to the facts of the case appears to be an extraterritorial application of the statute.

By contrast, the trafficking provision, Section 1590, is more broadly stated than the forced labor provision. Proof of Section 1590 is not reliant on evidence of specific types of threats. Rather, it sweeps in all those who "obtain[ ] by any means" a person for labor or services. Where Section 1589's focus is only on those who wield the prod, Section 1590's focus appears broad enough also to include those who urge and direct its use.

This Court has said previously that "Congress intended Sections 1589 and 1590 to be purely national solutions." 994 F.Supp.2d at 836–37. It does not alter that conclusion as to Section 1590 now. What the Court holds, instead, is that a domestic actor may participate so substantially in a trafficking scheme abroad that its activities come within the focus of Congress's concern when it enacted Section 1590. To hold otherwise would be to reward the scheme's mastermind for constructing layers of legal and organizational insulation.

Congress's purposes and findings in enacting the statute bear out this holding. 22 U.S.C. § 7101; Trafficking Victims Protection Act of 2000, Pub. L. 106–386, § 102 (2000). The statute was addressed to an international problem—the roughly 700,000 persons trafficked annually at the time, only 50,000 of whom were brought to the U.S. § 7101(b)(1). Congress

---

*   [*Eds.' Note*: The 2008 Amendment added a provision entitled "Additional jurisdiction in certain trafficking offenses." As amended, Section 1596(a) now provides: "In addition to any domestic or extra-territorial jurisdiction otherwise provided by law, the courts of the United States have extra-territorial jurisdiction over any offense (or any attempt or conspiracy to commit an offense) under section 1581, 1583, 1584, 1589, 1590, or 1591 if . . . ."]

described trafficking as a "growing transnational crime." § 7101(b)(3). It stated an intent "[t]o deter international trafficking and bring its perpetrators to justice. § 7101(b)(24). Congress evinced concern for harms and victims around the world, not just in the U.S. E.g., § 7101(b)(8) (noting "official corruption in countries of . . . destination, thereby threatening the rule of law" in those countries); (b)(20) (describing victims' lack of familiarity with "the laws, cultures, and languages of the countries into which they have been trafficked").

The decision of another district court, *Plaintiff A v. Schair*, 2014 WL 12495639 (N.D. Ga. Sept. 9, 2014), also lends credence to this Court's holding on Section 1590. In *Plaintiff A*, defendants based in the United States solicited American customers for fishing tours in Brazil. *Id.* at *5. Once in Brazil, the defendants' employees would coerce local women into sex acts with the defendants' customers. *Id.* at *2. Women caught in the scheme in 2005 and 2006 sued, arguing that the alleged trafficking violations entailed a domestic application of the TVPRA due to the defendants' American headquarters and customer base. *Id.* at *5. Though the court ruled that the defendants' connections to the United States were "not enough" to change the essentially foreign nature of the case," *id.*, it suggested that conduct outside the United States might still be actionable under the statute then in effect. *Id.* at *5 n.4. "When the prohibited trafficking activity occurred entirely outside the United States, defendants must engage in more substantial domestic actions to facilitate trafficking activity than merely residing in the United States." *Id.* at *5. Plaintiffs allege just that kind of substantial domestic action here.

To be legally valid, Plaintiffs' TVPRA claims must also survive the extraterritoriality analysis of Section 1595, the statute's civil remedy. *RJR Nabisco*, 136 S. Ct. at 2106–11, marks out the proper path for this analysis. In *RJR Nabisco*, the Supreme Court held that certain substantive provisions of the Racketeer Influenced and Corrupt Organizations Act (RICO) applied extraterritorially. *Id.* at 2101–06. It also held that the statute's civil remedy, 18 U.S.C. § 1964(c), must apply extraterritorially for foreign plaintiffs suffering injury abroad to have an actionable case. *Id.* at 2106. Section 1964(c) permits "[a]ny person injured in his business or property by reason of" a substantive RICO violation to sue the violator. Looking in vain for express indications of extraterritorial reach, and citing concerns about international friction, the Supreme Court concluded that Section 1964(c) applies only to "a *domestic* injury to [a plaintiff's] business or property." 136 S. Ct. at 2106 (emphasis in original). The Supreme Court did not say how to determine "whether a particular alleged injury is 'foreign' or 'domestic.'" *Id.* at 2111.[16] Its phrasing, however, indicates that it is the location where the injury was suffered, not where it was caused, that determines its character. *Id.* ("Respondents' . . . claims . . . rest entirely on injury suffered abroad and must be dismissed."); *Id.* at 2099 ("[D]oes RICO's private right of action, contained in § 1964(c), apply to injuries that are suffered in foreign countries?").

RJR Nabisco's general rule is clear: a civil remedy that lacks clear indications of extraterritorial reach will redress only injuries experienced domestically, no matter the substantive provisions' scope. Section 1595 lacks those clear indications. Thus, [with respect to] whether KBR's alleged domestic violations of Section 1590 caused remediable domestic injuries or irremediable foreign injuries, the court must conclude the latter. Plaintiffs' injuries, whatever their cause, were suffered only in foreign countries. They are, therefore, beyond the reach of the TVPRA that existed at that time.

The Court's regret in reaching this holding is tempered by its recognition that Congress later extended the remedies for forced labor and trafficking to apply extraterritorially. That amendment of the law might be taken as an indication of the scope that Congress always intended those prohibitions to have. One can imagine canons of construction that avoided the need for Congress so to act, resolving statutory ambiguity in ways that further Congress's purposes and erring on the side of justice. But, as the Supreme Court's recent rulings instruct, those are not our canons. And so Plaintiffs' TVPRA claims must be dismissed.

B. Alien Tort Claims Act (ATS)

Defendants challenge Plaintiffs' ATS claim on several grounds. Defendants argue that Plaintiffs' allegations are not sufficiently tied to the United States to make this a domestic, rather than extraterritorial, application of the ATS, which does not apply extraterritorially; that the ATS is preempted by the TVPRA; that the ATS claim is time-barred; and that there is no corporate liability under the ATS. For the reasons explained below, these arguments fail. Therefore the motion to dismiss is denied as to Plaintiffs' ATS claim.

---

16 The plaintiffs in *RJR Nabisco* waived their claims to domestic injuries, leaving only foreign injuries. 136 S. Ct. at 2111.

1. Domestic versus extraterritorial application of the ATS

Defendants first challenge the ATS claim on the ground that the claim does not sufficiently touch and concern U.S. territory. As noted above . . . , courts follow a two-step framework in determining whether to apply the presumption against extraterritoriality. The first step is to determine whether the statute clearly indicates extraterritorial application. The Supreme Court found in *Kiobel v. Royal Dutch Petroleum Co.*, 133 S. Ct. 1659, 1669 (2013) that the ATS does not do so. Second, the court must determine whether the case involves a domestic or extraterritorial application of the statute. To do that, the court examines whether the conduct that constitutes the focus of congressional concern occurred inside or outside the United States. *RJR Nabisco*, 136 S. Ct. at 2101. If that conduct occurred inside the United States, then the case presents a permissible domestic application of the ATS. In *Adhikari I*, the Fifth Circuit held that "the ATS's focus is the 'tort . . . committed in violation of the law of nations or a treaty of the United States.' " 845 F.3d at 197 (citing 28 U.S.C. § 1350). The Fifth Circuit found that the human trafficking and forced labor in *Adhikari I*—the alleged violations of international law—all occurred outside the United States. *Id.* The Fifth Circuit further found that the conduct that occurred within the United States—financial transactions and U.S. personnel's awareness of allegations of human rights abuses—did not suffice to create liability under the ATS. *Id.* at 198.

This case, however, includes additional allegations that were not part of *Adhikari I.* As detailed in the preceding section, Plaintiffs put forth a theory that KBR's domestic personnel aided and abetted the human trafficking and forced labor that occurred abroad. *Id.* Defendants do not dispute that liability for aiding and abetting is possible under the ATS. Rather, they argue that *Adhikari I* already rejected this theory. Defendants note that this Court denied the *Adhikari I* plaintiffs leave to amend their complaint to add an aiding and abetting theory on grounds that amendment would be futile, and that the Fifth Circuit affirmed that denial. *See Adhikari I*, 845 F.3d at 199–200. However, this is a new case with allegations and potentially new evidence. Therefore, the denial of leave to amend the *Adhikari I* complaint does not foreclose the possibility that the Plaintiffs here can prevail on an aiding and abetting theory.

[After reviewing the case law on what constitutes aiding and abetting, the court concluded that the plaintiffs had sufficiently alleged that the defendants knowingly aided and abetted human trafficking and forced labor.]

Therefore, the Court declines to dismiss Plaintiff's ATS claim as an extraterritorial application of the statute.

[In subsequent parts of this opinion the court held that the plaintiff's ATS claim was not preempted by the TVPRA and was not barred by the statute of limitations. The court also rejected the defendants' contention that corporations could not be held liable under the ATS. On the plaintiffs' claims under state law, the court dismissed the claim for intentional infliction of emotional distress, but allowed the negligence, negligent hiring and negligent supervision claims to go to discovery. The court also did not dismiss the plaintiff's claims under Iraqi law.]

COMMENTS AND QUESTIONS

1. The ATS was passed by the First Congress in 1789. The statute reads, in its entirety: "The district courts shall have original jurisdiction of any civil action by an alien for a tort only, committed in violation of the law of nations or a treaty of the United States." 28 U.S.C. § 1350. Between 1789 and 1980 the statute lay dormant. Beginning with *Filartiga v. Pena-Irala*, 630 F.2d 876 (2nd Cir. 1980), the statute found new life: providing jurisdiction over violations of the law of nations (*e.g.*, cases involving war crimes, piracy, crimes against humanity, and violations of international human rights laws). The import of the ATS was severely curtailed, however, in *Kiobel v. Royal Dutch Petroleum Co.*, 569 U.S. 108 (2013), when the Supreme Court found nothing in the ATS to overcome the presumption against extraterritoriality. "[E]ven where the claims touch and concern the territory of the United States, they must do so with sufficient force to displace the presumption against extraterritorial application." When the claim is against a corporation, "mere corporate presence" in the United States will not suffice. 569 U.S. at 124–25.

2. Is the presumption against extraterritoriality an ideologically "liberal" or "conservative" proposition? Is the logic the same for the enforcement of both civil and criminal laws?

3. If Congress passes statutes after the Supreme Court has articulated its presumption against extraterritoriality, does the absence of any statutory mention of extraterritoriality mean that Congress does not want that statute to have extraterritorial reach?

---

2. Federal Law Incorporation of State Law

Claims that arise under federal law ordinarily do not raise issues of state law.[9] Federal legislation typically imposes a single, national substantive mandate. For example, a statute might define the parameters of an intellectual property right and prescribe the remedy for any infringement of that right. One of the purposes of having federal legislation, after all, is to achieve a uniform standard. Yet below we describe two sets of circumstances under which cases that arise under *federal* law may integrate *state* law: the first involves federal statutes that incorporate state law and the second involves the incorporation of state law as federal common law. Whenever *state law* may be invoked, the lawyer who is trained in choice of law may be able to influence *whether* state law is invoked, *which* state's law is invoked, or *how much* state law to incorporate.

First, in some instances, the substantive mandate of a federal law may explicitly incorporate some other jurisdiction's law. For example, the Federal Torts Claim Act (FTCA) provides a federal cause of action against the United States government for certain individuals who were injured or whose property was damaged because of the wrongful or negligent act of an employee who was acting on behalf of the federal government. But rather than defining (or expecting the courts to define) the parameters of wrongful or negligent conduct, the statutory language extends jurisdiction to

> circumstances where the United States, if a private person, would be liable to the claimant in accordance with the law of the place where the act or omission occurred.[10]

---

9   To be sure, causes of action that arise under federal law are routinely joined in the same lawsuit with causes of action that arise under state law. (*E.g.* Count I of a complaint arises under a federal law and Count II arises under state law.) In that situation, which is *not* our focus, federal law would apply to Count I and a choice of law analysis would be undertaken to determine which state's law applied to Count II.

10   28 U.S.C. § 1346(b). *See also* The National Guard Claims Act, 32 U.S.C. § 715; Federal Railroad Safety Act, 49 U.S.C. § 28103.

That mandate thus folds the state law of the place where the act or omission occurred into the mandate of the federal law.[11]

In any such instance where the federal law incorporates by reference some other (non-federal) law, litigators who are trained in the art and science of conflict of laws will see an opportunity. Notice that the language from the FTCA that is quoted above contemplates application of the "law of the place where the act or omission occurred." But, which state's law do we use to determine *where* an act or omission occurred? Which law do we use to determine *which* act(s) or omission(s) matter[s]? And once we have determined in which state the act or omission occurred, do we apply the whole law (including the conflict of laws rules) of that state, or just the internal law? Is there a public policy exception?

The objective here is not to answer those questions for the FTCA nor other statutes like it. Rather, the goal is to make you aware of federal laws that, rather than imposing a single, uniform, national mandate, may instead expressly require dynamic conformity with some other jurisdiction's law. To be clear, federal statutes that incorporate state law are the exception, not the rule: indeed, the very purpose of most federal statues is to impose one mandate universally across the country.

For the same reasons that Congress might elect to incorporate state law into some federal legislation, courts might elect to incorporate state law into some federal common law. Most federal common law is interstitial lawmaking: courts resolve ambiguities, clarify vagueness and otherwise fill gaps that manifest in federal legislation. But in limited substantive areas of the law—most notably cases "concerned with the rights and obligations of the United States, interstate and international disputes implicating the conflicting rights of States or our relations with foreign nations, and admiralty cases"[12]—the federal judge-made law is much more open-ended.

This federal common law is *common law* in the sense that it is decisional law as opposed to statutory law. But it is not always common in the sense that the mandate is uniform throughout the country. Three examples of incorporation of state law into federal common law follow.

---

11   The FTCA is an example of using state law to define what is included within the scope of liability of the federal statute. *See also* The Outer Continental Shelf Lands Act, 43 U.S.C. § 1331 (incorporating law of the state adjacent to the dispute as the federal rule of law). Other statutes use state law to define what is *excluded* from the scope of liability of the federal statute. *See, e.g.,* McCarran-Ferguson Act, 15 U.S.C. §§ 1011–1015 (exemplifying a phenomenon sometimes referred to as reverse preemption).

12   *Texas Indus. v. Radcliff Materials,* 451 U.S. 630, 641 (1981).

Example 1: A federal statute uses the word employee but does not define it. In litigation arising under that statute, the precise contours of the meaning of that word are important. The judge's resolution of vagueness about who/what constitutes an employee under this statute is federal common law. The content of that federal common law, however, could be state law. In other words, instead of having the federal common law prescribe one, universal definition of employee for all instances nationwide, the federal common law might adapt to a local definition of who/what constitutes an employee.

Example 2: The passenger of a ship sues the owner for damages caused by negligence on the high seas. Much of the substantive content of admiralty law is federal common law. But that federal common law includes a set of choice of law principles that direct the court to apply the law of the selected state or country. Thus, instead of having the federal common law prescribe one, universal corpus of negligence law to all parties in admiralty cases, the federal common law might incorporate the substantive law of another jurisdiction (via federal common law choice of law rules).

Example 3: A federal court with diversity jurisdiction dismissed a lawsuit because the plaintiff's breach of contract claim was barred by the state's statute of limitations. That plaintiff then refiled the same suit against the same defendant in another state—a state in which the statute of limitations had not expired. Federal common law determines the claim preclusive effect of the earlier judgment. But rather than prescribing a single set of preclusion principles applicable to all federal court judgments in diversity cases, the federal common law could dynamically incorporate the law that would be applied by state courts in the state in which the federal diversity court that issued the judgment sat.

As stated above with respect to statutes, the incorporation of state law into federal common law is the exception, not the rule. Yet there are circumstances when the interest in intra-state uniformity (*i.e.,* uniformity between state and federal courts within a state) with respect to federal law is more compelling than the interest in inter-state uniformity (*i.e.,* uniformity among all federal courts across the country).

Hypothetical 19-2

Malek Dajani, a Coloradan, was insured through his employer by a Dover Life Insurance Company accidental death policy and a business travel accident policy. Dajani was the passenger on a small plane on a business trip when an in-flight fire and crash in Rhode Island killed Dajani and the pilot. Dajani's spouse, Luc Picard, has sued Dover in a Colorado federal court to recover benefits from the two policies in the amounts of $300,000 and $400,000, respectively. Dover disputes that Dajani's death was accidental, and denies any obligation to provide benefits to Picard.

Picard's claim against the insurance company is brought under the Employee Retirement Income Security Act of 1974 (ERISA), a federal law that establishes standards for pension and health plans. That law provides a federal claim for a participant or beneficiary to enforce rights—and to recover benefits due—under the terms of the plan. Federal common law has long held that, generally speaking, a plaintiff suing under this provision bears the burden of proving entitlement to benefits. But if the insurer claims that a specific policy exclusion applies, then the insurer generally must prove that the exclusion prevents coverage.

The policy covers any "injury" sustained while Dajani was on company business. The policy defines "injury" as an "accidental bodily injury which is direct and independent of any other cause." The policy contains a specific exclusion for suicide. Accordingly, Dajani's death will come within the terms of the policy unless the crash was not accidental.

There is some evidence that Dajani was suicidal, and some evidence to support the arson/suicide scenario presented by Dover. But there is also evidence that Dajani did not commit suicide, and some evidence that an electronic malfunction may have caused the fire that led to the crash. The evidence is essentially in equipoise.

In similar actions that arise under state law, a majority of states, including Rhode Island, recognize a presumption against suicide and in favor of accidental death, although these presumptions are rebuttable. In a minority of states, including Colorado, there is a view that suicide is never presumed. The ERISA statute is silent on the matter, and there is no binding precedent.

In a bench trial, should the judge recognize a (rebuttable) presumption against suicide and in favor of accidental death? Whether the presumption is recognized or is rejected, do you imagine that mandate of federal common law applying uniformly across the country, or is this federal common law incorporating state law?

FROM THE COURTS

S.H. BY HOLT v. UNITED STATES

U.S. Court of Appeals for the Ninth Circuit
853 F.3d 1056 (9th Cir. 2017)

LUCERO, CIRCUIT JUDGE.

In *Sosa v. Alvarez-Machain*, 452 U.S. 692 (2004), the Supreme court held that the foreign country exception to the Federal Tort Claims Act ("FTCA") bars all claims based on any injury suffered in a foreign country. *Id.* at 712. The Court left unanswered, however, the issue currently before us: How to determine where an injury is "suffered." We hold that an injury is suffered where the harm first "impinge[s]" upon the body, even if it is later diagnosed elsewhere. *See* Restatement (First) Conflict of Laws § 377 n.1.

Applying that test to the facts of this case, we conclude that the foreign country exception bars plaintiffs' claims. S.H., the daughter of William and Chantal Holt, was born prematurely while the family was stationed at a United States Air Force ("USAF") base in Spain. As a consequence of her premature birth, S.H. sustained a permanent injury to the white matter of her brain; she was diagnosed as suffering from cerebral palsy after the family returned to the United States. The Holts filed suit against the United States, contending that officials at a USAF base in California negligently approved the family's request for command-sponsored travel to a base in Spain ill-equipped to deal with Mrs. Holt's medical needs. They further argue that S.H.'s injury—the cerebral palsy diagnosis—first occurred upon their return to the United States. At trial, the district court agreed that the injury occurred in South Carolina and awarded damages of $10,409,700. Although we are sympathetic to the plaintiffs' situation, we agree with the United States that the injury at issue was suffered in Spain. We exercise jurisdiction under 28 U.S.C. § 1291 and reverse.

I

A

Mr. Holt is a Master Sergeant in the USAF. He and his wife have four children. In 2004, when the family was stationed at Edwards Air Force Base in California, Mr. Holt was informed that he was being transferred to the USAF Air Base at Rota Naval Station in Spain. Shortly thereafter, a pregnancy test at the Edwards Air Force Base medical clinic confirmed that Mrs. Holt was pregnant with their third child.

After learning he was to be transferred overseas, Mr. Holt requested command-sponsored travel for his family. To obtain approval for this program, family members must be screened to ensure that the overseas base is capable of addressing their medical needs. Dr. Richard Stahlman, chief of the medical staff at Edwards Air Force Base, approved the Holt family's command-sponsored travel to Spain. The district court found that Dr. Stahlman knew Mrs. Holt was pregnant and had experienced two prior preterm deliveries and a miscarriage at the time he cleared her for overseas travel.

In March 2005, when Mrs. Holt was approximately twenty weeks pregnant, the family relocated to Spain. There, Mrs. Holt was treated by Dr. Dennis Szurkus, a specialist in obstetrics and gynecology at Naval Hospital Rota. During an ultrasound appointment on May 11, 2005, Dr. Szurkus determined that Mrs. Holt was exhibiting signs of preterm labor and had her transferred by ambulance to an off-base hospital—Puerto Real Hospital—where she underwent an emergency cesarean section. S.H. was born on May 12, at approximately 31 weeks gestation. She had difficulty eating and breathing and was kept in the neonatal intensive care unit for seventeen days.

In the months following S.H.'s birth, the Holts saw several doctors in Spain regarding her medical issues and expressed concern that S.H. was not developing like her two older siblings, both of whom were also born preterm. Doctors told the Holts that S.H. had strabismus, poor head control, low tone in her abdominal muscles, and significant motor and developmental delays. S.H. also experienced seizure-like symptoms, for which she was prescribed phenobarbital. When she was approximately five months old, S.H. underwent an MRI, which showed periventricular leukomalacia, an injury to the white matter of her brain.

At around nine months of age, S.H. was evaluated by a neurologist, Dr. Lisa Smith, who found that S.H. had abnormally brisk reflexes and a mild increase in dynamic tone in her lower extremities. Dr. Smith did not rule out cerebral palsy at that time but declined to render a diagnosis. Two other doctors in Spain did conclude that S.H. had cerebral palsy.

The family returned to the United States in mid-2006. Late that year, S.H. was diagnosed with tetraplegia of all four extremities. At the age of two, while living in South Carolina, S.H. was definitively diagnosed with cerebral palsy. It is undisputed that S.H.'s premature birth was the cause of her cerebral palsy.

B

In June 2006, while the Holts were still in Spain, they filed an administrative claim seeking damages from the government for S.H.'s "catastrophic neurological injuries, seizures, learning deficits, physical limitations," and "cerebral palsy." They alleged that these injuries resulted from the negligent approval of Mrs. Holt's command-sponsored travel overseas. The administrative claim was denied.

Having exhausted administrative remedies, the Holts filed the instant action in district court. The government unsuccessfully moved for summary judgment, contending that the FTCA's foreign country exception barred the Holts' medical malpractice claims. Following a bench trial, the court awarded the Holts $10,409,700 in damages. The government filed a motion to alter or amend the judgment under Fed. R. Civ. P. 59(e). The court granted the motion in part but ultimately declined to alter the damages award. The government timely appealed the amended judgment and all related interlocutory orders.

II

We review a district court's findings of fact following a bench trial for clear error. However, "[w]hether the United States is immune from liability in a FTCA action is a question of federal law subject to de novo review." *Montes v. U.S.*, 37 F.3d 1347, 1351 (9th Cir. 1994).

The FTCA generally waives the United States' sovereign immunity from suits in tort, "render[ing] the Government liable in tort as a private individual would be under like circumstances." *Richards v. United States*, 369 U.S. 1, 6 (1962); *see also* 28 U.S.C. § 2674. But that waiver is subject to certain exceptions. *See generally* 28 U.S.C. § 2680. Under the foreign country exception, the FTCA's waiver of immunity does not apply to "[a]ny claim arising in a foreign country." *Id.* § 2680(k).

In *Sosa*, the Supreme Court held that the foreign country exception "bars all claims based on any injury suffered in a foreign country, regardless of where the tortious act or omission occurred." 542 U.S. at 712. The Court noted that the foreign country exception codified Congress' "unwilling[ness] to subject the United States to liabilities depending upon the laws of a foreign power." *Id.* at 707 (quoting *U.S. v. Spelar*, 338 U.S. 217, 221 (1949)). At the time the FTCA was passed, "the dominant principle in choice-of-law analysis for tort cases was *lex loci delicti*: courts generally applied the law of the place where the injury occurred." *Id.* at 705. Accordingly, the Court concluded that Congress likely intended the phrase "arising in" to have the same meaning in § 2680(k) as it did in state choice-of-law statutes: that is, to "express the position that a claim arises where the harm occurs." *Id.* at 711.[2]

The question at the center of this appeal is where S.H.'s injury was "suffered" for the purposes of the foreign country exception. The *Sosa* opinion offers various formulations of *lex loci delicti*, but provides little guidance on this specific issue. In the ordinary case, an injury will be experienced in the same place it is inflicted, thereby obviating the need for further analysis. *See, e.g., id.* at 698 (seeking damages for false arrest in Mexico). However, the inquiry becomes more complicated when, as in this case, plaintiffs allege injuries manifesting after the initial infliction of harm.

The district court concluded that state accrual law should determine where an injury is suffered. Relying on California law, it held that S.H.'s cerebral palsy occurred in the United States because it was not until the Holts arrived in South Carolina that doctors could identify S.H.'s symptoms as cerebral palsy. But as we have previously noted, "[q]uestions of interpretation under the [FTCA's] exclusion provisions are controlled by federal law." *Ramirez v. U.S.*, 567 F.2d 854, 856 (9th Cir. 1977). The district court acknowledged this principle as a general matter but concluded that because California law governed the United States' liability under 28 U.S.C. § 1346(b)(1), it also determined where the Holts' claims arose. However, § 2680(k) states that § 1346(b) "shall not apply to" any claim falling within the foreign country exception.

---

2   *Sosa* recognized that Congress' intent in enacting the foreign country exception was to prevent the United States from being subjected to liability under the laws of a foreign power. *See* 542 U.S. at 707. However, the Court also acknowledged that under its interpretation of the statute, the foreign country exception would apply even "when a State's choice-of-law approach would not apply the foreign law of place of injury." *Id.* at 711. In rejecting a more selective approach, the Court noted that Congress did not write the statutory language to bar claims only "when foreign law would be applied" but rather to all claims "arising in" a foreign country. *Id.* The Court further reasoned that even if such a meaning could be inferred from the language of the statute, it would result in "a scheme of federal jurisdiction that would vary from State to State, benefitting or penalizing plaintiffs accordingly." *Id.* Thus, a consequence of the Court's decision in *Sosa* is that the foreign country exception will sometimes bar suits that would not have triggered the application of foreign law.

The district court also failed to recognize that the question of when a claim accrues for statute of limitations purposes is analytically distinct from the question of where a claim arises under the foreign country exception. . . . [T]he statute of limitations inquiry is concerned with a plaintiff's knowledge, to ensure that a limitations period does not lapse before a reasonably diligent plaintiff is aware of her injury. In deciding where a claim arises under the foreign country exception, however, we are not concerned with the possibility of a blameless plaintiff losing a claim through delay. Thus, we ask only where "the last act necessary to establish liability occurred," *Sosa*, 542 U.S. at 705, without taking into account what the plaintiff knew or did not know.[3]

To determine where the Holts' claims arose for the purposes of the foreign country exception, we must therefore look to governing choice-of-law principles at the time Congress enacted the FTCA. And, as the Supreme Court held in *Sosa*, we must apply *lex loci delicti*. *Id*. The Restatement (First) of Conflict of Laws, upon which the Supreme Court relied in *Sosa*, provides that "[t]he place of wrong is . . . where the last event necessary to make an actor liable for an alleged tort takes place." § 377. The Restatement illustrates application of this rule when an individual "sustains bodily harm" as follows:

> Such a force is first set in motion by some human being. It is quite immaterial in what state he set the force in motion. It must alone or in cooperation with other forces harm the body of another. The person harmed may thereafter go into another state and die from the injury or suffer other loss therefrom. The place where this last event happens is also immaterial. The question is only where did the force impinge upon his body.

Id. at 377, n.1. Thus, an injury "occurs" where it is first suffered, even if a negligent act later results in further or more serious harm.

It is undisputed that S.H.'s cerebral palsy resulted from the brain injury she sustained in Spain as a consequence of her premature birth. The district court held that the Holts' claims arose in the United States because that is where S.H.'s cerebral palsy definitively manifested itself. In reaching that determination, the court distinguished between S.H.'s brain injury and

---

3   It is for this same reason that we reject any suggestion that the Holts' administrative claim, which lists "cerebral palsy" as an injury caused by the USAF's negligence, establishes that S.H. had cerebral palsy in Spain. Where an injury is suffered for the purposes of the foreign country exception is an objective inquiry, one that does not depend on what the Holts knew at a particular time.

her cerebral palsy diagnosis, reasoning that because plaintiffs were suing to recover for the latter harm, and cerebral palsy is not a disease but rather a collection of symptoms, plaintiffs' claims could not have arisen prior to those symptoms being present and diagnosable. But S.H.'s premature birth caused appreciable injury while the Holts were in Spain, even if cerebral palsy was not definitively diagnosed in that country. Under *lex loci delicti*, as it was interpreted at the time of the FTCA's passage, the fact that a plaintiff suffers some "other loss" in a different jurisdiction is "immaterial." Restatement (First) of Conflict of Laws § 377, n.1. "The question is only where did the force impinge upon [her] body." *Id.* The undisputed facts of this case indicate that the force—the brain injury S.H. suffered at or near the time of her birth—impinged upon her body in Spain; thus, that is where the Holts' claim arose. *See Sosa*, 542 U.S. at 705–06.[4]

Our conclusion is consistent with the application of the foreign country exception by other federal courts. In *Thompson v. Peace Corps*, 159 F.Supp.3d 56 (D.D.C. 2016), the court held that the foreign country exception barred the plaintiff's FTCA claims, which were based on injuries she sustained as a result of taking an anti-malarial drug in Burkina Faso. The court reasoned that although the plaintiff "complain[ed] of continuing side effects after her return home," as well as "a permanent brain injury," the court lacked jurisdiction because the "claims based on those injuries arose out of the administration of mefloquine in Burkina Faso." *Id.* at 58, 61. Similarly, the District of Columbia Circuit has twice held that a district court lacked jurisdiction over a plaintiff's claims for emotional or economic injuries occurring in the United States because those injuries were derivative of harm suffered abroad by the plaintiffs' spouses. *See Gross v. U.S.*, 771 F.3d 10, 13 (D.C. Cir. 2014) (holding that foreign country exception applied because wife's economic injuries in the United States were derivative of injuries husband suffered as a result of imprisonment in Cuba); *Harbury v. Hayden*, 522

---

4   We recognize that courts have sometimes interpreted *lex loci delicti* to different effect in the context of long-latency diseases. *See, e.g., Pounders v. Enserch E&C, Inc.*, 232 Ariz. 352 (2013) (noting that "[f]or long-latency diseases, the 'last event' takes place when the disease is discoverable because, until then, a legally compensable injury does not exist"); *Trahan v. E.R. Squibb & Sons, Inc.*, 567 F. Supp. 505, 507–08 (M.D. Tenn. 1983) (rejecting argument that "last event" occurred when plaintiff's mother ingested DES, absent any evidence that "improper development of the plaintiff's cervix occurred immediately upon her mother's ingestion of the drug"). But in those cases, there was no evidence that the plaintiffs' exposure to a toxic substance resulted in any immediate harm beyond the cellular level. By comparison, S.H.'s brain injury, resulting from her premature birth, had appreciable effects while the Holts were living in Spain. *See In re "Agent Orange" Prod. Liab. Litig.*, 580 F.Supp. 690, 707 (E.D.N.Y. 1984) (explaining, for purposes of *lex loci delicti*, that "harmful force" of Agent Orange affected military service members immediately, even though "many of the more serious symptoms did not manifest themselves until years later").

F.3d 413, 423 (D.C. Cir. 2008) (holding that foreign country exception applied to claims for emotional injuries that wife suffered in United States but that resulted from physical abuse and death of husband in Guatemala). In both cases, the court expressed concern that plaintiffs would be able to "plead around the FTCA's foreign-country exception simply by claiming injuries . . . that are derivative of the foreign-country injuries at the root of the complaint." *Harbury*, 522 F.3d at 423.

Like the injuries alleged in these cases, S.H.'s cerebral palsy is derivative of the harm she sustained at birth. As the Holts recognize, cerebral palsy is not itself a disease, but rather a group of non-progressive motor conditions. It is therefore a description of symptoms manifesting from S.H.'s brain injury, rather than a separate, compensable harm. Moreover, to hold that the Holts' claims did not arise until cerebral palsy could be definitively diagnosed would enable plaintiffs in similar circumstances to avoid application of the foreign country exception, either by pleading their injuries in a particular way or by relocating to the United States before obtaining a diagnosis. *Cf. Sosa*, 542 U.S. at 702–03 (rejecting idea that "allegations of negligent medical care . . . can . . . be repackaged as headquarters claims based on . . . the offering of bad advice" in the United States, even though harm is suffered overseas, because the practice would "swallow the foreign country exception whole" (citations omitted)); *Harbury*, 522 F.3d at 423 (prohibiting plaintiffs from "plead[ing] around" the foreign country exception by claiming domestic injuries "that are derivative of the foreign-country injuries at the root of the complaint"). Jurisdiction under the FTCA cannot turn on whether the Holts framed their suit as seeking damages for S.H.'s cerebral palsy or the brain injury she sustained at birth.

III

Because the Holts' claims against the United States arose in Spain, the FTCA's foreign country exception bars their suit. Accordingly, the district court's order is vacated, and we remand the case with instructions to dismiss for lack of subject matter jurisdiction.

COMMENTS AND QUESTIONS

1. The FTCA provides a (limited) federal cause of action for negligence against the United States government. But rather than prescribing one standard of negligence for all cases brought against the government, under the FTCA, the court applies the law (the *whole* law—including the choice of law principles) of the place of injury. The legislative history of the foreign country exception suggests that the exception was included because of Congress's unwillingness to subject the United States government to the laws of a foreign power. *Sosa v. Alvarez-Machain*, 452 U.S. 692, 707–08 (2004). The First Restatement (and the traditional choice of law methodology), dominant in the 1940s when the FTCA was passed, equated place of injury with applicable law. But if the Holts aren't arguing for the application of foreign law, why should the government enjoy the immunity of the foreign country exception?

2. To avoid the "foreign country exception" in the FTCA, the Holts argued that S.H. suffered injury not in Spain, but instead thereafter, in South Carolina where the baby was diagnosed with cerebral palsy. The appeals court rejected that argument. Is there a viable argument that S.H. suffered her injury in the United States *before* she was born in Spain? A damages judgment in excess of $10.4 million hangs in the balance.

B. Choice of Law When State Law Claims Are in Federal Court

Through diversity jurisdiction and supplemental jurisdiction, the limited subject matter jurisdiction of federal courts extends to certain claims that arise not under federal law, but rather under state (or a foreign country's) law. Consider, for example, a diversity action filed in a Wyoming federal court arising out of a contract dispute between Gould, who is a Wyoming domiciliary, and Lutz, a Californian. Their dispute arises out of a transaction that the parties never reduced to writing, and the two businesspersons now dispute the terms of their agreement. There is no relevant *federal* law of contracts. So what law applies when the claim is litigated in *federal* court?

Whether because you studied the *Erie* Doctrine in Civil Procedure or Federal Courts or because you read the earlier chapters in this book that referenced *Klaxon*

Co. v. Stentor Electric Manufacturing Co,[13] you already know that a federal court with diversity jurisdiction will apply the substantive law that would apply if that claim were instead pending in a state court of the forum state. In other words, in a *diversity* case pending in a Wyoming *federal* court, the federal judge must apply the same substantive law that a Wyoming *state* judge would apply if that action were pending in that state court. Of course the applicable law might be the substantive law of Wyoming. But if a Wyoming state judge, applying Wyoming's choice of rules, would instead apply the substantive law of, say, California, then the federal court must do likewise.

This approach has the virtue of intra-state uniformity: whether a plaintiff files in the state or federal court of Wyoming, the same substantive law will be applied.

> We are of the opinion that the prohibition declared in *Erie R. Co. v. Tompkins* against such independent determinations by the federal courts, extends to the field of conflict of laws. The conflict of laws rules to be applied by the federal court in Delaware must conform to those prevailing in Delaware's state courts. Otherwise, the accident of diversity of citizenship would constantly disturb equal administration of justice in coordinate state and federal courts sitting side by side. Any other ruling would do violence to the principle of uniformity within a state, upon which the *Tompkins* decision is based.[14]

In another case decades later, the Court added:

> A federal court in a diversity case is not free to engraft onto those state rules exceptions or modifications which may commend themselves to the federal court, but which have not commended themselves to the State in which the federal court sits. The [federal court of Texas] should identify and follow the Texas conflicts rule.[15]

Klaxon embraced the "principle of uniformity" enshrined in the *Erie* Doctrine. Understand, though, that there were, in a sense, two species of uniformity from which to choose. *Klaxon* required *intra-state uniformity.* Accordingly, then and now, the same choice of law principles apply within the state and federal courts of a state.

But the pursuit of intra-state uniformity came at the expense of *inter-district uniformity—i.e.,* uniformity throughout the system of federal courts. Federal judges in diversity cases in Wyoming apply Wyoming's state choice of law principles,

---

13   313 U.S. 487 (1941).

14   *Klaxon Co.,* 313 U.S. at 497.

15   *Day & Zimmerman, Inc. v. Challoner,* 423 U.S. 3, 4 (1975).

while federal judges in diversity cases in Iowa apply Iowa's state choice of law principles. This is unfortunate to the extent that a *system* of federal courts should share certain characteristics, including, one might argue, the approach for determining what law applies when a transaction or occurrence transcends state boundaries. Yet the federal court in Wyoming conforms to the state court in Wyoming, rather than to the federal courts in other states.

These two species of uniformity—intra-state and inter-district—are at odds with each either. If all federal courts instead applied the same set of choice of law rules in diversity cases, then there would be inter-district uniformity across the system of federal courts. But naturally this pursuit would undermine intra-state uniformity, because the choice of law rules could differ between the federal and state courts within the state.

Klaxon's endorsement of *intra-state* uniformity prevents forum shopping between the state and federal courts of a state. It prevents what is sometimes referred to as *vertical* forum shopping. But the *Erie/Klaxon* approach does not prevent so-called *horizontal* forum shopping. If California's choice of law principles are more favorable to a Wyoming plaintiff, then she can file in a California state or federal court; that state or federal court will apply California's choice of law methodology. Or if a plaintiff wants Wyoming's choice of law principles, then filing in either a federal or state court in Wyoming will suffice to invoke them.

If, contrary to contemporary practice, federal courts had one (federal) choice of law methodology that applied in all diversity cases, there would be less horizontal forum shopping: the same federal choice of law methodology would apply no matter in which federal court the case was pending, and most cases involving diverse parties would wind up in federal court because the federal methodology would be attractive (vis-à-vis state methodologies) either to the plaintiff, who could file the case in federal court, or to the defendant, who could remove the case from state to federal court.[16] But such an approach is still problematic when viewed from the perspective of two similarly-situated litigants, only one of whom has the option of filing in federal court. *Erie* thought it was an example of the unequal administration of justice when, by virtue of the fortuity of diversity, one plaintiff could file in the federal court and enjoy the benefit of a set of laws that a litigant who is trapped in state court could not also enjoy.

There is one more *What if?* to consider. There is a way to achieve comprehensive intra-state uniformity *and* inter-district uniformity. Indeed, there is a way to elimi-

---

16   Defendants who are not residents of the forum state may remove a state case to federal court if the federal court would have diversity jurisdiction. *See* 28 U.S.C. § 1441.

nate both vertical and horizontal forum shopping with respect to choice of law. The answer is federal choice of law rules *that also bind the states*. These rules could be the product of federal common law or of federal legislation. The constitutional justification for such federal law would be the uniquely federal interest in resolving the competition among state laws to regulate a transaction or occurrence that transcends state boundaries. The proposal is radical, not because of what it would achieve (to-wit, a uniform approach to a universal problem) but rather because of all that would need to be undone.

C. Litigating State Law Claims in Federal Court— The *Erie* Doctrine

In this part we delve more deeply into the law that applies when federal courts exercise jurisdiction over state law claims.

The seminal decision in this area of the law is *Erie Railroad Co. v. Tompkins*.[17] You may recall that, in that case, Harry Tompkins was walking along a footpath in a Pennsylvania town next to the Erie Railroad's train tracks. A train approached, and an object protruding from the train struck Tompkins, knocking him to the ground. When he fell, the wheels of the train crushed his arm.

Pennsylvania (state) common law provided that the Railroad owed a trespasser like Tompkins only the duty to refrain from wanton negligence. But in common law cases (as opposed to statutory claims, that is), federal courts with diversity jurisdiction did not then apply state common law. Instead, the federal courts had their own common law. And under that federal common law, a person walking along railroad tracks was owed the standard duty of care. Under the federal common law standard, Tompkins would likely prevail; under the state common law standard, Tompkins would surely lose. So Tompkins, a Pennsylvanian, sued the Erie Railroad, a New York corporation, in a New York federal court, invoking the court's diversity subject matter jurisdiction.

In *Erie*, however, the Supreme Court rejected the notion of a federal common law of torts, finding no authority in the Constitution for the federal courts to make such law. Emphasizing the importance of intra-state uniformity, Justice Brandeis's opinion for the Court required federal courts sitting in diversity to apply the law that would apply if the action were instead pending in a state court of that state. Justice Brandeis regretted how parallel federal and state court systems had encouraged forum shopping for different laws and outcomes. And he observed that it

---

17   304 U.S. 64 (1938).

574 • Learning Conflict of Laws •

was inequitable to allow the serendipity of in-state and out-of-state citizenship to produce different results.[18] *Erie* required federal courts with diversity jurisdiction to apply state law.

The *Erie* holding was consistent with the Rules of Decision Act which had long required federal courts sitting in diversity to apply "the laws of the several states. . . ."[19] Prior to *Erie*, the state "laws" that federal courts applied were state *statutes*, but not state *decisional* law. *Erie* redefined the meaning of "laws" in the Rules of Decision Act to include the decisional law as well as the statutory law of the state.

Immediately after *Erie*, the question for courts was *how much* of state law the federal courts had to apply. As we learned in Chapters 2, 10, and 14, courts have long applied their own *procedural* law even in circumstances when they apply some other jurisdiction's *substantive* law. That same principle surfaced in *Erie*, where Justice Reed, concurring, clarified that "no one doubts federal power over procedure."[20] Indeed, when federal courts sit in diversity cases, they apply the *substance* of the state law (the mandate of intra-state uniformity applied to *substantive* law), but use federal *procedure*.

Naturally, this leads to a characterization problem about what is *substantive* law and what is *procedural* law. Eight decades of case law since *Erie* have established some guidelines, yet this characterization problem, like others, is often more art than science—which is to say that the standard is flexible enough that advocacy can influence the outcome. At a generalized level the inquiry resembles the substance/procedure dichotomy examined in Chapter 10. In the *Erie* context, however, there are constitutional concerns that inform the distinction, whereas in the choice of law context the distinction is fundamentally practical.

Before we more closely examine the Court's seminal *Erie* decision, it is important—especially for a student of Conflicts—to appreciate the status of the law prior to 1938. Before the Court decided *Erie*, a federal court sitting in diversity would apply *federal* common law (not state common law). This meant, among other things, that there was essentially no *choice* of law to be made in these cases; rather than choosing between the common law of state *x* or state *y*, the court instead applied federal common law. This earlier, pre-*Erie* regime is often referred to

---

18   Imagine that Tompkins was accompanied by a friend on his walk that night. And imagine that the friend was a *New York*er who received injuries identical to Tompkins's. The inequity to which Justice Brandeis referred is the notion that Tompkins, by virtue of diversity, would be subject to a different law than his similarly situated companion.

19   *See* 28 U.S.C. § 1652.

20   304 U.S. at 92 (Reed, J., concurring).

by another seminal case, *Swift v. Tyson*.[21] The *Swift* Court held that, although the Rules of Decision Act required federal courts to apply "the laws" of the states, that mandate applied only to state *statutory* law or law linked to local matters, but not to matters of general common law. Accordingly, *Swift* endorsed a federal common law of contracts that applied when federal courts exercised diversity jurisdiction. Federal courts exercising diversity jurisdiction also developed a federal common law of *torts*; hence Tompkins' decision to file in federal court to get the benefit of the more favorable federal common law (and to avoid the less favorable state common law of Pennsylvania).

From the perspective of choice of law, this notion of a general federal common law had (and still has) some intuitive appeal. Remember that a federal court has diversity jurisdiction only when the parties are citizens of different states. Resort to a federal common law of contracts or torts in these circumstances avoided the technicalities and traps for the unwary that lurked in parochial state common laws; any chauvinism or complexity in the state common laws of either of the disputing parties was irrelevant because the laws of neither jurisdiction would apply. Parties could enter into interstate contracts with knowledge about the common law that would apply—generating *ex ante* predictability. And disputes about the common law applicable to interstate contracts were easily resolved—delivering *ex post* certainty.

Under this old regime, then, when transactions or occurrences crossed state boundaries, courts sitting in diversity could apply general federal common law, which reflected a neutral set of general principles and best practices. To the student of Conflicts who is less-than-impressed with the choice of law methodologies profiled in Chapters 3–8, the idea of applying federal common law may sound like an answer to a prayer for a fair and simple solution to the problem of what law to apply when some transaction or occurrence implicates multiple states.

But this regime of a general federal common law had a flaw: it was unconstitutional. In *Erie* the Supreme Court said that the federal courts lacked constitutional authority to create general federal common law.[22] The fact that the federal courts had engaged in this practice for at least a century was no excuse for its continuance. It was not that the practice violated a particular provision of the U.S. Constitution. Rather, it was that the federal government had limited authority, and there was no affirmative grant in the Constitution that enabled the judiciary to create a federal common law of torts or contracts.

---

21   41 U.S. 1 (1842).

22   General federal common law is distinguished from the (specialized) federal common law discussed in Part A.2, *supra*.

The old regime was premised on an increasingly outmoded jurisprudential mind-set. Prior to *Erie*, there was a sense that the common law was a transcendent body of law that courts *discovered*. The common law that was applied in a particular case represented a judge's best efforts to discern the ethereal truths of a common law that was omnipresent. In that line of thinking, it followed that there was no reason for federal common law to defer to state common law, because federal judges were as capable as state judges of unearthing these ultimate truths. By the 1930's, however, legal realism was ascendant, and *Erie* reflects that new thinking: law is not discovered by judges, but rather is *made* by judges. Federal judges were making law that they had no authority to make. Meanwhile, the Rules of Decision Act required federal courts sitting in diversity to apply the laws of the several states, and the common law decisions of state courts were among the *laws* that federal courts were obliged to follow.

Even from a choice of law perspective, the regime prior to *Erie* was not, in practice, a solution. A choice of law analysis (and the selection of one state law over another state's law) was still necessary with respect to *statutory* law, and it was often the statutory law where the technicalities and traps for the unwary were buried. Further, the content of the general federal common law of torts or contracts was not always known beforehand nor consistently applied across all federal courts.

Erie introduced a new era for the treatment of state law in federal court. In matters of substantive law, the federal court was obliged, in diversity cases, to replicate what a state court in that state would do. Yet it could apply its own procedure. The *Erie* Court's embrace of a federal *system* of procedure (i.e., *inter-district uniformity* on matters of *procedure*) in 1938 is no coincidence. The Supreme Court had just promulgated the Federal Rules of Civil Procedure (FRCP), which took effect in 1938.[23] Prior to the passage of the FRCP, the procedural law in the federal courts, in cases at law, required judges to apply the procedure of the state court in which they sat. The FRCP thus represented a shift away from intra-state procedural uniformity and toward inter-district procedural uniformity. Of course this shift occurred while the shift in *substantive* law was headed in the *opposite* direction—away from the inter-district substantive uniformity achieved by the general federal common law and toward intra-state substantive uniformity demanded by *Erie*.

The labels *substance* and *procedure* have bedeviled federal court practice then and since. We will emphasize three key Supreme Court cases in the development of that jurisprudence. First, *Guaranty Trust Co. v. York*,[24] focused on whether a state

---

23 308 U.S. 645, 649 (1938), pursuant to the Rules Enabling Act of 1934, Act of June 19, 1934, Pub. L. No. 73–415, 48 Stat. 1064.

24 326 U.S. 99 (1945).

statute of limitations applied to bar a claim that was otherwise timely under federal procedure. If the statute of limitations was *substantive*, then the state statute had to be respected in the diversity action. But if the statute of limitations was *procedural*, then the federal court could apply federal law. The Court held that matters that were *outcome-determinative* were, by virtue of that significance, matters of *substance*:

> In essence, the intent of [*Erie*] was to insure that, in all cases where a federal court is exercising jurisdiction solely because of the diversity of citizenship of the parties, the outcome of the litigation in the federal court should be substantially the same, so far as legal rules determine the outcome of a litigation, as it would be if tried in a State court.[25]

So, under the *Erie* Doctrine, statutes of limitations were (and still are) part of the substantive law that federal courts sitting in diversity are obliged to apply.[26]

The problem with an outcome-determinative test was that essentially all laws were *substantive* under that test. Indeed, even a trivial law—say, a requirement that pleadings filed with the court be fastened with a paper clip rather than a staple—could affect the outcome of litigation. If the failure to comply with that law was consequential (*e.g.,* rejection of the filing, sanctions, dismissal of the case), then the imposition of the penalty could affect the *outcome* of the case; thus the law could be labeled substantive. Such a caricature of outcome-determinativeness is not what the *Guaranty Trust* Court had in mind for its test. But for any state law that was worth fighting about, courts tended to err on the side of labeling it substantive. Accordingly, there was very little room for federal procedure under an outcome-determinative test.

Second, in *Byrd v Blue Ridge Rural Electric Cooperative, Inc.,*[27] the Supreme Court rescued federal procedure from obsolescence. In *Byrd,* the issue was whether a particular disputed issue of fact was an issue for the judge or for the jury. Most disputed issues of fact, in both federal and state court, are issues for the jury. But under the state law that created this particular cause of action, the disputed issue was to be decided by the judge. Because the nature of the factfinder could affect the outcome of the case, under *York's* outcome-determinative test, the issue would have been substantive; and, thus, the federal court would have been required to

---

25   326 U.S. at 109

26   In Chapters 10, 14, and 16, we learned that, for purposes of choice of law, statutes of limitations were traditionally labeled *procedural.* Thus the substance/procedure characterization varies by context.

27   356 U.S. 525 (1958).

apply the state law. Instead, the Court said that the court should apply federal (procedural) law:

> [The question is] whether the federal policy favoring jury decisions of disputed fact questions should yield to the state rule in the interest of furthering the objective that the litigation should not come out one way in federal court and another way in state court.[28]

The Court balanced the merits of intra-state uniformity against the merits of inter-district uniformity. Recognizing the strong federal policy interest in favor of a uniform approach to the judge-jury relationship, the Court applied the federal *procedural* law.

Third, *Hanna v. Plumer*,[29] involved a state law that required persons asserting claims against a decedent's estate to serve process upon the executor personally. Instead, the plaintiff who filed a diversity action in federal court served process upon the executor by leaving copies of the summons and the complaint with the executor's wife at their home; this service was permissible under Rule 4 of the Federal Rules of Civil Procedure but not under the relevant Massachusetts state law. The state law was outcome-determinative, but that was no longer the operative test for separating substance from procedure. If the Court had followed *Byrd*, there was, on one hand, strong policy reasons that rules for serving process should be uniform across all federal courts. But on the other hand, the law had some "substantive" characteristics, as it was uniquely tailored to permit an executor to distribute the estate without fear that further liabilities may be outstanding for which the executor can be held personally liable.

Writing for the Court, Chief Justice Warren essentially insulated the content of the Federal Rules from interference with conflicting state laws by labeling them as presumptively *procedural*.

> When a situation is covered by one of the Federal Rules, the question facing the court is a far cry from the typical, relatively unguided Erie choice: the court has been instructed to apply the Federal Rule, and can refuse to do so only if the Advisory Committee, this Court, and Congress erred in their prima facie judgment that the Rule in question transgresses neither the terms of the Enabling Act nor constitutional restrictions.

---

28   356 U.S. at 538.

29   380 U.S. 460 (1965).

Contemporary cases invoking *Erie* issues continue to use this notion of *guided* and *unguided* choices. The *Erie* analysis is guided when the state law addresses a situation that "is covered by one of the Federal Rules," and is unguided when the situation is not.

When there is no Federal Rule on point, federal courts engage in the balancing test announced in *Byrd*. Understand that even when there is no Federal Rule there is still some federal standard (or tradition) generating an *Erie* issue: one party identifies some state law that they would like the federal court to apply; the other resists, citing the contrary practice in federal court (though not dictated by a Federal Rule). As a threshold matter, the judge will determine whether

- the state law is outcome-determinative.

If the law is not outcome-determinative, the analysis ends: the federal courts will apply the federal standard and ignore the state law. If the threshold inquiry is satisfied, "*Byrd* balancing" follows. Litigators advocating for the federal court to apply the state law emphasize that:

- the difference between the state law and the federal standard would lead to (vertical) forum shopping;[30]

- the differential treatment of otherwise similarly-situated litigants solely because of diversity jurisdiction is inconsistent with the equal administration of justice;[31]

- the state law has prototypically substantive characteristics;[32] and/or

- there is no strong or clearly discernible federal policy at stake.[33]

Let us now consider the first track (*i.e.,* the guided *Erie*). The standard announced in *Hanna v. Plumer* (described above) made it sound easy to apply (If there is a

---

[30]   The question is whether differential treatment in federal court would *actually* lead to forum shopping. Is this something for which litigants would actually file in (or remove to) federal court to take advantage of? The more that the answer to that question is "yes," the more that the state law looks substantive. This is the first of the "twin aims" of *Erie*. Accordingly, it has the import of a Constitutional mandate.

[31]   Hypothesize a case exactly like the one that you are litigating, but with one exception: the parties are not diverse. Now compare the [plaintiff/defendant] in your case with the similarly situated [plaintiff/defendant] in the hypothetical case. How *unfair* is it that the [plaintiff/defendant] in your case gets to take advantage of the federal standard, if the [plaintiff/defendant] in the hypothetical case does not? The stronger the argument for unfairness, the more that the state law looks substantive. This is the second of the "twin aims" of *Erie*.

[32]   What is the prototypic substantive law? How closely can you analogize the law in your case to that prototype? Also, what are the characteristics of a substantive law? What are synonyms for substance? The Court is obliged to apply state *substantive* law.

[33]   The history behind federal "standards" can be long or short. Their origins may be more or less hallowed. The policies behind them may be sacrosanct or desultory. To the extent one is arguing for the application of ("substantive") state law, minimizing the other side of the balancing test is useful.

Federal Rule of Civil Procedure (FRCP) on point, apply it. Full stop!), but in fact, the test is much more nuanced—and is in flux. Lest this topic consume too much of a course where it is only tangentially relevant, we highlight here only the two major battle lines for the guided *Erie* analysis.

Battleground #1: Whether the FRCP is, in fact, directly on point.[34]

Often, it is not obvious whether a FRCP is directly on point. For example, FRCP 3 provides that an action "commences upon the filing of a complaint." Yet in *Walker v. ARMCO Steel Corp.*,[35] the Court applied a Minnesota state law which provided that, for purposes of tolling a limitations period, a case commenced upon *service*. The diversity plaintiff's complaint was timely under the Federal Rule, but was barred by the statute of limitations under the state law. Rather than concluding that the issue was covered by the Federal Rules, the Court held that the Federal Rule was not directly on point. In the Court's view, the Federal Rule was not intended "to toll a state statute of limitations, much less . . . to displace state tolling rules. . . . [The Federal Rule simply] governs the date from which various timing requirements of the Federal Rules begin to run. . . ." So the Court applied the state law *and* the Federal Rule, giving each law its own domain. On this battleground, then, the parties dispute how broadly or narrowly the text (and purpose) of the FRCP should be read; essentially, it is revisiting the question whether the *Erie* analysis is guided or unguided. Some justices are much more inclined than others to read the FRCP narrowly to accommodate important state regulatory interests; but only occasionally do those justices form a majority of the court.

Battleground #2: If the FRCP *is* directly on point, is the rule valid?

Federal Rules are promulgated under the Rules Enabling Act. Under this rulemaking authority, the Supreme Court may "prescribe general rules of practice and

---

34   As Professor Adam Steinman has elegantly summarized, this test is variously described by the Supreme Court as whether
- the issue "is covered by one of the Federal Rules";
- a Federal Rule "answers the question in dispute";
- there is a "direct collision between the Federal Rule and the state law";
- the "clash" between state law and a Federal Rule is "unavoidable";
- the scope of the Federal Rule in fact is sufficiently broad to control the issue before the Court;
- following state law would "command[ ] displacement of a Federal Rule by an inconsistent state rule";
- the Federal Rule "leav[es] no room for the operation of [state] law";
- the "purposes underlying the [Federal] Rule are sufficiently coextensive with the asserted purposes of the [state law] to indicate that the Rule occupies the [state law's] field of operation."

Adam N. Steinman, *Our Class Action Federalism:* Erie *and the Rules Enabling Act After Shady Grove*, 86 NOTRE DAME L. REV. 1131, 1135–36 (2011) (citations omitted).

35   *Walker v. Armco Steel Corp.*, 446 U.S. 740 (1980).

procedure . . . [that do] not abridge, enlarge or modify any substantive right."[36] Some justices read this mandate as imposing a very modest check on the rulemaking authority of courts. To this group of justices, who occasionally constitute a majority, if the Federal Rule purports to govern the manner and the means by which a litigants' rights are enforced, then it is valid. (The state law is wholly irrelevant to this analysis.)

A contrary view, embraced by other members of the Court, emphasizes the Rules Enabling Act's demand that application of the Federal Rule "not abridge, enlarge or modify any substantive [state] right." In their view, a Federal Rule is invalid if its application would supersede a state law that is so bound up with the state-created right or remedy that it defines the scope of that substantive right or remedy.[37] To this contingent, even a state law that is superficially procedural (*e.g.,* a state law that prohibits class actions) might be deemed part of the substantive law that a federal court is obliged to apply in diversity cases.

Although these battle lines are fairly easy to observe, predicting the outcome in individual cases is notoriously difficult. *Erie* disputes are highly fact-contingent.

Hypothetical 19-3

Diane Downey lived on her own until she was 90. Two years ago, Downey's three daughters moved her into a nursing home in Einstein, Oklahoma that was operated by Braintree Nursing Homes (Braintree), a national chain that is incorporated and has its principal place of business in Louisiana. Downey suffered from severe arthritis, and had difficulty communicating due to dementia.

Downey was seriously abused by two certified nursing assistants at Braintree. The daughters noticed bruises and behavioral changes; hidden cameras captured video of the assistants' physically-abusive acts. When the daughters showed the video to administrators at Braintree, the administrators called the police. The assistants were arrested, charged, and convicted of various crimes.

Downey's daughters moved her out of Braintree as quickly as possible, as her condition was failing. Downey died in another facility approximately three months after the abuse was discovered.

---

36   28 U.S.C. § 2072.

37   *See, e.g., Shady Grove Orthopedics Assocs., P.A. v. Allstate Insurance Co,* 559 U.S. 393 (2010) (Stevens, J., concurring).

The family filed a lawsuit against Braintree in an Oklahoma federal court. Evidence of Braintree's failures with respect to hiring, training, and supervising employees was appalling. After a trial, the jury found for plaintiffs on claims of negligence and negligence per se. The jury awarded $1.2 million in compensatory damages and $800,000 in punitive damages.

After the jury returned its verdict and the judge announced the entry of judgment in those amounts, Braintree moved to alter or amend the judgment. In a civil action arising from a claimed bodily injury, Oklahoma caps noneconomic damages on all tort claims at $350,000.

The trial judge announced that she is inclined to deny Braintree's motion, because "the damage cap is an affirmative defense that Braintree waived by failing to assert in its answer."

Braintree concedes that it did not plead the cap as an affirmative defense. But Braintree argues that it was not obliged to do so. Two years ago, the Oklahoma Supreme Court rejected the notion that the cap was tied to the assertion of an affirmative defense, holding "The legislature's unmistakable intent was to minimize exorbitant damage awards and the imposition of procedural technicalities could undermine that intention. A post-verdict motion that brings the matter to the attention of the judge is sufficient."

Federal Rule of Civil Procedure 8(c)(1) provides that when "responding to a pleading, a party must affirmatively state any avoidance or affirmative defense, including [eighteen defenses such as duress, estoppel, laches, and statute of limitations]." Damages caps are not on the list, but this list is non-exhaustive. It is well-settled law of the federal courts that, generally speaking, an affirmative defense that is not asserted is waived.

There is persuasive case law in the U.S. Court of Appeals for the Tenth Circuit (which includes Oklahoma) that a state's statutory limit on damages is substantive law that federal courts sitting in diversity must apply. The question here, however, is whether the classification of that substantive right as an affirmative defense that defendants must assert is also a matter of substantive state law. This is a question of first impression.

You clerk for the trial judge, who has asked for your help resolving this dispute.

FROM THE COURTS

OTTO v. NEWFIELD EXPLORATION CO.

U.S. District Court for the District of Montana
___ F.Supp.3d ___, 2017 WL 3616712 (D. Mont. Feb. 22, 2017)

WATERS, DISTRICT JUDGE.

Before the Court is Plaintiff Estate of Otto's Motion to Amend the Complaint to add a claim for punitive damages [under North Dakota law]. For the [following] reasons, the Estate of Otto's Motion is granted.

I. Facts

Blain Otto (Otto) was employed by a company that provided tank inspection services, among other things, to Newfield on a contract basis at various well sites in the Bakken Shale Oil Field. On July 18, 2013, Otto was found dead on the catwalk of an oil storage tank at a well site in McKenzie County, North Dakota.

Otto's estate filed suit, alleging Otto died of exposure to deadly hydrocarbon vapors due to intentional, malicious, and/or negligent conduct by Newfield. The complaint included a claim for punitive damages under Montana law. On July 26, 2016, the Court determined North Dakota law governed the case.

II. Law

Although not raised by either party, the Court notes the Estate of Otto's Motion is governed by both a federal rule and a state law. Under Fed. R. Civ. P. 15(a)(2), a party may amend its pleading with either the opposing party's written consent or the court's leave. The Court should grant leave to amend "when justice so requires." Fed. R. Civ. P. 15(a)(2). Under N.D.C.C. § 32–03.2–11(1),[*] a party may amend its complaint to include punitive

---

*   [Eds.' Note: Section 03.2–11 of Chapter 32 ("Judicial Remedies") of North Dakota's Code provides as follows: § 32–03.2–11. When court or jury may give exemplary damages

    1. In an action for the breach of an obligation not arising from contract, when the defendant has been guilty by clear and convincing evidence of oppression, fraud, or actual malice, the court or jury, in addition to the actual damages, may give damages for the sake of example and by way of punishing the defendant. Upon commencement of the action, the complaint may not seek exemplary damages. After filing the suit, a party may make a motion to amend the pleadings to claim exemplary damages. The motion must allege an applicable legal basis for awarding exemplary damages and must be accompanied by one or more affidavits or deposition testimony showing the factual basis

damages only by filing a motion with accompanying affidavits and deposition testimony showing the factual basis for the claim. The opposing party may then respond with affidavits and deposition testimony. The Court may grant the motion to amend if "there is sufficient evidence to support a finding by the trier of fact that a preponderance of the evidence proves" the elements of punitive damages. N.D.C.C. § 32–03.2–11(1).

The Court previously noted the motion to amend standard contained in § 32–03.2–11(1) when it determined North Dakota law applied to the case. However, the Court's choice of law analysis turned on the difference between Montana law and North Dakota law, not between North Dakota law and federal procedure. Furthermore, the Court's determination that a conflict existed between Montana law and North Dakota law was premised on the difference between the punitive damages caps, not the standard a party must meet to amend its complaint to add punitive damages. The Court is now faced with a conflict between North Dakota law and federal procedure and therefore must determine whether Rule 15(a)(2) or § 32–03.2–11(1) governs the Estate of Otto's Motion to Amend.

Federal courts apply state substantive law and federal procedural law to diversity cases. *Goldberg v. Pacific Indem. Co.*, 627 F.3d 752, 755 (9th Cir. 2010) (citing *Erie R.R. Co. v. Tompkins*, 304 U.S. 64 (1938)). But the line between procedural and substantive law is often hazy. *Erie*, 304 U.S. at 92 (Reed, J., concurring). A state procedural rule, though undeniably "procedural" in the ordinary sense of the term may exist to influence substantive outcomes. *Shady Grove Orthopedic Assocs., P.A. v. Allstate Ins. Co.*, 559 U.S. 393, 419–20 (2010) (Stevens, J., concurring). Thus, when a State chooses

---

for the claim. The party opposing the motion may respond with affidavit or deposition testimony. If the court finds, after considering all submitted evidence, that there is sufficient evidence to support a finding by the trier of fact that a preponderance of the evidence proves oppression, fraud, or actual malice, the court shall grant the moving party permission to amend the pleadings to claim exemplary damages. For purposes of tolling the statute of limitations, pleadings amended under this section relate back to the time the action was commenced.

2. If either party so elects, the trier of fact shall first determine whether compensatory damages are to be awarded before addressing any issues related to exemplary damages. Evidence relevant only to the claim of exemplary damages is not admissible in the proceeding on liability for compensatory damages. If an award of compensatory damages has been made, the trier of fact shall determine whether exemplary damages are to be awarded. . . .

4. If the trier of fact determines that exemplary damages are to be awarded, the amount of exemplary damages may not exceed two times the amount of compensatory damages or two hundred fifty thousand dollars, whichever is greater; provided, however, that no award of exemplary damages may be made if the claimant is not entitled to compensatory damages. In a jury trial, the jury may not be informed of the limit on damages contained in this subsection. . . .]

to use a traditionally procedural vehicle as a means of defining the scope of substantive rights or remedies, federal courts must recognize and respect that choice. *Shady Grove*, 559 U.S. at 420 (Stevens, J., concurring).

In *Shady Grove*, Justice Stevens formulated a two-step framework to negotiate this "thorny area." 559 U.S. at 421 (Stevens, J., concurring). Justice Stevens' concurrence controls the *Shady Grove* plurality because it concurred in the judgment on the narrowest grounds. *See Marks v. U.S.*, 430 U.S. 188, 193 (1977) (When "no single rationale explaining the result enjoys the assent of five justices, the holding of the Court may be viewed as that position taken by those Members who concurred in the judgments on the narrowest grounds."); *Baumann v. Chase Inv. Services Corp.*, 747 F.3d 1117, 1124 (9th Cir. 2014) (applying Justice Stevens' concurrence).

The first step is determining whether the federal rule and state law conflict. To do so, the Court considers whether the federal rule is "sufficiently broad to control the issue before the court, thereby leaving no room for the operation of seemingly conflicting state law." *Shady Grove*, 559 U.S. at 421 (Stevens, J., concurring). If a "direct collision" exists, the federal rule and state law conflict. *Shady Grove*, 559 U.S. at 422 (Stevens, J., concurring). The federal rule controls unless it violates the Rules Enabling Act. *Shady Grove*, 559 U.S. at 422 (Stevens, J., concurring).

The second step is determining whether the federal rule violates the Rules Enabling Act. A federal rule violates the Rules Enabling Act if it abridges, enlarges, or modifies any substantive right. *Shady Grove*, 559 U.S. at 422 (Stevens, J., concurring) (citing 28 U.S.C. § 2072(b)). The inquiry is not always simple because "it is difficult to conceive of any rule of procedure that cannot have a significant effect on the outcome of a case." *Shady Grove*, 559 U.S. at 422 (Stevens, J., concurring). Almost "any rule can be said to have substantive effects affecting society's distribution of risks and rewards." *Shady Grove*, 559 U.S. at 422 (Stevens, J., concurring). Because "one can often argue the state rule was really some part of the State's definition of its right or remedies," the bar for finding a Rules Enabling Act violation "is a high one." *Shady Grove*, 559 U.S. at 422 (Stevens, J., concurring). The mere possibility that a federal rule would alter a state-created right is not sufficient here, there must be little doubt. *Shady Grove*, 559 U.S. at 422 (Stevens, J., concurring).

Here, there is a "direct collision" between Rule 15(a)(2) and § 32–03.2–11(1). Under Rule 15(a)(2), the Estate of Otto may amend its complaint to add punitive damages "when justice so requires, whereas under § 32–03.2–11(1), the Estate of Otto may amend its complaint to add punitive damages when "a preponderance of the evidence" proves the elements of punitive damages. The two rules cannot coexist and the federal rule controls unless it violates the Rules Enabling Act.

Turning to the second step, the Court holds Rule 15(a)(2) does not violate the Rules Enabling Act because there is sufficient doubt that Rule 15(a)(2) alters North Dakota's rights or remedies.[1] First, Rule 15(a)(2) is facially valid under the Rules Enabling Act because it does not affect traditional aspects of substantive law such as the elements the Estate of Otto will have to prove at trial or the burden it must meet to prove them. *Shady Grove*, 559 U.S. at 426 n.10 (Stevens, J., concurring) ("It will be rare that a federal rule that is facially valid under [the Rules Enabling Act] will displace a State's definition of its own substantive rights.").

Second, the legislative history of § 32–03.2–11(1) does not clearly establish § 32–03.2–11(1) is part of North Dakota's definition of its rights and remedies. There was some discussion that § 32–03.2–11(1) would provide defendants protection from punitive damages claims. *See* House Standing Committee Minutes on House Bill 1297, January 21, 1997 (N.D. 1997). But that is not "particularly strong evidence" that § 32–03.2–11(1) was intended to define a defendant's rights and remedies because any procedure that places an obligation on the plaintiff accomplishes that purpose. *See Shady Grove*, 559 U.S. at 434 (Stevens, J., concurring) (legislative history that class action rule was adopted to avoid "annihilating punishment of the defendant" was not "particularly strong evidence" of intent to define rights because "[a]ny device that makes litigation easier makes it easier for plaintiffs to recover damages."). . . .

Furthermore, the legislature discussed the best point in the proceedings for judicial disposition of punitive damages claims.[2] *See* House Standing Committee Minutes on House Bill 1297, January 21, 1997 and March

---

1   There is a split among district courts that considered this question pre-*Shady Grove*. *See Belkow v. Celotex Corp.*, 722 F. Supp. 1547 (N.D. Ill. 1989) (state law procedural); *Citron v. Armstrong World Indus., Inc.*, 721 F. Supp. 1259 (S.D. Fla. 1989) (state law procedural); *NAL II, Ltd. v. Tonkin*, 705 F. Supp. 522 (D. Kan. 1989) (state law procedural); *Windsor v. Guarantee Trust Life Ins. Co.*, 684 F. Supp. 630 (D. Idaho 1988) (state law substantive); *Fournier v. Marigold Foods, Inc.*, 678 F. Supp. 1420 (D. Minn. 1988) (state law substantive); *McHugh v. Jacobs*, 450 F.Supp.2d 1019, 1021 (D.N.D. 2006) (state law substantive).

2   There was also discussion of whether § 32–03.2–11(1) violated the separation of powers because it regulated procedure. See House Standing Committee Minutes on House Bill 1297, January 21, 1997 and March 5–24, 1997, and attached letter of Frederick E. Saefeke (N.D. 1997).

5–24, 1997 (N.D. 1997). Pre- and post-judicial disposition of claims is the realm of procedure. *See* Fed. R. Civ. P. 12 (motion to dismiss); Fed. R. Civ. P. 50 (judgment as a matter of law); Fed. R. Civ. P. 56 (summary judgment). § 32–03.2–11(1) merely provides a different point than summary judgment for judicial disposition of a punitive damages claim because an order granting leave to amend under § 32–03.2–11(1) necessarily precludes summary judgment on the issue. *Compare* § 32–03.2–11(1) (preponderance of the evidence) *with* N.D. Civ. P. 56(c) (no genuine issue of material fact).

The Court holds Rule 15(a)(2) does not violate the Rules Enabling Act because it is facially valid and § 32–03.2–11(1)'s legislative history does not clearly show § 32–03.2–11(1) is part of North Dakota's definition of its rights and remedies. *Shady Grove*, 559 U.S. at 422–436 (Stevens, J., concurring). Rule 15(a)(2) therefore governs the Estate of Otto's motion to amend. . . .

COMMENTS AND QUESTIONS

1. Why would the court raise an *Erie* issue *sua sponte*?

2. Characterize the conflict wisely (strategically) when arguing an *Erie* issue. The court raised the *Erie* issue as a conflict between the state law and Fed. R. Civ. P. 15(a)(2). Is there also a conflict between the state law and Fed. R. Civ. P. 8(a)(3), which states that the complaint "must contain: . . . a demand for the relief sought"?

3. Does it matter that N.D.C.C. § 32–03.2–11(1) was part of a comprehensive tort reform package that was intended to lower insurance rates and improve the business climate within the state?

SAMPLE EXAM QUESTION

Question 19-4

Nebi Lazos, a citizen and resident of Las Cruces, New Mexico, sought medical treatment at nearby El Paso Community Hospital in El Paso, Texas. Doctors misread an x-ray, misdiagnosed her condition, and prescribed treatment that dramatically worsened her symptoms. Lazos nearly died before the doctor's errors were corrected and, after six months of misery, she is now nearly fully recovered.

Lazos has come to you seeking legal representation, and you conclude that she may have a viable claim for medical malpractice. Both New Mexico and Texas have identical statutes that require plaintiffs pursuing medical malpractice claims to file an "Affidavit of Merit" with respect to each named defendant. The Affidavit of Merit must include:

(i) A statement that the affiant has reviewed all medical records reasonably available to the plaintiff concerning the allegations contained in the complaint;

(ii) A statement that the affiant is familiar with the applicable standard of care;

(iii) The opinion of the affiant that the standard of care was breached by one or more of the defendants to the action and that the breach caused injury to the plaintiff.

If the plaintiff fails to include the Affidavit(s) of Merit with the initial filing of the Complaint, the complaint must be dismissed. These provisions were adopted by the states as part of comprehensive tort reform measures that were intended to eliminate frivolous lawsuits, reduce medical malpractice premiums, and streamline medical malpractice litigation.

Further, in Texas, the state court has a heightened pleading requirement that was added to the state's pleading rules as part of the same comprehensive tort reform measure mentioned above. The pleading rule provides as follows:

8.01 Medical malpractice.—Any complaint alleging medical malpractice by a health care provider in failing to comply with the applicable standard of care shall be dismissed unless the facts and circumstances giving rise to each element of the cause of action are pled with heightened specificity. Dismissals hereunder shall be without prejudice.

As plaintiff's counsel, your preliminary efforts to secure an Affidavit of Merit from an appropriate expert have been unsuccessful. But given the availability of diversity jurisdiction in federal court, would you need an Affidavit of Merit if you filed in federal court? And if you do file in (a New Mexico or Texas) federal court, will you need to satisfy Texas's heightened pleading requirement?

Quick Summary

- There is a strong (but rebuttable) presumption against extraterritorial application

- Occasionally, federal law does not impose a single, uniform, national mandate, and instead prescribes conformity with state (or even a foreign country's) law.

- Federal courts with diversity jurisdiction apply the choice of law methodology of the state in which the federal court sits

- Federal courts with diversity jurisdiction apply state substantive law, but may apply federal procedural law

- The substance/procedure dichotomy requires a species of characterization; yet the categories of substance and procedure are inherently neither mutually exclusive nor cumulatively exhaustive

20

Personal Jurisdiction

Key Concepts

- General jurisdiction: domicile, principal place of business, state of incorporation, and being "at home"
- Specific jurisdiction: relatedness, long-arm statutes, minimum contacts, and reasonableness
- Personal service (transient or tag jurisdiction)
- Waiver: intentional, inadvertent, and waiver by conduct
- Consent: forum selection clause
- Status
- 100-mile bulge rule
- Federal statute: nation- and world-wide service of process
- Federal question against foreign defendant under FRCP 4(k)(2)

Personal jurisdiction is one of the three major topics in a Conflict of Laws course. Personal jurisdiction is sometimes referred to as jurisdiction to adjudicate. *Adjudicative* jurisdiction regards the authority to host the litigation that determines the parties' rights and responsibilities. This is distinguished from *legislative* jurisdiction which regards the authority of a state or country to regulate those rights and responsibilities. A state may have both legislative and adjudicative jurisdiction; a state might have one of those forms of jurisdiction but not the other; or a state may have neither.[1]

Adjudicative jurisdiction can influence the outcome of litigation even if that state does not also have legislative jurisdiction. This is to say that there are reasons to file a case in, say, Oregon even if Oregon substantive law will not prescribe the

---

1   A third type of jurisdiction is *subject matter* jurisdiction. That doctrine constrains a court's ability to hear a specific type of claim. The subject matter jurisdiction of federal courts, for example, is limited.

parties' rights and responsibilities. First, litigating in an inconvenient place can add expense and complexity. For example, a party may need to hire local counsel with whom they have no prior relationship nor any realistic likelihood of a future relationship. Second, the court will apply forum *procedural* law. (Chapters 2 and 10.) Procedure is power, and procedural means can achieve substantive ends, whether intentionally or unintentionally. Third, the forum will apply that state's choice of law rules. Adjudicative jurisdiction thus includes the authority to determine which state (or states) has (have) legislative jurisdiction. Especially in light of the homeward trend that leads judges naturally to favor the application of familiar, forum law, the authority to adjudicate makes it more likely, as a practical matter, that the same state will also have the authority to legislate.

The plaintiff initially chooses the forum and there are six bases that can provide a state with adjudicatory jurisdiction—any one of which will suffice.

- General jurisdiction
- Specific jurisdiction
- Personal service within the forum
- Waiver
- Consent
- Status

When a case is pending in federal rather than state court, the above list expands to include three additional bases:

- Fed. R. Civ. P. 4(k)(1)(B) (the 100-mile bulge rule)
- Fed. R. Civ. P. 4(k)(1)(C) (nation- or world-wide service statutes)
- Fed. R. Civ. P. 4(k)(2) (federal questions against alien defendants)

We will consider all nine of these jurisdictional bases in turn.

General Jurisdiction

General jurisdiction allows the forum state to adjudicate the rights and responsibilities of a defendant who is "at home" in the forum state, even if the underlying claim has nothing to do with the forum state. General jurisdiction is frequently referred to as *all-purpose* jurisdiction, which is in contrast to the *specific* or *case-based* jurisdiction that we will study next.

An individual (*i.e.*, a natural person) is "at home" in their state of domicile. A corporation is "at home" in their state of incorporation and also in the state of their principal place of business (i.e., their corporate headquarters). These are the so-called paradigmatic bases for determining where a litigant is at home, which is to say: where they are subject to general jurisdiction.

Conceivably, an individual might also be "at home" in a state other than their state of domicile. Remember the definition of domicile. (Chapter 13.) Someone, let's call him Pat, might still be legally domiciled in Maine even if he has not lived there for years and even if he has no intention of returning to Maine. He might *reside* in West Virginia, where he has lived for years. West Virginia would not be Pat's domicile unless while present in West Virginia he also had the intention of remaining indefinitely in West Virginia. Under such circumstances one could argue—perhaps successfully—that Pat is "at home" in West Virginia.

Similarly, a corporation might be "at home" in a state other than its state of incorporation and the state of its principal place of business. The Boeing Corporation, for example, is incorporated in Delaware and has its corporate headquarters (and therefore its principal place of business) in Chicago, Illinois.[2] But Boeing also has an enormous manufacturing operation in Everett, Washington. According to its website, Boeing's campus "is big enough to encompass Disneyland with 12 acres left over for parking." The site includes "the largest manufacturing building in the world." To be clear, this muscular presence in Washington does not establish Washington as the company's principal place of business; a corporation's headquarters establishes the principal place of business.[3] But one could argue—perhaps successfully—that Boeing is "at home" in Washington.

Before the Supreme Court's decision in *Goodyear Dunlop Tires Operations, S.A. v. Brown*, 564 U.S. 915, 919 (2011), lower courts often found that a corporate defendant was subject to general jurisdiction if it had a systematic and continuous presence in the forum state. (In this earlier, now-outdated era, general jurisdiction was often referred to as "doing-business jurisdiction." A company was subject to general jurisdiction in any state where it had a systematic and continuous business presence.) In *Goodyear*, the Supreme Court rejected what it called a "sprawling view" of general jurisdiction, and introduced as a limited concept the notion that general jurisdiction is appropriate only where the defendant is "at home." Determining whether a defendant is "at home" requires more than an assessment of the *absolute* magnitude of the defendant's contacts with the forum state. The contacts

---

2   In the year 2001, Boeing moved its corporate headquarters from Washington to Illinois.

3   *See Hertz Corp. v. Friend*, 559 U.S. 77, 80 (2010) (holding that a company's principal place of business is "where the corporation's high level officers direct, control, and coordinate the corporation's activities").

with the forum state must, *relative* to the defendant's contacts with other states, demonstrate that the defendant is at home there. Accordingly, the ubiquitous presence of a company like McDonald's does not mean that they are "at home" in every state. Indeed, outside of the "exceptional case," general jurisdiction over a corporation will usually be limited to the two paradigm locations where a corporation is at home: its state of incorporation and its principal place of business.

Hypothetical 20-1

Dr. Harpreet Panesar was a research fellow at the distinguished Tulsa University Hospital in Tulsa, Oklahoma, when she was designated the Medical Researcher of the Year by the National Hemophilia Foundation (NHF). She received the award at the NHF annual awards banquet at NHF's headquarters (and its only place of business) in Minneapolis, Minnesota.

Shortly after Panesar received the award, Dr. Kevin Tsui, wrote to the NHF "on behalf of the University of District of Columbia Hospitals (UDCH)" and told them that Panesar lacked the credentials that she claimed to possess. According to Tsui's letter, UDCH discovered irregularities in Panesar's resume when, years earlier, she applied for a fellowship at UDCH.

In response to Tsui's letter, the NHF immediately posted a notice on its website that it had "just become aware of possible inaccuracies regarding Dr. Panesar's background, qualifications, and experience." The statement further provided that "NHF is taking all appropriate steps to preserve the integrity of its nominations and awards process, and apologizes for recent failures."

Shortly after the NHF published the statement on its website, Tulsa University Hospital decided not to extend Panesar's fellowship. Panesar found an inferior job with a medical research company in northern Virginia, where she now lives and works. Panesar claims that there is not even a typographical error on her resume, much less a factual misrepresentation. Accordingly, Panesar has a colorable defamation claim against Tsui, UDCH, and NHF.

Tsui lives in Virginia and is an associate professor at UDCH. UDCH is in the District of Columbia, but has many collaborative projects at hospitals, colleges, high schools, and community centers in Northern Virginia. NHF is incorporated in Virginia, but all of its assets and employees are in Minnesota. NHF scientists regularly attend conferences in Washington D.C., Virginia, and elsewhere.

Would the courts of D.C. have general jurisdiction over all three defendants? Would the courts of Virginia have general jurisdiction over the defendants?

FROM THE COURTS

WAL-MART STORES, INC. v. LEMAIRE

Court of Appeals of Arizona
242 Ariz. 357 (2017)

SWANN, JUDGE.

Kathi Buss sued Wal-Mart Stores, Inc., a company incorporated in Delaware with its principal place of business in Arkansas, in Arizona over a slip-and-fall accident that occurred at a store in Oregon. Wal-Mart filed a motion to dismiss for lack of jurisdiction, and the superior court, relying on our opinion in *Bohreer v. Erie Ins. Exc.*, 216 Ariz. 208 (App. 2007), denied it, finding Wal-Mart was subject to general jurisdiction in Arizona. Wal-Mart then filed a petition for special action.

Because the facts of the case have no connection to Arizona, Wal-Mart can be sued here only if the Arizona courts have general jurisdiction over it. Buss maintains that Wal-Mart's pervasive presence and substantial business activities in Arizona are sufficient to create general jurisdiction, and *any* claim against Wal-Mart is therefore cognizable in Arizona. We disagree. In keeping with *Goodyear Dunlop Tires Operations, S.A. v. Brown*, 564 U.S. 915 (2011) and *Daimler AG v. Bauman*, 571 U.S. 117 (2014), we hold that the magnitude of a corporation's business activities in Arizona is not sufficient to create general jurisdiction when that corporation is neither incorporated nor has its principal place of business in Arizona. We further hold that foreign corporations do not impliedly consent to general jurisdiction merely by registering as foreign corporations and appointing agents for service of process under A.R.S. §§ 10–1501 to –1510. Wal-Mart therefore is subject only to specific jurisdiction in Arizona, and actions against it in the Arizona courts must relate to its activities in the state. . . .

States may exercise two forms of personal jurisdiction. First, specific jurisdiction exists when the defendant establishes minimum contacts with the forum state by purposefully directing its activities to that state, and the litigation arises out of those activities. Second, general jurisdiction allows a forum state to hear any claim against the defendant, even when the facts giving rise to it have no connection to the forum. *Goodyear*, 564 U.S. at 919. General jurisdiction exists over a corporation in . . . a state in which its affiliations with the State are so continuous and systematic as to render it essentially at home in the forum State. . . .

Because this case arises entirely out of Wal-Mart's activities in Oregon, Arizona courts lack specific jurisdiction. The sole issue in this . . . action is the extent to which Arizona may exercise general jurisdiction over foreign corporations. Buss suggests two theories to support general jurisdiction over Wal-Mart in Arizona: (1) by appointing an agent for service of process, it has consented to general jurisdiction, and (2) the sheer magnitude of Wal-Mart's presence in Arizona relative to other corporations means that Wal-Mart is "at home" here. We address each argument in turn.

[First, t]he superior court concluded . . . that Wal-Mart impliedly consented to general jurisdiction in Arizona by registering and appointing an agent to receive process here. . . .

We hold that these provisions do not create general personal jurisdiction over foreign corporations, either by prescription or consent. . . . Buss argues that it would be "manifestly unfair to Arizonans" to hold that we lack general jurisdiction over Wal-Mart such that Arizona residents cannot sue for causes of action that arise in other states. But, it is settled law that the specific-jurisdiction analysis focuses exclusively on the "the relationship among the defendant, the forum, and the litigation," *Walden v. Fiore*, 571 U.S. 277 (2014), and the convenience to the *plaintiff* has no bearing on whether a *defendant's* due process rights are violated by subjecting it to general jurisdiction.

[Next,] Wal-Mart is not "at home" in Arizona.

A state has general jurisdiction over a foreign corporation when the corporation's "affiliations with the State are so 'continuous and systematic' as to render [it] essentially at home in the forum State." *Goodyear*, 564 U.S. at 919. But general jurisdiction requires more than continuous and systematic activity. *Id.* at 927–28; *see also Daimler*, 134 S. Ct. at 761 n.19 (general jurisdiction outside the state of incorporation or forum state may be permissible in an "exceptional case"). Wal-Mart argues that after *Daimler* and *Goodyear*, foreign corporations are subject to general jurisdiction *only* in their respective principal places of business and states of incorporation. We need not endorse Wal-Mart's broad reading of those cases to conclude that they do not support the exercise of general jurisdiction in Arizona on this record.

In *Goodyear*, the Supreme Court held that North Carolinians could not sue Goodyear's foreign subsidiaries in a United States court for a tire design defect that allegedly caused an accident in France. 564 U.S. at 920–21. The Court reasoned that placement of tires into the stream of commerce, some of which may end up in the forum, is not enough to confer general jurisdiction in that forum. *Id.* at 926–29.

In *Daimler*, Argentinian residents sued Daimler, a German company, in federal court in California over its Argentinian subsidiary's alleged collaboration with Argentinian security forces in the perpetration of human rights abuses in the 1970s and 1980s in Argentina. 134 S. Ct. at 750–51. The plaintiffs claimed that Daimler was subject to general jurisdiction in California based on the contacts of its subsidiary, Mercedes. *Id.* at 751. The Court reasoned that "[i]t was . . . error . . . to conclude that Daimler, even with [Mercedes's] contacts attributed to it, was at home in California, and hence subject to suit there on claims by foreign plaintiffs having nothing to do with anything that occurred or had its principal impact in California." *Id.* at 762.

Daimler did not categorically reject the possibility that a state may exercise general jurisdiction over a corporation for other reasons:

> We do not foreclose the possibility that in an exceptional case [such as *Perkins v. Benguet Consol. Mining Co.*, 342 U.S. 437 (1952)] a corporation's operations in a forum other than its formal place of incorporation or principal place of business may be so substantial and of such a nature as to render the corporation at home in that State. . . .

> [But] the general jurisdiction inquiry does not focus solely on the magnitude of the defendant's in-state contacts. . . . *General jurisdiction calls for an appraisal of a corporation's activities in their entirety, nationwide and worldwide.* A corporation that operates in many places can scarcely be deemed at home in all of them. Otherwise, "at home" would be synonymous with "doing business" tests framed before specific jurisdiction evolved in the United States.

Id. at 761 n.19 (internal quotation, modification, and citation omitted) (emphasis added).

Federal circuit courts have interpreted *Daimler* to mean that states other than a corporation's state of incorporation and principal place of business may exercise general jurisdiction over that corporation only in exceptional cases. *Brown*, 814 F.3d at 627 ("[I]n our view *Daimler* established that, except in a truly "exceptional" case, a corporate defendant may be treated as 'essentially at home' only where it is incorporated or maintains its principal place of business—the 'paradigm' cases."); *Carmouche v. Tamborlee Mgmt., Inc.*, 789 F.3d 1201, 1204 (11th Cir. 2015) (noting that general jurisdiction is appropriate "only in 'exceptional' cases"); . . . *Monkton Ins. Servs., Ltd. v. Ritter*, 768 F.3d 429, 432 (5th Cir. 2014) (noting that it is "incredibly difficult to establish general jurisdiction in a forum other than the place of incorporation or principal place of business"). . . .

The Supreme Court has acknowledged only one exceptional case that would give rise to general jurisdiction over a foreign corporation *Daimler*, 134 S. Ct. 746 at 761 n.19 (citing *Perkins*, 342 U.S. 437). In *Perkins*, the Supreme Court held that general jurisdiction was proper in Ohio when the defendant company's mining operation in the Philippines was shut down by the Japanese occupation, and the general manager, who was also the principal stockholder, relocated and ran the company's "necessarily limited wartime activities" in Ohio. 342 U.S. at 447–48.

Buss argues that Wal-Mart is subject to general jurisdiction based on its exceptionally substantial business activities in Arizona. As of January 2017, in Arizona Wal-Mart operates 127 retail locations and 4 distribution centers, employs 33,910 people, spent $1.5 billion with suppliers, collected $270.3 million in state sales taxes, and paid $91.5 million in state taxes. Wal-Mart was the largest employer in Arizona in 2014 and the second-largest in 2015. In 2015, it employed more Arizonans than the next two largest employers combined. But while Wal-Mart has a large economic presence in the state, there is nothing "exceptional" about its activities to give rise to general jurisdiction.

Were we to hold that Arizona, a state that is home to just under 34,000 of Wal-Mart's estimated 2.3 million global employees (1.5 million of whom are employed in the United States) has general jurisdiction over Wal-Mart, we would effectively confer general jurisdiction over every foreign corporation with a large commercial presence in Arizona. Such a rule would be neither fair, rational nor consistent with the reasoning of *Daimler* and *Goodyear*. Neither the facts of this case nor the nature of Wal-Mart's activities in Arizona give rise to the "exceptional case" envisioned by the Supreme Court—exigent circumstances that render traditional jurisdictional limits unworkable.

Moreover, a size-based approach would be both standard-less and malleable. There is no constitutional doctrine establishing a threshold level of commercial activity sufficient to create general jurisdiction. And if mere size were sufficient, the fluctuating levels of each foreign corporation's economic activity would have to be re-litigated in every case before jurisdiction could be determined. We view such an approach as constitutionally untenable.

Buss argues that Wal-Mart's presence here is more like *Perkins* by arguing it is a party to many suits in Arizona and is thus not prejudiced by having to defend this action in Arizona, and she notes that the former chairman of Wal-Mart's board of directors resides in Arizona. We disagree. First, Wal-Mart's contacts with the state are easily sufficient to subject it to specific jurisdiction in cases involving its activities in, or directed to, Arizona. The fact that such cases arise does not create jurisdiction over cases that have no connection to this state—as the Supreme Court noted, "[a] corporation that operates in many places can scarcely be deemed at home in all of them." *Daimler*, 134 S. Ct. at 762 n.20. . . .

In sum, subjecting Wal-Mart to general jurisdiction in Arizona based on the level of its commercial activity would wrongly conflate general jurisdiction with specific jurisdiction and provide an unworkable standard that would require extensive factual findings in every case. Even without general jurisdiction in Arizona, Buss has a forum readily available to seek redress for her injuries—Oregon. . . .

COMMENTS AND QUESTIONS

1. Buss was injured in Oregon. Why did she file suit in Arizona? Where would this defendant have been subject to general jurisdiction?

2. Who is this court protecting from Arizona's exercise of jurisdiction? Would Wal-Mart be unfairly prejudiced or inconvenienced by litigating in Arizona (instead of Oregon)? Would the taxpayers of Arizona be unfairly burdened by subsidizing litigation (maybe even staffing a jury) to resolve a dispute that doesn't affect them?

3. The court rejected plaintiff's argument that Wal-Mart should be subject to personal jurisdiction in Arizona because of the substantial business that it does there, noting that "[s]uch a rule would be neither fair, rational nor consistent with the reasoning of . . . *Goodyear*."

   In *Goodyear*, one of the defendants named in the North Carolina lawsuit was Goodyear USA, an Ohio corporation with a principal place of business in Ohio. Goodyear USA had physical plants in North Carolina and did substantial business there. Although the foreign affiliates of Goodyear moved to dismiss for lack of personal jurisdiction, Goodyear USA did not even challenge personal jurisdiction. Presumably Goodyear USA, in fact, thought that general jurisdiction was such a foregone conclusion that the company did not even object. Was it right?

4. If the Due Process Clause is about fairness, to what extent should the general jurisdiction calculus take into account fairness *to the plaintiff* in providing a forum that is convenient?

5. Imagine that you represented Wal-Mart. After voicing your concern about the lack of jurisdiction (but before preparing the motion papers) the plaintiff's counsel asked whether you would be willing to waive the jurisdictional objection in exchange for something. (Waiver is another basis for jurisdiction, as analyzed below.) Are you willing to deal? In exchange for what?

FROM THE COURTS

DAIMLER AG v. BAUMAN

Supreme Court of the United States
571 U.S. 117 (2014)

JUSTICE GINSBURG delivered the opinion of the Court, in which CHIEF JUSTICE ROBERTS and JUSTICES SCALIA, KENNEDY, THOMAS, BREYER, ALITO, and KAGAN joined.

[Twenty two Argentinian citizens and one Chilean citizen filed this suit against DaimlerChrysler Aktiengesellschaft ("Daimler"). Daimler, a German public stock company headquartered in Stuttgart Germany, manufactures Mercedes-Benz vehicles in Germany. The plaintiffs were former employees or relatives of employees of Daimler's Argentinian subsidiary. According to the plaintiffs, Daimler's subsidiary Mercedes-Benz Argentina collaborated with the military dictatorship in Argentina in kidnapping, detaining, torturing and killing the plaintiffs or their family members during the period of systematic human rights violations from 1976 to 1983 known as the Dirty War.

The plaintiffs asserted various theories of liability including claims under the Alien Tort Statute and the Torture Victim Protection Act which allow American federal courts to adjudicate international human rights claims. Plaintiffs contend that Daimler is vicariously liable for the actions of its Argentinian subsidiary.

Daimler's American subsidiary is Mercedez-Benz United States ("MBUSA"). MBUSA, a Delaware corporation with its headquarters in New Jersey, purchases vehicles from Daimler, imports them from Germany, and distributes them throughout the United States. The action was filed in the Northern District of California.]

[In *Goodyear Dunlop Tires Operations, S.A. v. Brown*, 564 U.S. 915 (2011), we emphasized] the essential difference between case-specific and all-purpose (general) jurisdiction. . . . [A] corporation's continuous activity of some sorts within a state is not enough to support the demand that the corporation be amenable to suits unrelated to that activity. . . . We have declined to stretch general jurisdiction beyond limits traditionally recognized. . . . As this Court has increasingly trained on the relationship among the defendant, the forum, and the litigation, *i.e.,* specific jurisdiction, general jurisdiction has come to occupy a less dominant place in the contemporary scheme. . . .

With this background we turn directly to the question whether Daimler's affiliations with California are sufficient to subject it to the general (all-purpose) personal jurisdiction of that State's courts. . . .

In sustaining the exercise of general jurisdiction over Daimler, the Ninth Circuit relied on an agency theory, determining that MBUSA acted as Daimler's agent for jurisdictional purposes and then attributing MBUSA's California contacts to Daimler. The Ninth Circuit's agency analysis [asks] whether the subsidiary performs services that are sufficiently important to the foreign corporation that if it did not have a representative to perform them, the corporation's own officials would undertake to perform substantially similar services.

This court has not yet addressed whether a foreign corporation may be subjected to a court's general jurisdiction based on the contacts of its in-state subsidiary. . . . But we need not pass judgment on invocation of an agency theory in the context of general jurisdiction, for in no event can the appeals court's analysis be sustained. . . . Even if we were to assume . . . that MBUSA's contacts are imputable to Daimler, there would still be no basis to subject Daimler to general jurisdiction in California, for Daimler's contacts with the State hardly render it at home there.

Goodyear made clear that only a limited set of affiliations with a forum will render a defendant amenable to all-purpose jurisdiction there. "For an individual, the paradigm forum for the exercise of general jurisdiction is the individual's domicile; for a corporation, it is an equivalent place, one in which the corporation is fairly regarded as at home." 131 S. Ct. at 2853–1854. With respect to a corporation, the place of incorporation and principal place of business are paradigm bases for general jurisdiction. Those affiliations have the virtue of being unique—that is, each ordinarily indicates only one place—as well as easily ascertainable. . . .

Goodyear did not hold that a corporation may be subject to general jurisdiction *only* in a forum where it is incorporated or has its principal place of business; it simply typed those places paradigm all-purpose forums. . . .

Here, neither Daimler nor MBUSA is incorporated in California, nor does either entity have its principal place of business there. If Daimler's

California activities sufficed to allow adjudication of this Argentina-rooted case in California, the same global reach would presumably be available in every other State in which MBUSA's sales are sizable. Such exorbitant exercises of all-purpose general jurisdiction would scarcely permit out-of-state defendants "to structure their primary conduct with some minimum assurance as to where that conduct will and will not render them liable to suit." *Burger King Corp.*, 471 U.S. at 472.

It was therefore error for the Ninth Circuit to conclude that Daimler, even with MBUSA's contacts attributed to it, was at home in California, and hence subject to suit there on claims by foreign plaintiffs having nothing to do with anything that had occurred or had its principal impact in California.[20] . . .

JUSTICE SOTOMAYOR, concurring in the judgment.

. . . Our personal jurisdiction precedents call for a two-part analysis. The contacts prong asks whether the defendant has sufficient contacts with the forum State to support personal jurisdiction; the reasonableness prong asks whether the exercise of jurisdiction would be unreasonable under the circumstances. . . . I would decide this case under the reasonableness prong. . . . [This case] involves Argentine plaintiffs suing a German defendant for conduct that took place in Argentina. . . . [I]t would be unreasonable for a court in California to subject Daimler to its jurisdiction.

COMMENTS AND QUESTIONS

1. The Court did not need to address the issue whether MBUSA's California contacts could be imputed to the parent company, Daimler AG. Generally speaking, courts have held that the jurisdictional contacts of one corporate entity can be imputed to another corporate entity (including an entity that is a subsidiary, parent, or affiliate) *only* when the latter is an alter ego of the former. Indeed, the separate identity of corporation is a hallowed principle of corporate law and our economic system. In *Daimler*, the U.S. Court of Appeals for the Ninth Circuit had adopted a less rigorous test,

---

[20] . . . [T]he general jurisdiction inquiry does not focus solely on the magnitude of the defendant's in-state contacts. General jurisdiction instead calls for an appraisal of a corporation's activities in their entirety, nationwide and worldwide. A corporation that operates in many places can scarcely be deemed at home in all of them. . . .

suggesting that a subsidiary could be an "agent" for some purposes, such as for establishing general jurisdiction over a foreign corporation, even if that company would not be an agent for all purposes. The Supreme Court did not need to reach that reasoning of the appeals court, and would almost certainly have rejected the reasoning if it had reached the issue. The law generally respects the separate identities of corporations so long as the corporations themselves respect those boundaries.

2. The Brussels Regulation that governs personal jurisdiction within the European Union similarly allows for personal jurisdiction over individuals who are domiciled in a member state to be sued in that member state (regardless of their nationality). Companies of member states are subject to general jurisdiction in the place of their statutory seat (incorporation), central administration (headquarters), or principal place of business.

FROM THE COURTS

BNSF RAILWAY CO. v. TYRRELL

Supreme Court of the United States
___ U.S. ___, 137 S. Ct. 1549 (2017)

JUSTICE GINSBURG delivered the opinion of the Court, in which CHIEF JUSTICE ROBERTS, and JUSTICES KENNEDY, THOMAS, BREYER, ALITO, KAGAN, and GORSUCH joined.

[Two railroad employees, Nelson and Tyrrell, sued their employer, BNSF Railway Co. ("BNSF"), in a Montana state court for workplace injuries. The employees were not residents of Montana and never worked for BNSF in Montana. BNSF is a Delaware corporation that has its principal place of business in Texas. About 6% of BNSF's 32,500 miles of railroad track, about 5% of its 43,000 employees, and less than 10% of its total revenue are in or from Montana.

The Montana Supreme Court asserted that the courts of that state had jurisdiction. It distinguished *Daimler AG v. Bauman*, 134 S. Ct. 746 (2014), by observing that *Daimler* involved foreign plaintiffs.

The Montana Supreme Court also asserted that it had personal jurisdiction over BNSF under 45 U.S.C. § 56 of the Federal Employers Liability

Act (FELA). The Supreme Court rejected this argument, finding that the language of Section 56, which provides that "an action may be brought in a district court of the United States," is a venue prescription that does not establish personal jurisdiction.]

Because FELA does not authorize state courts to exercise personal jurisdiction over a railroad solely on the ground that the railroad does some business in their States, . . . [we] inquire whether the Montana courts' exercise of personal jurisdiction under Montana law comports with the Due Process Clause of the Fourteenth Amendment. . . . [W]e have distinguished between specific or case-linked jurisdiction and general or all-purpose jurisdiction. . . . Because neither Nelson nor Tyrrell alleges any injury from work in or related to Montana, only the propriety of general jurisdiction is at issue here.

Goodyear Dunlop Tires Operations, S.A. v. Brown, 564 U.S. 915, 919 (2011), and *Daimler, supra,* clarified that "[a] court may assert general jurisdiction over foreign (sister-state or foreign-country) corporations to hear any and all claims against them when their affiliations with the State are so 'continuous and systematic' as to render them essentially at home in the forum State." *Daimler,* 571 U.S. at 127 (quoting *Goodyear,* 564 U.S. at 919). The "paradigm" forums in which a corporate defendant is "at home," we explained, are the corporation's place of incorporation and its principal place of business. *Daimler,* 571 U.S. at 137; *Goodyear,* 564 U.S. at 924. The exercise of general jurisdiction is not limited to these forums; in an "exceptional case," a corporate defendant's operations in another forum "may be so substantial and of such a nature as to render the corporation at home in that state." *Daimler,* 571 U.S. at 139. We suggested that *Perkins v. Benguet Consol. Mining Co.,* 342 U.S. 437 (1952), exemplified such a case. *Daimler,* 571 U.S. at 139, n.19. In *Perkins,* war had forced the defendant corporation's owner to temporarily relocate the enterprise from the Philippines to Ohio. 342 U.S. at 447–449. Because Ohio then became "the center of the corporation's wartime activities," *Daimler,* 571 U.S. at 130 n.8, suit was proper there. *Perkins,* 342 U.S., at 448.

The Montana Supreme Court distinguished *Daimler* on the ground that we did not there confront "a FELA claim or a railroad defendant." The Fourteenth Amendment due process constraint described in *Daimler,* however, applies to all state-court assertions of general jurisdiction over nonresident defendants; the constraint does not vary with the type of claim asserted or business enterprise sued.

BNSF, we repeat, is not incorporated in Montana and does not maintain its principal place of business there. Nor is BNSF so heavily engaged in activity in Montana "to render [it] essentially at home" in that State. As earlier noted, BNSF has over 2,000 miles of railroad track and more than 2,000 employees in Montana. But, as we observed in *Daimler*, "the general jurisdiction inquiry does not focus solely on the magnitude of the defendant's in-state contacts." *Id.*, at 139 n.20. Rather, the inquiry "calls for an appraisal of a corporation's activities in their entirety"; "[a] corporation that operates in many places can scarcely be deemed at home in all of them." *Ibid.* In short, the business BNSF does in Montana is sufficient to subject the railroad to specific personal jurisdiction in that State on claims related to the business it does in Montana. But in-state business, we clarified in *Daimler* and *Goodyear*, does not suffice to permit the assertion of general jurisdiction over claims like Nelson's and Tyrrell's that are unrelated to any activity occurring in Montana.

JUSTICE SOTOMAYOR, concurring in part and dissenting in part.

I concur in the Court's conclusion that the Federal Employers' Liability Act, 45 U.S.C. § 51 *et seq.,* does not confer personal jurisdiction over railroads on state courts. . . . I continue to disagree with the path the Court struck in *Daimler AG v. Bauman*, 571 U.S. 117 (2014), which limits general jurisdiction over a corporate defendant only to those States where it is "essentially at home." . . .

. . . This Court would do well to adhere more faithfully to the direction from *International Shoe Co. v. Washington*, 326 U.S. 310 (1945), which instructed that general jurisdiction is proper when a corporation's "continuous corporate operations within a state [are] so substantial and of such a nature as to justify suit against it on causes of action arising from dealings entirely distinct from those activities." *Id.*, at 318. Under *International Shoe* . . . courts were to ask whether the benefits a defendant attained in the forum State warranted the burdens associated with general personal jurisdiction. [Instead of following that holding,] the majority opinion goes on to reaffirm the restrictive "at home" test set out in *Daimler*—a test that . . . has no home in our precedents and creates serious inequities.

The majority's approach grants a jurisdictional windfall to large multistate or multinational corporations that operate across many jurisdictions. Under its reasoning, it is virtually inconceivable that such corporations will ever be subject to general jurisdiction in any location other than their principal places of business or of incorporation. Foreign businesses with principal places of business outside the United States may never be subject to general jurisdiction in this country even though they have continuous and systematic contacts within the United States. What was once a holistic, nuanced contacts analysis backed by considerations of fairness and reasonableness has now effectively been replaced by the rote identification of a corporation's principal place of business or place of incorporation.[1] The result? It is individual plaintiffs, harmed by the actions of a far-flung foreign corporation, who will bear the brunt of the majority's approach and be forced to sue in distant jurisdictions with which they have no contacts or connection.

Moreover, the comparative contacts analysis invented in *Daimler* resurfaces here and proves all but dispositive. The majority makes much of the fact that BNSF's contacts in Montana are only a percentage of its contacts with other jurisdictions. But *International Shoe*, which the majority agrees is the springboard for our modern personal jurisdiction jurisprudence applied no comparative contacts test. There the Court analyzed whether the Delaware corporation had "by its activities in the State of Washington rendered itself amenable to proceedings" in the State. 326 U.S., at 311. The Court evaluated whether the corporation had offices in the forum State, made contracts there, delivered goods there, or employed salesmen there. *See id.*, at 313. Despite acknowledging that the corporation maintained places of business in several States, the Court did not engage in a comparison between International Shoe's contacts within the State of Washington and the other States in which it operated. The Court noted that the corporation employed 11 to 13 salesmen in Washington but did not query how that number compared to the number of salesmen in other States. As well it should not have; the relative percentage of contacts is irrelevant. The focus should be on the quality and quantity of the defendant's contacts in the forum State.

The majority does even *Daimler* itself a disservice, paying only lip service to the question the Court purported to reserve there—the possibility of an "exceptional case" in which general jurisdiction would be proper in a forum State that is neither a corporate defendant's place of incorporation nor its principal place of business. Its opinion here could be understood to limit that exception to the exact facts of *Perkins v. Benguet Consol. Mining Co.*,

---

1   As many commentators have observed, lower courts adhered to the continuous-and-systematic standard for decades before *Daimler*, and its predecessor *Goodyear Dunlop Tires Operations, S.A. v. Brown*, 564 U.S. 915 (2011), wrought the present sea change. . . .

342 U.S. 437 (1952). That reading is so narrow as to read the exception out of existence entirely; certainly a defendant with significant contacts with more than one State falls outside its ambit. And so it is inevitable under its own reasoning that the majority would conclude that BNSF's contacts with Montana are insufficient to justify the exercise of personal jurisdiction here. This result is perverse. Despite having reserved the possibility of an "exceptional case" in *Daimler*, the majority here has rejected that possibility out of hand.

Worse, the majority reaches its conclusion only by departing from the Court's normal practice. Had it remanded to the Montana Supreme Court to reevaluate the due process question under the correct legal standard, that court could have examined whether this is such an "exceptional case." Instead, with its ruling today, the Court unnecessarily sends a signal to the lower courts that the exceptional-circumstances inquiry is all form, no substance. . . .

COMMENTS AND QUESTIONS

1. The two plaintiffs were injured in workplaces in North Dakota and South Dakota, respectively. Why might these plaintiffs have filed suit instead in Montana? If not in Montana, in what states would the defendant have been subject to general jurisdiction? Is *every* defendant *always* subject to general jurisdiction somewhere in the United States?

2. Justice Sotomayor alone laments the narrowing of the jurisprudence of general jurisdiction. Procedural reforms generate winners and losers. Who benefits and who loses from the narrowing of the scope of general jurisdiction?

Specific Jurisdiction

A second basis for establishing adjudicative authority over a defendant is specific jurisdiction. There are essentially four components necessary to establish specific (also called case-linked) jurisdiction. A plaintiff must establish all four components.

The threshold element for establishing personal jurisdiction is that the cause of action must *arise out of the defendant's contacts* with the forum state. In other words, there must be some affiliation between the forum and the underlying controversy, such as an activity or an occurrence by the defendant that takes place in the forum. If that connection does not exist, a court will not have specific jurisdiction regardless of the extent of a defendant's unconnected activities in the state. Accordingly even regularly occurring sales of a product in a state do not justify the exercise of specific jurisdiction over a claim that is *unrelated* to those sales.

A controversy that arises out of the defendant's contacts with the forum establishes the authority to adjudicate.[4] In order to determine whether the cause of action arises out of the defendant's contacts with the forum state, litigators often focus on the elements of the plaintiff's cause(s) of action. A cause of action establishes a narrative about the defendant's wrongdoing: the defendant breached a contract, acted negligently, misrepresented something, infringed on the plaintiff's intellectual property rights, trespassed, etc. Litigators parse the elements of the cause of action to identify the essential components of the conduct that is complained of. When enough of the defendant's allegedly wrongful conduct occurred *in the forum state*, this threshold element of specific jurisdiction is satisfied. Importantly, a cause of action does *not* arise out of the defendant's contacts with the forum simply because the *plaintiff* is in the forum state. Indeed, even if the defendant knew that the plaintiff was in the forum state, and if the defendant could foresee that the plaintiff would suffer harm in the forum state, and if the plaintiff in fact did suffer injury in the forum state, these conditions are not alone sufficient to establish the threshold element.[5] It is the *defendant's* conduct in the forum state that triggers the authority to adjudicate.

The second element for establishing specific jurisdiction is a state long-arm statute. In order for the state or federal courts of a state to adjudicate the rights and responsibilities of a foreign defendant the forum state's legislature must have authorized the "reach." Some long-arm statutes identify specific acts that give rise to jurisdiction. In Illinois, for example, the long-arm statute authorizes courts in that state to exercise jurisdiction over causes of action arising from "the transaction of any business within this State," "the commission of a tortious act within this State," "the ownership of an interest in any trust administered within this State," and eleven other specific acts.[6] In other states, the long-arm statute gives blanket authority

---

4   Do not confuse the authority to adjudicate with the authority to legislate or regulate. The former is personal jurisdiction; the latter is choice of law.

5   *See Bristol-Myers Squibb Co. v. Superior Court of California,* ___ U.S. ___, 137 S. Ct. 1773 (2017); *Walden v. Fiore,* 571 U.S. 277 (2014).

6   735 Ill. Comp. Stat. 5/2–209(a)(1)–(14).

to reach foreign defendants. For example, California's long-arm statute provides that "A court of this state may exercise jurisdiction on any basis not inconsistent with the Constitution of this state or of the United States."[7] Those Constitutional boundaries are represented in the third and fourth elements, discussed below. In jurisdictions where the long-arm statute gives blanket authority, then, this second element requires no analysis; you can skip to the third and fourth elements.

Even in jurisdictions where the long arm statute enumerates specific acts, there is often case law interpreting the list of enumerated acts to extend to the constitutional limits. Or, as in Illinois, another paragraph of the text of the long-arm statute includes a catch-all: "A court may also exercise jurisdiction on any other basis now or hereafter permitted by the Illinois Constitution and the Constitution of the United States."[8] In jurisdictions where a long-arm statute enumerates acts and the limitations of the statute are taken seriously, questions will arise: does a long-arm statute that reaches "transacting business in the state" include out-of-state charities who are soliciting donations with targeted Facebook ads? Is an out-of-state church that has its missionaries traversing the state "transacting business in the state"? These arguments require statutory construction and interpretation, and usually without the benefit (or burden) of case precedent.

The third element of specific jurisdiction introduces the constitutional component. The Due Process Clause protects persons from deprivations by governments of life, liberty, and property interests without due process of law. Courts may assert personal jurisdiction over persons and deprive them of life, liberty, and property interests, but those deprivations must be consonant with due process. You may recall from your Civil Procedure course that, since *International Shoe Co. v. Washington*,[9] due process has required that the defendant have *minimum contacts* with the forum state.

The standard of minimum contacts generally requires that the defendant have purposefully derived a benefit from its forum activities. A defendant that avails itself of the benefits of the forum state, the thinking goes, may fairly be subjected to the burden of litigating in that forum. Remember that the Due Process Clause is about fairness. A defendant that has deliberately created a connection to the forum state for its own benefit is on notice that it can be sued there, and it seems fair to allow the courts of that state to exert adjudicative authority over such a defendant.

---

7   Cal. Civ. Proc. § 410.10.

8   735 Ill. Comp. Stat. 5/2–209(c).

9   326 U.S. 310 (1940).

In previous decades the minimum contacts criterion was the primary litigation focus of most exercises of specific jurisdiction. Because some judges may still think of it this way (because of the imprint of their legal education), litigators should know some history. Until recently, the first element of specific jurisdiction (the requirement that the cause of action arise out of the defendant's contacts with the forum state) was very loosely applied: if the instant case was *related*[10] to the defendant's contacts with the forum state, the threshold test was usually satisfied. Because the second element of specific jurisdiction (the long-arm statute) was also often easily satisfied, the third element—minimum contacts or purposeful availment—was the gatekeeper. Accordingly, much time and effort was spent interrogating the meaning of minimum contacts.

But with the first element of specific jurisdiction now operating as a gatekeeper, minimum contacts will likely play a more modest role. Indeed, any court that reaches this third element (minimum contacts) will necessarily have already found (per the first element) that this defendant engaged in some activity or occurrence in the forum state and that that activity gave rise to the litigation. The *quantum* of contacts with the forum state thus will often be satisfied; attention, then, will shift to the *nature* of those contacts. Specifically, the Supreme Court may use the minimum contacts criterion to ensure that specific jurisdiction is allowed only when the defendant intentionally, deliberately, and directly *targeted* the forum state. In other words, one does not accidentally or indirectly have minimum contacts in some jurisdiction. Writing for a four-Justice plurality in *J. McIntrye Machinery, Ltd. v. Nicastro*, Justice Kennedy observed that minimum contacts requires that the defendant's activities "manifest an intention to submit to the power of a sovereign" or "target[ ] the forum."[11]

The fourth element of specific jurisdiction is the second half of the constitutional test established in *International Shoe Co. v. Washington*. The exercise of specific jurisdiction must not offend traditional notions of fair play and substantial justice. Very few cases of specific jurisdiction are denied because of a failure to satisfy this fourth element. But the Due Process Clause is about fairness, and circumstances can arise where it would be unfair to require a defendant to appear in the forum—even in circumstances that satisfied the first three elements of specific jurisdiction described above.

---

10   An action might be *related* to the defendant's in-state conduct yet not *arise out of* that conduct. Imagine a products liability case where neither the plaintiff nor the defendant is domiciled in Arizona; the product was not manufactured nor sold in Arizona, and the plaintiff may not have been injured in Arizona. The product that injured the plaintiff was part of a product line, some of which was stored in a warehouse in Arizona. The products liability action might be related to the defendant's conduct in Arizona even if the cause of action does not arise out of the conduct of storing the product in the warehouse.

11   564 U.S. 873 (2011) (Kennedy, J., with Chief Justice Roberts and Justices Scalia and Thomas).

Defendants emphasize the unfairness of the exercise of jurisdiction when appearing in court would be difficult as a practical matter (distance, expense, inconvenience) and when appearing in that particular forum would be prejudicial (because a jury or judge would not treat them fairly, or unfamiliar procedures would compromise the presentation of their case).[12] Imagine a defendant company that is located in some distant, obscure country and that may be treated unfairly if forced to defend in a city where the main employer in town faced competition from the defendant. But even this sort of inconvenience would often not be enough without more.

To offend traditional notions of fair play and substantial justice the facts would need to show not only some severe burden on the defendant, but also some inconvenience to the state and the court. For example, the state may not have an interest in the outcome of the litigation against that defendant: the plaintiff may not be from the forum state, forum law will not apply, and it would be a waste of judicial resources to burden the state with the suit. In *Asahi Metal Industry Co., Ltd. v. Superior Court of California, Solano County*,[13] for example, eight Justices of the Court agreed that it would offend traditional notions of fair play and substantial justice for the State of California to assert jurisdiction over a Japanese defendant on a third-party claim by a Taiwanese plaintiff regarding conduct in Japan and Taiwan involving issues of foreign law, where there was no evidence that it was easier or better to have the litigation occur in California, and California had no interest in the outcome of the litigation.

Hypothetical 20-2

Best Auto is a used car business outside of Seattle, Washington. Best Auto listed for sale on eBay a Mini Cooper that was eight years old with approximately 76,000 miles of wear. The advertisement described the excellent condition of the car's interior, exterior, and motor in great detail. The ad also said "I've driven it many miles over the past few weeks and freeway cruised at 75 mph. . . . I have every confidence this Mini Cooper could easily be driven cross-country tomorrow."

Best Auto lists at least half of its inventory on eBay, and the advertisement that attaches to every listing states that Best Auto sells to purchasers in

---

12   Courts consider (1) the burden on the defendant, (2) the forum state's interest in resolving the dispute, (3) the plaintiff's interest in receiving convenient and effectual relief, (4) the interstate judicial system's interest in obtaining the most efficient resolution of controversies, and (5) the shared interest of the several states (or nations) in furthering fundamental social policies.

13   480 U.S. 102 (1987).

North and South America, Europe, and Australia. The ad for the Mini Cooper also contained this paragraph:

> We've sold many cars here on eBay over the past few years and the one thing I'm questioned about again and again is shipping. Because we're up in Washington State, at the Northwestern tip of the country, many Midwesterners and folks on the East Coast sometimes are reluctant to bid due to distance. **DON'T BE CONCERNED!** We ship cars out almost weekly and are happy to arrange and/or work with the transporter of your choice. As outlined above, please contact me here at BEST AUTO with any questions or for suggestions. My name is Mark Thompson and my direct phone number is 206-914-1173.

William and Julie Brown live in Aledo, Texas. The Browns read the eBay description of the Mini Cooper. At the time, the "current bid" was listed as $12,000. On April 27 of last year, the Browns called Best Auto about the Mini Cooper. Best Auto agreed to sell the car directly to the Browns for $13,250. Best Auto withdrew the eBay listing.

On April 28, the Browns sent $13,250 by wire transfer to Best Auto. Best Auto faxed a "Vehicle Purchase Order" to the Browns. The Vehicle Purchase Order states the odometer "reads 076,115 miles." The Browns used one of the companies recommended by Best Auto to ship the Mini Cooper from Washington to a shipment center in Mesquite, Texas.

On May 13, the Browns went to Mesquite to pick up the Mini Cooper. After inspecting the exterior of the car, the Browns called Best Auto about "several trim items." Best Auto agreed to pay the cost to repair the trim items.

The Browns took possession of the Mini Cooper. Julie Brown drove the Mini Cooper. Less than 10 miles from the shipping center, Julie noticed the air condition was not working and the engine temperature gauge pointed to "HOT." Julie immediately pulled over and called a tow truck. The tow truck operator took the car to the nearest authorized Mini Cooper dealership, Moritz Mini of North Arlington, Texas.

The Browns asked the mechanic at Moritz Mini to inspect the car, identify the cause of the problem, and provide an estimate. The mechanic identified a number of necessary repairs, including the need to fix the cracked radiator and front panel, a leaking valve cover gasket, and the power steering pump. The estimated cost of repairs was $6,012.61. The Moritz Mini mechanic noted, "75% of Body Panels have been Repainted." The Browns faxed the repair estimate to Best Auto.

After communicating with Best Auto a number of times, the Browns demanded Best Auto take possession of the car and refund the purchase price. The Browns said Best Auto misrepresented the condition of the Mini Cooper and that it would cost nearly half of the purchase price to make the car run properly. Best Auto suggested the Browns auction the car in Texas. Best Auto assured the Browns the auction operator would be able to sell the Mini Cooper for the purchase price. Best Auto offered to help arrange the auction and pay $550 to repair the radiator. The Browns agreed to auction the Mini Cooper. The Browns paid an additional $1,000 to repair the car.

On May 27, the Browns drove the Mini Cooper from Moritz Mini to the auction site in Texas. The auction company attempted to sell the car at least two different times.

On June 18, William Brown contacted Thompson to demand Best Auto refund the purchase price, pay for repairs, and accept return of the car. William stated that "the car was nothing like you represented in the ebay ad." William told Thompson that another mechanic at a dealership in Fort Worth inspected the car and "found a long list of problems including a cracked radiator, failed power steering pump, a dead [air conditioning] unit, 75% replaced and repainted panels, and obvious signs that the car had been in a wreck, including frame damage." William also expressed concern about Best Auto's failure to send the title.

> Where did you get this from? You still haven't sent us the title. . . . Since we have not received the title, I am wondering if this is a salvage vehicle or if there is some other documented sign that this was deemed totaled from a wreck. Our estimates from the dealer here show it will take over $4,000 to repair just to get it on the road. In addition we have spent over $2,000 for related expenses.

In mid-July, Best Auto sent the Browns the "Vehicle Certification of Ownership (Title)" to the Mini Cooper. The title states that Best Auto transferred the Mini Cooper to the Browns on April 27. Contrary to Best Auto's representation that Thompson drove the Mini Cooper "many miles over the past few weeks and freeway cruised at 75 MPH," the disclosure and release of interest by the registered owner showed that when Best Auto purchased the car on March 29, the odometer reading was 76,114 miles, and it was 76,115 miles when Best Auto transferred title to the Browns on April 27.

On August 6, the Browns filed a lawsuit against Best Auto in Parker County, Texas. The complaint alleged breach of contract, unjust enrichment, promissory estoppel, fraud, and violations of the Texas Deceptive Trade Practices Consumer Protection Act (DTPA). The Browns sought economic damages for the purchase price of $13,250, reimbursement for repairs, gas, and shipping, and treble damages and attorneys fees and costs under the DTPA. The Browns served Best Auto through the Texas Secretary of State by certified mail. On August 20, the Texas Secretary State received proof of service and the return receipt from Best Auto.

Do the courts of Texas have personal jurisdiction on a theory of specific jurisdiction?

Hypothetical 20-3[14]

Ralph Hague died as a result of injuries he sustained in a motorcycle accident. Ralph's son was driving the motorcycle, on which Ralph was a passenger, when an automobile struck the motorcycle from behind. Ralph and his son were citizens of Wisconsin, as was the negligent driver. The two vehicles involved in the accident were registered in Wisconsin, and the fatal accident occurred in Wisconsin.

Both the negligent driver and Ralph's son were uninsured. Ralph carried uninsured motorist coverage on each of the three vehicles that he owned. Each of those three policies provided for up to $15,000 of coverage for injuries caused by the negligence of uninsured motorists, regardless of whether the accident involved the insured vehicles. Ralph's cars were registered in Wisconsin and were insured by a policy that Ralph obtained in Wisconsin from a Wisconsin branch of Allstate.

The decedent's personal representative, Ralph's widow, Lavinia Hague, filed a declaratory judgment action against Allstate in Minnesota. After the accident, she had moved twenty five miles to Redwing, Minnesota and married a Minnesota resident. In the suit, Lavinia sought a declaration that the uninsured motorist coverage on each of the decedent's automobile policies could be "stacked." The parties disputed whether the maximum recovery was $15,000 or instead (by stacking) $45,000.

---

14   This hypothetical is based on the case that we read in Chapter 7 and discussed again in Chapter 14.

Mr. Hague had been a member of Minnesota's work force for fifteen years. He lived in Hager City, Wisconsin, which was just 1.5 miles from the Minnesota border. Allstate is a Delaware with its principal place of business in Illinois. Allstate does substantial business in all states, including Minnesota.

Does the Minnesota court have personal jurisdiction over Allstate on a theory of specific jurisdiction?

FROM THE COURTS

KATZ v. SPINIELLO COS.

U.S. District Court for the District of Massachusetts
244 F.Supp.3d 237 (D. Mass. 2017)

CASPER, DISTRICT JUDGE.

I. Introduction

This case arises out of a May 31, 2014 airplane crash that occurred in Bedford, Massachusetts during the takeoff rotation of a Gulfstream G-IV aircraft, killing all passengers onboard. Plaintiffs Drew Katz and Melissa Silver ("Plaintiffs"), individually and as the co-personal representatives of the estate of Lewis A. Katz, a passenger on the flight, have filed this lawsuit against numerous defendants including Gulfstream Aerospace Corporation (Georgia) ("Gulfstream Georgia"), Gulfstream Aerospace Corporation (Delaware) ("Gulfstream Delaware"), Gulfstream Aerospace Services Corporation ("Gulfstream Services") and Rockwell Collins, Inc. ("Rockwell"),* alleging claims of wrongful death and conscious suffering predicated on theories of negligence and breach of the implied warranty of merchantability. Plaintiffs have also brought claims under Mass. Gen. Laws c. 93A. Rockwell, Gulfstream Services, Gulfstream Georgia and Gulfstream Delaware have all moved to dismiss for lack of personal jurisdiction. . . .

II. Standard of Review

In ruling on a motion to dismiss for lack of personal jurisdiction without holding an evidentiary hearing, a district court must apply the prima facie standard of review. Under the prima facie standard, Plaintiffs must "dem-

---

*   [Eds.' Note: Spiniello Companies, the named defendant, was the pilots' employer.]

onstrate the existence of every fact required to satisfy both the forum's long arm statute and the Due Process Clause of the Constitution," to meet their burden pursuant to Fed. R. Civ. P. 12(b)(2). The Court considers the facts alleged in the pleadings as well as the parties' supplemental filings. The Court will "take specific facts affirmatively alleged by the plaintiff as true (whether or not disputed) and construe them in the light most congenial to the plaintiff's jurisdictional claim." *Mass. Sch. of Law at Andover, Inc. v. Am. Bar Ass'n*, 142 F.3d 26, 34 (1st Cir. 1998). In doing so, the Court will not "credit conclusory allegations or draw farfetched inferences," *Ticketmaster-NY, Inc. v. Alioto*, 26 F.3d 201, 203 (1st Cir. 1994), and must keep in mind that Plaintiffs need to "do more than simply surmise the existence of a favorable factual scenario; [they] must verify the facts alleged through materials of evidentiary quality." *Killion v. Commonwealth Yachts*, 421 F.Supp.2d 246, 252 (D. Mass. 2006). . . . The Court is also required to "add to the mix facts put forward by the defendants, to the extent they are uncontradicted." *Mass. Sch. of Law*, 142 F.3d at 34.

III. Factual Allegations

These allegations are taken from the operative complaint and the affidavits filed by Gulfstream Services, Gulfstream Georgia, Gulfstream Delaware and Rockwell in support of their motions to dismiss. For the purposes of the instant motions, the Court presumes the allegations put forth by the Plaintiffs to be true and also considers the Defendants' uncontradicted factual allegations. The Court . . . only recounts facts relevant to the motions to dismiss of Gulfstream Georgia, Gulfstream Delaware, Gulfstream Services and Rockwell.

On May 31, 2014, a Gulfstream G-IV aircraft, Serial Number N121JM (the "G-IV") crashed during its takeoff rotation as it was departing from Laurence G. Hanscom Field in Bedford, Massachusetts. The accident resulted in the deaths of seven people, including Lewis A. Katz, his three companions, the flight attendant, and [two] pilots.

Gulfstream Georgia, a corporation organized and existing under the laws of the state of the Georgia, designed and manufactured the G-IV. Gulfstream Georgia neither has any design or manufacturing facilities in Massachusetts nor is it registered or authorized to do business in the Commonwealth. No agent for service of process exists for Gulfstream Georgia in Massachusetts and Gulfstream Georgia has not consented to jurisdiction in Massachusetts.

In addition, Gulfstream Georgia does not utilize a network of distributors or retailers in the sale of its aircraft, instead opting to sell its aircraft directly to consumers. The G-IV at issue here was sold by Gulfstream Georgia to Rim Air LLC, a Delaware corporation, in 2000. Rim Air LLC subsequently sold the G-IV to SK Travel LLC ("SK Travel"), a North Carolina corporation that is a separate defendant in this case, in 2007. Prior to the initial sale of the G-IV, Gulfstream Georgia never tested, operated or serviced the aircraft in Massachusetts. At present, Plaintiffs have filed suit in Georgia state court against Gulfstream Georgia that is a near-identical lawsuit to the instant action.

Gulfstream Delaware, the parent holding company of Gulfstream Georgia and Gulfstream Services, is not incorporated in Massachusetts and does not have its principal place of business in in Massachusetts. Additionally, Gulfstream Delaware is not registered or authorized to do business in Massachusetts, does not have an agent for service of process here and has never consented to jurisdiction in Massachusetts. Gulfstream Delaware did not design or manufacture the particular G-IV that crashed in Bedford, nor has it designed or manufactured any other G-IV or any other component of a G-IV aircraft.

Gulfstream Services is the wholly-owned subsidiary of Gulfstream Delaware and is organized under the laws of the state of Delaware. Gulfstream Services' corporate headquarters are in Georgia. Like Gulfstream Delaware, Gulfstream Services did not design or manufacture the particular G-IV that crashed in Bedford, nor has it designed or manufactured any other G-IV or any other component of a G-IV aircraft. Gulfstream Services has also never been the type certificate holder for the Gulfstream G-IV product line, which was instead held by Gulfstream Georgia. Rather, Gulfstream Services specializes in the repair and maintenance of Gulfstream aircraft and it has several service facilities located throughout the country, including one in Westfield, Massachusetts (the "Westfield Facility"). Gulfstream Services' business records reveal that employees from the Westfield Facility provided maintenance to the G-IV on a single occasion in January 2013. On that occasion, the G-IV's auxiliary power unit ("APU") was malfunctioning and, at the request of SK Travel, two technicians were sent from the Westfield Facility to repair the issue in Delaware.

Rockwell designed, manufactured and sold the G-IV's interlock mechanism and gust lock at issue in this case. Rockwell does not have an office in

Massachusetts; it has never had a principal place of business in Massachusetts; it does not maintain bank accounts in Massachusetts; nor has it ever manufactured any component of the gust lock system in Massachusetts or sold, marketed or distributed the gust lock system to a Massachusetts customer. Rockwell delivered the last pedestal assembly in 2004 and the last G-IV sector assembly in 2008 and neither was to Massachusetts. In 2001, Rockwell registered as a foreign corporation to do business in Massachusetts and also identified a registered agent in the Commonwealth. From 2001 until 2005, Rockwell leased property in Massachusetts, but it has not leased any property since that time, and does not own property in Massachusetts. Additionally, for one month—from January 1, 2013 until February 1, 2013—Rockwell had one employee, out of its 19,000 employees, who was located in Massachusetts.

IV. Procedural History

Plaintiffs filed an amended complaint in this action on May 27, 2016 in Suffolk Superior Court. The case was removed to this Court on July 1, 2016. Gulfstream Services, Gulfstream Georgia and Gulfstream Delaware subsequently filed motions to dismiss for lack of personal jurisdiction. Rockwell also filed a motion to dismiss for lack of personal jurisdiction. . . .

V. Discussion

The Court's personal jurisdiction over a defendant may derive from either general or specific jurisdiction. Plaintiffs do not maintain that this Court has general jurisdiction over Rockwell, Gulfstream Services, Gulfstream Georgia or Gulfstream Delaware and, as such, the Court must only determine whether Plaintiffs have asserted facts sufficient to exercise specific jurisdiction over these defendants. To establish specific personal jurisdiction, Plaintiffs "must demonstrate that the Massachusetts long-arm statute grants jurisdiction over [them] and that the exercise of that jurisdiction comports with the Due Process Clause of the Fifth Amendment." *Adelson v. Hananel*, 510 F.3d 43, 48 (1st Cir. 2007). The First Circuit, however, has "construed the Massachusetts long-arm statute as being coextensive with the limits permitted by the Constitution." *Adelson v. Hananel*, 652 F.3d 75, 80–81 (1st Cir. 2011). It is, therefore, acceptable to sidestep the statutory inquiry and proceed directly to the constitutional analysis.

Due process requires the Court to determine whether the defendant has maintained "certain minimum contacts" with the forum state "such that the maintenance of the suit does not offend 'traditional notions of fair play and substantial justice.' " *Int'l Shoe Co. v. Washington*, 326 U.S. 310, 316 (1945). Accordingly, "[t]he accepted mode of analysis for questions involving personal jurisdiction concentrates on the quality and quantity of the potential defendant's contacts with the forum." *Phillips Exeter Acad. v. Howard Phillips Fund, Inc.*, 196 F.3d 284, 288 (1st Cir. 1999). The specific jurisdiction inquiry is threefold: relatedness, purposeful availment and reasonableness. The Court must find that all three are present to assert personal jurisdiction over a defendant.

A. Rockwell

Plaintiffs allege no facts that would satisfy the relatedness prong as it pertains to Rockwell. The relatedness inquiry focuses on whether "the claim underlying the litigation . . . directly arise[s] out of, or relate[s] to, the defendant's forum-state activities." *Newman v. Eur Aeronautic Def. & Space Co. EADS N.V.*, 2011WL 2413792, at *4 (D. Mass. 2011). This is a "flexible, relaxed standard," *id.*, but still requires a causal relationship between Plaintiffs' claim and Defendants' forum-related conduct. Though not precisely proximate cause, "due process demands something like a 'proximate cause' nexus." *Harlow v. Children's Hosp.*, 432 F.3d 50, 61 (1st Cir. 2005). "[T]he defendant's in-state conduct must form an important, or [at least] material, element of proof in the plaintiff's case." *Id.* at 61. Furthermore, a court may have specific jurisdiction in situations where there is only a single contact with the forum state, but that contact must be "meaningful." *Nowak v. Tak How Invs., Ltd.*, 94 F.3d 708, 717 (1st Cir. 1996).

Here, Plaintiffs' claims against Rockwell are premised on the allegation that the G-IV's gust lock system, which the pilots had failed to disengage prior to takeoff and which allegedly contributed to the crash, contained "design defects, manufacturing defects, and inadequate and unreasonably dangerous instructions and warnings." Rockwell, however, has never manufactured any part of the gust lock system in Massachusetts, nor has it marketed, sold or distributed this component in this Commonwealth. Plaintiffs have not contested these facts. Although Rockwell registered as a foreign corporation to do business in Massachusetts and briefly rented space and had a single employee here, these limited contacts do not relate to Plaintiffs' allegations regarding the gust lock system. As such, the Court cannot conclude that any of Plaintiffs' claims against Rockwell relate to Rockwell's alleged negligence or misconduct in Massachusetts. . . .

B. Gulfstream Services

1. Relatedness

Again, to satisfy the relatedness prong, Plaintiffs would need to show that the cause of action either arises directly out of, or is related to, Gulfstream Services' forum-based contacts. In other words, "an injury is jurisdictionally relevant only insofar as it shows that the defendant has formed a contact with the forum State. The proper question is not where the plaintiff experienced the particular injury or effect but whether the defendant's conduct connects him to the forum in a meaningful way." *Walden v. Fiore*, 571 U.S. 277, 290 (2014). Plaintiffs contend that the Court has personal jurisdiction over Gulfstream Services on the basis that technicians from the company's Massachusetts facility performed maintenance on the G-IV prior to its crash in May 2014 "on at least one prior occasion."

Plaintiffs allege—and Gulfstream Services confirms—that in January 2013 two Gulfstream Services' employees traveled from the company's facility in Massachusetts to Delaware to perform maintenance on the G-IV. After servicing the G-IV, as Plaintiffs claim, the Gulfstream Services' technicians signed a "return to service" form which certified that the G-IV was airworthy. Plaintiffs argue that because the G-IV's gust lock system was faulty, the G-IV was not airworthy and, therefore, Gulfstream Services breached its duty of care in connection with any inspection, maintenance, service, repair and certification of the G-IV. Gulfstream Services counters, however, that the January 2013 service of the G-IV had nothing to do with the gust lock system which Plaintiffs allege to be a contributing cause of the crash. Specifically, the maintenance record from the January 2013 service of the G-IV shows that the Gulfstream Services' technicians were sent to Delaware to work on an issue related to the G-IV's APU system. Moreover, Gulfstream Services challenges the purported scope of the certification contained in the "return to service" form, claiming it certified only that "[t]he maintenance [completed] was performed in accordance with current Federal Aviation Regulations and [the G-IV was] approved for return to service with regards to the maintenance accomplished." That is, they maintain that the "return to service" form only certified that the aircraft met FAA regulations as relevant to the APU system.

In considering issues of personal jurisdiction, the Court may consider, as previously noted, "facts put forward by the defendant[ ], to the extent they are uncontradicted." *Stars for Art Prod. FZ, LLC v. Dandana, LLC*, 806 F.Supp.2d 437, 442 (D. Mass. 2011). Here, Gulfstream Services' proffer as to servicing of the APU system itself is uncontradicted. Moreover, Plaintiffs make no allegations in the operative complaint about the APU system or how it relates to the gust lock system that allegedly contributed to the crash. Instead, Plaintiffs contend, without specific support, that the APU and gust lock systems might be related. As to the certification, however, although Gulfstream Services insists that the certification only concerned the specific repairs performed in January 2013, this document does not, as Plaintiffs point out, clearly stand for such limited guarantee. Moreover, Gulfstream Services' factual claim regarding the scope of the certification is contradicted by Plaintiffs' allegations in the operative complaint. Therefore, in analyzing its jurisdiction, the Court considers the maintenance record proffered by Gulfstream Services to the extent it demonstrates that the January 2013 service of the G-IV concerned the APU system, but not the company's claim that the certification only concerned the APU system or that the certification only demonstrated the airworthiness of the APU system. Although it is perhaps a close question, but mindful of the prima facie standard applying here, it is at least plausible that the Gulfstream Services technicians' alleged conduct has a causal relationship to Plaintiffs' negligence claim against Gulfstream Services. The Court finds that Plaintiffs have adequately alleged a "meaningful" connection between their claim and Gulfstream Services' activities in Massachusetts.

2. Purposeful Availment

"In determining whether the purposeful availment condition is satisfied, [the] 'key focal points' are the voluntariness of the defendants' relevant Massachusetts contacts and the foreseeability of the defendants falling subject to Massachusetts's jurisdiction." *Copia Commc'ns, LLC v. AMResorts, L.P.*, 812 F.3d 1, 5 (1st Cir. 2016). Here, there is no dispute that Gulfstream Services has purposefully availed itself of the benefits and protections of Massachusetts law. Plaintiffs adequately allege numerous facts evidencing Gulfstream Services' voluntary connections to Massachusetts which make it foreseeable that the company could be haled into court here. . . . These allegations include: (1) the operation of the Westfield Facility that employs over 225 people; (2) the receipt of $4 million in tax-incentives from the Commonwealth since 2011 to expand the facility; and (3) more than $5 million in state-funded improvements to perimeter roads at the facility, provided at the request of the Gulfstream Services. Given that the alleged actions of the maintenance employees at the Westfield Facility have a direct link to the claims brought against Gulfstream Services, Plaintiffs have met their burden under the purposeful availment prong of the inquiry by sufficiently demonstrating that Gulfstream Services has "purposefully avail[ed] itself of the privilege of conducting activities within the forum State, [and has] thus invoke[ed] the benefits and protections of its laws." *Hanson v. Denckla*, 357 U.S. 235, 253 (1958).

3. Reasonableness

The Court also agrees with Plaintiffs that the balance of the Gestalt factors weigh in favor of exercising jurisdiction over Gulfstream Services.

First, considering Gulfstream Services' contacts with Massachusetts, the burden on the company of appearing before the Court is relatively low. Moreover, because it is "almost always inconvenient and costly for a party to litigate in a foreign jurisdiction . . . the defendant must demonstrate that the exercise of jurisdiction in the present circumstance is onerous in a special, unusual, or other constitutionally significant way." *Hilsinger Co. v. FBW Invs.*, 109 F.Supp.3d 409, 429 (D. Mass. 2015). Gulfstream Services has not done so here. Second, a state also has a heightened interest in obtaining jurisdiction where the alleged injury occurred within the state's borders. Although Katz was not a Massachusetts resident at the time of the crash, the Court nevertheless has an interest in exercising jurisdiction over claims arising from an incident that occurred within Massachusetts where it is alleged that employees from a facility within the Commonwealth may have been negligent in certifying the G-IV's airworthiness. Third, Plaintiffs' "choice of forum must be accorded a degree of deference," *Hilsinger*, 109 F.Supp.3d at 429, and so "the plaintiff[s'] interest in obtaining convenient and effective relief" also supports the Court exercising jurisdiction. Fourth, the First Circuit has recognized that the interest of judicial economy counsels against furcation of a dispute among several different jurisdictions. Plaintiff argue "this litigation will proceed in Massachusetts against the remaining defendants . . . with or without Gulfstream Services," suggesting that judicial economy, therefore, will be best served by the Court exercising jurisdiction. This argument is not entirely convincing because the Court dismisses the claims against Rockwell and the other Gulfstream entities and so there will likely be duplicative litigation even if the Court also dismisses the claims against Gulfstream Services. While the analysis of this factor does not favor the exercise of jurisdiction here, neither does it provide support for not exercising jurisdiction here against Gulfstream Services. Fifth, and finally, Plaintiffs argue that "Massachusetts has a powerful interest in regulating the safety of its airspace and in preventing deadly accidents at its airports," yet, as the Court has already noted, Plaintiffs' claims against other Defendants advances this interest. Like the fourth factor, then, the fifth Gestalt factor does not weigh clearly in favor of the exercise of personal jurisdiction or dismissal. In sum, the balance of the Gestalt factors supports the reasonableness of the Court exercising jurisdiction over Gulfstream Services.

While it is a close question whether Gulfstream Services' in-forum conduct is sufficiently related to Plaintiffs' cause of action, the other jurisdictional inquiries—purposeful availment and reasonableness—provide stronger support for an exercise of specific jurisdiction. For these reasons, the Court finds that it has personal jurisdiction over Plaintiffs' claims against Gulfstream Services and the Court denies Gulfstream Services' motion to dismiss.

C. Gulfstream Delaware and Gulfstream Georgia

In their briefing, Plaintiffs essentially concede that Gulfstream Delaware and Gulfstream Georgia do not have sufficient contacts with Massachusetts on their own to satisfy the relatedness and purposeful availment prongs of the First Circuit's specific jurisdiction test. For Gulfstream Delaware, Plaintiffs instead ask the Court to impute Gulfstream Services' Massachusetts contacts to Gulfstream Delaware on the basis that the companies are agents of one another. As to Gulfstream Georgia, Plaintiffs argue for specific jurisdiction on the basis of a "stream of commerce plus" theory. The Court is unpersuaded by either argument and finds that it lacks jurisdiction over both Gulfstream Delaware and Gulfstream Georgia.

1. Gulfstream Delaware

As an initial matter, both Plaintiffs and Gulfstream Delaware are uncertain about which law controls the question of whether to impute Gulfstream Services' Massachusetts contacts to Gulfstream Delaware. Gulfstream Delaware argues that the correct law to apply is Georgia law on piercing the corporate veil—although the company also fortifies its argument with support from Massachusetts and Delaware law on piercing the corporate veil. Plaintiffs counter that their theory for imputing Gulfstream Services' contacts to Gulfstream Delaware is rooted in agency law, not piercing the corporate veil or an alter ego test. Plaintiffs, however, do not address the choice of law problem raised by Gulfstream Delaware and instead rely on "basic principles" of agency law as applied in federal court opinions. . .

[After surveying Georgia, Delaware, and Massachusetts laws, the court concluded that, no matter which of those laws applies, there could be no imputation of Gulfstream Services' contacts with Massachusetts to Gulfstream Delaware. The motion to dismiss this defendant for lack of personal jurisdiction was granted.]

2. Gulfstream Georgia

Plaintiffs begin by arguing that the Court has jurisdiction over Gulfstream Georgia under the traditional First Circuit test of relatedness, purposeful availment and reasonableness. Plaintiffs, however, do not allege any facts to support a causal connection between their claims against Gulfstream Georgia and the company's Massachusetts contacts. Rather, Plaintiffs allege generally that "there is reason to believe that the negligent repairs conducted on the [G-IV] in January of 2013 were carried out by employees of Gulfstream, Georgia who were—under what circumstances, the Plaintiffs cannot now say—stationed at the Gulfstream Services facility in Westfield." Plaintiffs' argument, therefore, relies on the theory that Gulfstream Georgia and Gulfstream services are in fact operating as a single entity. After all, Plaintiffs have separately argued that the January 2013 repairs of the G-IV were carried out by Gulfstream Services employees. The Court has already rejected such a theory in connection with Gulfstream Delaware and Gulfstream Services and Plaintiffs have not alleged any additional facts specific to Gulfstream Georgia that would lead to a different outcome here. As to purposeful availment, Plaintiffs ask the Court to consider Gulfstream Georgia's marketing efforts directed at Massachusetts as well as the fact that the company has historically sold aircraft to Massachusetts residents. Yet, Plaintiffs have not shown how these facts relate to any claim in the present lawsuit.

[In support of their] stream of commerce argument[,] . . . Plaintiffs make a series of broad claims about Gulfstream Georgia's Massachusetts-directed commercial activity, Plaintiffs do cite the fact "that at least 10 Gulfstream Georgia aircraft are currently owned or operated by Massachusetts citizens or entities." . . . [T]he G-IV did not enter the state through a stream of commerce, but rather entered the Commonwealth's borders fortuitously during a scheduled flight. [C]onstruing the stream of commerce doctrine to reach defendants like Gulfstream Georgia would eliminate any limiting principle. Because Gulfstream Georgia took no actions that caused the G-IV to make its way to Massachusetts, any reliance upon the stream of commerce theory is unavailing. Moreover, Plaintiffs' allegation that Gulfstream Georgia knew that the G-IV had previously traveled into Massachusetts is insufficient because stream of commerce plus requires more than "mere awareness that a product may end up in the forum state." *Boit v. Gar-Tec Prods., Inc.*, 967 F.2d 671, 683 (1st Cir. 1992). . . .

COMMENTS AND QUESTIONS

1. The court states early in its opinion that "[i]n ruling on a motion to dismiss for lack of personal jurisdiction without holding an evidentiary hearing, a district court must apply the prima facie standard of review." If personal jurisdiction is seriously disputed, why wouldn't the court hold an evidentiary hearing? What would the "standard of review" be if the court held an evidentiary hearing? Do evidentiary hearings systematically benefit plaintiffs (or defendants) with respect to establishing that a court does (or does not have) personal jurisdiction?

2. The plaintiffs filed a nearly identical lawsuit against Gulfstream Georgia in a Georgia state court. Which of the following statements is the most accurate?: (A) Filing the Georgia action was a necessary action; it might have been malpractice if the plaintiffs had neglected to do so. (B) Filing the Georgia action was legally improper; the plaintiffs should have been sanctioned for filing parallel actions. (C) Filing the Georgia action was legally proper, but was a serious tactical mistake.

3. Each of the three Gulfstream entities had strong arguments that the Massachusetts court lacked personal jurisdiction. Why would plaintiff's counsel sue all three (thereby triggering three fights about personal jurisdiction) rather than suing only the (most) legally-responsible one?

4. With respect to the imputation of one Gulfstream entity's contacts to the other Gulfstream entities, the court concludes that because Georgia, Delaware, and Massachusetts laws are substantially similar, a choice is not necessary. If the choice had mattered (and for a good advocate the choice of law will almost always matter), what law should apply? The

corporate (including agency) law of the forum? The corporate law of the state(s) of incorporation? Generic corporate law? The corporate law of the state that will supply the substantive law regarding the negligence and warranty claims?

FROM THE COURTS

J. MCINTYRE MACHINERY, LTD. v. NICASTRO

Supreme Court of the United States
564 U.S. 873 (2011)

JUSTICE KENNEDY announced the judgment of the Court and delivered the opinion in which CHIEF JUSTICE ROBERTS and JUSTICES SCALIA and THOMAS joined.

Whether a person or entity is subject to the jurisdiction of a state court despite not having been present in the State either at the time of suit or at the time of the alleged injury, and despite not having consented to the exercise of jurisdiction, is a question that arises with great frequency in the routine course of litigation. The rules and standards for determining when a State does or does not have jurisdiction over an absent party have been unclear because of decades-old questions left open in *Asahi Metal Industry Co. v. Superior Court of Cal., Solano Cty.,* 480 U.S. 102 (1987).

Here, the Supreme Court of New Jersey, relying in part on *Asahi,* held that New Jersey's courts can exercise jurisdiction over a foreign manufacturer of a product so long as the manufacturer "knows or reasonably should know that its products are distributed through a nationwide distribution system that might lead to those products being sold in any of the fifty states." Applying that test, the court concluded that a British manufacturer of scrap metal machines was subject to jurisdiction in New Jersey, even though at no time had it advertised in, sent goods to, or in any relevant sense targeted the State.

That decision cannot be sustained. Although the New Jersey Supreme Court issued an extensive opinion with careful attention to this Court's cases and to its own precedent, the "stream of commerce" metaphor carried the decision far afield. Due process protects the defendant's right not to be coerced except by lawful judicial power. As a general rule, the exercise of judicial power is not lawful unless the defendant "purposefully avails itself of the privilege of conducting activities within the forum State, thus invoking the benefits and protections of its laws." *Hanson v. Denckla*, 357 U.S. 235, 253 (1958). There may be exceptions, say, for instance, in cases involving an intentional tort. But the general rule is applicable in this products-liability case, and the so-called "stream-of-commerce" doctrine cannot displace it.

I

This case arises from a products-liability suit filed in New Jersey state court. Robert Nicastro seriously injured his hand while using a metal-shearing machine manufactured by J. McIntyre Machinery, Ltd. (J. McIntyre). The accident occurred in New Jersey, but the machine was manufactured in England, where J. McIntyre is incorporated and operates. The question here is whether the New Jersey courts have jurisdiction over J. McIntyre, notwithstanding the fact that the company at no time either marketed goods in the State or shipped them from there. Nicastro was a plaintiff in the New Jersey trial court and is the respondent here; J. McIntyre was a defendant and is now the petitioner.

At oral argument in this Court, Nicastro's counsel stressed three primary facts in defense of New Jersey's assertion of jurisdiction over J. McIntyre.

First, an independent company agreed to sell J. McIntyre's machines in the United States. J. McIntyre itself did not sell its machines to buyers in this country beyond the U.S. distributor, and there is no allegation that the distributor was under J. McIntyre's control.

Second, J. McIntyre officials attended annual conventions for the scrap recycling industry to advertise J. McIntyre's machines alongside the distributor. The conventions took place in various States, but never in New Jersey.

Third, no more than four machines (the record suggests only one), including the machine that caused the injuries that are the basis for this suit, ended up in New Jersey.

In addition to these facts emphasized by respondent, the New Jersey Supreme Court noted that J. McIntrye held both United States and European patents on its recycling technology. It also noted that the U.S. distributor "structured [its] advertising and sales efforts in accordance with" J. McIntyre's "direction and guidance whenever possible," and that "at least some of the machines were sold on consignment to" the distributor.

In light of these facts, the New Jersey Supreme Court concluded that New Jersey courts could exercise jurisdiction over petitioner without contravention of the Due Process Clause. Jurisdiction was proper, in that court's view, because the injury occurred in New Jersey; because petitioner knew or reasonably should have known "that its products are distributed through a nationwide distribution system that might lead to those products being sold in any of the fifty states"; and because petitioner failed to "take some reasonable step to prevent the distribution of its products in this State."

Both the New Jersey Supreme Court's holding and its account of what it called "[t]he stream-of-commerce doctrine of jurisdiction," were incorrect, however. This Court's *Asahi* decision may be responsible in part for that court's error regarding the stream of commerce, and this case presents an opportunity to provide greater clarity.

II

The Due Process Clause protects an individual's right to be deprived of life, liberty, or property only by the exercise of lawful power. This is no less true with respect to the power of a sovereign to resolve disputes through judicial process than with respect to the power of a sovereign to prescribe rules of conduct for those within its sphere. As a general rule, neither statute nor judicial decree may bind strangers to the State.

A court may subject a defendant to judgment only when the defendant has sufficient contacts with the sovereign "such that the maintenance of the suit does not offend 'traditional notions of fair play and substantial justice.' " *International Shoe Co. v. Washington*, 326 U.S. 310, 316 (1945). Freeform notions of fundamental fairness divorced from traditional practice cannot transform a judgment rendered in the absence of authority into law. As a general rule, the sovereign's exercise of power requires some act by which the defendant "purposefully avails itself of the privilege of conducting activities within the forum State, thus invoking the benefits and protections of its laws," *Hanson v. Denckla*, 357 U.S. 235, 253 (1958), though in some cases, as with an intentional tort, the defendant might well fall within the State's authority by reason of his attempt to obstruct its laws. In products-liability cases like this one, it is the defendant's purposeful availment that makes jurisdiction consistent with "traditional notions of fair play and substantial justice."

A person may submit to a State's authority in a number of ways. There is, of course, explicit consent. Presence within a State at the time suit commences through service of process is another example. Citizenship or domicile—or, by analogy, incorporation or principal place of business for corporations—also indicates general submission to a State's powers. Each of these examples reveals circumstances, or a course of conduct, from which it is proper to infer an intention to benefit from and thus an intention to submit to the laws of the forum State. These examples support exercise of the general jurisdiction of the State's courts and allow the State to resolve both matters that originate within the State and those based on activities and events elsewhere. By contrast, those who live or operate primarily outside a State have a due process right not to be subjected to judgment in its courts as a general matter.

There is also a more limited form of submission to a State's authority for disputes that "arise out of or are connected with the activities within the state." *International Shoe Co., supra*, at 319. Where a defendant "purposefully avails itself of the privilege of conducting activities within the forum State, thus invoking the benefits and protections of its laws," *Hanson, supra*, at 253, it submits to the judicial power of an otherwise foreign sovereign to the extent that power is exercised power in connection with the defendant's activities touching on the State. In other words, submission through contact with and activity directed at a sovereign may justify specific jurisdiction "in a suit arising out of or related to the defendant's contacts with the forum." *Helicopteros Nacionales de Colombia, S.A. v. Hall*, 466 U.S. 408, 414 (1984).

The impression arising from *Asahi*, for the most part, results from its statement of the relation between jurisdiction and the "stream of commerce." The stream of commerce, like other metaphors, has its deficiencies as well as its utility. It refers to the movement of goods from manufacturers through distributors to consumers, yet beyond that descriptive purpose its meaning is far from exact. This Court has stated that a defendant's placing goods into the stream of commerce "with the expectation that they will be purchased by consumers within the forum State" may indicate purposeful availment. *World-Wide Volkswagen Corp. v. Woodson*, 444 U.S. 286, 298 (1980) (finding that expectation lacking). But that statement does not amend the general rule of personal jurisdiction. It merely observes that a defendant may in an appropriate case be subject to jurisdiction without entering the forum— itself an unexceptional proposition—as where manufacturers or distributors "seek to serve" a given State's market. *Id.* at 295. The principal inquiry in cases of this sort is whether the defendant's activities manifest an intention to submit to the power of a sovereign. In other words, the defendant must "purposefully avai[l] itself of the privilege of conducting activities within the forum State, thus invoking the benefits and protections of its laws." *Hanson*, *supra*, at 253. Sometimes a defendant does so by sending its goods rather than its agents. The defendant's transmission of goods permits the exercise of jurisdiction only where the defendant can be said to have targeted the forum; as a general rule, it is not enough that the defendant might have predicted that its goods will reach the forum State.

In *Asahi*, an opinion by Justice Brennan for four Justices outlined a different approach. It discarded the central concept of sovereign authority in favor of considerations of fairness and foreseeability. As that concurrence contended, "jurisdictions premised on the placement of a product into the stream of commerce [without more] is consistent with the Due Process Clause," for "[a]s long as a participant in this process is aware that the final product is being marketed in the forum State, the possibility of a lawsuit there cannot come as a surprise." 480 U.S. at 117. It was the premise of the concurring opinion that the defendant's ability to anticipate suit renders the assertion of jurisdiction fair. In this way, the opinion made foreseeability the touchstone of jurisdiction.

The standard set forth in Justice Brennan's concurrence was rejected in an opinion written by Justice O'Connor; but the relevant part of that opinion, too, commanded the assent of only four Justices, not a majority of the Court. That opinion stated:

> The 'substantial connection' between the defendant and the forum State necessary for a finding of minimum contacts must come about by an action of the defendant purposefully directed toward the forum State. The placement of a product into the stream of commerce, without more, is not an act of the defendant purposefully directed toward the forum State.

Id. at 112.

Since *Asahi* was decided, the courts have sought to reconcile the competing opinions. But Justice Brennan's concurrence, advocating a rule based on general notions of fairness and foreseeability, is inconsistent with the premises of lawful judicial power. This Court's precedents make clear that it is the defendant's actions, not his expectations, that empower a State's courts to subject him to judgment.

The conclusion that jurisdiction is in the first instance a question of authority rather than fairness explains, for example, why the principal opinion in *Burnham* "conducted no independent inquiry into the desirability or fairness" of the rule that service of process within a State suffices to establish jurisdiction over an otherwise foreign defendant. 495 U.S., at 621. As that opinion explained, "[t]he view developed early that each State had the power to hale before its courts any individual who could be found within its borders." *Id.* at 610. Furthermore, were general fairness considerations the touchstone of jurisdiction, a lack of purposeful availment might be excused where carefully crafted judicial procedures could otherwise protect the defendant's interests, or where the plaintiff would suffer substantial hardship if forced to litigate in a foreign forum. That such considerations have not been deemed controlling is instructive.

Two principles are implicit in the foregoing. First, personal jurisdiction requires a forum-by-forum, or sovereign-by-sovereign, analysis. The question is whether a defendant has followed a course of conduct directed at the society or economy existing within the jurisdiction of a given sovereign, so that the sovereign has the power to subject the defendant to judgment concerning that conduct. Personal jurisdiction, of course, restricts "judicial power not as a matter of sovereignty, but as a matter of individual liberty," for due process protects the individual's right to be subject only to lawful power. But whether a judicial judgment is lawful depends on whether the sovereign has authority to render it.

The second principle is a corollary of the first. Because the United States is a distinct sovereign, a defendant may in principle be subject to the jurisdiction of the courts of the United States but not of any particular State. This is consistent with the premises and unique genius of our Constitution. Ours is "a legal system unprecedented in form and design, establishing two orders of government, each with its own direct relationship, its own privity, its own set of mutual rights and obligations to the people who sustain it and are governed by it." *U.S. Term Limits, Inc. v. Thornton*, 514 U.S. 779, 838 (1995). For jurisdiction, a litigant may have the requisite relationship with the United States Government but not with the government of any individual State. That would be an exceptional case, however. If the defendant is a domestic domiciliary, the courts of its home State are available and can exercise general jurisdiction. And if another State were to assert jurisdiction in an inappropriate case, it would upset the federal balance, which posits that each State has a sovereignty that is not subject to unlawful intrusion by other States. Furthermore, foreign corporations will often target or concentrate on particular States, subjecting them to specific jurisdiction in those forums.

It must be remembered, however, that although this case and *Asahi* both involve foreign manufacturers, the undesirable consequences of Justice Brennan's approach are no less significant for domestic producers. The owners of a small Florida farm might sell crops to a large nearby distributor, for example, who might then distribute them to grocers across the country. If foreseeability were the controlling criterion, the farmer could be sued in Alaska or any number of other States' courts without ever leaving town. And the issue of foreseeability may itself be contested so that significant expenses are incurred just on the preliminary issue of jurisdiction. Jurisdictional rules should avoid these costs whenever possible.

The conclusion that the authority to subject a defendant to judgment depends on purposeful availment, consistent with Justice O'Connor's opinion in *Asahi*, does not by itself resolve many difficult questions of jurisdiction that will arise in particular cases. The defendant's conduct and the economic realities of the market the defendant seeks to serve will differ across cases, and judicial exposition will, in common-law fashion, clarify the contours of that principle.

III

In this case, petitioner directed marketing and sales efforts at the United States. It may be that, assuming it were otherwise empowered to legislate on the subject, the Congress could authorize the exercise of jurisdiction in appropriate courts. That circumstance is not presented in this case, however, and it is neither necessary nor appropriate to address here any constitutional concerns that might be attendant to that exercise of power. Nor is it necessary to determine what substantive law might apply were Congress to authorize jurisdiction in a federal court in New Jersey. *See Hanson*, 357 U.S., at 254 ("The issue is personal jurisdiction, not choice of law."). A sovereign's legislative authority to regulate conduct may present considerations different from those presented by its authority to subject a defendant to judgment in its courts. Here the question concerns the authority of a New Jersey state court to exercise jurisdiction, so it is petitioner's purposeful contacts with New Jersey, not with the United States, that alone are relevant.

Respondent has not established that J. McIntyre engaged in conduct purposefully directed at New Jersey. Recall that respondent's claim of jurisdiction centers on three facts: The distributor agreed to sell J. McIntyre's machines in the United States; J. McIntyre officials attended trade shows in several States but not in New Jersey; and up to four machines ended up in New Jersey. The British manufacturer had no office in New Jersey; it neither paid taxes nor owned property there; and it neither advertised in, nor sent any employees to, the State. Indeed, after discovery the trial court found that the "defendant does not have a single contact with New Jersey short of the machine in question ending up in this state." These facts may reveal an intent to serve the U.S. market, but they do not show that J. McIntyre purposefully availed itself of the New Jersey market.

It is notable that the New Jersey Supreme Court appears to agree, for it could "not find that J. McIntyre had a presence or minimum contacts in this State—in any jurisprudential sense—that would justify a New Jersey court to exercise jurisdiction in this case." 201 N.J. at 61. The court nonetheless held that petitioner could be sued in New Jersey based on a "stream-of-commerce theory of jurisdiction." *Ibid.* As discussed, however, the stream-of-commerce metaphor cannot supersede either the mandate of the Due Process Clause or the limits on judicial authority that Clause ensures. The New Jersey Supreme Court also cited "significant policy reasons" to justify its holding, including the State's "strong interest in protecting its citizens from defective products." *Id.* at 75. That interest is doubtless strong, but the Constitution commands restraint before discarding liberty in the name of expediency. . . .

Due process protects petitioner's right to be subject only to lawful authority. At no time did petitioner engage in any activities in New Jersey that reveal an intent to invoke or benefit from the protection of its laws. New Jersey is without power to adjudge the rights and liabilities of J. McIntyre, and its exercise of jurisdiction would violate due process. The contrary judgment of the New Jersey Supreme Court is reversed.

JUSTICE BREYER, with whom JUSTICE ALITO joined, concurring.

[This opinion agreed with the plurality that J. McIntyre had not purposefully availed itself of the New Jersey marketplace, but disagreed with what it described as the plurality's "strict no-jurisdiction rule." The concurrence suggests that jurisdiction would have been proper if, in fact, a stream of commerce brought J. McIntyre's goods into the forum state. In this case, however, a "single isolated sale" was not a stream but rather an "edd[y], i.e., an isolated occurrence."]

JUSTICE GINSBURG, with whom JUSTICES SOTOMAYOR and KAGAN joined, dissenting.

A foreign industrialist seeks to develop a market in the United States for machines its manufactures. It hopes to derive substantial revenue from sales it makes to United States purchasers. Where in the United States buyers reside does not matter to this manufacturer. Its goal is simply to sell as much as it can, wherever it can. It excludes no region or State from the market it wishes to reach. But, all things considered, it prefers to avoid products liability litigation in the United States. To that end, it engages a U.S. distributor to ship its machines stateside. Has it succeeded in escaping personal jurisdiction in a State where one of its products is sold and causes injury or even death to a local user?

. . . On October 11, 2001, a three-ton metal shearing machine severed four fingers on Robert Nicastro's right hand. Alleging that the machine was a dangerous product defectively made, Nicastro sought compensation from the machine's manufacturer, J. McIntrye Machinery Ltd. (McIntyre UK). . . . The machine that injured Nicastro a "McIntyre Model 640 Shear," sold in the United States for $24,900 in 1995, and a features a "massive cutting capacity." According to McIntyre UK's product brochure, the machine is "use[d] throughout the [w]orld." . . . The instruction manual advises "owner[s] and operators of a 640 Shear [to] make themselves aware of [applicable health and safety regulations]," including "the American National Standards Institute Regulations (USA) for the use of Scrap Metal Processing Equipment."

Nicastro operated the 640 Shear in the course of his employment at Curcio Scrap Metal (CSM) in Saddle Brook, New Jersey. . . . In 2008, New Jersey recycling facilities processed 2,013,730 tons of scrap iron, steel, aluminum, and other metals—more than any other State—outpacing Kentucky, its nearest competitor, by nearly 30 percent. . . .

From at least 1995 until 2001, McIntyre UK retained an Ohio-based company, McIntyre Machinery America, Ltd. (McIntyre America), "as its exclusive distributor for the entire United States." 399 N.J. Super. 539

(App. 2008).[2] Though similarly named, the two companies were separate and independent entities with "no commonality of ownership or management." *Id.* at 545. In invoices and other written communications, McIntyre America described itself as McIntyre UK's national distribution, "America's Link" to "Quality Metal Processing Equipment" from England. . . .

In a November 23, 1999 letter to McIntyre America, McIntyre UK's president spoke plainly about the manufacturer's objective in authorizing the exclusive distributorship: "All we wish to do is sell our products in the [United] States—and get paid!" Notably, McIntyre America was concerned about U.S. litigation involving McIntyre UK products, in which the distributor had been named as a defendant. McIntyre UK counseled McIntyre America to respond personally to the litigation, but reassured its distributor that "the product was built and designed by McIntyre Machinery in the UK and the buck stops here—if there's something wrong with the machine." Answering jurisdictional interrogatories, McIntyre UK stated that it had been named as a defendant in lawsuits in Illinois, Kentucky, Massachusetts, and West Virginia. And in correspondence with McIntyre America, McIntyre UK noted that the manufacturer had products liability insurance coverage. . . .

[Nicastro] alleges that McIntyre UK's shear machine was defectively designed and manufactured and, as a result, caused injury to him at his workplace. The machine arrived in Nicastro's New Jersey workplace not randomly or fortuitously, but as a result of the U.S. connections and distribution system that McIntyre UK deliberately arranged. . . .

[Justice Ginsburg did not disagree with the basic premise that a defendant must "purposefully avail[ ] itself" of the forum state in order to establish minimum contacts. But] McIntyre UK, by engaging McIntyre America to promote and sell its machines in the United States, "purposefully availed itself" of the United States market nationwide, not a market in a single State or a discrete collection of States. McIntyre UK thereby availed itself of the market of all States in which its products were sold by its exclusive distributor. . . .

[She criticized "the splintered majority [for turning] the clock back to the days before modern long-arm statutes when a manufacturer, to avoid being

---

2   McIntyre America filed for bankruptcy in 2001, is no longer operating, and has not participated in this lawsuit. . . .

haled into court where a user is injured, need only Pilate-like wash its hands of a product by having independent distributors market it."]

The Court's judgment also puts United States plaintiffs at a disadvantage in comparison to similarly situated complainants elsewhere in the world. Of particular note, within the European Union, in which the United Kingdom is a participant, the jurisdiction New Jersey would have exercised is not at all exceptional. The European Regulation on Jurisdiction and the Recognition and Enforcement of Judgments provides for the exercise of specific jurisdiction "in matters relating to tort . . . in the courts for the place where the harmful event occurred." Council Reg. 44/2001, Art. 5, 2001 O.J. (L.12) 4. The European Court of Justice has interpreted this prescription to authorize jurisdiction either where the harmful act occurred or at the place of injury. *See Handelskwekerij G.J. Bier B.V. v. Mines de Potasse d'Alsace S.A.*, 1976 E.C.R. 1735, 1748–1749. . . .

COMMENTS AND QUESTIONS

1. Where can Nicastro sue J. McIntyre Machinery, Ltd., if not in New Jersey?

2. How does Justice Kennedy distinguish a defendant's "actions" (vis-à-vis a state) from a defendant's "expectations"? In which states, if any, did J. McIntyre Machinery, Ltd., *act*?

3. Justice Kennedy warns that if expectations are relevant to the jurisdictional inquiry, then "the issue of foreseeability may itself be contested so that significant expenses are incurred just on the preliminary issue of jurisdiction. Jurisdictional rules should avoid these costs whenever possible." What is the marginal cost associated with the inquiry into the defendant's state of mind (—that is, beyond the inquiry into the defendant's actions)? When are the costs associated with fact-specific inquiries to be avoided and when are they instead a necessary evil? (What about other pre-trial motions? Choice of law inquiries? Discovery disputes?)

4. Supreme Court Justices may use oral argument to persuade their colleagues. The following transcript captures the opening minutes of the oral argument in *Nicastro*. Arthur Fergenson, now Senior Counsel with

Ansa Assuncao LLP, represented the defendant, J. McIntyre Machinery, Ltd. Fergenson is a former law professor and federal prosecutor turned big firm lawyer.

> Mr. Fergenson: Mr. Chief Justice, and may it please the Court. Because J. McIntyre did not direct any activity at residents of New Jersey either itself or by directing its distributor MMA to do so and had no awareness or knowledge that the distributor took the action that it did toward New Jersey. New Jersey lacked adjudicative jurisdiction.

> Justice Scalia: When you say "its distributor," was this distributor at all controlled by the defendant?

> Mr. Fergenson: No, Your Honor. It was not. And both under Ohio law and under the Restatement (Second) Agency, section 1–1, the right to control is essential to ascribe actions to create an agency, and it's on a per-purpose basis.

> Justice Scalia: It might be better to refer to it as the company that distributes its products, rather than calling it "its distributor."

> Mr. Fergenson: Very good, Your Honor.

> Justice Scalia: It's loaded, it seems to me.

> Justice Kagan: Mr. Fergenson, in your question presented to this court, you asked whether there's personal jurisdiction—and I'm quoting here—"solely because the manufacturer targets the United States market the sale of the product." So I'm taking from that, that you acknowledge that this manufacture, McIntyre, a British manufacturer, targeted the United States market for the sale of its product. That's correct, yes?

> Mr. Fergenson: Yes.

Transcript, Oral Argument pp. 3–5.

5. The U.S. Chamber of Commerce filed an amicus brief in support of the petitioner, J. McIntyre Machinery, Ltd. Why would American businesses be concerned about the exercise of personal jurisdiction over foreign businesses? (Wouldn't American businesses that are putative defendants benefit from having foreign businesses as additional or alternative defen-

dants? And wouldn't American businesses often be plaintiffs suing foreign businesses?)

6. A *foreign* business like J. McIntyre Machinery, Ltd. can evade personal jurisdiction (per Justice Kennedy) in the United States by employing an American distributor. What is the analogous blueprint for a *domestic* corporation?

Personal Service

Personal jurisdiction over a natural person is established by serving the defendant with process in the forum state. Although the seminal case, *Burnham v. Superior Court*, 495 U.S. 604 (1990), does not have a majority opinion, it unequivocally endorses the validity of jurisdiction by personal service. This technique is also referred to as *transient jurisdiction* or *tag jurisdiction*.

In *Burnham*, the court granted certiorari on the question whether personal service on a non-resident established jurisdiction as to a cause of action that was unrelated to the non-resident's activities within the forum state. The case involved Dennis and Francie Burnham, a married but separated couple. The couple had lived in New Jersey. But upon separation, Francie moved with the couple's two children to California. Francie sued for divorce and support in a California state court. Thereafter, Dennis, still a New Jersey domiciliary and resident, was in southern California on business. He then traveled north to visit his children in the San Francisco area. During that visit, Francie had him served with a summons and divorce petition.

All nine justices of the court agreed that California had personal jurisdiction. Justice Scalia's plurality opinion (writing for himself and three other members of the Court) recited the historical bases for jurisdiction and held categorically that personal service within the forum state established personal jurisdiction:

> Among the most firmly established principles of personal jurisdiction in American tradition is that the courts of a State have jurisdiction over nonresidents who are physically present in the State. The view developed early that each State had the power to hale before its courts any individual who could be found within its borders, and that once having acquired jurisdiction over such a person by properly serving him with process, the State could retain jurisdiction to enter judgment against him, no matter how fleeting his visit.

495 U.S. at 610. Justice Brennan (writing for himself and three other members of the Court) opined that personal service in the forum state warrants a "strong presumption" that the exercise of jurisdiction is constitutional. The exercise would typically be constitutional, he observed, because it aligns with the "reasonable expectations" of a defendant who is voluntarily present in the forum. 495 U.S. at 637.

Justice Scalia's analysis required no assessment of reasonableness, while Justice Brennan would preserve an "independent inquiry into the . . . fairness of the prevailing in-state service rule." 495 U.S. at 621, 629. The reasonableness inquiry contemplated by Justice Brennan is not especially rigorous, however. Justice Brennan noted that Dennis Burnham's use of state roads and his enjoyment of the state infrastructure of police and fire protection or medical care, if needed, constituted purposeful availment of benefits provided by the state justifying the "slight" burden that transient jurisdiction imposed. Still, litigators should be familiar with this notion that some Justices might demand that the establishment of personal jurisdiction through tag jurisdiction also be "reasonable" in order to satisfy the Constitution.

Also, although not necessarily a part of the Constitutional mandate, a state may impose constraints on tag jurisdiction as a method for establishing personal jurisdiction. Justice Scalia observed in his opinion that most states do not permit jurisdiction to be asserted over individuals who were brought into the forum by force or by fraud. Similarly, someone who is in the jurisdiction as a party or as a witness in an unrelated case may enjoy immunity from service. Accordingly, these three exceptions are likely arguments for resisting tag jurisdiction as a basis for personal jurisdiction.

In circumstances where one or more of these three exceptions would be helpful to your case, but the exception is not established by state law, you would need to argue that it is unconstitutional for the court to assert jurisdiction on such grounds. Justice Scalia's opinion does not provide that support. In fact, his opinion does not explicitly hold that presence must be voluntary for his rule to apply; he refers only to "personal service upon a physically present defendant." This might be the sort of circumstance that would trigger Justice Brennan's test that demands that the exercise of jurisdiction be reasonable.

Hypothetical 20-4

Tovino Stables, Inc. (Tovino), is an 800-acre thoroughbred horse breeding farm located in upstate New York. It is a New York corporation that was founded in 1954.

Carlo Soffia is an Argentine citizen and prominent businessman in South America. Soffia is actively involved in the promotion of horseracing throughout South America and Central America—facilitating the exchange of information and harmonizing protocols within countries across the region.

Soffia's relationships with South American breeders and investors led Tovino to propose a joint venture with Soffia. Tovino's familiarity with and reputation in the United States, in turn, was valuable to Soffia. Alas, the relationship broke down within 18 months, and Tovino claims that Soffia owes it $1.6 million. Tovino's lawyer has a rough draft of a complaint, but is worried about an expensive fight over personal jurisdiction. And Tovino does not want to sue Soffia in Argentina.

Soffia has no presence or assets in the United States. He rarely visits the United States, and whenever he does, he has a carefully orchestrated schedule with security that does not expose him to the public. Tovino recently received a flyer from an organization called the Latin American Horsebreeders Association (LAHA), which is hosting a special event at the upcoming Kentucky Derby Festival (an annual two-week festival in Louisville, Kentucky, that culminates with the world's most famous horse race). The LAHA event is an invitation-only affair with tight security, but this is the sort of event that Soffia might attend.

Tovino's counsel has a plan to serve Soffia at that special event. The plan involves having a process server impersonate a member of the wait staff to get close access to Soffia. If Soffia is served, will this establish personal jurisdiction in Kentucky? In New York?

NORTHERN LIGHT TECHNOLOGY, INC.
v. NORTHERN LIGHTS CLUB

U.S. Court of Appeals for the First Circuit
236 F.3d 57 (1st Cir.), cert. denied, 533 U.S. 911 (2001)

STAHL, CIRCUIT JUDGE.

This case involves a dispute over the simultaneous use of two similar Internet domain names by two separate entities. Defendants-appellants Northern Lights Club, Jeff Burgar and 641271 Alberta Ltd. appeal a preliminary injunction entered by the district court requiring the posting of a specified disclaimer on their World Wide Web site's portal page. The court entered the injunction after finding that plaintiff-appellee Northern Light Technology, Inc. ("Northern Light" or "plaintiff") was likely to prevail on the merits of its state and federal trademark claim and its claim under the Anticybersquatting Consumer Protection Act, 15 U.S.C. § 1125(d) ("ACPA").

Defendants assert . . . that the district court lacks personal jurisdiction. . . .

I. Background

On September 16, 1996, plaintiff registered the Internet domain name northernlight.com with Network Solutions, Inc. ("NSI"), which at that time was the organization exclusively entrusted with the task of registering domain names on the World Wide Web. Plaintiff also filed registration papers for the "Northern Light" service mark with the United State Patent and Trademark Office ("PTO") during that same month. Nearly a year later, in August 1997, plaintiff began its operation of the northernlight.com website (and, consequently, its use of the "Northern Light" mark in commerce) as a search engine. Search engines are popular Web-retrieval tools that match a search query submitted by an Internet user with the websites whose content best corresponds to the submitted search terms. The northernlight.com site has remained in continuous existence as a search engine since August 1997.

Defendant Jeff Burgar, a resident of High Prairie, Alberta, Canada is the president and principal shareholder of 641271 Alberta, Ltd., an Alberta corporation that owns the northernlights.com domain name. Burgar, a self-described "Internet entrepreneur," has, since the mid-1990s, registered thousands of "catchy" domain names i.e., Internet addresses appropriating, in identical or slightly modified form, the names of popular people and organizations. He is also the president of Northern Lights Club, an unincorporated association with a listed address in Las Vegas, Nevada. While Northern Lights Club's stated mission is to bring together devotees of the Northern Lights, or *aurora borealis*, including businesses that take their name from the famous celestial phenomenon, Burgar's testimony indicates that the club has no actual individual members.

In October 1996, approximately one month after plaintiff registered its northernlight.com website, Burgar, on behalf of Northern Lights Club, registered the northernlights.com domain name with NSI. Soon after registration, Burgar licensed the name to FlairMail, a vanity e-mail service that he manages and that is owned by a local Alberta newspaper. Burgar "believes" that this newspaper is owned by his wife. Under this arrangement with FlairMail, defendants offered e-mail accounts under the northernlights. com domain name that users could access through some other website, such as flairmail.com, although Internet users who attempted to visit the northernlights.com page on the World Wide Web would find that no such site existed.

The two similar domain-name registrations enjoyed a peaceful coexistence until March 2, 1999, when a USA Today story on Internet search engines erroneously identified plaintiff's website as northernlights.com. After ascertaining that defendants were the owners of this domain name, plaintiff's marketing director contacted Burgar to find out whether defendants might be interested in selling it. The parties exchanged a series of proposals and counterproposals by e-mail over a two-month period but ultimately no sales or licensing agreement was consummated. Soon thereafter, in April 1999, defendants posted an active page on the northernlights.com World Wide Web site. Visitors to the site saw, among other things, a site-search function near the top of the screen that enabled users to perform a search of the northernlights.com site for specific words or phrases, as well as links to FlairMail and other members of the "Northern Lights Community." Plaintiff's Web site was placed third in the list of the Northern Lights Community "Business Listings." Plaintiff had not agreed to this listing.

On July 14, 1999, plaintiff sent Burgar a cease-and-desist letter, demanding that the northernlights.com site be deactivated. Defendants chose not to respond to this letter. Fifteen days later, plaintiff asked NSI to strip defendants of their respective marks, but NSI declined, citing the one-letter discrepancy between the name of defendant's website and plaintiff's trademark. On August 6, 1999, plaintiff filed the instant lawsuit [in the U.S. District Court for the District of Massachusetts] under federal and state theories of unfair competition, trademark infringement, and trademark dilution. In its complaint, plaintiff sought both a temporary restraining order and a preliminary injunction. In December 1999, plaintiff amended its complaint to add a claim under the Anticybersquatting Consumer Protection Act, 15 U.S.C. § 1125(d) (which had been enacted into law less than one month earlier) and to abandon its federal trademark-dilution claim and its state-law claims of unfair competition and trademark dilution.

Moments before the district court hearing on September 1, 1999 to consider the merits of plaintiff's claims and the court's personal jurisdiction over defendants, plaintiff's agent physically served process upon Burgar, who had traveled voluntarily to Boston from Alberta to witness the proceedings and to make himself available for testimony if needed. Although the hearing itself focused largely on the convoluted issues of personal jurisdiction arising from Internet activities, it also touched upon the merits of plaintiff's request for preliminary injunctive relief. . . . [The district court granted the preliminary relief. This appeal followed.]

II. Personal Jurisdiction

Defendants . . . challenge the injunction entered by the district court on the ground that the court was without personal jurisdiction to order such a remedy. . . .

The district court expressly declined to consider the validity of personal jurisdiction based on physical service of process. On appeal, however, plaintiff continues to press its case that, under the doctrine of transient jurisdiction, it has satisfactorily created jurisdiction through its service of process on Burgar prior to the September 1, 1999 hearing. *See Burnham v. Superior Court of Cal.*, 495 U.S. 604 (1990) (plurality opinion); *Schinkel v. Maxi-Holding, Inc.*, 30 Mass. App. Ct. 41 (1991) (holding that personal jurisdiction in Massachusetts need not be predicated on Long-Arm Statute when defendant served with process while in forum under transient-jurisdiction doctrine). Defendants dispute this proposition, claiming that this method of service of process is fundamentally unfair in that it represents a trap for the unwary litigant who travels to the forum state solely to contest the issue of personal jurisdiction. Defendants also argue that permitting service of process under these circumstances is unwise from a public-policy perspective in that it discourages the litigant from actively assisting the district court in the jurisdictional discovery process.

[D]efendants' argument against personal jurisdiction essentially boils down to a request that Burgar be deemed immune from service of process since, at the time he was served, he was present in Massachusetts only for the purpose of attending a personal-jurisdiction hearing in this lawsuit. This argument enjoys some measure of historical pedigree, albeit in a related context. Long before the Supreme Court in *Burnham* affirmed that personal jurisdiction can be sustained against a defendant solely on the basis of his presence in the forum state at the time of service of process, it had recognized that *some* parties temporarily in the forum state enjoy immunity from service by virtue of their status as participants in ongoing litigation. For instance, in *Lamb v. Schmitt*, 285 U.S. 222 (1932), the Court noted the potential peril of allowing an individual who is attending a proceeding in one suit to be served with process in conjunction with another:

> [T]he due administration of justice requires that a court shall not permit interference with the progress of a cause pending before it, by the service of process in other suits, which would prevent, or the fear of which might tend to discourage, the voluntary attendance of those whose presence is necessary or convenient to the judicial administration in the pending litigation.

Id. at 225 (internal citations omitted). Similarly, Justice Scalia's plurality opinion in *Burnham* referred to several states' historical imposition of statutory or common-law prohibitions on the service of process of those individuals present in the forum as parties or witnesses in unrelated judicial proceedings, a practice that led him to conclude that transient jurisdiction comported with constitutional due process. *See* 495 U.S. at 613.

Accompanying the court's repeated recognition of the validity of the party/witness immunity exception, however, has been a persistent acknowledgment of the exception's limitations. The *Lamb* Court itself noted that, because the privilege exists for the convenience of the district court in its exercise of judicial administration, rather than to protect the individual seeking to avoid service of process, courts enjoy the discretion to confer (or deny) immunity in such instances. *See* 285 U.S. at 225 (citing *Stewart v. Ramsay*, 242 U.S. 128, 130 (1916)). Just as importantly, the extension of the privilege has been limited by the majority of courts to cases in which the party or witness was participating in an *unrelated* litigation at the time that he was served with process in the forum state. *See, e.g., ARW Exploration Corp. v. Aguirre*, 45 F.3d 1455, 1460 (10th Cir. 1995) (denying process immunity where party was served with process in second lawsuit while attending deposition in first lawsuit alleging similar facts); *In re Fish & Neave*, 519 F.2d 116, 118 (8th Cir. 1975) (similar); *LaCroix v. American Horse Show Ass'n*, 853 F. Supp. 992, 994–95 (N.D. Ohio 1994) (applying *Lamb* and denying defendants' claim of entitlement to immunity based on appearance in forum state solely to contest personal jurisdiction); 4 Charles A. Wright & Arthur R. Miller, *Federal Practice and Procedure* § 1080, at 511 (2d ed. 1987) ("There is generally no immunity from service of process when the suit in which immunity is sought is part of, or a continuation of, the suit for which the person claiming immunity is in the jurisdiction."); *see also Lamb*, 285 U.S. at 225 ("[T]he [process-immunity] privilege should not be enlarged beyond the reason upon which it is founded, and . . . should be extended or withheld only as judicial necessities require.").[9] The rationale for the differing-lawsuit prerequisite to process immunity in this context is relatively straightforward: while a court can, in cases before it, choose to protect the jurisdictional status of a party or witness who is reluctant to come to the forum state by issuing protective orders or subpoenas, it cannot wield such power in other cases. The process-immunity exception therefore fills the gap only where it needs to be filled, that is, in cases where a district court wishes to shield an individual from service of process to encourage his or her travel to the forum state, but would be unable to do so absent the power to grant immunity.

---

9   In their brief, defendants cite to other cases, such as *American Centennial Ins. Co. v. Handal*, 901 F. Supp. 892, 895 (D.N.J. 1995), which interpret *Lamb* differently. Those cases hold that process immunity should be granted to non-residents present in the forum state to participate in *any* litigation, whether or not related to the suit for which the disputed service has been effected, as long as such immunity does not obstruct justice in the first suit. *See, e.g., Shapiro & Son Curtain Corp. v. Glass*, 348 F.2d 460, 461–62 (2d Cir. 1965); *NASL Marketing, Inc. v. de Vries*, 94 F.R.D. 309 (S.D.N.Y. 1982); *United Nations v. Adler*, 90 F. Supp. 440, 441 (S.D.N.Y. 1950). We reject this view, as *Lamb* definitely retains the distinction between presence in the forum state for related and unrelated cases. *See* 285 U.S. at 225 ("[T]he due administration of justice requires that a court shall not permit interference with the progress of a cause pending before it *by the service of process in other suits* . . . .") (emphasis added).

Turning to the facts of this case, several features of defendants' litigation posture counsel against a finding that Burgar is entitled to process immunity. First, and most apparent, is the fact that defendants have never asked the district court for such immunity on behalf of Burgar, either prior to or following the hearing at which Burgar was served with process. In lieu of a specific request for immunity, defendants instead have asked this court to fashion a broad, *per se* rule precluding the exercise of personal jurisdiction whenever the served individual is in the jurisdiction to attend litigation-related proceedings that pertain to him or her. In light of the admonitions in *Lamb* and other cases that process-immunity should be meted out sparingly, we reject this suggestion. Moreover, the circumstances surrounding the service of process on Burgar are not those that would ordinarily favor a finding of immunity even in a case where it had been timely requested. Specifically, Burgar *voluntarily* entered into Massachusetts to attend proceedings as a spectator in the *same* case in which he was served with process. While we need not decide the issue, it seems apparent that under these facts, the district court would have faced a relatively heavy presumption against granting such immunity if it actually had been sought by Burgar.

For these reasons, we hold that the district court properly exercised personal jurisdiction over defendants in this case.[10]

COMMENTS AND QUESTIONS

1. Part of footnote 10 of the court's opinion is surely wrong. Remember that each defendant has its own personal jurisdiction objection, and the analyses must be conducted separately. Moreover, personal jurisdiction over entities like corporations cannot be established by personal service. Only a natural person has "hands" that can satisfy the requirement that a defendant be served in-*hand* within the forum state. Serving an officer or employee of a company (while the person is in the forum state) *may* constitute proper *service of process* upon the defendant-company, but it will

---

10 We believe that the service of process effected upon Burgar also conferred personal jurisdiction over the other defendants. Burgar serves as the president of both Northern Lights Club, an unincorporated association, and 641271 Alberta, Ltd., a foreign corporation. . . . In all events, defendants have attacked the efficacy of service of process only in general. They have not attacked its efficacy vis-à-vis particular defendants. Consequently, we deem waived any possible argument that personal service upon Burgar was ineffectual as a means of bringing Northern Lights Club and/or 641271 Alberta, Ltd. before the court.

not also establish personal jurisdiction over that defendant-company. Why not? Can you give a convincing explanation of the differential treatment?

2. Why does the plaintiff's counsel bother suing the Alberta corporation 641271 Alberta, Ltd. and the unincorporated association Northern Lights Club if the Massachusetts court has personal jurisdiction over Burgar? (Are the additional defendants worth the headache of fighting about personal jurisdiction?)

3. When does the appeals court contemplate that a defendant like Burgar should ask the district judge for process immunity: before they enter the state or immediately after being served with process in the state? And *why* is the appeals court confident that Burgar would have been denied process immunity even if he properly had asked for it?

4. The court presents Burgar as an unsympathetic character. The Northern Lights Club is a club ostensibly about the *aurora borealis* yet it is based in Las Vegas . . . and the club has no individual members. The court also mocks Burgar for "believ[ing]" facts, rather than admitting or denying them. Burgar was an email spammer and patent troll before either of those terms were entrenched. Does the distasteful nature of Burgar's business affect the court's conclusion about whether the Massachusetts courts have personal jurisdiction over Burgar and his entities? (Should it?)

5. Defendants argue that allowing service to establish personal jurisdiction is bad public policy because it discourages parties from attending court proceedings and from actively participating in the fact-finding process. Do arguments about what is "good" and "bad" public policy generally explain the contours of personal jurisdiction doctrine?

FROM THE COURTS

MANITOWOC WESTERN COMPANY, INC. v. MONTONEN

Supreme Court of Wisconsin
250 Wis.2d 452 (2002)

ANN WALSH BRADLEY, JUSTICE.

The petitioner, Allen Montonen, seeks review of a . . . court of appeal decision affirming a circuit court grant of summary judgment in favor of the respondent, Manitowoc Western Company. Montonen asserts that this court should extend the fraud exception to the transient rule of personal jurisdiction in order to prohibit service of a lawsuit on a person who comes to Wisconsin for settlement negotiations. . . .

. . . Manitowoc Western Company is a Wisconsin corporation that employed Montonen, a California resident, in its Benicia, California facility. In October 1994, Manitowoc Western sent a letter to Montonen outlining proposed terms for Manitowoc Western's sale of its Benicia Boom Truck Crane Dealership to Montonen. Manitowoc Western believed the letter to be a non-binding general expression of intent, but Montonen maintained that the letter was a binding and enforceable agreement.

Although the parties dispute many of the details surrounding events subsequent to the signing of the October letter, the following three facts are undisputed. First, Montonen came to Wisconsin with his attorney on April 30, 1996, to meet with representatives of Manitowoc Western to discuss their disagreement over the letter. Second, Manitowoc Western filed this lawsuit against Montonen in Wisconsin earlier that day. Third, Manitowoc Western served Montonen with process at the end of the meeting.

Montonen moved to set aside the service of process and asked the circuit court to declare that it lacked jurisdiction over the person. He argued that Manitowoc Western engaged in fraud and deceit by tricking or enticing him to come to Wisconsin for settlement negotiations, then subsequently serving him with process. The circuit court denied Montonen's motion and eventually granted summary judgment in favor of Manitowoc Western. . . . [T]he court of appeals affirmed the circuit court. . . .

We begin with a brief recitation of the relevant law of personal jurisdiction. . . . [A] court has jurisdiction over an individual who is a natural person served with process while voluntarily present within this state. Physical presence is, in fact, the traditional basis of personal jurisdiction. *Burnham v. Superior Court*, 495 U.S. 604, 612 (1990). Personal jurisdiction based only on physical presence within a state at the time of service has been referred to alternatively as "transient jurisdiction" or the "transient rule" of personal jurisdiction. *Burnham*, 495 U.S. at 629 n.1 (Brennan, J., concurring).

Of course courts may achieve personal jurisdiction over an individual on a basis other than physical presence within the state at the time of service. In this case, however, we address personal jurisdiction and service only under the transient rule.

The transient rule is not without exception. Where an individual is brought within a jurisdiction by fraud or trickery, service will be set aside upon the proper showing.

> If a person is induced by false representations to come within the jurisdiction of a court for the purpose of obtaining service of process upon him . . . it is an abuse of process, and, the fraud being shown, the court will, on motion, set aside the service.

Townsend v. Smith, 47 Wis. 623, 626 (1879); *see also Saveland v. Connors*, 121 Wis. 28, 31 (1904).

Montonen has consistently and forthrightly acknowledged that his position represents an expansion of the fraud exception to the transient rule. He concedes that he is unable to show actual fraudulent intent and thus does not fall within the fraud exception as it stands under *Townsend* and *Saveland*. Rather, he emphasizes the vintage of the two cases and asserts that it is time for the exception to expand and evolve.

Citing cases from other jurisdictions, Montonen asks that we extend the fraud exception by adopting a flat prohibition on service under the transient rule during settlement negotiations. In support of this rule, Montonen relies primarily on *El M Lubricants, Inc. v. Microfral*, 91 F.R.D. 235 (N.D. Ill. 1981); and *K Mart Corp. v. Gen. Star Indus. Co.*, 110 F.R.D. 310 (E.D. Mich. 1986).

The federal district court in *El M Lubricants*, 91 F.R.D. at 238, determined that the fraud exception should be extended to cover cases where a defendant "reasonably relies on plaintiff's agreement to discuss settlement and where, later, plaintiff, without notice to defendant, decides to sue." In such cases, the court explained, the duty is on the plaintiff to either (1) communicate to the defendant before the defendant enters the jurisdiction that pre-suit negotiations are no longer feasible or that the plaintiff has chosen a legal remedy, or (2) forego service on the defendant if the defendant is in the jurisdiction for the exclusive purpose of discussing settlement. *Id.*

Likewise in *K Mart*, 110 F.R.D. at 313, the district court concluded that service was prohibited during settlement talks unless the plaintiff either (1) warns the defendant before entering the jurisdiction that it may be subject to service, or (2) gives the defendant an opportunity to leave the jurisdiction after settlement talks fail. The court in *K Mart* characterized its standard as a "bright-line" rule that would eliminate "a determination of whether the plaintiff intended to file a complaint at the time the parties were arranging the settlement meeting." *Id.*

As an alternative, Montonen asserts that this court could expand the fraud exception to require the quashing of service when a plaintiff invites a defendant into Wisconsin for purposes of settlement talks and fails to inform the defendant of the possibility of service. Among other cases, he cites to *Coyne v. Group Indus. Trieme*, 105 F.R.D. 627 (D.D.C. 1985) and *Henkel Corp. v. Degremont*, 136 F.R.D. 88 (E.D. Pa. 1991), in support of this rule.

In *Coyne*, the district court applied the fraud exception and recognized a presumption of fraud, given certain facts. In essence, the court adopted an "invitation rule" that establishes an evidentiary presumption of fraud when a plaintiff invites a defendant into the plaintiff's jurisdiction to discuss settlement and then effects service. *Coyne*, 105 F.R.D. at 630.

Similarly, the district court in *Henkel,* relying on *Coyne*, concluded that service should be quashed "whenever a defendant enters a jurisdiction for settlement talks at the plaintiff's suggestion and the plaintiff has not clearly and unequivocally informed the defendant of the possibility of service should the settlement negotiations fail." *Henkel*, 136 F.R.D. at 96. Thus, the focus of the test under *Coyne* and *Henkel* is the plaintiff's role in initiating the settlement meeting in the plaintiff's jurisdiction and subsequently serving the defendant without forewarning.

Although the standards set forth under either approach have much in common, it is apparent that they are not the same. As we read the cases, the essential difference between the two is that under *Coyne* and *Henkel*, the plaintiff must have initiated the settlement meeting while *El Lubricants* and *K Mart* purport to apply a "bright-line" rule that makes irrelevant the inquiry into which party initiated the meeting.

Other cases Montonen cites illustrate further variations on the theme. *See TMF Tool Co. v. H.M. Financiere & Holding*, 689 F. Supp. 820 (N.D. Ill. 1988); *Commercial Bank & Trust Co. v. District Court*, 605 P.2d 1323 (Okla. 1980); *Western States Refining Co. v. Berry*, 6 Utah 2d 336 (1957). In *Western States*, for example, the Utah Supreme Court determined that a showing of actual fraudulent intent was unnecessary where the following conditions were met: (1) the plaintiff "extends an invitation" to the defendant to enter the jurisdiction for purposes of settlement; (2) the defendant was in the jurisdiction for the "sole purpose" of discussing settlement; (3) service was effected either during settlement negotiations or during a "reasonable period" involved in coming to the negotiations and returning therefrom; and (4) the plaintiff did not advise the defendant at the time of the invitation that the defendant would be served if settlement negotiations failed. 313 P.2d at 481–82.

In *TMF Tool*, the district court adopted a rule similar to that in *El M Lubricants* and *K Mart*, but framed it as a three-prong test. The court in *TMF Tool* determined that service may be quashed on a transient defendant when (1) the parties agree to have a settlement discussion; (2) the defendant entered the jurisdiction "only for that purpose"; and (3) the plaintiff failed to notify the defendant, before the defendant arrived, that it might be served.

The courts in the cases cited gave a variety of reasons for adopting their respective rules. Most of these reasons, however, may be distilled into two important public policy considerations.

First, the courts relied on the public policy of the promotion and encouragement of settlement negotiations. Second, the courts sought to avoid thorny factual inquiries, particularly where such inquiries amount to nothing more than "swearing matches about who said what to whom." *Henkel*, 136 F.R.D. at 94. Montonen echoes these considerations in his assertions, arguing that an extension of the fraud exception is necessary to promote these important public policies in Wisconsin.

We agree that encouraging the efficient resolution of disputes through settlement negotiations and avoiding factual inquiries that are certain to devolve into swearing matches are important public policy considerations. These public policy goals may, upon initial examination, appear to justify rules like the ones Montonen advances. Ultimately, however, we are not convinced that they are best achieved by an expansion of Wisconsin's fraud exception to the transient rule.

The rules as advanced by Montonen create at least as many factual inquiries as they eliminate. This is true even of the rule that Montonen, citing *K Mart*, characterizes as a bright-line rule. That rules leaves questions such as the following ripe for contention: What constitutes a settlement negotiation? Was the served party in the jurisdiction for the sole purpose of these negotiations? What happens if it is the primary purpose but not the sole purpose? When does one purpose end and another begin?

Under other variations of the rules, such as those adopted in *Coyne* or *Western States*, still further factual inquiries are added to the mix: Did the plaintiff "invite" or "suggest" the settlement negotiations? In any given case, what is a "reasonable period" of time before and after a settlement negotiation in which a person may expect to remain immune from service?

Indeed, the disputes that would arise from these types of questions are foreshadowed by the facts in this case. For example, Montonen asserts that Manitowoc Western "invited" him to Wisconsin although Manitowoc Western argues that it was Montonen who requested the meeting. Manitowoc Western also argues that the meeting in Wisconsin may not have constituted a "settlement discussion," yet Montonen maintains that it is beyond dispute that the purpose of the meeting was to "discuss settlement." Both parties submitted affidavits in support of their positions, each with competing versions of the facts.

In addition, we note that although Montanen helpfully has attempted to categorize cases expanding the fraud exception into essentially two rules, there is substantial variation among the cases cited as to the exact bounds of the rules. This further illustrates that an expanded fraud exception provides no more of a bright-line standard than does the fraud exception as it now exists.

We do not agree with Montanen that the fraud exception in its present form significantly discourages settlement negotiations, thus undermining the efficient resolution of disputes through settlement negotiations. Parties who wish to engage in face-to-face settlement negotiations without risking service are not without alternatives. As technologies such as internet video conferencing become increasingly commonplace, the benefits of face-to-face settlement negotiations may be realized without an in-person meeting.

Perhaps more significantly, parties may agree ahead of time that they will not attempt service during the settlement negotiations. Thus, a party who is fearful of service can be protected by simply insisting on a clear statement from the other party that service will not be attempted. At oral argument, Manitowoc Western conceded that service in violation of such a safe harbor agreement would fall within the traditional fraud exception as it is presently formulated under *Saveland* and *Townsend*.

The rules that Montonen advances also fail to account for another important public policy that provides a compelling reason to retain the present fraud exception's relatively narrow formulation. Wisconsin has a definite interest in providing a forum where its citizens may seek legal redress. Expanding immunity from service of process to cover parties in settlement negotiations may limit and obfuscate the availability of a Wisconsin forum for Wisconsin litigants. As the dissenting justice in *Western States* noted in criticizing Utah's version of the rule:

> This [rule] opens the door to the unscrupulous nonresident present in the state, who, on being served by a resident, need only conveniently to state that he is present in the state at the invitation of the plaintiff for the purpose of settling a claim, thus inoculating himself. . . . Before such immunity should be granted, there should be a finding of an allurement, enticement, trickery, fraud, legal or otherwise, or some other kind of bad faith on the part of him, who did the inviting to negotiate, as the great weight of authority requires.

313 P.2d at 482–83 (Henriod, J., dissenting)

We agree with the dissent in *Western States* that the better rule is to continue to require a showing of actual fraud when a party seeks to set aside service under the fraud exception to the transient rule. Montonen has failed to provide a compelling reason why this court should depart from the rule of *Saveland* and *Townsend*. . . . Accordingly, we affirm the court of appeals.

COMMENTS AND QUESTIONS

1. What relief is Manitowoc Western seeking in its suit against Montonen? Should the answer to that question have any effect on whether Wisconsin has personal jurisdiction over Montonen?

2. Manitowoc Western had already filed its complaint against Montonen (unbeknownst to him) before their meeting. Is that fact inconsistent with the statement that Manitowoc Western entered into its settlement negotiations (or meeting with Montonen) in "good faith"? Does the Court care whether Manitowoc Western acted in good faith? Is good faith the same thing as not acting fraudulently?

3. Montonen's counsel "concede[d] that he [wa]s unable to show actual fraudulent intent." What would evidence of actual fraudulent intent look like? (Think of specific examples.) How often will defendants have such evidence? Did defense counsel err in characterizing their position as advocating for an expansion of the fraud exception?

4. Why did the parties have an in-person meeting if, as the court suggests, video conferencing is a viable alternative?

5. The Court observed—and claims to be furthering—two public policies: (i) promoting and encouraging settlement negotiations, and (ii) avoiding thorny factual inquiries. Does the court's holding, in fact, advance these policies?

6. Did Montonen's counsel make a tactical mistake by giving the court too many alternative standards?

Waiver

A state has personal jurisdiction over a defendant who waives her right to object to the court's jurisdiction over her. Because waiver can happen inadvertently, it is important for a litigant to preserve the objection by asserting it timely and properly.

The notion that waiver could be a basis for personal jurisdiction was not always obvious. In the context of *subject* matter jurisdiction, for example, the lack of subject matter jurisdiction is not something that can be overcome by waiver nor can it be created by consent of the parties. But in *Insurance Corp. of Ireland v. Compagnie Des Bauxites de Guinee*, 456 U.S. 694 (1982), the Court established a fundamental proposition of *personal* jurisdiction doctrine by rejecting the formalism of a sovereignty approach and focusing instead on the defendant's liberty interest. Personal jurisdiction (unlike subject matter jurisdiction) is about the Due Process Clause, and due process is about fairness to the defendant; it is not about structural limitations on judicial authority. Accordingly, under conditions that are fair to the defendant, a defendant may be subject to personal jurisdiction because she failed to object.

The prospect of waiver means that litigators must be keenly aware of the rules. You may recall from your Civil Procedure course that a response to a complaint can be *either* a motion or an answer. *See* Fed. R. Civ. P. 12(a). In whichever of these the defendant files first, the objection to personal jurisdiction must be included or else it is waived. Moreover, as a practical matter, in whichever of these the defendant files second, the objection to personal jurisdiction must again be included, or else it is waived.

There are essentially two paths by which personal jurisdiction can be established by waiver. First, by procedural rule, a defendant must include the objection to personal jurisdiction in her first responsive filing, whether that filing be a motion or an answer. The rules of procedure allow for the assertion of multiple objections (lack of subject matter jurisdiction, improper venue, insufficiency of process, failure to state a claim, etc.), but if the court's lack of personal jurisdiction is not among the objections in that first filing, the objection is considered to be waived, and the court has personal jurisdiction.

Second, even if the defendant properly asserts the court's lack of personal jurisdiction, the defendant may, through her litigation conduct, waive the objection. This species of waiver is a product of case law rather than procedural rule, and thus is highly fact-bound with criteria that vary by jurisdiction. The extreme case is easy to resolve. Imagine a defendant includes lack of personal jurisdiction as one of a litany of defenses in an answer but, rather than moving promptly for dismissal of the case, instead participates in discovery for two years and then on the third day of trial moves the court to dismiss for lack of personal jurisdiction. The defendant will surely be deemed to have waived the objection. Any defendant who neglects to push the issue of personal jurisdiction or who begins to litigate the merits runs the risk of waiving the objection. The prudent course is to move the court to consider a personal jurisdiction objection first.

Hypothetical 20-5

Biggio LLC is an Ohio corporation with its principal place of business in Cincinnati, Ohio. Biggio is a small, local investment company that makes investments on behalf of its clients—almost all of whom are Cincinnatians. Robertson is a registered securities representative for Biggio, and is a resident of Ohio. Robertson manages a hedge fund at Biggio.

Hayward is a domiciliary of Utah. Hayward grew up in Cincinnati, Ohio and recently attended a 20th high school reunion, where she reunited with her old friend, Robertson. Conversation at the reunion led ultimately to an agreement, whereby Hayward agreed to (and did) invest $500,000 in the hedge fund managed by Robertson.

In a matter of months, the value of the investments in the Robertson account dwindled to $50,000. Hayward asserts that Robertson breached their agreement by allocating gains and losses inconsistently among Biggio's investors (with more losses being allocated to Hayward).

On April 15, Hayward filed a complaint against Robertson and Biggio in Utah state court alleging, in count one, breach of fiduciary duty based upon the allegation that defendants engaged in the illegal practice of "cherry-picking" by allocating gains and losses inconsistently among Biggio investors. Counts two and three alleged violations of federal and state securities laws, respectively.

Biggio and Robertson timely removed the action to federal court and moved to transfer the case from the federal court in Utah to the Southern District of Ohio. While the motion to transfer was pending, defendants filed an answer on July 2, asserting lack of personal jurisdiction as an affirmative defense. The federal district judge denied without argument the motion to transfer, and ordered a scheduling conference.

In anticipation of the scheduling conference, the judge ordered the parties to make their mandatory initial disclosures in accordance with the Federal Rules of Civil Procedure. The parties complied. The scheduling conference was a video teleconference and all of the parties participated. In the course of this conference, the defendants made passing reference to their jurisdictional objections. The judge largely ignored counsel for both parties, and was fixated instead on mediation as "the answer to suits like this." Both parties had to be cajoled into agreeing to a mediation; they ultimately agreed to participate in a video mediation program provided on a complimentary basis by the Utah Bar Association.

The mediation was postponed a couple of times by the mediator, and the mediation itself involved three video sessions of 2-hours each spread over three months. The mediation was unsuccessful.

In January, Hayward served interrogatories and document requests that were timely answered by the defendants. Defendants' moved for a protective order to protect certain confidential and proprietary information from disclosure; that motion was denied.

In March, approximately 11 months from the date that the complaint was filed, Defendants moved to dismiss for lack of personal jurisdiction. Assume that waiver would be the only basis for Utah's exercise of personal jurisdiction over these defendants. Will the court grant the defendants' motion to dismiss?

FROM THE COURTS

EMEKEKWUE v. OFFOR

**U.S. District Court for the
Middle District of Pennsylvania
2012 WL 5249414 (M.D. Pa. Oct. 24, 2012)**

SYLVIA H. RAMBO, DISTRICT JUDGE.

Before the court is Defendant's motion for summary judgment wherein Defendant argues that this court lacks personal jurisdiction over Defendant. The parties have briefed the issues, and the matter is ripe for disposition. For the reasons stated below, the motion will be denied.

I. Background

Plaintiff, Bertram Emekekwue, brought this action in response to comments made by Defendant, Chinwe Offor, in an e-mail dated July 19, 2011. Plaintiff's initial complaint brought claims of libel, intentional infliction of emotional distress, negligent infliction of emotional distress, and punitive damages. [Offor's email regarded the Obosi Community Association of New York Inc.'s (OCA) consideration of Plaintiff's application for financial benefits following the death of Plaintiff's ex-wife, Vanessa Emekekwue. Offor was a past president of the OCA. Bertram Emekekwue was a secretary of OCA and Vanessa was once a member of OCA's scholarship committee. Bertram argued that Offor's email to OCA contained malicious, false statements that harmed his reputation, mental and physical health, and economic status. In her email Offor claimed that Plaintiff terminated his ex-wife's medical insurance and that the interruption in medical services and the inferior medical care that followed was a cause of his ex-wife's death. The email asserted that the Plaintiff was underserving of money from the OCA, a charitable organization.]

On December 7, 2011, Defendant filed her initial motion to dismiss along with a brief in support. In that motion, Defendant argued for dismissal of Plaintiff's complaint based on lack of personal jurisdiction under Fed. R. Civ. P. 12(b)(2), as well as for failure to state a claim under Rule 12(b)(6).

[Before the court could rule on the defendant's motion to dismiss, Plaintiff filed an amended complaint on December 16, 2011. In response to the amended complaint, Defendant filed an amended motion to dismiss on January 3, 2012. The amended motion to dismiss focused exclusively on the plaintiff's failure to state a claim—and did not "re-raise, incorporate by reference, or otherwise mention" the lack of personal jurisdiction.]

On May 15, 2012, this court ruled on Defendant's [amended] motion to dismiss the [amended] complaint. [The court granted the 12(b)(6) as to all of the plaintiff's claims except for his claim for defamation.]

Following the issuance of the court's memorandum and order granting in part and denying in part Defendant's motion to dismiss, Defendant filed an answer to the amended complaint on June 1, 2012. In the section entitled "Affirmative Defenses," Defendant asserts that "[t]he court lacks personal jurisdiction over the Defendant." On July 24, 2012, Defendant filed the instant motion for summary judgment, raising the sole issue of personal jurisdiction. . . .

II. Discussion

Following a thorough review of the relevant authority, the court finds that Defendant, pursuant to the waiver provisions Fed. R. Civ. P. 12(g) and 12(h), has waived her right to raise personal jurisdiction arguments at this point in the case. Accordingly, for the following reasons, the motion for summary judgment will be denied.

a. Amended Pleadings

Plaintiff filed an amended complaint within 21 days after service of Defendant's initial motion to dismiss, as permitted under Fed. R. Civ. P. 15(a)(1). When a plaintiff amends their complaint, the amended complaint supersedes the original complaint and renders the original complaint a nullity. The amended complaint thus becomes the operative document which serves to shape the litigation.

The amendment of a complaint also may give rise to circumstances which serve to render a motion to dismiss, made in response to the superseded original complaint, moot. Defendants "are not required to file a new motion to dismiss simply because an amended pleading was introduced while their motion was pending. If some of the defects raised in the original motion remain in the [amended complaint], the court may simply consider the motion as being addressed to the amended pleading." *Jordan v. City of Phila.*, 66 F.Supp.2d 638, 641 n.1 (E.D. Pa. 1999).

If a defendant decides not to rest on its initial motion, the defendant may, as here, file an amended motion to dismiss. In the amended motion, defendants have the freedom to re-raise or incorporate by reference any and all issues asserted in their initial motion to dismiss. *See Pippett v. Waterford Dev., LLC*, 166 F.Supp.2d 233, 236 (E.D. Pa. 2001). However, upon submission of an amended motion to dismiss, the original motion to dismiss becomes moot, and the court is therefore constrained to address the arguments contained in the amended motion. *See Holiday Village East Home Owners Ass'n, Inc. v. QBE Ins. Corp.*, 830 F.Supp.2d 24, 28 (D.N.J. 2011). It is fair for the court to assume that the defendant thoughtfully raised the arguments he or she wished to preserve and omitted any arguments that he or she wished to leave out.[3]

b. Waiver

Unlike subject matter jurisdiction, which relates to the court's Article III constitutional power, personal jurisdiction flows from the due process clause. *Ins. Corp. of Ir., Ltd. v. Compagnie des Bauxites de Guinee*, 456 U.S. 694, 702–703 (1982). Accordingly, the defense of lack of personal jurisdiction may be waived through a defendant's personal actions, whether voluntary or involuntary.

Waiver of personal jurisdiction may occur in two ways. First, a defendant may waive personal jurisdiction by failing to comply with Fed. R. Civ. P. 12(g) and (h). Second, a Defendant waives personal jurisdiction when it submits itself to the jurisdiction of the court by seeking affirmative relief from the court. *Bel-Ray Co. v. Chemrite (Pty) Ltd.*, 181 F.3d 435, 443 (3d Cir. 1999) (citing *Adam v. Saenger*, 303 U.S. 59, 67–68 (1938)).

The first inquiry in this court's analysis is whether Defendant waived the defense of personal jurisdiction by failing to include it in her amended motion to dismiss. Fed. R. Civ. P. 12(g) and (h) provide the rules governing the waiver of certain defenses. Rule 12(h) provides in pertinent part:

(h) Waiving and Preserving Certain Defenses

  (1) When some are waived

    A party waives any defense listed in Rule 12(b)(2)–(5) [including a motion to dismiss for lack of personal jurisdiction pursuant to 12(b)(2)] by:

    (A) omitting it from a motion in the circumstances described in rule 12(g)(2); or

    (B) failing to either:

      (i) make it by motion under this rule; or

      (ii) include it in a responsive pleading or in an amendment allowed by Rule 15(a)(1) as a matter of course.

---

[3]   It is generally not proper for a district court to raise the defense of personal jurisdiction *sua sponte. See Zelson v. Thomforde*, 412 F.2d 56, 59 (3d Cir. 1969). Parties and their counsel are free to leave out viable arguments that they do not wish to assert and are also free to voluntarily submit to the jurisdiction of the court by waiving any personal jurisdiction defenses then available. *See Azubuko v. Eastern Bank*, 160 F. App'x 143, 146 (3d Cir. 2005).

Fed. R. Civ. P. 12(h)(1). Rule 12(g) provides, in relevant part:

> (g) Joining Motions
>
>> (1) Right to Join
>>
>>> A motion under this rule may be joined in any other motion allowed by this rule.
>>
>> (2) Limitation on Further Motions
>>
>>> Except as provided in Rule 12(h)(2) or (3), a party that makes a motion under this rule must not make another motion under this rule raising a defense or objection that was available to the party but omitted from its earlier motion.

Fed. R. Civ. P. 12(g).

In other words, Rule 12(g) requires a party who brings a Rule 12 motion to join all available Rule 12(b)(2)-(5) defenses in that motion. Fed. R. Civ. P. 12(g)[5]. . . . Thus, if a party fails to raise any defense listed in Rule 12(b)(2)–(5) in their motion, Rule 12(h)(1) provides that those defenses are waived. Fed. R. Civ. P. 12(h)(1); *see also Ins. Corp. of Ir.*, 456 U.S. at 704 (discussing framework for waiver of personal jurisdiction noting that failure to raise timely objection under Rule 12(h) constitutes waiver). Moreover, a party who fails to raise personal jurisdiction as a defense in a Rule 12 motion is precluded from raising that defense in an answer or in a subsequent motion. *Myers v. American Dental Ass'n*, 695 F.2d 716, 720 (3d Cir. 1982).

Succinctly stated,

> the message conveyed by the present version of Rule 12(h)(1) seems quite clear. It advises a litigant to exercise great diligence in challenging personal jurisdiction, venue, or service of process. If that party wishes to raise any of these defenses, that must be done at the time the first significant defensive move is made—whether by way of a Rule 12 motion or a responsive pleading.

5C Arthur R. Miller & Mary Kay Kane, *Federal Practice and Procedure* § 1391 (3d ed. 1998 & Supp. 2012).

---

[5]   The purpose of this requirement "is to afford an easy method for the presentation of defenses but at the same time to prevent their use for purposes of delay." 2A J. LUCAS & J. MOORE, MOORE'S FEDERAL PRACTICE ¶ 12.02, at 2225 (2d ed.1982).

This statement is further supported by the Advisory Committee's Note to the 1966 amendment to Rule 12(h), which states:

> Amended subdivision (h)(1)(A) eliminates the ambiguity and states that certain specified defenses which were available to the party when he made a pre-answer motion, but which he omitted from the motion, are waived. The specified defenses are lack of jurisdiction over the person, improper venue, insufficiency of process, and insufficiency of service of process (see Rule 12(b) (2)-(5)). A party who by motion invites the court to pass upon a threshold defense should bring forward all the specified defenses he then has and thus allow the court to do a reasonably complete job. The waiver reinforces the policy of subdivision (g) forbidding successive motions.

Fed. R. Civ. P. 12, Adv. Comm. Note (1966 Amendments).

It is clear that Defendant's personal jurisdiction defense has been waived by the operation of Rules 12(g) and (h). Initially, the court notes that Defendant's amended motion to dismiss is considered her first defensive move for legal purposes because the initial motion to dismiss is moot, as discussed above. The amended motion to dismiss only raised arguments for dismissal for failure to state a claim under Rule 12(b)(6). It did not raise, re-raise, incorporate or even reference the defense of lack of personal jurisdiction. Defendant's failure to even mention the court's alleged lack of personal jurisdiction in the amended motion rendered that defense waived under Rule 12(h)(1). Accordingly, Defendant is precluded from raising the defense in her answer or in a subsequent motion for summary judgment. Defendant's motion for summary judgment will therefore be denied.[6]

---

6   This holding is also consistent with the "waiver-by-conduct" rule, which states that even if a party complies with the procedural requirements of rules 12(g) and (h), a party may consent to personal jurisdiction if he or she "actually litigates the underlying merits or demonstrates a willingness to engage in extensive litigation in the forum." *In re Tex. Eastern Transmission Corp.*, 15 F.3d 1230, 1236 (3d Cir. 1994). "[W]here a party seeks affirmative relief from a court, it normally submits itself to the jurisdiction of the court with respect to the adjudication of claims arising from the same subject matter." *Bel-Ray*, 181 F.3d at 443. . . . The purpose behind the "waiver-by-conduct" rule is to foster compliance with the spirit of Rule 12(h) and to protect judicial economy by requiring parties to expeditiously bring preliminary defenses to the court's attention. Here, the court can reasonably conclude that by moving this court to rule on the sufficiency of the amended complaint before seeking a determination on the issue of personal jurisdiction, Defendant showed a willingness to litigate this case in this court. Thus, defendant's actions, when considered in conjunction with the rationale behind the "waiver-by-conduct" rule, supports the court's finding that defendant waived her right to assert the personal jurisdiction defense under the facts of this case.

COMMENTS AND QUESTIONS

1. Defending the notion of waiver, the judge says that "[i]t is fair for the court to assume that the defendant thoughtfully raised the arguments he or she wished to preserve and omitted any arguments that he or she wished to leave out." But why would the court assume that this defendant wished to abandon an objection that it had already properly asserted once? Could (Should) the judge instead have asked defense counsel?

   The typical waiver case involves a defendant who never raised the objection. Here, of course, the defendant objected, but then did not object again when the plaintiff filed an amended complaint. Is the difference between the typical case and the instant case a difference of degree or a difference in kind? Which of those two narratives is more compelling here?

2. The highly fact-bound inquiry associated with *specific* jurisdiction might lead courts to be especially eager to embrace bright-line tests for the other bases for establishing personal jurisdiction. How might an effective litigator raise this in an oral argument? (Would this broad policy argument augur in favor of plaintiffs or defendants?)

Consent

A party who enters into a contract that includes a forum selection clause has consented to personal jurisdiction in the selected forum. Indeed, this principle is so firmly established that it is rare even to see a challenge to personal jurisdiction in such a context, much less a successful challenge.

Instead, issues about forum selection clauses arise in contexts where one party to the contract has filed suit in some forum other than the one selected in the contract, and the other party is trying to enforce the forum selection clause. Because such disputes are about *venue*, rather than *personal jurisdiction*, we address them in a separate chapter. (*See* Chapter 21.)

When the litigation is filed in the forum selected by the parties, only standard contract defenses could disturb the finding of consent to jurisdiction. For example, assent cannot be obtained fraudulently or through duress. Similarly, a battle of the forms with countermanding forum selection clauses raises questions about whether the parties agreed to a forum selection clause, and if so, to which one.

If the claim arises under federal law, then federal law governs the validity and enforcement of forum-selection clauses. If the claim arises under state or foreign law, there is a circuit split about whether federal law or the law of the forum state (or, if the case also involves a choice of law clause, the law of the selected state) governs. Whatever the source of the governing law, courts are strongly inclined toward enforcement of the clause; this inclination manifests a general preference for validating rather than invalidating contractual obligations.

Finally, an emerging area of litigation involves state registration statutes. As a condition of doing business in a state, state laws require foreign (out-of-state) corporations to register and to satisfy certain conditions. Typically, one of those conditions is the appointment of a local agent for purposes of service of process. Historically, some states deemed the appointment of a local agent to be consent to personal jurisdiction. Plaintiffs' counsel still occasionally make the argument, but there are two reasons that the argument tends to fail. First, service and personal jurisdiction are conceptually distinct doctrines; consent to service in the jurisdiction does not necessarily mean that the courts of the state also have personal jurisdiction. Of course state legislatures could amend their registration statutes and include consent to personal jurisdiction as a condition of doing business in the state; and this leads to the second hurdle. If states could create consent to personal jurisdiction through their state registration statutes, this basis for establishing jurisdiction would seriously undermine the work that the Supreme Court has done in narrowing the scope of general (and specific) jurisdiction: a defendant corporation would be deemed to have consented to personal jurisdiction even if its contacts with the forum state were tenuous and unrelated.

Hypothetical 20-6

Allen Cemetery Association (Allen), a Nevada corporation located in Boulder City, Nevada, ordered a 54,000-pound granite monument from Bosse Granite Resources Corporation (Bosse), a California corporation with its principal place of business in Truckee, California. Bosse responded by faxing an invoice to Allen.

Bosse claims that its invoice contained terms and conditions on the back sides of its pages, including the following forum selection clause:

> Any unresolved legal disputes shall be submitted solely to courts of the State of Utah, and each party accepts Utah jurisdiction.

666 • Learning Conflict of Laws •

The terms and conditions also included a Utah choice of law clause. Bosse is a subsidiary of a corporation that is incorporated in Utah and that has its principal place of business there.

Allen admits that it received the faxed invoice. But Allen denies ever receiving the alleged terms and conditions on the back side of that document.

Bosse delivered the monument. Allen asked Bosse to wait for payment until the start of Allen's new fiscal year; Bosse acquiesced. Many months passed. Allen ultimately notified Bosse that it was not obligated to pay for the monument because it was cracked. Bosse investigated but concluded that the cracks were tiny, natural fissures that were not indicative of defect. Allen still refused to pay, and Bosse filed suit in a Utah federal court. Which jurisdiction's contract law governs the interpretation of this forum selection clause?

FROM THE COURTS

FLIPBOARD, INC. v. AMORPHOUS

U.S. District Court for the Northern District of California
2015 WL 8482258 (N.D. Cal. Dec. 10, 2015)

BETH LABSON FREEMAN, DISTRICT JUDGE.

Before the Court is Defendant's Motion to Dismiss for lack of personal jurisdiction. Defendant, a *pro se* Rhode Island resident, argues that the Court lacks jurisdiction over her, and that asserting such jurisdiction would offend traditional notions of fair play and substantial justice. Plaintiff responds that Defendant consented to personal jurisdiction in this forum. . . .

I. Background

Plaintiff Flipboard, Inc. alleges that its principal place of business is located in Palo Alto, California. Plaintiff describes itself as an online service that "allows users to view a variety of online content, including images . . . in interactive magazine-style layouts and, if they choose, share their personalized collections with others." Plaintiff alleges that it stores some of the content it makes accessible pursuant to a license, or the Digital Millenium Copyright Act ("DMCA"). Plaintiff alleges that the remaining content is served from other online locations, including websites like Flickr, Tumblr, and Bored Panda, through, among other things, application protocol interfaces.

Defendant Kalliope Amorphous is a visual artist residing in Rhode Island. She has posted her photographs on various online services, including Bored Panda, Flickr, and Tumblr.

Plaintiff alleges that, on June 5, 2015, Plaintiff received a letter from Barbara Hoffman, New York counsel for Defendant, at its Palo Alto office. The letter was addressed to Plaintiff's General Counsel in Palo Alto and described Plaintiff as a company "with its principal place of business in Palo Alto, California."

The letter claimed that Plaintiff was infringing Defendant's copyright on images she had posted on Bored Panda. In the letter, Defendant's New York Counsel stated, "[I]t would be simple enough for Ms. Amorphous, my client, to file suit against [Plaintiff] for copyright infringement and seek the maximum statutory damages." The letter claims that Defendant "is entitled to three million dollars."

On June 10, 2015, an attorney in New York representing Plaintiff responded. Over the next several days, Plaintiff's New York attorney and Defendant's New York Counsel exchanged four additional letters or emails and one call, in which Defendant's New York Counsel additionally accused Plaintiff of improperly taking Defendant's images from Flickr and Tumblr and continued to note the possibility of litigation.

On June 24, 2015, Defendant's New York Counsel wrote Plaintiff's New York attorney that she was "willing to settle for one million dollars." Plaintiff's New York attorney rejected the offer on June 30, 2015, and asked for additional information regarding the copyrighted works and registrations Defendant claimed Plaintiff was infringing. On July 8, Defendant's New York Counsel sent information about her client's works on Flickr and Tumblr, "along with some screenshots showing the ways that Defendant herself had used those works in connection with the Flipboard application." Plaintiff alleges that Defendant provided no evidence of any other Flipboard user accessing, incorporating, copying, or sharing those works through its services. On July 13, 2015, the attorneys spoke again and Defendant's New York Counsel allegedly repeated her one million dollar settlement offer while noting the possibility of court action.

Later that day, Plaintiff filed this action for declaratory judgment of noninfringement pursuant to the Declaratory Judgment Act, 28 U.S.C. §§ 2201–2202, the Copyright Act of 1976, 17 U.S.C. §§ 101 et seq., the Digital Millennium Copyright Act ("DMCA"), 17 U.S.C. § 1202, and the Lanham Act, 15 U.S.C. § 1051 et seq.

On July 27, 2015, Defendant, represented by her New York Counsel, filed an action for direct and contributory copyright infringement and violation of the DMCA in the Southern District of New York ("New York Case").

On September 21, 2015, Defendant filed the instant motion to dismiss for lack of personal jurisdiction. Plaintiff opposed on October 15, 2015 and Defendant replied on October 21, 2015. The Court heard oral argument on this motion on November 12, 2015, with Defendant appearing by phone. On October 16, 2015, Plaintiff moved to transfer the New York Case here. A decision on that motion has not yet been issued.

II. Legal Standard

Federal Rule of Civil Procedure 12(b)(2) authorizes a defendant to seek dismissal of an action for lack of personal jurisdiction. When a defendant challenges a court's personal jurisdiction, the plaintiff bears the burden of establishing that jurisdiction over the defendant is proper.

"Where, as here, the defendant's motion is based on written materials rather than an evidentiary hearing, the plaintiff need only make a prima facie showing of jurisdictional facts to withstand the motion to dismiss." *Ranza v. Nike, Inc.*, 793 F.3d 1059, 1068 (9th Cir. 2015). The plaintiff may meet that burden by submitting affidavits and discovery materials. A "plaintiff may not simply rest on the bare allegations of the complaint. But uncontroverted allegations must be taken as true, and conflicts between parties over statements contained in affidavits must be resolved in the plaintiff's favor." *Ranza*, 793 F.3d at 1068. . . .

A court may exercise personal jurisdiction over a defendant based on consent. "[I]t is settled . . . that parties to a contract may agree in advance to submit to the jurisdiction of a given court." *National Equip. Rental, Ltd. v. Szukhent*, 375 U.S. 311, 316 (1964). Where the defendant has consented to California jurisdiction, the "court need not embark on a 'minimum contacts' analysis." *Craigslist, Inc. v. Kerbel*, 2012 WL 3166798.

Plaintiff argues that Defendant's consent to Flipboard's terms of use ("TOU"), which include a California forum selection clause, suffices to establish the Court's personal jurisdiction over her. The TOU state, "we each agree that any [non-arbitrable] claims shall be litigated exclusively in a state court located in Santa Clara County, California, and you consent to personal jurisdiction in those courts."

Courts have applied the consent principle to forum selection clauses in website terms of use. *Id.* "Forum selection clauses [in TOUs] are presumptively valid." *Kerbel*, 2012 WL 3166798 at *6.

Defendant admits that she "adopt[ed] the role of 'user' " on Plaintiff's service. And she has exhibited a high level of familiarity with website terms of service and use. Defendant "relied on the protection of the . . . [terms of service] of Bored Panda, Flickr, and Tumblr," and asserts personal knowledge of the terms for the Flickr and Tumblr APIs. Defendant asserts that she chose Flickr and Tumblr as her "primary photo hosting services due to [their] strict copyright policies."

In the face of this consent, "the only issue for the court is whether the contracts are unfair or unreasonable." *Kerbel,* 2012 WL 3166798 at *6. "The party disputing the validity of a forum selection clause bears the burden of proving the clause is unenforceable." *Craigslist, Inc. v. Naturemarket, Inc.*, 694 F.Supp.2d 1039, 1052 (N.D. Cal. 2010).

Defendant first argues that enforcing Plaintiff's forum selection clause here would be "patently unreasonable" because she "had to access Flipboard" in order to document the alleged infringement. This left her with "an overreaching and deceptive Catch 22": she could either have proof of Plaintiff's infringement but be subject to suit in California, or she could reject the forum selection clause but deprive herself of the proof she needed to bring the New York case.

Plaintiff responds that Defendant joined Flipboard and agreed to its TOU not to document infringement, but to manufacture it. Specifically, Plaintiff argues that, to establish Plaintiff's secondary liability for copyright infringement, Defendant needed to show infringement by a third party but had no proof that any Flipboard user had accessed her work; to rectify this, Plaintiff contends, Defendant "used her own account on Flipboard to manufacture the supposed 'infringements' for which she seeks to hold Flipboard secondarily liable."

To the extent that the parties' affidavits have created a factual dispute, the Court must resolve the disagreement in Plaintiff's favor for the purposes of this motion. *See Bancroft & Masters, Inc. v. Augusta Nat. Inc.,* 223 F.3d 1082, 1087 (9th Cir. 2000). Thus, the Court assumes that Defendant joined Plaintiff's service in order to manufacture at least some of the alleged infringement and finds Defendant's catch-22 argument unavailing.

Defendant next contends that enforcing the forum selection here would be unfair or unreasonable as it would "effectively depriv[e] her of her day in court." But Defendant is, in fact, having her day in court, albeit as a defendant and in California.

Finally, Defendant argues that enforcing the forum selection clause would be unreasonable because litigating here would impose a "substantial and impossible" financial burden on her and would "wrest [her] from her long-time attorney in New York." But, "[w]ith the advances in transportation and telecommunications and the increasing interstate practice of law, any burden of litigation in a forum other than one's residence is substantially less than in days past." *CollegeSource, Inc v. AcademyOne, Inc.,* 653 F.3d 1066, 1080 (9th Cir. 2011). As demonstrated at the November 10, 2015 hearing, Defendant can minimize costs by e-filing and appearing by phone. With regard to access to counsel, Defendant employs a regular attorney in New York, "qualified for the service of the California Lawyers for the Arts but was not provided with an attorney with the appropriate qualifications given the short time frame." Thus, Defendant should be able to either redirect the financial resources she uses to hire her regular attorney in New York to find assistance here, or, with more time, she should be able to access an attorney through the California Lawyers for the Arts.

Given Defendant's high level of understanding of the TOU, and taking Plaintiff's contention that Defendant only joined Plaintiff's service to manufacture infringement for the purposes of litigation as true, the Court finds that enforcement of the forum selection clause here is neither unfair nor unreasonable. While the Court does not find that mere use of a website is sufficient to justify exercising personal jurisdiction over the user, the Court finds that, under the unique circumstances of this case, Defendant's consent to jurisdiction here is valid and binding. *Automattic Inc. v. Steiner,* 82 F.Supp.3d 1011, 1022 (N.D. Cal. 2015) [("In becoming a user of WordPress, Defendant accepted terms of service [that included] a forum selection clause selecting this forum. [T]his constitutes sufficient evidence that Defendant has consented to jurisdiction in this forum.")].

COMMENTS AND QUESTIONS

1. When a typical person accepts an application's terms of service and those terms include a forum selection clause, how meaningful is their consent to jurisdiction? Is it knowing? Willful? What do we mean when we say that a court may exercise personal jurisdiction over a defendant who "consents"?

2. The court observes that "with the advances in transportation and telecommunications and the increasing interstate practice of law, any burden of litigation in a forum other than one's residence is substantially less than in days past." But isn't this also a reason why corporations like Flipboard do not need to include forum selection clauses in their terms of service?

FROM THE COURTS

WILDERNESS USA, INC. v. DEANGELO BROTHERS LLC

U.S. District Court for the Western District of New York
265 F.Supp.3d 301 (W.D.N.Y. 2017)

ELIZABETH A. WOLFORD, DISTRICT JUDGE.

Introduction

Plaintiff Wilderness USA, Inc. ("Plaintiff") commenced this action in New York State Supreme Court, Monroe County, seeking various forms of relief arising out of a contractual dispute with defendant DeAngelo Brothers LLC ("Defendant"). On July 25, 2017, Defendant filed a notice of removal to this Court based on diversity jurisdiction.

Presently pending before the Court is Defendant's motion to dismiss for lack of *in personam* jurisdiction and improper venue. The central question governing the disposition of this motion is whether the Court has general jurisdiction over a party, such as Defendant, who is registered to do business as a foreign corporation in New York State, and, as such, has appointed the New York State Secretary of State as its agent for service of process. *See* N.Y. Bus. Corp. Law §§ 1301, 1304(a)(6). Defendant rightly acknowledges that New York courts have permitted the exercise of general jurisdiction over a foreign corporation upon no other basis but compliance with the registration statute. *See Steuben Foods, Inc. v. Oystar Grp.*, No. 10-CV-780S, 2013 WL 2105894, at *3 (W.D.N.Y. May 14, 2013). However, Defendant also contends that this method of acquiring personal jurisdiction is outmoded and has been rendered inapplicable in light of the Supreme Court's decision in *Daimler AG v. Bauman*, 571 U.S. 117 (2014), as well as the subsequent cases decided within this Circuit. Plaintiff recognizes that several federal district court cases have construed *Daimler* as Defendant suggests, but Plaintiff argues that these cases were wrongly decided and that the exercise of general jurisdiction pursuant to New York's business registration statute is still supported by good law. Because the Court agrees with Defendant that *Daimler* altered the landscape for acquiring personal jurisdiction in a case such as this, Defendant's motion to dismiss is granted, and Plaintiff's complaint is dismissed without prejudice.

Factual Background

Plaintiff, a New York corporation maintaining its principal place of business within this district in Monroe County, New York, operates a business specializing in "vegetation management." Plaintiff employs various individuals to assist in controlling overgrowth along highways and right-of-ways. According to Defendant's notice of removal, Defendant is a Pennsylvania limited liability company and maintains its principal place of business in Pennsylvania.

On February 15, 2016, Plaintiff entered into a subcontract with a nonparty contractor known as Mercier, Inc. ("Mercier"). Mercier agreed to bid on projects offered by the Georgia Department of Transportation ("GDOT"), and promised to assign Plaintiff as its sole subcontractor for vegetation management on any contracts it was awarded by the State of Georgia. Mercier obtained three contracts for vegetation management within three different GDOT districts (collectively, "GDOT Contract"). However, after learning that the owner of Mercier wished to sell the company to Defendant, Plaintiff engaged in negotiations with Mercier and Defendant to protect its rights under the subcontract.

On November 29, 2016, Plaintiff, Defendant, and Mercier entered into an "Assignment and Assumption and Release" agreement (the "Agreement"), which provided that Defendant would assume Mercier's responsibilities under the subcontract with Plaintiff. The Agreement also prevented Defendant from interfering with Plaintiff's work under the GDOT Contract. Plaintiff alleges that it has been competently performing its obligations under the GDOT Contract for over a year and a half.

In June and July of 2017, Defendant allegedly sent its employees to antagonize GDOT personnel about Plaintiff's job performance under the GDOT Contract. Plaintiff notified Defendant that it was interfering with Plaintiff's obligations under the GDOT Contract, and Defendant responded by terminating the subcontract for several material breaches of the subcontract and the GDOT Contract. Plaintiff alleges that Defendant manufactured these various contractual breaches to "squeeze [Plaintiff] out of the GDOT Contract so that it can take over the work itself." Plaintiff further alleges that it will suffer irreparable harm upon the termination of the subcontract, such as being forced to lay off 50 employees in Georgia, the loss of its goodwill and reputation with GDOT, and the loss of "substantial investments in acquiring materials and equipment" for the performance of the GDOT Contract.

Plaintiff filed this action in New York State Supreme Court, Monroe County, seeking a declaration that it has not materially breached the subcontract or the GDOT Contract, a declaration that Defendant's purported termination of the subcontract is void, injunctive relief enjoining Defendant from seeking to terminate the subcontract or otherwise interfere with Plaintiff's performance of the GDOT Contract, and, alternatively, monetary damages for Defendant's alleged breach of the subcontract and the Agreement. On July 20, 2017, the state court entered a temporary restraining order preventing Defendant from terminating the subcontract or otherwise interfering with Plaintiff's performance of the GDOT Contract.

Defendant has since filed a notice of removal, and a motion to dismiss/transfer of venue. Defendant claims that this Court does not have the authority to exercise either general or specific jurisdiction over Defendant, and thus, the action must be dismissed for lack of personal jurisdiction. Plaintiff responds only to Defendant's argument regarding general jurisdiction, and contends that personal jurisdiction has been established because Defendant has registered to do business in New York State as a foreign corporation and has appointed the New York State Secretary of State as its agent for service of process in the state. . . .

Discussion

. . ."In general, a 'district court's personal jurisdiction is determined by the law of the state in which the court is located.' " *Mrs. U.S. Nat'l Pageant, Inc. v. Miss U.S. Org., LLC*, 875 F.Supp.2d 211, 219 (W.D.N.Y. 2012) (quoting *Spiegel v. Schulmann*, 604 F.3d 72, 76 (2d Cir. 2010)). "There are two ways that New York exercises personal jurisdiction over non-residents: general jurisdiction pursuant to N.Y. CPLR § 301 . . . or specific jurisdiction pursuant to N.Y. [CPLR] § 302." *Thackurdeen v. Duke Univ.*, 130 F.Supp.3d 792, 798 (S.D.N.Y. 2015) (quotations omitted), *aff'd*, 660 Fed.Appx. 43 (2d Cir. 2016). "Specific jurisdiction is available when the cause of action sued upon arises out of the defendant's activities in a state. General jurisdiction, in contrast, permits a court to adjudicate any cause of action against the corporate defendant, wherever arising, and whoever the plaintiff." *Brown v. Lockheed Martin Corp.*, 814 F.3d 619, 624 (2d Cir. 2016).[3] . . .

The Supreme Court has held that "[a] court may assert general jurisdiction over foreign (sister-state or foreign-country) corporations to hear any and all claims against them when their affiliations with the State are so 'continuous and systematic' as to render them essentially at home in the forum State." *Goodyear Dunlop Tires Operations, S.A. v. Brown*, 564 U.S. 915, 919 (2011) (citing *Int'l Shoe Co. v. State of Wash., Office of Unemployment Comp. & Placement*, 326 U.S. 310, 317 (1945)). "With respect to a corporation, the place of incorporation and principal place of business are paradig[m] . . . bases for general jurisdiction." *Daimler AG v. Bauman*, 571 U.S. 117, 137 (2014); *see Brown*, 814 F.3d at 627 ("*Daimler* established that, except in a truly 'exceptional' case, a corporate defendant may be treated as 'essentially at home' only where it is incorporated or maintains its principal place of business—the 'paradigm' cases."). . . .

Defendant argues that this Court cannot exercise general jurisdiction pursuant to *Daimler* and its progeny because it is not incorporated under the laws of New York State and it does not maintain its principal place of business in

3 It is clear that the Court does not have specific jurisdiction over Defendant. The complaint alleges that the asserted causes of action arise from conduct occurring in Georgia, not New York. Indeed, Plaintiff does not even respond to Defendant's argument that specific jurisdiction does not exist in this matter. As Plaintiff fails to allege that its causes of action arise out of any conduct by Defendant in New York State, the Court cannot exercise specific jurisdiction over Defendant pursuant to CPLR 302(a)(1).

this state. Defendant submitted an affidavit of William Hartman ("Hartman"), Defendant's Executive Vice President, who averred that Defendant is not incorporated in New York and does not maintain its principal place of business in this state, and further, that Defendant "has no agents or subsidiaries located in New York" or any other business office. Plaintiff does not controvert these assertions; rather, Plaintiff focuses solely upon an alternative consent-by-registration theory of personal jurisdiction. . . .

Plaintiff argues that because Defendant is a foreign corporation that is registered to do business in New York and has appointed the New York State Secretary of State as its agent for service of process, Defendant has consented to the exercise of general jurisdiction. It appears that every other federal district court in New York to squarely address whether a foreign corporation's registration with the secretary of state constitutes consent to general jurisdiction has held that this doctrine has been invalidated by the Supreme Court's decision in *Daimler. See, e.g., Famular v. Whirlpool Corp.*, No. 16 CV 944 (VB), 2017 WL 2470844, at *5 (S.D.N.Y. June 7, 2017); *Justiniano v. First Student Mgmt. LLC,* No. 16 CV 02729 (ADS) (AKT), 2017 WL 1592564, at *6 (E.D.N.Y. Apr. 26, 2017); *Minholz v. Lockheed Martin Corp.*, 227 F.Supp.3d 249, 264–65 (N.D.N.Y. 2016); *Bonkowski v. HP Hood LLC*, No. 15 CV 4956 (RRM) (PK), 2016 WL 4536868, at *3 (E.D.N.Y. Aug. 30, 2016); *Chatwal Hotels & Resorts LLC v. Dollywood Co.*, 90 F.Supp.3d 97, 105 (S.D.N.Y. 2015). Although Plaintiff has offered this Court with an appendix of cases that have confirmed New York's consent-by-registration doctrine of general jurisdiction, all of the cases were decided prior to *Daimler.*

In its opposition papers, Plaintiff points to several more recent state trial court opinions and a federal district court decision in support of its position. Specifically, Plaintiff relies upon *Beach v. Citigroup Alternative Invs. LLC,* No. 12 CIV. 7717 (PKC), 2014 WL 904650 (S.D.N.Y. Mar. 7, 2014), which appears to state that "[n]otwithstanding these limitations [in *Daimler*], a corporation may consent to jurisdiction in New York under CPLR § 301 by registering as a foreign corporation and designating a local agent." *Id.* at *6. This language has been criticized by a more recent decision out of the same district for relying upon outdated precedent. *Famular*, 2017 WL 2470844, at *5. The Court concurs with *Famular*'s assessment of *Beach*, and finds that *Beach*'s cursory one-sentence statement offered little-to-no insight into how *Daimler* has affected the viability of the cases cited therein. Moreover, this language appears as mere dicta in *Beach*, which ultimately held that the plaintiff failed to make a *prima facie* showing of personal jurisdiction under CPLR 301. *Beach*, 2014 WL 904650, at *7; *see Famular*, 2017 WL 2470844, at *5. Therefore, the Court does not find Plaintiff's reliance upon *Beach* to be persuasive.

Similarly, the Court does not find the state trial court opinions cited by Plaintiff to be persuasive given their brief and incomplete analytical treatment of this issue. [Citations]

Plaintiff also relies upon *Gucci Am., Inc. v. Weixing Li*, 768 F.3d 122 (2d Cir. 2014) and *Tiffany (NJ) LLC, Tiffany & Co. v. China Merchs. Bank*, 589 Fed. Appx. 550 (2d Cir. 2014), *as amended* (Sept. 23, 2014), to support its position. Again, the Court finds this reliance unpersuasive. Plaintiff notes that in both cases the Second Circuit instructed the district court that, upon remand, it "may also consider whether [the defendant] ha[d] consented to personal jurisdiction in New York by applying for authorization to conduct business in New York and designating the New York Secretary of State as its agent for service of process." *Gucci Am., Inc.* 768 F.3d at 137 n.15; *see Tiffany (NJ) LLC, Tiffany & Co.*, 589 Fed. Appx. at 553. However, if anything, the Second Circuit's directive indicates that the conflict between *Daimler* and the registration statute was not squarely before it in either case. *See Tiffany (NJ) LLC, Tiffany & Co.*, 589 Fed. Appx. at 553 ("[T]he district court *had no reason to consider, or to develop the record as to* . . . whether the [defendants] consented to jurisdiction by applying for authorization to conduct business in New York and designating the New York Secretary of State as their agent for service of process." (emphasis added)); *Gucci Am., Inc.*, 768 F.3d at 137 n.15 ("The district court *may also consider* whether BOC has consented to personal jurisdiction in New York by applying for authorization to conduct business in New York and designating the New York Secretary of State as its agent for service of process." (emphasis added)).

Had it been otherwise, the Second Circuit would have faced the legal issues that arose in *Brown* two years later, and then, even had it found that New York's registration statute could be interpreted to warrant the exercise of general jurisdiction post-*Daimler*, the Second Circuit would have had to square this construction with the strictures of constitutional due process. *See Brown*, 814 F.3d at 640 ("Were the Connecticut statute drafted such that it could be fairly construed as requiring foreign corporations to consent to general jurisdiction, we would be confronted with a more difficult constitutional question about the validity of such consent after *Daimler*.").

Observing no such factual development or legal analysis in *Gucci* or *Tiffany*, this Court declines to view the Second Circuit's suggestion upon remand in either case to be controlling on the instant issue, especially in light of the Second Circuit's own cautionary advisement against an "overly expansive view of general jurisdiction." *Gucci Am., Inc.*, 768 F.3d at 135.

Plaintiff further contends that *Brown* does not completely foreclose its argument, and in fact, actually bolsters its position. In *Brown*, the Second Circuit distinguished the Connecticut registration statute from Pennsylvania's registration statute. *See Brown*, 814 F.3d at 637, 640. In doing so, *Brown* indicated that Pennsylvania's registration statute "more plainly advise[d] the registrant that enrolling in the state as a foreign corporation and transacting business w[ould] vest the local courts with general jurisdiction over the corporation." *Id.* at 640. The court then stated that "[t]he registration statute in the state of New York has been definitively construed to accomplish that end. . . ." *Id.* After citing to two decisions from other circuits that have upheld the exercise of general jurisdiction arising from a foreign corporation's compliance with state registration statutes,[5] the Second Circuit suggested, in dicta, "that a carefully drawn state statute that expressly required consent to general jurisdiction as a condition on a foreign corporation's doing business in the state, at least in cases brought by state residents, might well be constitutional." *Id.* at 641.

Here, it is clear that New York's registration statute does not provide an express requirement of consent to general jurisdiction as a condition for a foreign corporation to become authorized to transact business within the state. *See* N.Y. Bus. Corp. Law §§ 1301, 1304. Plaintiff argues that because the New York courts have interpreted the registration statute to achieve this end since the early twentieth century, the reasoning in *Brown* is not applicable since the Second Circuit was absent "a clear legislative statement and a definitive interpretation by the Connecticut Supreme Court" on this issue. *Id.* at 641.

Plaintiff cites to no case decided by the New York Court of Appeals in recent years that squarely addresses this issue, let alone a decision post-dating *Daimler*. Moreover, the two New York Court of Appeals cases Plaintiffs relies upon predate *International Shoe* and its progeny, and interpret an earlier version of New York's business registration statute. *See Pohlers*, 293 N.Y. at

---

5   Notably, both cases predate *Daimler*. *See Bane v. Netlink, Inc.*, 925 F.2d 637, 640 (3d Cir. 1991); *Knowlton v. Allied Van Lines, Inc.*, 900 F.2d 1196, 1199–1200 (8th Cir. 1990).

280; *Bagdon*, 217 N.Y. at 437. . . . Indeed, Plaintiff points to no cases decided even by New York's intermediate appellate courts that have addressed the viability of the consent-by-registration theory of general jurisdiction in the wake of *Daimler*, and this Court has found none. . . .

"*Daimler* suggests that federal due process rights likely constrain an interpretation that transforms a run-of-the-mill registration and appointment statute into a corporate 'consent'—perhaps unwitting—to the exercise of general jurisdiction by state courts. . . ." *Brown,* 814 F.3d at 637. "After *Daimler,* with the Second Circuit cautioning against adopting 'an overly expansive view of general jurisdiction,' the mere fact [that a defendant is] registered to do business is insufficient to confer general jurisdiction in a state that is neither its state of incorporation [n]or its principal place of business." *Chatwal Hotels & Resorts LLC*, 90 F.Supp.3d at 105 (quoting *Gucci Am., Inc.*, 768 F.3d at 135). "Because New York Business Corporations Law § 1301 is absent an explicit indication that registration subjects a registrant to general jurisdiction in New York, an exercise of general personal jurisdiction based on registration alone would be counter to the principles of due process articulated in *Daimler.*" *Minholz*, 227 F.Supp.3d at 264.

The Court acknowledges that Plaintiff's argument is not without some support. Preceding *Daimler,* the decisions issued by the courts of New York and this Circuit indicated that consent-by-registration was a viable theory upon which to assert general jurisdiction. *See STX Panocean (UK) Co. Ltd. v. Glory Wealth Shipping Pte Ltd.*, 560 F.3d 127, 131 (2d Cir. 2009). . . . As Plaintiff has correctly articulated, Judge Cardozo's declarations in *Bagdon* as well as the Supreme Court's decisions in *Pennsylvania Fire* and *Neirbo* have not been explicitly overruled. However, this Court concurs with its sister courts in this Circuit that to blindly follow these pre-*International Shoe* and pre-*Daimler* decisions from the first half of the 20th century would be to ignore the monumental changes to the legal principles of general jurisdiction that have since taken place. As such, it may be time for New York's highest court to revisit its holding in *Bagdon* in light of *Daimler.*[7] Until a clearer expression of the post-*Daimler* viability of New York's consent-by-registration doctrine is settled by the New York State legislature or the New York Court of Appeals, this Court agrees with and, indeed, is bound by

---

[7]   The Court notes that the Supreme Court of Delaware, in light of *Daimler* and *Goodyear*, has recently overruled its longstanding precedent that held foreign corporations to have implicitly consented to the exercise of general jurisdiction thorough its business registration statute. *See Genuine Parts Co. v. Cepec*, 137 A.3d 123, 148 (Del. 2016).

Brown's prudence and declines to interpret New York's business registration statute as providing consent-by-registration jurisdiction "in the absence of a clear legislative statement and a definitive interpretation by the [New York Court of Appeals]." *Brown*, 814 F.3d at 640.

Lastly, at oral argument counsel for Plaintiff produced two additional post-*Daimler* federal district court cases in support of Plaintiff's position. However, *Plumbers' Local Union No. 690 Health Plan v. Apotex Corp.*, No. 16–665, 2017 WL 3129147 (E.D. Pa. July 24, 2017) applied the Third Circuit's pre-*Daimler* decision in *Bane v. Netlink, Inc.*, 925 F.2d 637 (3d Cir. 1991), which interpreted the Pennsylvania business registration statute. *Apotex Corp.*, 2017 WL 3129147, at *10–11. As already noted, Pennsylvania enacted a business registration statute that expressly notifies foreign corporations that the designation of Pennsylvania's secretary of state as agent for service of process constitutes consent to general jurisdiction. *See* 42 Pa. Cns. Stat. § 5301(a)(2) (i)-(ii); *see also Brown*, 814 F.3d at 627. The District of New Jersey also held in favor of exercising consent-by-registration jurisdiction in *Senju Pharm. Co., Ltd. v. Metrics*, 96 F.Supp.3d 428 (D.N.J. 2015). Nonetheless, unlike the federal district courts in New York, which have unanimously concluded that *Daimler* and *Brown* have compromised the validity of consent-by-registration in New York, the District of New Jersey has issued diverging opinions on this point. *See Display Works, LLC*, 182 F.Supp.3d at 175. Notably, a very recent decision from an intermediary appellate court of the State of New Jersey has rejected *Senju*'s analysis. *Dutch Run-Mays Draft, LLC v. Wolf Block, LLP*, 450 N.J. Super. 590 (Ct. App. 2017) (rejecting the application of prior precedent that permitted the exercise of general jurisdiction "solely based on the fiction of implied consent by a foreign corporation's compliance with New Jersey's business registration statute"). These two out-of-circuit district cases do not warrant a different result.

Therefore, because Defendant does not maintain its principal place of business in New York and is not incorporated under the laws of New York, the Court concludes that the exercise of general jurisdiction would be inappropriate as Defendant cannot be considered "essentially at home" in New York. *See Daimler*, 134 S. Ct. at 760. . . . In other words, the Court is absent authority to exercise general jurisdiction over Defendant and, as such, Defendant's motion to dismiss for lack of personal jurisdiction is granted, and Plaintiff's complaint is dismissed without prejudice. . . .

COMMENTS AND QUESTIONS

1. Compare/contrast the nature of the consent that is established pursuant to a registration statute with consent that is established by accepting the terms of service of an application or website. Which of these two species of consent is more knowing, willful, and meaningful? What do we mean when we say that a court may exercise personal jurisdiction over a defendant who "consents"?

2. Courts are somewhat less inclined to enforce forum selection clauses that are contained in "browsewrap agreements." Browsewrap agreements describe circumstances where the webpage or application provides a hyperlink to the terms of service. "Clickwrap agreements," by contrast, put the terms in front of the user and require her to affirmatively click a box acknowledging acceptance. Is that a meaningful distinction?

Status

A court may have personal jurisdiction over a case that involves only a determination of the plaintiff's *status*. This basis is usually referred to as the status *exception*—because it constitutes an exception to the typical requirements for establishing personal jurisdiction. The status exception allows a court to determine the legal status of a person properly before the court, even if that status impacts another person over whom the court does not (otherwise) have personal jurisdiction. As a practical matter, it applies only in the context of family law. But even in that realm, the status exception has limited applicability. It applies in divorce, adoption, child custody, and parental termination cases,[15] but only to the extent that the court is making a status determination.

Status was a part of personal jurisdiction doctrine even before the Supreme Court decided *Pennoyer v. Neff*,[16] the materfamilias of personal jurisdiction jurisprudence. The Court held that exercises of personal jurisdiction by state courts were subject to the limitations of the Due Process Clause. But it added:

> To prevent any misapplication of the views expressed in this opinion, it is proper to observe that we do not mean to assert, by any thing we have said, that a State may not authorize proceedings to deter-

---

15   Some courts have also used the status exception to issue a domestic violence restraining order against an out-of-state defendant.

16   95 U.S. 714 (1877).

mine the *status* of one of its citizens towards a non-resident. . . . The jurisdiction which ever State possesses to determine the civil *status* and capacities of all its inhabitants involves authority to prescribe the conditions on which proceedings affecting them may be commenced and carried on within its territory.[17]

The status exception has been used to justify the adjudication of divorce actions and child custody actions over out-of-state defendants who have an immediate interest in the status determination. The typical justification is that a sovereign state requires the authority to determine the status of its citizens in relation to something so essential as marriage and child custody. Thus, even in divorce cases, jurisdiction is exercised even if the defendant-spouse has no contacts with the forum state. The court will often review the fairness factors to ensure that the exercise of jurisdiction does not offend traditional notions of fair play and substantial justice, but this is usually more of a genuflection as opposed to a rigorous inquiry.

Jurisdiction over these actions is limited, however, to the status determination. Accordingly, for ancillary matters such as alimony or support orders, some *other* basis for personal jurisdiction over the foreign defendant is necessary.

Hypothetical 20-7

In an Ohio domestic relations court, Medina Wicklow filed a complaint for divorce, child custody, and support against her husband Aidan Matthews. Matthews has moved to dismiss, claiming that the court lacks personal jurisdiction.

The parties were married in Dayton, Ohio, on August 22, 1994. Both were born and raised in Ohio. The couple resided in Ohio from August 22, 1994 until September 11, 1994, living in an in-law apartment in the home of Wicklow's parents. In September 1994, the couple moved to Rome, Italy, where Wicklow attended graduate school. The parties were in Italy for three years. While in Italy, the parties listed Ohio as their state of residence on their federal income tax forms, maintained Ohio driver's licenses, and kept Ohio bank accounts open. In 1997, the couple moved to South Bend, Indiana. In 1999, the couple moved to Lincoln, Nebraska. And in 2004, the couple moved to Norman, Oklahoma. During the marriage, the couple had two children, one of whom is now emancipated.

Last year, Wicklow moved to Columbus, Ohio, with the couple's minor child. Matthews stayed in Oklahoma, where he has lived since 2004.

---

17   95 U.S. at 734.

Ohio's long-arm statute authorizes the exercise of personal jurisdiction over nonresident defendants in domestic relations matters that

> arise out of a marital relationship within this state notwithstanding subsequent departure from this state, as to all obligations arising for spousal support, custody, child support, or property settlement, if the other party to the marital relationship resides in this state.

Will the courts of Ohio have personal jurisdiction over Matthews? If yes, will it include jurisdiction to enter a divorce decree, a child custody order, alimony, and child support?

FROM THE COURTS

IN RE TERMINATION OF PARENTAL RIGHTS TO THOMAS J.R.

Supreme Court of Wisconsin
262 Wis.2d 217 (2003)

ANN WALSH BRADLEY, JUSTICE.

The petitioner, Tammie J.C., seeks review of an unpublished decision of the court of appeals reversing an order that terminated the parental rights of the respondent, Robert T.R. The court of appeals determined that a court could terminate a person's parental rights only if it had personal jurisdiction over the person, and that the court's exercise of jurisdiction over Robert in this case had no basis because Robert, a resident of Arizona, lacked minimum contacts with Wisconsin.

We recognize that personal jurisdiction through minimum contacts is generally necessary for a judgment to bind any out-of-state person. We conclude, however, that the status exception to the general personal jurisdiction requirements, as employed in the Uniform Child Custody Jurisdiction Act (UCCJA), provides a basis for the exercise of jurisdiction in a child custody case. Such an exercise of jurisdiction is consistent with notions of fair play and substantial justice. We also conclude that Wis. Stat. § 801.05(11), which references the UCCJA, provides sufficient due process protection to out-of-state parents based on notice and an opportunity to be heard. Accordingly, we reverse the court of appeals and remand the case for a determination on the remaining issues previously raised in that court, but not briefed or argued here.

I

Tammie and Robert were married in Wyoming in 1987. Thomas J.R. was born in Wyoming in 1988, during the marriage. Tammie's daughter from a previous marriage (Robert's step-daughter) lived with the family throughout their marriage. The family moved to Arizona in 1991. In 1992, after Robert was accused of sexually assaulting Tammie's daughter, Tammie moved back to Wyoming with her daughter and Thomas, leaving Robert in Arizona. Robert accepted a plea bargain related to the sexual assault charge, and he was sentenced to a ten-year prison term in Arizona.

Subsequently, Robert filed for divorce. The Arizona court awarded sole custody of Thomas J.R. to Tammie and denied Robert all visitation rights. It found such visitation would seriously endanger Thomas' physical, mental, and emotional health.

Tammie moved to Nebraska with Thomas and her daughter in 1993, and then in 1996, they moved to Wisconsin. Tammie did not disclose either move to Robert, but he was aware of Tammie's general location while she was living in Nebraska.

Robert did not contact Thomas during his time in prison because Thomas lived with Robert's step-daughter, the victim of the sexual assault. Arizona law prohibited anyone convicted of sexual assault from contacting any person at the address belonging to the sexual assault victim. Robert began to send mail to Thomas after this rule was changed in 1998, but the Arizona Department of Corrections curtailed his mailings after Tammie complained about the correspondence.

Tammie remarried her daughter's biological father in Wisconsin, and on January 13, 2000, she filed a petition in Lafayette County Circuit Court to terminate Robert's parental rights. At the same time, Tammie's husband petitioned the court to adopt Thomas following termination of Robert's parental rights.

The circuit court issued a summons notifying Robert of the pending termination action and ordering him to appear on February 2, 2000. The court continued the matter to February 28, because of difficulties serving Robert, who was in prison in Arizona. Robert was served on February 14,

2000. On March 8, Robert moved, through his Wisconsin counsel, for an order requiring Tammie to pay his expenses in appearing personally at the termination trial, or alternatively, for a delay in the proceedings until he was released from prison. The court found good cause to delay the trial, and noting that Robert was to be released from prison on August 28, 2000, it set the matter for a jury trial on September 19, 20, and 21, 2000.

Robert moved to dismiss, asserting that Wisconsin lacked personal jurisdiction over him, and that he had not received required statutory notice that the child custody decree in Arizona could lead to termination of parental rights in Wisconsin. Robert claimed that the petition for termination did not afford him due process. The circuit court denied the motion. Robert moved for reconsideration after the case was transferred to a different judge, but the successor judge denied the motion.

Before issuing a final ruling in the termination of parental rights proceeding, the circuit court afforded the parties an opportunity to seek resolution of the jurisdictional question in the Arizona courts. Tammie filed a motion requesting that the Arizona court decline jurisdiction. Robert filed a separate motion to modify visitation, asking the Arizona court to grant him "reasonable periods of visitation with his son." Pointing to A.R.S. § 8–532, an Arizona statute requiring that a child at issue in a termination proceeding be present in the state, the Pima County Juvenile Court granted Tammie's motion, declining to exercise jurisdiction over an action to terminate Robert's parental rights.

The circuit court in Wisconsin then determined that termination would be in the best interest of the child in this case and terminated Robert's parental rights on the ground of "continuing denial of periods of physical placement and visitation," under Wis. Stat. § 48.415(4) (1999–2000).

Robert appealed the order, again asserting that the circuit court lacked personal jurisdiction over him to terminate his parental rights and that he had not received the proper notice that the Arizona child custody decree could lead to termination in Wisconsin. The court of appeals determined that a parent must be provided with fundamentally fair procedures, including an adequate basis for exercising personal jurisdiction, in any action to terminate parental rights. Because it concluded that Wisconsin did not have personal jurisdiction over Robert, the court reversed the termination order.

II

This case presents us with an issue involving the interpretation and application of the jurisdictional provisions of the UCCJA and Wisconsin's jurisdiction statutes, in the context of an action to terminate the parental rights of a person who is not a Wisconsin resident and does not have minimum contacts with the state. A circuit court's determinations of whether statutory and constitutional bases exist for jurisdiction over a non-resident in a termination of parental rights proceeding present questions of law, subject to independent appellate review.

In addressing whether the court in this case had jurisdiction to terminate Robert's parental rights, we first discuss the general requirement of minimum contacts to establish personal jurisdiction, and the exception to the requirement for cases involving determinations of status under the UCCJA. We then consider Wis. Stat. § 801.05(11) which provides that child custody determinations are binding on persons who receive notice under § 822.05 and are afforded an opportunity to be heard. Finally, we address the requirement that an exercise of jurisdiction satisfies the due process standard of fair play and substantial justice, and assess the exercise of jurisdiction.

III

A

The court of appeals in this case determined that the termination of parental rights order issued by the circuit court was not binding on Robert because the circuit court lacked personal jurisdiction over him. . . .

Wisconsin has codified the "minimum contacts" doctrine in its statute governing personal jurisdiction, . . .

There is no dispute that in this case, Robert was not served while in Wisconsin, does not live in Wisconsin, and is not engaged in substantial activities in Wisconsin. In fact, he has never been to Wisconsin. The only tie Robert has to Wisconsin is that his son and ex-wife live here. Robert does not have minimum contacts with Wisconsin, and Wisconsin did not have personal jurisdiction over him under Wis. Stat. § 801.05(1).

B

While we have determined that Wisconsin does not have personal jurisdiction over Robert by virtue of minimum contacts, our determination does not necessarily mean that Wisconsin does not have jurisdiction to enter an order terminating Robert's parental rights. The answer lies in an exception to the requirement of minimum contacts for personal jurisdiction, applicable to determinations of status.

A "status" exception to the general requirement of minimum contacts for personal jurisdiction has long been recognized by the Supreme Court:

> To prevent any misapplication of the views expressed in this opinion, it is proper to observe that we do not mean to assert, by anything we have said, that a State may not authorize proceedings to determine the *status* of one of its citizens towards a non-resident, which would be binding within the State. . . .

Pennoyer, 95 U.S. at 734 (emphasis in original). The *Pennoyer* Court excluded certain types of actions, such as marriages and divorces, from the minimum contacts requirement, explaining that each state has jurisdiction to "determine the civil *status* and capacities of all its inhabitants," even if an involved non-resident cannot be served within the state. *Id.* at 734–35.

In 1977, the Supreme Court reasserted the validity of the status exception it had recognized in *Pennoyer*. The Court stated that a minimum contacts analysis under *International Shoe* is generally required when determining personal jurisdiction. *Shaffer*, 433 U.S. at 208. In a footnote, however, the *Shaffer* court emphasized that an exception exists for "particularized jurisdiction rules governing adjudications of status": "We do not suggest that jurisdictional doctrines other than those discussed in the text, such as the particularized jurisdictional rules governing adjudications of status, are inconsistent with the standard of fairness." *Id.* at 208 n.30.

The Supreme Court has long required that for an exercise of personal jurisdiction not to offend the Due Process Clause of the Fourteenth Amendment, it must comply with "traditional notions of fair play and substantial justice." *International Shoe*, 326 U.S. at 316. In *Burnham v. Superior Court*, 495 U.S. 604 (1990), the Court stated that any method of assuming jurisdiction over a person must satisfy the same due process standard required for personal jurisdiction based on minimum contacts: "For new procedures, hitherto unknown, the Due Process Clause requires analysis to determine whether

'traditional notions of fair play and substantial justice' have been offended."
Burnham, 495 U.S. at 622.

The status exception to the minimum contacts requirement has commonly been applied in the context of divorce actions. For instance, the Supreme Court has held that states can enter divorce decrees binding on a non-resident spouse so long as the other spouse lives in the state. *See, e.g., Estin v. Estin*, 334 U.S. 541, 544 (1948); *Williams v. North Carolina*, 317 U.S. 287, 298–99 (1942). The Court reasoned in *Williams* that divorce decrees

> are more than in personam judgments. They involve the marital status of the parties. Domicile creates a relationship to the state which is adequate for numerous exercises of state power. . . . The marriage relation creates problems of large social importance. Protection of offspring, property interests, and the enforcement of marital responsibilities are but a few of commanding problems in the field of domestic relations with which the state must deal.

Williams, 317 U.S. at 298. The Court concluded that "each state by virtue of its command over its domiciliaries and its large interest in the institution of marriage can alter within its own borders the marriage status of the spouse domiciled there, even though the other spouse is absent." *Id.* at 298–99.[5]

Jurisdiction for the termination of parental rights actions in this case was determined under the UCCJA.[6] It governs child custody proceedings that determine the status of children, and bases the exercise of jurisdiction on the status exception to personal jurisdiction. "Termination of parental rights" actions are not specifically included in the UCCJA's definition of "child custody proceedings," which are "proceedings in which a custody determination is one of several issues, such as an action for divorce or separation, and includes child neglect and dependency proceedings." Wis. Stat. § 822.02(3). This court has explicitly concluded, however, that termination of parental rights actions are child custody proceedings under the UCCJA. *A.E.H.*, 161 Wis.2d at 298–99.

---

5   The Supreme Court has made clear, however, that subjects such as alimony and child support are not covered by the status exception, and awards or changes in awards made in divorce decrees re not binding on a non-resident spouse. *Kulko v. Superior Court*, 436 U.S. 84, 91–92 (1978).

6   The UCCJA, or the closely-related Uniform Child Custody Jurisdiction Enforcement Act (UCJEA), has been adopted in each of the 50 states. *David S. v. Laura S.*, 179 Wis.2d 114, 138 (1993). Wisconsin adopted the UCCJA in 1975, effective May 28, 1976, as chapter 822 of the statutes. *See* ch. 283, Laws of 1975.

A comment to section 12 of the UCCJA, Binding Force and Res Judicata Effect of Custody Decree, adopted in Wisconsin as Wis. Stat. § 822.12 explains that the drafters of the UCCJA intended that jurisdiction under the UCCJA need not be based on technical personal jurisdiction, but rather on the theory that child custody proceedings are "proceedings in rem or proceedings affecting status." The drafters noted that there must be strict compliance with the due process mandates of notice and the opportunity to be heard:

> This section deals with the intra-state validity of custody decrees which provides the basis for their interstate recognition and enforcement. The two prerequisites are (1) jurisdiction under section 3 of this Act and (2) strict compliance with due process mandates of notice and opportunity to be heard. There is no requirement for technical personal jurisdiction, on the traditional theory that custody determinations, as distinguished from support actions . . . are proceedings in rem or proceedings affecting status.

See Commissioners' comment on § 12 of the UCCJA, 9 U.L.A. 557.

The purpose behind the UCCJA is explained in a prefatory note to the UCCJA stating why a uniform law regulating child custody jurisdiction was necessary when the UCCJA was drafted in 1968:

> There is growing public concern over the fact that thousands of children are shifted from state to state and from one family to another every year while their parents or other persons battle over their custody in the courts of several states. . . .

> There is no certainty as to which state has jurisdiction when persons seeking custody of a child approach the courts of several states simultaneously or successively. . . .

UCCJA Prefatory Note, 9 U.L.A. 262–63 (1999).

The UCCJA was enacted to address these concerns. Among the objectives of the UCCJA is to: "avoid jurisdictional competition and conflict with courts of other states in matters of child custody," and to "assure that litigation concerning the custody of a child takes place ordinarily in the state with which the child and family have the closest connection." Wis. Stat. § 822.01(1)(a) and (c).[8] Moreover, "jurisdiction exists only if it is in the *child*'s interest,

---

8 Wisconsin Stat. § 822.01(1) provides that:

not merely the interest or convenience of the feuding parties, to determine custody in a particular state." *See* Commissioners' comment on § 3 of the UCCJA, 9 U.L.A. 309 (emphasis in original).

The UCCJA has been the subject of numerous constitutional challenges, on the grounds that it does not require minimum contacts. Most courts that have considered the validity of jurisdiction under the UCCJA have determined that the status exception applies to child custody cases under the UCCJA, and that personal jurisdiction based on minimum contacts is not required. *See, e.g., In re Marriage of Leonard*, 122 Cal.App.3d 443, 450–60 (Cal. App. 1981); *People ex rel. State of Wyoming ex rel. Watson v. Stout*, 969 P.2d 819, 821 (Colo.App. 1998); *Balestrieri v. Maliska*, 622 So.2d 561, 563 & n.1 (Fla.App. 1993) (listing states which had made such determinations); *Thompson v. Thompson*, 241 Ga.App. 616 (1999); *Bartsch v. Bartsch*, 636 N.W.2d 3 (Iowa 2001). . . .

A review of commentary regarding the constitutionality of relying on the status exception for jurisdiction under the UCCJA reaches varying conclusions. *See* Rhonda Wasserman, *Parents, Partners, and Personal Jurisdiction*, 1995 U. Ill. L. Rev. 813, 816 n.15 (listing commentary on each side of the issue). Some commentators have determined that the UCCJA's reliance on the status exception passes constitutional muster. *See, e.g.,* Anthony Dorland, *Civil Procedure—Orders for Child Protection and Nonresident Defendants: The UCCJA Applies and Minimum Contacts are Unnecessary*, 25 Wm. Mitchell

---

(1) The general purposes of this chapter are to:
  (a) Avoid jurisdictional competition and conflict with courts of other states in matters of child custody which have in the past resulted in the shifting of children from state to state with harmful effects on their well-being;
  (b) Promote cooperation with the courts of other states to the end that a custody decree is rendered in that state which can best decide the case in the interest of the child;
  (c) Assure that litigation concerning the custody of a child takes place ordinarily in the state with which the child and family have the closest connection and where significant evidence concerning the child's care, protection, training, and personal relationships is most readily available, and that courts of this state decline the exercise of jurisdiction when the child and family have a closer connection with another state;
  (d) Discourage continuing controversies over child custody in the interest of greater stability of home environment and of secure family relationships for the child;
  (e) Deter abductions and other unilateral removals of children undertaken to obtain custody awards;
  (f) Avoid relitigation of custody decisions of other states in this state insofar as feasible;
  (g) Facilitate the enforcement of custody decrees of other states;
  (h) Promote and expand the exchange of information and other forms of mutual assistance between the courts of this state and those of other states concerned with the same child; and
  (i) Make uniform the law of those states which enact it.

690 • Learning Conflict of Laws •

L. Rev. 965 (1999); Brigitte M. Bedenheimer & Janey Neeley-Kvarme, *Jurisdiction over Child Custody and Adoption After* Shaffer *and* Kulko, 12 U.C. Davis L. Rev. 229, 240–41 (1979). Others have concluded that minimum contacts-based personal jurisdiction is necessary notwithstanding the UCCJA. *See, e.g.,* Wasserman, *supra*, at 818 (concluding that "the status exception should not be used to sanction divorce or child custody proceedings in states that lack in personam jurisdiction over all interested parties").

We agree with the majority of the courts and many of the commentators that have considered the validity of jurisdiction under the UCCJA, that traditional personal jurisdiction is not required in child custody proceedings. We find persuasive the cases and commentary concluding that child custody proceedings under the UCCJA are valid even in the absence of minimum contacts over an out-of-state parent. A contrary determination fails to acknowledge the interests and rights of the child. We also note that while child custody proceedings determine the "status" of children, they also implicate "the rights and obligations of the state in its parens patriae role to consider the welfare of the child subject to its jurisdiction and to make a determination that is in the best interests of the child." *Leonard,* 122 Cal.App.3d at 454.

A conclusion that minimum contacts are necessary for child custody determinations ignores the realities of child custody proceedings and leaves children in the position of Thomas J.R. with no practical forum to have their status adjudicated. A requirement of minimum contacts would necessitate that a child travel to the state in which his or her parent resides. Under the UCCJA, the child would have to reside in the parent's state for six months for that state to have jurisdiction. *See* Wis. Stat. §§ 822.02(5), 822.03(1)(a). In the case of an abandoned child whose parents live in different states, the child might be required to travel to both states to have his or her rights determined. Custody determinations involving parents living in foreign nations would pose further complications.

Children in the position of Thomas J.R. need a forum in which their status can be determined. Requiring minimum contacts would often make termination of parental rights and the subsequent adoption proceedings impractical or impossible. Such a child would essentially be left in "limbo," unable to have a court adjudicate his or her status.

For these reasons we join the many states that have concluded that the status exception to the general personal jurisdiction requirements, as employed in the UCCJA, provides a basis for the exercise of jurisdiction in a child custody case. Such an exercise of jurisdiction, for reasons more fully set forth below, is consistent with notions of fair play and substantial justice.

C

Subsection (11) of Wis. Stat. § 801.05 relies on the status exception to provide a basis for jurisdiction in the context of child custody proceedings under the UCCJA, by conditioning jurisdiction not on minimum contacts over the out-of-state parent, but on the parent receiving notice and an opportunity to be heard. . . .

The text of Wis. Stat. § 822.12 specifically provides that a child custody decree is binding on out-of-state persons who received sufficient notice of the child custody action and who were afforded the opportunity to be heard. . . .

D

Having determined that the status exception and Wis. Stat. § 801.05(11) provides a basis for jurisdiction over a person absent minimum contacts, we must examine the statute's requirement of notice of the exercise of jurisdiction, and an opportunity to be heard, and assess them in the context of this case.

Wisconsin Stat. § 822.12 requires that notice of an exercise of jurisdiction be given to out-of-state parties pursuant to § 822.05, which governs the mechanics of giving of notice. Section 822.05 is entitled "Notice to persons outside this state; submission to jurisdiction," and lists the different methods for serving notice of a child custody action on an out-of-state person.[12]

In this case, there is no dispute regarding compliance with the notice requirements of § 822.05. In fact, Robert received actual notice of the proceedings,

---

12 Wisconsin Stat. § 822.05(1) provides:

    (1) Notice required for the exercise of jurisdiction over a person outside this state shall be given in a manner reasonably calculated to give actual notice, and may be:

        (a) By personal delivery outside this state in the manner prescribed for service of process within this state;

        (b) In the manner prescribed by the law of the place in which the service is made for service of process in that place in an action in any of its courts of general jurisdiction;

        (c) By any form of mail addressed to the person to be served and requesting a receipt; or

        (d) As directed by the court, including publication, if other means of notification are ineffective.

and successfully requested that the court delay action on the petition to terminate until he was released from prison.

There also is no dispute that Robert was given an opportunity to be heard, as required by § 822.12. Section 822.12 explains that if in addition to notice under § 822.05, a party is afforded an opportunity to be heard, "a custody decree rendered by a court of this state which had jurisdiction under § 822.03" is binding on the party. Robert was afforded an opportunity to be heard under § 822.05, and participated by telephone in the trial and another hearing.

We conclude that in this case Robert received notice and an opportunity to be heard as required by Wis. Stat. § 822.12. Statutory compliance alone, however, does not render an exercise of jurisdiction constitutional. By requiring an opportunity to be heard, in addition to the notice requirement under § 822.05, section 822.12 codifies a recognition that child custody determinations, especially those involving parents or guardians in different states, involve important rights and require additional procedural protections. Safeguards must be in place to protect against potential abuses.

As noted above, the Due Process Clause requires that any exercise of jurisdiction comport with "traditional notions of fair play and substantial justice." *Burnham*, 495 U.S. at 622 (quoting *International Shoe*, 326 U.S. at 316). A determination of the validity of an exercise of jurisdiction based on minimum contacts or some other jurisdictional rule requires an evaluation of the reasonableness of the exercise of jurisdiction. *Asahi Metal Indus. Co. v. Superior Court*, 480 U.S. 102, 113 (1987); *World-Wide Volkswagen Corp. v Woodson*, 444 U.S. 286, 292 (1980). Reasonableness depends on several factors, including (1) the burden on the defendant; (2) the interests of the forum state; (3) the plaintiff's interest in obtaining relief; (4) the interest of the interstate judicial system in obtaining the most efficient resolution of controversies; and (5) the shared interest of the several states in furthering fundamental social policies. *Id.* [After evaluating each factor the court concluded that the] exercise of that jurisdiction was not unreasonable. . . .

The decision of the court of appeals is reversed and the cause remanded to the court of appeals.

[The concurring opinion of JUSTICE WILCOX and the dissenting opinion of JUSTICE SYKES are omitted.]

COMMENTS AND QUESTIONS

1. Is the broad adoption by states of the UCCJA relevant to the due process question (i.e., whether status is constitutionally sufficient basis to exercise jurisdiction)?

2. The court defends its judgment by observing that a "minimum contacts" requirement for child custody determinations would "ignore[ ] the realities of child custody proceedings. . . ." We have not seen the "realities" of litigation as a relevant criterion in our study of other bases of personal jurisdiction. In *Nicastro*, *supra*, for example, the reality was that the New Jersey plaintiff injured by the metal shearing machine who was denied a forum in New Jersey could sue the manufacturer only in England. Are some plaintiffs more deserving of an accommodation for the practical realities of their situations?

3. Courts can use the status exception to establish personal jurisdiction over someone who has no contacts with the forum state, but the exercise of jurisdiction on that basis extends only to the determination of status. So, for example, the court can terminate a parent's rights, but it cannot order the payment of alimony (when jurisdiction is based solely on status). Is this distinction justified because the payment of alimony is a more substantial deprivation of the foreigner's rights?

100-Mile Bulge

Federal Rule of Civil Procedure 4(k)(1)(B) allows a federal court to exercise personal jurisdiction over a Rule 14[18] or Rule 19[19] party who is served in the United States within 100 miles of the court. Very rarely would a defendant be subject to personal jurisdiction under this 100-mile bulge rule and not *also* subject to personal jurisdiction under some other basis (*e.g.,* specific jurisdiction, consent, etc.). But good litigators will be aware of this basis—and will remember also that it can be utilized *only* when the case is pending in *federal* court.

---

18 Fed. R. Civ. P. 14.

19 Fed. R. Civ. P. 19.

The 100-mile bulge rule is applicable only to Rule 14 and Rule 19 parties. You will recall from your Civil Procedure course that a Rule 14 defendant is a third-party defendant: if A sues B, and B, in turn, brings a claim against C, then C is a third-party defendant. In the typical situation, the claim by B against C might be a claim for contribution by one tortfeasor against a joint tortfeasor, or a claim by an insured against their insurer. The 100-mile bulge rule allows a federal court to exercise personal jurisdiction over that third-party defendant, provided the defendant is served within 100 miles of the courthouse. Accordingly, a case pending in the U.S. District Court for the Northern District of Illinois (Chicago, Illinois) would have personal jurisdiction over a third-party defendant who lives in Milwaukee, Wisconsin (approximately 90 miles away). This would be true even if the Wisconsin defendant had never been to Illinois and had no contacts in Illinois.

The 100-mile bulge rule also applies to Rule 19 parties. Rule 19 very narrowly defines three categories of persons who are necessary to the litigation.[20] The Rule protects unjoined but interested parties by assuring that their interests will not be prejudiced without their participation, and it protects active parties by assuring that issues will not have to be relitigated. Typically, defendants invoke Rule 19 to urge dismissal of the plaintiff's case; they argue that the plaintiff has failed to join a necessary party. If the absentee is a necessary party, Rule 19 requires that that party be joined when joinder is feasible. When joinder is not feasible, the judge must choose between two ugly options: proceed without the necessary party or dismiss the case for failure to join someone that plaintiff could not feasibly join. One reason that it may not be feasible to join someone is that that person is not subject to personal jurisdiction; the 100-mile bulge rule puts Rule 19 parties within the scope of the court's personal jurisdiction, provided that person is served within 100 miles of the courthouse. Accordingly, the U.S. District Court for the Southern District of New York (in New York City) would have personal jurisdiction over a Rule 19 defendant who lives in Philadelphia, Pennsylvania (approximately 90 miles away). This would be true even if the Pennsylvania defendant had never been to New York and had no contacts in New York.

The justification for the 100-mile bulge rule is the efficiency gained when related disputes are resolved in one litigation package. In the above scenario(s), allowing the court to exercise personal jurisdiction over the Wisconsin (or Pennsylvania) defendant prevents multiple litigation. By limiting the bulge to 100 miles, the federal court also limits the extent to which it can accommodate an efficient litigation package. Query whether it would satisfy the Due Process Clause (of the *Fifth*

---

20 The three categories are (1) persons needed to accord complete relief to the existing parties; (2) persons whose interests will be practically impaired or impeded if not joined; and (3) persons who are needed to make sure that the existing parties are not exposed to multiple or inconsistent obligations. *See* Fed. R. Civ. P. 19(a).

Amendment, not the Fourteenth Amendment) if the Rule authorized a reach of 200 miles, 500 miles, or a reach that was nationwide.

Hypothetical 20-8

Spuckies, Inc. (Spuckies), is a franchisor of sandwich shops along the Eastern Seaboard of the United States. Spuckies is a Delaware corporation that has its principal place of business in Quincy, Massachusetts.

Two years ago, Spuckies entered into a franchise agreement with Jaclyn Piechocki to open a Spuckies store at a truck stop outside of Manchester, New Hampshire. A clause in the franchise agreement promises Piechocki that, for a period of three years, her Spuckies would be the "exclusive" Spuckies franchise "for a 43-mile stretch along Interstate 93 from a southern point at Exit 37 in Massachusetts to a northern point at Exit 15 in New Hampshire, hereinafter 'the exclusive I-93 territory.' "

Piechocki recently learned that Spuckies entered into a franchise agreement with Roy Adams to open a Spuckies restaurant outside of Lawrence, Massachusetts, in a shopping mall about two miles east of Interstate 93. In response to a letter from Piechocki's lawyer, Spuckies admitted that the new franchise is "near" the exclusive I-93 territory, but denied that it is "along" Interstate 93 since it is two miles east of the interstate.

Piechocki, a lifelong resident of New Hampshire, worries that the new franchise will destroy her business. Piechocki advertises heavily along Interstate 93 with signs that count down the number of miles to her Spuckies. She is justifiably worried that a new Spuckies, in Lawrence, Massachusetts, will siphon away a considerable amount of her business. The city of Lawrence is approximately the midpoint between the start and end of Piechocki's exclusive I-93 territory.

Piechocki's lawyer filed a complaint against Spuckies in the federal court in Concord, New Hampshire. Piechocki has not suffered any damages yet because Adams has not opened his store. But damages, once incurred, will be difficult to prove with reasonable certainty. Accordingly, Piechocki's complaint seeks (only) equitable relief in the form of specific performance of the exclusivity clause.

A junior associate in your law firm observes that your case against Spuckies has a Rule 19 problem. Roy Adams, the new franchisee, is almost certainly a Rule 19(a) (or a "necessary) party, and Spuckies will move to dismiss this case for failure to join him. Adams is a Rule 19 party because either (i)

Adams' interests could be substantially prejudiced or (ii) Spuckies could face inconsistent obligations.

The problem is that, if (without Adams joined as a defendant) we win our case and Spuckies is ordered by this court to ensure that Piechocki has the exclusive franchise, Spuckies will have to renege on its franchise agreement with Adams. When that happens, Adams will sue Spuckies for enforcement of its franchise agreement (in a future suit #2). At that point, the judge in suit #2 may feel some sympathy for Spuckies who is obliged by the order in suit #1 to prevent the Adams franchise from opening. If the judge is influenced by the outcome of suit #1 to the detriment of Roy Adams in suit #2, this is to say that Adams' interests were prejudiced in suit #1. If, instead, the judge in suit #2 is in no way influenced by the outcome of suit #1, then the judge in suit #2 might order Spuckies to specifically perform its franchise agreement with Roy Adams. And at that point, Spuckies would face inconsistent obligations.

We could have avoided the Rule 19 problem by requesting only monetary relief in our complaint against Spuckies; in that scenario, Adams would not be a Rule 19(a) (necessary) party, notwithstanding the inefficiency of multiple suits and the potential for inconsistent verdicts. But our client wants equitable relief.

We could have avoided the Rule 19 problem by naming Roy Adams as a defendant. Naming an additional defendant almost always adds cost: more research, more motions to defend, more lawyers to deal with, etc. But, to our knowledge, Roy Adams has no contacts with New Hampshire. He is a lifelong Massachusetts resident who has no assets, property, employees, businesses, or investments in New Hampshire.

Assume that Spuckies will file a 12(b)(7) motion to dismiss for failure to join a Rule 19 party. Assume that Roy Adams is a Rule 19(a) (necessary) party who must be joined if it is feasible. It is not feasible to join Adams if the court lacks personal jurisdiction over him. Is Adams subject to personal jurisdiction in New Hampshire?

FITZGERALD v. WAL-MART STORES EAST, LP

U.S. District Court for the District of Maryland
296 F.R.D. 392 (D. Md. 2013)

ALEXANDER WILLIAMS, JR., DISTRICT JUDGE.

Pending before the Court is Third Party Defendant's Motion to Dismiss the Third Part Complaint for lack of personal jurisdiction. The Court has reviewed the motion papers and concludes that no hearing is necessary. For the reasons articulated below, Third Party Defendant's Motion to Dismiss will be denied.

I. Background

This personal injury action arises from an incident on December 21, 2009, when Plaintiff Christel Fitzgerald fell on a patch of ice in a parking lot adjacent to a Wal-Mart store in Alexandria, Virginia. On December 20, 2012, Fitzgerald filed suit in the Circuit Court for Prince George's County, Maryland against six different Wal-Mart entities which she claimed owned, operated, or were responsible for the premises. She also named USM, Inc. ("USM" or "Third Party Plaintiff") as a Defendant, alleging that it had a contract with one or more Wal-Mart entities to perform or oversee snow removal at the premises.

Defendants removed the action to this Court on February 11, 2013. On June 13, 2013, USM filed a Third Party Complaint against MCHI, Inc. d/b/a Snow Patrol, Inc. ("Snow Patrol" or "Third Party Defendant"). Third Party Defendant was the company contracted by USM to perform snow removal services at the Alexandria location on the date of Plaintiff's fall. USM seeks indemnification and/or contribution from Snow Patrol in an amount equal to any damages awarded against USM in Plaintiff's first party action.

On September 20, 2013, Third Party Defendant filed its Motion to Dismiss for lack of personal jurisdiction pursuant to Rule 12(b)(2) of the Fed. R. Civ. P. The Motion has been fully briefed and is ripe for the Court's consideration.

II. Analysis

When a court's power to exercise personal jurisdiction over a nonresident defendant is properly challenged by a motion under Rule 12(b)(2), "the jurisdictional question is to be resolved by the judge, with the burden on the plaintiff ultimately to prove grounds for jurisdiction by a preponderance of the evidence." *Carefirst of Md., Inc. v. Carefirst Pregnancy Ctrs., Inc.,* 334 F.3d 390, 396 (4th Cir. 2003). If the existence of jurisdiction turns on disputed factual questions the court may resolve the motion on the basis of an evidentiary hearing. *See Combs v. Bakker,* 886 F.2d 673, 676 (4th Cir. 1989). "However, if the court rules on the motion without conducting an evidentiary hearing and relies solely on the basis of the pleadings, allegations in the complaint, motion papers, affidavits, and discovery materials, the plaintiff need only make a prima facie showing of personal jurisdiction." *Metro. Reg'l Info. Sys., Inc. v. Am. Home Realty Network, Inc.,* 888 F.Supp.2d 691, 697 (D. Md. 2012) (citations and internal quotations omitted). "In deciding whether the plaintiff has made the requisite showing, the court must take all disputed facts and reasonable inferences in favor of the plaintiff." *Carefirst of Md.,* 334 F.3d at 396.

The analysis in this case is governed by Rule 4(k)(1) of the Federal Rules of Civil Procedure, which provides:

> (1) In General. Serving a summons or filing a waiver of service establishes personal jurisdiction over a defendant:
>
>   (A) who is subject to the jurisdiction of a court of general jurisdiction in the state where the district court is located;
>
>   (B) who is a party joined under Rule 14 or 19 and is served within a judicial district of the United States and not more than 100 miles from where the summons was issued; or
>
>   (C) when authorized by a federal statute.

Fed. R. Civ. P. 4(k)(1) (emphasis added). As Snow Patrol was impleaded as a third party defendant under Rule 14 of the Federal Rules, it is subject to the "100-mile bulge" of Rule 4(k)(1)(B). *Hollerbach & Andrews Equip. Co., Inc. v. S. Concrete Pumping, Inc.,* 1995 WL 604706, at *2 (D. Md. Sept. 29, 1995). "Rule 4(k) extends the territorial jurisdiction of the federal courts; thus, whether or not the forum state could exercise jurisdiction over the party in the same circumstances is immaterial." *Id.* The rationale underlying the bulge rule was aptly summarized by Judge Kaufman in an opinion from this District:

> The fundamental federal policy underlying the 100-mile bulge pro-vision of [Rule 4(k)(1)(B)] is that the benefits that may be obtained from the disposition by a federal court of an entire controversy far outweigh the burden of requiring an appearance in a federal court located in a state other than his own, by an impleaded party properly served within the modest bulge area around the forum. The fact that the state, in which a federal district court sits, does not adopt that policy, insofar as its own state courts are concerned, cannot be permitted to affect the duty of a federal court, which is part of an independent system for administering justice, to effectu-ate the federal policy enunciated in a rule whose constitutionality is established. Indeed, were the application of the 100-mile bulge provision of [Rule 4(k)(1)(B)] to turn on standards set by the fo-rum state, that provision would be a dead letter in any state which chose not to have any long-arm statute—a result which would clearly thwart federal policy. In order fully to effectuate federal policy, the 100-mile bulge provision of [Rule 4(k)(1)(B)] must be applied independently of the service provisions of the forum state.

McGonigle v. Penn-Central Transp. Co., 49 F.R.D. 58, 62 (D. Md. 1969)

However, application of the 100-mile bulge rule may still be limited by the Due Process Clause. For the Court to exercise personal jurisdiction over the Third Party Defendant in this action, it must find that Snow Patrol established sufficient minimum contacts with the bulge area. *See, e.g., Hol-lerbach*, 1995 WL 604706, at *2 (requiring finding that third party defendant "purposefully availed itself of the benefits and protections of the bulge state"; *Quinones v. Penn. Gen. Ins. Co.*, 804 F.2d 1167, 1177 (10th Cir. 1986) ("[A] federal district court may exercise personal jurisdiction over a Rule 14 . . . party if that party has sufficient minimum contacts with the area defined by a 100-mile radius from the courthouse, regardless of whether that limited area is within one state or spans several states."); *Sprow v. Hartford Ins. Co.*, 594 F.2d 412, 417 (5th Cir. 1979) (requiring a "meaningful nexus" with the bulge area or forum state). Furthermore, the exercise of jurisdiction over Snow Patrol "must not offend traditional notions of fair play and substantial justice." *Hollerbach*, 1995 WL 604706, at *2.

USM has successfully made a prima facie showing that the Court has jurisdiction over Third Party Defendant, as the record demonstrates that Snow Patrol had the requisite minimum contacts within the bulge area to alleviate any due process concerns. Snow Patrol was incorporated in Virginia, its business address was in Fairfax, Virginia, and its registered agent is located in Broad Run, Virginia. It is not disputed that these addresses are within 100 miles of both the Greenbelt and Baltimore federal courthouses.[5] The underlying accident involving Plaintiff occurred at a Wal-Mart store in Alexandria, Virginia, also within 100 miles of the courthouses.[6] Snow Patrol does not dispute that it contracted with USM to provide snow removal services at the Alexandria site. It is therefore clear from the record that Snow Patrol purposefully availed itself of the privilege of conducting business activities within the bulge area such that the Court may exercise specific jurisdiction. In circumstances similar to those present in this case, courts in this District have determined that the exercise of personal jurisdiction was appropriate. *See, e.g., Hollerbach*, 1995 WL 604706, at *3 (third party defendant conducted continuous business and marketing efforts within the bulge area); *Paxton*, 93 F.R.D. at 505 (third party defendant's principal place of business was within the bulge area); *McGonigle*, 49 F.R.D. at 63 (third party defendants' principal office and the location of the underlying accident were within the bulge area). Accordingly, the Court discerns no unfairness, undue burden, or surprise in its exercise of jurisdiction over the Third Party Defendant.[8]

---

5   USM's exhibits show the driving distance between the relevant locations. In *Pierce v. Globemaster Baltimore, Inc.*, 49 F.R.D. 63, 65 (D. Md. 1969), Judge Kaufman adopted the "air mile approach" rather than the driving distance approach. Under either approach, however, it is clear that the locations of Snow Patrol's office and relevant business activities were within 100 miles of the federal courthouses in Maryland.

6   The Court may take judicial notice of distance calculations. *See, e.g., U.S. v. Franklin*, 2012 WL 71018, at *1 n.3 (D. Md. Jan. 9, 2012).

8   Snow Patrol asserts that it would be "unconscionable" to subject it to the jurisdiction of this Court because Maryland has a different statute of limitations for personal injury actions than does Virginia, the only state in which it ever directed its business. Snow Patrol maintains that although the Plaintiff filed her action against Defendants within the three-year Maryland statute of limitations, the same suit could not have been filed in Virginia. However, it cannot be said that Snow Patrol is "being haled into the bulge area solely as a result of random, fortuitous, or attenuated contacts." *Hollerbach*, 1995 WL 604706, at *3 (quoting *Burger King*, 471 U.S. at 475). Nor can it be said that Snow Patrol is being haled into the bulge area by the "unilateral activity of another party or a third person." *Burger King*, 471 U.S. at 475. As discussed herein, Snow Patrol has deliberately engaged in significant activities within and created a substantial connection with the bulge area. In these circumstances, "it is presumptively not unreasonable to require [it] to submit to the burdens of litigation in that forum as well." *Id.* at 476. Furthermore, Plaintiff's interest in obtaining "convenient and effective relief" and "the interstate judicial system's interest in obtaining the most efficient resolution of controversies" counsel in favor of the Court's exercise of jurisdiction in this case. *Id.* at 477.

III. Conclusion

For the foregoing reasons, Third Party Defendant's Motion to Dismiss will be denied.

COMMENTS AND QUESTIONS

1. Snow Patrol complains that Maryland's (longer) statute of limitations will apply if Snow Patrol must litigate there. This accident happened in Virginia. Snow Patrol has only done business in Virginia. Is the fact that Snow Patrol "deliberately engaged in significant activities within and created a substantial connection with the bulge area" (footnote 8 of Judge Williams' opinion) sufficient justification to subject them to personal jurisdiction in Maryland (and all that that entails, including the application of forum procedural law)?

2. What would have been the outcome of Snow Patrol's motion if this action had not been removed from state to federal court?

3. Imagine that Snow Patrol had been named by Fitzgerald as an additional defendant (i.e., a joint tortfeasor) in the original action. USM still could have asserted an indemnification claim against its co-defendant, Snow Patrol. What result if Snow Patrol moved to dismiss the claims of both Fitzgerald and USM because Maryland lacked personal jurisdiction?

Federal Statute

Federal statutes routinely create substantive causes of action. Occasionally, a statutory regime will also provide for nationwide or even worldwide service of process. Under Fed. R. Civ. P. 4(k)(1)(C) service "authorized by a federal statute" also "establishes personal jurisdiction."

The topics for which Congress has legislated about service range from antitrust and securities to pension plans and the environment.[21] The False Claims Act, for

21 See, e.g., Antiterrorism Act, 18 U.S.C. § 2334; Clayton Act, 15 U.S.C. §§ 5, 22, 25; CERCLA, 42 U.S.C. § 9613(e); Employment Retirement Income Security Act (ERISA), 29 U.S.C. §§ 1132(e)(2), 1453(d); False Claims Act, 31 U.S.C. § 3732(a); Interpleader Act, 28 U.S.C. § 2361; RICO, 18 U.S.C. § 1965; Securities Act of 1933, 15

example, creates a cause of action against contractors who defraud the federal government. But it also contains a worldwide service provision:

> A summons as required by the Federal Rules of Civil Procedure shall be issued by the appropriate district court *and served at any place within or outside the United States.*[22]

Of course compliance with a legislative statute and a rule of procedure does not mean that the exercise of personal jurisdiction is also constitutional. Although the Supreme Court has not squarely addressed the scope of the Fifth Amendment Due Process under such circumstances, the circuit courts generally require that the defendant have *minimum contacts* with the United States *as a whole.* The courts thus borrow the concept of minimum contacts from specific jurisdiction but expand the relevant geographic area from one state to the entire country.

Hypothetical 20-9

Amana Life Insurance Co. (Amana) issued a policy insuring the life of Harriet Finkel, a lifelong resident of Sacramento, California. Amana is a Nevada corporation that has its principal place of business in Winters, California.

Harriet Finkel died while hiking in Yosemite National Park in Mariposa, California. Harriet's $1 million policy named "Hank Finkel" as the beneficiary. Two individuals have contacted Amana, each claiming to be the relevant "Hank Finkel." One of the claimants, Henry Finkel, is Harriet Finkel's ex-husband. The other claimant, Harry Finkel, is Harriet Finkel's only grandson; because Harry is a minor, his parents are asserting the claim on Harry's behalf. Both of these claimants, Henry and Harry, are commonly referred to as "Hank Finkel."

Henry Finkel has lived in Tijuana, Mexico since he and Harriet divorced three years ago. Harry Finkel's parents have lived in Eugene, Oregon for eighteen years.

Amana has contacted your California law firm because both Henry Finkel and Harry Finkel have threatened to sue. Henry has hired a San Diego law firm. And Harry's parents have hired a lawyer in Portland. Amana could face separate lawsuits and, in theory, could lose both. Amana wants you to help them avoiding paying the million dollars *twice.* In fact, Amana disputes whether it even must pay *once.* On her application for life insurance,

---

U.S.C. § 77v; Securities Exchange Act of 1934, 15 U.S.C. § 78aa.

22   31 U.S.C. § 3732 (emphasis added).

Harriet lied about her age, claiming to be 7 years younger; this material misrepresentation could void or substantially reduce Amana's obligation to pay the $1 million.

The partners at your firm are contemplating an interpleader action. An interpleader is appropriate when two or more parties claim the same thing. The stakeholder (here: Amana) initiates an interpleader action naming the adverse claimants (here: Henry and Harry) as defendants. The stakeholder can also name itself as an additional defendant if it, too, is an adverse claimant.

But an interpleader action still requires that the court have personal jurisdiction over the defendants. The partners have told you that Harry and Harry's parents do not have minimum contacts with California. Henry may or may not have minimum contacts with California. Henry does not have minimum contacts with Oregon.

The federal court has *subject matter* jurisdiction over an interpleader action provided the amount in controversy exceeds $500 and there is minimal diversity between or among the adverse claimants. 28 U.S.C. § 1335. That is satisfied here.

You are asked to determine whether a federal court would have *personal* jurisdiction. Section 2361 of Title 28 provides:

> In any civil action of interpleader or in the nature of interpleader under section 1335 of this title, a district court may issue its process for all claimants and enter its order restraining them from instituting or prosecuting any proceeding in any State or United States court affecting the property, instrument or obligation involved in the interpleader action until further order of the court. Such process and order shall be returnable at such time as the court or judge thereof directs, and shall be addressed to and served by the United States marshals for the respective districts where the claimants reside or may be found.

> Such district courts shall hear and determine the case, and may discharge the plaintiff from further liability, make the injunction permanent, and make all appropriate orders to enforce its judgment.

Is this a federal statute that, pursuant to Fed. R. Civ. P. 4(k)(1)(C) would give a California federal court personal jurisdiction over Henry and Harry? If the interpleader action were instead filed in a New York federal court, would that court have personal jurisdiction?

U.S. SEC. & EXCH. COMM. v. LINES OVERSEAS MGMT., LTD.

U.S. District Court for the District of Columbia
2007 WL 581909 (D.D.C. Feb. 21, 2007)

RICHARD W. ROBERTS, DISTRICT JUDGE.

Respondents Lines Overseas Management, Ltd. ("LOM") and one of its officers, Scott Lines ("Lines"), have filed objections to, and seek modification of, a magistrate judge's order enforcing four administrative investigative subpoenas issued by the Securities and Exchange Commission ("SEC"). Respondents argue, among other things, that this court lacks personal jurisdiction over them. . . .

Background

In early 2003, the SEC ordered two investigations into possible violations of securities laws. Related to these investigations and under the authority of 15 U.S.C. § 78u(b), the SEC issued a total of four subpoenas commanding Lines and LOM to produce certain documents and to submit to deposition. The next day, the four subpoenas were served personally on Lines, a Bermuda citizen and resident, at the Miami International Airport, where he had arrived after seeking medical attention in Boston and before returning to Bermuda. Lines is an officer and managing director of LOM, which is a Bermuda financial services corporation with no offices in the United States.

Lines and LOM disobeyed the subpoenas. The SEC filed an Application for an Order to Show Cause and for an Order Requiring Obedience to the Subpoenas ("SEC Application"). After reviewing voluminous submissions and hearing argument, the magistrate judge ordered LOM and Lines to comply with the subpoenas, and respondents objected.

LOM and Lines filed separate objections to the magistrate judge's determination, but presented substantially similar arguments. Both argue that this court lacks personal jurisdiction over them, that compliance would put them in conflict with foreign law to which they are subject, and that the subpoenas are overbroad and, in Lines' case, impossible to obey. LOM argues in addition that the subpoena relating to [one] investigation is void for defect because it did not correctly state LOM's corporate name.

Discussion

Respondents argue that the SEC subpoenas are unenforceable because respondents did not have the minimum contacts with either the District of Columbia or the United States that the Constitution requires for personal jurisdiction. The SEC counters by citing the multiple declarations and many documents it submitted that provide facts supporting its allegations of personal jurisdiction.

The SEC as the movant has the burden of establishing that the court has personal jurisdiction. In its moving papers, the SEC need make only a prima facie showing of personal jurisdiction. If discovery on the issue has been taken or the issue is raised in an evidentiary hearing or a trial, a heightened standard of a preponderance of the evidence is employed. *Mwani v. bin Laden*, 417 F.3d 1, 6 (D.C. Cir. 2005). Magistrate Judge Kay, in his discretion, employed the heightened standard of preponderance of the evidence in determining the factual matters relating to personal jurisdiction.

Congress has authorized nationwide service of SEC investigative subpoenas issued under 15 U.S.C. § 78u(b).[6] Congress has also authorized worldwide service of a summons in an action to enforce a subpoena that is issued under § 78u(b). *See* 15 U.S.C. § 78u(c);[7] *see also In re Application to Enforce Admin. Subpoenas Duces Tecum of the SEC v. Knowles*, 87 F.3d 413, 417 (10th Cir. 1996) ("*Knowles*") ("Congress has provided for worldwide service of process in cases of enforcement of subpoenas issued by the SEC.") (citing 15 U.S.C. § 78u(c)). Given these statutory provisions, service under Fed. R. Civ. P.

---

6   The authorizing statutory text is: "For the purpose of any investigation, or any other proceeding under this chapter, any member of the Commission or any officer designated by it is empowered to administer oaths and affirmations, subpoena witnesses, compel their attendance, take evidence, and require the production of any books, papers, correspondence, memoranda or other records which the Commission deems relevant or material to the inquiry. Such attendance of witnesses and the production of any such records may be required from any place in the United States or any State at any designated place of hearing." 15 U.S.C. § 78u(b).

7   The statutory text, in pertinent part, states: "In case of contumacy by, or refusal to obey a subpoena issued to, any person, the Commission may invoke the aid of any court of the United States within the jurisdiction of which such investigation or proceeding is carried on, or where such person resides or carries on business, in requiring the attendance and testimony of witnesses and the production of books, papers, correspondence, memoranda, and other records. And such court may issue an order requiring such person to appear before the commission or member or officer designated by the Commission, there to produce records, if so ordered, or to give testimony touching the matter under investigation or in question; and any failure to obey such order of the court may be punished by such court as a contempt thereof. All process in any such case may be served in the judicial district whereof such person is an inhabitant or wherever he may be found." 15 U.S.C. § 78u(c).

[4(k)(1)(C)] "establishes personal jurisdiction . . . subject to constitutional limits." *Knowles*, 87 F.3d at 417.

In this case, the constitutional limits stem from the Fifth Amendment's due process protections. *See Steinberg v. Int'l Criminal Police Org.*, 672 F.2d 927, 930 (D.C. Cir. 1981) (noting that a federal action requires personal jurisdiction sufficient to satisfy the Fifth Amendment's due process clause). The Supreme Court has never squarely defined Fifth Amendment due process limits on personal jurisdiction. However, with respect to the identically-phrased due process clause in the Fourteenth Amendment, the Supreme Court has required that persons, whether individuals or corporations, haled into court in a particular forum "have certain minimum contacts with [the forum] such that the maintenance of the [judicial proceeding] does not offend traditional notions of fair play and substantial justice." *Int'l Shoe Co. v. State of Washington*, 326 U.S. 310, 316 (1945). In this circuit, following the Supreme Court's Fourteenth Amendment personal jurisdiction jurisprudence, "certain 'minimum contacts' must exist between the person and the jurisdiction to be consistent with the Due Process Clause of the Fifth Amendment." *Gilson v. Rep. of Ireland*, 682 F.2d 1022, 1028 (D.C. Cir. 1982). The contacts should be such that based on the person's "conduct and connection with the forum . . . he should reasonably anticipate being haled into court there." *World-Wide Volkswagen v. Woodson*, 444 U.S. 286, 297 (1980). Where a person has "purposefully directed his activities at the residents of the forum" and the court proceeding results from alleged injuries that "arise out of or relate to those activities," the minimum contacts required by the constitution are satisfied. *See Burger King Corp. v. Rudzewicz*, 471 U.S. 462, 472–73 (1985). A person's minimum contacts may be established by evidence of his virtual presence in the state. "Presence in the [forum] in this sense has never been doubted when the activities of the [person] there have not only been continuous and systematic, but also give rise to the liabilities sued on, even though no consent to be sued or authorization to an agent to accept service of process has been given." *Int'l Shoe,* 326 U.S. at 317.

"This circuit has held that the requirement of 'minimum contacts' with a forum state is inapplicable where the court exercises personal jurisdiction by virtue of a federal statute authorizing nationwide service of process. . . . In such circumstances, minimum contacts with the United States suffice." *SEC v. Bilzerian*, 378 F.3d 1100, 1106 n.8 (D.C. Cir. 2004). Specifically with respect to 15 U.S.C. § 78u(c), "[w]hen the personal jurisdiction of a federal court is invoked based upon a federal statute providing for nationwide or worldwide service, the relevant inquiry is whether the respondent has had sufficient minimum contacts with the United States. . . . Specific contacts with the district in which enforcement is sought . . . are unnecessary." *Knowles*, 87 F.3d at 417 (interpreting 15 U.S.C. § 78u(c));[9] *see also FTC v. Compagnie De Saint-Gobain-Pont-A-Mousson*, 636 F.2d 1300, 1324 (D.C. Cir. 1980) (interpreting a similar statute, 15 U.S.C. § 49, and concluding that "[s]hould the FTC be able to obtain personal service upon . . . an officer . . . of [a non-resident foreign corporation] within the territorial boundaries of the United States, it could validly obtain a judicial enforcement order for that subpoena"); *NGS Am. Inc. v. Jefferson*, 218 F.3d 519, 524 (6th Cir. 2000) (noting that one of the ERISA statutes provides nationwide service of process and personal jurisdiction could arguably be founded on minimum contacts with the United States). Here, then, the SEC need not show that Lines and LOM had minimum contacts with the District of Columbia, and respondents' argument to the contrary is incorrect.

The SEC has submitted documents and sworn statements that provide specific, detailed evidence of Lines' and LOM's many telephonic, email, and mail contacts with persons and entities in the United States in order to make or omit representations regarding certain securities, and to buy and sell thousands of U.S. securities in the U.S. securities market during the period between January and July 2003. Lines' declaration states that he does not "currently" place trades "on behalf of LOM," and draws various legal conclusions such as "I do not conduct business in the United States[ ]" and "I do not maintain numerous purposeful contacts with the United States," but does not refute the specific evidence submitted by the SEC. LOM's compliance manager filed a declaration on behalf of LOM stating that "[i]n January 2003 [LOM] maintained brokerage accounts with the United States brokerage firms" and at Schwab Capital Markets LLC and Sterne, Agee Capital Markets, Inc. He explained that LOM places trades with these U.S. brokerage firms and provides "back office" functions related to those trades for other LOM-related entities. These statements confirm evidence of LOM's contacts with U.S. securities markets that was submitted by the SEC. Neither Lines nor LOM have offered evidence that refutes or compromises the substantial documentary and testimonial evidence of their contacts and activities related to trading in the U.S. securities market in 2003.

9   The Fifth Amendment may proscribe personal jurisdiction in the highly unusual case where the chosen forum is so inconvenient that it actually infringes a liberty interest. *See Peay v. Bellsouth Med. Assistance Plan*, 205 F.3d 1206, 1212 (10th Cir. 2000). Respondents have not made, and under the circumstances cannot make, such an argument.

The SEC's submissions reveal conduct by Lines and LOM involving specific sales and purchases of specific securities, and specific representations to purchasers and omissions from those representations. This conduct gave rise to the matters under investigation for which the SEC issued the subpoenas. The SEC's evidence supports a conclusion that Lines and LOM were purposefully directing activities toward the United States securities market, and did so for a sustained period of time in 2003, such that they could reasonably expect to be haled into court in the United States for matters pertaining to their activities in the U.S. securities market.

Respondents' contention that the Constitution requires "some physical manifestation in the forum, such as permanent local offices, locally based agents, or, at the very least, a continuous flow of such agents into the forum" construes the law too narrowly. As the D.C. Circuit has recently said:

> Although "the constitutional touchstone remains whether the defendant purposefully established 'minimum contacts' in the forum," *Burger King*, 471 U.S. at 474 . . . (quoting *International Shoe*, 326 U.S. at 316 . . .), the "foreseeability" of causing injury in the forum can establish such contacts where "the defendant's conduct and connection with the forum . . . are such that he should reasonably anticipate being haled into court there." *Id.* (quoting *World-Wide Volkswagen* . . . , 444 U.S. at 295 . . .). "Jurisdiction in these circumstances may not be avoided merely because the defendant did not physically enter the forum." *Id.* at 477. . . . Rather, "[s]o long as [an] actor's efforts are 'purposefully directed' toward residents of another [forum]," the Supreme Court has "consistently rejected the notion that an absence of physical contacts can defeat personal jurisdiction there." *Id.* at 476 . . . (quoting *Keeton* [*v. Hustler Magazine, Inc.*], 465 U.S. [770,] 774 . . . [(1984)]); *see GTE* [*News Media Servs., Inc. v. Bellsouth Corp.*], 199 F.3d [1343,] 1349 [(D.C. Cir. 2000)] (noting that "jurisdiction may attach if the defendant's conduct is aimed ato or has an effect in the ofrum state" (quoting *Panavision Int'l, LP v. Toeppen*, 141 F.3d 1316, 1321 (9th Cir. 1998))).

Mwani, 417 F.3d at 12–13.

In light of the evidence submitted by the SEC, this court's exercise of personal jurisdiction over Lines and LOM does not offend traditional notions of fair play and due process, and falls well within constitutional limits. Because the SEC has established that respondents had sufficient minimum contacts with the United States to satisfy the constitutional requirements of the Fifth Amendment and respondents have not shown that the inconvenience of litigating these judicial proceedings in the District of Columbia rises to a constitutional level, *see Peay*, 205 F.3d at 1212, respondents' objections to this court's exercise of personal jurisdiction will be overruled. . . .

Conclusion

Because respondents' contact with the United States is sufficient to support an exercise of personal jurisdiction within constitutional limits, and because respondents' other objections are unavailing, respondents' objections seeking modification of Magistrate Judge Kay's January 7, 2005 Order enforcing the subpoenas will be overruled. . . .

COMMENTS AND QUESTIONS

1. The exercise of jurisdiction pursuant to Fed. R. Civ. P. 4(k)(1)(C) must be consistent with the due process guaranteed by the Fifth Amendment. Should we expect the scope of that guarantee to mimic the ebb and flow of the guarantee under the Fourteenth Amendment, or do the two clauses protect fundamentally different concerns? Put another way, do *Goodyear Dunlop Tires Operations, S.A. v. Brown, supra, Walden v. Fiore, supra,* and *Nicastro v. McIntyre Machinery, Ltd., supra,* make it harder for plaintiffs to establish the constitutionality of an exercise of personal jurisdiction pursuant to a federal statute?

    Is the quote from *Mwani v. bin Laden* near the end of Judge Roberts' opinion still an accurate statement of the law of minimum contacts?

2. Imagine a foreign defendant does enough business in the United States that it would be considered to have "minimum contacts" with the (aggregated) United States. Further, imagine that that defendant is being sued in a United States federal court for acts that trigger liability under a federal statute. If that federal statute authorized worldwide service of process, would the court have personal jurisdiction *only if* the defendant's conduct *arose out of* its minimum contacts with the United States, or would the court have personal jurisdiction even if the claim under the federal

statute was *unrelated* to the defendant's contacts with the United States? Put another way, are the categories of "general jurisdiction" and "specific jurisdiction" relevant with respect to exercises of jurisdiction pursuant to federal statutes? *See, e.g., Siswanto v. Airbus Americas, Inc.*, 2016 WL 7178459 (N.D. Ill. 2016).

Federal Question Against Foreign Defendant Under FRCP 4(k)(2)

The final basis for establishing personal jurisdiction regards situations where a plaintiff has a *federal* cause of action, but that statutory regime does not also authorize nationwide or worldwide service of process. Even for plaintiffs in federal court with federal causes of action this basis is available only if the defendant could not be subject to personal jurisdiction in any state. And, as we have seen repeatedly now, the exercise must also be consistent with the Fifth Amendment's guarantee of due process for defendants.

As a practical matter, only foreign-country defendants will fall within the scope of personal jurisdiction authorized by Fed. R. Civ. P. 4(k)(2). Although this rule does not mention foreign (or domestic) defendants, a prerequisite for its exercise is that "the defendant is not subject to jurisdiction in any state's courts of general jurisdiction."[23] Conceptually, then, every exercise of personal jurisdiction under Fed. R. Civ. P. 4(k)(2) requires the court to ensure that the defendant is not subject to personal jurisdiction in any state from Alabama, Alaska, Arizona, and Arkansas, to Washington, West Virginia, Wisconsin, and Wyoming. This prerequisite is sometimes referred to as the negation requirement. Because a domestic defendant will, at a minimum, be subject to personal jurisdiction in the state of their domicile (if a natural person), or their state of incorporation and the state of their principal place of business (if a corporation), only a foreign-country defendant could satisfy this criterion.[24]

This basis for jurisdiction will not reach all claims against foreign-country defendants, however. Many foreign defendants will be subject to personal jurisdiction in some state, thereby failing to satisfy Fed. R. Civ. P. 4(k)(2)(A). Further, claims against foreign defendants often arise under state, not federal law. For example, claims for negligence, defective products, breach of contract, fraud, libel, tortious interference with contractual relations, and misappropriation of a trade secret are

---

[23]   Fed. R. Civ. P. 4(k)(2)(A).

[24]   An American citizen who is domiciled abroad could meet this definition.

state law claims; Rule 4(k)(2) can manufacture personal jurisdiction against a defendant only "[f]or a claim that arises under federal law." Claims that arise under a foreign country's law also cannot satisfy this prerequisite of Rule 4(k)(2).

And finally, the foreign-country defendant's "national contacts" or "aggregate contacts" must be substantial enough to satisfy the Fifth Amendment. This means that the defendant must have "minimum contacts" with the United States as a whole. As the Second Circuit observed:

> Rule 4(k)(2) was specifically designed to "correct[ ] a gap" in the enforcement of federal law in international cases. The gap arose from the general rule that a federal district court's personal jurisdiction extends only as far as that of a state court in the state where the federal court sits. . . . The pre-1993 [version of Federal Rule 4], the Advisory Committee noted, left a significant lacuna "when the defendant was a non-resident of the United States having contacts with the United States sufficient to justify the application of United States law and to satisfy federal standards of forum selection but having insufficient contact with any single state to support jurisdiction under state long-arm legislation or meet the requirements of the Fourteenth Amendment limitation on state court territorial jurisdiction.

Porina v. Marward Shipping Co., 521 F.3d 122, 126–27 (2d Cir. 2008) (citing Fed. R. Civ. P. 4 advisory committee's note, 1993 Amendment). By amending Rule 4(k)(2), the drafters closed that gap.

Rare is the case that meets all three criteria of this rule: (1) plaintiff's cause of action arises under federal law; (2) the defendant is not subject to the jurisdiction of the courts in any state; and (3) the defendant's total contacts with the United States as a whole are sufficient to confer the court with personal jurisdiction without offending the Fifth Amendment.

Hypothetical 20-10

AMFIB plc is a British company that provides offshore drilling services on a contract basis. The company's headquarters are in London.

Rex Mondrake is a technical specialist who, born and raised in Texas, has worked in the oil industry for decades. A little less than a year ago, Mondrake was finishing up a three-week consulting gig in the Persian Gulf when he was hired by AMFIB for a three-month project there.

On the first day of his employment with AMFIB, Mondrake was required to participate in a water survival training course. The course, which was taught ashore in Saudi Arabia, included participating in a simulated at-sea escape from a downed helicopter and boarding life rafts. Mondrake, who was then fifty-eight years old, had great difficulty getting out of the helicopter and into the life raft. During this exercise, Mondrake suffered serious cervical neck injuries when he was grabbed by fellow participants and was roughly hauled aboard the raft.

Unable to work, Mondrake immediately returned to Texas, where doctors performed a lumbar fusion operation. His recovery has been slow, and AMFIB has refused to pay medical expenses and has not offered any other compensation.

AMFIB has no presence in Texas but has an office in New Orleans, Louisiana, and two employees there who operate what AMFIB's website describes as its "North American Outpost." AMFIB has a substantial bank account in New York City, and it routinely engages lawyers and accountants there for professional advice.

Your firm represents Mandrake. The senior partner has asked you to focus exclusively on the question whether the courts of Texas would have personal jurisdiction over AMFIB. Outline the steps you would take to formulate an answer to that question.

FROM THE COURTS

SYNGENTA CROP PROTECTION, LLC v. WILLOWOOD, LLC

U.S. District Court for the Middle District of North Carolina
139 F.Supp.3d 722 (M.D.N.C. 2015)

CATHERINE C. EAGLES, DISTRICT JUDGE.

Syngenta Crop Protection, LLC, has sued four business entities alleging patent infringement, copyright infringement, and unfair and deceptive trade practices. Syngenta's claims relate to the defendants' roles in the registration and sale of fungicide products that include the chemical azoxystrobin. Defendant Willowood Limited is a Chinese corporation whose only presence in the United States is through its sales of azoxystrobin to a United

States affiliate. Willowood Limited asserts that the Court lacks personal jurisdiction and has brought a motion to dismiss. Because it established an affiliate specifically to market and sell products to customers in the United States and sold the allegedly infringing chemical to that affiliate for sale in the United States, Willowood Limited has sufficient connections to the United States for the exercise of jurisdiction to be fair and just. The Court will deny the motion.

Standard

When a defendant challenges personal jurisdiction by Rule 12(b)(2) motion, "the jurisdictional question is to be resolved by the judge, with the burden on the plaintiff ultimately to prove grounds for jurisdiction by a preponderance of the evidence." *Carefirst of Md., Inc. v. Carefirst Pregnancy Ctrs., Inc.*, 334 F.3d 390, 396 (4th Cir. 2003). All jurisdictional allegations are taken in the light most favorable to the plaintiff, and all inferences must be in favor of jurisdiction. *New Wellington Fin. Corp. v. Flagship Resort Dev. Corp.*, 416 F.3d 290, 294 (4th Cir. 2005). If there is no evidentiary hearing, "the plaintiff need only make a prima facie showing of personal jurisdiction." *Carefirst*, 334 F.3d at 396.

Although the standard may be lenient, a court "need not credit conclusory allegations or draw farfetched inferences." *Masselli & Lane, PC v. Miller & Schuh, PA*, 2000 WL 691100, at *1 (4th Cir. 2000). Blanket conclusory allegations as to multiple defendants are insufficient. The plaintiff must base its claim for personal jurisdiction "on specific facts set forth in the record." *Magic Toyota, Inc. v. Se. Toyota Distribs., Inc.*, 784 F. Supp. 306, 310 (D.S.C. 1992). Further, a parent-subsidiary relationship does not by itself support jurisdiction. *Saudi v. Northrop Grumman Corp.*, 427 F.3d 271, 276 (4th Cir. 2005).

The allegations of the complaint are taken as true only if evidence from the defendant does not contradict them. Once the defendant presents evidence indicating that the requisite minimum contacts do not exist, the plaintiff must come forward with affidavits or other evidence in support of its position. *Clark v. Remark*, 1993 WL 134616, at *2 (4th Cir. Apr. 29, 1993) (per curiam). Where both sides present evidence, a court resolves factual conflicts in favor of the party asserting jurisdiction. *Id.*

Facts

The movant, Willowood Limited ("W-Limited"), is a Chinese entity with its principal office in Hong Kong. It buys and sells pesticides, including azoxystrobin, outside the United States. W-Limited maintains its records in China and does not have any assets, bank accounts, offices, agents, or employees in the United States. Its website is available worldwide, but it does not target any specific customer or location in North Carolina or anywhere else in the United States. It is not registered to do business anywhere in the United States.

The other defendants are limited liability companies registered and based in Oregon. The defendant Willowood USA, LLC ("W-USA") is the parent company, while the defendants Willowood, LLC, and Willowood Azoxystrobin, LLC are W-USA's wholly owned subsidiaries.

W-Limited formed W-USA to expand into the United States market and knew that the azoxystrobin it sold W-USA would end up in products sold in the United States. W-Limited announced the formation of W-USA in a 2010 press release on W-USA's website. It stated that the new company "will operate as a wholly owned subsidiary of Willowwood [sic] Limited of Hong Kong, China" and that it is "very excited about this new opportunity to expand and grow our company in the United States." This press release was available on W-USA's website until Syngenta cited it in an opposition brief to this motion, after which W-USA removed the "wholly owned subsidiary" language. W-Limited is the sole supplier of azoxystrobin to W-USA.

The websites of W-USA and W-Limited frequently refer to W-USA as an affiliate of W-Limited. W-Limited's website describes W-USA as an "affiliate" or an "affiliate office," provides the address and phone number to W-USA's office, and includes a link to W-USA's website. A news update on the W-Limited website announcing the launch of W-USA states that "Willowood Limited, launches its U.S. business (Willowood USA LLC) based out of Oregon, USA, please contact us . . . for more information and business opportunities in the US." W-USA's website shows similar connections. It describes W-Limited's business and contains a link to W-Limited's website. W-USA's website also has a page called "Meet the Team" that prominently displays a picture and biography of Vijay Mundhra, founder, majority owner, and manager of W-Limited.

W-USA buys azoxystrobin from W-Limited in China and then imports it into the United States, where it is processed in St. Louis, Missouri, for sale in the form of fungicide products. W-USA has sold products containing azoxystrobin throughout the United States, including in North Carolina. W-Limited was not involved in either the processing or the sales of these fungicide products by W-USA.

W-Limited does not hold any registrations from the EPA for sale of azoxystrobin in the United States and is not involved in registering any of W-USA's products in the United States. The documents attached to the complaint show that Willowood, LLC, a subsidiary of W-USA, filed applications for registration with the EPA, and registered the azoxystrobin products with the North Carolina Department of Agriculture.

Discussion

Federal Circuit law applies. The parties agree that the law of the Federal Circuit applies to personal jurisdiction in connection with the patent claims. W-Limited contends that the law of the Fourth Circuit, not the Federal Circuit, applies to personal jurisdiction in connection with the copyright and unfair trade practices claims. While this may be correct, it is irrelevant, because the complaint cannot plausibly be read to assert copyright and unfair trade practices claims against W-Limited.

The complaint often does not distinguish between and among the various defendants, lumping them all together as "Willowood." The exhibits attached to the complaint, however, show that the actions in the copyright and unfair trade practice claims are attributable only to W-USA and its subsidiaries, and not to W-Limited.

Counts V and VI allege copyright infringement based on two fungicide product labels. According to Syngenta's exhibits to the complaint, the labels were sent to the EPA on behalf of Willowood, LLC, and refer to W-USA and Willowood, LLC, only. Nothing in the complaint indicates that W-Limited had a specific role in registering these labels.

Count VII alleges unfair and deceptive trade practices based on false representations made to the EPA and early entry into the generic azoxystrobin market. Again, Syngenta's exhibits indicate that these representations to the EPA and sales within the United States were made by or on behalf of W-USA and its subsidiaries only. The complaint contains no specific allegations that

W-Limited made representations to the EPA or sold products containing azoxystrobin within the United States.

Since Counts I to IV allege patent infringement based on alleged conduct that is attributable to W-Limited, the Court will follow Federal Circuit law in analyzing personal jurisdiction.

I. Personal Jurisdiction

An out-of-state defendant is subject to personal jurisdiction of a district court only if both the forum state's long-arm statute and due process are satisfied. *Avocent Huntsville Corp. v. Aten Intern. Co.*, 552 F.3d 1324, 1329 (Fed. Cir. 2008). "North Carolina's long-arm statute is construed to extend jurisdiction over nonresident defendants to the full extent permitted by the Due Process Clause" *Christian Sci. Bd. Of Dirs. v. Nolan*, 259 F.3d 209, 215 (4th Cir. 2001). Therefore, the North Carolina long-arm statute limit merges into the due process question.

There are two different types of personal jurisdiction. *See, e.g., Avocent*, 552 F.3d at 1330. Syngenta has not contended that the Court can exercise general jurisdiction over W-Limited, so the Court will limit its analysis to specific jurisdiction.

A court may assert specific jurisdiction over a foreign defendant when "the defendant has purposefully directed [its] activities at residents of the forum and the litigation [then] results from alleged injuries that arise out of or relate to those activities." *Burger King Corp. v. Rudzewicz*, 471 U.S. 462, 472–73 (1985). "Due process requires that a defendant be haled into court in a forum State based on his own affiliation with the State, not based on the 'random, fortuitous, or attenuated' contacts he makes by interacting with other persons affiliated with the State." *Walden v. Fiore*, 571 U.S. 277 (2014). To determine whether the contacts with the forum state were sufficient, a court looks to whether the defendant "should reasonably anticipate being haled into court there." *Burger King*, 471 U.S. at 474.

Even after a plaintiff shows that a defendant purposefully directed activities at a forum, a court must consider "whether the assertion of personal jurisdiction would comport with fair play and substantial justice." *Burger King*, 471 U.S. at 476. The factors to consider under fair play and substantial justice are "(1) the burden on the defendant, (2) the forum's interest in adjudicating the dispute, (3) the plaintiff's interest in obtaining convenient and effective relief, (4) the interstate judicial system's interest in obtaining the most efficient resolution of controversies, and (5) the shared interest of the states in furthering fundamental substantive policies." *Touchcom, Inc. v. Bereskin & Parr*, 574 F.3d 1403, 1417 (Fed. Cir. 2009).

Syngenta contends that purposefully directed activities can be shown using the stream-of-commerce theory. As set forth in *Beverly Hills Fan Co. v. Royal Sovereign Corp.*, the stream-of-commerce theory allows a court in a patent case to exercise specific jurisdiction over an out-of-state actor who "purposefully shipped" the allegedly infringing item into the forum state "through an established distribution channel." 21 F.3d 1558, 1565 (Fed. Cir. 1994). Later case law created doubts about how to apply this doctrine. *See Celgard, LLC v. SK Innovation Co.*, 792 F.3d 1373, 1381 (Fed. Cir. 2015) ("The precise requirements of the stream-of-commerce theory of jurisdiction remain unsettled."); *Prototype Prods., Inc. v. Reset, Inc.*, 844 F.Supp.2d 691, 702 n.3 (E.D. Va. 2012) (summarizing stream-of-commerce plurality opinions).

At its most basic level, jurisdiction based on stream-of-commerce requires "the movement of goods from manufacturers through distributors to consumers," ending in the forum state. *See J. McIntyre Mach., Ltd. v. Nicastro*, 564 U.S. 873 (2011) (plurality opinion). Syngenta has proven this basic requirement. It is undisputed that W-Limited sold azoxystrobin to a distributor, W-USA, who then used that azoxystrobin in fungicide products available for sale in North Carolina.

It is uncertain whether a plaintiff must also show that the defendant "targeted" a specific forum and had "an intention to benefit from and thus an intention to submit to the laws of the forum State," *Nicastro*, 564 U.S. at 881, or whether only awareness plus some additional "act . . . purposefully directed toward the forum State" is required. *Asahi Metal Indus. Co. v. Super. Ct.*, 480 U.S. 102, 112 (1987) (O'Connor J., writing for a plurality). The Federal Circuit's solution to this uncertainty has been to simply use the original *Beverly Hills Fan* test and disregard the later fractured Supreme Court decisions. *See AFTG-TG, LLC v. Nuvoton Tech. Corp.*, 689 F.3d 1358, 1363–64 (Fed. Cir. 2012).

By any of these standards, Syngenta has not made a prima facie showing of specific jurisdiction as to North Carolina. Syngenta alleges that, because W-Limited "intentionally established a distribution channel" to sell the infringing azoxystrobin in the United States, it has purposefully directed its activities toward North Carolina. However, W-Limited's website makes no mention of North Carolina, and W-Limited has no physical or business presence in North Carolina. There is no evidence or specific allegation that W-Limited's management directed W-USA to make sales in North Carolina. Only W-USA and Willowood, LLC, have registered azoxystrobin products in North Carolina and made those products available for sale in the state. Nor is there any showing that the acts of W-USA can be imputed to W-Limited. W-Limited has neither targeted nor purposefully directed any act at North Carolina, and so specific jurisdiction is inappropriate as to North Carolina.

II. Rule 4(k)(2)

Alternatively, Syngenta contends that personal jurisdiction is available under Rule 4(k)(2). Fed. R. Civ. P. 4(k)(2). In appropriate circumstances, an out-of-state defendant that lacks sufficient contacts to a particular forum state can still be subject to personal jurisdiction in that state based on contacts with the United States as a whole. Rule 4(k)(2), which acts as a "federal long-arm statute," authorizes personal jurisdiction over a defendant if "(1) the plaintiff's claim arises under federal law, (2) the defendant is not subject to personal jurisdiction in the courts of any state, and (3) the exercise of jurisdiction satisfies due process requirements." *Merial Ltd. v. Cipla Ltd.*, 681 F.3d 1283, 1294 (Fed. Cir. 2012); Fed. R. Civ. P. 4(k)(2). For due process analysis Rule 4(K)(2), the relevant forum state is the United States as a whole. *Merial*, 681 F.3d at 1294.

Claim arises under federal law. The first requirement is "relatively straightforward" in a patent case. *Synthes (U.S.A.) v. G.M. Dos Reis Jr. Ind. Com. de Equip. Medico*, 563 F.3d 1285, 1294 (Fed. Cir. 2009). Because Syngenta's patent claims arise under federal laws, and W-Limited does not disagree, this requirement is satisfied.

Negation requirement. The second requirement under Rule 4(k)(2) is that the defendant must not be subject to personal jurisdiction in any individual state. *Merial*, 681 F.3d at 1294. This requirement is satisfied "if the defendant contends that he cannot be sued in the forum state and refuses to identify any other where suit is possible." *Id.* at 1294. Specifically, the burden is on the defendant to "identify [ ] . . . a forum where jurisdiction would have been proper at the time of filing, regardless of consent." *Id.*

Here, W-Limited has not identified another forum where suit is possible. While W-Limited identified Oregon as a potential alternate forum state,

W-Limited has not conceded that it is subject to personal jurisdiction there. W-Limited says only that personal jurisdiction "may" be available in Oregon.

When a plaintiff directly asserts Rule 4(k)(2) jurisdiction, as Syngenta has done here, this tepid response of "maybe" by a defendant is not enough. In *Merial*, the defendant consented to jurisdiction in another state while litigation was pending, and the Federal Circuit held this "*ex post* consent" was insufficient because jurisdiction in the new state would not have been proper at the time of filing. 681 F.3d at 1294. Here, W-Limited did not even fully concede jurisdiction. A defendant who seeks to avoid Rule 4(k)(2) by alluding to jurisdiction in another state, but not fully conceding jurisdiction there, is "playing jurisdiction hide-the-ball" and should not benefit. *See Snap-On Inc. v. Robert Bosch, LLC*, 2013 WL 5423844, at *6 (N.D. Ill. 2013). Because W-Limited has not affirmatively identified a state where personal jurisdiction is appropriate, and because W-Limited's own evidence shows that it has not purposely directed acts toward any state, the negation requirements means the exercise of jurisdiction via Rule 4(k)(2) is appropriate.

Due process as to United States as a whole. The third requirement asks whether the extension of personal jurisdiction to this defendant is compatible with due process. This uses the same test for personal jurisdiction described *supra* except it "contemplates a defendant's contacts with the entire United States, as opposed to the state in which the district court sits." *See Synthes*, 563 F.3d at 1295.

For specific jurisdiction under Rule 4(k)(2), Syngenta must show three things: that W-Limited has "purposefully directed [its] activities at residents of the forum," that the claim "results from alleged injuries that arise out of or relate to those activities," and that "the assertion of personal jurisdiction would comport with fair play and substantial justice." *Avocent*, 552 F.3d at 1330–31.

Here, taking all inferences in favor of the plaintiff, Syngenta has shown such purposefully directed activities. W-Limited created an affiliated company in the United States for the purpose of broadening its sales to the United States. This affiliation with W-USA was prominently displayed on W-Limited's website under the company's "News updates" heading. W-Limited described that affiliation as "its U.S. business" and "for . . . business opportunities in the U.S.," which shows a continuing intent to target the United States. By posting W-USA's contact information and links on its website, W-Limited sought to channel business opportunities in the United States to W-USA.

Mr. Mundhra's declaration establishes that W-Limited's management was aware that the azoxystrobin it sold to W-USA would later be sold in the United States, and W-USA did actually sell azoxystrobin products to the United States market.

These facts establish purposefully directed activities, regardless of the standard used. W-Limited "targeted" the United States under *Nicastro. See* 564 U.S. at 882. It conducted an "act . . . purposefully directed toward" the United States under *Asahi. See* 480 U.S. at 112. It sent azoxystrobin "through an established distribution channel" to the forum state under *Beverly Hills Fan. See* 21 F.3d at 1565. Because W-Limited established and used W-USA specifically as a distributor for sales to the United States market, and because it publicly announced and maintained that connection, it has purposefully directed activities at the United States sufficient for specific jurisdiction.

Syngenta's claims also arise out of or are related to those activities. As discussed *supra,* the claims attributable to W-Limited are the patent claims described in Counts I to IV of the complaint. Those claims allege "selling" and "importing" infringing products and inducing others to do the same. The purposeful activities of W-Limited towards the United States resulted in the creation of an affiliate, W-USA. That affiliate imported and sole the allegedly infringing azoxystrobin products in the United States.

In considering whether "fair play and substantial justice" supports jurisdiction, the Court considers "(1) the burden on the defendant, (2) the forum's interest in adjudicating the dispute, (3) the plaintiff's interest in obtaining convenient and effective relief, (4) the interstate judicial system's interest in obtaining the most efficient resolution of controversies, and (5) the shared interest of the states in furthering fundamental substantive policies." *Touchcom*, 574 F.3d at 1417.

Defending a case in the United States will be a burden on W-Limited, which is halfway around the world. Nonetheless, "progress in communications and transportation has made the defense of a suit in a foreign tribunal less burdensome," *World-Wide Volkswagen Corp. v. Woodson*, 444 U.S. 286, 294 (1980), and that progress is even more evident today than when *World-Wide* was decided. Documents can be sent electronically, depositions can be taken by videoconferencing, and communication is less expensive and virtually instantaneous with email, texts, and modern phones. Syngenta, the alleged injured party, is based in the United States and the alleged injury is here. The courts of this country have "a substantial interest in enforcing the federal patent laws." *Synthes*, 563 F.3d at 1299. No one has identified another forum for Syngenta to enforce its rights or any reason this Court cannot efficiently determine the issues. Finally, the United States has a strong interest in preventing a foreign entity from evading patent laws and prematurely exploiting a patent-holder's rights, as alleged here.

W-Limited chose to direct the allegedly infringing product to the United States market by selling to an affiliate formed explicitly for that purpose. Thus, W-Limited purposefully directed its activities to citizens in the United States. No individual state would have personal jurisdiction over W-Limited for these patent claims, and the exercise of personal jurisdiction over W-Limited for patent infringement arising out of the sale of those products is fair and in the interest of justice. Jurisdiction is appropriate under Rule 4(k)(2).

Conclusion

Syngenta has not established that Willowood Limited has the minimum contacts with North Carolina necessary for this Court to exercise personal jurisdiction. However, Syngenta has shown that personal jurisdiction is appropriate under Fed. R. Civ. P. 4(k)(2). The motion to dismiss will be denied.

COMMENTS AND QUESTIONS

1. Why would plaintiff's counsel make the personal jurisdiction argument even harder to win by suing in North Carolina rather than in Oregon?

2. What policy justifies the prerequisite of Rule 4(k)(2)(A) that the plaintiff must demonstrate that "the defendant is not subject to jurisdiction in any state[ ]"?

3. What did defense counsel hope to achieve by conceding only that it "may be" subject to jurisdiction in Oregon?

4. The majority of cases that cite Federal Rule 4(k)(2) involve intellectual property or maritime claims.

A Concluding Note on Pendent Personal Jurisdiction

Of the nine possible bases for establishing personal jurisdiction, five include some attention to the plaintiff's cause of action.

In order to establish **specific jurisdiction** over a defendant, the claim must arise out of the defendant's contacts with the forum state.

A defendant may **consent** to personal jurisdiction, but the scope of the forum selection clause must include the plaintiff's claim.

Personal jurisdiction may be obtained through the **status exception**, but the plaintiff's claim must seek a determination of status.

A **federal statute** can create personal jurisdiction under Rule 4(k)(1) (C), but the plaintiff's claim must arise under that statutory regime.

A **federal question claim against a foreign defendant** can create personal jurisdiction under Rule 4(k)(2), but the plaintiff's claim must raise a federal question.

By contrast, the other four bases for establishing personal jurisdiction are indifferent to the plaintiff's claim.[25]

When the nature of the plaintiff's claim is an essential component of the personal jurisdiction analysis we must anticipate situations where the plaintiff has joined causes of action that satisfy the test for personal jurisdiction with causes of action that do not. Take specific jurisdiction, for example. A plaintiff with a cause of action for patent infringement could obtain personal jurisdiction over a defendant, provided the plaintiff's cause of action arose out of the defendant's contacts with the forum state. But what if this plaintiff added a breach of contract claim against the same defendant that did not arise out of the defendant's contacts with the forum state?

In the interest of efficiency, the avoidance of piecemeal and potentially-inconsistent litigation outcomes, and the overall convenience of the parties, courts have developed the concept of pendent personal jurisdiction. As a general rule, courts allow plaintiffs to append additional claims, provided that the pendent claims arise out of the same basic factual predicate. In the above example, the breach of

---

25   If the defendant is "at home" in the forum state, **general jurisdiction** exists. If the defendant is **personally served** in the forum state, the courts of that state have personal jurisdiction. If the defendant fails to properly object to the court's lack of personal jurisdiction, **waiver** establishes it. A Rule 14 or Rule 19 party who is served within the **100-mile bulge** area is subject to personal jurisdiction.

contract (pendent) claim could be more or less *related* to the patent infringement claim. The more related the pendent claim, the more obvious it is that it should be permitted to tag along with the claim that established personal jurisdiction in the forum state. Borrowing from the terminology of pendent *subject matter* jurisdiction, courts sometimes ask whether the claims arise out of "a common nucleus of operative facts."[26]

Of course pendent personal jurisdiction is unavailable when personal jurisdiction is obtained through the status exception. Claims that seek something other than a determination of status require an independent basis for personal jurisdiction.

The doctrine of pendent personal jurisdiction is a creature only of common law, and the Supreme Court has not defined its contours in the myriad circumstances that arise in litigation. The exercise of pendent personal jurisdiction is always discretionary.[27] Accordingly, and especially when the pendent claim is unrelated to the claim that established personal jurisdiction, defense counsel can argue to the court that the plaintiff's causes of action should be analyzed separately for purposes of personal jurisdiction.

SAMPLE EXAM QUESTIONS

Question 20-11

Plaintiff Phyllis Plotz (Plotz) is a U.S. citizen who is domiciled in Oregon. Defendant Drone Manufacturing, Inc. (Drone) is incorporated in Delaware and has its principal place of business in Arlington, Virginia. Drone designs, manufactures, and sells drones. A drone is an unmanned airplane that can be navigated remotely.

Defendant Distant Shores Photos, Inc. (DS Photos) is incorporated in California and has its principal place of business in San Francisco, California. DS Photos is a business that uses drones to photograph luxury yachts off of the coast of California. DS Photos charges between $5,000 and $10,000 for a high definition video of owners piloting their boats on ocean waves.

---

26 *United Mine Workers of America v. Gibbs*, 383 U.S. 715, 725 (1966) (allowing pendent subject matter jurisdiction over a state-law cause of action when the state and federal claims arise from a "common nucleus of operative fact").

27 *See, e.g., Action Embroidery Corp. v. Atlantic Embroidery, Inc.*, 368 F.3d 1174, 1181 (9th Cir. 2004) (court has discretion to dismiss the pendent claims "where considerations of judicial economy, convenience and fairness to litigants so dictate").

Plotz was seriously injured last November 30th, when a Model S-3 drone manufactured and sold by Drone, and owned and operated by DS Photos, struck her in the head, neck, and shoulders while she was gardening in her backyard in Oregon. On the date of the accident, the yacht being photographed by the DS Photos' drone was owned and operated by California resident Brian Wall, who paid DS Photos $8,000 for the video service.

The Wall yacht was approximately 40 miles off the California coast when the drone failed to respond to the instruction of its pilot, and inexplicably veered north, traveling 200 miles toward the California/Oregon state border, and then another 50 miles into Oregon, until it either ran out of gas or, for some other reason, plummeted from the sky and struck Plotz. The drone was launched from the California coast and was operated by a DS Photos employee in California.

As a result of multiple injuries caused by defendants, Plotz has suffered $3,000,000 in damages through medical bills, lost wages, and pain and suffering. Plotz's lawyer is preparing to file suit in a Oregon federal court, seeking damages against Drone for defective design and against DS Photos for negligence.

Drone, one of the world's major drone manufacturers, is incorporated in Delaware, and has its corporate headquarters in Virginia. It has manufacturing facilities in only two states: about 80% of its drones are manufactured in Oregon, and the rest in Texas. All of the drones that are manufactured in Oregon are manufactured for sale to the United States government for military purposes. All of the drones that are manufactured in Texas, including the Model S-3, are manufactured for commercial or personal use. Prior to January 2016, and starting in May 2006, Drone was a manufacturer of ordinary airplanes. At that time, its headquarters and all of its manufacturing were located in Oregon.

But in 2016, Drone became a major defense contractor, focusing exclusively on drones; it then changed its name from Ace Aircraft, Inc. to Drone Manufacturing, Inc., and moved its corporate headquarters to Virginia. The Chief Financial Officer of Drone, however, stayed in Oregon and still lives there. Drone made substantial changes to its Oregon manufacturing facility to comply with security mandates required by the U.S. Department of Defense.

To facilitate the design, manufacture, and sale of drones to the public, Drone then opened the new facility in Texas. The drone in question was sold in Texas to DS Photos for $40,000. Drone has hundreds of millions of dollars of profits each year, with about 80% of those profits derived from its military drones in Oregon. Drone has savings accounts with more than $5,000,000 cash in Oregon banks. In addition to the manufacturing facilities, Drone also owns a large building in Oregon that it operates as a showroom for military drones.

Since 2016, a forum selection clause in all of Drone's sales contracts provides that "In any dispute or action arising out of or related to this transaction, the parties agree that the courts of Virginia shall be the exclusive forum for litigation

Do Oregon courts have personal jurisdiction over Drone and/or DS Photos?

Question 20-12

Dafoe is a social activist who grew up in Princeton, New Jersey. Just over a year and a half ago, Princeton's law school hosted a prominent intellectual property conference for the country's leading law professors of patent law. Neither a lawyer nor a law student, the then-twenty-six-year-old Dafoe attended this conference with the sole purpose of making a point about the sexism that inheres in American intellectual property law. During one of the question and answer sessions, he entered the room and made his point: he told the audience that it was unfair and sexist that creative people in traditionally female fields have long been denied patents for their inventions. His 90-second remarks included the following: "Think about it. Software code is patentable. But recipes are not. That's called sexism, you morons. You might be good law students but you don't know anything about the real world because you're trapped in here reading your expensive books. Make a difference! Think consciously about what are American values."

Dafoe made these comments at the conference wearing a very memorable and distinctive costume. Essentially, it was a homemade mini-dress that was made from the front covers of two dozen cookbooks that were pieced and sewn together like a puzzle.

Although neither Princeton nor the media was broadcasting or taping the conference, several of the law professors in attendance from other schools were tweeting and otherwise sharing various details about the conference on the internet. Dafoe's protest got their attention, and comments and pictures circulated quickly. One picture that got the most traction showed Dafoe defiantly pointing his finger at the audience, with the cover of one cookbook in particular prominently displayed around his neck. The cookbook in this picture of Dafoe that went viral is titled "The American Values Recipe Book" (hereafter, the "Cookbook"); it has the book's title and an American flag on its cover.

Dafoe's protest re-ignited a national conversation and debate about sexism in our society more generally. One consequence of this national conversation was a public boycott of the Cookbook. Indeed, on dozens of social media websites thousands of people denounced the Cookbook—some burned copies of the Cookbook that they long had owned; others mocked the Cookbook through songs and cartoons; many people publicly announced that they would never buy the Cookbook; the Cookbook became the butt of many jokes on late-night television shows. This ridicule and boycott of the Cookbook occurred even though the Cookbook (and its publisher) didn't really represent either position in the debate; indeed, both sides of the debate about sexism in society were mocking and urging their supporters to boycott the Cookbook.

Throughout the decade prior to the incident at Princeton Law, the Cookbook consistently generated profits of approximately $75,000 per year. As is true of most traditional cookbooks, the majority of the purchases were from people who lived along the East Coast of the United States (specifically, the northeastern, mid-Atlantic, and southeastern states). The Cookbook was/is authored, published, and sold by a company called Publication Inc. (Publication). Both the front and back covers of the Cookbook prominently indicate that its author and publisher is "Publication Inc.—Dallas, Texas." Publication is a company that was incorporated in Delaware in 1989. Since its founding, Publication's corporate headquarters have been in Dallas, Texas. Its warehouse and only property is also in Dallas. Since the incident at Princeton Law, the Cookbook has generated $0 in profits.

Dafoe's social activism has taken him around the country. Migrating to various points of social foment over the past 11 years since dropping out of Princeton High School, he has spent months at a time rotating between locations in Illinois, Massachusetts, Washington DC, Delaware, and far more than any of these other states: California. Essentially, wherever there is a significant protest regarding women's rights or income inequality in one of those states, he either is there or is hitchhiking his way there. His parents have continued to live in Princeton, and over the past 11 years, he has returned there briefly and reluctantly whenever he is out of money and has nowhere else to go.

Publisher filed a lawsuit again Dafoe in a Texas state court. The lawsuit claims that Dafoe intentional provoked the crowd at Princeton Law and that he deliberately drew negative and unwarranted attention to Publisher and the Cookbook. The complaint asserts only one cause of action: tortious interference with contractual relations. Publisher alleges that Dafoe knew and intended that customers would cancel purchases, return purchases, and discontinue efforts to purchase the Cookbook.

If Dafoe moves to dismiss the complaint for lack of personal jurisdiction, how likely is the court to grant that motion?

Question 20-13

DangerMyn is a triathlon race for male and female endurance athletes. This triathlon requires competitors to swim for 2.4 miles, then bike for 112 miles, and then run for 26.2 miles—all in a single day. The entry fee for these races is $750. DangerMyn selects a charity for each event and donates 10% of the entry fees to that charity. DangerMyn is a for-profit corporation with four full-time employees that is incorporated in Colorado and has its principal place of business in Las Vegas, Nevada. DangerMyn schedules races once every few months—with the host cities alternating between Las Vegas (NV) and Phoenix (AZ). DangerMyn used to schedule races at various sites around the country, including in Indianapolis (IN), Portland (OR), Denver (CO), Boston (MA), and Oakland (CA). But four years ago, DangerMyn's legal counsel advised the company to schedule races only in Las Vegas (NV) and Phoenix (AZ).

The DangerMyn races have become increasingly popular and have a distinctive brand. For example, DangerMyn sells t-shirts and gear—but only at its races and never online. Stories in two national triathlon magazines cover DangerMyn races extensively, and those magazines also regularly report the statistics of the top finishers of each race. DangerMyn also shares with these magazines (at no charge to the magazines) the exquisite photographs and professional video race footage that DangerMyn edits for its own website. On only a few occasions (though not recently), DangerMyn purchased ads in the two triathlon magazines; but all of these advertisement purchases were essentially favors by DangerMyn, which was simply buying the ads to financially support the magazines; DangerMyn's employees are friends with the folks in Los Angeles (CA), where the magazines are produced. DangerMyn does not need to advertise. Each race is limited to 1,000 competitors and, for the last three years, each race has sold out within hours of the opening of online registration. The races are expensive to host because DangerMyn has to hire dozens of contractors for each race: permits need to be secured to close all of the roadways; security needs to be hired to protect the competitors; guides are needed for participants and spectators; videographers and photographers need to be hired for marketing, etc. But the brand is now huge: DangerMyn makes at least $100,000 in profits with each race. There are other triathlon companies in this field (IronMan," for example), but DangerMyn is recognized as the most grueling and the most prestigious among them.

Last year, DangerMyn hosted one of its competitions in Las Vegas. Tragically, one of the competitors—Paula Pennsky—was struck by a car during her run and was killed. The driver of that car was Drake Driver, a drunk driver who smashed through a security barrier at the intersection of Grassley and Harkin Streets and struck Pennsky just six miles from the finish line. She was leading the race at the time of the accident. Competitors must finish the race within the 12-hour race window (6 a.m. to 6 p.m.), and this accident took place around 2:30 p.m.

Pennsky was a successful lawyer who had her own small practice, and was also a world-class endurance athlete. She lived with her family in Indiana and trained primarily in Colorado. She was an extremely likeable athlete whose success and personality played a big part in growing the popularity of triathlons generally and DangerMyn in particular. (She had elegant and prominent DangerMyn tattoos on her legs and her arms.) Because of her popularity among fans and fellow competitors, Pennsky hadn't filled out a registration form or paid an entry fee for many years; DangerMyn always invited her to participate in their races, assuring her by telephone that registration forms and payment of fees was unnecessary. Leading up to the Race, Pennsky had even suggested to DangerMyn that she might require an "appearance fee"—to be paid for her appearance at future events; DangerMyn indicated that they were open to that discussion.

For at least the past three years, the standard registration forms for Danger-Myn races have included a choice of law clause that provides "DangerMyn's liability hereunder shall be governed and construed under and in accordance with the laws of the state where the race is scheduled to take place." There is also a release clause for claims arising from negligence, stating: "In consideration for being permitted to participate in this event, I agree to release DangerMyn from any liability resulting from my participation in this event, regardless of the cause, including negligence on the part of DangerMyn." These clauses were added to the standard registration forms upon the advice of DangerMyn's counsel, who worried that liability under the laws of other states was too risky. Nothing else contained in the form or release is implicated here.

No one from Pennsky's family was present at the Race. However, Pennsky's surviving spouse filed suit against DangerMyn in the U.S. District Court for the Southern District of Indiana. The courthouse is in Indianapolis (IN), where Pennsky and her family resided.

Would this case survive a motion to dismiss for lack of personal jurisdiction?

Quick Summary

- The text describes nine bases for establishing personal jurisdiction over a defendant, any one of which will suffice

- The scope of general jurisdiction has been curtailed to establish jurisdiction only where the defendant is at home; an individual is at home in their state of domicile; the paradigmatic cases for general jurisdiction over a corporation are its state of incorporation and the state of its principal place of business

- The scope of specific jurisdiction has been curtailed to establish jurisdiction only where the cause of action arises out of the defendant's contacts with the state, the state's long-arm statute authorizes jurisdiction, the defendant has minimum contacts with the state, and the exercise of jurisdiction would not offend traditional notions of fair play and substantial justice

- Personal service can establish personal jurisdiction when an individual defendant is served in-hand within the forum state; most states recognize exceptions if the defendant's presence in the state is procured by force of by fraud and when the defendant is in the forum state to testify in an unrelated matter

- Defendants can waive their objection to lack of personal jurisdiction; failure to preserve the objection or the failure to pursue it may constitute waiver

- Courts routinely enforce forum selection clauses, which constitute a litigant's consent to personal jurisdiction in the selected state

- In cases involving only the determination of status (e.g., divorce), a court may have personal jurisdiction over a non-resident defendant who has no connection with the forum state

- Personal jurisdiction analysis is substantially the same whether the case is filed in federal or state court; in federal court, however, there are three additional bases that are not available in state court

- The 100-mile bulge rule allows federal courts to exercise personal jurisdiction over a Rule 14 or a Rule 19 defendant that is within 100 miles of the court

- Congressional statutes may authorize federal courts to issue nation- or world-wide service of process, thereby establishing personal jurisdiction over a defendant that has no connection with the forum state

- Federal courts with federal question jurisdiction have personal jurisdiction over foreign defendants who have minimum contacts with the United States as a whole; provided, however, that if the foreign defendant has minimum contacts with any one (or more) of the United States, then that Rule does not authorize personal jurisdiction

21

Venue Transfers and Forum Non Conveniens

Key Concepts

- Transfers: 28 U.S.C. §§ 1404 and 1406
- Dismissals: FRCP 12(b)(3) and *forum non conveniens*

In this Chapter we consider two doctrines that recognize judicial discretion to decline to hear a case even when the court has subject matter jurisdiction over the dispute and personal jurisdiction over the defendant(s). Rather than proceeding with the case and adjudicating the parties' rights and responsibilities, a judge might *transfer* the case to a more appropriate forum or she might *dismiss* (or *stay)* the case pursuant to the doctrine of forum non conveniens. We will focus in this chapter primarily on *federal* court practice and procedure with respect to venue transfers and forum non conveniens dismissals. Many state courts have analogues to these doctrines that more or less resemble their federal counterparts, but we address them only peripherally here.

The federal venue statute provides that a civil action may be brought in

(1) a judicial district in which the defendant resides, if all defendants are residents of the State in which the district is located;

(2) a judicial district in which a substantial part of the events or omissions giving rise to the claim occurred, or a substantial part of property that is the subject of the action is situated; or

(3) if there is no district in which an action may otherwise be brought as provided in this section, any judicial district in which any defendant is subject to the court's personal jurisdiction with respect to such action.[1]

---

[1] 28 U.S.C. § 1391(b)(1)-(3).

As a practical matter there is a fourth basis that is not enumerated in the statute: waiver. If a defendant fails to properly object to improper venue, venue is proper.[2]

This Chapter is about circumstances when venue is proper. When venue is <u>proper</u>, the court may proceed with the case or, under certain circumstances may transfer or dismiss it. But in an effort to minimize confusion, we remind you of what you probably learned in your Civil Procedure course about how courts handle a case where venue is <u>improper</u>. When venue is improper, a court has two options:

> *Transfer* the case to pursuant to 28 U.S.C. § 1406; or

> *Dismiss* the case pursuant to 12(b)(3).

Although we will also be focusing on "dismissals" and "transfers" in circumstances where venue is proper, those dismissals and transfers invoke different authorities and are governed by different standards.

Transfers

Even when venue is proper in a district, a federal judge has the authority to transfer the case to another district. Pursuant to Section 1404(a) of Title 28,

> For the convenience of parties and witnesses, in the interest of justice, a district court may transfer any civil action to any other district or division where it might have been brought or to any district or division to which all parties have consented.

Accordingly, a judge hearing a case in, say, Virginia, may transfer that case to Delaware. She might do so for any number of reasons, including because Delaware law applies and, in her estimation, the parties and justice would be better served by having a Delaware judge apply Delaware law. Similarly, the Virginia judge might transfer the case because a forum selection clause indicates that the parties agreed to litigate in Delaware.

There are several prerequisites to a transfer under 28 U.S.C. § 1404. First, the instant (the "transferor") forum must be a *federal* court. Although state courts have analogous statutory authority for intra-state transfers (between counties, for example), a state court cannot transfer a case to another state.[3] Second, Section

---

2   *See* Fed. R. Civ. P. 12(b)(3) and 12(h)(1).

3   In 1991 the National Conference of Commissions on Uniform State Laws crafted the Uniform Transfer of Litigation Act which would facilitate the transfer of cases between state courts. No state has adopted the model law. In complex litigation matters, Congress has expanded the scope of federal subject matter jurisdiction to facilitate the consolidation of related cases that would otherwise be litigated in multiple state courts. *See, e.g.,* Multiparty,

1404 authorizes transfers only to other federal district courts; in other words, both the transferor and the transferee courts must be federal district courts. Third, the transferee court must be a court where the action could originally have been filed (or is a forum to which the parties now consent); this means that the transferee court must have subject matter jurisdiction, personal jurisdiction, and be a proper venue.

When all three of those conditions are satisfied, the judge will consider the wisdom of a transfer. Judges have broad discretion. Factors that influence that decision are sometimes characterized as clusters of "public" and "private" interest. Factors relating to the parties' private interests include:

> relative ease of access to sources of proof; availability of compulsory process for attendance of unwilling, and the cost of obtaining attendance of willing, witnesses; possibility of viewing of premises, if viewing would be appropriate to the action; and all other practical problems that make trial of a case easy, expeditious and inexpensive.[4]

Public interest factors, in turn, include:

> the administrative difficulties flowing from court congestion; the local interest in having localized controversies decided at home; and the interest in having the trial of a diversity case in a forum that is at home with the law.[5]

Any combination of factors can move the court to transfer the case. Occasionally a plaintiff files her case in a jurisdiction where venue is technically proper, yet there is a more obvious (or "natural") forum where the litigation could occur.

> **Example:** Judith Moran, a Massachusetts native, suffered severe injuries as a result of ingesting Soutshora, a pharmaceutical drug that was prescribed by her treating physician in Massachusetts. In a federal district court in Delaware, Moran filed a negligence and products liability action against Eli Lilly & Co., the drug's manufacturer. Eli Lilly is a Delaware corporation with a principal place of business in Indianapolis, Indiana.
>
> The Delaware federal court is a proper forum to the extent that (1) the court's subject matter jurisdiction is founded in diversity (28 U.S.C.

Multiforum Trial Jurisdiction Act, 28 U.S.C. § 1369; Class Action Fairness Act, 28 U.S.C. § 1332(d).

4   *Piper Aircraft Co. v. Reyno*, 454 U.S. 235, 241 n.6 (1981).

5   *Id.*

§ 1332); (2) courts of the state of Delaware have personal jurisdiction because the defendant, which is incorporated there, is "at home" and therefore subject to general jurisdiction; and (3) the District of Delaware is a proper venue under 28 U.S.C. § 1391(b)(1) and 1391(c)(2).

Transfer may be appropriate, however, in light of the fact that, presumably, none of the relevant events occurred in Delaware, none of the witnesses live in Delaware, none of the evidence is located in Delaware, and Delaware law is unlikely to apply. Whether the court would be more likely to transfer to Indiana or, instead, to Massachusetts could turn on where the witnesses and evidence are located.[6]

The most common explanation for a transfer is that the witnesses and documentary evidence are located in another district. But because this is a Conflict of Laws course, we home in two other possible triggers: (1) pursuant to the forum state's choice of law methodology, the court is obliged to apply another jurisdiction's substantive law (*see* Chapters 4–9); and/or (2) a forum selection clause identifies some other jurisdiction as the designated forum (*see* Chapter 20).

The mere fact that another state's law applies is usually not alone sufficient to initiate a transfer. This factor can be dispositive when the case raises complex or novel questions about the other state's law. But for more ordinary applications of another state's law, there is only a modest advantage in having the court in the other state apply that state's law. In combination with other factors, of course, the prudence of (and preference for) allowing a local court to determine local law could justify a transfer.

Importantly, when a federal district court transfers a case pursuant to 28 U.S.C. § 1404, the transferee court applies the substantive law that would have applied if the case had stayed in the transferor court. This is sometimes referred to as the "plaintiff's venue privilege."[7] In other words, if the Delaware federal district judge in the above example transferred Moran's product liability action against Eli Lilly to a federal district court in Indiana, the Indiana court must apply the same substantive law that the Delaware would have applied. Imagine that Delaware's choice of law methodology required, in tort cases, application of the law of the place of injury, to-wit: Massachusetts. Accordingly, upon transfer under 28 U.S.C. § 1404, the Indiana federal court must likewise apply the substantive law of Massachusetts.

---

6   With respect to the prospect of a transfer to a Massachusetts federal district court, remember that the transferee court must be a court where the action could originally have been filed. Would courts in Massachusetts have personal jurisdiction over Eli Lilly?

7   *Van Dusen v. Barrack*, 376 U.S. 612, 635 (1964). As discussed later in this chapter, plaintiffs may not enjoy this privilege when the transfer is occasioned by a forum selection clause.

The Indiana federal court must apply Massachusetts substantive law under these circumstances even if, under Indiana's choice of law methodology, Indiana or some other state's substantive law would apply.

A second common trigger for a transfer under 28 U.S.C. § 1404 is a choice of forum clause that identifies some other state as the parties' contractually-negotiated situs of litigation. When a forum selection clause designates an alternative forum (that satisfies the three conditions above), judges have a near obligation to transfer.

> In the typical case not involving a forum-selection clause, a district court considering a § 1404(a) motion . . . must evaluate both the convenience of the parties and various public-interest considerations. Ordinarily, the district court would weigh the relevant factors and decide whether, on balance, a transfer would serve "the convenience of parties and witnesses" and otherwise promote "the interest of justice." § 1404(a).

> The calculus changes, however, when the parties' contract contains a valid forum-selection clause, which "represents the parties agreement as to the most proper forum" *Stewart Org., Inc. v. Ricoh Corp.*, 487 U.S. 22, 31 (1992). The "enforcement of valid forum-selection clauses, bargained for by the parties, protects their legitimate expectations and furthers vital interests of the justice system." *Id.* at 33 (Kennedy, J., concurring). For that reason, and because the overarching consideration under § 1404(a) is whether a transfer would promote "the interest of justice," "a valid forum-selection clause [should be] given controlling weight in all but the most exceptional cases." *Id.* at 33. The presence of a valid forum-selection clause requires district courts to adjust their usual § 1404 analysis in three ways.

> First, the plaintiff's choice of forum merits no weight. Rather, as the party defying the forum-selection clause, the plaintiff bears the burden of establishing that transfer to the forum for which the parties bargained is unwarranted. Because plaintiffs are ordinarily allowed to select whatever forum they consider most advantageous (consistent with jurisdictional and venue limitations), we have termed their selection the "plaintiff's venue privilege." *Van Dusen v. Barrack*, 376 U.S. 612, 635 (1964). But when a plaintiff agrees by contract to bring suit only in a specified forum—presumably in exchange for other binding promises by the defendant—the plaintiff has effectively exercised its "venue privilege" before a dispute arises. Only that initial

choice deserves deference, and the plaintiff must bear the burden of showing why the court should not transfer the case to the forum to which the parties agreed.

Second, a court evaluating a defendant's § 1404(a) motion to transfer based on a forum-selection clause should not consider arguments about the parties' private interests. When parties agree to a forum-selection clause, they waive the right to challenge the preselected forum as inconvenient or less convenient for themselves or their witnesses, or for their pursuit of the litigation. A court accordingly must deem the private-interest factors to weigh entirely in favor of the preselected forum. . . . As a consequence, a district court may consider arguments about public-interest factors only. Because those factors will rarely defeat a transfer motion, the practical result is that forum-selection clauses should control except in unusual cases. . . .

Third, when a party bound by a forum-selection clause flouts its contractual obligation and files suit in a different forum, a § 1404(a) transfer of venue will not carry with it the original venue's choice-of-law rules—a factor that in some circumstances may affect public-interest considerations. *See Piper Aircraft Co. v. Reyno*, 454 U.S. 235, 241 n.6 (1981) (listing a court's familiarity with the "law that must govern the action" as a potential factor).

Atlantic Marine Const. Co. v. U.S. Dist. Court for Western Dist. of Texas, 571 U.S. 49, 62–65 (2013). Justice Alito wrote this opinion for a unanimous Court.

As the Court said in *Atlantic Marine*, it would certainly be an unusual case for the public interest factors to militate against a transfer. The better argument against a transfer, then, is to argue that the forum selection clause is unenforceable. (In *Atlantic Marine*, the Court presupposed a contractually valid forum selection clause.) These arguments, too, are hard to win, but one or some combination of the following are occasionally successful:

(1) The forum selection clause was the product of "fraud or overreaching." To prove fraud, a party must meet the high bar of showing an intent to mislead. Plaintiff must prove that the forum selection clause itself was procured by fraud—as opposed to the contract as a whole. The word *overreaching* suggests something less than fraud may suffice, but even contracts of adhesion among parties with a dramatic imbalance of bargaining power do not constitute over-

reaching. There must be some element of coercion, misrepresentation, or trickery.

(2) Enforcement of the forum selection clause would effectively deprive the plaintiff of her day in court. Sometimes a forum selection clause—in combination with a choice of law clause—would, as a practical matter, foreclose a meaningful remedy. A different and inferior remedy does not necessarily deprive the plaintiff of a remedy. But a profoundly different remedy—or no remedy at all—*could* be a reason to find the forum selection clause unreasonable and, therefore, unenforceable.

(3) Enforcement of the forum selection clause would contravene a strong public policy of the forum. Public policies explicitly relating to venue or procedural mechanisms that are favored under forum law and would be unavailable in the transferee forum are the most compelling policies. Remember that you don't need this argument if the public policy of the forum is embedded in a localizing statute that can trump a choice of law clause. (*See* Chapter 16.)

Hypothetical 21-1

Best Collegiate Marketing Inc. (BCM) is an Illinois corporation with a principal place of business in Carbondale, Illinois. Ultimate Universals Co. (UUC) is a Michigan corporation with a principal place of business in Ann Arbor, Michigan. BCM is a sales representative company for a number of products targeted at college students. BCM uses brand ambassadors and media campaigns on university and college campuses. UUC is a manufacturing company that produces various products, including liquid energy shots that are sold across the country.

UUC hired BCM, and the parties entered into a five-year marketing agreement (Agreement). In the Agreement, UUC contracted to pay BIM commissions monthly pursuant to a payment schedule that varied both by state and by type of seller (college bookstore, convenience store, discount store, etc.). In the Agreement, UUC also agreed to send BCM commission statements that displayed commission calculations and a list of invoices covered by the commission statement.

For six consecutive months, BCM claimed that the commissions it earned on products sold by Wal-Mart were not properly calculated by UUC. Wal-Mart's principal place of business is Bentonville, Arkansas. After six months of complaints, UUC unilaterally terminated the entire Agreement and refused even to communicate with BCM.

BCM filed suit against UUC in the U.S. District Court for the Western District of Arkansas. BCM alleges that UUC breached its agreement with BCM, breached the implied covenant of good faith and fair dealing, and violated the Arkansas Sales Representative Commission Act (ASRCA). UUC answered the complaint, denied all of BCM's allegations, asserted lack of jurisdiction, and moved to transfer the case to the U.S. District Court for the Eastern District of Michigan.

The Agreement contained the following clause:

> This Agreement shall be construed and governed in accordance with the laws of the State of Michigan and the federal laws of the United States applicable therein, without regard to principles of conflict of law, and any action arising out of this Agreement shall be brought either in a state court in Michigan or in the federal district court located in the Eastern District of Michigan.

Although admitting that the Agreement contains a forum selection clause, BCM contends that the forum selection clause is void due to the application of the ASRCA. The ASRCA imposes a number of requirements on sales contracts, including requirements about how sales commissions must be computed and paid. The statute creates a safe harbor for those who comply with the statute's requirements, but imposes severe adverse consequences for those who do not comply. Included among the statute's provisions is a statement that the mandate constitutes a fundamental public policy of the state that cannot be waived and should not be subordinated to the laws of another state. The ASRCA also provides that any contract establishing venue in another state is void.

How likely is the court to grant the defendant's motion to transfer?

––––––––––

Forum Non Conveniens Dismissals

A transfer under Section 1404(a) is not available if one (or more) of the three prerequisites identified above is (are) not satisfied. Accordingly, a state court judge cannot transfer a case to a court outside of her own state. And even a federal court judge cannot transfer a case to a *state* court, a court in some other country, or to an arbitral panel. In any of these circumstances, then, the alternative to transfer is *dismissal*. The common law doctrine of forum non conveniens is the doctrinal basis for dismissal.

The analytical framework for a dismissal on grounds of forum non conveniens tracks the analysis for transfers. In fact, the ellipsis in the first paragraph of the lengthy block quote from *Atlantic Marine* above indicates the removal of these words that appeared in parentheses in Justice Alito's opinion: "or a forum non conveniens motion." Accordingly, upon a motion to dismiss for forum non conveniens, the court will consider the public and private interest factors.

As with transfers, in circumstances where there is a forum selection clause selecting a foreign court (or arbitral forum), there is a strong preference for enforcement. It bears noting that the Court's embrace of forum selection clauses generally is a relatively recent and stunning jurisprudential turnabout. Prior to the 1970s, forum selection clauses were viewed very skeptically. Much like the Court's aversion to choice of law clauses (discussed in Chapter 9), forum selection clauses were viewed as interfering with the judicial function.

A discussion of modern jurisprudence on forum selection clause typically begins with *M/S Bremen v. Zapata Off-Shore Co.*[8] In this case, Zapata Off-Shore Company contracted with a German company, Unterweser Reederei, GmBH, to transport The Chaparal, Zapata's oil-drilling rig, from Louisiana to a location off the coast of Italy. During the tow, a severe storm in the Gulf of Mexico damaged the rig, causing its legs to break off. At Zapata's direction, Unterweser's deep-sea tug, The Bremen, towed the rig from international waters to Tampa Bay, Florida. The Texas oil company brought an admiralty suit in a Florida federal court seeking $3.5 million in damages against Unterweer for negligence and breach of contract. Relying on the forum-selection clause in their contract, the defendant moved to dismiss the suit. Both the trial court and, later, the Circuit Court instead sided with the Texas oil company, refusing to enforce a clause that would oust the courts of jurisdiction.

In its landmark decision, the Supreme Court (essentially) enforced the clause. Six key facts framed that decision:

(1) This transaction was "far from routine." It contemplated "the tow of [an oil-drilling rig, an] extremely costly piece of equipment," to a destination six thousand miles away.

---

8   407 U.S. 1 (1972).

(2) The contract was an "arm's-length [transaction] by experienced and sophisticated businessmen" with "equal . . . bargaining power."

(3) The contract was actually negotiated.

(4) This clause "was clearly a reasonable effort to bring vital certainty to this international transaction." The uncertainty was as remarkable as it was looming, and in this sense, the clause "was a vital part of the agreement."

(5) This clause "was clearly a reasonable effort . . . to provide a neutral forum experienced and capable in the resolution of admiralty litigation."

(6) The claim involved the breach of a private agreement.

In sum, then, for the (1) uncommon transaction (2) where commercial parties (3) freely negotiate a contract with a forum selection clause (4) where the clause resolves profound uncertainty about the situs of litigation that bedevils both parties, (5) their selection of a neutral arbiter (6) for the resolution of disputes about a private agreement should be respected.

The enforcement of forum selection clauses did not remain limited to these narrow circumstances. Through a series of decisions after *The Bremen*, the Court enforced forum selection clauses even in (1) routine transactions (2) involving customers and other vulnerable parties who (3) entered into contracts of adhesion (4) where the choice of forum had nothing to do with resolving uncertainty, (5) the drafter of the clause chose the forum, and (6) the claims concerned statutory rights. Thus in contemporary litigation, not one of the *The Bremen*'s six conditions is necessary to enforce a forum selection clause.

The consequences of a *dismissal* (per forum non conveniens) are potentially much more severe than a *transfer* (per 28 U.S.C. § 1404). When a case is transferred, the case file is sent to the transferee court and a new judge picks up the litigation where it left off in the transferor court. By contrast, when a case is dismissed, it is up to the plaintiff to initiate a new action. There are hurdles to filing a new action. Typically, this means hiring a new lawyer, paying another filing fee, navigating another set of procedural rules, repeating service of process, researching and invoking new substantive law, and dodging new defenses like statute of limitations. These hurdles are more pronounced if the new action must be filed in Denmark or Djibouti, rather than in Delaware.

Forum non conveniens dismissals thus raise specific concerns that transfers do not. Specifically, federal courts consider whether, if an action is dismissed, the plaintiff has an *adequate alternative forum.*

The alternative forum is inadequate if the defendant is not amenable to service or subject to jurisdiction there. To address this concern, a defendant seeking a forum non conveniens dismissal will typically waive service of process in the alternative forum. The judge dismissing the case on grounds of forum non conveniens may also condition the dismissal on the defendant's waiver of any jurisdiction objection.[9]

The alternative forum is also inadequate if it "would in substance provide 'no remedy at all.' "[10] The plaintiff bears an initial burden of producing some evidence of inadequacy (*e.g.,* corruption, delay, lack of basic due process), but the defendant bears the ultimate burden of persuasion as to the adequacy of the alternative forum. The alternative forum may be adequate even if the substantive law is different, the procedural law singular, the available remedies constrained, and the prospect and amount of plaintiff's recovery significantly inferior. In fact, the Supreme Court has said that the adequate alternative forum requirement will

> [o]rdinarily . . . be satisfied . . . [absent] rare circumstances . . . where the remedy offered in the other forum is clearly unsatisfactory. . . . Thus, for example, dismissal would not be appropriate where the alternative forum does not permit litigation of the subject matter of the dispute. *Cf. Phoenix Canada Oil Co., Ltd. v. Texaco, Inc.,* 78 F.R.D. 445 (Del 1978) (court refuses to dismiss, where alternative forum is Ecuador, it is unclear whether Ecuadorean tribunal will hear the case, and there is no generally codified Ecuadorean legal remedy for the unjust enrichment and tort claims asserted).

Piper Aircraft Co. v. Reyno, 454 U.S. 235, 254 n.22 (1981).

The conceit is that the plaintiff whose claim is dismissed for forum non conveniens will initiate a new action in the alternative forum. But, as a practical matter, a forum non conveniens dismissal is frequently outcome determinative. "The reality, on many occasions, is that the case will never be heard at all in the identified forum

---

9 Occasionally, a judge will stay the action rather than dismiss it. In either instance the plaintiff must pursue the case elsewhere if she seeks a remedy. But if the court issues a stay, the plaintiff might return to the forum if the alternative forum is profoundly inadequate—if, for example, the defendant challenges personal jurisdiction in the foreign forum after promising not to do so.

10 *In re Gen. Elec. Co.,* 271 S.W.3d 681, 685 (Tex. 2008) (quoting *Piper Aircraft Co. v. Reyno,* 454 U.S. 235, 254 (1981)).

conveniens, and a cheerful wave from the U.S. courtroom ends the action."[11] In this sense the analogue to a transfer is only ironic.

Many of the plaintiffs whose claims are dismissed for forum non conveniens are foreign-country plaintiffs suing American defendants (in American courts). In fact, one recent empirical study suggested that foreign plaintiffs are twice as likely to have their suits dismissed.[12] Courts take pains to emphasize that such dismissals are not based on a dislike of foreign nationals or their claims. Rather "the presumption in favor of [plaintiff's choice of forum applies] with less than maximum force when the plaintiff . . . [is] foreign."[13] Courts instead focus their inquiry on what is most convenient for the parties and the court.

This notion of foreign plaintiffs suing American defendants in American courts has led some foreign countries to discourage American courts from invoking forum non conveniens. By enacting a so-called *blocking statute* a foreign country mandates that when one of its citizens files suit in the United States, the non-U.S. forum relinquishes all jurisdiction. Accordingly, if Nigeria had a blocking statute, and a Nigerian initiated an action in the United States, the courts of Nigeria could no longer hear the case. Thus, when the defendant moved to dismiss the U.S. action on grounds of forum non conveniens, the American judge must deny it because the Nigerian courts would provide "no remedy at all" for that plaintiff.

Hypothetical 21-2

Louis Higgins died in the Bahamas eighteen months ago when the landing gear of an airplane that he was servicing at the Lynden Pindling International Airport in Nassau collapsed on him. Higgins is an American citizen who lived in the Bahamas and worked for the airport for the past twenty two years.

---

11   Alan Reed, *Venue Resolution and Forum Non Conveniens: Four Models of Jurisdictional Propriety*, 22 Transnat'l L. & Contemp. Probs. 369, 399 (2013) (citing Jacqueline Duval-Major, *One-Way Ticket Home: The Federal Doctrine of Forum Non Conveniens and the International Plaintiffs*, 77 Cornell L. Rev. 650, 671–72 (1982) (highlighting that the forum non conveniens dismissal constitutes "the end of the line for many foreign plaintiffs").) *See also* David W. Robertson, *Forum Non Conveniens in America and England: A Rather Fantastic Fiction*, 103 Law Q. Rev. 388, 418–19 (1987). Professor Robertson mailed surveys to the lawyers in 180 reported cases dismissed by federal courts and received 85 responses. Of these, eighteen plaintiffs abandoned further effort, in twelve cases the lawyer did not know what happened, and in three the lawyer had not yet decided on a next step. Thirty-six cases settled; of these, fifteen settled for less than 30% of their estimated value, seven settled for between 31% and 50% of their estimated value, nine settled for more than 50%, and five were for an unspecified amount. Ten cases were pending in a foreign court and three in a state court. Three cases had been lost in foreign courts, and none had been won in either a foreign or a state court. *Id.*

12   *See* Christopher A. Whytock, *The Evolving Forum Shopping System*, 96 Cornell L. Rev. 481, 502–03 (2011).

13   *Piper Aircraft Co. v. Reyno*, 454 U.S. 235, 236 (1981)

Last week, a lawyer for Higgins's estate filed suit in a Florida state court against Island Air Servicers, Inc. (Island Air) for its failure to maintain the aircraft properly which, in turn, caused the landing gear to collapse. Island Air, an airplane service and repair company, is incorporated in Texas and has its principal place of business in Fort Lauderdale, Florida. Island Air has assets, employees, and business partners at fourteen airports across the Bahamas.

You work for the law firm representing the plaintiff's estate. According to Emerson Freer's *Bahama Law in Nutshell* (2004), Bahamian courts recognize negligence actions like the plaintiff's. However, the statute of limitations probably is 12 months (18 months have elapsed) and total damage recovery may be capped at (US) $100,000.

The senior partner in your firm has asked you to prepare for what she characterizes as inevitable, to-wit: defendant's motion to transfer or to dismiss for forum non conveniens. (Focus your attention only on matters relevant to that motion.) The partner is meeting tomorrow with the decedent's brother, who also worked at the airport and who is the only known eyewitness to the accident. The partner has asked you for a list of questions that you would like her to ask this brother. She has also asked you to describe your research agenda.

––––––––––

Finally, although this is not an arbitration course, you should be aware that the Supreme Court treats an arbitration clause as a specialized type of forum selection clause. Courts are even *more* likely to enforce a clause requiring arbitration than one selecting a foreign court. This may seem counterintuitive in light of the fact that an arbitral forum is usually a private provider of dispute resolution services with less formality and transparency than the public courts of a foreign sovereign. But the Federal Arbitration Act (9 U.S.C. § 1 *et seq.*) embodies a federal policy favoring arbitration (and there is no analogous federal statute endorsing litigation in foreign courts). The Supreme Court has severely curtailed the grounds upon which a court can refuse to enforce an arbitration clause.[14] In the cases that follow, however, the forum selection clauses select courts, not arbitration.

---

14   *See generally AT&T Mobility LLC v. Concepcion*, 563 U.S. 333 (2011); *Marmet Health Care Ctr., Inc. v. Brown*, 565 U.S. 530 (2012); *Nitro-Lift Techs., L.L.C. v. Howard*, 568 U.S. 17 (2012); *Kindred Nursing Centers, Ltd. Partnership v. Clark*, ___ U.S. ___, 137 S. Ct. 1421 (2017). In *Mitsubishi Motors Corp. v. Soler Chrysler-Plymouth, Inc.*, 473 U.S. 614, 637 (1985), the Court stated that "in the event [an arbitration clause] and a choice of law clause operated in tandem as a prospective waiver of a party's right to pursue statutory remedies," the Court "would have little hesitation in condemning the [arbitration] agreement as against public policy." *See, e.g., Dillon v. BMO Harris Bank, N.A.*, 856 F.3d 330 (4th Cir. 2017) (invalidating an arbitration agreement).

FROM THE COURTS

COOPER v. SLICE TECHNOLOGIES, INC.

U.S. District Court for the Northern District of California
__ F.Supp.3d __, 2017 WL 4071373 (N.D. Cal. Sept. 14, 2017)

LAUREL BEELER, MAGISTRATE JUDGE.

This is a motion to transfer a class-action data-privacy lawsuit to the Southern District of New York under 28 U.S.C. § 1404(a) based on a forum selection clause. The plaintiffs signed up for UnrollMe's free web-based email-management service and claim that UnrollMe impermissibly scraped data, which its parent company Slice Technologies sold to third parties, in violation of federal and California statutes. Unroll Me requires users to agree to its Terms of Use as a precondition to creating an account. The Terms of Use include a forum-selection clause for federal or state courts in New York. The court grants the motion, enforces the forum-selection clause, and transfers the case to the Southern District of New York.

Statement

1. UnrollMe's Email-Management Service

UnrollMe is a free service for consumers to "purportedly rid their email inboxes of junk by using UnrollMe's 'email management' service to mass unsubscribe from spam messages and to group categories of emails into a single email digest that would be sent to the user daily." "In exchange, UnrollMe could display daily advertisements to the users via the digest and offer them new productivity products or services over time."

Slice Technologies bought UnrollMe in 2014. It is a data-mining company. UnrollMe then began selling access to data from its "unwitting users' email accounts," and Slice Technologies sells the data to third parties. For example, Slice Technologies sold emails from users who used the Lyft ridesharing application to Lyft's competitor Uber. "UnrollMe does not adequately disclose its true business model" to users. Instead, UnrollMe disguises itself as an email-management service to mislead users to sign up for the service so that it (and Slice) can access their data. The plaintiffs acknowledge the disclosure about data collection in UnrollMe's Privacy Policy, but they contend that the disclosure is inconsistent with UnrollMe's representations that access to users' emails is to manage spam and advertisements to achieve "a cleaner inbox." For this reason, the plaintiffs claim that the defendants' access to their emails for data scraping exceeded the scope of their permissions.

2. UnrollMe's Registration Process and the Forum-Selection Clause

Users—including the named plaintiffs—create a free account by registering with a valid email address and expressly assenting to UnrollMe's Terms of Use.

During the registration process, the plaintiffs "[were] presented with a screen with a box next to the statement 'I agree to the <u>terms</u> and the <u>privacy policy</u>.' " UnrollMe embedded hyperlinks to the Terms of Use and Privacy Policy in that statement. Users had to "check the box next to the statement 'I agree to the terms and the privacy policy' to enable the 'Continue' button and be able to create an account.". . .

A user cannot register for UnrollMe without (1) checking the box next to "I agree to the terms and privacy policy" to affirm assent to the Terms of Use and Privacy Policy and (2) separately clicking the "Continue" button to complete the sign-up process. [The plaintiffs] Ms. Parikh and Mr. Cooper both completed this process.

The Terms of Use have the following forum-selection clause:

> The laws of New York, U.S.A., excluding New York's conflict of laws rules, will apply to any disputes arising out of or relating to these terms or the Website. All claims arising out of or relating to these terms or the Website will be litigated exclusively in the federal or state courts of New York, New York, USA, and you and we consent to personal jurisdiction in those courts.

3. The Plaintiffs' Lawsuit Against UnrollMe and Slice Technologies

The two named plaintiffs are Jason Cooper (from Michigan) and Meghan Parikh (from California). They assert federal claims on behalf of themselves and national classes for violations of (1) the Electronic Communications Privacy Act ("ECPA"), 28 U.S.C. § 2510 et seq., for the defendants' alleged interception of their communications and (2) the Stored Communications Act ("SCA"), 18 U.S.C. § 2701 et seq., for the defendants' alleged accessing of their stored communications. Ms. Parikh asserts a California claim on behalf of herself and a California subclass for a violation of California's Invasion of Privacy Act, Cal. Penal Code § 630 et seq. Both plaintiffs allege

state-law claims on behalf of themselves and national classes for unjust
enrichment and violations of privacy based on intrusion.

Governing Law

A defendant may file a motion under 28 U.S.C. § 1404(a) to enforce a
forum-selection clause and transfer the case to the contractually agreed-upon
forum. *Atlantic Marine Const. Co. v. U.S. Dist. Court for the W. Dist. of Tex.*,
134 S. Ct. 568, 580 (2013). "Section 1404(a) is merely a codification of the
doctrine of *forum non conveniens* for the subset of cases in which the transferee forum is within the federal court system. . . ." *Id.* at 580. The analyses
under § 1404(a) and *forum non conveniens* are substantively identical. *See
id.* ("Section 1404(a) 'did not change "the relevant factors" which federal
courts used to consider under the doctrine of *forum non conveniens*. . . .' ")
(quoting *Stewart Org., Inc. v. Ricoh Corp.*, 487 U.S. 22, 37 (1988) (Scalia,
J., dissenting)).

Normally, *forum non conveniens* analysis requires the court to evaluate the
parties' "private interests," along with "public-interest considerations," and
to decide whether, "on balance," sending the case to a new venue would
serve "the convenience of parties and witnesses" and otherwise promote
"the interest of justice." *Atlantic Marine*, 134 S. Ct. at 579, 581 (citing
§ 1404(a)). "The calculus changes, however," when transfer is sought under
a "valid forum-selection clause." *Id.* at 581. In such a case, the court "should
not consider arguments about the parties' private interests." *Id.* at 582. The
Supreme Court has held:

> When parties agree to a forum-selection clause, they waive the
> right to challenge the preselected forum as inconvenient or less
> convenient for themselves or their witnesses, or for their pursuit
> of the litigation. A court accordingly must deem the private-in-
> terest factors to weigh entirely in favor of the preselected forum.

Id. "As a consequence, a district court may consider arguments about public-
interest factors only." Id. There are five public-interest factors considered by
courts in this circuit:

> (1) Local interest in the lawsuit; (2) the court's familiarity with
> the governing law; (3) the burden on local courts and juries; (4)
> congestion in the court; and (5) the costs of resolving a dispute
> unrelated to a particular forum.

Bridgemans Serv. Ltd. v. George Hancock, Inc., 2015 WL 4724567, at *4 (W.D. Wash. Aug. 7, 2015) (citing *Boston Telecomm. Group v. Wood*, 588 F.3d 1201, 1211 (9th Cir. 2009)). The Supreme Court has identified essentially the same set of public interests. *See Atlantic Marine*, 134 S. Ct. at 581 n.6. . . .

"The party challenging a valid forum selection clause must show that the public interest factors 'overwhelmingly disfavor' enforcement. . . ." *Bridgemans*, 2015 WL 4724567, at *4 (quoting *Atlantic Marine*, 134 S. CT. at 583). "A proper application of § 1404(a) requires that a forum selection clause be given controlling weight in all but the most exceptional cases." *Atlantic Marine*, 134 S. Ct. at 579; *see id.* at 575, 581 (When a party moves to enforce such a clause, "a district court should transfer the case unless extraordinary circumstances unrelated to the convenience of the parties clearly disfavor a transfer."). . . .

"The Ninth Circuit has identified three 'compelling' reasons that would permit a court to disregard a forum selection clause. . . ." *Premiere Radio Networks, Inc. v. Hillshire Brands Co.*, 2013 WL 5944051, at *2 (C.D. Cal. Nov. 4, 2013) (citing *Murphy*, 362 F.3d at 1140). These reasons are:

(1) its incorporation into the contract was the result of fraud, undue influence, or overweening bargaining power;

(2) the selected forum is so inconvenient that the complaining party will be practically deprived of its day in court; or

(3) enforcement of the clause would contravene a strong public policy of the forum in which the suit is brought.

Bridgemans, 2015 WL 4724567, at *2. These departures from presumed validity are "construed narrowly." *Argueta v. Banco Mexicano, S.A.*, 87 F.3d 320, 325 (9th Cir. 1996). "Public policy," moreover, "strongly favors the enforcement of forum selection clauses." *Koken v. Stateco Inc.*, 2006 WL 2918050, at *8 (N.D. Cal. Oct. 11, 2006). "The party challenging the clause [thus] bears a 'heavy burden of proof' and must 'clearly show that enforcement would be unreasonable and unjust, or that the clause was invalid for such reasons as fraud or over-reaching.' " *Murphy*, 362 F.3d at 1140; *accord, e.g., Manetti-Farrow, Inc. v. Gucci Am., Inc.*, 858 F.2d 509, 514 (9th Cir. 1988) ("Forum selection clauses are *prima facie* valid, and are enforceable absent a strong showing by the party opposing the clause. . . .").

Analysis

The plaintiffs do not dispute that they assented to UnrollMe's Terms of Use and its forum-selection clause. Instead they advance three arguments against transfer. First, they argue transfer is against California public policy because the choice-of-law provision selects New York law, New York has less robust privacy laws than California's Invasion of Privacy Act (with its statutory and actual treble damages), and transfer denies the California subclass the ability to pursue the California claim. Second, they argue the forum-selection clause is imbedded in an adhesion contract. Third, they assert that transfer is otherwise against the public-interest factors at play in the transfer/*forum non conveniens* analysis.

First, the forum-selection clause determines where the case is heard and is separate and distinct from choice-of-law provisions that are not before the court. "Courts in the Ninth Circuit have generally agreed that the choice-of-law analysis is irrelevant to determining if the enforcement of a forum selection clause contravenes a strong public policy." *Rowen v. Soundview Commc'n, Inc.*, 2015 WL 899294, at *4 (N.D. Cal. Mar. 2, 2015). The transferee court decides the choice-of-law issues.

The California plaintiff asserts that it is unlikely that a New York court will adjudicate the California statutory claim because, under New York's choice-of-law rules, it is significantly likely that the transferee court will apply New York substantive law based on UnrollMe's principal place of business in New York. (The plaintiff contends that the test is a reasonable-relationship test, meaning the court enforces a choice-of-law clause if the chosen law bears a reasonable relationship to the parties or the transaction.) The defendants counter with examples of district courts in New York adjudicating the California statutory claim on the merits.

The court is not convinced. The plaintiff's argument is speculative. Slice Technologies—the seller of the data—has its principal place of business in California. The remedies under the ECPA provide similar and maybe larger relief. In any event, the plaintiff's speculation about the transferee court's application of the choice-of-law rules does not meet the "heavy burden" of establishing that the forum-selection clause is unenforceable. The issue is for the transferee court.

Moreover, the California plaintiff has not established that having her case heard in New York contravenes a strong public policy of California. She cites *Doe 1 v. AOL LLC*, 552 F.3d 1077 (9th Cir. 2009) (per curiam). There, the Ninth Circuit held that AOL's subscription agreement, which required subscribers to file lawsuits in Virginia state court, violated public policy when it was applied to California residents who brought a class-action lawsuit under California consumer-protection laws. 552 F.3d at 1079–1080, 1083–84. Virginia did not allow consumer disputes to be tried as class actions, which foreclosed the lawsuit entirely. This violated California's strong public policy favoring consumer class actions and disallowing waiver of consumer remedies. *Id.* at 1083–84 & n.12. By contrast, there is no foreclosure of remedies here given the overlapping federal and state violations (including a claim under N.Y. Gen. Bus. Law § 349).

Second, the plaintiffs' unequal bargaining power does not render the forum-selection clause unenforceable. Unequal bargaining power is routine in form contracts. *Carnival Cruise Lines, Inc. v. Shute*, 499 U.S. 585, 593 (1991). The issue is whether a consumer has adequate notice. *Id.* at 590; *Tompkins v. 23andMe, Inc.*, 840 F.3d 1016, 1029 (9th Cir. 2016). The Ninth Circuit has enforced forum-selection clauses in online consumer contracts like the one here. *Tompkins*, 840 F.3d at 1020–21 (consumers could—but did not have to—click on a link to read the Terms of Service and had to click on a box agreeing to the Terms of Service). The plaintiffs do not charge fraud or overreaching. *Tompkins* drives the outcome here.

That brings us to the [transfer] analysis itself. This inquiry weighs the public-interest factors that the Supreme Court and the Ninth Circuit have identified: local interest in the lawsuit, familiarity with the governing law, burden on the courts, and costs. *See, e.g., Bridgemans*, 2015 WL 4724567, at *4; *Atlantic Marine*, 134 S. Ct. at 581–84. To block the transfer, the plaintiffs must show that these factors "overwhelmingly disfavor" enforcing the forum-selection clause. *Bridgemans*, 2015 WL 4724567, at *4. Public interest will "rarely defeat" a motion to enforce a forum-selection clause, however, so that the latter must be "given controlling weight in all but the most exceptional cases." *Bridgemans*, 2015 WL 4724567, at *4 ("rarely defeat"); *Atlantic Marine*, 134 S. Ct. at 579, 581 ("exceptional"). . . .

The public-interest factor here is California's interest in enforcement of its laws. As discussed above, it does not defeat the enforcement of the forum-selection clause. The claims are mostly federal, and the district court in New York is capable of applying California law. As for burdens on the court and costs, the court deems the factors neutral.

Ultimately, these public-interest factors do not "overwhelmingly disfavor" enforcing the forum-selection clause. *See Atlantic Marine*, 134 S. Ct. at 583. This is not a "rare[ ]" and "most exceptional" case in which the court should ignores such a clause. *See id.* at 579, 582. . . .

The court grants the defendants' motion to transfer and transfers the lawsuit to the Southern District of New York.

COMMENTS AND QUESTIONS

1. Customers who purchased or received a product or service subject to certain terms (including choice of law and choice of forum clauses) are not especially sympathetic when they later try to escape those terms of service. After all, if the customer didn't want the product subject to those terms, she should have purchased or used somebody else's product. But what result in a case where the defendant is the *only* provider of the service or product, and that service or product is *essential*? (*E.g.,* the electric company, an employer in a specialized field.)

2. Some courts are rather dogmatic about refusing to consider the law that the putative transferee court would apply as part of the decisional calculus for determining whether transfer is appropriate. If the standard for transfer under 28 U.S.C. § 1404 is the "interest of justice," how could any issue be off limits?

From the courts

JIANGSU HONGYUAN PHARM. CO., LTD. v. DI GLOBAL LOGISTICS INC.

U.S. District Court for the Southern District of Florida
159 F.Supp.3d 1316 (S.D. Fla. 2016)

Darrin P. Gayles, District Judge.

This cause comes before the Court on Defendant DI Global Logistics, Inc.'s ("DI Global") Motion to Dismiss Plaintiff's First Amended Complaint. This case concerns the scope and effect of a forum selection clause designating China, contained in a contract between a Florida corporation and a Chinese company (drafted by the Chinese company), on a forum non conveniens analysis. The Plaintiff, Jiangu Hongyuan Pharmaceutical Co., Ltd. ("Hongyuan"), has brought both contractual and noncontractual claims against DI Global, alleging that DI Global has failed to remit payment for shipments of chemical products. DI Global has moved to dismiss the action, inter alia, under the doctrine of forum non conveniens, arguing that the forum selection clause mandates that this dispute be resolved in China.

This Court has reviewed the pleadings, the briefs, the record, and the applicable law, and has considered the arguments advanced by counsel at two different hearings on the motion. For the reasons that follow, the motion to dismiss shall be granted.

I. Background

Plaintiff Hongyuan is a company registered to do business in China. Defendant DI Global is a Florida corporation. In or around April or May 2013, Hongyuan and DI Global executed an Agency Agreement (the "Agreement"), originally drafted by Hongyuan, through which Hongyuan—for a term of five years—granted DI Global exclusive rights to sell its chemical products in a territory designated as Colombia, Trinidad & Tobago, Brazil, Venezuela, and the United States. The Agreement also granted DI Global "all exclusive rights and power of attorney to connect, communicate, negotiate and finalize import and distribution contracts with all private and public establishments" in the prescribed territory. Hongyuan agreed not to sell its products directly to any customers in that territory or indirectly through any brokers or resellers inside or outside the territory. Hongyuan also granted DI Global the right to sell its products to customers outside the territory who buy those products for use in production of a finished product that is marketed and sold inside the territory.

According to the Amended Complaint, DI Global requested that Hongyuan ship certain chemical products to it. Hongyuan alleges that, pursuant to that request, it remitted "Invoice Number 72" for the shipment of Titanium Dioxide Anatase 3100, seeking payment in the amount of $210,000.00. DI Global allegedly accepted the invoice but did not pay it in full. Hongyuan states that it has repeatedly demanded payment from DI Global, but that

DI Global has refused to pay the amount due and has "default[ed] under the terms of the sales purchase agreement."

On June 26, 2015, [plaintiff] filed a three-count complaint against DI Global, alleging claims for breach of contract, account stated, and unjust enrichment. . . . DI Global filed a . . . motion to dismiss on August 17, 2015, pursuant to Fed. R. Civ. P. 12(b)(3), alleging improper venue, and 12(b)(6), alleging that the Amended Complaint fails to state a claim for which relief can be granted. In its reply, DI Global acknowledged that a Rule 12(b)(3) motion for improper venue was not the appropriate vehicle through which to move for dismissal and requested that the Court view its motion as a motion to dismiss under the doctrine of forum non conveniens. In support of the forum non conveniens argument, DI Global pointed to the text of Article 6 of the Agreement, titled "Governing Law," which provides:

> This agreement shall only be governed by Chinese law. In the event of any disputes between the parties the People's Court of Jiangsu (China) shall be empowered to take cognizance of it, unless coercive law prescribes another court.

DI Global contends that this language constitutes a forum selection clause that mandates that this action be heard in China. Hongyuan made no argument in its opposition against DI Global's forum non conveniens allegation, other than that "there is no legal or contractual obligation forcing Plaintiff to sue in China." . . .

II. Legal Standard

"Under the doctrine of forum non conveniens, a district court has the inherent power to decline to exercise jurisdiction even when venue is proper." *Vanderham v. Brookfield Asset Mgmt., Inc.*, 102 F.Supp.3d 1315, 1318 (S.D. Fla. 2015) (citing *Gulf Oil Corp. v. Gilbert*, 330 U.S. 501–506–07 (1947), *superseded by statute on other grounds as recognized in Am. Dredging Co. v. Miller*, 510 U.S. 443 (1994)). Although a court may consider matters outside the pleadings in ruling on a motion to dismiss based on forum non conveniens, it "must draw all reasonable inferences and resolve all factual conflicts in favor of the plaintiff." *Id.* (quoting *Wai v. Rainbow Holdings*, 315 F.Supp.2d 1261, 1268 (S.D. Fla. 2004)). To obtain dismissal for forum non conveniens, the moving party must demonstrate that (1) the public and private factors weigh in favor of dismissal, (2) an adequate alternative forum is available, and (3) the plaintiff can reinstate his suit in the alternative forum without undue inconvenience or prejudice. *GDG Acquisitions, LLC v. Government of Belize*, 749 F.3d 1024, 1028 (11th Cir. 2014).

III. Discussion

A. Viability of the Forum Selection Clause

DI Global, relying on the premise that the language in Article 6 of the Agreement constitutes a valid forum selection clause, argues that this case should be dismissed on forum non conveniens grounds. Before the Court can proceed to the forum non conveniens analysis, however, it must determine whether Article 6 contains a valid, enforceable, and mandatory forum selection clause, as well as whether that clause applies to the dispute in this case.

1. Validity and Enforceability

Forum selection clauses contained in international contracts are presumptively valid and enforceable. *M/S Bremen v. Zapata Off-Shore Co.*, 407 U.S. 1 (1972). Under *Bremen*, forum selection clauses in international contracts will be found *un*enforceable "only when: (1) their formation was induced by fraud or overreaching; (2) the plaintiff effectively would be deprived of its day in court because of the inconvenience or unfairness of the chosen forum; (3) the fundamental unfairness of the chosen law would deprive the plaintiff of a remedy; or (4) enforcement of such provisions would contravene a strong public policy." *Lipcon v. Underwriters at Lloyd's, London*, 148 F.3d 1285, 1292 (11th Cir. 1998).[2]

DI Global argues that the forum selection clause in Article 6 withstands all four Bremen exceptions. Given that "[f]or each category, the complaining party bears a heavy burden of demonstrating unreasonableness," *Davis v. Avvo, Inc.*, No. 10–2352, 2011 WL 4063282, at *2 (M.D. Fla. Sept. 13, 2011) (citing *Carnival Cruise Lines, Inc. v. Shute*, 499 U.S. 585, 592 (1991)), and that Hongyuan has advanced no argument on any category, the Court agrees. First, the Agreement was not induced by fraud or overreaching because it was drafted by Hongyuan. Second, Hongyuan will not be deprived of its day in court due to any alleged inconvenience or unfairness because

---

2   The Agreement and underlying transactions here are "'truly' and 'fundamentally' international," and thus the *Bremen* analysis applies. *Liles v. Ginn-Law W. End, Ltd.*, 631 F.2d 1242, 1246 (11th Cir. 2011). Hongyuan, the seller, is a Chinese company; DI Global, the buyer, is a Florida corporation whose president is a Venezuelan resident; and, "perhaps most importantly," the subject matter of the Agreement concerns the sale of chemicals to third parties located in Colombia, Trinidad & Tobago, Bazil, Venezuela, and the United States, as well as the potential for sale to third parties in other countries not specifically listed. *See Liles*, 631 F.2d at 1246.

Hongyuan drafted the Agreement and chose to include a clause designating China as the forum. Therefore, Hongyuan either foresaw or should have foreseen any inconvenience it would suffer by being forced to litigate in China at the time it elected to include Article 6 in the Agreement. Third, the chosen law will not deprive Hongyuan of a remedy, because Article 6 clearly states that the agreement shall be governed only by Chinese law, so "the remedy will be determined under the same set of rules no matter where the case is heard"—China or Florida. And fourth, enforcement of the forum selection clause would not contravene a strong public policy. DI Global has a legitimate interest in limiting the fora in which it can be sued, given the "international character" of the Agreement. In light of the realities of present-day commercial international trade, a "forum clause should control absent a strong showing that it should be set aside." Bremen, 407 U.S. at 13–14, 15.

Because the forum selection clause passes muster under all four categories of the Bremen analysis, the clause is both valid and enforceable.

2. Mandatory or Permissive Character of the Forum Selection Clause

The Court must next determine whether the forum selection clause is mandatory. The Eleventh Circuit enforces "only those clauses that unambiguously designate the forum in which the parties must enforce their rights under the contract." *Fla. Polk Cnty. v. Prison Health Servs., Inc.*, 170 F.3d 1081, 1083 n.8 (11th Cir. 1999). A "permissive" forum selection clause "authorizes jurisdiction in a designated forum but does not prohibit litigation elsewhere. A mandatory clause, in contrast, 'dictates an exclusive forum for litigation under the contract.' " *Global Satellite Commc'n Co. v. Starmill U.K. Ltd.*, 3378 F.3d 1269, 1272 (11th Cir. 2004). . . .

To review, the provision at issue states: "In the event of any disputes between the parties the People's Court of Jiangsu (China) shall be empowered to take cognizance of it, unless coercive law prescribes another court." (Emphasis added). Upon first glance, the use of the term "shall," under Global Satellite and Cornett, characterizes the clause as mandatory, not permissive. However, the Court would be remiss in not considering what effect, if any, the phrase at the end of the clause—"unless coercive law prescribes another court"—has on the clause's mandatory or permissive character as a whole. DI Global affords this phrase no argument whatsoever, while Hongyuan argues that the phrase is "utterly vague on its own terms" because the Agreement does not define either "coercive law" or "another court." Further, Hongyuan contends that because the Agreement is "clearly subject to the limitations of other 'coercive' courts it is far from an absolute bar on litigation in other jurisdictions."

[Judge Gayles reasoned that there would have been no need for a forum selection clause identifying China as a possible forum: neither party could have objected to jurisdiction there. The clause was needed, however, "to require suit in China because alternative possible fora for suit exist." Accordingly, she concluded that the clause was mandatory.]

3. Applicability

Finally, the Court must determine whether the forum selection clause applies to the dispute at issue. Hongyuan urges the Court to adopt a limited view of the scope of the Agreement. . . It argues that because the Agreement does not clearly state that "any and all transactions between" the parties are governed by the Agreement, the Agreement is, at best, ambiguous as to its application to "other disputes," including this dispute.

In this Circuit, . . . "[c]lauses referencing 'any lawsuit regarding this agreement' and 'any action brought by either party in any court' have been broadly construed to include contract claims 'arising directly or indirectly from' the contractual relationship, as well as tort and extra-contractual claims." *Pods, Inc. v. Paysource, Inc.*, No. 05–1764, 2006 WL 1382099, at *2 (M.D. Fla. May 19, 2006). . . It is clear from the language of the agreement that the forum selection clause encompasses any dispute arising out of or in connection with the distributor-manufacturer relationship. . . . Such a conclusion "is consistent with the Supreme Court's directive in *The Bremen* to encourage commercial reliance on forum selection clauses and thus keep intact the usefulness of these agreements." *Stewart*, 810 F.2d at 1070.

B. Forum Non Conveniens Analysis

The existence of a valid, enforceable, mandatory, and applicable forum selection clause—like the clause contained in the Agreement—is not alone dispositive in the forum non conveniens analysis. In *Atlantic Marine Constr. Co. v. U.S. Dist. Ct. for the Western Dist. of Texas*, 571 U.S. __, 134 S. Ct. 568 (2013), the Supreme Court explained that a viable forum selection clause carries *near*-determinative weight: "When parties agree to a forum-selection clause, they waive the right to challenge the preselected forum as inconvenient or less convenient for themselves or their witnesses, or for their pursuit of the litigation." *Id.* at 582. Following *Atlantic Marine*, this Court must "adjust [its] usual forum non conveniens analysis in three ways":

> First, "the plaintiff's choice of forum merits no weight." Second, the district court "should not consider arguments about the parties['] private interests" because when a plaintiff agrees to a forum-selection clause, the plaintiff waives the right to challenge the pre-selected forum as inconvenient. Third, when a party bound by a forum-selection clause files suit in a different forum than the one pre-selected, the plaintiff's chosen venue's choice-of-law rules will not apply.

Vanderham, 102 F.Supp.3d at 1318–19 (quoting *Atlantic Marine*, 134 S. Ct. at 581–82). Post-*Atlantic Marine*, the Eleventh Circuit has ruled that "[a] binding forum-selection clause requires the court to find that the forum non conveniens *private factors* entirely favor the selected forum." *GDG Acquisitions*, 749 F.3d at 1029. (emphasis added).[7] What remains to be determined under this modified analysis prior to any consideration of dismissal, then, is (1) whether the public interest factors weigh in favor of dismissal, (2) whether an adequate alternative forum is available, and (3) whether the Plaintiff can reinstate its suit in the alternative forum without undue inconvenience or prejudice. *Id.* at 1028.

1. Public Interest Factors

The relevant public interest factors include "the familiarity of the court(s) with the governing law, the interest of any foreign nation in having the dispute litigated in its own courts, and the value of having local controversies litigated locally." *Pierre-Louis v. Newvac Corp.*, 584 F.3d 1052, 1056 (11th Cir. 2009) (quoting *Liquidation Comm'n of Banco Intercont'l, S.A. v. Renta*, 530 F.3d 1339, 1356–57 (11th Cir. 2008)). The *Atlantic Marine* Court opined that "[b]ecause [these] factors will rarely defeat a transfer motion, the practical result" of a court's finding that a viable forum selection clause exists is that the clause "should control except in unusual cases." 134 S. Ct. at 582. "In all but the most unusual cases," the Court continued, "the interest of justice is served by holding parties to their bargain." *Id.* at 583.

---

7   The "private factors" include "'relative ease of access to sources of proof; availability of compulsory process for attendance of unwilling, and the cost of obtaining attendance of willing, witnesses; possibility of view of premises, if view would be appropriate to the action; and all other practical problems that make trial of a case easy, expeditious and inexpensive.' " *Atlantic Marine*, 134 S. Ct. at 581 n.6 (quoting *Piper Aircraft Co. v. Reyno*, 454 U.S. 235, 241 n.6 (1981)).

The public interests all weigh in favor of dismissal here. First, according to Article 6, this dispute is governed by Chinese law, with which Chinese courts are infinitely more familiar than this Court. Next, China has a stronger interest in having this dispute litigated in its courts, as the parties contracted to litigate in China, and China doubtlessly wants its citizens to be empowered to seek redress in its courts when they contract to have their claims heard there. And finally, the aggrieved party is a Chinese entity, and "[t]here is 'a local interest in having localized controversies decided at home.'" *Piper Aircraft Co. v. Reyno*, 454 U.S. 235, 260 (1981) (quoting *Gilbert*, 330 U.S. at 509.).

Hongyuan's arguments on this point—(1) that DI Global has not demonstrated that the public interest factors strongly favor a Chinese forum because it has not provided data regarding the congestion of Chinese and U.S. Courts, (2) that it has not demonstrated China has a greater interest in the dispute than the United States, and (3) that the application of Chinese law to this dispute does not overcome the deference to its own chosen forum—are unavailing. On the first two points, Hongyuan inappropriately foists onto DI Global a burden it is not subject to. "[A]s the party defying the forum-selection clause," it is "the *plaintiff* [who] bears the burden of establishing that transfer to the forum for which the parties bargained for is unwarranted" and "showing why the court should not transfer the case to the forum to which the parties agreed." *Atlantic Marine*, 134 S. Ct. at 581–82 (emphasis added). Hongyuan cannot argue based on a lack of evidence from DI Global that the public interest factors weigh against transfer. And on the third point, under *Atlantic Marine*, a finding of a valid and enforceable forum selection clause vitiates any deference owed a plaintiff's choice of forum. *Id.* at 581.[8] In sum, there is no indication this is one of the "unusual cases" in which the public factors outweigh a valid forum selection clause.

2. Adequacy and Availability of the Alternative Forum

The next factor in the forum non conveniens analysis involves two inquiries, each of which "warrant[s] separate consideration." *Leon v. Millon Air, Inc.*, 251 F.3d 1305, 1311 (11th Cir. 2001): whether the alternative forum is "adequate" and whether the alternative forum is "available," *Aldana v. Del Monte Fresh Produce N.A.*, 578 F.3d 1283, 1290 (11th Cir. 2009).

---

8 Even prior to *Atlantic Marine*, the Supreme Court in *Piper Aircraft* ruled that foreign plaintiffs (like Hongyuan) are entitled to less deference in their choice of forum. *See Piper Aircraft*, 454 U.S. at 255–56.

a. Adequacy

"An alternative forum is adequate if it provides for litigation of the subject matter of the dispute and potentially offers redress for plaintiffs' injuries." *King v. Cessna Aircraft Co.*, 562 F.3d 1374, 1382 (11th Cir. 2009). "An adequate forum need not be a perfect forum." *Satz v. McDonnell Douglas Corp.*, 244 F.3d 1279, 1283 (11th Cir. 2001). Courts need ask "only whether some remedy exists; whether the remedy afforded is less favorable in the foreign forum is not determinative." *Neuralstem, Inc. v. ReNeuro, Ltd.*, 365 Fed. Appx. 770, 771 (9th Cir. 2010) (per curiam). The adequacy of the forum also "does not depend on the existence of the identical cause of action in the other forum." *Norex Petrol. Ltd. v. Access Indus., Inc.*, 416 F.3d 146, 158 (2d Cir. 2005). On the other hand, an alternative forum is *in*adequate "if the remedy provided by th[at] alternative forum is so clearly inadequate or unsatisfactory that it is no remedy at all." *Piper Aircraft*, 454 U.S. at 252; *see also Aldana*, 578 F.3d at 1290 (stating that only in "rare circumstances" will "the remedy offered by the forum [be] clearly unsatisfactory" such that the forum would be considered inadequate).

Hongyuan argues that DI Global bears the burden to demonstrate that China is an adequate forum in this case. According to Hongyuan, DI Global failed to meet that burden by failing to provide the Court with a sworn affidavit of an individual familiar with Chinese law or provide proof of (1) the availability of a comparative cause of action for Hongyuan's claim, (2) the accessibility of Chinese courts to disputes involving American defendants, or (3) whether the statute of limitations in China bars Hongyuan's claim. Hongyuan asserts that, without such proof, the Court must find DI Global has not proven adequacy and its forum non conveniens motion must be denied.

But Hongyuan's is only a partially correct view of the law. In this Circuit, an alternative forum is "presumed 'adequate' unless the plaintiff makes some showing to the contrary," through, for example, "'substantiated . . . allegations of serious corruption or delay.' " *J.C. Renfroe & Sons, Inc. v. Renfroe Japan Co.*, 515 F.Supp.2d 1258 (M.D. Fla. 2007) (quoting *Leon*, 251 F.3d at 1312). . . . Therefore, the Court must decide whether Hongyuan has proffered significant evidence of partiality, corruption, or delay before deciding whether DI Global has any burden to establish adequacy at all and, if it does, whether it has met that burden.

Hongyuan asserts that scholarly articles have noted the Chinese legal system's "potential for excessive trial delays, obstructive legal counsel, corruption, lack of legal safeguards, [and] undue influence by political leadership" and cites a single law review article that discusses China's purported suitability, or lack thereof, as an alternative forum in forum non conveniens cases. However, "[a]bsent a showing of inadequacy by a plaintiff, 'considerations of comity preclude a court from adversely judging the quality of a foreign justice system.'" *Abdullahi v. Pfizer, Inc.*, 562 F.3d 163, 189 (2d Cir. 2009) (quoting *PT United Can Co. v. Crown Cork & Seal Co.*, 138 F.3d 65, 73 (2d Cir. 1998)). The great weight of authority holds that "generalized, anecdotal complaints of corruption are not enough for a federal court to declare that [a nation's] legal system is so corrupt that it can't serve as an adequate forum." *Stroitelstvo Bulgaria Ltd. v. Bulgarian-Am. Enter. Fund*, 589 F.3d 417, 421–22 (7th Cir. 2009); *see also Tuazon v. R.J. Reynolds Tobacco Co.*, 433 F.3d 1163, 1179 (9th Cir. 2006) (finding that the plaintiff's anecdotal evidence of corruption and delay" in courts in the Philippines was insufficient to show inadequacy); *In re Arb. between Monegasque De Reassurances S.A.M. v. Nak Naftogaz of Ukr.*, 311 F.3d 488, 489 (2d Cir. 2002) (refusing "to pass value judgments on the adequacy of justice and the integrity of Ukraine's judicial system on the basis of no more than . . . bare denunciations and sweeping generalizations"); *El-Fadl v. Cent. Bank of Jordan*, 75 F.3d 668, 678 (D.C. Cir. 1996) (ruling that the plaintiff's general allegations of the lack of impartiality in Jordanian courts was insufficient to render the forum inadequate), *abrogated on other grounds by Samantar v. Yousuf*, 560 U.S. 305 (2010); *Mercier v. Sheraton Int'l, Inc.*, 981 F.2d 1345, 1351 (1st Cir. 1992) (holding that Turkish courts were adequate despite the plaintiff's unsubstantiated complaints of bias against foreign litigants and women). *Cf. Bhatnagar v. Surrendra Overseas Ltd.*, 52 F.3d 1220, 1228 (3d Cir. 1995) (finding that a delay of at least eighteen to twenty-six years in Indian courts, supported by evidence that included a quote from the former Chief Justice of India saying that the Indian legal system is "almost on the verge of collapse," rendered the remedy there "clearly inadequate").

A district court in California rejected arguments like Hongyuan's in *CYBERsitter, LLC v. People's Republic of China*, No. 10–0038, 2010 WL 4909958 (C.D. Cal. Nov. 18, 2010). There, the plaintiff proffered a declaration from a law professor in support of its opposition to the defendant's forum non conveniens motion seeking dismissal in favor of a Chinese forum. The professor argued that the Chinese government could easily control the outcome of a judicial proceeding, meaningful judicial independence does not exist in China, and political authorities could interfere in any lawsuit in which they took an interest. *Id.* at *4. The court, however, concluded that those allegations were too "speculative" to convince it that China would not provide an adequate forum. *Id.* at *5. This Court sees neither need nor justification to find otherwise here, as Hongyuan's generalized, anecdotal, and unsubstantiated allegations are similarly speculative.

Hongyuan also argues that China is not an adequate forum because the Chinese courts would not provide a "practical remedy." It contends that because DI Global does not own property or attachable assets in China, a judgment against DI Global would cause Hongyuan "extreme difficult in collecting a damages award." The Court reminds Hongyuan that it establishes the inadequacy of the foreign forum based on inadequacy of that forum's remedy only by showing that the remedy the forum provides is, in actuality, "no remedy at all," *Piper Aircraft*, 454 U.S. at 252, not that the remedy is "impractical" or "difficult." And while recognition of a foreign forum's adequacy does not require the Court to "conduct[ ] complex exercises in comparative law," even a cursory consultation of Chinese law resolves any doubt that the remedy it provides is a far cry from "no remedy at all." *Id.* at 251–52. . . . At bottom, "[t]his case presents a straightforward contractual dispute with similarly uncomplicated ancillary [noncontractual] claims that a Chinese court can adequately manage." *Huang v. Advanced Battery Techs., Inc.*, No. 09–8297, 2010 WL 2143669, at *5 (S.D.N.Y. May 26, 2010).

Based on its own review of the relevant provisions of Chinese law, the Court is sufficiently satisfied that some remedy for the causes of action alleged here exists in China. Whether this remedy is "practical" or whether Hongyuan may be inconvenienced trying to enforce a judgment does not bear on the Court's analysis.[11] Because Chinga provides for litigation of the subject matter of this dispute and potentially offers redress for Hongyuan's injuries, *see King*, 562 F.3d at 1382, and because Hongyuan has not substantiated its allegations of corruption or delay in the Chinese legal system, this Court finds that China is an adequate alternative forum.

---

11   The Court is hard-pressed to see how Hongyuan would have, as it contends, "extreme difficulty collecting a damages award" should they prevail against DI Global, a Florida corporation, when Florida's Uniform Out-of-Country Foreign Money-Judgment Recognition Act exists to govern that exact factual scenario. *See* Fla. Stat. § 55.601-.607.

b. Availability

An alternative forum is "available" to a plaintiff "when the foreign court can assert jurisdiction over the litigation sought to be transferred." *Leon*, 251 F.3d at 1311. . . . DI Global, through its counsel, agreed to submit to China's jurisdiction and accept service of process. . . . The Court therefore concludes that the availability requirement is satisfied.

3. Undue Inconvenience or Prejudice

Turning to the final forum non conveniens requirement, the Court finds that Hongyuan can reinstate its claim in China without undue inconvenience or prejudice. *See GDG Acquisitions*, 749 F.3d at 1028. The burden to satisfy this requirement is not onerous. *See, e.g., Seguros Universales, S.A. v. Microsoft Corp.*, 32 F.Supp.3d 1242, 1252 (S.D. Fla. 2014). Hongyuan admits that the cost of refiling suit in China is insignificant, and the Court has already addressed and rejected its arguments regarding alleged delays and corruption in the Chinese legal system. . . .

IV. Conclusion

Based on the foregoing, it is ordered and adjudged that . . . the Defendant's motion to dismiss is granted, conditioned on the Defendant's agreement, as stated in its Supplemental Brief, to submit itself to the jurisdiction of China and to accept service of process from the courts of China. . . .

COMMENTS AND QUESTIONS

1. If you were defense counsel, could you keep a straight face while arguing, on behalf of your Florida client, that the case belongs not in Florida but in China? Why doesn't the court even mention this?

2. The court's reliance on conditions to ensure (or to manufacture, as the case may be) that the alternative forum is adequate is a very common yet also curious practice. Should we assume that Chinese law is like American law in that it allows a defendant to "submit" to jurisdiction or to "accept" service? Maybe those are jurisdictional issues that constrain the authority of the courts and cannot be waived by the parties. What happens then?

3. One dilemma that plaintiffs have when arguing against forum non conveniens motions is that they must describe how awful (i.e., "inadequate") litigation in the alternative forum will be. This is problematic because it gives your opponent a playbook of how to defeat you in the event that litigation ultimately occurs there. And even if the motion to dismiss is denied, you have spent considerable time describing the worthlessness of your case according to another court system—leading the judge or any other reasonable person to wonder whether maybe you just don't have a very good case.

4. The judge mentions "burdens" eight times in this excerpt. Burdens become more relevant when evidence is scarce.

5. Does an account of corruption within a country's court system suggest that that country's courts are inadequate, or is that story instead evidence of noble transparency?

SAMPLE EXAM QUESTIONS

Question 21-3

Oregon-Idaho Utilities, Inc. (OIU) is a provider of broadband DSL services in parts of Oregon and Idaho. A few years ago, OIU and Skitter Cable TV, Inc. (Skitter) entered into a Franchise Agreement based on Skitter's representations that it had a working platform that would enable OIU to provide its customers with a full television channel lineup. Skitter is a Georgia company with its principal place of business in Atlanta.

The parties' Franchise Agreement includes a forum selection clause which states:

> The parties . . . agree that litigation brought by either party against the other party in connection with rights or obligations arising out of this Agreement shall be instituted in a federal or state court of competent jurisdiction in the State of Georgia.

The agreement also provides that "[t]he validity and effect of this Agreement are to be governed by and construed and enforced in accordance with the laws of the State of Georgia."

OIU filed suit against Skitter in a federal district court in Idaho. Pursuing claims in tort, contract, and restitution, the complaint alleges that Skitter made various ongoing misrepresentations of fact and other false statements in the course of their dealings with plaintiffs, inducing plaintiffs to enter into the Franchise Agreement, to wire $495,000 to Skitter for equipment, services, and content, to purchase equipment, and to perform its own obligations under the Franchise Agreements.

Skitter has moved the court to transfer the case to the U.S. District Court for the Northern District of Georgia. What is the likelihood that the Idaho federal court will grant the defendant's motion?

Question 21-4

Elizabeth Burch is a British econometrician who was a guest lecturer eighteen months ago at Dokuz Eylul University in Izmir, Turkey. During that 3-day visit she stayed at a nearby resort owned by Marriott International, Inc. (Marriott), a Delaware corporation with its principal place of business in Bethesda, Maryland. While a guest at the Izmir Marriott, Burch slipped on a cracked and broken area of the pool deck and fell. As a result, she suffered a fracture of the left proximal humerus and median nerve compression. Her injuries required two surgeries, one of which occurred in Turkey shortly after the accident, and the second which occurred in London after she returned home.

Burch, who is now a visiting research fellow at Johns Hopkins University in Baltimore, Maryland, has filed a lawsuit against Marriott in a Maryland federal district court. She seeks compensatory damages, including, inter alia, special damages for past and future medical expenses and lost wages, and costs.

Marriott's counsel has moved to dismiss on grounds of forum non conveniens. Which side is more likely to win this motion, and why?

Quick Summary

- When venue is improper under 28 U.S.C. § 1391, federal courts may transfer the case to a federal district court where venue would be proper (28 U.S.C. § 1406) or may dismiss the case (FRCP 12(b)(3))

- When venue is proper under 28 U.S.C. § 1391, federal courts may transfer the case to a federal district court where the action could have been brought; the court considers public interest and private interest factors

- Federal courts have a near-obligation to transfer the case when a valid forum selection clause identifies another state as the forum selected by the parties

- When venue is proper under 28 U.S.C. § 1391, federal courts may dismiss the case pursuant to the common law doctrine of forum non conveniens; the court considers public interest and private interest factors, and also whether the alternative forum is adequate

- Federal courts frequently dismiss the case on grounds of forum non conveniens when a valid forum selection clause identifies another country as the forum selected by the parties

- Arbitration clauses are a specialized type of forum selection clause and are routinely enforced by courts

22

Enforcement of Foreign Judgments

Key Concepts

- Final judgment
- Judgment creditor; judgment debtor
- Issuing or rendering court (F1); enforcing or recognizing court (F2)
- Recognition; enforcement
- Full Faith and Credit Clause
- Collateral attack (personal jurisdiction)
- Extrinsic fraud

The enforcement of foreign judgments is one of the three major topics in a Conflict of Laws course. The topic regards the circumstances under which a judgment issued in one court will be recognized and enforced by a court in some other jurisdiction.

Enforcement of foreign judgments is an important topic for litigators. Prevailing in a lawsuit means only that you receive a piece of paper called a final judgment. When a plaintiff prevails, a "Final Judgment" with a caption that names the parties, the court, and the civil action number is docketed with text that would look something like this:

> This action was tried by Judge Colatrella without a jury and the following decision was reached:
>
> It is ordered that Plaintiff AAA Inc. recover from the Defendant ZZZ Co. $200,000, plus prejudgment interest from <prior date> to this day in the amount of $14,150, plus costs in the amount of $850, with postjudgment interest to accrue hereafter at the rate of 5.25% per annum."
>
> <Date>   <Signature of Clerk of Court>

If the defendant prevailed, the text would say that the plaintiff recovers nothing, that the action is dismissed on the merits, and that the defendant recovers costs from the plaintiff.

When a plaintiff wins, the plaintiff is then a *judgment creditor* who is owed a sum by the defendant, the *judgment debtor*. But like any creditor, the fact that the plaintiff is owed money does not necessarily mean that it will be paid. The defendant ZZZ Co. might write AAA Inc. a check for $215,000—in which case the judgment will be satisfied (and so will the plaintiff!). Or the defendant might tell the plaintiff that it (ZZZ Co.) is judgment-proof and thus unable to make any payment. Or the defendant might tell the plaintiff that ZZZ Co. will write a check for $100,000 and waive its right to appeal the judgment if plaintiff agrees to surrender collection of the other $115,000. Or ZZZ Co. may not talk to plaintiff at all.

The judgment for $215,000 gives you some legal rights to collect the money owed. Generally speaking, it is fairly easy to collect on a judgment if the defendant has (i) identifiable assets (ii) that are not exempt from collection and (iii) are located in the jurisdiction that issued the judgment. Assets that can be located and described are seized by the sheriff and sold, with the proceeds satisfying the debt. Judgment creditors can also obtain liens. Judgment creditors may also garnish the debtor's wages or other money that is flowing to the debtor. The procedures for collecting a judgment vary by state, but usually involve a writ of execution. Discovery may also be available to help creditors locate the defendant's assets. (*See, e.g.,* Fed. R. Civ. P. 69(a)(2).) Finally, different jurisdictions exempt certain types of property from collection efforts; for example, clothing, household furnishings, work tools, a vehicle, and the debtor's homestead may be exempt.

Frequently the defendant will not have identifiable assets in the jurisdiction that issued the judgment. But that defendant may have identifiable assets in some other jurisdiction. And it is at this point—as we contemplate taking a judgment from one state into another state—that the discipline of conflict of laws becomes relevant. Under these circumstances we refer to the state or court that entered the final judgment as the *rendering* (or *issuing*) state or court. The rendering jurisdiction is also occasionally referred to as the F_1, an abbreviation for "Forum #1," meaning the first forum. As we take that final judgment across a territorial boundary to enforce it in another jurisdiction, we refer to that second jurisdiction as the *enforcing* (or *recognizing*) state or court, or as F_2 (Forum #2). This process is also sometimes referred to as *domesticating* or *registering* the judgment in F_2.

The Full Faith and Credit Clause of the U.S. Constitution imposes an obligation on F_2:

> Full Faith and Credit shall be given in each State to the public Acts, Records, and judicial Proceedings of every other State. And the Congress may by general Laws prescribe the Manner in which such Acts, Records and Proceedings shall be proved, and the Effect thereof.

U.S. Const. art. IV, § 1. With respect to the second sentence of the Full Faith and Credit Clause, Congress has not prescribed the manner by which states must recognize another's judgments. But the states individually have done so, by enacting uniform legislation.

"The Uniform Law Commission (ULC, also known as the National Conference of Commissioners on Uniform State Laws), established in 1892, provides states with non-partisan, well-conceived and well-drafted legislation that brings clarity and stability to critical areas of state statutory law."[1] Members of the ULC are members of the bench, bar, and the academy appointed by state governments to research, draft and promote the enactment of uniform state laws in areas of state law where uniformity is desirable and practical. The Enforcement of Foreign Judgments Act (EFJA or UEFJA), originally enacted in 1948 and revised in 1964, is an example of this model legislation.

Almost all states have enacted the uniform law. Under the uniform law, the creditor can domesticate the F_1 judgment in F_2 by filing proof of the judgment, providing the last known address of the debtor, and paying a filing fee. Once the correct papers are filed, the clerk of the court (in F_2) notifies the judgment debtor that they have a certain number of days to respond and to dispute enforcement.

Disputes about enforcement of the judgment are severely constrained by the fact that the enforcing court must give "full faith and credit" to the judgment of the rendering court. Accordingly, as a general proposition, returning to the hypothetical above, if F_1 has already decreed that Plaintiff AAA Inc. is entitled to recover $215,000 from ZZZ Co, then F_2 must give full faith and credit to that determination. There are a few exceptions to that general proposition and these exceptions are enumerated below. But bear in mind that the Supreme Court has characterized F_2's obligation under the Full Faith and Credit Clause as being to obey the nearly absolute command of the clause.

Before we address those exceptions, we must lay more foundation. Notice that the text of the Full Faith and Credit Clause prescribes full faith and credit only where *both* F_1 and F_2 are *state* courts; the text addresses neither the rendering nor the enforcement of *federal* court judgments. The UEFJA, the model legislation adopted

---

1   *See* www.uniformlaws.org.

by most states, does not differentiate between federal and state court judgments. Accordingly, under the UEFJA, F_2 must be a *state* court, but the foreign judgment could have been rendered by either a federal or a state court. This leaves as an open question only the enforcement in federal court of state and federal court judgments

To ensure that *federal* courts gave full faith and credit to the acts, records, and proceedings of state courts, Congress (acting in furtherance of the second sentence of the Full Faith and Credit Clause quoted above) passed a statute that now provides:

> The Acts of the legislature of any State, Territory, or Possession of the United States, or copies thereof, shall be authenticated by affixing the seal of such State, Territory or Possession thereto.
>
> The records and judicial proceedings of any court of any such State, Territory or Possession, or copies thereof, shall be proved or admitted in other courts within the United States and its Territories and Possessions by the attestation of the clerk and seal of the court annexed, if a seal exists, together with a certificate of a judge of the court that the said attestation is in proper form.
>
> Such Acts, records and judicial proceedings or copies thereof, so authenticated, shall have the same full faith and credit in every court within the United States and its Territories and Possessions as they have by law or usage in the courts of such State, Territory or possession from which they are taken.

28 U.S.C. § 1738.

Of the four possible combinations of rendering and enforcing jurisdictions that involve American state and federal courts, only one combination remains: the enforcement of federal court judgments by other federal courts. Because this chapter regards only the enforcement of foreign judgments, you might wonder whether a federal court judgment can be *foreign* to another federal court; after all, all federal courts are part of one court system. Nevertheless, 28 U.S.C. § 1963 contemplates the registration of a judgment issued by another federal district court, and that judgment will be enforced according to the laws of the state in which the judgment is registered.

When enforcement proceedings take place in federal court, Rule 69 of the Federal Rules of Civil Procedure further emphasizes that the execution of money judgments should proceed in accordance with the state procedure of the state where the court is located, absent some specific federal statute. With very few exceptions, the practice and procedure for enforcing judgments in federal court incorporates by reference the law of the state in which the federal court sits.

Now let us focus more intently on what it means to enforce—to give full faith and credit to—the judgment of some other court. On one hand, one might expect the F_2 jurisdiction to vigorously enforce the F_1 judgment without hesitation. After all, because some other jurisdiction has already determined the respective rights and responsibilities of these parties, a rubber-stamp may seem appropriate. But on the other hand, one might expect the F_2 jurisdiction to be suspicious of the F_1 judgment. After all, why should F_2 lend its legitimacy and authority to seize local assets in support of a judgment that it did not issue, and that is the product of litigation that it did not host? For example, the citizens of Texas will wonder why a Texas court is seizing the assets of Texans to satisfy a judgment issued by some court in Massachusetts. This chapter is about the circumstances under which F_2 can second-guess or, instead, must rubber-stamp the F_1 judgment

The enforcement of foreign judgments is also important for *defendants* who prevail in litigation in F_1. The judgment is important to a defendant because the plaintiff in F_1 might initiate the same or a similar action against that defendant in F_2. And when that case is filed in F_2, the defendant will produce the judgment from F_1, and the question for the court will be the extent to which the F_2 court will *recognize* (not *enforce*, but recognize) the judgment from F_1 to preclude (or to allow, as the case may be) re-litigation.

We will focus here on the ten most likely exceptions to enforcement of a foreign judgment. We are assuming throughout this discussion that the enforcing court is an American federal or state court and that the foreign judgment was rendered by some other American federal or state court. If F_1 were instead, say, a judgment of the superior court in Vietnam you would look elsewhere to determine the enforceability of that foreign judgment in an American federal or state court. (See Chapter 23).

1. Lack of Personal Jurisdiction

If the F_1 court did not have personal jurisdiction *and* the defendant did not appear in that F_1 proceeding, then the courts of F_2 are not obliged to enforce the F_1 judgment. You may remember from your Civil Procedure course that one way to challenge the lack of personal jurisdiction is to refuse to appear. When a defendant refuses to appear in F_1, a default judgment enters. When the plaintiff presents that default judgment in F_2 the defendant can challenge the lack of personal jurisdiction in F_1. One of the risks of such a collateral attack is that if the collateral attack is unsuccessful (i.e., if the F_2 court determines that the courts of F_1 had personal jurisdiction), the defendant will be deemed to have waived its challenges to the merits of the plaintiff's case.

The F_2 court will not relitigate issues of personal jurisdiction. If a defendant appears in the F_1 litigation, then that defendant may not dispute enforcement in F_2 by contending that F_1 lacked personal jurisdiction. Rather, the determination by F_1 that the defendant was subject to personal jurisdiction will be given full faith and credit. Thus the only way that a defendant can invoke this exception to enforcement is if she did not appear in F_1, and is challenging the enforcement of a default judgment.

2. Lack of Subject Matter Jurisdiction

If the F_1 court did not have subject matter jurisdiction, then in some rare circumstances the courts of F_2 are not obliged to enforce it. Unfortunately, the contours of these circumstances are not entirely clear. Two general principles emerge from the key Supreme Court decisions:

> If the subject matter jurisdiction issue was not actually litigated[2] in F_1, then the values of accuracy and fairness militate in favor of denying the F_1 judgment full faith and credit.

> If the limits on F_1's jurisdiction involve matters regarding that court's jurisdictional competence,[3] then the integrity of the allocation of jurisdiction may be as or more important than the policies behind full faith and credit.

When the facts of your case implicate *both* of these principles, the issue of subject matter jurisdiction can be invoked to resist enforcement in F_2. If the facts of your case implicate *neither* of these principles, the F_2 court should give full faith and credit to the F_1 judgment.

If the facts of your case implicate only *one* of these principles then unfortunately the Supreme Court's case law is dated and irreconcilable.[4] Section 12 of the Restatement (Second) of Judgments characterizes the law as follows:

---

2   Actual litigation means that the issue was raised and argued by the parties.

3   Jurisdictional competence requires you to examine the reason(s) that jurisdiction is limited. Matters within the exclusive jurisdiction of federal courts, for example, may be intended to protect the integrity of some federal policy from interference by hostile state courts. The more deliberate (as opposed to casual) and policy-driven (as opposed to etiquette) the jurisdictional limit, the easier it is to conclude that the limitation speaks to jurisdictional competence.

4   *See Durfee v. Duke*, 375 U.S. 106 (1963); *Sherrer v. Sherrer*, 334 U.S. 343 (1948); *Kalb v. Feuerstein*, 308 U.S.

Restatement (Second) of Conflict of Laws

§ 12. Contesting Subject Matter Jurisdiction

When a court has rendered a judgment in a contested action, the judgment precludes the parties from litigating the question of the court's subject matter jurisdiction in subsequent litigation except if:

(1) The subject matter of the action was so plainly beyond the court's jurisdiction that its entertaining the action was a manifest abuse of authority; or

(2) Allowing the judgment to stand would substantially infringe the authority of another tribunal or agency of government; or

(3) The judgment was rendered by a court lacking capability to make an adequately informed determination of a question concerning its own jurisdiction and as a matter of procedural fairness the party seeking to avoid the judgment should have opportunity belatedly to attack the court's subject matter jurisdiction.

3. Extrinsic Fraud

The courts of F_2 are not required to enforce an F_1 judgment that was obtained fraudulently. This exception pertains only to *extrinsic* (also called *collateral*) fraud. The type of fraud necessary to invoke the exception regards conduct undertaken in the very act of obtaining the judgment—fraudulent conduct that thwarted the unsuccessful party from fully presenting their case. By contrast, fraudulent conduct that is intertwined with the underlying dispute is *intrinsic* fraud; these incidents may not be used as a bar to enforcement of a foreign judgment because they should have been raised during the course of the litigation in F_1.

The paradigm examples of extrinsic fraud are situations where someone is deliberately kept in ignorance of the action or is otherwise fraudulently induced not to appear in the F_1 litigation: the defendant did not present its case because the plaintiff promised to drop the suit; the plaintiff notified the defendant that the proceeding had been dismissed; the plaintiff did not serve the defendant but then represented to the court that the defendant was served. These circumstances are in contrast to fraud occurring in the course of an adversary hearing—e.g., perjured testimony, false documents, concealing evidence—which are instances of *intrinsic* fraud and do not trigger this exception.

---

433 (1940); *Chicot County Drainage Dist. v. Baxter State Bank*, 308 U.S. 371 (1940).

4. Penal Claims

The courts of F_2 are not required to enforce F_1 judgments that are based on penal claims. The malleability of the concept of punishment could allow this exception to swallow the rule. Are awards for punitive damages penal? How about statutory or presumed damages? Even ordinary damages in tort can have a punitive dimension. In fact, however, this exception is read very narrowly. As a practical matter, a judgment is penal only when (i) the purpose of the underlying law is to punish (as opposed to compensate) *and* (ii) the recovery is in favor of a government (rather than an individual). When interrogating the purpose of a law, focus on how the damages are calculated: if the damages are focused on the plaintiff's loss, this suggests that they are compensatory.

5. Title to Land

The courts of F_2 are not required to enforce F_1 judgments that directly affect title to land in the state of F_2. This exception, once known as the land taboo, is invoked infrequently today because it is so easily avoided. In the case most directly associated with this exception, *Fall v. Eastin*,[5] a court in the State of Washington issued an order requiring the defendant to convey Nebraska real estate to the plaintiff. When the defendant refused, the Washington court appointed a commissioner to execute a deed to the plaintiff on the defendant's behalf. The plaintiff then took that deed to Nebraska and initiated an action to quiet title to the property. The Nebraska court refused to recognize the deed, and the Supreme Court affirmed. The exception was triggered (only) because the Washington court *directly* affected the title to Nebraska land. If it had only indirectly affected the land, the acts of F_1 would have been entitled to full faith and credit. Accordingly, if the Washington court had simply held the defendant in contempt (e.g., put him in jail) until he executed the deed, the land taboo would not have been implicated.

6. Interference with Official Acts

The courts of F_2 may not be required to enforce F_1 judgments that purport to accomplish an official act within the enforcing state or that directly interfere with litigation over which the rendering state has no authority.[6]

In the ordinary course, an F_1 judgment that contains equitable relief (instead of or in addition to monetary relief) is entitled to full faith and credit. The enforcing

---

5   215 U.S. 1 (1909).

6   *Baker v. General Motors*, 522 U.S. 222 (1998).

court must give the judgment the same effect that it would have in the rendering court.

However, some Justices of the Supreme Court have recognized that an equitable order could go too far. Although the Full Faith and Credit Clause requires that F_1's respect F_1's determination of the parties' rights and responsibilities, including entitlement to legal and equitable relief, the F_1 court cannot dictate the judicial process in F_2. For example, the F_1 court cannot tell the F_2 court how to enforce its order or otherwise alter the procedural rules of F_2.

7. Deprivation of Day in Court

Full faith and credit is a constitutional mandate fueled by concerns of efficiency, uniformity, and fairness. But full faith and credit should not unfairly steamroll a litigant and deprive them of their day in court.

The unfair denial of an opportunity to be heard is more likely an argument that you will make in conjunction with one of the other exceptions. When F_1 lacks personal jurisdiction, it would be unfair to *require* the defendant to appear in that court for the sake of arguing that she should not have to appear in that court. So the system allows her to ignore that proceeding. But because she has not had her day in court, we allow her to argue to the F_2 court at the enforcement stage that F_1 lacked jurisdiction. The exception for fraud likewise worries that fraud will deprive someone of meaningful notice of the stakes of litigation and the right to be heard.

We include it here as a separate exception as a placeholder for circumstances that may not fall neatly into the other exceptions. Looming in the background here is the Due Process Clause, which promises fairness. Giving full faith and credit to the judgment of another jurisdiction should not be unfair. Importantly, however, this exception is no escape from bad lawyering, bad arguments, or strategic miscalculations.

8. Unenforceable in the Rendering State

The mandate of "full faith and credit" uses the rendering state as the baseline for enforceability. In other words, F_2 is not obliged to give a judgment *more* faith or credit than would the rendering jurisdiction. Accordingly, litigators at the enforcement stage can resist enforcement with any argument that would justify denying enforcement in F_1. For example, a judgment may not be enforceable in the rendering (nor, therefore, in the enforcing) state because it is not a *final* judgment.[7]

---

7   Unlike countries in the Civil Law tradition, in the United States a final judgment refers only to its "finality"

9. Inconsistent Judgments

This exception is for circumstances where the enforcing forum is F_3 and there are *two* prior (inconsistent) judgments, rather than just one. Imagine, for example, that litigation in F_1 led to a final judgment. The prevailing party in the F_1 litigation then sought recognition or enforcement in F_2. However, for one of the reasons enumerated above, the F_2 forum refused to enforce the F_1 judgment. At this point there are now two judgments that involve these parties, and those judgments may be mutually exclusive. One or both of these judgments could be presented in a *third* forum, at which point the question would be: should F_3 give full faith and credit to the F_2 judgment or the F_1 judgment? The typical answer is F_2. The court has adopted a last-in-time rule that allows the F_3 court to deny full faith and credit to the F_1 judgment.[8]

10. Federal Legislation

The second sentence of the Full Faith and Credit Clause authorizes Congress to prescribe the manner of proof and the effect of acts, records, and judgments. In 28 U.S.C. § 1738, for example, Congress extended the scope of full faith and credit to include federal, territorial, and state courts. In 28 U.S.C. §§ 1738A and 1738B Congress also clarified the enforceability of child custody and child support orders; prior to the legislation, the modifiability of custody and support orders made their finality (and, hence, their enforceability) uncertain. These acts of legislation expanded the scope of full faith and credit.

Although some commentators argue that the second sentence of the Full Faith and Credit Clause should be used only to expand the scope of full faith and credit, Congress has also acted to limit its scope. In the context of habeas corpus, 28 U.S.C. § 2254(d) specifies the extent to which states' decisions must be respected in collateral attacks on criminal judgments. Congress also passed the Defense of Marriage Act, which (until it was rendered unconstitutional[9]) allowed states to deny effect to a marriage license of another state if the marriage was between persons of the same sex.

---

in the *trial* court, not the appellate court. In fact, in the ordinary course, the appellate process does not even begin until the judgment is "final."

8   *See* Restatement (Second) of Conflict of Laws § 114 ("A judgment rendered in a State of the United States will not be recognized or enforced in sisters States if an inconsistent, but valid, judgment is subsequently rendered in another action between the parties and if the earlier judgment is superseded by the later judgment under the local law of the State where the later judgment was rendered."). *See also Treines v. Sunshine Mining Co.*, 308 U.S. 66, 74–75 (1939).

9   *See U.S. v. Windsor*, 570 U.S. 744 (2013); *Obergefell v. Hodges*, __ U.S. __, 135 S. Ct. 2584 (2015).

* * *

Notably absent from the above list is a public policy exception. This can be confusing for students and lawyers because, you will remember, in the context of *choice of law*, the Full Faith and Credit Clause tolerates a public policy exception. Yet there is no public policy exception to full faith and credit with respect to the enforcement of judgments.

The absolute nature of the Full Faith and Credit Clause is captured in, *Fauntleroy v. Lum*,[10] a famous opinion of the U.S. Supreme Court that is more than a century old. In 1893, a cotton dealer in Vicksburg, Mississippi entered into a contract with Lum that speculated on the price of cotton. Lum was caught short, and could not cover his margin. Lum's debt was guaranteed by Searles, who covered Lum's debt to the cotton dealer. (The cotton dealer was Searles' brother, to whom Searles had sold the business shortly before these events.) Lum refused to reimburse Searles, and the two agreed to submit the matter to arbitration. Lum argued that his debt to the cotton dealer was a gambling transaction that, under Mississippi law, was unenforceable. Lum was correct on his statement of Mississippi law, but the arbitration panel nevertheless ordered Lum to reimburse his guarantor, Searles. Again, Lum did not pay the debt.

Years later, Searles sought to enforce the arbitration award in the courts of the state of Missouri, where Lum was visiting. Lum again argued that the underlying transaction was a gambling contract that was unenforceable. The Missouri court distinguished repayment of a guaranty from payment of a gambling debt, and converted the arbitrator's award into a final judgment. Searles then assigned the judgment to Fauntleroy; but other than changing the name of the plaintiff, this assignment is immaterial.

Fauntleroy then initiated an enforcement action back in Mississippi, where Lum had assets. The Mississippi courts refused, noting the illegality of the underlying obligation and the unenforceability also of the guaranty under Mississippi law.

> Until the supreme court of the United States shall expressly so declare, we will not hold that a contract condemned by our civil and criminal laws as immoral, and which the courts of this state are prohibited from enforcing, is sanctified, and purged of its illegality, by a judgment rendered in another state against a citizen of this state, sued and served with process on being found temporarily in the jurisdiction of

---

10   210 U.S. 230 (1908).

the court, so that in a suit here on such judgment the illegal character of the cause of action may not be inquired into...

If this be law, all that is necessary to free the most corrupt transaction from all objection is to obtain service on a party, and get judgment in another state, and then come into a court of this state, and obtain judgment by virtue of article 4, § 1, Const. U.S., and the act of congress in pursuance of it. . . .

Lum v. Fauntleroy, 80 Miss. 757 (1902).

The United States Supreme Court took Fauntleroy's appeal. The Court acknowledged that the guaranty was against Mississippi's public policy—noting even that the gambling transaction was a misdemeanor under Mississippi law. Yet the Full Faith and Credit Clause did not allow Mississippi to invoke its own policies or interests. Rather, provided the Missouri court had personal jurisdiction over Lum (a fact not contested here, because Lum was personally served while visiting Missouri), the Mississippi courts were obliged to give to the Missouri judgment (F_1) the faith and credit that a Missouri court would give its own judgment.

But, as the jurisdiction of the Missouri court is not open to dispute, the judgment cannot be impeached in Mississippi even if it went upon a misapprehension of the Mississippi law. . . . We feel no apprehensions that painful or humiliating consequences will follow upon our decision. No court would give judgment for a plaintiff unless it believed that the facts were a cause of action by the law determining their effect. Mistakes will be rare. In this case the Missouri court no doubt supposed that the award was binding by the law of Mississippi. If it was mistaken, it made a natural mistake. The validity of its judgment, even in Mississippi, is, as we believe, the result of the Constitution as it always has been understood, and is not a matter to arouse the susceptibilities of the states, all of which are equally concerned in the question and equally on both sides.

Fauntleroy v. Lum, 210 U.S. 230, 237 (1908) (Holmes, J.). A four-Justice dissent lamented that the "ruling so enlarges the [Full Faith and Credit C]lause as to cause it to obliterate all state lines, since the effect will be to endow each state with authority to overthrow the public policy and criminal statutes of the others, thereby depriving all of their lawful authority." 210 U.S. at 239 (White, J., dissenting).

Fauntleroy is still good precedent, and there are very exceptions to the general principle that F_1 judgments must be rubber-stamped (i.e., not revisited) when presented in the courts of F_2.

Hypothetical 22-1

Schmitt Network Service LLC filed a complaint against Virding Co. for breach of a services contract. Schmitt had billed Virding monthly over the course of two years, and Virding was $75,000 in arrears when Schmitt filed suit in a Nevada state court, where Schmitt was located. Virding was properly served in New Hampshire, where that business is located. Virding did not answer the complaint, and a default judgment promptly entered.

Virding has clients in Nevada, but no assets nor employees. Schmitt hired counsel to domesticate the judgment in New Hampshire. Virding challenges enforcement, claiming that it is entitled to vacate the judgment on grounds of excusable neglect. In both Nevada and New Hampshire, Rule 60 of the state rules of civil procedure allow the court to vacate a judgment for "mistake, inadvertence, surprise, or excusable neglect," provided the motion is made not more than a year after entry of the judgment.

Virding's chief executive offer has persuasive evidence that the company missed the relevant deadline because of a tragic collision of two events: (i) a fire that destroyed a significant part of the business; and (ii) the death of the Nevada lawyer that they hired to represent them. The default judgment was entered less than two months ago.

How should the New Hampshire court rule on Virding's motion?

Hypothetical 22-2

Horizon Telephone Inc. is a major telecommunications company that is incorporated in Delaware and has its principal place of business in Virginia. Horizon was looking for corporate talent to hire and targeted Doris Christopher, who worked for a rival company in Phoenix, Arizona. Executives in Horizon's southwest regional office in Los Angeles recruited and ultimately hired Christopher, who moved to Los Angeles and worked there for ten months before she quit.

Christopher's employment agreement with Horizon provided that in the event Christopher terminated the contract without cause within the first twelve of months of her employment she would be obligated to repay the signing bonus ($45,000) and moving expenses ($20,000) that she received, and would also reimburse Horizon for certain enumerated expenses incurred with her recruitment ($15,000). The agreement also contained a forum selection clause with the parties identifying Virginia as the exclusive forum for all disputes arising out of the employment relationship.

When Christopher refused Horizon's demand for $80,000, Horizon filed suit in a state court in Virginia. Christopher was properly served, but did not appear. She has absolutely no connection to or contacts in Virginia. The court entered a default judgment.

Horizon filed an enforcement action in California, where Christopher lives and has assets. Under California law, unlike other states' laws, forum selection clauses are viewed with suspicion—especially in the employment context where employees have little bargaining power. California courts rarely enforce a forum selection clause that selects a forum other than the employee's place of hire or place(s) of work.

Christopher objects to enforcement asserting lack of personal jurisdiction. Christopher also objects on the grounds that the Virginia state court lacked subject matter jurisdiction; the parties to that suit were diverse and the amount in controversy exceeded $75,000.

How should the California court rule when Christopher moves to vacate the Virginia judgment?

Hypothetical 22-3

Stippich Jewelry Inc. is an independent sales representative company for jewelry manufacturers. Stippich is a Delaware corporation that has its principal place of business in Illinois.

Mattern Imports Co. is an importer, seller, and distributor of silver jewelry to retail and department stores throughout the United States. Mattern is a New York corporation that has its principal place of business in New York.

Stippich and Mattern entered into an oral agreement whereby Stippich agreed to secure new accounts for Mattern. Each time that Stippich secured a new account, Stippich and Mattern would agree on a commission schedule. Each month Mattern would send Stippich a statement detailing items shipped to retailers, and Stippich would send Mattern an invoice detailing the commissions due from those orders. The relationship went smoothly for about a year, but then Mattern quit paying all of the invoiced amounts. Mattern is in turmoil amidst internecine fights, financial troubles, and a public relations mess.

Stippich eventually filed suit in Illinois. Mattern was served but did not appear. A default judgment entered. The trial judge ordered a separate hearing to determine the amount of damages. In that hearing Stippich submitted copies of invoices, witness testimony, and an accounting showing $194,500 in unpaid invoices.

Stippich now seeks to domesticate the judgment in New York. Mattern challenges enforcement with evidence that Stippich lied to the Illinois judge. Specifically, Stippich failed to provide copies of four checks that Mattern had sent to Stippich and that Stippich had cashed. Each of these checks corresponded with a specific amount on an invoice that Stippich presented to the Illinois court as unpaid. The four checks totaled $104,500.

Assume that Mattern's evidence is correct and that it was only $90,000 in arrears. Should the New York court enforce all, part, or none of the Illinois judgment?

FROM THE COURTS

ADDINGTON v. VIRGIN GREEN FUND I, L.P.

Court of Appeals of Kentucky
2014 WL 3714615 (Ky. Ct. App. July 25, 2014)

TAYLOR, JUDGE.

Robert R. Addington brings this appeal from an October 2, 2012, Order of the Fayette Circuit Court granting the motion to domesticate a foreign judgment and to execute thereupon filed by Virgin Green Fund I, L.P. We affirm.

Addington executed a personal guaranty (Amended and Restated Guaranty Agreement) of a promissory note in favor of Virgin Green Fund I, L.P. (Virgin Green). The promissory note was for the principal amount of $15,000,000, and the primary debtor was DTX Oil, LLC (DTX). Addington was the principal officer of DTX.

Eventually, DTX defaulted upon the terms of the promissory note and entered into bankruptcy proceedings. Virgin Green filed an action against Addington upon the personal guaranty in Superior Court of the State of Delaware. Despite being properly served Addington neither responded nor appeared in the Delaware action. As a consequence, a default judgment was entered against Addington on April 19, 2012, in the amount of $20,276,052.50 plus 5.75 post-judgment interest.

Virgin Green then filed a Notice and Affidavit of Foreign Judgment Recognition in the Fayette Circuit Court in Kentucky pursuant to Kentucky Revised Statutes (KRS) 426.955. Virgin Green sought to domesticate the Delaware default and execute thereupon in Kentucky. Addington filed an "answer" and subsequently filed motions to dismiss or quash domestication of the Delaware default judgment.

By order entered October 2, 2012, the circuit court held that the Delaware default judgment was valid and domesticated the judgment in Kentucky. The court also granted Virgin Green's motion to execute upon the default judgment in Kentucky. This appeal follows.

Addington contends that the circuit court erred by domesticating the Delaware default judgment and permitting execution upon the judgment in Kentucky. Addington raises various defenses to Virgin Green's entitlement to collect upon the personal guaranty.

The Kentucky Legislature adopted the Uniform Enforcement of Foreign Judgments Act codified in KRS 426.950–990. A foreign judgment is defined as "any judgment, decree, or order of a court of the United States or any other court which is entitled to full faith and credit in this Commonwealth." KRS 426.950. The procedure for the domestication of a foreign judgment is set forth in KRS 426.955:

> A copy of any foreign judgment authenticated in accordance with the Act of Congress or the statutes of this state may be filed in the office of the clerk of any court of competent jurisdiction of this state. The clerk shall treat the foreign judgment in the same manner as a judgment of any court of this state. A judgment so filed has the same effect and is subject to the same procedures, defenses and proceedings for reopening, vacating, or staying as a judgment of a court of this state and may be enforced or satisfied in like manner.

And, our Court has recognized that "a sister state's judgment is entitled to full faith and credit and to registration if the judgment is valid under that state's own laws." *Sunrise Turquoise, Inc. v. Chemical Design Co., Inc.*, 899 S.W.2d 856, 857–58 (Ky. App. 1995).

In the case at hand, Addington does not argue that the Delaware default judgment is invalid under Delaware law. And, Addington does not argue that the default judgment should be set aside [for mistake, inadvertence, excusable neglect, newly discovered evidence and fraud.] Instead, Addington asserts that Virgin Green is not entitled to collect upon the personal guaranty and sets forth various "defenses" upon the merits. However, a default judgment is not granted upon the merits of a claim under either Delaware law (Rule 55) or Kentucky law (CR 55.01). But, a default judgment is granted based upon a party's failure to enter an appearance. It is undisputed that Addington received proper notice of the Delaware proceeding and failed to enter an appearance therein. Addington does not dispute these facts. Consequently, Addington has failed to demonstrate that the default judgment was invalid under Delaware law (Rule 55).

Accordingly, we hold that the circuit court properly domesticated the Delaware default judgment and permitted enforcement thereof in Kentucky. . . .

COMMENTS AND QUESTIONS

1. Addington's defense on the merits could be, for example, that his signature was forged, or that conditions to his obligation were not satisfied, etc. When will his merits arguments be evaluated by a court?

2. What result in this case if Virgin Green filed in Delaware *because* it was an especially inconvenient forum for Addington?

FROM THE COURTS

BROWN v. GARRETT

Court of Appeals of Washington
175 Wash. App. 357 (2013)

SCHINDLER, JUDGE.

. . . Rod J. Garrett d/b/a Best Auto Limited and Mark A. Thompson d/b/a Best Auto (collectively Best Auto) own a used car business in Washington. In April 2008, Best Auto listed for sale on eBay a 2004 Mini Cooper with approximately 76,000 miles. The eBay advertisement states that Best Auto sells to purchasers in North and South America, Europe, and Australia. The advertisement describes the condition of the 2004 Mini Cooper as follows:

> THIS CAR RUNS AS SMOOTH AS SILK. . . In total, this is a clean, well cared for, smoke-free, great-driving MINI. I take great pride in the vehicles we sell and feel that you should know as much about the car as possible. Accordingly, here is a list of the good and also things needing attention: All the glass is in great shape—no cracks or delam[ination] spots. Hop in, fire her up and this car starts instantly, even when cold. It idles, runs and drives as it should—strong oil pressure, strong battery and charging system, no overheating, no brake pull or alignment issues! I've driven it many miles over the past few weeks and freeway cruised at 75 MPH.
>
> Please look again at the interior [pictures]. The dark grey leather upholstery is all-original with the pictures giving a very accurate view of its clean, soft condition. You'll feel comfortable sitting on these firm seats for hours and they can be adjusted for height as well as forward/back and, when needed, they're heated too! The electric window lifts and [air conditioning] system all work great. Push a button and roll back the large power moonroof for that open-air drive! . . . The car is equipped with Dynamic Stability Control (DSC) operated by a dash switch that enables you to take corners on those twisty country roads at 90+ MPH! As you can probably guess from the photos, the original rubber factory mats have done a great job of protecting the clean carpets

beneath. It is a bit difficult to tell from the photos, but I can see several body panels have had paintwork done sometime in the past. Don't know why as there's no history of accidents or other negatives, but my professional eye catches it on a close inspection all the same. . . . I have every confidence this MINI Cooper could easily be drive cross-country tomorrow.

We've sold many cars here on eBay over the past few years and the one thing I'm questioned about again and again is shipping. Because we're up in Washington State, at the Northwestern tip of the country, many Midwesterners and folks on the East Coast sometimes are reluctant to bid due to distance. DON'T BE CONCERNED! We ship cars out almost weekly and are happy to arrange and/or work with the transporter of your choice. As outlined above, please contact me here at BEST AUTO with any questions or for suggestions. My name is Mark Thompson and my direct phone number is 206/914–1173. [A]nd, yes, it is for sale locally before this auction ends if you'd like to make an offer.

William and Julie Brown live in Aledo, Texas. The Browns read the eBay description of the Mini Cooper. At the time, the "[c]urrent bid" was listed as $10,000. On April 27, the Browns called Best Auto about the Mini Cooper. Best Auto agreed to sell the car directly to the Browns for $11,250. On April 27, the eBay advertisement states that "[t]he seller ended this listing early because the item is no longer available for sale."

On April 28, the Browns sent $11,250 by wire transfer to Best Auto. Best Auto faxed a "Vehicle Purchase Order" to the Browns. The Vehicle Purchase Order states the odometer "reads 076,115 miles." The Browns used a company recommended by Best Auto to ship the Mini Cooper from Washington to a shipment center in Mesquite, Texas.

On May 13, the Browns went to Mesquite to pick up the Mini Cooper. After inspecting the exterior of the car, the Browns called Best Auto about "several trim items." Best Auto agreed to pay the cost to repair the trim items.

The Browns took possession of the Mini Cooper. Julie Brown drove the Mini Cooper. Less than 10 miles from the shipping center, Julie noticed the air condition was not working and the engine temperature gauge pointed to "HOT." Julie immediately pulled over and called a tow truck. The tow truck operator took the car to the nearest authorized Mini Cooper dealership, Moritz Mini of North Arlington, Texas.

The Browns asked the mechanic at Moritz Mini to inspect the car, identify the cause of the problem, and provide an estimate. The mechanic identified a number of necessary repairs, including the need to fix the cracked radiator and front panel, a leaking valve cover gasket, and the power steering pump. The estimated cost of repairs was $4,012.61. The Moritz Mini mechanic noted, "75% of Body Panels have been Repainted." The Browns faxed the repair estimate to Best Auto.

After communicating with Best Auto a number of times, the Browns demanded Best Auto take possession of the car and refund the purchase price. The Browns said Best Auto misrepresented the condition of the Mini Cooper and that it would cost nearly half of the purchase price to make the car run properly. Best Auto suggested the Browns auction the car in Texas. Best Auto assured the Browns the auction operator would be able to sell the Mini Cooper for the purchase price. Best Auto offered to help arrange the auction and pay $350 to repair the radiator. The Browns agreed to auction the Mini Cooper. The Browns paid an additional $800 to repair the car.

On May 27, the Browns drove the Mini Cooper from Moritz Mini to the auction site in Texas. The auction company attempted to sell the car at least two different times.

On June 18, William Brown contacted Thompson to demand Best Auto refund the purchase price, pay for repairs, and accept return of the car. William stated that "the car was nothing like you represented in the ebay ad." William told Thompson that another mechanic at a dealership in Fort Worth inspected the car and "found a long list of problems including a cracked radiator, failed power steering pump, a dead [air conditioning] unit, 75% replaced and repainted panels, and obvious signs that the car had been in a wreck, including frame damage." William also expressed concern about Best Auto's failure to send the title.

> Where did you get this from? You still haven't sent us the title. . . . Since we have not received the title, I am wondering if this is a salvage vehicle or if there is some other documented sign that this was deemed totaled from a wreck. Our estimates from the dealer here show it will take over $4,000 to repair just to get it on the road. In addition we have spent over $2,000 for related expenses.

In mid-July, Best Auto sent the Browns the "Vehicle Certification of Ownership (Title)" to the Mini Cooper. The title states that Best Auto transferred the Mini Cooper to the Browns on April 27, 2008. Contrary to Best Auto's representation that Thompson drove the Mini Cooper "many miles over the past few weeks and freeway cruised at 75 MPH," the disclosure and release of interest by the registered owner showed that when Best Auto purchased the car on March 29, 2008, the odometer reading was 76,114 miles, and it was 76,115 miles when Best Auto transferred title to the Browns on April 27.

On August 6, 2008, the Browns filed a lawsuit against Best Auto in Parker County, Texas. The complaint alleged breach of contract, unjust enrichment, promissory estoppel, fraud, and violations of the Texas Deceptive Trade Practices Consumer Protection Act (DTPA). The Browns sought economic damages for the purchase price of $11,250, reimbursement for repairs, gas, and shipping, and treble damages and attorney fees and costs under the DTPA. The Browns served Best Auto through the Texas Secretary of State by certified mail. On August 20, the Texas Secretary State received proof of service and the return receipt from Best Auto.

On September 2, an attorney representing Best Auto informed the attorney for the Browns that Best Auto "has contacted an attorney in Texas to seek dismissal of this action" based on the forum selection clause in the Vehicle Purchase Order. The state of Washington is designated as the forum to enforce the contract in the section addressing "Attorney's Fees and Costs." But Best Auto did not file a notice of appearance or otherwise participate in the Texas proceedings.

The Browns filed a motion for a default judgment. The Texas court entered a judgment against Best Auto that includes treble damages under the DTPA, as well as prejudgment interest, attorney fees, and costs. The judgment states, in pertinent part:

> The Court determined it had jurisdiction over the subject matter and the parties to this proceeding. No jury having been demanded, all matters in controversy, legal and factual, were submitted to the Court. Defendants, although having been duly and legally cited to appear and answer, failed to appear and answer, and wholly made default.

> Citation was served upon the Texas Secretary of State according to law and the Certificates of Service were returned to the Clerk

where they remained on file for more than ten days as required by law. The court has read the pleadings and the papers on file, and is of the opinion that the allegations of Plaintiffs' Original Petition have been admitted, including the Defendants' knowing violation of the Texas Deceptive Trade Practices Act, that the causes of action are liquidated and proven by an instrument in writing as to Plaintiffs' actual damages, and that the causes of action are unliquidated as to Plaintiffs' costs and reasonable attorneys' fees and, on good and sufficient evidence presented to the Court, finds that the Defendants are jointly and severally indebted to Plaintiffs in the trebled sum of Thirty Nine Thousand Four Hundred Seventeen and 00/100 Dollars ($39,417.00), plus prejudgment interest at the rate of five percent (5%) per annum beginning on July 3, 2008 (the last date an element of damage was incurred) in the amount of Four Hundred Forty Two and 76/100 Dollars ($442.76) as of September 23, 2008, accruing at the rate of $5.39 per day until the date of entry of this Judgment, and that Plaintiffs should recover a reasonable and necessary attorneys' fee, which the court finds to be Seven Thousand Five Hundred Ninety Three and 75/100 ($7,593.75), and costs incurred in the amount of Six Hundred Ninety Nine and 00/100 ($699.00).

The Browns filed the Texas judgment in King County Superior Court, and obtained a write to garnish the funds of Best Auto at Banner Bank.

Best Auto filed a motion to vacate the Texas judgment and quash the writ of garnishment. Best Auto argued that because the Texas court did not have jurisdiction, the judgment was void. The Browns argued the Texas court had jurisdiction under the Texas long-arm statute and Best Auto did not file a motion in the Texas court to enforce the forum selection clause. The Browns also disputed whether the forum selection clause was enforceable.

The superior court entered an order vacating the Texas judgment and quashing the writ of garnishment. The Browns appeal.

Analysis

The Browns contend the King County Superior Court order vacating the Texas judgment violates the Full Faith and Credit Clause of the federal constitution, article IV, section 1, and the Uniform Enforcement of Foreign

Judgments Act (UEFJA), [Revised Code of Washington (RCW)] chapter 6.36. The Browns assert the Texas court had jurisdiction under the Texas long-arm statute, and Best Auto cannot collaterally attack the judgment based on the forum selection clause. We review de novo the decision to grant or deny a motion to vacate a default judgment for lack of jurisdiction.

UEFJA

Under the Full Faith and Credit Clause of the United States Constitution, a judgment rendered by one state is entitled to recognition in Washington. U.S. Const. art. IV, § 1 ("Full faith and credit shall be given in each state to the public acts, records, and judicial proceedings of every other state."). . . . "The Full Faith and Credit Clause provides a means for ending litigation by putting to rest matters previously decided between adverse parties in any state or territory of the United States." *State v. Berry*, 141 Wash.2d 121, 127 (2000).

The UEFJA codifies the Full Faith and Credit Clause. Under the UEFJA, creditors holding a judgment against a debtor from another jurisdiction can enforce that judgment in Washington. RCW 6.36.025. Once the foreign judgment is filed in superior court, it becomes a registered foreign judgment in this state. RCW 6.36.010(1), (2); RCW 6.36.025(1), (2).

A party can collaterally attack a foreign judgment only if the court did not have jurisdiction or the judgment violates a constitutional right, such as notice and the opportunity to be heard. Absent these grounds, "a court of this state must give full faith and credit to the foreign judgment and regard the issues thereby adjudged to be precluded in a Washington proceeding." *In re Estate of Tolson*, 89 Wash. App. 21, 30 (1997).

We review de novo whether the superior court erred in refusing to accord full faith and credit to a foreign judgment. A party attacking a foreign judgment has the burden of establishing lack of jurisdiction. *Williams v. Steamship Mut. Underwriting Ass'n, Ltd.*, 45 Wash.2d 209, 213 (1954) (Washington courts presume a court of general jurisdiction in a sister state has jurisdiction over the cause and the parties "unless disproved by extrinsic evidence or by the record itself.").

Jurisdiction Under the Texas Long-Arm Statute

The Browns contend the Texas court had jurisdiction under the Texas long-arm statute and the foreign judgment was entitled to full faith and credit in Washington. We apply the law of Texas to determine whether the Texas court had jurisdiction over the parties.

The Texas long-arm statute authorizes the exercise of jurisdiction over a nonresident defendant "doing business" in the state of Texas. Tex. Civ. Prac. & Rem. Code Ann. § 17.042. Personal jurisdiction under the Texas long-arm statute is valid to the extent allowed by due process under the federal constitution.

The Texas court had the authority to exercise personal jurisdiction over Best Auto if it "purposefully established 'minimum contacts' in the forum State," and requiring Best Auto to litigate in the forum state did not offend "traditional conception[s] of fair play and substantial justice." *Burger King Corp. v. Rudzewicz*, 471 U.S. 462, 474, 464 (1985) (quoting *Int'l Shoe Co. v. Wash.*, 326 U.S. 310, 316, 320 (1945)).

The requirement that a defendant purposefully establish minimum contacts ensures that a defendant "will not be haled into a jurisdiction solely as a result of . . . the 'unilateral activity of another party or a third person.' " *Burger King*, 471 U.S. at 475 (quoting *Helicopteros Nacionales de Colombia, S.A. v. Hall*, 466 U.S. 408, 417 (1984)). . . .

Here, the record establishes Best Auto purposely availed itself of the privilege of conducting business activities in Texas. The advertisement Best Auto placed on eBay for the Mini Cooper states that Best Auto sells cars to purchasers throughout North America. It is undisputed that Best Auto communicated with the Browns in Texas by telephone, email, and fax to negotiate the sale of the Mini Cooper, to obtain the wire transfer of the purchase price, and to send the Vehicle Purchase Order and title to the Browns. And after shipping the Mini Cooper to Texas, Best Auto continued to communicate with the Browns about repairs to the Mini Cooper, and coordinated with the auction company in Texas in an effort to sell the Mini Cooper at auction.

The case Best Auto relies on to argue the Texas court did not have jurisdiction under the long-arm statute is distinguishable. In *Mink*, a Texas resident sued a Vermont corporation for an alleged patent violation. *Mink v. AAAA Dev. LLC*, 190 F.3d 333, 335 (5th Cir. 1999). The Texas court dismissed for lack of personal jurisdiction. The Fifth Circuit affirmed on the grounds that the sole contact the corporation had with Texas was through a website that did not allow the user to order or purchase products or services on-line. *Mink*, 190 F.3d at 336–37.

In determining whether to subject Best Auto to litigation in the forum state, the court examines (1) the defendant's burden, (2) the forum state's interests, (3) the plaintiff's interest in convenient and effective relief, (4) the judicial system's interest in efficient resolution of controversies, and (5) the shared interest of the several states in furthering fundamental social policies. *World-Wide Volkswagen Corp. v. Woodson*, 444 U.S. 286, 292 (1980); *Asahi Metal Indus. Co., Ltd. v. Superior Court of Cal.*, 480 U.S. 102, 113 (1987). Because Texas has a strong interest in adjudicating a dispute that involves the sale of goods to consumers residing in Texas, requiring Best Auto to litigate in Texas does not offend "traditional conception[s] of fair play and substantial justice." *Int'l Shoe*, 326 U.S. at 320. We conclude that Texas had jurisdiction over the parties under the Texas long-arm statute.

Forum Selection Clause

Best Auto asserts that even if the Texas court had jurisdiction under the long-arm statute, "the forum selection clause outweighs the long arm statute jurisdiction." Best Auto claims it can collaterally attack enforcement of the Texas judgment based on the forum selection clause in the Vehicle Purchase Order. The Browns argue that because Best Auto did not file a motion in Texas to enforce the forum selection clause, it cannot collaterally attack enforcement of the judgment.

The Vehicle Purchase Order contains a forum selection clause in the paragraph addressing Attorney's Fees and Costs.

> 7. Attorneys' Fees and Costs. If this contract is placed in the hands of an attorney by reason of Purchaser's default or to enforce any provisions of this contract, the prevailing party shall be entitled to recover its reasonable attorney's fees and costs. The parties agree that the venue for any suit, action, or proceeding relating to the enforcement of this contract shall be in the county in which the Dealer's principal place of business is located within the State of Washington. The laws of the State of Washington shall be applied in the interpretation and construction of this Agreement.

Without regard to minimum contacts, parties can enter into an agreement consenting to personal jurisdiction. *RAHCO Int'l, Inc. v. Laird Elec., Inc.*, 502 F.Supp.2d 1118, 1122 (E.D. Wash. 2006) ("[P]arties may consent to the jurisdiction of a particular court through the use of a forum-selection clause in a contract, regardless of minimum contacts.").

In *The Bremen v. Zapata Off-Shore Co.*, 407 U.S. 1 (1972), the United States Supreme Court held that a forum selection clause is prima facie valid and should be enforced unless enforcement would be "unreasonable and unjust." *The Bremen*, 407 U.S. at 10, 15. . . .

Under the UEFJA, the Texas judgment "is subject to the same procedures [and] defenses . . . as a judgment of a superior court of this state." RCW 6.36.025(1). A party must timely raise a forum selection clause in a motion to dismiss. *Voicelink Data Servs., Inc. v. Datapulse, Inc.*, 86 Wash. App. 613, 618 (1997); *Deep Water Slender Wells, Ltd. v. Shell Int'l Exploration & Prod., Inc.*, 234 S.W.3d 679, 687 (Tex. App. 2007).

In *Voicelink*, we held that a party seeking to enforce a forum selection clause must file a motion to dismiss under CR 12(b)(3).

> [D]etermination of the enforceability of forum selection clauses under CR 12(b)(3) furthers judicial economy and efficiency by requiring assertion of the venue defense at a relatively early stage of the proceeding. . . . Furthermore, a determination under CR 12(b)(3) is consistent with the standard articulated by the U.S. Supreme Court and our courts for resolving motions to dismiss based on a forum selection clause, which requires submission of evidence by the party challenging its enforceability.

Voicelink, 86 Wash. App. at 624. Likewise, in *Deep Water*, the Texas court held that a motion to dismiss "is the proper procedural mechanism for enforcing a forum-selection clause that a party to the agreement has violated in filing suit." *Deep Water*, 234 S.W.3d at 687.

Here, there is no dispute that Best Auto was properly served but did not file a motion in the Texas court to enforce the forum selection clause. Nonetheless, Best Auto claims it can collaterally attack enforcement of the Texas judgment on this ground for the first time in Washington. . . .

COMMENTS AND QUESTIONS

1. Does a forum selection clause identifying Washington as the exclusive forum for resolution of the parties' contractual disputes *oust* other states from exercising jurisdiction or, instead, merely give those states a strong

reason to transfer the case to a Washington court? The answer to that question determines whether the Texas judgment must be enforced.

2. On what bases other than the Texas court's lack of personal jurisdiction could Best Auto have challenged the enforceability of the Texas judgment?

3. Notice how the Full Faith and Credit Clause restricts a court's ability to protect residents of the forum from aggressive (albeit lawful) actions taken by foreign courts. This Washington court must enforce a foreign (Texas) judgment to the benefit of a Texas resident and to the detriment of a Washington resident.

FROM THE COURTS

DOCRX, INC. v. EMI SERVS. OF NORTH CAROLINA, LLC

Supreme Court of North Carolina
367 N.C. 371, cert. denied, 135 S. Ct. 678 (2014)

PARKER, CHIEF JUSTICE.

The issue in this case is whether the Court of Appeals erred by holding that the Full Faith and Credit clause precludes the use of intrinsic fraud to defeat a foreign monetary judgment pursuant to North Carolina's Uniform Enforcement of Foreign Judgment Act and N.C.G.S. § 1A-1, Rule 60(b) (3). For the reasons stated herein, we modify and affirm the decision of the Court of Appeals.

DocRx, Inc. (plaintiff), an Alabama corporation, filed a breach of contract action against EMI Services of North Carolina, LLC (defendant) in Mobile County, Alabama on 6 August 2010. The complaint alleged that the defendant failed to pay plaintiff the agreed upon commission from defendant's pharmaceuticals sales under a contract the parties entered on June 28, 2010. Specifically, the complaint alleged that defendant failed to pay plaintiff "25% of all net profits of [defendant's] sales made of products supplied . . . by an [an intermediate company]" located by plaintiff. The complaint sought, *inter alia*, "compensatory damages, plus interest and costs" but did not allege a specific monetary amount of damages. Defendant did not respond to the complaint, and an initial default judgment was entered on 24 September 2010.

During the default proceedings in Alabama, Brian Ward (Ward), the President and CEO of plaintiff corporation, filed an affidavit with the court in which he stated that defendant sold 3,504 units "for $500 per unit, for a total profit of $475 per unit." Plaintiff's counsel filed a Motion to Enter Default Judgment Amount adopting Ward's statement. Plaintiff's counsel calculated that defendant's total net profits for the sale of the units was $1,664,400 and that plaintiff was entitled to a commission payment of $416,100, which represented 25% of defendant's total net profits. Plaintiff's counsel also alleged that plaintiff was entitled to recover reasonable attorneys' fees in the amount of $12,587.14 and interest on the breach of contract claim in the amount of $24,996. On 1 April 2011, the Circuit Court of Mobile County, Alabama entered a second default judgment against defendant for $453,683.14 (the Alabama judgment). . . .

The central issue in this case is whether the Full Faith and Credit Clause requires North Carolina courts to enforce the Alabama monetary judgment. This issue involves a question of law, which we review de novo.

To determine this issue, we look first to the language of the Full Faith and Credit Clause and the United States Supreme Court's jurisprudence interpreting this constitutional provision. The Full Faith and Credit Clause of the United States Constitution provides that "Full Faith and Credit shall be given in each State to the public Acts, Records, and judicial Proceedings of every other State. And the Congress may by general Laws prescribe the Manner in which such Acts, Records and Proceedings shall be proved, and the Effect thereof." U.S. Const. art. IV, § 1. Pursuant to that clause Congress has prescribed:

> Such Acts, records and judicial proceedings or copies thereof, so authenticated, shall have the same full faith and credit in every court within the United States and its Territories and Possessions as they have by law or usage in the courts of such State, Territory or Possession from which they are taken

28 U.S.C. § 1738 (2012). The purpose of the full faith and credit command

> was to alter the status of the several states as independent foreign sovereignties, each free to ignore obligations created under the laws or by the judicial proceedings of the others, and to make

them integral parts of a single nation throughout which a remedy upon a just obligation might be demanded as of right, irrespective of the state of its origin

Baker v. Gen. Motors Corp., 522 U.S. 222, 232 (1998).

Under United States Supreme Court decisions, the test for determining when the Full Faith and Credit Clause requires enforcement of a foreign judgment focuses on the validity and finality of the judgment in the rendering state. *See Morris v. Jones*, 329 U.S. 545 (1947). . . :

> A judgment of a court having jurisdiction of the parties and of the subject matter operates as res judicata, in the absence of fraud or collusion, even if obtained upon a default. Such a judgment obtained in a sister State is . . . entitled to full faith and credit in another State, though the underlying claim would not be enforced in the State of the forum. It is no more important that the suit on this underlying claim could not have been maintained in [the enforcing state] than the fact that a statute of limitations of the State of the forum might have barred it. . . . The full faith and credit to which a judgment is entitled is the credit which it has in the State from which it is taken, not the credit that under other circumstances and conditions it might have had.
>
> Under [the law of the rendering state] petitioner's judgment was a final determination of the nature and amount of his claim. That determination is final and conclusive in all courts. . . .
>
> The command [of the federal statute implementing the Full Faith and Credit Clause] is to give full faith and credit to every judgment of a sister State. And where there is no jurisdictional infirmity, exceptions have rarely, if ever, been read into the constitutional provision or the Act of Congress in cases involving money judgments rendered in civil suits.

Id. at 550–53. . . .

Thus, if the foreign judgment is valid and final in the rendering state, it is conclusive in the forum state and is entitled to receive full faith and credit. If the foreign judgment can be modified in the rendering state, it is not conclusive and can be modified by the forum state.

The UEFJA enacted in North Carolina sets out the procedure for filing a foreign judgment. N.C.G.S. §§ 1C-1701 to -1708 (2013). Section 1C-1703(c) states that "[a] judgment so filed has the same effect and is subject to the same defenses as a judgment of this State and shall be enforced or satisfied in like manner." N.C.G.S. § 1C-1703(c). A foreign judgment debtor may seek relief from the foreign judgment on the grounds that it "has been appealed from" or "stayed by" the rendering court "or on any other ground for which relief from a judgment of this State would be allowed." N.C.G.S. § 1C-1705(a).

Defendant contends that the phrase "is subject to the same defenses as a judgment of this State," N.C.G.S. § 1C-1703(c), entitles it to challenge the Alabama judgment under Rule 60(b) of the North Carolina Rules of Civil Procedure and that the trial court was, therefore, correct in denying plaintiff's motion to enforce the Alabama judgment on the ground that it was obtained by "intrinsic fraud, misrepresentation and misconduct of the plaintiff," namely, false testimony as to the amount of defendant's indebtedness to plaintiff. Defendant asserts that because Rule 60(b)(3) of the Alabama Rules of Civil Procedure, like Rule 60(b)(3) of the North Carolina Rules of Civil Procedure, provides for relief from a judgment for "fraud (whether heretofore denominated intrinsic or extrinsic), misrepresentation, or other misconduct of an adverse party," Ala. R. Civ. P. 60(b)(3), both the Full Faith and Credit Clause and the UEFJA are satisfied. *See* N.C.G.S. § 1A–1, Rule 60(b)(3) (2013).

This Court has not previously addressed the interplay among the Full Faith and Credit Clause, North Carolina's UEFJA, and Rule 60(b) of the North Carolina Rules of Civil Procedure. However, other state supreme courts that have considered the interplay between the Full Faith and Credit Clause and the UEFJA have rejected the argument that the judgment of the rendering state can be reopened in the forum state under Rule 60 of the Rules of Civil Procedure. For example, in *Matson v. Matson*, the Minnesota UEFJA provided that *"[a] judgment so filed has the same effect and is subject to the same procedures, defenses and proceedings for reopening, vacating, or staying a judgment of a district court or the supreme court of this state, and may be enforced or satisfied in like manner."* 333 N.W.2d 862, 867 (Minn. 1983) (en banc) (quoting Minn. Stat. § 548.27 (1982) (emphasis added)). Interpreting this provision, the Supreme Court of Minnesota stated:

> Appellant is under the misconception that the above-emphasized language allows the courts of this state to apply Minn. R. Civ. P.

60.02 to foreign judgments in the same manner it is applied to judgments of the courts of this state. It has been settled by the United States Supreme Court and courts of other states that the power of a state to reopen or vacate a foreign judgment is more limited than under the rules of civil procedure and that a foreign judgment cannot be collaterally attacked on the merits. After a foreign judgment has been duly filed, the grounds for reopening or vacating it are limited to lack of personal or subject matter jurisdiction of the rendering court, fraud in procurement (extrinsic), satisfaction, lack of due process, or other grounds that make a judgment invalid or unenforceable. The nature and amount or other aspects of the merits (i.e., defenses) of a foreign judgment cannot be relitigated in the state in which enforcement is sought. *See Morris v. Jones*, 329 U.S. 545 (1946).

Id. at 867–68 (citations omitted). . . .

This interpretation of the UEFJA also finds support in the Prefatory Note to the 1964 Revised Uniform Enforcement of Foreign Judgments Act, stating that the UEFJA as revised

adopts the practice which, in substance, is used in Federal courts. It provides the enacting state with a speedy and economical method of doing that which it is required to do by the Constitution of the United States. It also relieves creditors and debtors of the additional cost and harassment of further litigation which would otherwise be incident to the enforcement of the foreign judgment. This act offers the states a chance to achieve uniformity in a field where uniformity is highly desirable. Its enactment by the states should forestall Federal legislation in this field.

Rev. Unif. Enforcement of Foreign Judgments Act prefatory note (1964), 13 U.L.A. 156–57 (2002). . . . The federal statute, after providing for the registration of judgment in any other district, mentions only one defense, satisfaction, but does allow that "[t]he procedure prescribed under this section is in addition to other procedures provided by law for the enforcement of judgments." 28 U.S.C. § 1963 (2012). . . .

We hold that the defenses preserved under North Carolina's UEFJA are limited by the Full Faith and Credit Clause to those defenses which are directed to the validity and enforcement of a foreign judgment. The language of the UEFJA that a foreign judgment "has the same effect and is subject to the same defenses as a judgment of this State and shall be enforced or satisfied in like manner," N.C.G.S. § 1C-1703(c), does not refer to defenses on the merits but rather refers to defenses directed at the enforcement of a foreign judgment, such as, that the judgment creditor committed extrinsic fraud, that the rendering state lacked personal or subject matter jurisdiction, that the judgment has been paid, that the parties have entered into an accord and satisfaction, that the judgment debtor's property is exempt from execution, that the judgment is subject to continued modification, or that the judgment debtor's due process rights have been violated. To permit a party to relitigate matters that could have and should have been litigated in the rendering court is inconsistent with decisions of the United States Supreme Court holding that judgments that are valid and final in the rendering state are entitled to enforcement in the forum state under the Full Faith and Credit Clause. Further, to permit a party to collaterally attack a foreign judgment on the merits would be contrary to the rationale underlying the UEFJA, which is to streamline the procedure for enforcing a foreign judgment and eliminate the need for additional litigation. . . .

Therefore, we hold that the Alabama judgment is a final judgment, and . . . it is entitled to the same credit in North Carolina that it would be accorded in Alabama. The defenses to a foreign judgment under the UEFJA are limited by the Full Faith and Credit Clause to those defenses that are directed to the enforcement of the foreign judgment, and Rule 60(b) of the North Carolina Rules of Civil Procedure has no applicability.

Defendant's argument that the Court of Appeals decision should be reversed because a foreign judgment creditor would get better treatment than a North Carolina judgment creditor is misplaced. . . . The UEFJA is not on a parity with the Full Faith and Credit Clause. In the present case the Alabama monetary judgment was valid and final in Alabama, and North Carolina cannot give the Alabama judgment less credit than it would be given in Alabama.

For the reasons stated herein, the decision of the Court of Appeals is affirmed, as modified. This case is remanded to the Court of Appeals for further remand to the trial court for additional proceedings not inconsistent with this opinion.

COMMENTS AND QUESTIONS

1. How can the North Carolina Supreme Court disallow defenses to enforcement that are available under the UEFJA that was passed by the North Carolina state legislature?

2. The difference between intrinsic and extrinsic fraud can be elusive. Some jurisdictions describe intrinsic fraud as fraud that deceives the court in obtaining a judgment, and extrinsic fraud which happens outside of court, but which deprives an adversary of the opportunity to present its case. As with any issue of characterization, skilled litigators will manipulate the labels.

FROM THE COURTS

HONEYWELL INT'L, INC. v. KILGORE

Court of Appeals of Arizona
2015 WL 1044587 (Ariz. Ct. App. March 10, 2015)

OROZCO, JUDGE.

Honeywell International Inc. appeals from the trial court's decision dismissing its action to domesticate a New York default judgment and vacating that judgment against Jared Kilgore on the grounds that New York lacked personal jurisdiction over Kilgore. . . .

Facts and Procedural History

In December 2010, Honeywell obtained a default judgment for more than $830,000 against Kilgore, American Alarm Company, Inc., and Danielle Paletz in the Supreme Court of the State of New York, County of Suffolk. As to Kilgore, the default judgment was based on Honeywell's claim that Kilgore signed a guarantee to pay Honeywell by American Alarm Company. In January 2012, Honeywell filed a copy of the judgment in Maricopa County Superior Court, along with an Affidavit Substantiating a Foreign Judgment.

Kilgore filed a Notice of Limited Appearance and Motion to Vacate Default Judgment and Motion to Dismiss. Kilgore argued that judgment was void based on lack of due process because he was never properly served and never had actual notice of the New York action and disputed Honeywell's allegations of its attempts at service. Kilgore denied having signed the guarantee that was the basis of the judgment and argued that, New York never had personal jurisdiction over him.

Honeywell disputed Kilgore's claim that he did not sign the guarantee and argued that New York had personal jurisdiction based on a provision in the guarantee declaring that New York would have jurisdiction to adjudicate any disputes arising out of the guarantee. Honeywell further argued that Kilgore was properly served in Maricopa County, Arizona with the summons and verified complaint in the New York action under New York law by "nail and mail" service effectuated by the end of August 2010.

Without objection, the court held an evidentiary hearing to address the alleged forgery of Kilgore's signature on the guarantee and the "nail and mail" service. At the hearing, Kilgore testified that Danielle Paletz owned two separate companies, American Alarm Company, Inc., and American Alarm Partners of Arizona, Inc. He acknowledged doing consulting work for American Alarm Partners, but testified that he never worked for American Alarm Company and that he had never been an officer, director, or owner of either company. Kilgore denied signing the guarantee, alleging that the handwriting on the document was that of Paletz's colleague and then-fiancé, whom Kilgore knew to have forged other documents. He also noted that the guarantee did not identify any particular account number. For the New York action, Kilgore denied receiving personal service, service by mail, or service by attachment of the complaint to his residence. He argued that he would have been home and his wife was also at home when service was allegedly attempted and, accordingly, could not explain not having received the documents if service was in fact attempted as indicated on an affidavit of service.

Joshua Foster, an attorney for Honeywell, testified that he was unaware that American Alarm Company and American Alarm Partners were two separate companies. He also acknowledged that no account number was listed on the guarantee where it should have been and could not state from personal knowledge that the guarantee was affiliated with any particular account.

Based on the evidence and argument provided, the court found that Honeywell failed to prove that the guarantee was related to American Alarm Company, whose debt was the subject of the lawsuit. Because personal jurisdiction over Kilgore was based entirely on provisions in the guarantee and the guarantee was not found to be related to the debt, the court found that New York never acquired personal jurisdiction over Kilgore. The court vacated the default judgment as void. . . . Honeywell timely appealed. . . .

Discussion

. . . The Full Faith and Credit Clause of Article 2, Section 1 of the United States Constitution requires that a judgment rendered in a state court be accorded the same validity and effect in every other court in the United States as it has in the state rendering it. *Springfield Credit Union v. Johnson*, 123 Ariz. 319, 322–23 (1979). An authenticated foreign judgment is prima facie evidence of the rendering court's jurisdiction to enter it. Such a judgment filed in Arizona is treated in the same manner, has the same effect and is subject to the same procedures, defenses and proceedings for reopening, vacating, or staying as a judgment of a superior court of this state. A.R.S. § 12–1702 (West 2015).

A foreign judgment may be attacked on grounds of lack of personal or subject matter jurisdiction, lack of due process, incompetency of the foreign court, extrinsic fraud, and the invalidity or unenforceability of the judgment. The party attacking the judgment has the burden of proving that the judgment is not entitled to full faith and credit.

Whether a foreign judgment is entitled to full faith and credit is a question of law we review de novo. We are bound by the trial court's findings of facts unless clearly erroneous. We view the evidence and reasonable inferences from that evidence in the light most favorable to the prevailing party. We do not reweigh conflicting evidence and defer to the trial court's determination of witness credibility.

Honeywell argues that Kilgore's testimony was self-serving and not credible and that the evidence presented did not support the court's finding that Kilgore did not sign the guarantee. However, the court did not make such a finding. The court instead found that Honeywell failed to show that the guarantee was "related to American Alarm Company, Inc., the entity that apparently incurred the debt to" Honeywell. Because the provisions in the guarantee governing jurisdiction and choice of law were the only basis on which Honeywell claims New York had jurisdiction over Kilgore, the court found that New York lacked personal jurisdiction. The court did not resolve Kilgore's claims that he did not sign the guarantee and did not receive service.

The record supports the court's findings. As noted in the testimony of both Kilgore and Foster, the guarantee includes a blank for the applicable account number, but no account number appears in the document, and the guarantee does not otherwise identify the entity for whose debt the guarantee was given. When asked whether he had personal knowledge that the guarantee was associated with any particular account, Foster testified that he had personal knowledge that Honeywell had sought guarantees from three individuals to continue credit for the American Alarm Company account. He could not, however, connect the guarantee document to American Alarm Company.

Honeywell has not challenged on appeal the court's finding that Honeywell failed to prove that the guarantee was connected to the debt or the court's legal reasoning that the failure to show such a connection meant that the New York court lacked personal jurisdiction over Kilgore.[3] Consequently, we affirm the trial court's decision finding that New York lacked personal jurisdiction over Kilgore.

Honeywell argues that the trial court lacked the authority to vacate the underlying New York judgment except for its application in Arizona. Honeywell cites three cases in support. None of these cases is on point. Each recognizes that a foreign judgment may be attacked and vacated for lack of personal jurisdiction, but does not distinguish between the judgment's being vacated in the originating state versus the judgment's being vacated only in Arizona. *Phares v. Nutter*, 125 Ariz. 291, 293–94 (1980); *Springfield Credit Union,* 123 Ariz. at 323; *Stephens v. Thomasson*, 63 Ariz. 187, 194 (1945). The Uniform Enforcement of Foreign Judgments Act, which both Arizona and New York have adopted, provides that a filed foreign judgment is subject to the same procedures, defenses and proceedings for vacating as a judgment of the court in which it is filed. A.R.S. § 12–1702; N.Y.C.P.L.R. § 5402 (McKinney 2015). Thus, New York has recognized that judgments by its courts are subject to certain procedures (including being vacated) in other states, including Arizona. This statutory directive is consistent with the common law concept that a foreign judgment entered by a court lacking personal jurisdiction is not entitled to full faith and credit because it

---

3   In its reply brief, Honeywell asserts for the first time that the court had not ruled on whether Kilgore had signed the guarantee but decided New York lacked jurisdiction because the guarantee was not shown to be related to the debt. Honeywell argues that the court's actions and decision constituted an unpermitted retrial of the merits of the case. Arguments first raised in a reply brief are waived. We therefore do not consider it.

is void. Restatement (Second) of Conflict of Laws § 104 cmt. a (1971). We are not persuaded that the court erred in vacating the judgment. . . . We affirm the judgment of the trial court.

COMMENTS AND QUESTIONS

1. Is the issue whether the (unnumbered) guarantee executed by Kilgore was related to Alarm Company's obligation about the merits or about the court's jurisdiction?

2. If Kilgore did not receive *actual* notice of the New York litigation, why is this fact alone not sufficient to deny enforcement of the New York judgment?

3. What is the practical significance of this judgment being vacated also in the originating state (versus the judgment being vacated only in Arizona)?

FROM THE COURTS

EWING OIL, INC. v. JOHN T. BURNETT, INC.

Superior Court of New Jersey
441 N.J. Super. 251 (2015)

LIHOTZ, PRESIDING JUDGE, APPELLATE DIVISION.

This matter examines the enforceability of a sister-state judgment entered pursuant to a cognovit provision contained in a guaranty agreement against individual guarantors of a corporate debt. . . .

[Ewing Oil Co., Inc. ("Ewing Oil" or "Plaintiff"), is a Maryland corporation that is a wholesale supplier of petroleum products to gas stations in Maryland, New Jersey, and other Mid-Atlantic states. On March 18, 2009, Ewing Oil entered into a ten-year commercial supply agreement ("CSA") with John T. Burnett, Inc. ("JTB, Inc."), a New Jersey corporation, to supply JTB, Inc.'s retail gasoline service station in Monmouth County, New Jersey, with gasoline and other petroleum products.

The CSA required JTB, Inc. to make a $20,000 security deposit to Ewing Oil. The CSA granted Ewing Oil a security interest in the gas station's equipment. And the CSA demanded a personal guaranty from John T. Burnett for JTB, Inc.'s financial obligations "of every kind and nature".] The CSA contained the following forum selection clause:

> This Agreement shall be governed and construed in accordance with the laws of the State of Maryland and the courts of the State of Maryland shall have exclusive jurisdiction over any claims or controversies which arise under this Agreement. However, the courts of the [S]tate of New Jersey shall have jurisdiction in connection with any collection or enforcement action that [plaintiff], at its option, may elect to bring. . . .

The Guaranty also contained a cognovit provision, which stated:

> 3. Waiver of Notices, Confession of Judgment, Jurisdiction. Without notice to Guarantor, [plaintiff] may waive or modify any of the terms of the Agreement relating to [JTB, Inc.]'s performance without discharging or otherwise affecting Guarantor's obligations hereunder. Guarantor waives demand, diligence, presentment, protest[,] and notice of every kind. Guarantor acknowledges that the Agreement is governed by Maryland law and establishes Maryland as the appropriate jurisdiction for any actions arising out of, or relating to, the Agreement. Guarantor also hereby acknowledges, consents[,] and agrees that the provisions of this Guaranty and the rights of all parties mentioned herein shall be governed by the laws of the State of Maryland and interpreted and construed in accordance with such laws, and any court of competent jurisdiction of the State of Maryland shall have jurisdiction in any proceeding instituted to enforce this Guaranty and any obligations to venue are hereby waived. However, the courts of the [S]tate of New Jersey may have jurisdiction in connection with any enforcement and/or collection action that [plaintiff], at its sole option, may elect to bring in that state. GUARANTOR FURTHER IRREVOCABLY AUTHORIZES AND EMPOWERS ANY ATTORNEY-AT-LAW OR CLERK OF ANY COURT OF COMPETENT JURISDICTION OF THE STATE OF MARYLAND, OR ELSEWHERE, TO APPEAR AT ANY TIME FOR GUARANTOR IF ANY ACTION BROUGHT AGAINST GUARANTOR ON THIS GUARANTY TO CONFESS OR ENTER

JUDGMENT AGAINST GUARANTOR FOR HIS OBLIGATIONS
UNDER THE GUARANTY, INCLUDING COURT COSTS AND
REASONABLE ATTORNEYS' FEES.

[JTB, Inc. breached its duties and obligations under the CSA. On November
30, 2011, when JTB, Inc. was $225,197.34 in arrears, Ewing Oil commenced
an action in the Circuit Court for Washington County, Maryland against
JTB, Inc. for the outstanding debt plus attorney's fees.

On December 6, 2011, plaintiff obtained a default judgment against JTB,
Inc. for $258,976.94. Invoking the cognovit note, the Maryland court also
entered a judgment by confession against Burnett and the other guarantors
on the same day.

On July 24, 2012, Plaintiff Ewing Oil recorded the Maryland judgment
in New Jersey. On August 13, 2012, Burnett passed away. His widow was
named executrix of his estate.]

Burnett's estate (the Estate), through its executrix, moved to vacate the
default judgment against Burnett, pursuant to *Rule* 4:50–1(d), asserting
pre-judgment notice was not waived and the judgment's domestication
in New Jersey violated due process. The Estate also sought to collaterally
attack the judgment, maintaining New Jersey had plenary authority to
exercise jurisdiction over its enforcement, pursuant to the contract's forum
selection clause.

The Law Division denied the motion and the Estate filed this appeal, reas-
serting its challenges against New Jersey's recognition of the foreign judgment. . . . On appeal, the Estate [argues]: (1) the absence of pre-judgment
notice violates basic due process and cannot be remedies by an opportunity to
a post-judgment hearing; (2) pre-judgment notice rights under the cognovit
provision of the surety agreement were not voluntarily, intelligently, and
knowingly waived; and (3) New Jersey is the only forum with jurisdiction
to determine compliance with due process requirements and the enforceability of the confession of judgment clause, thus allowing the Estate to
assert available meritorious defenses against its enforcement. . . .

Whether the Maryland judgment may be registered in New Jersey implicates
the Full Faith and Credit clause of the United States Constitution, which
mandates "Full Faith and Credit shall be given in each State to the public
Acts, Records, and judicial Proceedings of every other State." U.S. Const.

art. IV, § 1. The clause requires a foreign judgment "properly entered in accordance with local procedure is entitled to full faith and credit in any other state provided . . . the judgment is not entered in violation of due process of law." *Sec. Ben. Life Ins. Co. v. TFS Ins. Agency, Inc.* 279 N.J. Super. 419, 424 (App. Div.), *certif. denied*, 141 N.J. 95 (1995). *See* N.J.S.A. 2A:49A–27. Thus, any judgment properly executed in a foreign state, which complies with the requirements of the due process clause is entitled to full faith and credit in New Jersey. *See In re Triffin*, 151 N.J. 510, 524 (1997). On the other hand, a foreign judgment entered without providing the necessary protections safeguarded by the Fourteenth Amendment of the United States Constitution and the fundamental rights clause of Article 1, paragraph 1 of the New Jersey Constitution, may not be enforced. . . .

When viewed through the prism of due process protections, a foreign judgment will not be entitled to full faith and credit in New Jersey if a defendant can demonstrate the forum state lacked personal or subject matter jurisdiction. *Tara Enters., Inc. v. Daribar Mgt. Corp.*, 369 N.J. Super. 45, 56 (App. Div. 2004), or if a defendant was denied adequate notice and a reasonable opportunity to be heard. *Sonntag Reporting Serv., Ltd. v. Ciccarelli*, 374 N.J. Super. 533, 538 (App. Div. 2005). "[A]bsent such due process defenses, . . . litigation pursued to judgment in a sister state is conclusive of the rights of the parties in the courts of every state as though adjudicated therein." *Ibid.* . . .

Although confessed judgments are viewed with "judicial distaste" in New Jersey, *Ledden v. Ehnes*, 22 N.J. 501, 510 (1956), constitutional and public policy challenges against their enforcement have been advanced and found legally untenable. *See United Pac. Ins. Co. v. Estate of Lamanna*, 181 N.J. Super. 149, 155–56 (Law Div. 1981) ("New Jersey courts have long recognized foreign judgments by confession and have held that they are entitled to full faith and credit. . . . No public policy [in New Jersey] denies recognition to a foreign judgment by confession."). Rather, the law is clear: "Entry of judgment based upon a warrant to confess judgment does not . . . necessarily offend due process, as long as the due process requirements of reasonable notice and opportunity to be heard are knowingly and voluntarily waived." *Tara Enters., supra*, 369 N.J. Super. at 56. . . . *See also D.H. Overmyer Co. v. Frick Co.*, 405 U.S. 174, 187 (1972) (holding confessed judgments are "not, [per se], violative of the Fourteenth Amendment due process" protections, as reasonable notice and opportunity to be heard could be waived).

Maryland Court Rule 2–611 governs confessed judgments in that state. The rule provides such judgments "may be entered by the circuit court clerk upon the filing of a complaint accompanied by the original or a copy of the instrument authorizing the confessed judgment and an affidavit specifying the amount due and stating the address of the defendant." *Schlossberg v. Citizens Bank*, 341 Md. 650, 655–56 (1996).

> Upon entry of a judgment by confession, the clerk is required to notify the defendant of the entry of judgment and of the deadline for filing a motion to "open, modify or vacate" the judgment. Md. Rule 2–611(b).

> If the defendant so moves, the circuit court must determine whether there is a "substantial and sufficient basis for an actual controversy as to the merits of the action." Md. Rule 2–611(d). In other words, the court must determine whether the defendant has a potentially meritorious defense to the confessed judgment complaint. The court does not, however, decide the merits of the controversy at this stage. [Paul V. Niemeyer & Linda M. Schuett, Maryland Rules Commentary 466 (4th ed. 2014).] If the court finds that a basis for a defense exists, the rule requires the court to order the confessed judgment be opened, modified, or vacated so that the defendant can file a responsive pleading to the plaintiff's complaint and the merits can be determined. Md. Rule 2–611(d).

Id. at 656.

Applications to open, modify, or vacate entry of default must be filed within sixty days of service. *See* Md. Rule 2–611(d) & 2–321(b)(1) ("A defendant who is served with an original pleading outside of the State [of Maryland] but within the United States shall file an answer within [sixty] days after being served.").

Further, Maryland law does not presuppose a waiver is valid. In fact, Maryland Rule 2–611(b) requires the trial court to determine, among other things, "the pleadings and papers demonstrate a factual and legal basis for entitlement to a confessed judgment."

In this matter, the Estate suggests the motion judge erred in concluding plaintiff fully complied with Maryland procedures in entering its judgment against Burnett. However, the Estate does not dispute the same complaint contained separate requests for judgment against JTB, Inc. and to confess judgment against the guarantors. The pleading appended all documentation necessary to identify the rights and responsibilities of the respective parties. Plaintiff filed and served its complaint against JTB, Inc. and the other defendants; no response or objection was filed. Once judgment was entered against the corporation, plaintiff was free to request relief against the guarantors.

The Estate also suggests Burnett's waiver of pre-judgment notice contained in the Guaranty was uncounseled and, therefore, uninformed. We cannot agree.

There is no statement of personal knowledge by the executrix stating whether Burnett consulted with legal counsel prior to executing the CSA or Guaranty. Plaintiff certified JTB, Inc. defaulted under the CSA and provided the documents supporting entry of judgment against it. JTB, Inc. never challenged the action or the relief sought. Proof of the Guaranty and its execution by Burnett was also provided to support judgment under the cognovit provision.

Moreover, the Guaranty is clearly written and its waiver provisions are boldly identified, as is the confession of judgment clause. Importantly, plaintiff's action was based on the Guaranty, not the terms of its CSA with JTB, Inc. *See Tara Enters., supra*, 369 N.J. Super. at 59 (holding a guarantee of a note that contains a cognovit provision alone is insufficient to permit confession of judgment against the guarantors). Further, the provision contains a succinct statement that Maryland law governs enforcement and that any attorney so appointed may enter judgment against the guarantors.

Maryland law recognizes:

> *Overmyer* does not require an evidentiary hearing to determine whether [the] defendant's waiver was voluntarily, knowingly, and intelligently made before a confessed judgment may be entered by the court. Rather, the burden is on [the] defendant in its motion to vacate and in any hearing thereon to set forth fully the evidence showing either than the alleged amount owed had no basis in fact (e.g., was miscalculated) or that the agreement was not knowingly and voluntarily entered.

Atl. Leasing & Fin. Inc. v. IPM Tech., Inc., 885 F.2d 188, 193 (4th Cir. 1989).

The Estate has failed to meet this burden. After reviewing all the documents and considering the executor's certification, we find no support for concluding Burnett's execution of the Guaranty was involuntary or unknowing.

We also reject the Estate's due process challenge. The Maryland judgment was entered and plaintiff served Burnett, individually, as mandated by Maryland Rule 2–611(a). The post-judgment process affords additional notice and an opportunity to challenge the confessed judgment's validity within sixty days of its entry. This fully complies with the rigors of due process. *See Tara Enters., supra*, 369 N.J. Super., at 56 (recognizing "[i]n certain contexts . . . a post-judgment hearing may afford the requisite due process"). Despite the availability of a constitutionally valid post-judgment procedure to challenge entry of the judgment in Maryland, which could include whether Burnett's waiver was knowing and voluntary, Burnett did not act within the permitted sixty-day period. Thereafter, plaintiff properly filed its complaint to domesticate the Maryland judgment in New Jersey, attaching all requisite documents. . . .

In this state action to domesticate the Maryland judgment, the Estate cannot now raise substantive claims collaterally attacking the enforceability of the cognovit provision or its voluntary acceptance, as these issues could and should have been presented in the Maryland post-judgment process. Burnett was given notice of the judgment and had the right to petition the Maryland court to open, modify, or vacate the judgment if a valid basis to do so was presented. For reasons not disclosed, he chose not to do so. . . . Affirmed.

COMMENTS AND QUESTIONS

1. Cognovit notes have a controversial, although ancient history. Justice Harry Blackmun stated, "[L]ong ago, the cognovit method was described by the Chief Justice of New Jersey as the 'loosest way of binding a man's property that ever was devised in any civilized country.'. . . The cognovit has been the subject of comment, much of it critical." *See D.H. Overmyer Co. v. Frick Co.*, 405 U.S. 174, 178 (1972). By their very nature, the cognovit judgment limits due process rights. Accordingly, even in circumstances when they are allowed, the waiver of due process rights must be voluntary, knowing, and intelligently made. Some states, like Massachusetts, ban them. But how can a state protect its domiciliaries (like

Burnett) from the evils of judgments entered by confession if a choice of forum and choice of law clause require litigation in Maryland under Maryland law, and then every other state must give full faith and credit to the Maryland judgment?

2. Did the death of John Burnett make it harder or easier for Ewing Oil to enforce the judgment on the guaranty? (Is that fair?)

FROM THE COURTS

XTRA LEASE LLC v. GENESIS TRUCKYARD, LLC

Court of Appeals of Texas
2014 WL 6997326 (Tex. Ct. App. Dec. 11, 2014)

BILL MEIER, JUSTICE.

Appellant XTRA Lease LLC appeals the trial court's order vacating a foreign judgment that it had domesticated in Texas pursuant to the Uniform Enforcement of Foreign Judgments Act (UEFJA). *See* Tex. Civ. Prac. & Rem. Code Ann. §§ 35.001-.008 (West 2008 & Supp. 2014). We will affirm.

In July 2012, XTRA entered into an Equipment Lease Agreement (ESL) with Genesis Express, Inc. One of the ESL's provisions stated that the parties "hereby submit to the jurisdiction of the Circuit Court of St. Louis County, Missouri for purposes of adjudicating any action arising out of or related to the Lease."

In January 2013, XTRA sued Express in a St. Louis County, Missouri circuit court to recover damages for Express's alleged breach of the ESL. XTRA also named Appellee Genesis Truckyard LLC as a defendant to the suit. XTRA alleged that Express had defaulted on its obligations under the ESL but also that it had "stopped doing business" and had transferred its assets to Truckyard in order to defraud its creditors. According to XTRA, Truckyard had retained the same customers and equipment as Express and had impliedly agreed to assume Express's liability under the ESL; consequently, Express's liability under the ESL extended to Truckyard because it was "a mere continuation" or "a successor liability company" of Express. Several months later, the circuit court signed a default judgment in favor of XTRA and against Truckyard in the amount of $289,811.98. The judgment recited that although duly served, Truckyard had failed to plead or otherwise defend against XTRA's petition.

In June 2013, pursuant to the UEFJA, XTRA domesticated the Missouri judgment against Truckyard by filing an authenticated copy of the judgment with the clerk of the Tarrant County [Texas] district court and by providing Truckyard with notice of the filing. Truckyard promptly filed a motion to vacate the Missouri judgment on the ground that the circuit court had lacked personal jurisdiction over Truckyard. Specifically, Truckyard argued that because Truckyard had no contacts with Missouri and had never had any business dealings with XTRA, XTRA was constrained to aver in its Missouri petition that Truckyard was liable for Express's alleged breach of the ESL under the theory of successor liability. Truckyard also challenged XTRA's invocation of successor liability, contending that it did not apply—and that the trial court therefore lacked any basis upon which to exercise personal jurisdiction over Truckyard—because Truckyard did not assume any liability of Express under the ESL, did not assume possession of any equipment that Express had leased from XTRA under the ESL, had never purchased or acquired any assets from Express, and was not a continuation of Express.

The trial court granted Truckyard's motion after conducting an evidentiary hearing and later entered findings of fact and conclusions of law, finding in part that "Truckyard has not purchased or acquired any asset from Express" and that "Express has not agreed to sell, assign or transfer any assets to Truckyard." The trial court concluded in part that "Truckyard is not a successor liability company to Express," that "Truckyard is not a continuation of Express," and that "[t]he Missouri court did not have the requisite jurisdiction to enter the Missouri Judgment against Truckyard."

XTRA argues in its only issue that the trial court abused its discretion by vacating the properly domesticated Missouri judgment. XTRA acknowledges that its Missouri petition relied solely upon Missouri's successor liability law to impose liability upon Truckyard for Express's breach of the ESL, but it contends that the legal theory applied because there are a number of similarities between Express and Truckyard. Because Express had contractually agreed to submit to Missouri's jurisdiction and because Truckyard was Express's successor in liability, XTRA contends that the Missouri circuit court had personal jurisdiction over Truckyard.

Truckyard responds that it is neither a continuation of nor a successor to Express because it did not acquire all, or substantially all, of Express's assets. Because successor liability did not apply to impose liability on Truckyard for Express's breach of the ESL, Truckyard contends that Express's submission to Missouri jurisdiction under the ESL did not apply to Truckyard and that the trial court correctly granted the motion to vacate because the Missouri circuit court had no personal jurisdiction over Truckyard.

Accordingly, as the parties have developed the issue and presented it on appeal, whether the trial court properly vacated the Missouri judgment on jurisdictional grounds depends on whether Truckyard was liable under the ESL as a successor entity of Express.

The United States Constitution requires that full faith and credit be given in each state to the public acts, records, and judicial proceedings of every other state. U.S. Const. art. IV, § 1. In Texas, enforcement of foreign judgments is governed by the Texas version of the UEFJA. *See* Tex. Civ. Prac. & Rem. Code Ann. § 35.002; *Tri-Steel Structures, Inc. v. Hackman*, 883 SW.2d 391, 393 (Tex. App.-Fort Worth 1994, writ denied). When a judgment creditor files an authenticated copy of a foreign judgment, the judgment creditor satisfies its burden to present a prima facie case for enforcement of the judgment. The burden then shifts to the judgment debtor to prove why the sister state's judgment should not be given full faith and credit. A well-established exception to the requirement that a foreign judgment be afforded full faith and credit is the defense that the sister state lacked personal jurisdiction over the judgment debtor. The presumption of validity that accompanies a foreign judgment can only be overcome by clear and convincing evidence, and the law of the state rendering the judgment determines its validity.

We . . . review the record to determine whether the trial court misapplied the law to the established facts in concluding that Truckyard established an exception to the full faith and credit doctrine.

[According to Missouri law, a corporation does not assume the debts and liabilities of a corporation from which it purchases assets. One exception to that rule is "when the purchaser is merely a continuation of the seller."]

Four people testified at the hearing on Truckyard's motion to vacate. Beatrice Ogango testified that she purchased Seacom Freight LLC in November 2012 for $10,000, that she changed the name of the company to Genesis Truckyard LLC, and that she is the manager of Truckyard. Truckyard operates online as a broker for businesses that need freight shipped and owners of trucks seeking to transport freight. Truckyard has an office, but it does not have customer accounts or own any trucks or trailers, nor are the owners or operators of the trucks and trailers that transport the freight the employees of Truckyard.

Ogango testified that Truckyard had not conducted any business in Missouri, had never maintained an office in Missouri, had never had any employees in Missouri, had never initiated litigation in Missouri, and had never owned any property in Missouri. Contrary to XTRA's allegations in its Missouri petition, Ogango explained that Truckyard had never assumed or agreed to assume any debt or liability of Express, had never acquired any property or assets from XTRA, had never paid any debts that Express owed, and had never entered into any contacts with Express. Ogango also disputed that Truckyard had ever had any control of any equipment (trailers) that belonged to Express.

On cross-examination, Ogango agreed that her husband, Thomas Ondari, had been the owner of Express, that Truckyard's business is similar to the business that Express had operated, that Truckyard had begun doing business around the same time that Express had ceased doing business, that several truck drivers who drove for Express had applied to drive for Truckyard, and that she had previously worked as a nurse's aide and at a gas station. Ogango testified that Ondari is not an owner of, nor does he participate in managing, Truckyard.

Celestine Andrews testified that she had formed Seacom Freight but later sold it because it "didn't work out." Andrews's boyfriend, Bill Owuou, testified that Ondari had contacted him about selling Seacom Freight, that he had conducted the buy-sale transaction, and that he thought Ondari was the one who had purchased Seacom Freight.

Ondari testified that he is Ogango's husband, that he was the owner of Express, and that he now works in a shop fixing big trucks. Ondari said that the "the Government" had "shut down" Express because "the insurance company could not get us a policy." Ondari acknowledged that Express had ceased doing business on or about December 7, 2012, that Express's business model was similar to Truckyard's business model, and that Truckyard is a tenant in the building that he owns. XTRA questioned Ondari about a

$7,500 payment that he had received from Truckyard, but Ondari explained that it was repayment for a loan.

Directing us to the pertinent parts of the record, XTRA argues that Truckyard "is nothing more than a continuation of and successor to" Express because Truckyard "conducted exactly the same business as [Express], at the same location, with the same people." We disagree. XTRA's analysis is inconsistent with Missouri law because it largely ignores the requirement that as a prerequisite to impose corporate successor liability, there must have been a transfer of all or substantially all of the assets of one corporation to another. *See Edwards*, 418 S.W.3d at 520–21. We cannot overlook the requirement of a substantial asset transfer and proceed to consider one or more exceptions to the general rule of nonliability—as XTRA implicitly advocates—because the asset transfer is the underlying occurrence that provides the impetus for considering whether one entity is a continuation of the other. Further, predicating successor liability upon mere similarities between two separate entities without requiring a substantial asset transaction would compromise, or effectively render meaningless, each entity's separate legal identity.

Here, while XTRA offered evidence of similarities between Truckyard and Express, it presented no evidence that Truckyard had acquired all or substantially all of Express's assets. To the contrary, Ogango's uncontroverted testimony was that Truckyard had never acquired any property or assets from XTRA, had never assumed or agreed to assume any debt or liability of Express, had never paid any debts that Express owned, and had never entered into any contracts with Express. Consequently, any exceptions to the general rule of nonliability, including whether a purchaser of assets is merely a continuation of the seller of assets, were never triggered. *See id.*

A Missouri court of appeals decision demonstrates our point precisely. *See Roper Elec. Co. v. Quality Castings, Inc.*, 60 S.W.3d 708 (Mo. App. S.D. 2001). Roper performed work for Quality, but Quality never paid Roper. *Id.* at 710. Around the same time, Quality and Bagby Enterprises, Inc. entered into a "Sale of Assets Agreement," whereby Quality sold all of its assets to Bagby for certain consideration. *Id.* Roper subsequently sued both Quality and Bagby to recover the money that it was owed from Quality and prevailed. In concluding that the evidence amply supported the trial court's judgment imposing liability on Bagby for Quality's debt under the corporate continuation doctrine, the court of appeals reasoned as follows:

> All of the assets of [Quality] were transferred to Bagby; Bagby retained all of [Quality's] employees without notifying them of any change in ownership; neither Bagby nor [Quality] notified [Roper], as a creditor, of the change in ownership; Bagby continued the exact same business using the same equipment and had the same customers as [Quality], but never notified them of the change; Bagby held itself out to the public as [Quality] by utilizing the same trade name. . . ; Bagby retained the key employees in management positions. . . ; [and] Bagby took over the works in progress of [Quality], collected the accounts receivable, operated in the same location, and had the same phone number as [Quality]. . .

Id. at 713 (emphasis added). The court of appeals thus analyzed facts that were relevant to whether Bagby was merely a continuation of Quality, but unlike the evidence involving Express and Truckyard in this case, the court had before it undisputed evidence that one defendant (Quality) had transferred its assets to the other defendant (Bagby)—a prerequisite to corporate successor liability under any of the four exceptions to the general rule of nonliability. *Id.* at 710; *Edwards*, 418 S.W.3d at 520–21. . . .

Because Truckyard could not have been liable under the ESL as a successor entity of Express and because XTRA relied upon no other facts or theories to support the Missouri circuit court's exercise of personal jurisdiction, the Missouri court had no basis by which to exercise personal jurisdiction over Truckyard. Truckyard therefore met its burden to prove by clear and convincing evidence that full faith and credit should not be afforded to the Missouri judgment. We hold that the trial court did not abuse its discretion by granting Truckyard's motion to vacate. . . .

COMMENTS AND QUESTIONS

1. Is the issue whether Truckyard is a mere continuation of Express about the merits or about jurisdiction? What difference does that characterization make?

2. One policy justification for full faith and credit is familiarity with the relevant substantive law. When issues of substantive law arise at the enforce-

ment stage, the enforcing court will often be applying the substantive law of the rendering state. Query whether Texas correctly applied Missouri's law of successor liability.

3. If you represent XTRA Lease, what is your next move with respect to collecting the three hundred thousand dollars that your client is owed?

FROM THE COURTS

ELMO GREER & SONS, INC. v. CITIZENS BANK, INC.

Court of Appeals of Kentucky
2013 WL 2450524 (Ky. Ct. App. June 7, 2013)

DIXON, JUDGE.

Appellants, Elmo Greer & Sons, Inc. and Elmo Greer & Sons, LLC, appeal from an order of the Bell Circuit Court granting full faith and credit to an amended judgment of a Tennessee Court thereby authorizing enforcement of the judgment in Kentucky by Appellee, Citizens Bank, Inc. Because we conclude that the Tennessee Court was without jurisdiction to enter the amended judgment, the same must be considered void in Kentucky. Accordingly, this matter is remanded to the Bell Circuit Court for an order of dismissal.

In 2009, Citizens Bank filed suit in Claiborne County, Tennessee, against Elmo Greer & Sons, Inc. ("Greer, Inc.") for a returned check from one of Greer, Inc.'s customers. Summons was duly issued to the registered agent for Greer, Inc. On April 28, 2010, after Greer Inc. failed to respond, the Tennessee court entered a default judgment in favor of Citizens Bank in the amount of $15,523.67. Subsequently, on June 11, 2010, the Tennessee court entered an amended judgment, modifying the original judgment against Greer, Inc. "to include also Elmo Greer & Sons, LLC ["Greer, LLC"] in the amount of $15,523.67 plus court costs." On August 11, 2011, Citizens Bank proceeded to register the June amended judgment in Kentucky pursuant to Kentucky's Uniform Enforcement of Judgment Act, Kentucky Revised Statutes (KRS) 426.960. . . .

On August 30, 2011, Greer, Inc. and Greer, LLC filed a motion to dismiss, arguing that Citizens Bank's complaint in the Tennessee action only named Greer, Inc., which had been inactive since 1999. Further, Citizens Bank did not file an amended complaint in Tennessee to name Greer, LLC as a party and, as a result, service of process was never perfected on that entity. Finally, Greer, Inc. and Greer, LLC argued that the amended judgment was void as it was entered in violation of Tennessee Civil Rule 59.04, and was thus not entitled to enforcement in Kentucky. Citizens Bank responded that Greer Inc. and Greer, LLC were essentially one and the same, and that their "arguments about the Tennessee procedure for amending the judgment would have been better heard in Tennessee. . . ."

On October 31, 2011, the circuit court entered an order ruling:

> The Court finds and concludes Elmo Greer & Sons, Inc. and Elmo Greer & Sons LLC are, for all intents and purposes, one and the same entity. These entities merged in 1999; they share the same offices and agent; and the LLC endorsed and deposited a check payable to the corporation in the sum of $15,523.67, which is the check that is the subject of the Tennessee action being enforced herein. Summons in the Tennessee action was duly issued to and served upon the appropriate agent. . . The Tennessee judgment is valid and enforceable in all respects against both Elmo Greer & Sons. Inc. and Elmo Greer & Sons LLC.

Greer, Inc. and Greer, LLC thereafter appealed to this Court. On appeal, Greer, Inc. and Greer, LLC argue that the amended Tennessee judgment is void and thus not entitled to full faith and credit in Kentucky. Greer, Inc. and Greer, LLC also contend, as they did below, that Citizens Bank neither filed an amended complaint naming Greer, LLC nor offered any proof that the LLC was properly served in the Tennessee action. Both entities note that simply because they share the same agent for service of process does not necessarily mean that both entities were served simultaneously.

The law in Kentucky is that a sister state's judgment is entitled to full faith and credit if the judgment is valid under that state's own laws. *Sunrise Turquoise, Inc. v. Chemical Design Co., Inc.*, 899 S.W.2d 856, 857–58 (Ky. App. 1995). As such, the question before us is whether the default judgment as amended is valid in Tennessee. We must conclude that it is not. Tennessee Civil Rule 59.04 provides that "[a] motion to alter or amend a judgment shall be filed and served within thirty (30) days after entry of the judgment."

As in Kentucky, if a post-trial motion is not timely, the trial court lacks jurisdiction to rule on the motion. *See Binkley v. Medling*, 117 S.W.3d 252, 255 (Tenn. 2003). The record indicates that the original Tennessee default judgment was entered on April 28, 2010. Entry of the amended judgment was on June 11, 2010, which was clearly outside of the thirty-day window for amendment of the April judgment. Accordingly, because the Tennessee court was without jurisdiction to enter the amended judgment, a Kentucky court cannot afford it full faith and credit.

Interestingly, Citizens Bank has never addressed the jurisdictional defect of the amended judgment. In the trial court, Citizens Bank erroneously argued that any issue of the judgment's validity should have been raised in the Tennessee Court. Such is not the law in Kentucky. "It is well-established that the issue of subject matter jurisdiction can be raised at any time, even *sua sponte*, as it cannot be acquired by waiver, consent, or estoppel." *Gossett v. Kelley*, 362 S.W.3d 379, 380 (Ky. App. 2012).

Finally, Citizens Bank has asserted for the first time on appeal that the Tennessee Court had the authority to amend the judgment under Tennessee Rules of Civil Procedure 60.01 or 60.02 to correct a clerical mistake. As Citizens Bank failed to present this argument to the lower court, it is not properly preserved for appellate review. It is well settled that "a question not raised or adjudicated in the court below cannot be considered when raised for the first time in this court." *Flag Drilling Co., Inc. v. Erco, Inc.*, 156 S.W.3d 762, 767–68 (Ky. App. 2005). Notwithstanding, whether the amendment adding Greer LLC to the judgment constituted the correction of a clerical error under Tennessee law is not a determination properly made by this or any other Kentucky court.

Because we are compelled to conclude that the Tennessee amended judgment was procedurally void, we need not address the parties' arguments as to whether Greer, Inc. and Greer, LLC are, in fact, one and the same for purposes of determining proper party and service of process issues.

For the reasons set forth herein, this matter is remanded to the Bell Circuit Court for entry of an order dismissing the instant action.

COMMENTS AND QUESTIONS

1. The Kentucky court concluded that the Tennessee judgment was procedurally void under Tennessee law. Which state's court is the better authority on Tennessee Civil Rule 59.04: Kentucky or Tennessee? Does that matter in a federal system governed by the Full Faith and Credit Clause?

2. Assuming that the Tennessee court erred in amending the judgment outside the 30-day window allowed by Tennessee Civil Rule 59.04, did the Tennessee trial court act without "subject matter jurisdiction," as the Kentucky court suggests? Is there a strategic reason to characterize the Tennessee court's action as acting without subject matter jurisdiction as opposed to say, failing to rigidly adhere to a procedural technicality?

3. Why did the bank initially sue the defendant in Tennessee if the Greer family's assets were in Kentucky?

4. The parties and the courts in this matter are all located on the Kentucky-Tennessee state border. Should the close geographic proximity of these events influence the analysis one way or the other?

SAMPLE EXAM QUESTIONS

Question 22-4

Tatum owned a home in Atlanta, Georgia that he was looking to sell. Irving, an interested buyer, ultimately entered into a "Residential Lease With Option to Purchase" with Tatum. The contract included a provision stating that Tatum would be entitled to attorney fees and costs if he prevailed in a dispute between the parties. There was no reciprocal clause in favor of Irving should he prevail in a dispute.

Irving breached the contract, and Tatum filed suit in Georgia. The contract included a clause identifying Georgia as the exclusive forum for lawsuits arising out of the dispute. In a case that went to a bench trial, the court determined that Irving breached the contract. Tatum proved the following damages: $18,000 for missed payments, $32,000 in property damage, and attorney fees of $56,000. The court entered a judgment for

$106,000. Irving has no assets in Georgia, but shortly after the final judgment entered, Irving wrote a check to Tatum for $50,000 in satisfaction of the amounts due for the missed payments and the property damage.

Irving claims he is not obligated to pay Tatum's attorney fees. Indeed, a Georgia landlord-tenant statute provides that a fee-shifting clause that is not reciprocal (i.e., is a one-way fee shift) is unenforceable. Seeking to collect on the outstanding $56,000, Tatum domesticated the judgment in South Carolina, where Irving has a boat and other assets. Irving challenges enforcement of the Georgia judgment, citing the Georgia court's incorrect application of Georgia law. Irving has produced copies of trial transcripts demonstrating Irving's objection to that trial court's ruling and preserving the issue.

Does the Full Faith and Credit Clause require the South Carolina court to enforce the Georgia judgment?

Question 22-5

Young purchased eight condo units in the Yacht Harbor Village in Palm Coast, Florida. As a result of this purchase, Young became a member of the condominium association and subject to the association's Declaration of Covenants and Restrictions. As part of the Declaration, Young was required to pay assessments to the condominium association.

Young refused to pay the assessments, and the association ultimately filed a complaint in a Florida state court to recover a money judgment. Young did not respond to that suit, and a default judgment entered in the amount of $442,000 plus interest.

The association seeks to domesticate the judgment in Dayton, Ohio, where Young lives and has substantial assets. Young resists enforcement on the ground that the association must instead foreclose on the Florida property and recover the assets from the sale; only if there remains a deficiency thereafter would the association be able to recover from Young's other assets. Provisions in the Declaration support Young's argument.

You clerk for a judge in the Ohio court before whom the enforcement proceeding is pending. She asks you to research whatever she needs to know. Do you research Florida and/or Ohio law? (What is your research question?)

Question 22-6

Veena Rao was a passenger in an automobile that was involved in a one-car accident in Salt Lake City Utah. She was riding in a car that was driven by her roommate. Rao ordinarily took the bus to work, but on this day her roommate offered to give her a ride. The roommate was a driver for a rideshare company, but Rao did not pay for the ride and the ride was not booked nor registered through the rideshare app.

Rao was seriously injured in the accident and incurred significant expense. The driver had an auto insurance policy with Major Insurance Co. (Major), and was insured for up to $500,000 of personal injury protection (PIP) benefits. With the roommate-driver's cooperation and assistance, Rao submitted a claim to Major. But Major denied coverage, relying on an exception in the policy that disclaimed coverage for injuries suffered while the car is offered as "transportation for hire, including ride-share and similar commercial purposes."

Rao and her roommate contacted a lawyer to help get coverage from Major. Major argued that these circumstances fell within the scope of the exception. Major closed its file on the incident and took no other action on the claim.

Major is a Delaware corporation that has its principal place of business in Connecticut. Major has no employees nor physical presence in Utah, but it does substantial business in all 50 states. The driver purchased her policy over the internet.

Rao and the roommate eventually sued Major in Utah for coverage. Major defended the suit, again invoking the policy exception. The judge granted plaintiff's motion for summary judgment, determining that the defendant was liable for $150,000 in compensatory damages.

The plaintiffs then amended the complaint to add a claim for treble damages and attorney fees incurred as a result of Major's willful and wanton failure to pay the PIP benefits. Following a trial on this claim, a jury determined that Major's refusal to pay PIP benefits was willful and wanton. The trial court entered judgment for plaintiffs and awarded treble damages pursuant to a Utah state statute that provides for an automatic trebling of compensatory damages upon proof of willful and wanton conduct by an insurer.

The insurance policy contained neither a choice of law nor a choice of forum clause.

You represent the insurance company which has no identifiable assets in Utah. Evaluate your client's options and offer a recommendation. Would a Connecticut court enforce the $450,000 judgment of the Utah state court?

Quick Summary

- Generally speaking, every American federal or state court is obligated to recognize and enforce the judgment of any other American federal or state court

- There are several exceptions to the recognition and enforcement of a foreign judgment, but these exceptions are read narrowly

- The most common exception to the recognition and enforcement of a foreign judgment involves a judgment that was issued by a court that did not have personal jurisdiction over the defendant; a defendant who does not appear in the court that issued the judgment may collaterally attack the judgment in an enforcement action

- Other exceptions to the recognition and enforcement of a foreign judgment include: lack of subject matter jurisdiction, extrinsic fraud, penal claims, title to land, interference with official acts, deprivation of day in court, judgment is unenforceable in the rendering state, inconsistent judgments, and federal legislation

- There is no exception for a foreign judgment that violates the public policy of the forum state

23

Enforcement of Foreign-Country Judgments

Key Concepts

- Final judgment
- Judgment creditor; judgment debtor
- Issuing or rendering court (F1); enforcing or recognizing court (F2)
- Recognition; enforcement
- Comity; reciprocity

The recognition and enforcement of foreign-country judgments is guided by different considerations than those that apply to sister-state judgments. It requires a balance of interests. On one hand, even though neither the Full Faith and Credit Clause nor 28 U.S.C. § 1738 requires the recognition or enforcement of foreign-country judgments, the same basic policy urges enforcement: the United States is a member of a community of nations, and if all countries respected each other's judgments the arrangement would be efficient and mutually beneficial. But on the other hand, the rights and assets and integrity of persons in the United States could be in jeopardy if American courts enforced the judgment of foreign courts without an independent review with respect to such matters as whether the judgment debtor was accorded due process. This Chapter charts the practice of American courts which recognize and enforce some, but not all foreign-country judgments. It should be noted at the outset, however, that American courts are viewed as being generally hospitable to foreign-country judgments, perhaps because they have considerable experience with the enforcement of sister-state judgments.

There is a threshold matter about the rationale for recognizing and enforcing *any* foreign-country judgment. Well over a century ago, the Supreme Court, in *Hilton v. Guyot*,[1] identified comity as a rationale for such recognition and enforcement. Comity is a principle that is not derived from obligation, but rather from mutual

---

[1] 159 U.S. 113 (1895).

respect, convenience, and good will.[2] While it is more general and flexible than reciprocity, a country that enforces another country's judgments based on comity could justifiably expect the other country to return the favor. Comity is part of the voluntary law of nations that promotes commerce and good relations. But comity is not a firm rule of law. Rather it is a rule of practice, convenience, and efficiency that can be applied on a case-by-case basis. A foreign judgment is inadmissible when it is contrary to the forum's policy or is prejudicial to the forum's interest.

And yet always in the background is the fundamental principle of *res judicata*: once a matter has been adjudicated, it should not be re-adjudicated. Within the United States, the Full Faith and Credit Clause carries with it an implicit presumption that we trust the courts of sister states to adjudicate disputes in an impartial way, according to proper procedures—in short, within a *system* that has these attributes. If a judgment of a foreign country is presented for recognition or enforcement, a U.S. state or federal court would naturally want to satisfy itself that the same would be true of the rendering court in the foreign country. If so, the basic policy of *res judicata* would normally click in, leading to recognition and enforcement.

With respect to *monetary* judgments, over half of the United States have adopted the Uniform Foreign-Country Money Judgment Recognition Act (UFCMJRA), another project of the Uniform Law Commission.[3] (Injunctions—equity decrees—are generally not enforced, though the judgments giving rise to them would be *res judicata* as to the matters adjudicated.) States that have not adopted the UFCMJRA use different mechanics, but generally follow the same approach. The enforcement of foreign-country judgments is typically a matter of state, not federal law. There is no treaty or federal statute that preempts state authority, and federal courts generally apply the law of the state where the judgment is sought to be enforced.[4]

The scope of the UFCMJRA is limited to money judgments that are final, conclusive, valid, and enforceable under the law of the foreign country where rendered.

---

2   *Id.* at 163–164 ("'Comity,' in the legal sense, is neither a matter of absolute obligation, on the one hand, nor of mere courtesy and good will, upon the other.").

3   Chapter 22 described the model Enforcement of Foreign Judgments Act (EFJA), which is limited to the enforcement of domestic judgments. *See* Revised Uniform Enforcement of Foreign Judgments Act § 1 (defining "foreign judgment" as "any judgment, decree, or order of a court of the United States or of any other court which is entitled to full faith and credit in this state.")

4   In extremely rare circumstances, the presence of a federal question or of some uniquely federal interest can create federal question jurisdiction. *See, e.g., Wilson v. Marchington*, 127 F.3d 805, 813 (9th Cir. 1997) ("[T]he quintessentially federal character of Native American law, coupled with the imperative of consistency in federal recognition of tribal court judgments, by necessity require that the ultimate decision governing the recognition and enforcement of a tribal judgment by the United States be founded on federal law.").

The Act excludes from its scope judgments for taxes, fines or other penalties, and domestic relations matters.

The UFCMJRA prescribes that a court "*shall* recognize a foreign-country judgment" unless it falls within one of the two tracks of exceptions.

A court of this state may not recognize a foreign-country judgment if:

(1) the judgment was rendered under a judicial system that does not provide impartial tribunals or procedures compatible with the requirements of due process of law;

(2) the foreign court did not have personal jurisdiction over the defendant;[5] or

(3) the foreign court did not have jurisdiction over the subject matter.

A court of this state need not recognize a foreign-country judgment if:

(1) the defendant in the proceeding in the foreign court did not receive notice of the proceeding in sufficient time to enable the defendant to defend;

(2) the judgment was obtained by fraud that deprived the losing party of an adequate opportunity to present its case;

(3) the judgment or the cause of action on which the judgment is based is repugnant to the public policy of this state or of the United States;

(4) the judgment conflicts with another final and conclusive judgment;

(5) the proceeding in the foreign court was contrary to an agreement between the parties under which the dispute in question was to be determined otherwise than by proceedings in that foreign court;

(6) in the case of jurisdiction based only on personal service, the foreign court was a seriously inconvenient forum for the trial of the action;

---

5   [*Eds.' Note*: Another section of the UFCMJRA clarifies that a foreign-country judgment may not be refused recognition for lack of personal jurisdiction if the defendant was personally served in the foreign country, made a general appearance in the foreign proceeding, consented to the jurisdiction of the foreign court, was at home in the jurisdiction, was doing business in the jurisdiction and the cause of action arose out of that business, or the defendant operated a motor vehicle or airplane in the foreign country and the cause of action arose out of that operation.]

(7) the judgment was rendered in circumstances that raise substantial doubt about the integrity of the rendering court with respect to the judgment; or

(8) the specific proceeding in the foreign court leading to the judgment was not compatible with the requirements of due process of law.

UFCMJRA § 4 (b), (c). Naturally, even a state that adopts the model legislation can tailor it. Some states, for example, include reciprocity as a factor: judgments of the foreign country are treated in the same fashion that the foreign country treats American judgments.

The category of foreign-country judgments that *may not* be enforced (*i.e.,* the *mandatory* grounds for non-enforcement) are limited to extreme circumstances, such as where the judgment was rendered under a system which does not provide impartial tribunals or procedures compatible with the requirements of due process of law. But exactly what constitutes impartiality and compatibility with due process are debatable: Must the judiciary be "independent"? What if legal counsel is not formally or not practically available? Does evidence of a recent effort to end judicial corruption militate in favor of (or against) enforcing a judgment from that system? Which, if any, of the following are *essential* to due process: jury trial, discovery, right to cross-examine witnesses, oral (as opposed to written) presentation, right to appeal?

The answer to all of these questions is some version of "It depends." It depends on the country, the context, and your ability to frame a persuasive narrative around the unique facts of your case and the specific foreign country involved. Think about *why* some foreign countries' judgments are more likely than others to be enforced in the United States. For example, even without knowing the specifics of a particular case, consider what foreign country's judgments are *most* likely to be enforced (England? Canada? Mexico?), and why? Use the list of reasons as creative inspiration as you craft the narrative to persuade a judge to enforce some other foreign country's judgment; emphasize the right details, mollify the likely reservations.

For counsel representing the party that is *resisting* enforcement, the same exercise should be done in reverse. What is the foreign country whose judgments are *least* likely to be enforced, and why? That list of reasons becomes a springboard for you to resist the enforcement of any foreign country's judgment. Generally speaking, the party challenging the validity of a foreign judgment has the burden of presenting the evidence of its invalidity.

The second category of exceptions—the *discretionary* grounds for non-enforce-ment—includes many of the justifications for refusing enforcement of a domestic (foreign) judgment (as we saw in Chapter 22). The fraud exception again is limited to *extrinsic* fraud. Intrinsic fraud is not a basis for disturbing enforcement because the foreign court either was or should have been the place for the allegations of fraud to be ventilated. Extrinsic fraud denies a litigant the opportunity to argue; intrinsic fraud is intertwined within the argument.

Items (7) and (8) on the list of discretionary grounds are more particularized ver-sions of the inquiry captured in Item (1) from the list of mandatory grounds. Even if the country's *system* is not pathologically flawed, the specific *litigation* at issue in that system might be suspect.

The public policy exception in Item (3) deserves emphasis because you will recall that there is no public policy exception to the enforcement of foreign (sister-state) judgments: because of the Full Faith and Credit Clause, by definition, a judgment of a sister state cannot violate the enforcing court's public policy. But in order for the principle of comity to have any meaning, the public policy exception must require something more than the mere fact that the law or procedure of the foreign country is different than that of the enforcing state. Notice that the foreign judg-ment must be "repugnant," not merely reflective of a public policy that is different from that of the enforcing state.

In an oft-cited opinion of the U.S. Court of Appeals for the Seventh Circuit, Judge Posner enforced a judgment of the English courts notwithstanding differences in both substance and procedure between the Illinois and English courts.

> Not that the English concept of fair procedure is identical to ours; but we cannot believe that the Illinois statute [adopting the UFC-MJRA] is intended to bar the enforcement of all judgments of any foreign legal system that does not conform its procedural doctrines to the latest twist and turn of our courts regarding for example, the circumstances under which due process requires an opportunity for a hearing in advance of the deprivation of a substantive right rather than afterwards.[6]

The opinion also quoted Justice Cardozo's famous observation that "[w]e are not so provincial as to say that every solution of a problem is wrong because we deal with it otherwise at home."[7]

---

6   *Society of Lloyd's v. Ashenden*, 233 F.3d 473, 476 (7th Cir. 2000).

7   *Loucks v. Standard Oil Co. of New York*, 224 N.Y. 99 (1918).

The public policy exception is a frequent battle-ground because, inevitably, there are significant policy differences between the laws of the rendering and enforcing jurisdictions. Litigators have stock arguments to expand or narrow the scope of this exception. For example, there is overlap between the public policy exception and the other exceptions. Litigators arguing in favor of enforcement of a foreign-country judgment use this overlap to constrain the scope of the public policy exception: "Your Honor, the list includes matters of fraud, lack of due process, lack of jurisdiction. Those are the kinds of 'public policy' concerns that are implicated here." But litigators who are arguing against enforcement use this overlap to broaden the scope of the public policy exception: "Your Honor, the list specifically includes a public policy exception for circumstances that the exceptions for fraud, lack of due process, lack of jurisdiction do not already capture."

In most circumstances, the enforcement of a foreign-country judgment in the United States involves a foreign-country plaintiff and an American defendant. In order to collect the judgment, the plaintiff needs to file where the defendant's assets are located; a defendant who has assets in the United States but not elsewhere is likely to be an American. But that configuration is not the only possibility: both litigants might be Americans; both litigants might be foreigners; or the plaintiff might be an American who couldn't get jurisdiction over a foreign defendant in the United States for the underlying litigation but can enforce a foreign-country judgment in the United States because that foreign defendant has American assets. The likelihood that foreign-country judgment debtors will have assets in the United States is enhanced by the fact that many businesses maintain U.S. bank accounts, often in New York.

Recognition and enforcement practice can compromise the rights and assets and integrity of persons in the United States. The stakes can be very high. In 2011, in an action brought by 30,000 indigenous villagers living in the Lago Agrio region of Ecuador against Texaco/Chevron for polluting the Amazon rainforest for years, an Ecuador court issued a 188-page ruling ordering Texaco/Chevron to pay $8.6 billion in compensation and an additional $860 million to the Amazon Defense Front trust. The order also ordered a doubling of those damages (to $18 billion) if Chevron failed to issue a public apology within fifteen days of the order. The award was affirmed by an intermediate appeals court in Ecuador. The Ecuador National Court of Justice also affirmed, but cut the award in half. In 2014, a federal district court in New York refused to enforce the award on the ground that the judgment was the product of fraud and racketeering.[8]

---

8 *Chevron Corp. v. Donziger*, 974 F.Supp.2d 362 (S.D.N.Y. 2014), *affirmed,* 833 F.3d 74 (2d Cir. 2016), *cert. denied,* 137 S. Ct. 2268 (2017).

A foreign-country judgment may also be invoked *defensively* to prevent re-litigation. A plaintiff who sues a defendant in some foreign country and loses, could bring a second action against that defendant in a United States court. Under these circumstances, the defendant would ask the American forum to *recognize* (rather than *enforce*) the foreign judgment. The plaintiff seeking re-litigation would need to show that the foreign judgment was invalid in order to avoid preclusion.

Finally, because the practice of recognizing and enforcing foreign-country judgments is not subject to an over-arching mandate like the Full Faith and Credit Clause, the practice with respect to certain types of cases can be tailored by policy-makers to achieve certain objectives. We emphasize three of those types here:

First, Foreign judgments in defamation causes are very difficult to enforce in the United States. The practice of "libel tourism"[9] that chilled free speech led Congress in 2010 to pass the Securing the Protection of Our Enduring and Established Constitutional Heritage Act (the SPEECH Act), 28 U.S.C. § 4102. Under the SPEECH Act, foreign defamation judgments are not enforceable in the United States unless the judgments satisfy the protections of freedom of speech and press guaranteed by both the First Amendment to the U.S. Constitution and also the state constitution of the state in which the domestic court is located.

Second, child custody matters fall within the scope of a specialized international treaty that provides a framework for assigning jurisdiction and returning children in accordance with foreign custody decrees. *See* Hague Convention on the Civil Aspects of International Child Abduction, and implementing legislation at 42 U.S.C. §§ 11601 et seq.

Third, foreign judgments that emanate from a jurisdiction that was knowingly and willfully consented-to by parties to a contract should ordinarily be enforced. The Hague Convention on Choice of Courts Agreement entered into force on October 1, 2015. The United States has signed the convention, but has not yet ratified it, meaning that it is not in force for the United States.

---

9   "Libel tourism" refers to a form of international forum-shopping in which a plaintiff chooses to file a defamation claim in a foreign jurisdiction with more favorable substantive law. England is the best-known example, because with few exceptions, any alleged defamatory statement that adversely affects an individual's reputation is prima facie defamatory; the defendant then shoulders the burden to prove the truth of that statement. English law also does not impose any standard of fault; a statement that the speaker believed to be true can be defamatory.

Hypothetical 23-1

Plaintiff Revero Boat Rentals Inc. (Revero) a Barbados corporation obtained a default judgment for (US) $7,764.00 in the small claims division of the Barbados Magistrates Court against the Defendant Ian Bartrum, who is a resident of Vermont. Bartrum rented and damaged Revero's party boat while visiting Barbados, causing Revero to pay for repairs. Revero properly served Bartrum who did not appear in the Barbados action. After obtaining the default judgment, Revero sought enforcement of the Barbados judgment in a Vermont court.

In the Vermont action, Bartrum filed a motion for relief from the judgment. Defendant Revero correctly observes that (i) the Barbados small claims division has jurisdiction over all civil actions where the amount in controversy does not exceed (US) $9,000; (ii) the procedure in the small claims division is, by statute, "informal and summary as is consistent with justice"; (iii) "neither party may be represented by counsel, and all parties shall appear in person" in the small claims division; and (iv) appeals from the small claims division may be taken to the Magistrates Court, but "no additional evidence shall be taken or considered" in those appeals.

Bartrum does not dispute that Revero complied with the UEFJA by filing a properly authenticated copy of the judgment and an accompanying affidavit in the Vermont court. But defendant argues that he was deprived of his right to due process by the rules of the Barbados court and therefore was not obliged to defend that action.

Is a Vermont court likely to enforce this judgment?

Hypothetical 23-2

While on a week's vacation in Austria, Adrienne Brungess, an Idaho domiciliary, met with Wilhelmine Siedler, an antiques dealer who lived in Salzburg, Austria. Brungess inspected several items that Siedler was selling, but made no immediate purchase. At Siedler's urging, Brungess agreed to leave with Siedler a small, rare, and extremely valuable antique porcelain figurine owned by Brungess that she (Brungess) had purchased earlier that month in Turkey; Siedler wanted to show the figurine to another collector who, Siedler assured Brungess, would pay top dollar. Brungess returned to the United States to await communication from Siedler.

The following month Siedler showed the figurine to Werner Goebl, a collector who specialized in figurines of this vintage and style. Goebl was thrilled with the rare and unique piece, and asked about its provenance. When Siedler explained that it was an Idaho collector named Brungess, Goebl was aghast. According to Goebl, Brungess had purchased a different item from him less than a year earlier at a show in Paris, France, and refused to pay him the 45,000 euros (approximately $53,000) that he was still owed.

Goebl is preparing to file a lawsuit in Austria against Brungess to recover the 45,000 euros. Under Austrian law the courts have personal jurisdiction over a foreign defendant who, like Brungess, has property in the forum state. You are a lawyer in Idaho. Goebl's attorney in Austria has called you to discuss whether a judgment obtained in Austria would be enforceable in Idaho. What is your advice? (What are your questions for her? Prepare for that conversation.)

Hypothetical 23-3

Jon Wolgamuth is an Iowa domiciliary and a recently-retired professional hockey player. Last year, Wolgamuth played for HC Davos in the Switzerland National Hockey League. During a mid-season game with the ZSC Lions, Wolgamuth "checked" a Lions player, Darren Key, from behind, hitting Key in the head and neck. As a result of Wolgamuth's hit, Key fell and hit his head on the ice, suffering a non-localized concussion and other injuries. Key was hospitalized for several weeks.

Shortly after the incident, the hockey league commenced disciplinary proceedings against Wolgamuth and ultimately suspended him for eight games for violating a hockey federation regulation that prohibits "malicious conduct intended to cause injury to another player." Wolgamuth complied with the suspension and also waived his right to appeal that decision. Unbeknownst to Wolgamuth, the finding from the disciplinary proceeding created a rebuttable presumption in a subsequent criminal proceeding, which the public prosecutor in the Canton of Zurich then filed. Wolgamuth vigorously defended himself against the criminal charge but was ultimately found guilty of intentional bodily harm and gross negligence. The court ordered Wolgamuth to pay the court a fine of 75,000 Swiss Francs (approximately $77,200).

Key then filed a separate civil action against Wolgamuth in the District Court of Zurich for past and future medical expenses, wage loss, and other amounts Wolgamuth was required to pay under Swiss law. The civil court was not bound by the criminal finding of guilt, but instead was obligated to take a fresh look at the issues of culpability and damages. The court received extensive evidence from both sides, including expert witnesses. Under Swiss civil procedure, witnesses are not subject to oral cross-examination by the parties, but must answer written questions submitted in advance of trial. The court entered judgment in the amount of one million Swiss Francs (approximately $1,029,000) plus interest at the rate of five percent, court costs of sixty-one thousand five hundred Swiss Francs (~$64,000), court disbursements of five hundred fifty Swiss Francs (~$566), and attorney fees and costs of sixty-two thousand eight hundred Swiss Francs (~$64,600). Wolgamuth did not appeal this judgment.

Wolgamuth's substantial assets are in Iowa, not Switzerland. Is an Iowa court likely to enforce the Swiss judgment?

––––––––––––

Finally, although this is not an arbitration course, you should be aware that courts are also frequently asked to enforce foreign arbitral awards. The United States has ratified and implemented the United Nations Convention on the Recognition and Enforcement of Foreign Arbitral Awards. *See* 9 U.S.C. §§ 201–208. The Convention, often referred to as the "New York Convention" is the primary legal basis for enforcing international commercial arbitration awards. There is a very strong presumption that arbitrations are valid and that the award should be enforced when the prevailing party seeks to convert the arbitral award into a court judgment. Although the Convention identifies a few specific and very limited grounds upon which an arbitral award may be denied recognition, the pro-enforcement bias is renowned and is much stronger even than the pro-enforcement bias with respect to the enforcement of foreign-country judgments. This may seem counterintuitive in light of the fact that an arbitral forum is usually a private provider of dispute resolution services with less formality and transparency than the public courts of a foreign sovereign. But the Federal Arbitration Act (9 U.S.C. § 1 *et seq.*) embodies a federal policy favoring arbitration (and there is no analogous federal statute endorsing enforcement of the judgments of foreign courts). In the cases that follow, however, American courts are asked to enforce the judgments of foreign countries, not arbitration awards.

FROM THE COURTS

WEIR FOULDS LLP v. RESTIVO

Court of Appeals of Ohio
2014 WL 1345497 (Ohio Ct. App. Mar. 24, 2014)

CARR, JUDGE.

. . . I

This matter arises out of a dispute over legal fees between Restivo and appellee, Weir Foulds, LLP, a law firm located in Ontario, Canada. Restivo hired Weir Foulds in relation to a prospective real estate [development on Pelee Island in Ontario, Canada. Restivo refused to pay, disputing the work and the fairness of the cost of that work.] In 2009, Weir Foulds obtained a judgment against Restivo in the Ontario Superior Court of Justice. On April 22, 2010, Weir Foulds filed a notice of filing the foreign judgment in the Lorain County [Ohio] Court of Common Pleas. . . .

II

. . . Restivo challenges the validity of the Canadian judgment on the basis that the case was resolved by way of a summary trial instead of a jury trial. . . .

Restivo further contends that the Canadian master's decision at the pretrial conference to have a summary trial instead of a jury trial was influenced by favoritism toward Weir Foulds.

"Like sister-state judgments, foreign judgments have a strong presumption of validity in United States courts." *Samyang Food Co., Ltd. v. Pneumatic Scale Corp.*, 2005 WL 2711526, *5 (Oct. 21, 2005) (citing *Clarkson Co. v. Shaheen*, 544 F.2d 624, 631 (2d Cir. 1976)). "The party challenging the validity of a foreign judgment has the burden of presenting evidence of its invalidity." *Id.* American courts have long recognized that "mere divergence from American procedure does not render a foreign judgment unenforceable." *Canadian Imperial Bank of Commerce v. Saxony Carpet Co., Inc.*, 899 F. Supp. 1248, 1252 (S.D.N.Y. 1995).

"Unless some federal statute or treaty is involved, the recognition and enforcement of foreign country judgments is a matter of state law. Actions to enforce a foreign country judgment do not arise under the laws of the United States. Therefore, federal courts apply state law in deciding whether foreign judgments should be recognized." *Samyang*, at *5, citing *Erie v. Tompkins*, 304 U.S. 64 (1938).

As noted above, Ohio's Foreign Money-Judgments Recognition Act is codified in R.C. 2329.90 through R.C. 2329.94. R.C. 2329.91 states, in part:

(A) Except as provided in sections 2329.92 and 2329.93 of the Revised Code, any foreign country judgment that is final, conclusive, and enforceable where rendered shall be recognized and enforced by the courts of this state, even though an appeal from the judgment is pending or the judgment is subject to an appeal. Such a foreign country judgment is enforceable in this state in the same manner as a judgment of another state that is entitled to full faith and credit.

(B) For purposes of division (A) of this section, a foreign country judgment is conclusive between the parties to the extent that it grants or denies the recovery of a sum of money, except that, if any of the following applies, a foreign country judgment is not conclusive:

(1) The judgment was rendered under a system that does not provide impartial tribunals or procedures that are compatible with the requirements of the due process of law;

(2) . . . [T]he foreign court did not have personal jurisdiction over the defendant.

(3) The foreign court did not have jurisdiction over the subject matter.

R.C. 2329.92(A)(3) states that "A foreign country judgment shall not be recognized and enforced pursuant to [R.C. 2329.91] if the judge determines that . . . [t]he claim for relief on which the foreign country judgment is based is repugnant to the public policy of the state."

In *Samyang, supra*, the United States District Court for the Northern District of Ohio conducted an in-depth examination of Ohio's Foreign Money-Judgments Recognition Act. The *Samyang* court concluded that even though the Korean judicial system did not provide for the right to a civil jury trial under any circumstances, the foreign country judgment was enforceable in

Ohio because the Korean judicial system had legal procedures that generally comported with notions of due process and basic fairness. *Samyang*, at *6–*7. Unlike the Korean judicial system, the Canadian judicial system, like the American judicial system, does employ jury trials to resolve civil disputes. In this case, however, the parties appeared for a pretrial conference where the master decided that the matter could be resolved with a "summary trial" pursuant to Rule 76 of the Rules of Civil Procedure as set forth in the Ontario Courts of Justice Act. Rule 76 governs "Simplified Procedure."

"Ohio law do[es] not contemplate that foreign judgments only become enforceable when exact Ohio[ ] procedures are followed. Instead, the statute concerns itself with whether the foreign court offers a fair procedure generally compatible with the due process obligations of notice and opportunity to be heard." *Samyang* at *6. "In affording jury trials in civil cases, the United States is the exception, not the rule." *Id.* at *7. A foreign legal system that does not offer a jury trial in civil proceedings can comport with due process if notice and an opportunity to be heard by a neutral magistrate is permitted. *Id.*, citing *Hilton v. Guyot*, 16 S. Ct. 139, 159 (1895). In setting forth this standard, the *Samyang* court adopted the reasoning espoused in *Society of Lloyd's v. Ashenden*, 233 F.3d 473 (7th Cir. 2000), where Judge Posner wrote that the judicial processes of civilized nations should be deemed valid when "the foreign procedures are 'fundamentally fair' and do not offend against 'basic fairness.' " *Samyang* at *6, quoting *Ashenden*, 233 F.3d at 476–477.

Thus, while Restivo argues that the *Samyang* decision fails to recognize the place of the jury trial under Ohio law, Ohio does not require identical procedure in order for a foreign country judgment to be considered valid. "[P]rocedural differences alone are not grounds for setting aside a foreign judgment." *Burgan Express for Gen. Trading and Contracting Co. v. Atwood*, 2012 WL 4473210, at *6 (Sept. 26, 2012). "[T]he overall thrust of Ohio and federal law concerning recognition of foreign judgments is that the foreign court's procedures must broadly comport with due process as defined in the United States. The procedures need not exactly mirror procedures of United States courts, provided the differences do not render the proceedings fundamentally unfair." *Id.* Moreover, while the Canadian judicial system does not precisely mirror the procedures in Ohio, we note that "the judicial systems of Canada and the United States are rooted in the same common law traditions." *Theunissen v. Matthews*, 935 F.2d 1454, 1462 (6th Cir. 1991).

As an initial matter, we note that while Restivo broadly asserts that the decision to hold a summary trial in this case was influenced by favoritism toward Weir Foulds, he may not challenge the foreign judgment by attempting to relitigate specific legal issues that arose during the foreign litigation. R.C. 2329.94(B) states that Ohio's Foreign Money-Judgments Recognition Act "shall be construed so as to effectuate the general purpose to make uniform the laws of the states that enact similar provisions." Allowing parties to collaterally attack foreign country judgments would undermine the purpose of the Foreign Money-Judgments Recognition Act. *Samyang* at *5, citing *Clarkson Co. v. Shaheen*, 544 F.2d 624, 631 (2d Cir. 1976) ("A foreign judgment may not be collaterally attacked upon the mere assertion of the party that the judgment was erroneous in law or in fact, much less upon a mere assertion of fraud. . . ."). Thus, in order to prevail on his claim that Ohio should not recognize the Canadian judgment, Restivo must demonstrate that the procedures available in the foreign legal system were fundamentally unfair and failed to even generally comport with American notions of due process.

Restivo's central argument is that the Canadian judgment should be deemed invalid because he was not afforded a jury trial, thereby rendering the judgment unacceptable in light of both Ohio due process standards, as well as Ohio public policy. This argument is without merit. Ohio courts will recognize a foreign country judgment absent a right to a jury trial provided that the foreign court offered a fair procedure generally compatible with the due process obligations of notice and opportunity to be heard. *Samyang* at *7. Pursuant to the summary trial procedure set forth in Rule 76, each party is provided with an opportunity to present evidence, as well as challenge any evidence offered by a party opponent. After the presentation of evidence, each party is permitted to make an oral argument prior to the time the judge renders judgment. Restivo has failed to explain how the summary trial procedure in the Ontario Superior Court of Justice is not a fair procedure which generally comports with basic notions of due process. Under these circumstances, we cannot say that the trial court erred in concluding that the procedures available to Restivo in the Canadian court were sufficient to render the foreign country judgment final, conclusive, and enforceable under R.C. 2329.91. . . . [This assignment of error is overruled.]

COMMENTS AND QUESTIONS

1. Why wouldn't Weir Foulds sue Restivo in Ohio from the outset to avoid the hassle of enforcing a foreign-country judgment?

2. The opinion doesn't mention the amount of the Ontario judgment. Is the enforcement analysis the same whether the judgment is $300,000 or $30,000?

3. The court is confident that the Canadian summary trial procedure "comports with basic notions of due process," even if it does not incorporate juries. If not juries, what are the basic notions of our due process tradition? (What is absolutely *essential*?)

4. Restivo claims that the Canadian judge unfairly favored the local law firm, Weir Foulds. But the Ohio court says that it will not "relitigate specific legal issues that arose during the foreign litigation." Does this mean that, as a practical matter, favoritism is not a basis for refusing enforcement of a foreign-country's judgment?

FROM THE COURTS

ALBERTA SEC. COMM'N v. RYCKMAN

Superior Court of Delaware
2015 WL 2265473, *affirmed* 127 A.3d 399 (Del. 2015)

JOHNSTON, JUDGE.

Procedural Context

This case presents an issue of first impression in Delaware. The Alberta Securities Commission ("ASC"), the judgment creditor, brought this action against Lawrence G. Ryckman, the judgment debtor, to enforce an Arizona judgment, which originated in Canada. The ASC is a duly authorized and constituted administrative body for the Canadian government in Alberta. At the time of the Canadian judgment, Ryckman resided in Alberta, Canada. At the time of the Arizona judgment, Ryckman resided in Scottsdale, Arizona.

Ryckman has moved to vacate the ASC's action to enforce the Arizona judgment in Delaware pursuant to Superior Court Rule 60. Ryckman argues the Arizona judgment is not entitled to full faith and credit under the United States Constitution and Delaware's Uniform Enforcement of Foreign Judgments Act ("UEFJA") because the Arizona judgment is a domesticated Canadian judgment. It is undisputed that Delaware could not directly domesticate the Canadian judgment because it would violate Delaware's Uniform Foreign-Country Money Judgment Recognition Act ("UFCMJRA").

In response, the ASC contends that even if Delaware could not directly domesticate the Canadian judgment, Delaware must enforce the Arizona judgment under the full faith and credit clause and the UEFJA.

On December 17, 2014, the ASC served a subpoena *duces tecum* directed to garnishee Studio One Media, Inc. ("Studio One") requesting: (1) a corporate designee for a deposition in Delaware pursuant to Superior Court Civil Rule 30(b)(6); and (2) certain documents pursuant to Superior Court Civil Rules 30(b)(6) and 45. On December 30, 2014, Studio One filed objections to every item requested. On January 5, 2015, the ASC filed a motion to compel the subpoena. On January 29, 2015, Studio One filed a motion to quash the subpoena. [Ryckman is the President and CEO of Studio One.]

Undisputed Facts

A hearing was held before the ASC in January 1996. The ASC found that Ryckman had violated the Alberta Securities Act in his role as director and chairman of Westgroup when he deliberately engaged in a complex scheme that created a false and misleading appearance of trading designed to deceive investors to trade at artificial prices. The ASC ordered Ryckman to resign any positions that he held as director or officer for any issuer; to cease serving as a director or officer for any issuer for 18 years; to cease trading in all securities for any issuer for 18 years; and to pay $492,640.14 (Canadian Dollars) in costs to the ASC. On January 18, 1996, the ASC obtained a valid judgment against Ryckman in Canada ("Canadian Judgment").

In January 1997, Ryckman moved his residence from Canada to Scottsdale, Arizona. The Superior Court of Arizona considered the pleadings and heard argument on the ASC's action to domesticate the Canadian Judgment in Arizona. The Arizona court granted the ASC's Motion for Summary Judgment and ordered judgment against Ryckman and his wife. The court ordered judgment for $485,140.14 (Canadian Dollars) for the principal owed plus 10 percent per annum interest from the date of the Arizona judgment; $87,222.23 (Canadian Dollars) in past due interest; and $202.50 (U.S. Dollars) for recoverable court costs plus 10 percent per annum from the date of the Arizona judgment ("Arizona Judgment").

Ryckman then appealed the lower court's decision to the Arizona Court of Appeals. The court of appeals affirmed the trial court's holding based on principles of comity. The court of appeals found that the Canadian Judgment was final, on the merits, and not procured by prejudice, fraud, unfairness, or irregularities in the foreign-country proceedings. For purposes of the motions at issue, the validity of the Arizona Judgment is not disputed.

On July 31, 2013, the ASC filed a copy of the Arizona judgment in Delaware, seeking to enforce the judgment pursuant to the UEFJA.

It is undisputed that Delaware could not directly domesticate the Canadian Judgment for two reasons. First, the Canadian Judgment violates the UFCMJRA's statute of limitations. Delaware's UFCMJRA imposes a 15-year statute of limitations on foreign-country judgment recognition. The Canadian Judgment was issued in 1996 and the instant action was filed in Delaware in 2013—a 17-year gap.

Second, the Canadian Judgment constitutes a fine or penalty. The UFCMJRA "does not apply to a foreign-country judgment . . . to the extent that the judgment is: . . . [a] fine or other penalty."[12] The Canadian Judgment is a fine or penalty because the ASC ordered a pecuniary judgment on Ryckman to punish him for his Securities Act violations.

Analysis

Motion to Vacate

The narrow issue presented is a matter of first impression in Delaware. Ryckman argues the enforcement action violates Delaware's UFCMJRA because the Canadian Judgment was not domesticated in Arizona under the UFCMJRA. Consequently, he contends the Arizona Judgment should be analyzed as a foreign-country judgment under the UFCMJRA, not a sister-state judgment entitled to full faith and credit. . . .

---

12 . . . Arizona's foreign-country judgment act equivalent does not impose such a limitation.

Full Faith and Credit Clause

Article IV, Section 1 of the United State Constitution states, in pertinent part: "Full Faith and Credit shall be given in each State to the public Acts, Records, and judicial Proceedings of every other State." The Full Faith and Credit Act provides, in pertinent part:

> The records and judicial proceedings of any court of any . . . State
> . . . shall have the same full faith and credit in every court within
> the United States and its Territories and Possessions as they have
> by law or usage in the courts of such State . . . from which they
> are taken.[16]

Relevant Delaware Statutes

Delaware's statutory framework reflects a distinction between the circumstances that Delaware may enforce a sister-state judgment (pursuant to the UEFJA) and those in which Delaware may recognize a foreign-country judgment (pursuant to the UFCMJRA).

UEFJA

The UEFJA governs enforcement of sister-state judgments. The UEFJA is Delaware's version of a uniform act that nearly all states have adopted. The UEFJA applies to any United States judgment, decree, or order which is entitled to full faith and credit. Rather than subjecting a sister-state judgment to further judicial review, the UEFJA allows a judgment creditor simply to file an authenticated copy of the foreign judgment with the Prothonotary. Once the foreign judgment is filed, the Prothonotary must treat the foreign judgment in the same manner as a judgment of this Court. By its express provisions and purpose, however, the UEFJA does not apply to foreign-country judgments.

UFCMJRA

The UFCMJRA governs recognition of foreign-country judgments. The UFCMJRA only applies to judgments rendered outside of the U.S. The UFCMJRA applies when the foreign-country judgment "(1) [g]rants or denies recovery of a sum of money; and (2) [u]nder the law of the foreign country where rendered, is final, conclusive, and enforceable." The UFC-MJRA does not apply if the foreign-country judgment constitutes a fine or

---

16   28 U.S.C. § 1738.

other penalty. Similarly, recognition is not granted if the action seeking to recognize the foreign-country judgment is commenced more than 15 years from the effective date of the foreign-country judgment.

Once a foreign-country judgment is recognized *under the UFCMJRA*, it is entitled to the same full faith and credit as a sister-state judgment. However, Delaware's UFCMJRA is silent on whether a sister-state judgment that domesticates a foreign-country judgment—under recognition procedures *other than the UFCMJRA*—is entitled to the same full faith and credit.

The UFCMJRA "does not prevent recognition under principles of comity or otherwise of a foreign-country judgment not within the scope of [the UFCMJRA]." Additionally, when interpreting the UFCMJRA, "consideration must be given to the need to promote uniformity of the law with respect to its subject matter among states that enact it."[31]

Competing Public Policy Considerations

This Court must be concerned with establishing appropriate precedent and avoiding unintended consequences. There are several competing public policy considerations at issue in the instant litigation.

If the Court finds in favor of Ryckman, Delaware only could enforce a foreign-country judgment if the domestication originally is sought in Delaware. The ASC first filed the Canadian Judgment under Arizona's more lenient foreign-country judgment recognition procedures. The ASC then brought the Canadian Judgment to Delaware, arguing that it is a sister-state judgment entitled to full faith and credit. If the Court were to permit this procedure, future judgment creditors simply could file a judgment in a state that has not enacted the UFCMJRA, obtain a valid judgment, then rely on the UEFJA to obtain full faith and credit in a sister state.

Finding in favor of Ryckman would avoid this type of forum-shopping and "bootstrapping" a foreign-country judgment "through the back door" in Delaware. However, finding in favor of Ryckman potentially could require this Court to "pierce the veil" of an otherwise valid sister-state judgment entitled to full faith and credit. Such a ruling would disturb Delaware's clear

---

31 10 Del. C. § 4808. Thirty-two states enacted the 1962 Act. *Foreign-Country Money Judgment Recognition Act*, Uniform Law Commission, http://www.uniformlaws.org/Act.aspx?title=Foreign-Country Money Judgments Recognition Act (last visited Apr. 6, 2015). Twenty states enacted the revised 2005 Act, including Delaware. As of the date of this opinion, Arizona has not adopted either the 1962 Act or the 2005 Act.

precedent instructing this Court to respect sister-state judgments without relitigating the case on the merits.

The purpose of the UEFJA is to recognize sister-state judgments without requiring courts to look beyond undisputed validity. Finding in favor of the ASC would promote this purpose by granting full faith and credit to the Arizona Judgment without time- and resource-consuming inquiry into whether the Canadian Judgment could have been domesticated in Delaware in the first instance. However, such a ruling could risk increased forum-shopping and bootstrapping when a party seeks domestication of a foreign-country judgment.

Relevant Non-Delaware Case Law

A jurisdictional split exists as to whether a sister-state judgment domesticating a foreign-country judgment is entitled to full faith and credit in another state. . . .

In *Reading & Bates Construction Co. v. Baker Energy Resources Corp.*, [976 S.W.2d 702 (Tex. Ct. App. 1998),] the Texas Court of Appeals refused to give full faith and credit to a Louisiana judgment obtained by domestication of a Canadian judgment, reasoning that it would interfere with important interests of Texas. [We will not] "permit a party to clothe a foreign country judgment in the garment of a sister state's judgment and thereby evade the . . . [Texas] recognition process." [*Id.* at 715.] . . .

Conversely, in *Standard Chartered Bank v. Ahmad Hamad Al Gosaibi & Bros.* [, 9 A.3d 936 (Pa. Super. 2014),] the Pennsylvania Superior Court gave full faith and credit to a New York judgment obtained by domestication of a Bahraini judgment. In *Standard Chartered*, the trial court did not discuss the merits of New York's recognition of the Bahraini judgment. Instead, the trial court focused on full faith and credit principles to enforce the sister-state judgment. The appellate court affirmed the trial court's ruling, noting that "judgments recognized as valid after a full hearing in a sister-state are *res judicata.*" *Id.* at 945. Consequently "[s]tates must give full faith and credit to sister-state judgments 'even where the judgment violates the policy or law of the forum where enforcement is sought.' " *Id.* . . .

Delaware Case Law

While no Delaware court has considered the precise issue presented in this case, the Delaware Supreme Court recently examined considerations similar to those stated by the *Standard Chartered* Court. In *Pyott v. Louisiana Municipal Police Employees' Retirement System*, [74 A.2d 612 (Del. 2013)], the Delaware Supreme Court reversed the Court of Chancery's refusal to dismiss a stockholder derivative action after a California federal court had dismissed a similar action against the same directors, and essentially the same complaint. The Delaware Supreme Court focused on principles of full faith and credit.

The *Pyott* Court reasoned that even if enforcing another state's judgment is repugnant to Delaware law and policy, the sister state's judgment is entitled to full faith and credit. The Court reasoned:

> Under this Court's precedents, the undisputed interest that Delaware has in governing the internal affairs of its corporations must yield to the stronger national interests that all state and federal courts have in respecting each other's judgments. The United States Supreme Court has held that the full faith and credit obligation is "exacting" and that there is "no roving 'public policy exception' to the full faith and credit due judgments."[64] . . .

Pyott controls the issue presented in this case. Even though Delaware could not directly domesticate the Canadian Judgment, this Court's analysis is guided by the Delaware Supreme Court's ruling that Delaware public policy must yield to the stronger national interest in giving full faith and credit to sister-state judgments. The ASC obtained a valid judgment on the merits against Ryckman in Canada. The ASC then obtained a valid domestication of the Canadian Judgment in Arizona. Accordingly, the Court finds that the Arizona Judgment is entitled to full faith and credit in Delaware pursuant to the UEFJA. . . .

Additionally, judgments recognized as valid after a full hearing in a sister-state are *res judicata*. Ryckman had a full and fair opportunity to present his case challenging domestication in Arizona. There, Ryckman presented various pleadings and argument before the Arizona Superior Court. Subsequently, Ryckman presented argument before the Arizona Court of Appeals challenging domestication. The Arizona Court of Appeals rejected Ryckman's position, and affirmed the Arizona Superior Court's domestication of the Canadian Judgment. Therefore, the Arizona Judgment should be given full faith and credit based on *res judicata*. . . .

---

64   *Id.* (quoting *Baker v. Gen. Motors Corp.*, 522 U.S. 222, 232–33 (1998)).

Ryckman argues the ASC is attempting to "back door" the Canadian Judgment into Delaware by unlawfully circumventing the UFCMJRA. However, the facts of this case compel a contrary conclusion. Ryckman voluntarily moved his residence from Canada to Arizona. Thus, Arizona was a forum chosen by Ryckman—not the ASC. Therefore, there is no evidence that the ASC engaged in any improper forum-shopping. . . .

The ASC simply seeks to collect on a judgment through assets allegedly held by Ryckman in a Delaware corporation. There is no evidence that the ASC's enforcement is motivated by an improper purpose. The situs of a corporation's stock is the place of incorporation. Delaware is interested in disputes regarding stockholders of a Delaware corporation when the ownership of stock is at issue in the litigation. Studio One is a Delaware corporation. The ASC seeks to determine the amount of assets or shares held by Ryckman in Studio One, in order to execute the Arizona Judgment. Therefore, Delaware has an interest in the instant dispute.

Granting full faith and credit to the Arizona Judgment is consistent with important public policy considerations. First, enforcing the Arizona Judgment promotes the national interest in giving full faith and credit to sister-state judgments. This national interest outweighs Delaware's interest in enforcing foreign-country judgments under the UFCMJRA. Second, applying full faith and credit to the Arizona Judgment avoids the necessity of looking behind an otherwise valid judgment. Such an examination of a valid judgment would involve potentially needless, expensive, and time-consuming litigation. Further, such a process would disturb Delaware's clear precedent to respect sister-state judgments without relitigating the case on the merits. Once a creditor domesticates a foreign-country judgment, the Court finds that the UEFJA permits the creditor to seek enforcement in a sister state.

Therefore, the Court finds that full faith and credit applies. The Arizona Judgment should be domesticated and enforced pursuant to Delaware law, as codified by the UEFJ.

Motion to Compel & Motion to Quash

The ASC served a subpoena *duces tecum* on Studio One to: (1) produce a corporate designee pursuant to Superior Court Civil Rule 30(b)(6); and (2) produce certain documents for the deposition pursuant to Rules 30(b)(6) and 45. . . .

The Court finds that Studio One must respond to the subpoena pursuant to Rule 26(b)(1). The ASC is entitled to know what Ryckman-controlled companies own the other 5,879,904 shares of Studio One common stock that are listed under Ryckman's name. Studio One must produce any requested non-privileged documents in its possession and must state which, if any, documents are not in its possession. . . .

Discovery in aid of execution is broad. A judgment creditor may discover a debtor's assets and tax returns through a party other than the judgment debtor. To the extent that ASC is seeking privileged information, Studio One has discovery tools, such as a privilege log, at its disposal. Therefore, the Court finds the discovery sought pursuant to Rule 45 is not unduly burdensome. . . .

COMMENTS AND QUESTIONS

1. The UFCMJRA does not prevent recognition or enforcement on other grounds. The enforcement of a foreign court's equitable order, for example, falls outside the scope of the UFCMJRA. Comity is the basis for accepting or refusing to enforce a foreign court's equitable order.

2. The court relies heavily on *Pyott*. Does the policy and function of the Full Faith and Credit Clause apply equally to a sister-state judgment and to a sister-state judgment domesticating a foreign-country judgment?

3. Why do you think the ASC was unable to collect the judgment in Arizona if Ryckman lived there. A google search of Lawrence Ryckman suggests that he is not averse to controversy or litigation.

TROUT POINT LODGE, LTD. v. HANDSHOE

U.S. Court of Appeals for the Fifth Circuit
729 F.3d 481 (5th Cir. 2013)

JENNIFER WALKER ELROD, CIRCUIT JUDGE.

This case requires us to construe the newly-enacted Securing the Protection of our Enduring and Established Constitutional Heritage Act (the "SPEECH Act"), 28 U.S.C. § 4102. Appellants Trout Point Lodge, Ltd. ("Trout Point Lodge"), Vaughn Perret ("Perret"), and Charles Leary ("Leary") (collectively, "Trout Point") seek to enforce a defamation-based default judgment that they obtained against Appellee Doug K. Handshoe ("Handshoe") in Nova Scotia, Canada. We agree with the district court that Trout Point cannot satisfy its burden under the SPEECH Act to show that either (A) Nova Scotian law provided at least as much protection for freedom of speech and press in Handshoe's case as would be provided by the First Amendment and relevant state law, or (B) Handshoe would have been found liable for defamation by a Mississippi court. 28 U.S.C. § 4102. Accordingly, we affirm.

I

Handshoe, a Mississippi citizen, owns and operates Slabbed.org, a public-affairs blog with the tagline "Alternative New Media for the Gulf South." He describes Slabbed.org as a "forum for local residents and other interested parties to gather and share information regarding various political and legal issues that impact the Gulf Coast."

One of the blog's focal points over the last few years has been Aaron Broussard, the former Parish President of Jefferson Parish, Louisiana.[1] Broussard was indicted in the United States District Court for the Eastern District of Louisiana and pleaded guilty to charges of bribery and theft in September 2012. Handshoe claims that Slabbed.org has been "instrumental" in reporting the "ongoing corruption scandal, indictment, and guilty plea" involving Broussard.

---

[1] In addition to his blog, the record indicates that Handshoe engages in several other forms of internet communication. For example, he maintains a Twitter account for Slabbed.org and posts comments on several other web sites.

During his time in office, Broussard owned property in Nova Scotia. The property sat on Trout Point Road, very close to Trout Point Lodge, a hotel that Perret and Leary own and operate. In about January 2010, Handshoe began publishing entries on Slabbed.org alleging a link between Broussard and Trout Point Lodge, Perret, and Leary. At or near the same time, the *Times-Picayune*, a New Orleans newspaper, published an article indicating that Broussard had an ownership interest in Trout Point Lodge and that Jefferson Parish contractors had paid to rent the premises. The *Times-Picayune* retracted this assertion and issued a correction after Perret and Leary alerted the paper to purported "factual error in [its] reporting." It appears that the corporate parent of the *Times-Picayune* also took the Slabbed.org blog offline after Perret and Leary demanded this retraction. The district court determined that Handshoe, "apparently in reaction to his blog being taken offline," found another web host for his site and "began an internet campaign to damage Perret and Leary."[3] Specifically, Handshoe posted several updates regarding Trout Point Lodge, Perret, and Leary, which the district court noted "can be characterized as derogatory, mean spirited, sexist, and homophobic."

Trout Point filed suit in the Supreme Court of Nova Scotia (the "Nova Scotia Court") on September 1, 2011, alleging defamation and related claims. Trout Point's First Amended Statement of Claim referred to publications on Slabbed.org and related third-party web sites, which it asserted "were directly defamatory and were also defamatory by both true and false innuendo in that they would tend to lower the opinion or estimation of the plaintiffs in the eyes of others who read the defamatory publications as a series, or alternatively, in parts." At the outset, the First Amended Statement of Claim asserted four primary sources of reputational harm: (1) content linking Trout Point with the "Jefferson Parish Political Corruption Scandal," the "sting" of which was that "Trout Point Lodge and its owners were somehow involved in corruption, fraud, money laundering, and 'pay to play' schemes involving Jefferson Parish President Aaron Broussard and his administration"; (2) the "clear imputation" that Trout Point "misled investors and court officials in litigation" with the Atlantic Canada Opportunities

---

3   In April 2011, Handshoe wrote: "I think by now even our most casual readers know our successor website, Slabbed.org was knocked offline courtesy of the Times Picayune's corporate parent Advance Publications and this started a chain of events that resulted in Slabbed temporarily being moved back to WordPress. I'd submit this was a miscalculation of gargantuan proportions for several reasons, which will become clear as I roll out this series of posts on Aaron Broussard's connections to Trout Point Lodge and its purported owners. . . ."

Agency ("ACOA"), the "sting" of which was that "Leary perjured himself, investors were misled, businesses nefariously changed ownership, and that the ACOA litigation is ongoing, with the plaintiffs [losing] every step of the way"; (3) the "imputation" that the "Trout Point Lodge business is actively failing, near bankruptcy, having once relied on the good graces of Aaron Broussard," along with the "related imputation" that Perret and Leary "have had a series of failed businesses that used other people's money, creating a pattern" the "sting" of which was that Trout Point's "13-year-old business is on the verge of bankruptcy, that the plaintiffs will take the money and run, and that the plaintiffs are either con artists or have no business acumen whatsoever"; and (4) the "unabashed anti-gay, anti-homosexual rhetoric and rants of the defendant," used to "amplify and support the three other stings listed above" and "support[ ] and shore[ ] up all the other defamatory imputations."

The First Amended Statement of Claim continued to describe several specific blog posts on Slabbed.org, reciting much of the offensive language that Handshoe used to refer to Perret and Leary. Some of the alleged defamatory statements indicated Handshoe's poor opinion of Perret and Leary, for example, that they "had Champagne taste on a beer budget," "work as a unit grift their way through life," and were either "first-class b-tches, common thugs, or plain ol' morons."

In stating its defamation claim, Trout Point generically alleged that Handshoe's publications were false and malicious. It did not, however, make any specific statements to refute the truth of the individual blog posts at issue.[4] For example, the First Amended Statement of Claim included no information regarding Trout Point's actual connection to Broussard, if any, or its financial solvency.

Trout Point purportedly served Handshoe with a notice of the First Amended Statement of Claim in Mississippi, but Handshoe did not appear in the Nova Scotia action. In December 2011, the Nova Scotia Court entered a default

---

4   Specifically, Trout Point made the blanket assertion that the Slabbed.org posts were "replete with inaccuracies and an apparent inattention to basic ethics and duties to check facts before publishing," and that "the false statements west forth in the defendants' publications exposed the plaintiffs to public contempt, ridicule, aversion, and disgrace, and induced an evil opinion of the plaintiffs in the minds of right-thinking persons and deprived the plaintiffs of their friendly intercourse in and commerce with society." The First Amended Statement of Claim further alleged that Handshoe acted in a "reckless and malicious manner without due consideration for the standards of information gathering and dissemination ordinarily followed b responsible writers, editors, and publishers," disregarding whether the published content was "true or false."

judgment against Handshoe (the "Nova Scotia Judgment"). The Nova Scotia Judgment provided: "In accordance with the Civil Procedure Rule 31.12(4), Douglas K. Handshoe is now taken to have admitted, for the purposes of this action, the claims made against him in the Statement of Claim."

The Nova Scotia Court set the matter for a hearing to assess damages. At the hearing, Perret and Leary testified and offered additional evidence regarding Handshoe's allegedly defamatory statements and the damage that they inflicted on Trout Point Lodge, and Perret and Leary individually. Following the hearing, the court issued an oral decision summarizing the relevant Canadian law, the content of the publications at issue, and the harm that Trout Point purportedly suffered. Ultimately, the court awarded Trout Point Lodge $75,000 in general damages, and Leary and Perret each $100,000 in general damages, $50,000 in aggravated damages, and $25,000 in punitive damages. It also awarded $2,000 in costs.[5]

Trout Point enrolled the Nova Scotia Judgment in the Circuit Court of Hancock County, Mississippi, in March 2012 in an attempt to collect its damages award. Handshoe removed the action to the United States District Court for the Southern District of Mississippi pursuant to the SPEECH Act. The parties agreed that all issues were strictly legal in nature and, therefore, elected to submit the matter the district court on cross-motions for summary judgment.

The district court entered summary judgment in Handshoe's favor, finding that Trout Point failed to meet its burden under the SPEECH Act to show that "Handshoe was afforded at least as much protection for freedom of speech in [the Nova Scotia] action as he would have in a domestic proceeding or, alternatively, that Handshoe would have been found liable for defamation by a domestic court." Trout Point timely appealed.

II

We review *de novo* a district court's grant of summary judgment, applying the same standard as the district court. . . . On cross-motions for summary judgment, we review each party's motion independently, viewing the evidence and inferences in the light most favorable to the nonmoving party.

---

5   In addition to monetary relief, the Nova Scotia Court entered a permanent injunction against Handshoe, "restraining him from disseminating, posting on the Internet or publishing, in any manner whatsoever, directly or indirectly, any statements about the plaintiffs, Trout Point Lodge, Charles L. Leary, and Vaughn] J. Perret." . . . Trout Point does not seek to enforce the injunction in this action. . . .

III

This action depends on our interpretation of the SPEECH Act. The task of statutory interpretation begins and, if possible, ends with the language of the statute. When the language is plain, we must enforce the statute's plain meaning, unless absurd. . . .

[T]he SPEECH Act provides that a domestic court "shall not recognize or enforce a foreign judgment for defamation" unless it satisfies both First Amendment and due process considerations. *See* 28 U.S.C. § 4102. We focus our inquiry on the statute's "First Amendment considerations" provision.

Under the "First Amendment considerations" provision of the SPEECH Act, a foreign defamation judgment is unrecognizable and unenforceable unless

> (A) the defamation law applied in the foreign court's adjudication provided at least as much protection for freedom of speech and press in that case as would be provided by the [F]irst [A]mendment to the Constitution of the United States and by the constitution and law of the State in which the domestic court is located; or

> (B) even if the defamation law applied in the foreign court's adjudication did not provide as much protection for freedom of speech and press as the [F]irst [A]mendment to the Constitution of the United States and the constitution and law of the State, the party opposing recognition or enforcement of that foreign judgment would have been found liable for defamation by a domestic court applying the [F]irst [A]mendment to the Constitution of the United States and the constitution and law of the State in which the domestic court is located.

§ 4102(a)(1).

Although there is no case law directly interpreting these two prongs, the plain language of the statute suggests two distinct options for a party seeking to enforce a foreign defamation judgment: one focused on the law applied by the foreign forum and one focused on the facts the parties presented in the foreign proceeding. Put differently, a party may enforce a foreign defamation judgment in a domestic court if either (A) the law of the foreign forum, as applied in the foreign proceeding, provides free-speech protection that is coextensive with relevant domestic law, or (B) the facts, as proven in the foreign proceeding, are sufficient to establish a defamation claim under domestic law. We address each prong in turn.

A

There is no meaningful dispute that the law applied by the Nova Scotia Court provides less protection of speech and press than First Amendment and Mississippi law. Canadian defamation law is derivative of the defamation law of the United Kingdom, which has long been substantially less protective of free speech. . . .

The most critical legal difference here is that a Canadian plaintiff—unlike a plaintiff subject to First Amendment and Mississippi state law—need not prove falsity as an element of its prima facie defamation claim. Rather, in Canada, truth is a defense that a defamation defendant may raise and, if so, must prove. . . . In comparison, . . . American laws both seem to show a certain bias towards freedom of expression and freedom of the press; the burden of proof of the wrongful nature of the injury to reputation lies in both cases with the person defamed." Thus, Trout Point cannot satisfy the first prong of the First-Amendment considerations inquiry; that is, the law applied in the Nova Scotia proceeding did not provide at least as much protection for freedom of speech and press as Handshoe would have received under domestic law.

B

The more challenging question in this case arises from the statute's second prong: whether a Mississippi court presented with the same facts and circumstances would have found Handshoe liable for defamation. The answer depends on whether the facts Trout Point proved in the Nova Scotia proceeding were sufficient to demonstrate falsity under the United States Constitution and Mississippi state law. In Mississippi, "[t]he threshold question in a defamation suit is whether the published statements are false. Truth is a complete defense to an action for libel. The plaintiff bears the burden to prove such falsity." *Armistead v. Minor*, 815 So.2d 1189, 1194 (Miss. 2002). Significantly, statements that are "substantially true" are not defamatory in Mississippi. *Id.* "As the United States Supreme Court has noted, minor inaccuracies do not amount to falsity so long as the substance, the gist, the sting, of the libelous charge be justified." *Id.* (quoting *Masson v. New Yorker Magazine, Inc.*, 501 U.S. 496, 517 (1991)). . . .

[T]he First Amended Statement of Claim is unclear regarding whether all, or just some, of Handshoe's statements are false. At the outset, it indicates that Handshoe's statements were "defamatory by both *true* and false innuendo." (emphasis added). In explaining the particular statements at issue, the First Amended Statement of Claim repeatedly emphasizes that the statements were "defamatory," in that they would tend to lower one's opinion of Trout Point. But it specifically alleges falsity with respect to only a limited few of the statements, and offers no facts to rebut or undermine most of Handshoe's statements.[18] Although Trout Point includes some generic allegations of falsity towards the end of its defamation claim . . . this catch-all language offers little guidance regarding whether some or all of the statements are allegedly false, especially in light of the First Amended Statement of Claim's earlier reference to "true innuendo" as a source of harm.

For this reason, Trout Point cannot show that a state or federal court in Mississippi would grant a default judgment based on the First Amended Statement of Claim. . . .

Second, some of the publications at issue are statements of unverifiable opinion. For example, Trout Point based its defamation claim, in part, on the allegation that Handshoe used "unabashed anti-gay, anti-homosexual rhetoric and rants of the defendants" intended to "engender[ ] discrimination and hatred." The First Amended Statement of Claim complains that Handshoe referred to Perret and Leary as "'girls,' 'blow buddies,' queer f-g scum,' and 'b-tches,' published more than one reference to a gay-themed movie, and posted video clips of movies and music videos commonly associated with gay stereotypes." While less grotesque, many of the other statements at issue also involve expressions of opinion; for example, that True Point had "Champagne taste on a beer budget," that Perret and Leary were a "litigious bunch," and that the Nova Scotia action was "foolish and frivolous."

---

18   Compare, for example, paragraph 54 of the First Amended Statement of Claim with paragraph 100. Paragraph 54 alleges: "Publishing that Trout Point Lodge was not doing well financially is defamatory of the corporate plaintiff. Public reports of poor business performance would tend to lower the esteem of the corporate plaintiff in the eyes of a reasonable person." Trout Point does not specifically allege that the statement is false, nor does it claim that, for example, its financial performance had not declined. Paragraph 100, on the other hand, states: "Defendant Handshoe states that the Plaintiff Trout Point Lodge advertises heavily on Trip Advisor. This is defamatory, and *untrue*, designed to make it appear as though plaintiff is in dire economic straights [sic] and has resorted to drastic measures to advertise." (emphasis added).

Though offensive, these statements generally are not actionable in Mississippi. The Mississippi Supreme Court has recognized that "name calling and verbal abuse are to be taken as statements of opinion, not fact, and therefore will not give rise to an action for libel." *Johnson v. Delta-Democrat Pub. Co.*, 531 So.2d 811, 814 (Miss. 1988). "[N]othing in life or our law guarantees a person immunity from occasional sharp criticism, nor should it. . . . [N]o person avoids a few linguistic slings and arrows, many demonstrably unfair." *Ferguson v. Watkins*, 448 So.2d 271, 276 (Miss. 1984). Thus, statements of opinion are actionable "only if they clearly and unmistakably imply the allegation of undisclosed false and defamatory facts as the basis for the opinion." *Id.* . . . Here, although some of Handshoe's opinions certainly imply facts (*e.g.,* that Trout Point was involved in the Aaron Broussard scandal), his bare "linguistic slings and arrows" do not. Indeed, counsel for Trout Point conceded at oral argument that Handshoe's offensive insults and opinion statements would not be actionable in Mississippi. Thus, Trout Point cannot show that a state or federal court in Mississippi would grant a default judgment on these opinion-based allegations. . . .

Trout Point failed to show that the allegations in the First Amended Statement of Claim, standing alone and taken as true, would be sufficient to support a defamation claim in a Mississippi court. Trout Point asserts a second ground to establish falsity, however: the Nova Scotia Court's purported factual findings that Handshoe's statements were false and malicious. We turn next to that issue.

The critical question is not whether the Nova Scotia Court found falsity, but rather whether a state or federal court in Mississippi faced with the allegations in the First Amended Statement of Claim would have done so. *See* § 4102(a)(1)(B). . . .

But even assuming, *arguendo*, that the Nova Scotia Court's factual findings have some bearing on the enforceability inquiry, they are insufficient to demonstrate falsity. As the district court summarized, the Nova Scotia Court's oral decision "does not contain specific findings of fact with respect to the falsity of Handshoe's statements." Indeed, despite repeated entreaties at oral argument, Trout Point could not identify a single specific allegation in the Statement of Claim that the Nova Scotia Court found was actually false. Rather, the Nova Scotia Court noted generically that some statements were "erroneous," but remained silent as to the truth of others.[24] The only statement with arguably global reach is that Handshoe's conduct was "outrageous" in the "face of true facts" about Trout Point. This simply is not direct enough to constitute a meaningful factual finding that *all* of Handshoe's statements were false.[25] . . .

Moreover, the Nova Scotia Court awarded damages based on the name-calling and verbal abuse discussed above, which is not actionable in Mississippi. In sum, much of the conduct that underlies the Nova Scotia Court's oral opinion and damages award would not give rise to relief in Mississippi.

IV

Before we conclude, we note that the SPEECH Act also contains a "jurisdictional considerations" provision, which requires "the party seeking recognition or enforcement of the foreign judgment" to show that "the exercise of personal jurisdiction by the foreign court comported with the due process requirements that are imposed on domestic courts by the Constitution of the United States." § 4102(b).

Handshoe asserts that Trout Point also failed to satisfy this provision because the Nova Scotia Court's exercise of personal jurisdiction over him did not comport with our nation's due process requirements. He makes a strong argument that Nova Scotia was not the "focal point" of the statements that preceded the First Amended Statement of Claim. *Cf. Calder v. Jones,* 465 U.S. 783, 788–90 (1984). But we, like the district court, need not resolve whether Handshoe had the requisite minimum contacts with Nova Scotia at the time that Trout Point filed suit, as Trout Point's failure to satisfy the First Amendment considerations provision of the SPEECH Act is fatal to its claim. . . . We affirm.

---

24 *Compare, e.g.,* "The plaintiffs were erroneously identified as being connected with Mr. Broussard in a business venture and Mr. Broussard was named in error as owning Trout Point Lodge," *with* "The defamation continued with statements that Trout Point Lodge was losing business or going bankrupt because of the investigation of Mr. Broussard and his inability to continue to support it. . . . The statements also contained anti-gay rhetoric and homophobic comments."

25 Trout Point emphasized that certain evidence, specifically, affidavits and testimony by Perret and Leary, demonstrated the falsity of Handshoe's statements. But this evidence, like the purported factual findings, was admitted at the damages hearing *after* the Nova Scotia Court had already issued the Nova Scotia Judgment. Even if we consider this evidence, it still does not establish that *all* of the alleged statements were, in fact, false. Moreover, it refers to numerous statements of opinion and publications that post-dated the First Amended Statement of Claim. Thus, for essentially the same reasons discussed above, we hold that the evidence Trout Point cites is insufficient to show that Trout Point would have been entitled to relief in a Mississippi court.

COMMENTS AND QUESTIONS

1. Very few foreign-country judgments awarding damages on defamation claims could survive the exacting standard of 28 U.S.C. § 4102. How should Trout Point Lodge have litigated the case differently in Nova Scotia if it knew then that it would ultimately be trying to enforce a defamation judgment in the United States?

2. Free speech and a free press are cherished ideals in the United States. But does it follow that protection of those rights extends to the point of denying enforcement to judgments of foreign countries whose citizens were injured there by Americans?

SAMPLE EXAM QUESTIONS

Question 23-4

Moran, an Oregonian, claimed that he suffered personal injury as he walked past a construction site in Gibraltar. He sued the owner of the site, PartyGaming Ltd., a Gibraltar corporation, in the Supreme Court of Gibraltar (the country's trial court of general jurisdiction). Moran was never hospitalized yet claimed £ 2 million ((US) $2.6 million) in damages for serious personal injury, pain and suffering, and lost business opportunities. Moran formally represented himself in the litigation, but he was assisted throughout by Camille Fignon, an Oregon attorney who is Moran's business partner.

After eighteen months of litigation, the court dismissed Moran's action as "fraudulent and frivolous litigation." The court noticed a hearing to consider sanctions against Moran and/or Fignon. At the hearing PartyGaming Ltd. submitted evidence of its legal bills for the Moran matter totaling £ 225,000 ((U.S.) $ 300,000). Under the laws of Gibraltar, an award of sanctions including the payment of attorney fees may be imposed on a party and/or its lawyer if its claims are wholly lacking in merit or for representations to the court that are known to be false. After three days of testimony, the court ordered Moran and Fignon to be jointly and severally liable for a sanctions award to be paid PartyGaming Ltd. in the full amount of the defendant's legal fees. A final judgment entered. On an appeal by Moran and Fignon, the Supreme Court of Gibraltar noted an absence of precedent for an order sanctioning a non-party, but affirmed the trial court's award "given the unusual circumstances of the case and the abhorrent behavior of the appellants." Moran and Fignon have since left Gibraltar, leaving no assets behind.

PartyGaming Ltd. filed an enforcement action in Oregon that Moran and Fignon are resisting. As a British possession, Gibraltar is a common law jurisdiction with a judicial infrastructure that fairly resembles American courts. Accordingly, Moran and Fignon are not challenging the "judicial system" of Gibraltar. Rather, they are arguing that the circumstances of this specific proceeding are problematic. Are Moran and (or) Fignon likely to persuade the Oregon court to vacate the Gibraltar judgment?

Question 23-5

Killion International Development, Inc. (Killion) is a company that was formed in Texas by its sole owner, Robert Killion, a Texan, to fund an oil exploration and technology project in Morocco. Under Moroccan law, all business ventures and development projects require a local partner or shareholder. Maghreb Energy Explorations S.A. (Maghreb) was interested in a joint venture and, based upon Killion's representations, agreed to invest hundreds of millions of dollars in exchange for a 50% stake in all assets, including exploration licenses, technology licenses, inventories, supplies, real property, and personal property.

The joint venture had a promising future. The Kingdom of Morocco is located on the northwestern tip of the African continent and sits next to some of Africa's largest oil and gas producing nations. While its neighbors on the African coast have emerged as major producers of energy, Morocco had not discovered a reliable domestic source of oil and gas. The Killion-Maghreb venture intended to change that. The venture captured the imagination of the public and the government. Morrocco's King Mohammed, whose relatives are corporate officials of Maghreb, gave a nationally televised speech during which he announced that the discovery of enough oil to supply the Kingdom for at least 30 years was imminent.

The project did not find oil. Morocco's natural resources proved to be less plentiful than the King or others suggested—a reality which adversely affected both the King's credibility and the joint venture's business prospects.

Displeased that their investment in the joint venture proved fruitless, Maghreb filed suit in Morocco. Maghreb claimed that Killion (i) misrepresented and even falsified data; (ii) fraudulently represented the value of the company to induce Maghreb to invest; (iii) lied to government officials; and (iv) mismanaged the company. On Twitter the King blamed Killion for this debacle and promised that the interest of the people would surely be vindicated. Killion defended the suit and, just over a year ago, the court entered a judgment in favor of Maghreb for 969,832,062 Moroccan Dirhams (approximately $120 million).

Maghreb has filed an enforcement action in Texas, a state that has adopted the Uniform Foreign Country Money Judgment Recognition Act. Maghreb has complied with the technical provisions of that statute. The act presumes recognition and mandates enforcement unless the opposing party proves to the Court that it cannot or should not enforce the judgment. Your firm represents Killion. What is your litigation strategy for resisting enforcement?

Quick Summary

- Because the Full Faith and Credit Clause does not prescribe the treatment of a foreign country's judgment, the recognition and enforcement of foreign-country judgments is a matter of comity

- Federal and state courts routinely recognize and enforce foreign-country judgments

- Model state laws and common law recognize mandatory and discretionary grounds for non-enforcement

- Because the United States has ratified and implemented the New York Convention, arbitral awards are especially likely to be enforced

SUBJECT MATTER INDEX